THE SOUL OF LIFE

THE COMPLETE NEFFESH HA-CHAYYIM

Rav Chayyim of Volozhin

Translated by Eliezer Lipa (Leonard) Moskowitz

ISBN-13: 978-0615699912
ISBN-10: 061569991X

Rev. 1.4 (January 2014)

New Davar Publications, Teaneck, NJ

Distributed by:
Amazon.com, Inc.
www.amazon.com

Original cover illustration: Jeffrey Packard
Book design and layout: Jana Rade

Printed in USA

ישיבת רבנו יצחק אלחנן
Rabbi Isaac Elchanan Theological Seminary
An Affiliate of Yeshiva University

בס"ד

כ"ח אייר תשע"ב

The classic work Nefesh Hachayim – "The Soul of Life" written by R' Chayim of Volozhin is a seminal work which has had profound impact upon Jewish scholarship especially in the Lithuanian Yeshiva world. Until now, only Torah scholars had access to it.

I want to congratulate R' Eliezer Moskowitz shlita for his excellent translation into English. This will enable a much larger audience to explore and fathom the profound ideas of the work and will increase our awareness of G-d Almighty, of the supernal impact of human actions, and the importance of Torah study.

יישר כחו, להגדיל תורה ולהאדירה.

Rav Hershel Reichman

RABBI HERSHEL REICHMAN
P: 212.960-5304 F: 212.568.7380 Email: hreichman@yu.edu Website: www.yu.edu/riets
500 West 185th Street, Furst Hall, Room 325, New York, NY 10033-3201

Reviewer Comments

It is a very exact and literal translation. I wish you bracha and hatzlacha.

—Rabbi Dovid Miller, Rosh Yeshiva, Mashgiach Ruchani and Gottesfeld Chair in Talmud at Yeshiva University's Rabbi Isaac Elchanan Theological Seminary (RIETS)

It is very difficult for the average laymen to comprehend the meaning and significance of Philosophy books. It is even more so when the author uses kabbalistic phrases and ideas to illuminate the philosophical meaning of a particular text. R' Chaim Voloshin's Nefesh haChayim certainly fits that description. Lenny Moskowitz's full translation and footnotes allow the reader to gain a glimpse of this author's most famous work.

—Rabbi Yosef Adler, mara d'atra of Congregation Rinat Yisrael in Teaneck, New Jersey and Rosh HaYeshiva of Torah Academy of Bergen County

---

Rabbi Moskowitz' erudite translation will introduce Reb Chayim's master work to a new generation of disciples. It can only increase their Ahavat HaShem and Ahavat HaTorah.

—Rabbi Steven Pruzansky, mara d'atra of Congregation Bnai Yeshurun in Teaneck, New Jersey

The Translator

Eliezer (Leonard) Moskowitz is completing the s'mikha program at Yeshiva University's Rabbi Isaac Elchanan Theological Seminary (RIETS) in New York. He holds a Bachelor of Science degree in Psychology from the City University of New York, a Master of Science in Electrical Engineering from NYU Polytechnic, and worked in the defense and aerospace industries for twenty years. He is married to Deborah Teplow and lives in Teaneck, New Jersey. They have six children whom they love and of whom they are inordinately proud.

Contents

TRANSLATOR'S INTRODUCTION

The *Neffesh Ha-chayyim* is Rav Chayyim Volozhiner's explanation, in four sections, of: 1) man's nature and purpose; 2) how prayer is an essential expression of that nature and purpose; 3) how, while the nature of the Infinite Creator is essentially unknowable, His manifestation into creation carries with it a mandate for mankind; and 4) how involvement with Torah[1] is the ultimate fulfillment of man's purpose and the vehicle of his connection with God.

Early during my translation effort I contacted a few Jewish publishers to discuss publication. Most responded that they felt that, because it was so full of kabbalistic knowledge, the *Neffesh Ha-chayyim* should not be translated.

I was later surprised when in Elul 5769 (September 2009), Judaica Press published Rabbi Avraham Yaakov Finkel's excerpted colloquial translation. I was less surprised that they left out the translations of the many sections they deemed too sensitive. After all, when I once approached Rav Meyer Twersky (Rosh Yeshiva at Yeshivat Rabbeinu Yitzkhak Elchanan and a direct descendant of Rav Chayyim Volozhiner) with a question

---

1 Heb.: *eisek ha-Torah.* See the footnote at the beginning of Gate 4 for a discussion of what "involvement with Torah" means to Rav Chayyim.

about one word in Gate 3 of the *Neffesh Ha-chayyim,* he responded that the contents of that part of the book are *d'varim ha-ome-dim b'roomo shel olam* (literally "words whose positions are at the world's pinnacle"; less literally "subjects of extreme holiness") and shouldn't be carelessly spoken.

When asked how I can justify offering this complete translation, I point out Rav Chayyim Volozhiner's own words at the end of Gate 3, Chapter 3:

However, I reconsidered and noted that while this was proper for them in their generation, now a very long time has elapsed without a guide, and the ways of man are to follow the path that, led by his rational intellect, seems right, and the inclination of a person's heart/mind's thoughts is exclusively to fly-off in fantasies to wherever his heart/mind leads him. The most important reason is that this teaching has reached the general public, and is a metaphor espoused even by fools saying that every place and everything is absolute Godliness. And they aim constantly to deepen their understanding and to study it, to the point that it captures the heart/minds of the young and immature, and they determine their actions and behavior based on this rationale.

*... A person must exercise extreme caution in this matter and constantly guard his soul-*Neffesh. *For if (heaven forefend) our heart/mind would fixate on this idea*[2]*, to permit ourselves to act based on this idea, it's possible for the effect of this (heaven forefend) to be the destruction of many of the holy Torah's basic principles (may the Merciful save us).*

... This is what brought me to initiate a discussion of this matter and to caution and distance others from errors that could be caused by this (heaven forefend), and to thoroughly

2 Heb.: *likbo-ah lah-noo makh-shah-va zoo*

understand what our sages (OBM[3]) hinted at on this topic. And they are like all of God's righteous ways, this being an era with a pressing and urgent need[4].

What was true in Rav Chayyim's day is now, to our great sadness, even truer. Rarely a week goes by when I don't encounter less-educated Jews who have been exposed to the concepts of *Ma-kome* and *Ein Ode Milvado*, not in a Jewish context, but rather in the context of popular culture adaptations of Kabbala, and Eastern religions. They have no sense of what our holy Torah and sages have to say on these topics. Their curiosity demands a response from a deeply Jewish perspective, and if we ignore their needs they will (and do) go elsewhere for answers. And they will (and do) act based on what they learn.

In his introduction to this book, Reb Itzele (Rav Chayyim's son) further elaborated on Rav Chayyim's purpose in writing this book, including how Rav Chayyim saw the *Neffesh Ha-chayyim* both as a book that would benefit the masses and as an entry way into the hidden aspects of Torah for those who had that capacity. Indeed, Rav Yosef Shani (Shabtai) recommended the *Neffesh Ha-chayyim* to my peers as an entry way.

I consulted some of the greatest Torah scholars of our community (including Rav Aharon Lichtenstein), and they did not oppose the publication of a translation.

In addition, this text has already been translated into a Western language, so I am not breaking new ground: Benjamin Gross published a French translation in 1986 [Verdier], with a Forward by the eminent philosopher Emmanuel Levinas.

---

3 Of blessed memory

4 Heb.: *v'eit la-ah-sote*

TRANSLATOR'S RECOMMENDATION FOR ORDER OF STUDY

AFTER repeated journeys through this peerless book, I recommend that the reader skip directly to Gate 1 to learn the four Gates in order. After completing them, go back to learn the Chapters that can be found between Gates 3 and 4, then Reb Itzele's long Annotation (*Hagaha Ha-MHRY"tz*) and finally Reb Itzele's Introduction.

BIOGRAPHICAL INFORMATION ABOUT RAV CHAYYIM OF VOLOZHIN

For biographical information about Rav Chayyim of Volozhin I recommend Rabbi Norman Lamm's book "Torah Lishmah: Torah for Torah's Sake in the Works of Rabbi Hayyim of Volozhin and his Contemporaries", and the chapter on Rav Chayyim of Volozhin in Immanuel Etkes' book: "The Gaon of Vilna: The Man and His Image".

TRANSLATION NOTES

In the interest of offering the reader a clearer sense of how Rav Chayyim expressed himself, and in an effort to bring us closer to understanding his mental processes, I've tried to preserve his literary style. In most cases I've retained his sentence structures, and changed them only when the semantics would have been corrupted or compromised by its preservation. At first reading this may stress a reader of modern English, but I've found that after a while, Rav Chayyim's style becomes familiar and pleasant.

As Rav Chayyim discusses at length, Hebrew has many names for God. In English I translate them as "God" followed by the Hebrew name in italics (e.g. God-*YHV"H)*.

In Hebrew, there are at least five names for the English word "soul." I translate them as "soul" followed by the specific Hebrew word in italics (e.g. soul-*Neffesh*).

In some cases the Hebrew text includes implicit meaning. In these situations I've made the implicit explicit by adding a few words in square brackets.

When Rav Chayyim cites a book, I've included the Hebrew version of the book's title in the translation's text. To give the reader a sense of what those books are about, the first time they are mentioned I usually provide a footnote with an English translation of the title. This is not meant to imply that English translations of those books are available.

There are cases where a Hebrew word's gender and number are important to the meaning of the text. When that is so I include the word's gender and number in square brackets (e.g., "it [fem., plural]"). And when a Hebrew word is used in emphatic form (usually by being repeated), I include the note "emphatic" in square brackets.

When a Hebrew word or phrase is included, I've transliterated it in a contrasting font (e.g., *ahtzmoot*). Within each transliterated word, when neighboring transliterated syllables would not affect each individual syllable's pronunciation, I leave them attached to each other (e.g., *neffesh)*. When, by being attached, two syllables could possibly affect each other's transliterated pronunciations (e.g., *rakhoom*), I separated the one from the next by a hyphen (e.g., *ra-khoom*); each syllable is then written out as sounded in a manner that I felt was clear to me, a New York-born Jew. I did not include per-syllable accent/emphasis notations.

In a small number of cases, where a single English word didn't suffice to sufficiently capture the meaning of a single Hebrew word, I translated them as two words separated by a forward slash (e.g., *lev* as heart/mind, *ei-vehr* as limb/organ, and *yir-ah* as awe/fear).

When I felt that my translation of a word or phrase had a particularly subjective element, I included a footnote that provides the original Hebrew or Aramaic text. The reader then has the opportunity to translate the text on their own.

Whenever Rav Chayyim mentions God or the sages of past generations, he generally appends an honorific (e.g., "God-*YHV"H* (blessed be He)", and "the sages (OBM)"). In all cases, out of respect for Rav Chayyim's sensibilities and somewhat to the detriment of English readability, I've left them in place.

Rav Chayyim occasionally extends the length of a single sentence well beyond what's common in current English. Sometimes I've broken the lengthy sentence into a few shorter sentences. In others, I've divided the sentence into numbered sections that represent the structure of the original.

I've corrected a number of errors in the chapter and verse citations. I've noted when Rav Chayyim's quotation from a citation differs from what is found in current editions.

I've also added numerous footnotes with explanatory commentary.

In creating this translation I drew on five editions of the Neffesh Ha-chayyim: the 1824 first edition, the 1837 second edition, the 1861 third edition, the 1873 fourth edition, and Issacher Dov Rubin's 1989 edition. Rubin's edition, with its punctuation, in-line citations and Hebrew/Aramaic translations, was especially helpful. This translation sometimes differs from it in how the text is broken into individual sentences and punctuated.

For reference, I've included the 1837 second edition. It can be found at the end of the translation.

ACKNOWLEDGMENTS

I offer warm thanks to my friend and chevruta Chaim Dolinko, who first introduced me to the Neffesh Ha-chayyim more than twenty years ago. I'm certain that he had no idea that he was changing my life in such a profound way.

Thanks to Yeshiva University's Rabbi Isaac Elchanan Theological Seminary (RIETS) for the use of their beit midrash and libraries, and especially the Mendel Gottesman Library for the use of a first edition of the Neffesh Ha-chayyim, and manuscripts and early editions of the texts that Rav Chayyim cited.

Thanks to Rav Meyer Twersky, Rosh Yeshiva at RIETS, for his shiurim in Sha-ar Alef (only) of the Neffesh Ha-chayyim at Congregation Bnai Yeshurun (Teaneck NJ), and for his willingness to provide me with the benefit of his understanding of many key phrases.

Thanks to Rav Aharon Kahn, Rosh Yeshiva and my Talmud rebbe at RIETS, for his support in this effort.

Thanks to Rav Gideon Lipovsky, who long ago introduced me to the Ariza"l's Torah.

Thanks to my good friend Anna Olswanger, whose love of Jewish books inspired me to start on this translation.

Thanks to my good friend Sheri Prupis, whose encouragement provided incentive to continue working on this translation when doubts and difficulties arose.

Thanks to Rabbi Yechiel Wiener and Rabbi David Pahmer, Shoalim U'meishivim in the RIETS beit midrash, for their openness, good humor, availability and for their always thoughtful responses to my somewhat unusual questions.

Thanks to Donald Lewis Lively for his help in editing this book. Motivated solely by his love for Torah, his enthusiastic and professional assistance significantly improved this book.

Thanks to the respected rebbeim of my youth: Rav Yisrael Chait and Rav Zevulun Lieb. They taught me to love Torah and how to learn.

I offer my deepest thanks to my dear parents, my teachers, Joseph and Marcia Moskowitz (OBM), who spared no effort or expense to ensure that I grew up in a *ma-kome Torah*, and who provided me with a Torah education.

And lastly, thanks from the bottom of my heart to my dear wife Deborah Teplow for her unflagging encouragement and support for this project (and many others).

ERROR REPORTING

If you note an error in this book or have a recommendation for its improvement, please send a note to:

moskowit@panix.com
or
lenmoskowitz@optonline.net
or
lmoskowi@yu.edu

AN INTRODUCTION BY THE AUTHOR'S SON

The motivation for this is that everyone who authors a text starts with an introduction at the beginning of his book. Some have the custom to inform us what to expect to unfold in the book. Some inform us of the book's key purpose and the intention of its utility. Some follow the path of expressing that humility and fear of God-*H'* precedes their wisdom, to humble himself using words of Torah, so as not to boast about his composition. And if he should appoint his son to arrange its printing, lo, it falls to the son to recount the fatherly author's valor and to make known the text's glory. Each is praiseworthy in its own way[5].

And I, how shall I start? I am a young man. I don't know any reason that my words should be set down in a book. And it's even that I don't have it within me to choose a direction of how I should start, other than to praise what is stated in the book *Yir'aht H' La-chayyim*[6] and their purpose, because excess speech only results

5 Paraphrasing *Mishlei* 27:21

6 This is the original title of the collection of essays that we now call the *Neffesh Ha-chayyim*.

in loss[*7] when dealing with things that are clearly apparent to the eye, and when discussed between those who fear God-*H'*, who desire to grow close to God-*Elohi"m.* And anyone who reads his book—who reads it sincerely[8]—regarding him is said "blessed is He who distributed His wisdom to those who fear Him".

> **Annotation:** *It could be possible that the meaning of this verse ("excess speech only results in loss") is that when, from our world-view, it appears that there is something lacking, it requires words to correct. But when there is no lack, why add more words?*

And if I should seek to state the correct amount of praise for the honor of my father—the genius, the righteous, the famous (his soul rests in Eden)—I am naked of the power of understanding to evaluate the extent of his Torah and his righteousness. It's not within my capacity to adequately recognize it myself, nor to acquaint others with it. My elders, scholars of Torah and geniuses, the greatest of the rabbis of our nation (may their lights continue to illuminate), who knew the powers of his accomplishments in the revealed and the hidden, for them it was pleasant to retell their memories of him, for that is vast. And about his book all will write. And indeed, the righteousness of his ways will fill the earth, and his actions will speak for him.

---

7 The asterisk denotes that the following annotation addresses this text. All of the annotations were authored by Rav Chayyim other than the ones in this introduction and the long one between Gates 1 and 2. Those were authored by Rav Chayyim's son, the compiler and editor of the Neffesh Ha-chayyim, the fine scholar Reb Itzele.

8 Paraphrasing *T'hillim* 145:18

Is there anyone who hasn't had his attention drawn to note[9] the praiseworthy acts that he did in the land, and the strength and power given him in the true Torah, and good and truthful acts that he performed—how additional greatness was awarded him[10], as if he stands among God's legions in heaven?

He was the man who took upon himself the yoke of Torah in his time, in his land, as an expression of compassion. And he taught wisdom to hundreds of students. And he merited enlarging Torah, to teach and to explain. He heard and researched and corrected. And he built a great institution of learning that stands on three foundations: Torah, service[11] and compassion[12].

And it's not surprising that he earned merit for himself and enabled the public to be worthy of merit, for from his youth he bore the yoke of Torah with tremendous assiduousness. And at the age of fourteen he learned fixedly with his older brother, the genius, our teacher Simkha (OBM). And he acquired knowledge day and night. And our elders told us the story of how when the light of candles was not available, the light of the moon was enough for them to learn at night. And at that time they received the path of Torah from the rabbi of rabbis, genius of geniuses, the lion of the supernal residence, Rabbi Aryei Leib (in Eden is his resting place), the author of the *Shaagaht Aryei[*]*.

Annotation: *And the genius, the author of the* Shaagaht Aryei *(OBM) was for some years the chief justice of our court here in this holy community, and was known to my father,*

---

9 Heb.: *ah-sheir lo sha-ma kawl mahs-roo-keeta*—Lit.: heard the whistling sound

10 Aram.: *hawt-k'naht b'r'voo yateera*—Ref.: *Daniel* 4:33

11 Heb.: *avoda*

12 Heb.: *oo-g'mee-loot cha-sa-deem*

> *my master's (OBM) family. While he was here he authored his valuable composition* Responsa of the Shaagaht Aryei. *And when he left here to print it, my respected father (his resting place is in Eden) was young. When he traveled through here after publishing his book, he stayed over at my grandfather's (OBM) home for a few weeks, graced the city with his presence, and taught here. My father, my master (OBM) was then fifteen years old, and out of love for him and his older brother (his resting place is in Eden), he directed their studies so that they should be well-organized.*

By the time he was twenty-five he had completed the entire Talmud, and early and late *po-skim*, and he would learn Torah with his brother—the genius who is like the residents of heaven—our teacher Rav Shlomo Zalman[*] (his resting place is in Eden). How pleasant was the joining of brothers together[13] in Torah and service. The two of them, as one, learned Torah from the rabbi who resembles God-*YHV"H-Tz'va-ote*'s angel, spiritual guardian and holy from heaven, our great rabbi, the rabbi of all who live in exile, the genius, our master and teacher Eliyahu, the pious (may the memory of the righteous and holy be a blessing) of the holy community of Vilna. And he (OBM) emanated from his spirit-*Ruakh* upon them a spirit-*Ruakh* of wisdom[14]… . Fortunate is the eye that saw all of this[15]. Those who saw, looked and rejoiced. And those who heard with their ears, their souls-*Neffesh* craved more.

---

13 Paraphrasing *T'hillim* 133:1

14 Paraphrasing *B'midbar* 11:17

15 Paraphrasing the *Yom Kippur Mahkhzore*, regarding those who witnessed the service in the *Beit Ha-mikdash*

Annotation: *And he is famous in Judah and known as a genius among Israel*[16]*. A short description of his holy ways are recorded in the book* Tole-dote Ha-ahdahm, *parts one and two, authored by the Rav-par-excellence, the great preacher, our teacher Yekhezkel Feivel (preacher of correctness) from the great city Vilna. And he still has the third part in manuscript form. My father, my master (OBM) was older than his brother the genius, our teacher Rav Shlomo Zalman (his resting place is in Eden) by seven years and nine days, and was born in 5509, the second day of the holiday of Shavuot, the day that the Torah was given to Israel, and ascended from among us at the age of 72 on the day he was freed, the 14th day of Sivan during the week that* B'ha-ah-lote-kha *is read, in the year 5581.*

And beyond his learning, greater still was his service to his teacher (his resting place is in Eden). During the long period that he waited upon him, he illuminated to him the paths of revealed Torah and the wondrous paths in the recondite—this [emphatic] being the "seeing your Teacher before you"[*]. And the sections of the Talmud were revealed to him and wisdom shined brightly for him. And to him it seemed as only a short time that he learned before him in reverence and awe/fear, with trembling and great physical effort. From the River Dinoor[17] he would draw and then take his leave. In that same way he taught and informed his children and students about the great oceans that stood before him. Reverence for his teacher was upon him as a wondrous awe/fear, as if he was standing

---

16 Paraphrasing *T'hillim* 76:2

17 After death, souls immerse in the River Dinoor—a river of fire—to purify themselves. Reb Itzele likens Rav Chayyim's learning with the Vilna Gaon to drawing from that river of fire.

before him in the heavens. And when he began discussions of halakha and recalled the name of his teacher, his entire body would tremble and his appearance would change dramatically as a result of the flashing fire in his heart/mind when he would think about his ways of righteousness and piousness, and his purity of holiness. And he acquired the light of Torah because his powers were strong in the qualities by which Torah is acquired. And from Eliyahu's mantle[18] he donned humility and awe/fear.

Annotation: *Perhaps this matter that is mentioned in* Eruvin *13b: "...and if your eyes could see before you... 'and your eyes will behold your teacher'"* (Y'shaya *30:20) is like the matter mentioned in the verse* (Sh'mote *33: 23) "and you will see my back, but my face may not be seen". It can be interpreted per* Midrash Sh'mote, *chapter 3 on "I will be what I will be"—My names reflect My actions (and all of the details of the final outcome were included in the initial conception in thought). For that reason the initial conception in thought is called "face", for it precedes. And the action comes later. And even within the conception in thought itself there's the initial and overall/abstract [thought] which is hidden internally, and [also] the later thought that flows from the internal which is expressed as speech or action. (This is the knowledge that unfolds within the personality characteristics[19].) And it [emphatic] is recognized as the effect of action or in speech (which is action). But the earlier internal thought is impossible to express as speech, as in the context of "honey and milk under your tongue" (refer to* Chageega *13a [for*

---

18 Heb.: *ah-deh-ret eliyahu*—Referring to the prophet Eliyahu's mantle which he cast upon Elisha when God selected him to be a prophet (*M'lakhim Alef* 19:19).

19 Heb.: *mee-dote*—which can also be understood as the lower seven s'feerote.

more details]). And that is the supernal knowledge, as per the context of "a person can't understand his teacher..." (Avoda Za-ra *6b): that a student can't grasp it unless his teacher illuminates the subject to a scholar who is then capable of understanding on his own. All of this are about thoughts in a person's heart/mind, but in reference to Him (blessed be His name), for whom "My thoughts are not your thoughts"* (Y'shaya *55:8)—no one can conceive in any manner the general form of His thoughts, even supernal beings. And it's only His thoughts that unfold to accomplish His actions that are recognizable from His action by each prophet depending on their level. And this is "and you shall observe* et *my back", the* "et" *meaning to include the thought that unfolds to accomplish the action. And it is recognizable via the power of His actions, and it is described relative to the action. "And you will not see My face"—even via the powers of His actions, which come later than what precedes them, (and per the lessons about the word* yeir-oo*).*

And great was the humility of my honored father, the genius (his resting place is in Eden). And he was clothed with all of its[20] ways and paths. I will tell a few of his ways related to the path of humility, in being with the despondent or extolling being with the humble (*Sota* 5a). Both of these were apparent in him to any who are worthy, for from his youth through his old age he gave his soul-*Neffesh* to revive the spirit-*Ruakh* of the lowly, financially and with the righteousness of his generosity, and to be with the oppressed. And it was his crowning jewel, because the desperately poor rejoiced, because he drew them close with his right hand, and expanded their hearts/minds with soothing words, and with graceful words that arose from his lips

20 The Torah's

Additionally, among the ways of genuine humility are to genuinely despise and be repulsed by anything that has to do with the physical, to the point that they are considered as being nothingness and void, and not to experience any pleasure or attachment. And also to regard highly only God's ways, so that their heart/minds would be open to Torah and service and holiness, so that they would rejoice only in God and so that they would prepare their heart/minds to be a pleasant dwelling place for Him (blessed be His name), as is written (*Y'shaya* 29:19): "The meek will increase their joy in God-*YHV"H*", and per the verse that is often upon our lips when we stand in prayer saying: "And to those who curse me, may my soul-*Neffesh* be silent, and may my soul-*Neffes*h be like dust to all." And further on: "Make my heart/mind receptive to your Torah and then my soul-*Neffesh* will pursue your commandments". So too, anyone who knew my honored father the genius (OBM) can testify and tell of his great humility, that he would be offended rather than be offending, and was lowly in spirit before everyone. And regarding physical pleasures—he would be careful to absolutely minimize them, and he set about his ways without feeling pleasure. And even when old age arrived and he was afflicted with afflictions-of-love[21] in his property and his soul-*Neffesh,* he accepted them with joy and a jubilant expression, without expressing sighs (as our sages state [*B'rakhote* 62a] about those who accept affictions in silence), and he was in a happy frame of mind all those years when he accepted afflictions. And that righteous man only regretted that he had to support his physical needs responding to his illness. And behind closed doors his eyes would drop tears (and my eyes witnessed this, not a stranger). And even though

21 Heb.: *yee-soo-rei ah-ha-va*

his heart/mind was pained over it, he happily accepted his affliction that allowed him to minimize his perception of physical pleasure, to the extent that he paid no mind to pleasure or wounds[22].

Anyone who witnessed the Sun at its peak saw it and was amazed. For despite subjugating his body and reducing his spirit-*Ruakh* relative to wordly values, in the same way his heart/mind took the opposite position regarding heaven's values, donning an aspect of boldness and splendor, even unto the last shovelful of dirt thrown on his grave[23]. His heart/mind was attentive to create a pleasant dwelling place for Torah, service and compassionate action. How very proud he was to advance God's ways, to fight the Torah's battles. And any *mitzva* that he began with a spirit-*Ruakh* of wisdom and boldness, he completed with a spirit-*Ruakh* of understanding and awe/fear of God. He regretted not one of his words, and publicized his fine thoughts before the nation's multitudes. And all was done calmly and with words that were full of wisdom and which were received with ease.

A central feature of humility is not to be moved by one's good actions nor by the merit of the high standing that one has achieved. And to the extent that one's actions and standing grow great, his intellect increasingly recognizes God's (blessed be His name) greatness. In a similar way the spirit-*Ruakh* of God-*Elohi"m* increases his ability to be aware of his lack of abilities, and silences the sensation of the greatness of his own standing. And

---

22 Heb.: *l'oh-neg v'lo l'neh-ga*—Reb Itzele expresses these opposing physical states using two words spelled with the same three letters: *ayin*, *nun* and-*gimmel*.

23 Paraphrasing *B'rakhote* 8a

when he observes that others find it valuable to honor him, it's too much[24] and the behavior is repugnant to him[*], and reminds him of his lack of abilities, and to belittle himself so that his heart/mind doesn't become proud (as we found in the case of Rav—*Yoma* 87a—when he saw large groups of people following him to honor him).

Annotation: *And using an homiletic approach, perhaps this is the second intention of what Rabbee Eliezer stated to his students (*B'rakhote *28b): "Be mindful of your friends' honor"—that they should be careful that their own hearts/minds don't become prideful beyond the degree of honor that their friends use in relating to them.*

And anyone who didn't witness how my honored father-the-genius (OBM) behaved wouldn't believe it when told about it. All of his strategies and plotting that he set in place for himself—he made it a habit that all of the novel interpretations of Torah that he developed, whether in *G'mara,* RaSh"Y's commentary and *Tosafote,* or in Responsa, he evaluated whether he was becoming happy as a result of the intellectual effort. He was concerned about gaining pleasure from the words of Torah, and he would carefully examine if his novel interpretation perhaps wasn't a genuine expression of Torah. [We learn from] the statements of the sages (OBM, start of the *perek eiloo d'varim*) that anyone who becomes egotistical loses his wisdom (and as a kind of joke he would say that he considered it as a kind of bribe, that he bribes himself with the joy of success). And he would make the effort to disprove his own

24 Heb.: *mitz-ta-meik*—paraphrasing *Shabbat* 37b

words and to change his words, and to weigh on the balance scales of his intellect how to genuinely establish a correct theory, and the correct reasoning. And anyone who observed would see and understand in his wisdom that he accomplished it. How he would denigrate his opinion of his own knowledge. His opinion of what he knew would be lowly to him, as the sages stated (*Taanit* 7a): "Words of Torah only survive in someone whose opinion of his own knowledge is lowly".

He loved ethical admonition[25], and all of his words were like fire. They flamed from his mouth [like] the flame of God-*Y"H* with love, and flashes of fire with awe/fear[26]. Anyone who heard them, his hearts/minds melted like liquefying wax, and they were drawn after his charming words[27] of *Aggad'ta* that he would expound from time to time. And as a result of his humility he didn't find the courage to admonish others—he honestly admonished himself with all his words. And when he started to teach, the result was that he learned[*]. The majority of his admonishments were to reduce inflated ego[28].

> **Annotation:** *And maybe this was the intention of the verse* (Y'shaya *50:4*): *"God-ADN"Y God-YHV"H has granted me a tongue able to teach... He arouses my ear to be able to hear what the students perceive." Meaning that God-H' (blessed be His name) gave me the ability to teach mussar to others. And He (blessed be His name) aroused his ear so that he also could teach himself mussar, like the lessons that he teaches to others.*

---

25 Heb.: *toe-kh'khote moosar*
26 Paraphrasing *Shir Ha-shirrim* 8:6
27 Paraphrasing *Gittin 7a*
28 Heb.: *l'hahsh-peel gahv-hoot ha-lev*

[29]And while most of what he stated in his teachings was among the most profound, based on the *Zohar* and the writings of the Ariza"l (as those who understood were able to glean), he, out of his humble righteousness, clothed them, simplified them[30] and hid them—avoiding expounding the concealed parts of Torah in public[31]—so as to:

- sweeten them like honey and milk under his tongue, and like perfume under their garments,
- not expound them in public to the masses and to the crowds who hadn't filled their bellies with *Talmud*[32],
- to [motivate them to] purify their behaviors with proper attitudes of awe/fear of God-*H'* so that they shouldn't be caused to fail by the vanities of the world of falsehood.

---

29 In this paragraph and the next Reb Itzele explains how Rav Chayyim permitted himself to include direct quotes from the *Zohar*, the Ariza"l's writings and other sources not normally permitted to be taught in public.

30 Heb.: *hil-be-shahm v'hifsheetahm*—Reb Itzele employs a play on words here: *Hil-be-shahm* means "he clothed them", while *hifsheetahm* has two possible meanings. In the context of clothes it means "unclothed them". But the word could also be understood as being derived from the root word *pa-shoot* (simple), with *hifsheetahm* meaning "he simplified them".

31 Heb.: *l'vahl yahgdeel d'va-rav k'doe-reish ba-nistarote*—It is prohibited to expound the secrets of the Torah in public.

32 The R'MA in *Yoreh Dei-ah* 246:4, citing the RaMBa"M (in *Sefer Ha-ma-da,* at the end of chapter 4 of *Hilkhote Y'sodei Ha-Torah*) states that one should not study the recondite parts of Torah until one's belly is filled with knowledge of what is prohibited and what is permitted, and the laws pertaining to the *mitzvote* (i.e., *Talmud* and *poskim*). Reb Itzele may be referring here to the Chassidim whose study halls Rav Chayyim said held books of *Mussar* and didn't even have a full set of *Talmud.*

But when the situation demanded it he would say things without concealing them. He'd declare to himself: "the main thing is not study, but rather the practice"[33]. And it seems that he was referring to the last part of this *Mishna*: "...and one who speaks excessively...[34]" (these being the words of my teacher, the king[35])—that he cites esoteric sources directly[36], [37] so as to impress those who hear them[38] to take them seriously.[39] Refer to *Midrash Shmuel* comments on that [for more details][40].

In everything he did he would minimize his own honor so as to increase heaven's honor, in public affairs and specifically in matters of general concern. It's well known

---

33 *Mishna Ahvote* 1:17

34 This concludes with "...causes sin."

35 Who is Reb Itzele referring to here?

36 Heb.: *sheh-m'ma-leil mee-leen l'tzahd ma-ah-la*—paraphrasing *Daniel* 7:25

37 And as concisely and as powerfully relevant as he was able

38 Heb.: *b'ei-nei ha-shome-im* (literally: in the eyes of those who hear)—Here Reb Itzele makes a reference to the experience of synesthesia during the giving of the Torah at Sinai, where Israel "saw the thunder and the flames" (*Sh'mote* 20:15).

39 Rav Chayyim veered from his normal practice of hiding the deep meanings of what he taught only when the seriousness of how badly people were behaving demanded that he teach using the sources directly. And then he would remind himself that what is critical is how people behave and not the teachings that are used to teach them, and that in certain dire situations it is justified to publicly teach what is not normally taught in public. This was especially so when addressing the Chassidim, who held the *Zohar* and the writings of the Ariza"l in the highest esteem. By doing so, he would be able to limit to a minimum what he needed to say.

40 In Rav di Uzeda's *Midrash Shmuel*, near the end of his commentary on this section of *Mishna Ahvote*, he quotes Rav Yosef ben Nakh-mee-ahsh: "'for the body': for the uneducated masses who are called 'body'."

that he cast his own life aside[41] and engaged himself to the extreme limits of his abilities. Even when he was old, he acted reliably to the end[42]. And even when his energies were depleted (may the Merciful save us), even on his bed during his illness, he contemplated the future[43], and he would be gazing heavenward to associate heaven's Name with the suffering of the masses and the individuals, with groans and the sighs of extreme exertion, and his many sighs would distress all who heard them. (He would regularly reprove me about not being involved with the sufferings of others, and he would always tell me that man was not created to care only for himself, but rather to be helpful to others to the maximum extent of his abilities.) He would offer judgment and instruct; a lover of peace and a seeker of peace. He loved all beings and brought them closer to Torah.[*]

Annotation: *In that same vein we had the habit of expressing King Shlomo's prayer (*M'lakhim Alef *8:27): "If only God-*Elohi"m *would truly dwell on Earth"*[44]*—that You should deign to bestow all possible compassion. If a person should sin against another, [may You] act compassionately within the framework of compassionate justice to save the oppressed from the hand of his oppressor; to return a man's property from the one who took it; if they are thirsty for water, provide them with*

---

41 Paraphrasing *Shofe-tim* 9:17

42 Heb.: *ha-ya ya-dahv ehmoona ahd bo ha-sheh-mehsh*—Paraphrasing Exodus 17:12 where Moses reliably held his hands aloft during the battle with Amalek all night long, until the sun rose the next morning.

43 Aram.: *ra-ai-yo-nahv sleekoo*—Paraphrasing *Daniel* 2:29

44 This sentence is an actual quote of the start of Shlomo Ha-mellekh's prayer to God when the construction of the Temple was completed. The rest of the annotation is a paraphrased condensation of the remainder of the prayer.

> *rain; if there be starvation, provide food; to the ill and sickly*[45] *provide healing; to anyone who is heartsick, attend to their melancholy. And the land will be filled with Your good ways in order to bestow goodness in all possible ways.*

This was the way he taught holiness from when he was very young. Whether it was related to Torah or any of the other pathways of God that he would teach, he would set aside his own honor and decide to teach whatever would benefit others, children or adults, drawing from the reservoir of Torah that he merited, and by which he enabled the public to gain merit. He never ceased teaching those who lived in his town, after morning prayers, daily, something about the weekly Torah reading. All who entered the study hall exited full of his words, each one retaining according his ability. Those who loved learning the plain meaning of the text absorbed his deep understanding of the plain meaning of Scripture. And those who expounded commentaries were able to expound based on what they heard him say in his concise statements. All who heard him rejoiced in the sweetness of his words which were so clear it was as if he were reciting the section before very young children learning from their teacher. Fulfilling this *mitzva* was so dear to him that he would finish his prayers and would rush off to the study hall while the rest of the congregation were still praying, young and old. And he expressed perfect joy when he taught something that required teaching, something that few had learned. And this Torah, all of it was equal in value, and beneficial to all. And his heart/mind would rejoice in it. Let the humble learn from his ways[46].

---

45 Aram.: *l'k'tzeeree u-m'eeree* (see *Rosh Ha-shanna* 16a and *N'darim* 49b)

46 Paraphrasing *T'hillim* 25:9

And it's understood that his heart/mind witnessed much wisdom[47], and he enlarged the Torah[48] and contributed effort. As a result of his many actions, his wisdom was expressed[49] in every field of knowledge, to create novel understandings of Torah in *G'mara*, RaSh"Y's commentary and *Tosafote* that are sweeter than honey (and this is despite that in the fragments that his students recorded they wrote that he wasn't comfortable authoring a book that wasn't related to applied *Halakha*). And he responded generously, from his youth until his old age, to all of the great rabbis of our nation and the geniuses of our time, and they were all accepted as applied *Halakha*. (And it's due to our sins that most of the responsa that he stored away were destroyed by fire—due to our sins—in the fire that was sent from heaven on Wednesday, the 14th of Iyar in the year 5575, and nearly half the city was burned—may the Merciful save us—and his home was among those that the fire claimed. And only his teaching hall[50]—God's mercies flamed within the fire that consumed around it and at its edges—and it remained, like a brand saved from the fire[51]. And the books also survived—blessed be He who performed a miracle in this place. However, many of them remained with the students who were copying them for themselves, and many are scattered around the world[52]. May God assist those who collect and compile them.)

---

47 Paraphrasing *Kohelet* 1:16

48 Paraphrasing *Y'shaya* 42:21

49 Heb.: *chokh-ma-toe nit-ka-yeh-met*, paraphrasing *Ahvote* 3:11: "Anyone whose fear of sin has priority over his wisdom, his wisdom will endure."

50 The Volozhin Yeshiva

51 Paraphrasing *Z'kharya* 3:2

52 Presumably with Rav Chayyim's respondents.

And though my father (OBM) intended to gather them, he never, however, directed me to publish any of them. It's only this that he explicitly commanded me about, with fearsome words, issued from his lips on the day he ascended to the heavens: to use all my abilities to preserve his teaching hall so that Torah shouldn't disappear (heaven forefend). And also regarding these essays he instructed me, from the depths of his heart, that I shouldn't change any of his words, to leave them as written, and I was commanded to publish them quickly.

Bring a book and observe his modesty, for he set aside his own opinions in favor of the great texts, and played himself down so as to set down his understanding in these few concise essays, lowly in comparison to his very high worth. It's well known that God's word came to Eliyahu the pious[53] (may his soul-*Neshama* rest in Eden), and the concealed aspects of wisdom were revealed to him—his illuminating words have already been published. And he had command of ten times[54] more of the recondite texts, as my father the genius (OBM—may his soul-*Neshama* rest in Eden) described at length in his introduction to the *Sifra D'tznee-oota.* (And my father, the genius (OBM) told me that all of our teacher Eliyahu's writings on the recondite aspects of Torah were written before he reached the age of forty, for then he received an additional measure of *Beena*[55] and no longer had the time to record all that was revealed to him.) And my father (OBM) collected the finely refined flour from all of his teacher's (OBM) treasure houses[56], so

53 The Vilna Gaon

54 Paraphrasing *Shmuel Bet 19:44*

55 Ref.: Ahvote 5:25

56 Reb Itzele seems to make a play on words here, using the phrase *beit n'kha-ote* (perfumery) while perhaps implying *beit n'khote* (treasure house)

as to understand, based on his own efforts, the hints to the hidden meanings of the Ari's (OBM) *Derekh Etz Chayyim*[57], and they were engraved on the most immediately accessible parts of his heart/mind. In his humility, he spread and inserted the tiniest amount into these essays. And he created an opening the size of the eye of a needle, which for one whose heart is open, is an entrance to a great hall. With the breadth of his understanding he engraved and quarried[58] these words. He weighed them, converted them and refined them towards the way of Torah and service and fear/awe of God, so as to teach the path on which they should walk and what they should do. All along his soul-*Neffesh* desired to provide merit for the masses by creating something suitable for all people. Truthfully, his soul-*Neffesh*'s mission was still single-minded when it ascended to the heavens.[59]

And one who didn't observe his strength and humility on the day when he was taken from us, never observed courage and humility. From the time of the morning prayers until his soul-*Neshama* departed for the heavens, each and every hour he renewed his strength. One minute he would reduce his physical body with his words, when he felt it would return to the dust, to the earth where it originated, and his face was dark like a raven. And in the next moment gather his strength in attachment, and his face would shine like the light of

---

57 This is the book that is now known as the *Etz Chayyim.*

58 Heb.: *cha-kahk v'cha-tzahv*—Reb Itzele here uses descriptors from the meditative text *Sefer Y'tzeera*

59 In this paragraph Reb Itzele seems to say that Rav Chayyim wrote the *Neffesh Ha-chayyim* for two purposes: to help the masses learn how to behave, and also to provide an acceptable entrance to the recondite aspects of Torah for those whose hearts are open to that potential.

the living King, to connect his soul-*Neffesh* with his soul-*Ruakh*, so that he would return to God-*Elohi"m* in purity, until his soul-*Ruakh* and soul-*Neshama* was gathered back to Him (blessed be His name) with a kiss, and they were bound up with the *tz'rore ha-chayyim* with God-*H'*.

Before God-*Elohi"m* took him, on that same day he pulled himself together[60] and set his face with a quiet voice, a speaking soul-*Ruakh*[61], arising from a living soul-*Neshama*. And this is what he (OBM) said: "*Ahf B'ree*[62] will make an effort to publish the essays quickly. And you, my son, know that although I did not merit to learn[63], heaven rewarded me to teach others, and to cause involvement with Torah to persist. Truly, even if I didn't merit holding God in fear/awe[*] perhaps heaven will consider me meritorious enough to accept my words in these essays, so that they cause fear/awe of God and unsullied service to take root in the hearts/minds of those upright hearts/minds who seek God's ways[64]." These are the words that he spoke to me.

---

60 Heb.: *ahz-eer gahrmei*—This phrase is difficult to translate. Reb Itzele seems to have used an initial *alef* preceding an Aramic word as a reflexive indicator—doing something to oneself. *Z'eer* could be translated as compact, draw together, or young. So the first word of the phrase could mean "caused himself to be compacted", or "rejuvenated". *Gahrmei* could be translated as "his bones" or "himself". So I've translated itself as "pulled himself together". It might also have been translated as "revived himself". I've guessed as to its meaning.

61 Paraphrasing Onkeloos's translation of *neffesh chaya* in *B'reisheet* 2:7

62 Heb.: *ahf bree*—The name of the angel responsible for rain. Rav Chayyim refers to his son by this most affectionate name.

63 Rav Chayyim, though a truly great scholar, considered his level of knowledge to be small.

64 Paraphrasing *Divrei Ha-yamim 1 16:10*

Annotation: *And anyone who knew that because of his humility he still considered himself to be conceited, won't be surprised that he perceived himself as not understanding fear/awe of God-*H'*. This is per our sages (OBM) statement (*B'rakhote *33b): "Is fear/awe*[65] *an insignificant small matter? ... Yes! For Moshe Rabbeinu it was an insignificant matter. This is analogous to the case of someone from whom a large utensil is demanded, and he has it available. For him the large utensil is considered to be just like a small one. But if a small utensil is demanded from someone who doesn't have one, even that small utensil is considered to be like a large one." And the situation is that someone who is greatly humble doesn't perceive his humility. On the contrary, he considers himself conceited, and he considers his peers to be humble. And Moshe Rabbeinu, who was more humble than any other person, it's certain that he considered himself to be conceited while considering all the rest of Israel, in comparison, to be humble. And this [verse]*[66] *is in the context of Moshe who was exceedingly humble and considered Israel to be humble. He stated that for them fear/awe was an insignificant matter, for it is the effect of humility, as they (OBM) stated "what wisdom accomplished... humility accomplished; it's the result of a precursor". It was only in reference to himself that he perceived fear/awe as a significant matter, because he perceived himself as conceited still. And maybe it's for that reason that the* G'mara *brings the second metaphor about one who lacks even a small utensil, so as to expound the word in the text "from you"*[67].

---

65 Our editions of *B'rakhote* have "Is fear/awe *of heaven* an insignificant matter?"

66 The perspective of the cited verse in *D'varim* 10:12

67 Heb.: *mei-eemkha*

After hearing these words, wouldn't anyone who is in fear/awe of God cry tears, when these words that came from the heart/mind pierce the heart/ mind, as the final product of humility and awe/fear of God for life[68]? And if the person is great in Torah, and his effort was in Torah, and all his life he gave pleasure to his Former, it will seem to him as if he has no awe/fear of God. And if he said that, what could we say[69] about ourselves?

And I am at fault that I haven't rushed to fulfill my father's words, to quickly do what he commanded me.

(And I have been punished two-fold via my children for this mortal sin. First, the following year, on the fourteenth of Sivan 5582, the day that my father (OBM) passed away, a son was born to me, and I entered him into the covenant via circumcision. He was named after the *Neffesh Ha-chayyim.* And he is no longer with us for God-*Elohi"m* took him on the third day after his circumcision. And this year, on the fifth of Kislev, on the holy Shabbat, *parsha va-yeitzei,* my splendor left me[70], an eight-year old son, handsome, lovely and beloved. He already knew how to give and take about *G'mara* like an adult: Simkha Naftali Hertz[71]. "God is righteous, for his words I have disobeyed."[72] "And nevertheless, He is merciful and is forgiving of iniquity."[73] "And they will not continue to agonize any longer."[74])

---

68 Heb.: *v'yir-aht hashem l'chayyim*—This is what Reb Itzele entitled this collection of essays. It might be translated variously as "Chayyim's fear/awe of God" (where "Chayyim" refers to his father), "Fear/awe of God to Enable Life" or "Fear/awe of God for the Living".

69 Paraphrasing *B'rakhote* 31a

70 Paraphrasing *Eikha* 1:6

71 His name

72 *Eikha* 1:18

73 *T'hillim* 78:38

74 *Yirmiya* 31:11

However, it was not my own idea, but rather a result of circumstance, caused as a result of our many sins. For from the day that the crown was caused to ascend[75] we've no longer observed good, and I was left stunned, broken hearted, left behind and straggling. And I didn't find an instant in which I was free from heaven's labor, that I was commanded regarding his house of teaching[76], as everyone knows. And to decide how to allocate my effort, I considered my father's (OBM) desires, that perhaps it wouldn't be acceptable to him to defer the great cause of enabling the many to be involved with Torah over this commandment.

And I also intended to compile some of his texts about his commentaries on *Ahvote* that he'd deliver each week on Shabbat, that I titled (referring to his name) as soul-*Ruakh Chayyim*, in that they are full of the soul-*Ruakh* of advice, and the soul-*Ruakh* of understanding and knowledge, and they are life[77] to those who encounter them.

And I also intended to assemble his responsa and to organize them, and to entitle them soul-*Nishmaht Chayyim*, for with his words he would provide soul-*Neshama* and deep understanding[78] to those capable of understanding, as per the verse (*Ee-yove* 26:4): "Whose breath issued from you?" (And I entitled these essays *Neffesh Ha-chayyim*, as my father (OBM) signed his responsa and all his letters.) But there was no space left unoccupied[79] due to the many responsibilities and tasks that were incumbent upon me (may God expand them). And for those reasons I was delayed until now. And if I erred, may God atone. (And

75 Probably meaning the day of his father's passing.

76 The Volozhiner yeshiva

77 Heb.: *chayyim*

78 Heb.: *t'voona*

79 Paraphrasing *Tikkoonei Zohar* 70

two great geniuses who are in the holy congregation of Volozhin—may God-*Elohi"m* shield them—offered me their opinions that they agreed with me that I shouldn't delay what my respected father—the genius (may he rest in Eden)—wanted done first until after assembling the responsa that were scattered around the world.)

And now, after heaven aroused me to do the will of my righteous and respected father (the genius—may he rest in Eden), may it be Your will to attract the desire of those who fear/awe God, who yearn for the Torah of life[80]. May God find it pleasant to confirm our handiwork[81] so as to bring to light what was until now only in manuscripts. May heaven strengthen the powers (with heaven's assistance) of the very fine rabbi, the one who seeks the concealed aspects of fear/awe of God, the crown of Torah, our teacher Avraham Simkha (may he live on), who toiled and labored in righteousness for life[82] involved in the publication of these essays. And may God treat in a goodly way those who, out of their goodness, contributed to help. And may those who physically assisted receive blessing from God. And may the merit of my respected father, the genius (may his memory be a blessing in the life of the world-to-come) assist all those who carry out his goodly will, so as to bring them a blessing of good and still more good.

And you, the House of Israel, go out and witness the straight path to which a person should cleave. Pay attention to everything stated in the *Yir'aht Ha-shem L'chayyim*, for they are worthy of the one who stated them, and to whom they were stated. May it be Your will that these words

80 Alternately: who yearn for Chayyim's Torah
81 Paraphrasing *T'hillim* 90:17
82 Alternately: in righteousness for Chayyim

be considered significant among those who fear/awe God, to influence the hearts of our brothers, the House of Israel, towards a Torah of compassion, and to total service, and a high level of prayer, and to righteous activity resulting in life, for he devoted his soul-*Neffesh* during his lifetime to Torah and service. May anyone who desires life be strengthened in Torah and service with all their hearts and souls-*Neffesh*, to arouse the goodly treasure in soulful[83] compassion and mercy upon the souls-*Neffesh* of the House of Israel (may they live on), and may the soul-*Neffesh* receive a response.

Yitzkhak, the son of the genius, the author,
our teacher, the Rav Chayyim (may his memory
be a blessing in the world-to-come)
from Volozhin

83 Heb.: *n'feesheen*

Gate 1

CHAPTER 1

It is written (*B'reisheet* 1:27): "God-*Elohi"m*[84] [thus] created man with His *tzellem*[85]; with the *tzellem* of God-*Elohi"m*, He created him."[86] And it is also written (*B'reisheet* 9:6): "... for with the *tzellem* of God-*Elohi"m* He made man."

This is a reference to the deep inner meaning of *tzellem*, it being one of the loftiest concepts in creation, containing within it most of the *Zohar*'s innermost secrets. That said, herein we will address the term *tzellem* in the manner of the early plain-text commentators on the verse "Let us make man with our *tzellem* and per our *d'moot*" (*B'reisheet* 1:26).

The use of the words *tzellem*[87] and *d'moot*[88] are not per their simple meanings, for it is explicitly written (*Y'shaya* 40:18): "And what likeness will you compare unto Him." Rather, their meanings imply a similarity in

---

84 While the English translation of all these names is usually rendered simply as "God," in Hebrew God has many names, each of which denotes a specific Godly attribute or way of manifesting in the world. We will therefore include the Hebrew form of the Name, for later in the text the author will address the meanings of a few specific Names.

85 Heb.: *b'tzalmo*, often translated as "in His image". For the moment we leave it untranslated, as Rav Chayyim immediately addresses its meaning.

86 Translations of text from the Tanakh are rendered by the translator with assistance from a range of popular English language translations including Rabbi Aryeh Kaplan's "The Living Torah" (Maznaim, New York/Jerusalem, 1981), "The Stone Edition" (Mesorah Publications, Brooklyn 1998), the Jewish Publication Society (Philadelphia, 2003), and the Soncino Books of the Bible (Rev. Dr. A. Cohen, editor—The Soncino Press, London, 1949)

87 We translate *tzellem* here simply as "image", though it has a much more complex and technical definition.

88 We translate *d'moot as* "likeness".

some feature, as in (*T'hillim* 102:7): "I am like a desert pelican." It's not that he was given wings and a beak, and not that his physical appearance was transformed into a pelican, but rather that he is described in that instance by his actions, that he wandered from place to place like the pelican in the desert (a lone bird that flies from place to place). This is per the early plain-text commentators (OBM).

And so this is what is meant by *tzellem*: that the one resembles the other in some fashion.

CHAPTER 2

However, to understand why He specifically stated "in the image of God-*Elohi"m*" and not some other name, it is because the meaning of the name *Elohi"m* is well understood, that it implies that He (blessed be His name) is the Master of All Powers, as explained in the *Toor, Orakh Chayyim, siman* 5[89].

The matter of why He (blessed be He) is called "Master of All Powers," is because the attributes of the Holy One (blessed be He) are not like those of flesh and blood. For man, when he builds a structure (for example: of wood), the builder doesn't create and materialize the wood from his own powers; rather, he takes pre-existing lumber and organizes it into a structure. After he completes arranging it according to his will, if he ceases his efforts and departs, the structure still persists.

89 The "*Toor*" (formally known as the *Arba-ah Toorim*), authored by Rabbi Yaakov ben Asher, is an early code of Jewish Law.

In contrast, He (blessed be His name), as during the time when all of the worlds were created[90], created and materialized them ex nihilo, with His infinite powers. So it continues since then, every day and truly every moment: all of the powers that make them exist, structure them and sustain them are dependent only on what He (blessed be He) impresses upon them via His will at each moment, via the power and the influence of newly created light[91]. And if He (blessed be He) removed the

---

90 When the author speaks of worlds, he uses the context described by Rabbi Yitzkhak Luria (who is referred to as the *Ari Ha-kadosh* or *Ariza"l).* The Ariza"l describes four accessible worlds, one above (so to speak) the other, through which God's influence flows. This lowest physical world is referred to as the World of Action (Heb.: *olahm ha-ahseeya).* Above this world is the World of Formation (Heb.: *olahm ha-y'tzeera*). Above that is the World of Creation (Heb.: *olahm ha-breeya*) and above that is the World of Emanation (Heb.: *olahm ha-ahtzeeloot*). What is above/before the World of Emanation is generally inaccessible and is considered to be beyond discussion, except in rare and constrained circumstances.

91 Rav Chayyim, in accordance with the convention of the Ariza"l, uses the word "light" (Heb.: *ore*). In explanation, Rabbi Yosef Chayyim of Baghdad (also known as the Ben Ish Chai), in the second forward to his book *Da-at U-t'voona* states: "However, it being true that you'll find that in the books of the Kabbalists that they assign the name 'light' to the activities of the *Ein Sofe* and the *s'feerote,* it is not because they are really light. Rather it's only because of the limitation of our intellect while it is still clothed in the physicality of the body to grasp the true nature and the essence of the spiritual, and so it is impossible to describe spiritual actions as they are, so as to assign them a sufficiently descriptive name; for that reason they assigned it the name 'light', for it is the most precious of the perceivable." Also, the *g'matria* (the sum of the number values of the letters) of the word *Ore* (light) is the same as *Ein Sof* ("Without End", a way we refer to the One infinite source of all creation).

power of His influence for even one moment, in that moment everything would revert to nothingness and chaos.

And as the Notables of the Great Assembly[92] canonized in the blessing of "forms the light"[93]: "He constantly renews the act of Creation." [*] The specific term used is "constantly[94]", to denote every instant and moment, and the proof is explained in what is written (*T'hillim* 136:7): "to the One who actualizes the great luminaries." It wasn't written as "actualized" but rather as "actualizes."

Annotation: *Even if the renewal is not apparent to the eye. Truly, the four supernal elements, they who are the ancient roots, the precursors of all—as is written in the* Zohar *(*Va-eira *23b) that they are the root of all the events associated with creation and their inner aspect—and they are the four letters of the YHV"H (blessed be He). Their combining and assembling at every moment and instant in their root of roots is not perceived at all, and He (blessed be His name) renews them in every instant according to His will.*

And the matter of their combining in every instant, they are the one-thousand and eighty permutations of the Name (blessed be He), according to the variation in their punctuation[95] during the one-thousand and eighty divisions of the

92 Heb.: *ahn-shei k'nesset ha-g'doe-la*

93 Heb.: *yotzeir ore*

94 Heb.: *ta-meed*

95 Heb.: *n'koo-doe-tei-hem.* Hebrew words have four parts: the letters themselves (*o-tee-yote*), their punctuation (*n'koo-dote*), their trup (*ta-ahmim*), and the crowns upon select letters (*tahgim*). In the Torah scroll, only the letters and crowns are included in the written text; the punctuation and trup are not.

hour[96]*. And they vary even more so each hour to still other permutations, and also that the quality of the day is not equivalent to the quality of the night, no day resembles the one before or after it in any way. That is why it is specifically written "who actualizes... the event of creation."*

And this is why He (blessed be His name) is called "the God-*Elohi"m*", Master of all powers [*]. All powers found in any of the worlds—every one of them—He (blessed be His name) is Master over their power. He impresses within them the power and constrained strength during every moment, and they are constantly dependent upon Him to change and organize them according to His (blessed be He) will.

Annotation: *Even so, it is a name that is shared with all those who wield power in the world, and all the ministers of the upper and lower worlds are called* "elohim"*, as is written in* T'hillim *96:5,* "elohei ha-ah-mim"[97]*, "for all the nations shall go each in the name of their* elohim*"* (Mee-kha *4:5). And also refer to the* Zohar (Va-yikra *8a and in the section for* Ba-lahk *208b), in the context of* "va-ya-vo elohim" *as is written in the context of Avi-meh-lekh and La-vahn and Bil-ahm, where it means "his minister". For they are appointed over them to supervise them, and the same is true with judges in this world who are called* "elohim"*, and in* Savvah[98] *(96:1): "and the name is one of their alternative names". Refer there [to the* Zohar*, for more detail].*

96 For halakhic purposes, the hour is split into 1080 parts called *cha-la-kim.*

97 Those wielding power among the nations

98 Part of the *Zohar*

Truly, none of them have intrinsic power, only what was made permanent within them by Him (blessed be He), so that they should have the power and the constrained strength[99] *to be rulers... . Therefore He (blessed be His name) is called* "Eloh"ei ha-elohim"[100] (T'hillim *136:2), and so it also written* (Sh'mote *18:11): "For God-*YHV"H *is greater than all the* elohim", *"bow before Him all the* elohim" (T'hillim *97:7), and the pagans too call Him (blessed be He) the* "Elohi"m *of the* elohim" (Daniel *2:47).*

Therefore they are called "other elohim"[101]*, as if to say that they have no intrinsic power on their own, only the power from the one who is above him. And the one who is above him also draws his power from the power above him, until the Master of the true power for them all, He (blessed be His name).*

And therefore it says (Yirmiya *10:10) "and* God-YHV"H *is the true* Elohi"m", *that He is the true Master of all their power, that all of them receive their power from Him (blessed be His name), as is written* (M'la-khim Alef *18:39) "And they prostrated themselves on their faces and declared* YHV"H *is the* Elohi"m".

99 Heb.: *ko-akh u'g'voora*

100 Lit: the *Elohi"m* of the *elohim*

101 Heb.: *eh-lo-him ah-khei-rim*

CHAPTER 3

According to this model, He (blessed be He), as it were[102], created man and appointed him to rule over the multitude of powers and numberless worlds, and assigned them to him so that he should be their spokesman and govern them via all the minute details of his actions, speech, thoughts,[103] and the larger scale aspects of his behavior[104], whether for good, or (heaven forefend) for the opposite.

For via his positive actions, speech and thoughts he fulfills and invests strength in a number of supernal and holy powers and worlds, and adds holiness and light to them, as is written (*Y'shaya* 51:16): "and I will place my words in your mouth... to plant the heavens and lay the foundations of the earth." And in the words of the sages: (*B'rakhote* 64a): "Call them 'your builders'[105] rather than 'your sons'[106]" for they arrange the lofty worlds as a builder arranges his structure and invests it with great strength.

And the opposite (heaven forefend) [is also true, that] via his negative actions, speech or thoughts he destroys (may the Merciful save us) a number of powers, and the supernal, holy worlds without number and measure, as is written (*Y'shaya* 49:17): "your destroyers

---

102 Heb.: *ki'v'ya-khol.* This word is used when we attempt to explain God's actions in a human context, and realize our descriptive limitations.

103 Rav Chayyim here describes three ways that man affects the worlds. From lower to higher they are: actions, speech and thoughts. He addresses each of them in some detail in chapters 12 through 14. As Rav Chayyim discusses in chapter 15, they correspond to the inner aspects of soul-*Neffesh*, soul-*Ruakh* and soul-*Neshama.*

104 Heb.: *v'khol sidrei hanha-go-tahv*

105 Heb.: *bo-nie-yikh*

106 Heb.: *ba-nie-yikh*

and those who lay waste to you shall go forth from you," or darken or lessen their light and holiness, and add power to their opposites in the realms of impurity (may the Merciful save us).

This is what is meant by (*B'reisheet* 1:27): "And God-*Elohi"m* created man with His image. In the image of God-*Elohi"m*...", and (*B'reisheet* 9:6) "for God-*Elohi"m* made man..."—for just as He (blessed be His name) is the *Elohi"m,* Master of the powers found in the totality of all the worlds, and organizes and governs them each instant per His will, so too did His (blessed be He) will rule that man should be the enabler and disabler[107] of many multitudes of powers and worlds via all of the detailed patterns of his large scale behavior, in every situation, literally in every instant and moment, according to his supernal root[108], which includes his actions, speech and thought, as if he too is the master of their power, as it were.

And the sages said in *Ei-kha Rabba*[109] (1:33, on verse 1:6): "Rabbi Azarya said in the name of Rabbi Yehuda the son of Rabbee Seemon: 'When Israel performs God's will, the Almighty's power increases, as is written (*T'hillim* 60:14): "through God-*Elohi"m* we will make valor[110]." And when Israel doesn't perform God's will, it is as if they weaken the great power of heaven, as is written (*D'varim* 32:18): "Rock, your children weaken You" '."

107 Heb.: *ha-po-tei-ahkh v'ha-so-geir*—literally the "opener and closer"

108 Rav Chayyim here mentions in passing that we are not only our physical bodies: we have a root in the upper worlds. He elaborates on this theme in the following chapters.

109 Sources with the term "Rabba" in their title are Midrashic.

110 Heb.: *ba-Elohi"m na-ah-seh cha-yeel*

And in a few citations in the holy *Zohar* we find that the sins of man cause blemishes above, and similarly the opposite occurs too, as we mentioned. And this is what the Torah says (*T'hillim* 68:35): "Give strength to God-*Elohi"m*[111]." And in the *Zohar*, at the beginning of *Parshat Bo* (32b) it says: "(*Eeyove* 1:6) '...And it was the day and they came... to stand before God'—When they want to denounce Israel's actions, it is God they certainly denounce, because when Israel performs improper actions it is as if they weaken God's power, and when they perform proper actions they add force and power to the Holy One (blessed be He). And regarding this it is written 'Give strength to God-*Elohi"m*'. In what way? Via proper actions."

This is why it says: 'to God-*Elohi"m*', and similarly: 'through God-*Elohi"m* we will make valor', because its definition is 'Master of all powers'.

CHAPTER 4

And this is the law of man—each person in Israel should not say in his heart/mind (heaven forefend): "what am I, what power do I have to effect anything in the world via my lowly actions?"

Truthfully, one should understand and know and fix in his heart/mind's[112] thoughts, that every detail of his actions, speech and thoughts, in each instant and moment, are not for naught (heaven forefend). And how many are his actions and how great and exalted,

---

111 Heb.: *t'noo ohz leh-eh-lo-hi"m*

112 Heb.: *leebo.* Literally: his heart, but with the connotation of having both cognitive and emotional functions, and so we render it as heart/mind.

that each one rises according to its root[113], to effect its result at the loftiest heights, in the worlds and highest levels of the heavenly lights[114] [*].

Annotation: *And it's likely that this too is included in their (OBM) intention in* Ahvote *(2:1) "know what is above you[115]", as if to say that your eyes don't see the awesome situations caused by your actions. However, know reliably that all that is caused above in the higher worlds, highest of the highest, all is "from you", according to inclination of your actions—by their commands[116] they go and come[117].*

And verily, for the wise man who understands the veracity of this, his heart/mind will shiver within him with fear and trembling when he regards his no-good actions (heaven forefend), whence they arrive to ruin and destroy with a minor sin (heaven forefend) much more than Nebuchadnezzar and Titus[118].

For surely Nebuchadnezzar and Titus, via their actions, didn't cause a single blemish or ruination above, because they have no place or root in the higher worlds that they

---

113 Rav Chayyim states here that each of our actions, spoken words and thoughts has a connection to a "root" located in the upper worlds, and that its effect in the upper worlds is based on that root.

114 Heb.: *ba-o-la-mote v'tzahkh-tza-khote ha-o-rote ha-elyoneem. Tzakh-tza-khote* may refer to the only partially accessible world of *Ah-dahm Kadmone,* which is above the world of *Ahtzeeloot.*

115 Heb.: *meem-kha*

116 Heb.: *pee-hem* . Literally "their mouths".

117 Alluding to *B'midbar* 27:21

118 Nebuchadnezzar and Titus were the generals in charge of the armies that destroyed the first and second Holy Temples respectively.

could affect in any way via their actions[119]. It was only because of *our* sins that the greatness of heaven lessened and weakened (so to speak), God's Temple was defiled (so to speak)—the heavenly Temple—and by way of this, Nebuchadnezzar and Titus were given power to lay waste to the earthly Temple, which is the counterpart of the heavenly Temple. As the sages said (*Kohelet Rabba* 1:43): "pre-milled flour did you mill." After all, our sins ruined the upper dwelling, the lofty holy worlds, while they ruined only the lower dwelling.

And King Dovid (OBM) who prayed (*T'hillim* 74:5): "and it seemed as when men wielded upward their axes in a tree thicket,"—he[120] requested that it be thought of as if he destroyed up there (in the highest heavens); but in truth his actions didn't have any effect there at all, as we discussed above.

The heart/mind of a man who is of the holy nation[121] shall also tremble over this, that in his form he is comprised of all the powers and worlds, all of them, [*] as will be explained (God willing) later on in chapter 6 and in Gate 2 chapter 5, that they [emphatically] are the holy and the heavenly Temple[122]. And man's heart/mind, the body's center, integrates it all, corresponding to the interior of the Holy of Holies, Center of the Settlement, the Foundation Stone, all of

---

119 Rav Chayyim differentiates here between the effects of those individuals who are considered as part of Israel and those who are not.

120 "He" being the enemy.

121 Rav Chayyim makes a more pointed distinction between the spiritual makeup of Israel and those who are not Israel.

122 Rav Chayyim states here that man's form integrates all the powers and worlds, and corresponds directly to the form of the Holy Temple. He emphasizes this point in the following narrative.

which integrate all the roots of holy sources just as it[123] does. And the sages (OBM) hinted at this in the *Mishna,* in the chapter dealing with morning prayers (*B'rakhote* 28a): "intend your heart/mind towards the interior of the Holy of Holies."

In the *Zohar* (*Sh'lakh* 161a, end of page): "Come see that when the Holy One (blessed be He) created man in the world, He designed him according to a lofty and glorious plan, and gave him His power and driving force via his body in which therein rests his heart/mind. By this plan the Holy One (blessed be He) organized the world and made it one body. And the heart/mind that resides in the center, it is the driving force of everything and on it everything depends, and the hall in which resides the interior of the Holy of Holies, wherein is found the *Sh'kheena*[124], the ark cover, the cherubs and the ark. And here is the heart/mind of the entire earth and the world, and from there they are nourished." (Refer to the source for the complete quote.)

This being so, at the moment when a man strays to think in his hearts/minds[125] [plural] a thought that isn't pure, related to adultery (God save us), he introduces a prostitute, the symbol of envy[126] in the house of the heavenly Holy of Holies, dreadful, in the holy, lofty worlds (heaven forefend), and increasing (God save us) the power of impurity and the "other side[127]" in the house of the heavenly Holy of Holies, much more and even more

123 "It" here meaning the heart/mind.

124 The *Sh'kheena* (literally: "The Indwelling"—feminine gender) is God's perceivable manifestation into this world.

125 Echoing *D'varim* 6:5, the first paragraph of the Sh'ma.

126 Heb.: *kin-ah*

127 The term *sitra akh-ra* ("other side") refers to the powers that oppose holiness in the world.

than what the powers of impurity caused by Titus when he installed a prostitute in the interior of the Holy of Holies in the earthly Temple.

And so it is with every sin that a person in Israel inserts into his heart/mind (heaven forefend), an unauthorized fire[128], via expressions of anger or other evil desires (may the Merciful save us), surely it is exactly as the matter about which is written (*Y'shaya* 64:10): "Our Temple of holiness and beauty, where our fathers praised You, became a raging fire," the Merciful One (blessed be His name) save us.

And this is what God said to *Y'khezkel* (43:7): "[this is] my throne's place..., there I will dwell within Israel forever, and no longer will the house of Israel defile My holy name..., in their prostitution..., now they will distance themselves from their prostitution..., ...and I will dwell within them forever."

Annotation: *For the Tabernacle and the Holy Temple integrated all of the powers and worlds, and all the arrangements of holiness, all the buildings and treasuries, upper floors and rooms, and all the holy utensils, all are per an exalted template:* tzellem, d'moot, *model of the holy worlds, and the organization of the components of the Vehicle, they are those that Dovid and Shmuel the seer set in place, "all this in writing from God-*YHV"H*'s hand upon me, having made me understand all the works of the design" (Divrei Ha-yahmim 1 28:19).*

128 Heb.: *eish za-ra* (unauthorized fire) is a reference to Aharon's sons Nahdahv and Ahvihu who died as a result of bringing unauthorized fire (see *Va-yikra* 10:1–3).

And the sages (OBM) said in Chapter Ei-zeh-hu M'ko-mahn (Z'vahkhim *54:2): "why is it written 'and he and Shmuel traveled and settled in Na-yote... in Ra-ma'? What is the matter of the relationship between Na-yote and Ra-ma? It's that they settled in Ra-ma*[129] *and occupied themselves with the world's beauty*[130]*. And what is written in* Tahn-khooma *(at the beginning of* P'koodei*) that it is equal in importance to the creation of the world, and it enumerates there, in order, the general cases that occurred during creation, that they occurred also in the [construction of the] Tabernacle, and therefore the text wrote about B'tzal-el: "and I will fill him [with] the spirit-*Ruakh *of* Elohi"m, *with wisdom, understanding and knowledge" (*Sh'mote *31:3). For with these three items the worlds were created, as is written (*Mishlei *3:19)* "YHV"H *with wisdom founded the earth, established the heavens with understanding, [with knowledge the depths were split]...". And refer to* Zohar *(*P'koodei *221a and 231b) and in* Zohar Cha-dash *(*T'rooma *35c)—refer there at length. And therefore the sages (OBM,* B'ra-khote *55a) stated that B'tzal-el knew*[131] *to refine/combine*[132] *the letters with which the heavens and earth were created.*

And therefore a man from the holy nation, who is also comprised of all the structures and processes of creation, and all the structures and processes of the Vehicle[133]*, the totality of creation, he is also the model and plan of the Tabernacle and the Temple and all its utensils, organized according to the plan of the organs/limbs and components and sinews and all its powers. And therefore the* Zohar

---

129 Literally "a high place". RaSh"Y explained: to determine from the Torah the place for the Holy Temple.

130 Heb.: *noy-o*

131 Heb.: *ya-da*—using the term used for intimate knowledge

132 Heb.: *l'tzareif*

133 Heb.: *merkava*

details the entirety of the plans of the Tabernacle and its utensils, for they are all hinted at in man, a one-to-one correspondence.

For this reason, definitely the focal point of holiness and the Holy Temple, and the appearance in a particular place of the Sh'kheena, *is man. For if he makes himself as holy as is possible by fulfilling all of the commandments (for they are also dependent on their upper roots, in the components of the organs/limbs of the Stature*[134]*, so to speak, of the entirety of all the worlds taken together, and refer to* Zohar T'rooma *162b "and you shall make the Tabernacle... this is the secret of the unity... ",—refer there in depth), then he becomes the actual Holy Temple, and within him is* YHV"H *(blessed be He), as is written* (Yirmiya *7:4):" They [emphatic—three times] are the abode of* YHV"H. *And as they (OBM) said: "and I will dwell within them"– it does not say "among them" but rather "within them."*

And this is what they (OBM) stated (K'toobote *5a): "The handiwork of the righteous is greater than the creation of the heaven and the earth. For about the handiwork of the heaven and the earth it is written* (Y'shaya *48:13) 'Also, My hand has laid the foundation of the earth, and My right hand has measured out the heavens"*[135]*, while regarding the righteous is written* (Sh'mote *15:17): 'With your hands You set up God's-*ADN"Y *Holy Temple*[136]*'." They began with the actions of the righteous and concluded their proof with the Holy Temple, for in truth it is the righteous, as a result of their desirable actions before Him (blessed be He), that they [emphatic] are, in actuality, God's Holy Temple.*

---

134 Heb.: *Shee-oor koma*—the Stature is a description of the structure of creation in a manner that corresponds to the various parts of man's upright form.

135 This verse describes one hand being used.

136 This verse describes both hands being used.

compare 1Cor 3:16-17, 1Cor 6:19, 2Cor 6:16 Eph 2:19-22

*And based on this approach we can address the text (*Sh'mote *25:8)"And they shall make me a Holy Temple... according to all that I have shown you... and so you shall do". And our rabbis (OBM) derived (*Sanhedrin *16:2) "and so you shall do for all generations."*

And according to our method we can say also that it desires to convey: don't think that My focus of intention is the external Holy Temple. Rather, you should know that the whole point of My intention regarding the physical design of the Tabernacle and all its utensils is only to provide a hint for you so that you should see, and then you should do likewise to yourselves, that you should in your actions be completely holy and worthy and ready for My Sh'kheena *to actually settle within you. This is specifically "And they shall make me a Holy Temple and I will dwell within them"; [And regarding the verse] "that all I show you, the plans of the Tabernacle..."—My entire intention is that you should do the same with yourselves.*

*And this is also what He (blessed be His name) said to Solomon after the building of the Holy Temple was completed (*M'la-khim Alef *6:12): "this house that you are building" is only specifically "if you shall keep my commandments... and [then] I shall dwell within my nation Israel".*

And for this reason, when they ruined the inner aspect of the Holy Temple within them, then the external Holy Temple no longer served its purpose and its foundations were destroyed (may the Merciful save us).

And this is what the Name said to Yekhezkel *(43:10-11): "Tell the House of Israel about the Temple, and let them be ashamed of their iniquities..., and if they become ashamed of all that they have done, then make known to them the form of the Temple and its designs, its exits and entrances and all its forms and all of its laws, all its designs and all its teachings, and write them down in front of them, so that they*

> *may safeguard its entire form and all its rules and fulfill them." And this is clear, and is according to his[137] translation: "and if they should be ashamed about all they have done in beholding the form of the Temple and its appearance... ."*

And from this will be understood what is written (*B'reisheet* 2:7): "And God-*Elohi"m* formed man [from] dust..., and blew into his nostrils the soul-*Neshama*[138] of life, and man became a living soul-*Neffesh*." The plain meaning of the text is definitely according to his translation: "and it was within man a speaking soul-*Ruakh*", desiring to convey that when he was just a body, he was still actually dust without any life or movement. And when the soul-*Neshama* of life was blown within him, then he became a living person able to move about and speak. Refer to Nakhmanides'[139] commentary on the Torah.

However, the text does not say "and it was *in* man" but rather "and it was *the* man." For this reason there is room to explain it as we did, that the man with the living soul-*Neshama* that is within him, he becomes a living soul-*Neffesh*[140] for a multitude of worlds without number. For just as all the details of the body and its movements are by the power of the soul-*Neffesh* within him, so too man is the power, the living soul-*Neffesh* for all the higher and lower worlds without limitation, that he drives all of them.

---

137 Onkeloos, the author of the most widely used Aramaic translation of the Torah.

138 Man's soul consists of multiple parts. The *Neffesh* is the lowest part; it animates the body, allowing movement and action. The *Ruakh* is the next higher part; it relates to speaking. The *Neshama* is next higher; it relates to thought. They are rooted in successively higher spiritual worlds. Whenever a term is translated with the generic term "soul" we will also include the specific Hebrew term.

139 Nakhmanides is Rabbi Moshe ben Nakhman (the RaMBa"N).

140 Heb.: n*effesh chayya*

CHAPTER 5

And what arose in the blessed-be-His-name's will was to attach the lower man to the tops of the upper worlds, so that he should drive them.

For it is known in the *Zohar* and the writings of the Ariza"l,[141] in the description of how the worlds unfold one from another and how they are connected, that each world behaves in the arrangement of its matters and all the details of its concerns, according to the inclination of the power of the world above it, that guides it as a soul guides the body. And this pattern is replicated, higher and higher, until He (blessed be His name) is the soul of all of them.

Refer to the *Zohar* (*B'reisheet* 20a): "And all worlds..., above and below, from the heights of the secret of the upper singularity down to the final of all the levels, all of them, this is a garment for that, and that for that... ."

And in the *Idra*[142] (*Zoota* 291b): "And all of the lights grasp each other, this light to that light , and that light to that light, and they radiate one to the other... the light that is revealed is called the "garment of the King," and the light that is within all... ." Refer to the source there.

And the details of the matter are described in the *Etz Chayyim*[143] (*Sha-ar P'nimiyoot V'khitzoniyut, Drush Bet*), and

141 Ariza"l is an acronym signifying Rabbi Yitzkhak Luria, one of the foremost kabbalists of all time.

142 The *Idra* is a portion of the *Zohar*

143 The *Etz Chayyim* was authored by Rabbi Chayyim Vittal, the Ariza"l's primary student and principle compiler of the Ariza"l's teachings. It contains the Ariza"l's teachings.

in the *Pri Etz Chayyim*[144] in the introduction to the *Sha-ar Ha-shabbat* (chapters 7 and 8) and in *Sha-ar Ha-shabbat* (chapter 24), that the exterior of each *Partzoof*[145] and world flows down and clothes itself with the world below it, and becomes its interior and soul-*Neshama.*

And all the worlds are comprised of and split into four[146], as is known. They are: *Ophanim*[147], *Chayyot*[148], the Throne of Glory[149], and Emanation of His holiness[150] (blessed be He).

And the soul of each one is the world that is above it, as is written (*Y'khezkel* 1:19): "And when the *Chayyot* alighted..., the *Ophanim* would rise by their effect, because the soul-*Ruakh* of the *Chayya* is in the *Ophanim*—when they travel, so do they, and when they stop, so do they... ." And the *Chayyot* also are guided by the world of the Throne above them, as the sages (OBM) said that the Throne lifts those who transport it. And in the *Zohar*

---

144 The *Pri Etz Chayyim* is one of the texts written by Rabbi Chayyim Vittal that contains the Ariza"l's teachings related to rituals and holidays.

145 In the Ariza"l's description of the worlds' components, each world is comprised of five *partzoofs,* (faces/aspects/presentations/recognized features) [Heb.: *partzoofim*]. The concise English terms are inadequate so we will use the Hebrew.

146 According to the Ariza"l, there are four worlds that are accessible to human consciousness. This does not limit the possibility of the existence of yet others that are inaccessible. Another set of names for the four worlds (from lower to upper) are Action (Heb.: *Ahseeya*), Formation (*Y'tzeera*), Creation (*B'reeya*) and Emanation (*Ahtzeeloot*).

147 The *Ophanim* (plural, literally "wheels") are spiritual beings in the world of *Ahseeya.*

148 The *Chayyot* (plural, literally "living creatures") are spiritual beings in the world of *Y'tzeera.*

149 The "Throne of Glory" refers to the world of *B'reeya.*

150 The "emanation of His holiness" refers to the world of *Ahtzeeloot.*

Chaddash[151] (*Yitro,* in the description of the Vehicle Event[152], 33a): "the *Chayyot* lift up those who transport it... , and the holy Throne lifts up the *Chayyot.*"

And the living soul-*Neshama* of the Throne is the secret of the supernal root of the entirety of souls-*Neshama* of Israel together-as-a-whole[153], for it is much higher and raised far above even the Throne, for He is the Man above the Throne, as is written there "and on the likeness of the Throne... [*]."

Annotation: *For man's essence is planted above in the root of his soul, and for this reason the body is called "shoe"*[154] *(refer to the* Tikkoonim*) in relation to the Soul-*Neshama. *For only the quality of the heels of the root enter into man's body*[155].

And by way of this will be understood what they (OBM) said in B'reisheet Rabba *chapter 12, and in* Va-yikra

151 *Zohar Chaddash* is part of the *Zohar*

152 Heb.: *Ma'aseh Merkava*—This refers to the first chapter of *Y'khezkel,* one of the two key mystical narratives in the Torah, often translated as "the Account of the Chariot." We translate it here as "the Vehicle Event" because the term "chariot," while evocative, is archaic and doesn't convey the key sense of a *merkava* being a form of transport. We do the same for the *Ma'aseh B'reisheet* (the initial chapters of *B'reisheet*) in referring to it as "the Creation Event."

The Vehicle Event is a description of the structure of the worlds that comprise creation and that are potentially accessible to human consciousness.

153 The collective soul-*Neshama* of Israel. In some texts (e.g., *Tanya*) it is described as being below the Throne, but here Rav Chayyim makes clear that it is the soul-*Neshama* of the Throne, and therefore originates at the level above the Throne, in the world of *Ahtzeeloot.*

154 Heb.: *na-al*

155 Rav Chayyim states clearly that man's essence is the part that is rooted in the upper world, and that the body in this physical world is like a garment for that essential part.

*chapter 9, that the Holy One blessed be He did not desire to interject [the quality of] envy into the Creation Event, and during the first day He created heaven and earth, and during the second the sky, and during the third "send forth vegetation," and so in this manner during the fourth and fifth, and during the sixth he intended to create man. He said: If I create him only from the heavenly [plural] there won't be peace on the earth, and if I create him only from the lower [plural]...; rather, behold, I create him from the heavenly [plural] and the lower [plural], ..."dust from the ground, and breathed into his nostrils a breath" (*B'reisheet *2:7).*

And on the face of it, won't envy dominate now more than if He had created him from the lower [plural] alone? For now there is within him a part from the heavenly [plural] and he is entirely below, with the heavenly part that is within him.

However the situation is, that the man who is as perfect as he should be[156]*, his essential part is planted above in the root of his upper soul-*Neshama, *and it passes via myriad worlds until the other end of it enters into the body of the man below, and this is: "But His own nation remained God's-YHV"H portion; Jacob was the rope of His heritage" (*D'varim *32:9), for his key part is connected to and planted above, part of* YHV"H *actually (as it were), and it flows like rope until it arrives to the body of the man (refer ahead to chapter 17), and all his actions arrive to awaken his upper root, as with the situation of a rope that if you shake its lower end, its upper end's edge also awakens and shakes*[157]*.*

(And a wise man will understand this easily, that it is also the same situation (metaphorically) in the root of things

---

156 Note that Rav Chayyim says this description applies only to a person who has truly perfected himself.

157 Rav Chayyim says that everything a perfected person does flows upward to affect the root of his soul in the upper worlds.

above, according to the secret of the "supernal man"[158]*. Refer to the* Idra Rabba *141:2 in the verse: "And God-*YHV"H/ Elohi"m *formed the man..."* (B'reisheet *2:7) regarding the secret of the "supernal man". And it concluded with: "And all this, why? To exclude and include within it the most hidden of the hidden, to the extreme of all the hidden, that it is written: 'And He breathed into his nostrils a breath [soul-*Neshama*] of life', a soul-*Neshama *upon which the existence of all the upper [plural] and lower [plural] are dependent upon that soul, and are sustained from it [fem.]. "And the man became a living soul-*Neffesh*", to be influenced by and to enter into the rectifications in this manner, and to draw that specific soul-*Neshama *from level to level until the last of all levels, so that soul-*Neshama *would be present in all and flow into/through all", refer there.)*

And this is what is said in the [*Zohar*] *Yitro* (70b) in the matter of the verse: "Front and back they hemmed me in...". "Back"—relative to the Creation Event. And "front"—relative to the Vehicle Event. From the perspective of the body it's "back" relative to the Creation Event. And from the perspective of the supernal source of its life soul-*Neshama* it's "front" relative to the Vehicle Event. And also the soul-*Neshama* of life is the secret of the breath of His mouth (so to speak), as we'll explain with God's help further on in chapter 15, refer there.

Therefore all the worlds are guided by the actions of man, because they, according to their motions, awaken the root of his supernal soul above them that is their living soul-*Neffesh*: when it moves they move, and when it stands still, they stop.

158 For some information regarding the secret of the "supernal man", see the section of the *Idra* that Rav Chayyim cites here.

This is what he said: that when the soul-*Neshama* of life was blown into his nostrils—it being higher than all the worlds and their interiors—then "and the man became a living soul-*Neffesh*"—to the worlds. And our Rabbi Chayyim Vittal (OBM) also wrote the same thing in *Sha-ar Ha-k'doosha*, part 3, *Sha-ar* 2, that man's soul-*Neshama* is the innermost of them all.

CHAPTER 6

However, the matter still requires explanation, for he (OBM), in his holiness, spoke in his concise manner as was his manner in all of his holy writings relating to the hidden aspects of Torah, as he himself wrote in his introduction there, that he reveals a hand's breadth and conceals a thousand cubits. Its meaning is not literal per his (OBM) words there, that man is actually the soul-*Neffesh* of the worlds, as the soul-*Neffesh* is placed and attached inside man's body, so that anything the soul-*Neffesh* does is only via the vessel of the body, so that in that specific moment the body too does it—this is absolutely impossible [*].

Annotation: *And also according to this it would be necessary, that at the moment we say the* K'doosha[159] *in the lower world, obviously at the same moment the angels also would say* K'doosha *in the heavens with us, as one. And our sages (OBM) say in the chapter of* Gid Ha-na-sheh *(*Choolin *91:2) that the attending angels*[160] *don't utter Song above*

159 Heb.: The part of the prayer service that includes the verses from *Y'shaya* 6:3: "And one would call to another and say: holy, holy, holy…".

160 Heb.: *mahl-ah-khei ha-sha-reit*

until Israel [says it] below, as it says Eeyove *38:7): "When the morning stars sing together...", and continued "and all the angels of God-*Elohi"m *shout". And the phrasing of "and they continued and they shouted", its meaning is that they don't begin in any way to sanctify their Former until Israel finishes their threefold sanctification below. And the Notables of the Great Assembly arranged it in the same way in the blessing of the Holiness of the Name "Thou art holy"*[161] *... and afterwards "and holy ones each day praise Thee." Also from the phrasing of the* Zohar (parshat T'rooma *129b, top, and there 164b, top) apparently to indicate that the angels sanctify their Sanctification with us as one, because their Sanctification occurs immediately after the finish of our utterance, so it is essentially said as one.*

So the essential point of the matter, is that He (blessed be His name), after He created all the worlds, created man, last of all creations, an amazing creation, the final integrating power for all the camps, that included in him all of the highest levels of amazing lights, and worlds, and lofty palaces that preceded him, and every pattern of lofty honor according to the design of the parts of the Vehicle [*], and all the detailed powers found in all the upper and lower worlds. All of them gave him power and a part of their essence during his assembly, and were integrated into him in a number of the details of the powers that are within him.

As they said in the *Zohar* (*Yitro* 75b): "When the Holy One (blessed be He) created man, he arranged within him all of the likenesses of the heavenly secrets of the supernal world, and all the likeness of the lower secrets of the lower world, and all of them are engraved in man, for

161 Heb.: *ah-ta kadosh*

he stands in the image of God-*Elohi"m.*" Refer there [for more detail].

And in *parshat Tazria* (48a): "We learn that once man was created... ." And in the beginning of *parshat B'midbar*: "Rabbi Abba began: 'And God-*Elohi"m* created man with His image'—Come see...". And in the *Idra Rabba* (135a): "Like the appearance of man... ." And there on page 141a at the end: "the likeness that includes all of the likenesses... ." And in the *Raa-ya M'hemna*[162] in *parshat Pinkhas* (238b) and so they said in this language more at length in the *Tikkoonei Zohar Chaddash* (89a), see the reference there. And in the *Zohar Chaddash Yitro* in the Vehicle Event (32c): "Man's likeness is that likeness that includes all the likenesses... ." And there on page 33a (top). And there in *Shir Ha-shirrim* (58b): "And God-*Elohi"m* said: We will make man in Our image... ." (Research all the citations we mentioned well.) And see the *Etz Chayyim, Sha-ar Ha-tzellem* (chapter 1), and in the *Likutei Torah*[163], *parshat Teesa* and in *parshat Ha-ah-zeenu*

And this is all of man, that every specific power in him corresponds to one world and a specific power from the Stature. The Stature is the most general description of the powers and worlds, organized (as it were) based on the pattern of man's upright form, as will be explained (God willing) in Gate 2, chapter 5.

Annotation: *And this was before the sin. He was comprised only of all the worlds and powers of holiness alone, and not from the powers of evil. However, after the sin, the powers of*

162 The *Raa-ya M'hemna* ("Faithful Shepherd") is a part of the *Zohar.*

163 The *Likutei Torah V'Ta-ahmei Ha-Mitzvot* was written by Rabbi Chayyim Vittal and contains (along with the *Etz Chayyim* and the Eight Gates) some of the Ariza"l's key teachings.

impurity and evil were also integrated and mixed into him. And as a result, they were also mixed by this into the worlds, based on the fact that he is comprised of and integrates them all, and they are aroused and change according to the inclination of his actions; this is the matter of the Tree of the Knowing Good and Evil.

And the situation is that before the sin, he certainly had the absolute freedom of choice to incline himself towards anything he desired, to do good or the opposite (heaven forefend), for this was the primary intention of the entirety of creation, and also [we can confirm that this is so], for later he sinned.

However, it's not that the matter of his choice was the result of the powers of evil being an internal part of him, for he was a completely righteous[164] *person, comprised only of the structures and processes of the powers of holiness alone, and all of his interactions were totally righteous, holy and refined, absolute good, without any admixture or inclination to the opposite side in any way; the powers of evil stood off to the side and were independent, external to him.*

And he had the freedom of choice to engage with the powers of evil (heaven forefend), just as man has the freedom of choice to enter in the midst of the fire. Therefore when the other side desired to cause him to sin, the serpent had to come from the outside to seduce. It's not like it is now, that the urge that seduces the person is within the person himself, and makes it appear to the person as if he himself, he is the one who desires and lusts to do the iniquity, and not that another outside himself seduces him.

And when he sins because he is lured by the other side's seduction, then the powers of evil are actually mixed into him, and so too within the worlds. This is the Tree of Knowing Good and Evil—that they, the good and the evil, became

---

164 Heb.: *ya-shar*

attached and mixed within him and the worlds, one actually within the other, because the definition of "knowledge"[165] *is attachment*[166]*, as is known.*

And the matter is clear to one who understands the Etz Chayyim, sha-ar Kleepaht Noga[167] *(chapter 2), however there he was very concise. Refer carefully in* Gilgoolim[168] *(chapter1), and what our rabbis (OBM) stated (*Shabbat *146a): "When the serpent came upon Eve, it injected her with pollution", wishing to convey "actually within her".*

From then on this caused a great blending in his behavior, that all of a person's actions are [emphatic] mixed and with very many variations, at one moment good and at another evil; it continuously changes from good to evil and from evil to good.

And even a good action, it's almost impossible, for most of the world, that it should be completely holy, pure, and completely spotless, without any inclination to a turning away or frivolous indirect thought. So too the opposite, in relation to an action that's not good, sometimes it also has mixed into it some thought for good related in its conception.

*And even the absolutely righteous person, who all his days never did any action that's not good, who never had a frivolous conversation that wasn't good (heaven forefend), even so it's almost impossible that his good actions, in themselves, all his life, will all be completely in genuine perfection, and that there shouldn't be in at least one of them any deficiency or blemish at all. And what the text stated (*Kohelet *7:20): "For man, there is no righteous person on earth who is so wholly righteous that he does good and does not sin", intending to convey that it's impossible*

---

165 Heb.: *da-aht*

166 Heb.: *hit-khab-root*

167 Glowing husks

168 *Sha-ar Ha-gilgoolim*, of the Ariza"l,

that there won't be, in some manner, a minimal deficiency in the good action itself that he does, because the definition of "sin" is "deficiency".

*For that reason, when the person is brought to judgment before Him (blessed be His name), it requires an endless number of calculations, regarding all the details of all his actions, speech and thoughts, and all the details of his behaviors regarding the manner of their inclination, to where they were inclined. And what the text stated (*Kohelet *7:29): "that God-*Elohi"m *has made man straight"—as we discussed above; "and they [emphatic]"—with their sins, "sought many intrigues". Refer to* Zohar *(*Eh-more *107a, end), and it is explained there according to our words.*

*And this matter proceeded in this way until the giving of the Torah. Then that pollution ceased from within them, as our rabbis (OBM) stated (*Shabbat *op. cit.). And therefore after that, in the sin of the calf, the rabbis (OBM) stated (ibid 89a): "that the Satan came and mixed...", that is, that he came from the outside as in the situation of the sin of First Adam as we mentioned above, for "from within them" was he expelled. And because of the sin of the calf, the same pollution returned and "became mixed into them" as in the beginning. And this is what the text stated (*Hosea *6:7): "And they [emphatic] are like Adam, broke the covenant, there they betrayed me".*

*And this is what He (blessed be He) said to Adam (*B'reisheet *2:17): "for on the day that you eat from it, you will [emphatic] die". It's not that it was the case of a curse and punishment, for "is it not from the mouth of the Most High that evil and good issue..." (*Eikha *3:38). But rather its explanation is that, as a result of eating from it, the pollution of evil will be mixed into you, and there will be no other rectification afterwards to separate it from you so that it will be better for you afterwards, if not via death and the rotting in the grave.*

*And this is also the context of why He (blessed be He) said later (*B'reisheet *3:22): "Behold, man has become…, and now, lest he put forth his hand and take also of the Tree of Life, and eat and live forever". For after all, isn't God's (blessed be His name) desire to bestow good on his creations? So why should He care if he lives forever?*

However, it desires to convey that when he will eat from the Tree of Life and lives forever, he will remain (heaven forefend) without rectification, that the evil will never be separated from him (heaven forefend), and he won't see the luminaries nor good his entire life. For this reason, for his own good, he was expelled from the Garden of Eden, so that he would be able to arrive at a complete rectification when the evil will separate itself from him via death and rotting in the grave.

And this is the matter of the four who died because of the serpent's counsel[169] *(*Shabbat *55b), that even though they themselves didn't sin at all, even so they had to die as a result of the initial admixture of evil caused by the sin of Adam because of the serpent's counsel.*

*And so this situation will proceed until the end of days—"He will eliminate death forever" (*Y'shaya *25:8). And there will be another advantage then, that evil will be eliminated from the world in the fact of its very existence, as is written (*Z'kharya *13:2): "and the spirit of impurity from the land".*

And so all of the commandments are connected to and dependent upon the source of the supernal root in the structures and processes of the components of the Vehicle, and the Stature of all the worlds taken together, that each specific commandment in its root integrates

169 Heb.: *b'etyo shel na-khash*

tens upon tens of thousands of powers and lights in the structures and processes of the Stature.

It is as is written in *Zohar Yitro* (85b): "All of the commandments in the Torah are unified in the lofty Holy King, some in the King's head and some in the torso and some of them in the hands of the King, and some of them in His legs." And the topic is explained further in the *Tikkoonim* (*Tikkoon* 70, 129b, 130a), refer there [for more detail].

And in *Zohar T'rooma* (165b):"The Torah's commandments are all limbs/organs of the body according to the lofty secret, and when they are bound together as one they all amount to one secret."

And there on page 165b: "In that Name are integrated the 613 commandments that are the principles of all the secrets, lofty and lowly... and all the commandments are parts and limbs to display through them the secret of faith/reliability. One who does not watch and observe the secrets of the Torah's commandments, doesn't know and doesn't observe how the limbs are mended according to the lofty secret: the limbs of the body are all mended by way of the secret of the Torah's commandments." Refer there [for more detail]. And so wrote the Ariza"l in the *Sha-ar Ha-yikhoodim*[170], chapter two.

---

170 *Sha-ar Ha-yikhoodim* (Gate of the Unifications) is one of the Ariza"l's works, but is not currently included in the standard collections of the Ariza"l's writings. Current editions of the book include only the third section (*Sha-ar Tikkoonei Ah-vonote*) and fourth section (*Sha-ar N'vooah V'ruakh Ha-kodesh)* of the book known as *Pri Etz Chayyim*. In Rav Chayyim's time, it apparently also included the second section, which is called *Sha-ar Ha-mitzvote*; that is the section Rav Chayyim references. (The edition of the *Pri Etz Chayyim* found in the standard collections includes only the first section: *Sha-ar Ha-t'feela*.)

[171]And when man performs his Master's (blessed be His name) will, and fulfills one of God's commandments with a specific limb and the power within it, the mending that is caused relates to that world or lofty power that receives it, to:

- mend it or to uplift it, or
- to add light and holiness upon its holiness from the lofty desire and will (blessed be His name),

according to:

- the quality and manner of the performance, and
- the majority quality of the refinement and purity of the holiness of his thoughts at the time of the performance of the commandment, that joins for good with the essential action, and
- the quality of the level of that lofty world and power.

From there the holiness and life-force is directed also on that power of man [*] corresponding to it, with which he fulfilled his Creator's commandment.[172]

Annotation: *And this is how they codified the wording of the blessings associated with commandments[173]: "who sanctified us via His commandments", and so too: "and You sanctified us with Your commandments". For from the moment it occurs to a person to do a commandment, immediately its impression*

---

171 This very long sentence is difficult to parse. I've attempted to make it clearer by separating out the disjunctive (*or*) and conjunctive (*and*) clauses typographically.

172 Rav Chayyim says that performance of a mitzva mends the root of the mitzva in the upper worlds, and also mends the corresponding power or limb/organ within the person who performed the mitzva.

173 Heb.: *noo-sahkh bir-kaht ha-mitzvote*

is made above in the supernal source of its root, and it draws upon itself from there an encompassing light[174]*, and a heavenly holiness that hovers over him and surrounds him.*

And it states plainly (Va-yikra *20:7): "You shall sanctify yourselves and you will be holy", and as they stated (OBM)* (Yoma *39a): "Everyone who makes himself holy from below, they make him holy from above", wishing to convey that holiness is drawn upon him from above, from the commandment's supernal root.*

And as it's stated in the Zohar (Tzav *31b, top), it's written: "'You shall sanctify yourselves and you will be holy'—One who sanctifies himself from below, they make him holy from above…, that God-*YHV"H*'s holiness settles upon him… . If his actions from below are in holiness, the supernal holiness is awakened and comes and settles upon him and he is sanctified by it." Refer there.*

And in parshat K'doshim *86b: "When a person does his actions below conforming to the straight path… a supernal spirit-*Ruakh *of holiness is drawn out, issues and rests upon him…, and as a result of those same actions a spirit-*Ruakh *of holiness settles upon him, a supernal spirit-*Ruakh *to be sanctified thereby. If he comes to be sanctified, they sanctify him, as is written 'you shall sanctify…'." And in* parshat Nahso *(128, top): "that he draws upon himself the supernal spirit-*Ruakh *of holiness, as was stated* (Y'shaya *32:15) 'until a spirit-*Ruakh *from on high will be poured out upon us", refer there [for more details].*

*And via this holiness and the encompassing light, he is attached (so to speak) to Him (blessed be He) even during his life. And this is what the text stated: "And you who are attached to God-*YHV"H *your God-*Elohi"m*", even while "you are all alive today".*

174 Heb.: *ore meikeef*

*And this encompassing light, is for him an aid to complete the commandment, and as a result of the completion, the light strengthens more and raises [his] head upwards, and on this they (OBM) stated (*Yoma *38b): "One who approaches to be purified, they aid him".*

And it also appeals to and attracts his heart/mind to treasure a few more commandments, until he is actually sitting now in the Garden of Eden, sheltered in the shade of the wings of holiness in the supernal concealment[175]*—there's no room for the evil inclination to rule over him and to incite and seduce him from involvement with the commandments. About this they stated (*Ahvote *4:2): "commandment attracts commandment".*

*And when he pays attention to it during the performance of the commandment, he will understand and sense in his soul-*Neffesh *that he is surrounded and clothed that moment in the holiness, and a willing spirit-*Ruakh *is renewed within him. And this is what the text (*Va-yikra *18:5) stated: these are the commandments "which man shall carry out and within which*[176] *he shall live"—"within them", namely actually within them, for he is surrounded then with the holiness of the commandment and encompassed by the atmosphere of the Garden of Eden.*

*And so too the opposite (heaven forefend). At the moment that he transgresses one of God-*YHV"H*'s commandments, they (OBM) also stated in their statements (mentioned previously) that "all who impurify themselves below, are impurified from above", the meaning of which is also as we mentioned previously: that from the root of that transgression above in the powers of impurity, he draws (may the Merciful save us) a spirit-*Ruakh *of impurity upon himself, and it hovers over him and surrounds him.*

---

175 Heb.: *b'sei-ter elyone*
176 Heb.: *ba-hem*

As it's written in the statement in parshat Tzav *(mentioned previously): "...and if he defiles himself below, a spirit*-Ruakh *of defilement is awakened above and comes and settles upon him and he is defiled within it, for you can't have good and evil, holiness and impurity, that don't have their primary presence and root above, and the action below awakens an action above", refer there. And in* parshat K'doshim *that was mentioned previously: "When he performs an action below in a crooked manner..., then another kind of spirit*-Ruakh *issues and settles upon him"—refer there.*

And about this the text stated (Va-yikra *11:43): "you become defiled within them*[177]*", namely, actually within them (heaven forefend), for he is attached to and surrounded that moment by the spirit*-Ruakh *of impurity, and the atmosphere of* Gehinnom *envelopes and surrounds him even while he is still alive in the world, as the sages (OBM) stated* (Avoda Za-ra *5:1): "Anyone who transgresses one transgression in this world, it envelopes him and precedes him to the day of judgment, for it was stated (Eeyove 6:18): 'they determine...'—, Rabbee Elazar stated: 'it is attached to him...', and this is what King Dovid (OBM) stated: 'the transgressions that I trod upon surround me'* (T'hillim *49:6)."*

And through this is understood their (OBM) statement in Perek Yom Ha-kippurim (Yoma, *86b): "Great is repentance, for willful transgressions are accounted for them as merits, for it is stated* (Yekhezkel *33:19): 'And if a wicked person repents from his wickedness and acts with justice and righteousness, he shall live for [his acts]'." On the face of it, the proof is not conclusive, for with a liberal reading we can explain "he shall live for [his acts]" here to refer to the justice and righteousness that he did after he repented.*

---

177 Heb.: *v'nit-mei-tem bahm*

And according to what I've written, his proof is correct about what the text specifically teaches here, that if "he shall live for [his acts][178]" refers to justice and righteousness, he would have stated "he shall live within[179] them", as it states (Va-yikra *18:5): "and live within them[180]", and as was previously explained[181]. And because it stated "for [his acts]", it definitely refers to his wickedness and his previous transgressions, that as a result of his repentance in abandoning his original behavior and his doing thereafter justice and righteousness, they [emphatic] overcome his original actions to transform them too into merits and everlasting life[182].*

And when he:

1. perfectly fulfilled all of the commandments, in all their details and exactitude in the essential action, and
2. added upon them is the enormity of the purity and holiness of the thought,

thus he mends all of the worlds and lofty structures, and he becomes:

3. a vehicle for them with all of his powers and limbs, and
4. they are made holy from their supernal holiness, and

178 Heb.: *ah-lei-hem*
179 Heb.: *ba-hem*
180 Heb.: *ba-hem*
181 A few paragraphs back.
182 Rav Chayyim explains this verse to mean that it's not his current acts of justice and righteousness, within whose effects he now lives, that give him life, but rather that his previous sins are actually transformed by repentance into merits, and they give him life.

5. God's glory[183] hovers over him always.

Refer to *T'rooma* (155a): "'Everything that is called by my Name, and I created it for my glory...' (*Y'shaya* 43:7)—I created it for My glory specifically, and this secret... we learned that this 'glory'... is mended above in response to the emendments of those in this world, as when people are just and pious and know how to effect emendments." Refer there at length [for more detail]. And refer carefully to the *Raa-ya M'hehmna, Pinkhas* 239a. And this is what the sages (OBM) said (*B'reisheet Rabba* 47): "the Patriarchs, they [emphatic] are the Vehicle."

And so too the converse (God forefend): when he blemishes one of his powers or organs/limbs via his sin that he sinned, the blemish also reaches according to its root to that specific world and lofty power that corresponds to it in the structure of the Stature (so to speak), to demolish and destroy (heaven forefend), or to lower it, or to blemish it, or to darken or shrink the brilliance of its light, and to sap and weaken and to lessen the power of the purity of its holiness (heaven forefend), everything according to the quality of the sin and the context of its performance, and according to the quality and the situation of that world and the height of its level.

For all the worlds are not equivalent in their stature with regard to blemish and ruin. In the lower, it is demolition and destruction (so to speak), and above it is blockage of the light. In the yet loftier, it causes only a lessening of the flow of light or its reduction, and in the still higher

183 The term "God's glory" (Heb.: *k'vode ha-Shem*) is used in the Torah to denote God's perceivable manifestation in a specific place in the physical world, as when the Tabernacle was completed and God's glory manifested in it (*Sh'mote* 40:34).

and hidden, causes a reduction in the degree of the light's brilliance and the purity of its marvelous holiness. In this way there are many different aspects.

And this is why our sages (OBM), in a number of places, referred to the blemish caused by a sin as the "blemish on the King's image[184]." And in *Zohar Yitro* (85b): "and because of this, one who commits a crime relating to the commandments of the Torah, it is as if he committed a crime against the King's person, as is written (*Y'shaya* 66:24): 'And they went out and saw the dead bodies of the people who committed the crime in Me[185]'—in Me literally. Woe to those guilty ones who trespass on the words of Torah and don't realize what they are doing." And in the *Tikkoonim* (*Tikkoon* 70, 129b): "All who commit a crime against the commandments are as if they committed a crime against the image of the King." As we described above, the blemish is drawn out and contacts the parts and structures of the powers and worlds of the Stature, from the perspective that all are integrated in it and give a part of their essence to its assembly and creation.

Annotation: *And this is the plain meaning of this matter in the text (*B'reisheet *1:26): "let us make man"—using a plural syntax, wishing to convey that all of them should donate their power and material to construct him, so that he should integrate and be comprised of all of them, as is explained in his lengthy commentary in* Tikkoonei Zohar Chaddash *(86a) and in* Raa-ya M'hemna Pinkhas *219b. Rav Chayyim*

184 Aram.: *p'gahm eekonin shel mehlekh*
185 "...in Me" corresponds to the Hebrew word "bee," implying that the crime affects the (so to speak) "Person" of God.

Vittal (OBM) also wrote thusly in Sha-ar Ha-k'doosha[186] (khelek three, sha-ar *2), and in* Likutei Torah *(*parsha Teesa*) and* parsha Ha-ahzeenu, *refer there.*

And what is written in B'reisheet Rabba, *parsha 8: "'And God-*Elohi"m *said, let Us make man' (*B'reisheet *1:26)—Over whom was He declared Sovereign? Rabbee Yehoshua stated in the name of Rabbee Leivee: 'Over the labor of heaven and earth was He declared Sovereign'. Rabbee Shmuel bar Nakhman stated: 'In the labor of creating each day was He declared Sovereign'." And in* Kohelet Rabba (perek 2, pasuk 12*): "'that which was already completed in him?' (*Kohelet *2:12)—It's not written here 'He completed', but rather 'completed[187] in him[188]', as if to say that the Holy One (blessed be He) and His court were appointed over each and every of your organs/limbs, and sets you up in the way you were designed. And if you should assert that there are two domains[189], did it not already state (*D'varim *32:6): 'has He not created you and established you?'"—thus it is explained.*

CHAPTER 7

Now we have an explanation of the matter discussed previously in chapter 5, that man is called the soul-*Neffesh* and soul-*Neshama* of the multitudes of the worlds. It's not a

---

186 From the context, the cited text (*Sha-ar Ha-k'doosha*), appears to be the text we know as *Sha-ahrei K'doosha.* That text is divided up into *chalakim* and *sh'arim* per the citation, and the contents of section 3, sha-ar 2 corresponds well to Rav Chayyim's current context. Concurring with this conclusion, in a footnote for this citation, Issachar Dov Rubin's edition of the *Neffesh* Ha-chayyim brings text from *Sha-ahrei K'doosha.*

187 Heb.: *ah-sa-hoo*

188 Heb.: *ah-soo-hoo*

189 Heb.: *shtei r'shoo-yote*—two gods that share ultimate power

soul-*Neffesh* like the soul-*Neffesh* that literally is situated and adheres inside man's body, for that's not plausible.

However, just as all the detailed movements and tendencies of the body's limbs are caused by the living soul-*Neshama* within it according to the movement of its life force and tendencies, so too all the tendencies of the powers, worlds and structures of the Vehicle, their correction, assembly and destruction (heaven forefend) are (1) only according to the arousal from the actions of man below, and (2) because he is comprised of and integrated into a number of its details, powers and structures, according to the order of their unfolding and interconnection between all the powers and worlds, supernal and terrestrial. This is from the perspective of his soul-*Neshama*'s lofty root that is the highest and innermost of all the created worlds, as we described in chapter 5, therefore he integrates them all.

And the reason provided in chapter 5—that because the *root-of-the-soul-Neshama*[190] is the most lofty and innermost of the worlds—and the reason that was explained in the last chapter—because it is comprised of all of the worlds—both are identical, as was explained.

And for this reason, to him alone was given the power of free will, to direct himself and the worlds to whichever side he desires. Or even if he already caused and brought about (heaven forefend) via his sins the demolition of the worlds and the structures of the Vehicle, and their destruction and descent (heaven forefend), he has the power and opportunity to correct what he perverted, and to rebuild the demolished, from the perspective that he integrates and is in partnership with all of them.

And what King Dovid (OBM) said (*T'hillim* 121):

190 Also know as the *Chayya*

"God-*YHV"H* is your shadow on your right side," that is to imply that how an object's shadow moves is only per the movements of that object, in what direction it moves. By this same metaphor it's as if He (blessed be His name) joins in to move the worlds based on the movements and intentions of man's actions below.

And so it is explained in the *Midrash*: "The Holy One (blessed be He) said to Moshe: go and say to them, to Israel, that my Name is 'I will be as I will be'[191]". What is 'I will be as I will be'? Just as you are with Me, in that same way I am with you. And so said Dovid: 'God-*YHV"H* is your shadow on your right side'—What is 'God-*YHV"H* is your shadow? Like your shadow. As your shadow, when you play with it, it plays with you, and if you cry, it cries opposite you, and if you show it an angry or a cordial face, it does the same to you, so too the Holy One (blessed be He) 'God-*YHV"H* is your shadow'—just as you are with Him, He is with you." The quote ends here.

And in the portion of the *Zohar parshat T'tza-veh* (184b): "Come and see that the lower world always stands ready to receive... and the lofty world gives only according to how he stands. If he stands with a shining face looking upwards from below, then for that reason he is enlightened from above. And if he stands in sadness then he is given that same judgment in response, kind of as in "serve God joyously," for man's joy draws to him another supernal joy. So too this lower world, whatever it arouses, so it draws from above... ."

---

191 Heb.: *A-H-Y-H ah-sher A-H-Y-H*

And this is the matter of the cherubs[192] who were attached "like the embrace of a man and his wife"[193] (*M'la-khim Alef* 7:36), "their faces pointed to each other" [*Sh'mote* 25:20]. And by Shlomo's cherubs it is written (*Divrei Ha-yamim II* 3:13): "and their faces pointed outward to the walls", as we'll describe with God's help.

CHAPTER 8

And so the sages (OBM) stated in the context of the cherubs[194] (*Bava Batra* 99:1): "How were they situated? Rabbi Yokhanan and Rabbi Elazar—one said that they faced each other and one said they faced outward. For the one who said that they faced each other, how does he reconcile it being written 'and they faced outwards'? It's not a difficulty. Here it's when Israel does God's-*Ma-kome*[195] will, and there it's when they do not do God's-*Ma-kome* will." (Refer to RaSh"Y[196] [for more details].) And the one who said that they faced outwards, that it's written

---

192 The two cherubs stood atop the Ark of the Covenant's cover. Shlomo Ha-Meh-lekh added a second pair of large cherubs standing on the floor (per RaSh"Y, *M'lakhim Aleph,* 6:23) in the Holy of Holies. There were other images of cherubs on the walls, worked into the design of the curtains and on certain accessories.

193 This verse in *M'la-khim* is difficult to translate. Rav Chayyim seems to accept the explanation found in *Yoma* 54a and 54b (see RaSh"Y there) that we use here.

194 Two cherubs stood atop the Ark of the Covenant's cover (the *Kaporet*) in the Tabernacle and later in Solomon's Temple.

195 The appellation *Ma-kome* literally means "place" or "space." It implies that God is the space of Creation. See Gate 3 for a discussion of this.

196 RaSh"Y is Rabbi Shlomo Yitzkhaki (11th Century), one of the foremost of the early commentators on TaNa"Kh and Talmud.

that they faced each other means that they faced to the side, intending to convey: a little to each other and a little outwards—refer to RaSh"Y (OBM). And here it's impossible to explain it as above (e.g., "here it's when Israel does..."), that because the essential fact is that they made them face outwards, they shouldn't have done that, it being a sign that Israel were not doing God's-*Ma-kome* will. And this is what Tosafote[197] wrote there in the commentary beginning with the words "to the side"[198], that plainly they set them up initially as if they were doing God's-*Ma-kome* will. Seemingly that would question as to why they initially set Shlomo's cherubs up to face to the side and not facing each other directly.

And the matter is, as they said in the Chapter *Kei-tzad M'vor-khim* (*B'rakhote* 35b): "The Rabbis taught about 'You shall gather in your grain...'[199] (*D'varim* 11:14). What does it come to teach us in light of what is written (in *Y'hoshua* 1): 'This book of the Torah shall not cease from your mouth...'? Could the words be taken literally, to teach: '"you shall gather in your grain"—'behave in them per the ways of the world[200]'—these being Rabbee Yishmael's words? Rabbee Shim'on Bar Yo-khai said: 'Is it possible that a person should plow when it's the season for plowing... what will then become of Torah?' Rather, when Israel does God's-*Ma-kome* will, their labors are performed by others for them...; and when Israel doesn't do God's-*Ma-kome* will, they perform their own labor, as it is said "And you shall gather in your grain..."'."

197 Tosafote is a collection of rabbinic commentaries on the Talmud, beginning in roughly the 12th century.

198 Aram.: *d'mitz-doddi*

199 Heb.: *V'ah-saf-ta d'ga-neh-kha*

200 Rabbee Yishmael's words could be interpreted as: "spend time away from involvement with Torah to harvest your grain".

It seems surprising to explain the text "you shall gather in your grain..." as applying when [Israel] doesn't do God's-*Ma-kome* will, for just before that is written (*D'varim* 11:13): "If you are careful to pay heed to my commandments... to love... and to serve Him with your entire hearts/minds." It was in this context that "and you shall gather in your grain" was stated.

Rather the matter is, that Rabbee Yishmael's view is definitely not that permission is given to a person to separate himself (heaven forefend) even a short time from being involved with Torah[201], to be involved [instead] with earning a living, during which time he would be completely lacking involvement with Torah (heaven forefend). However, Rabbi Yishmael hinted in his holy statement: "behave in them per the ways of the world," to imply "with them" i.e., with the words of Torah—that at the same brief moment and time that you occupy yourself with earning a living to the extent necessary to stay alive, even so, in your thoughts you should be preoccupied only with the words of Torah.

And so did Ravah say to his students[202]: during the months of Nissan and Tishrei they shouldn't appear before him, shouldn't come to his Beit Midrash, but certainly Ravah's students weren't completely lacking involvement with Torah (heaven forefend) when at their homes during those periods.

And there it is stated that many did per Rabbee Yishmael's directions and they succeeded, and many did per Rabbee Shim'on Bar Yo-khai's words and they did not

---

201 Heb.: *ei-sek ba-torah*. See the footnote at the beginning of Gate 4 for a discussion of what "involvement with Torah" means to Rav Chayyim.

202 *B'ra-khote* 35b

succeed. It says specifically "many" because definitely, for most of the masses it's nearly impossible that they could dedicate all of their time only to involvement with Torah, to not turn away from it even a brief time for the sake of earning a living sustenance[203]. And about this the sages stated in *Ahvote*: "that all Torah that is not accompanied by labor...". But an individual, if it's possible for him to only be involved his entire lifetime with his Torah and his service to the One (blessed be His name), the obligation is definitely upon him to not separate even a brief time from Torah and service to earn a living (heaven forefend), in accordance with Rabbee Shim'on Bar Yo-khai's opinion [*].

And the verse "and you shall gather in your grain..." is found in the context of the section that starts "If you are..." that is stated wholly in the plural, while the verse "and you shall gather..." is stated in the singular. Therefore you should read it that one is not doing God's-*Ma-kome* will when he turns himself away even for a moment to earn a living.

Annotation: *And for that reason in the first paragraph of the* kree-aht sh'ma *it's written "and with all your [singular] resources*[204]*", and in parsha "v'ha-ya"*[205] *it doesn't say "and with all your [plural] resources", because the* parsha *of* sh'ma *is stated totally in the singular, and an individual who is capable, is required to fulfill "this document of Torah shall not cease from your mouth"* (Y'hoshua *1:8)—these words are to be taken literally. For that reason it's stated "and with all your [singular] resources", defined as with all your financial means, as is stated in* Mishna *at the end of* B'rakhote, *intending to convey that one shouldn't be involved in earning a living at all.*

---

203 Heb.: *par-na-saht m'zo-note*

204 Heb.: *m'oh-deh-kha*

205 *V'ha-ya* is the second paragraph of the *kree-aht sh'ma.*

But the parsha v'haya *that is stated in the plural form—for the many—it's almost an imperative to be involved in some minimal way also with earning a living, for that reason its not written there "and with all your [plural] resources."*

*And even though, according to the opinion of Rabbee Shim'on Bar Yo-khai, this is still not the way and the level that's the highest of the high, corresponding to the reality of His (blessed be His name) will, even so, for him it's not a case of (heaven forefend) that by doing this they are not doing God's-*Ma-kome *will when they dedicate a small amount of their time to also earn a living. While they are earning a living, their heart/minds are practicing wisdom and are reflecting on words of Torah and fear of God -*YHV"H. *And for Rabbee Yishmael this is His (blessed be He) primary will regarding the behavior of the public masses, and their argument is about what is His (blessed be He) primary will and the level that's highest about how the public masses behave.*[206]

And it's known that the cherubs, one of them hints at Him (blessed be His name), and the second at Israel, His chosen. And how close Israel is and how well they cling to Him (blessed be His name) (or the opposite, heaven forefend), this is revealed in the cherubs' postures, by way of a miracle and wonder. If their faces were faced directly toward Him (blessed be His name), the cherubs too then stood facing each other. Or if they turned their faces away somewhat to the side, so too, the situation was obvious immediately in the cherubs. Or if (heaven forefend) they turned completely away, the cherubs too instantly rotate and turn their faces away from each other completely (heaven forefend).

---

206 Rav Chayyim here makes a clear distinction between the obligations of the individual and the masses.

And also relating to the context relative to which our sages (may their memory be blessed) said (*Yoma* 54:1) that they would pull aside the curtain [that divided off the Holy of Holies] for those who made the pilgrimage to Jerusalem for the three holidays, and showed them the cherubs who were attached one to the other, and said to them: observe the affection that God-*Ma-kome* has for you... .

And in *T'rooma* 152b: "When is she in compassion? He said: during the time when the cherubs turn back... and stare face-to-face, so that when the cherubs stare face-to-face, then all of the colors[207] are rectified... just as Israel organizes all of their rectifications toward the Holy One (blessed be He), so everything occurs. And in this way all is put in order... ."

And in the section of *Ah-kha-rei* (59b, top): "'When brothers sit...'—For when they would stare face-to-face it is written 'how good and how pleasant...'; but when the male turns its face away from the female, woe to the world."

And in the *Zohar Chaddash*, at the end of *parshat T'rooma* 43a: "When Israel is righteous, the cherubs would cleave to each other face-to-face. And when they would sin, they would turn their faces away from each other... and in this way at that time when Israel was righteous the cherubs faced each other... and via these secrets Israel would know if they were righteous or not... . It is written 'serve God

207 Colors: This section of the *Zohar* addresses the meanings of colors when they appear in dreams. When the *Malkhut* (referring to the Throne in this case) appears in the color of *t'khei-let* (the blue/purple color used for *tzitzit*/fringes and in the *Mishkan*/Tabernacle), this implies capital judgment. When the cherubs turn to face each other, the *t'khei-let* changes to another color, implying a tendency away from judgment.

in joy', the joy of the two cherubs... when it would settle upon/permeate[208] them they would return to being in joy and the world would return to exist in compassion." And refer there for more information.

CHAPTER 9

And we know that the generation of the desert, who merited to dine from an exalted table on bread from the heavens each day in turn, and their clothing didn't wear out upon them, and who didn't require any involvement with earning a living in the world at all, everyone agreed that they were not referred to as performing God's-*Ma-kome* will unless they were staring upwards with absolute sincerity, and subjugated their hearts/minds only to Torah and service to God, and awe/fear of Him (blessed be His name), day and night it would not depart their mouths, the words exactly as written, without veering off to the side in any manner, even a single hour for the sake of earning a living. And as the sages (OBM) said in *M'khilta*[209] (*B'sha-lakh* 17 and others): "The Torah was not given to any except those who ate the *mahn*[210]. For that reason they set the cherubs in place according to how they performed God's-*Ma-kome* will—directly face-to-face—to show that they perceived His (blessed be He) face directly, face-to-face with His holy nation."

However, in Shlomo's time, when most of the Nation of Israel's masses were required by necessity to turn aside slightly to earn a living, even if it was just to sustain their lives, this is the essence of the truth of the Blessed One's will according to Rabbee Yishmael's opinion, who concluded

---

208 Heb.: *kei-vahn d'sh'aree ah-lie-hoo*

209 The *Mekhilta* is part of the midrashic literature.

210 Manna

that for the masses that it is more worthy to do thusly. As is said in *Ahvote*: "The study of Torah is better with an occupation..." and "All Torah that is not accompanied by labor...". And all the statements of *Ahvote* are statements of piety, [expressing] only that during the period that they are involved with earning a living, their hearts/minds should behave with wisdom, reflecting on words of Torah. For that reason at that time they first set up the cherubs according to how they would do God's-*Ma-kome* will, their faces turned aside a little, and even so they were attached "as a man and woman joined by their arms" (*M'la-khim Alef* 7:36), with expressions of affection, to exhibit His (blessed be He) affection for us, for this is the crux of His blessed will, as we described above. (And his opinion is per Rabbee Yishmael. And the one who said that Shlomo's cherubs also were set up initially according to how they would perform God's-*Ma-kome* will, absolutely facing each other, his opinion agrees with Rabbee Shim'on bar Yo-khai.)

And on the face of it, still, why was it necessary to set up the two cherubs turned aside slightly, for wasn't the one that hinted at Him (blessed be His name), shouldn't they have set it up absolutely straight?

However the matter is as we wrote, that His (blessed be He) relationship (so to speak) to all the worlds and powers and all their processes/structures and connections, and so too all the processes/structures of His (blessed be He) interactions with us, is based on the amount of movement and awakening that arrives to them as a result of our actions below. Based on that amount, aspects that are joyful and kind also flow and are drawn to us below. Therefore, the cherub corresponding to Him (blessed be His name) should also have been set in place turned slightly aside, to the same degree of turning aside of the cherub that corresponds to us, for that same reason.[*]

Annotation: *And according to this is understood their (OBM) statement in chapter 9 of* Shabbat *(86a): "Rabbee Chamma b'Rebbee Chaneena stated: 'Why is it written (*Shir Ha-shirrim *2:3) "like an apple among the trees of the forest...", why is Israel likened to an apple*[211]*...?' And Tosafote asked a difficult question there: "There in that text it's not Israel who is likened to an apple, but rather the Holy One (blessed be He), for it concludes with 'thus is my Beloved among the sons'."*

And it can be reconciled (with God's help) based on what I wrote. For later when Israel perceived Him and likened Him in the form of the apple, it is certain that it is because Israel is likened and compared in their actions to the matter of an apple. And just as we appear to Him (blessed be His name), so too He (blessed be His name) appears to the worlds, in the same gradation and degree, and for that reason it asks in what way and manner are Israel compared to and likened in their desirable actions to an apple, that because of this they perceived Him (blessed be His name) in the context of the apple.

Therefore, at the time of the splitting of the Sea of Reeds, He (blessed be He) said to Moshe (*Sh'mote* 14:15): "Why are you crying out to Me? Speak to the Israelites that they should start moving", as if to say that it depends on them. That if they will be in the mode of faith and belief, and they would travel, going and proceeding to the Sea absolutely certain and without fear, out of their mighty belief that it will undoubtedly split before them, then as a result they will cause an awakening above, so that a miracle should happen and it will split before them.

211 Israel is likened to an apple because just as the apple tree's fruit is visible before its leaves appear, so too, Israel agreed to abide by the Torah even before they examined it.

And this is (*Shir Ha-shirrim* 1:9): "I compared thee, my love, to Par-oh's chariot steed" meaning that Par-oh's horses reversed the normal order of the driver guiding the horse, for with Par-oh and his army the horse would lead the driver. And the sages (OBM) said (*Sh'mote Rabba* 23, and *Shir Ha-Shirrim Rabba* 1:50): "This is how I described and compared you, my beloved, in this specific manner: that just as I 'ride the highest heavens' even so, it is as if you lead Me according to your actions, for the essence of My interactions with the worlds is only according to what your actions stimulate, to where they tend." And this is what the text states (*D'varim* 33:26): "rides the heavens with your aid," and also what the sages stated (*Tractate Shabbat* 116:2, *Y'va-mote* 5:2, and *M'na-khote* 64:1): "the service is a high purpose."

CHAPTER 10

So based on this will be reconciled the matter of the different opinions of the early great ones[212] (OBM), whether the man from Israel is greater than an angel, or angel greater than him. The holders of the two opinions each bring explanatory proofs from proof texts, and based on our previous discussion it will be explained that both are the words of the living God, only from different perspectives.

For an angel is certainly greater than man, whether considered from the essence of his nature, whether considered from the greatness of his holiness and wondrous abilities, there's no comparison or resemblance between them at all.

And as is written in the *Zohar Chaddash, B'reisheet,* in the *Midrash Ha-neh-eh-lahm,* in the section dealing with "And

212 Heb.: *g'doe-lei ha-rishonim*

God-*Elohi"m* called the light 'day'": "The angels' accomplishment is a great accomplishment, which is not the case below them, a secondary level of accomplishment..., and the tertiary level of ability is the achievement at the lower level that has Dust[213] as its elemental, and that is Man's level of accomplishment." And there (16b): "The angels nearby receive the abundance of the heavenly lens'[214] power first, and from them it descends to the heavens and all of its hosts, and from them to man"—refer there [for more details]. And in *Zohar T'rooma* (129b): "High angels, they are much holier than we".

However, in one situation man has a great advantage over the angels, and that is in elevating and connecting the worlds and the powers and lights one to another, that is completely beyond the power of any angel.

This is because of the reason we discussed above, that the angel is, in essence, only one specific power that does not have within it the integration of all the worlds together. (And so it is written in the *Etz Chayyim, Sha-ar P'nimiyut V'khi-tzoniyut,* at the beginning of the tenth *droosh,* that the angel is a specific aspect of the world in which it exists, while man's soul-*Neshama,* in all three of its parts (*Neffesh, Ruakh* and *Neshama*), is comprised of all the worlds—refer there [for more details]. Therefore it's not within the ability of the angel in any way to elevate, connect or to unify a world with the world that is outstretched above their heads, because it is not integrated within them nor partnered with them.

---

213 Dust (or Earth) is one of the four elementals of creation, the others being Fire, Water, Air

214 The flow of heavenly influence from its Source to this lowest of worlds is often described as being similar to light that passes through a sequence of lenses of various qualities of clarity, some more clear and some less.

Also, the ascent of the angel's essence to its level, so as to connect to the world above him, does not depend on him by himself. For that reason the angels are referred to as "standing", as is written (*Y'shaya* 6:2): "*seraphim* standing" and (*Z'khar-ya* 3:7): "I will give you free access among these who stand".

Only man alone, he is the one who elevates and connects and unifies the worlds and the lights via the power of his actions, because he integrates them all, and then the angel too achieves an ascent and an increase in holiness over his holiness. That happens as a result of man's actions, because he [the angel] too is included in man. (Refer to something similar to this in the *Etz Chayyim, Sha-ar Ha-iburim,* at the beginning of chapter 4[215].)

Also, the three components (*Neffesh, Ruakh* and *Neshama*) of man himself are not given the power of elevation and connection of all the worlds and among themselves, until they descend into this world of action in the body of man, as is written (*B'reisheet* 2:7): "and He breathed into his nostrils a breath of life... ," about which is said (*B'reisheet* 28:12): "and he dreamed and lo, there was a ladder...". The ladder is definitely the living soul-*Neshama...* ," refer there, and as will be explained (with God's help) further on in Chapter 19. And via this "and lo, angels of God-*Elohi"m* ascended and descended upon it", as if to say via the living soul-*Neshama* that is positioned on the earth, its lowest edge clothing itself in man's body.

---

215 This section of the *Etz Chayyim* discusses how when a sage passes on to the next world, angels often accompany the soul, appearing as if they are transporting the soul, while in fact it is the other way around, that the soul transports the angels upward.

CHAPTER 11

And this is the reason that the angels who sanctify [God's name] in the heights of the heavens wait to say the three-fold Sanctification[216] until after we below say the three-fold Sanctification (as was discussed on Chapter 6 in the Annotations[217]) even though their holiness is higher than our holiness. It's not that they render honor to Israel [by waiting], but rather that it is not in their power to, by themselves, to open their mouths to sanctify their Former until the sound of Israel's Sanctification rises to them from below.

For the context of the saying of the Sanctification involves the elevation of the worlds and their interconnection, each world with the world above it, to increase its holiness and the brilliance of its light.

Refer to the *Heikhalot* of *parshat P'koodei*,[218] the second *Heikhal* (247b, end) in the context of the holiness of the angels that results from the power of our saying the Sanctification. It says: "And those on the right say song and elevate the will above and say 'Holy', and those on the left say song and elevate the will above and say 'Blessed', ... and join together in holiness all those who know how to sanctify their Master in unification ..., and all are integrated with one another into one unit and become interconnected one with another until all are performing one connection and one spirit, and connect to those who are above so that all are one, integrated one with the other."

---

216 Heb.: *K'doosha*—the three-fold Sanctification that begins with the words: "Holy, holy, holy... ."

217 Heb.: *ha-ga-hote*

218 Part of the *Zohar*

And refer to the *Pri Etz Chayyim* in all of Chapter 3, from the Gate of the Repetition of the Ahmeeda, it's explained there the intention of the matter of the saying of the Sanctification, that it is the elevation and interconnection of the upper worlds, to cause an increase in them via this addition of holiness and supernal light. (And it's possible that from this resulted the custom in Israel to elevate themselves at the moment when they say the Sanctification[219].)

And it is not in the power of any angel or seraph to start it by itself, as we said above. For this reason it does not open its mouth until the utterance from the mouths of Israel's Sanctification ascends from those who are gathered below.

And if it would happen that all of Israel, from one extreme end of the world to the other, were silent (heaven forefend) from saying the Sanctification, automatically they too would be absolutely silenced from sanctifying their Sanctification. And refer to the *Zohar Ba-lahk* (190b). And this is what the prophet said (*Yekhezkel* 1:24 and 25): "when they stood, their wings would stop," saying that when Israel below stand silent, automatically the wings of the multitudes above are silenced, for the matter of their saying the Sanctification is also with their wings. And per the sages' (OBM) words (*Khageega* 13b): "one source says... which one of them[220] was excluded? Rav Cha-nahn-el said in the name of Rav: "those with which

---

219 During certain parts of the *K'doosha*, it is currently a custom to rise from a full-footed position to tip-toes and then back down again.

220 One verse in *Y'shaya* (6:2-3) says that angels have six wings while another in *Y'khezkel* (1:6) says they have four. In *Chageega* this is reconciled by saying the smaller number was after the Temple was destroyed, silencing one set of wings. The Talmud discusses which pair of wings was lost.

they say song... ." And refer *Zohar Chaddash B'reisheet* (13b, top): "(*Yekhezkel* 1:24) 'a noise of tumult... '"—that there however, they explained the word "wings" using another word root meaning "gang."

And for this reason, the multitude of hosts above, are divided into groups. One says "Holy," and those are the *seraphim*, as is written in the *Heikhalot* of *B'reisheet* and *P'koodei*, in the second *Heikhal* there (42a, and there in 247a, end), and as is written (*Y'shaya* 6:2): "*Seraphim* stand above Him... ," "And one calls to the other and says: 'Holy'... ." And a second group, opposite, praise and say: 'Blessed'[221], and they are the *Ophanim* and the *Chayyot*, as our sages (OBM) wrote (*Choolin* 91a) at the beginning of the chapter *Gid Ha-na-sheh*: "Is there '*Ba-rookh*?' *Ba-rookh*—the *Ophanim* are the ones who say it." And as the Notables of the Great Assembly composed in the Sanctification of *Yotzeir*[222], that each group sanctifies according to its source and root in the worlds.

In contrast, Israel, those who are gathered below, say both: "Holy" and "Blessed", inasmuch as they integrate together all the sources and roots.

---

221 Heb.: *ba-rookh*—The Sanctification consists of a first part that begins "Holy, holy, holy... ," a second part: "Blessed is the glory of God-*YHV"H* from His place," and a third part that begins: "God-*YHV"H* will reign forever... ."

222 The Sanctification of *Yotzeir* is part of the morning prayer service, found between *Bor-khoo* and the recitation of the *Sh'ma*. It begins after the *Bor-khoo* with the blessing that includes the words: "...forms the light" [Heb.: *yotzeir or*]. For details about its significance see the relevant section in siddur *Chemdat Yisrael*, edited by R. Shmuel Vittal, son of R. Chayyim Vittal. Also see the Ariza"l's *Sha-ar Ha-kavvanot*, (*Inyan Kavvanat Chazzarat Ha-Ahmeeda, D'roosh Bet, Gimmel* and *Dalet*), where he describes the meaning and function of each of the prayer service's sanctifications in its place.

And this is also the context of the saying of the *Perek Sheera*[223], that our sages (OBM) said: "All who say *Perek Sheera*[224] each day... ," that when a person says it, that he integrates *all* [emphatically] of the powers, he gives power to the angels and the angels-assigned-to-all-the-creations[225] so that they may say these songs, and via this they draw their life force and flow so as to influence in all the lower beings. You can research this further in the *Likootei Torah V'ta-ahmei Ha-mitzvote,* in the section on *V'et-kha-nan.*

CHAPTER 12

And man's soul-*Neffesh,* soul-*Ruakh* and soul-*Neshama* are unable to interconnect the worlds until they descend below into man's body, as we discussed above in Chapter 10, for to rectify the World of Action it was absolutely necessary that they clothe themselves in the body in the World of Action. And we found this in several sources that discuss the three divisions of the soul we mentioned above.

Regarding the matter of arousal in the worlds above via the quality of action[226], King Dovid (peace is upon him) said (*T'hillim* 33): "He who forms together their hearts/minds and understands the direction of all their actions... [227]." According to the plain meaning it would have been appropriate to say "understands all their actions." And he said "*the direction* of

---

223 Chapter of Song

224 *Perek Sheera* (Chapter of Song) is the section of the liturgy that describes how each creation praises its Creator in its own manner.

225 Heb.: *sarim*

226 There are three ways for Man to affect the worlds: action, speech and thought. R. Chayyim addresses each of these in turn.

227 Heb.: *Ho-yotzeir ya-khad leebam ha-mei-veen el kall ma-ah-seihem*

all their actions," as if to say all the things that are relevant to their actions, to say that He who formed them (blessed be His name) is the One who knows and understands to where [the results of] their actions[228] reach and relate to in rectifying the worlds, or the opposite (heaven forefend).

And as Kohelet stated (12:14): "For every action, God-*Elohi"m* will bring to judgment, relative to all that is hidden... ." And it doesn't say: "For God-*Elohi"m* will bring to judgment every...". The reason for this is that the definition of "Elohi"m" is "Master of All Powers", and when a man stands in judgment before Him (blessed be His name), the specific action won't be judged in isolation; rather all the effects and results of his actions will be taken into account, be they good or bad, in all the powers and worlds. This is why he states: "...action, God-*Elohi"m*... ."

And he said: "for every action"[229] and not "relative to every action"[230]. It is as was stated (*Eeyove* 34): "For a man's action will he be recompensed." And it is as was explained above (in chapter 6, in the notes), that from the instant it enters into the purity of a man's thoughts to perform a commandment, immediately its impression is made above, in its lofty root, to build and to plant a number of worlds and lofty powers, as is written (*Y'shaya* 51): "And I will place my words in your mouth..." and "to plant the heavens...". And as they (OBM) stated (at the end of tractate *B'rakhote*): "Don't read it as 'your children'[231] but rather as 'your builders'[232]" as we mentioned above.

---

228 I.e., the effects of their actions

229 Heb.: *kee et call ha-ma-ah-seh*

230 Heb.: *kee al call ha-ma-ah-seh*

231 Heb.: *ba-nahyikh*

232 Heb.: *bo-nahyikh*

And of itself, it arouses and draws upon itself too an encompassing light from the lofty holiness, and it assists him to complete it. And after he finishes the commandment, the holiness and the light withdraws to its root.

And this is the matter of reward in the world-to-come, it being man's own actions. When after the soul-*Neffesh* separates from the body, he ascends to delight and satiate his soul-*Neffesh* in the glow of the holy lights, powers and worlds that were increased and multiplied as a result of his good works.

And that the sages (OBM) said (in *Mishna Ahvote*): "All Israel, there is for them, a portion *for* the world-to-come," and didn't say "*in* the world-to-come," whose meaning would be that the world-to-come is prepared from the time of creation, a subject and a thing by itself, and if a person is pious he will be given a portion from it as his reward. Rather, the truth is that the world-to-come is [emphatically] a result of a person's own actions, that a portion is expanded and added to and refined for himself via his actions. And therefore they said that all Israel, there is for them, for each one, a portion of the holiness and the lights and the brightness that he refined and to which he added *for* the world-to-come, via his good actions.

And so too the punishment of *Gehinnom*[233], its explanation is the same: that the sin itself is his punishment, and as is written (*Mishlei* 5:22): "His sins will trap him and in the ropes of his sins will he be held," and (*Yirmiya* 2:19): "Your own wickedness will afflict you," as will be explained, that when a person performs one of God's

---

233 *Gehinnom* (lit.: Valley of Hinnom) is a name used for the spiritual location used for repentance via a kind of suffering or intense embarrassment. Colloquially it is called Hell.

commandments that shouldn't be done, the defect and the destruction is recorded (heaven forefend) immediately above, at its root.

And in contrast to this (*Y'khezkel* 26:2) "I will be filled for it has been destroyed," [when a person sins] he sets upright and emboldens powers and legions of the defiled and the *kleepote*[234], may the Merciful (blessed be His name) save us.

And from there he draws also upon himself the spirit-*Ruakh* of impurity that wraps itself around him at the moment he performs the offense. And after performing it, the spirit-*Ruakh* of impurity withdraws to its place. And he, during his life, is literally in the *Gehinnom* that surrounds him at the moment he performs the sin, only that he doesn't sense it until after he dies, and is then trapped in the net that he prepared, they being the powers of impurity and the destructive forces that were created from his actions.

Annotation: *However, virtues outweigh..., with a major difference and degree of benefit. For the brilliance and increase in holiness that was added by his good deeds are eternal and exist forever, and his soul-*Neffesh *delights in them an everlasting pleasure.*

But the powers of impurity and the harmful entities that were created and multiplied as a result of his sins, after he receives the complete punishment decreed for him, by their nature they die and perish by themselves.

---

234 The *kleepote* ("shells" or "husks") are the remnants of the *kei-leem* (containers, vessels) that were broken at the time of creation, when they could not contain the "light" that was placed within them. They are associated with the world of impurity, and derive their sustenance by drawing light from sources of holiness, acting as a kind of parasite on the holiness in the world.

For the essence of their existence is only from the sin's blemish and the damage that it caused in the holy powers and the worlds, that from this is drawn to them a minimal amount of vital energy and sparks of light via long, crooked pipes, as in the context of "I will be filled for it has been destroyed" (M'gilla *6a), and because he received his judgment from them, "he swallowed wealth and vomited it out*[235]*", and the flow of life was stopped and in this case, naturally perish. This is the context in which* Gehinnom *is called "leech*[236]*"* (Eiruvin *19a), for the leech sucks out the bad bloods and as a result it [fem.] dies immediately; so it is with* Gehinnom *as mentioned above.*

And this is what our sages (OBM) said (*Eiruvin* 19:1): "The evil deepen *Gehinnom* for themselves," conveying that they themselves deepen *Gehinnom* for themselves, and expand it and ignite it with their sins, and as is written (*Y'shaya* 50:11): "Behold all you who kindle a fire... be gone in the flames of your fire and among the sparks that you kindled—from my hand shall this be for you... ."

Therefore when the Notables of the Great Assembly seized the evil inclination, then *Gehinnom* was thereby quenched, as it is written in *Zohar* (*T'rooma* 109b, top): "as the evil ones warm themselves by the fire of the evil inclination... in every warming and warming... this is the degree to which the fire burns in *Gehinnom*, when once the evil inclination was absent from the world..., and all during that period the fire of *Gehinnom* was extinguished and didn't burn at all. When the evil inclination returned to its place and the evil in the world began to warm themselves

---

235 *Eeyove* 20:15

236 Heb.: *ah-loo-ka.* Leeches were used in medical treatments to suck out the bad humors responsible for illness.

from it, the fire of *Gehinnom* began to burn, for *Gehinnom* doesn't burn except fueled by the power of the evil one's evil inclination."

This is what the text said (*Eeyove* 34:11): "for a man shall be paid for his actions"—that the action itself, whether it be good or evil (heaven forefend) it [emphatic] itself is his compensation, as we explained (and refer to *Zohar Korakh* 177a). And this is what is said in *Mishna Ahvote* (4:2): "The reward of [fulfilling] a commandment is another commandment, and the reward of a transgression is another transgression," and this is what is written (*Kohelet* 12:14): "For every action, God-*Elohi"m* will bring to judgment," to say it is the action itself that endures and is recorded as it is, as was explained above.

Therefore our sages (OBM) said (*Bava Kamma* 50a): "All who say that the Holy One (blessed be He) makes concessions[237], his life will be conceded[238]". And so it is in the *Yerushalmi* (the fifth chapter of *Sh'kalim*), and in *B'reisheet Rabba* (chapter 67), and in *Tahn-khooma* (*parshat Teesah*), and the *Shokhar Tov* (*T'hillim*). And on the face of it this seems surprising, for a kind person acts according to the characteristic of leniency.

However, it is as we wrote above, that this is not a method of punishment or revenge (heaven forefend), only that (*Mishlei* 13:21): "Evil pursues sinners," that the sin itself is the punishment. For from the moment of creation, He (blessed be His name) fixed the order of how the worlds behave, that they should be dependent on what a person's actions arouse, whether good or evil (heaven forefend), that all of his actions and situations create their own effects, each one in its source and root.

---

237 Heb.: *vaht-rahn*

238 Heb.: *yee-va-troo khay-yahv*

And he necessarily receives judgment via the powers of impurity that he empowered with his actions, according to the degree and severity of the defect. And by this, of itself, will be rectified the defect in the worlds and his soul-*Neffesh*.

Or, via the power of repentance that reaches to its very highest root—the world of repentance—a world of complete freedom and light: from there the additional supernal holiness and brilliant light emanates and makes its impression, to finish and obliterate all impurity and to rectify the worlds back to their earlier state via the benefit of the new light from the world of repentance[239] that appears over them.

For that reason, leniency doesn't enter into it. And this is what they said in *Ahvote* (2:41): "and all of your actions are written in a book," that they are written by themselves and recorded above.

CHAPTER 13

And similarly with the subject of the arousal above via the quality of "speech"—the Prophet Amos (peace be upon him) said (4:13): "For lo, He that forms[240] the mountains and creates[241] the wind[*], and tells[242] man what his words... ." For they stated in the *Zohar* (*Lekh L'kha,* 6:2; *Va-y'khi* 234:4 and 249:1; *Yitro* 80a; *Tazria* 50b; *Sh'lakh* 161:1; and in *Idra Zoota* 293; and in *Zohar Chaddash, Shir Ha-Shirrim* 55d) that the term "*ha-ga-da*" relates to the secret of language[243].

---

239 Heb.: *olahm ha-t'shoova*

240 Heb.: *yotzeir*

241 Heb.: *u-vorei*

242 Heb.: *oo-ma-geed*

243 Aram.: *ra-za d'milta*

Here it warns man, that because he is currently in this lowly world and doesn't perceive the constructive effects or damage (heaven forefend) caused in the worlds above as an effect of each of his utterances, that it might occur to him (heaven forefend) to assert: "what possible importance could each utterance and simple conversation have, that it could cause any effect or situation in the world," but it's taken for granted that each of his utterances and light conversations, anything that he expresses with his lips, is not for naught and does not go to waste.

Annotation: *And according to the ordering of the four worlds ABY"A*[244]*, it would have been correct to first state the phrase about Creation-*B'reeya *and afterwards Formation-*Y'tzeera[245].

*However, the context is that the phrase "Formation-*Y'tzeera"*, means the giving of form to something already existing*[246]*, and the expression "Creation-*B'reeya*" means a completely new thing that comes into existence from nothingness"*[247]*, as all the plain text commentators agreed (and as it is also stated in the* Zohar Chaddash, B'reisheet *in the* Midrash Ha-neh-eh-lahm *17a, top).*

It's written in this order because even though it appears to us that now, after the creation, that He only forms *mountains, a thing that exists from another thing that already exists, (for the novel act of creating a thing from nothingness was completed during the six days of creation), rather the truth is that as it was then, so it is now, that at every instant and*

---

244 ABY"A is an acronym for the four worlds of *Ahtzeeloot, B'reeya, Y'tzeera, Ahseeya*

245 The verse from Amos reverses the order of the worlds, Formation-*Y'tzeera* first and Creation-*B'reeya* second.

246 Heb.: *yesh mee-yesh*

247 Heb.: *yesh mee-ayin*

*moment He creates them and recreates what is existent out of the nothingness, using the life force of the soul-*Ruakh *that impinges upon them anew via His will (blessed be He) each moment*[248]*. And so it was stated in* Ahvote *(4:29): "He is the Former, He is the Creator", and this is as discussed above.*

From the source of these words, one who delves into it will understand plainly the matter of the four worlds being called Emanation- Ah'tzeeloot, *Creation-*B'reeya, *Formation-*Y'tzeera, *Action-*Ahseeya.

For it's understood that the worlds unfolded in step-wise fashion, from level to level, and what unfolded and descended further down became more dense[249]*. And the totality of the worlds can be split into four divisions, differing according to their level (exclusive of the supernal "transparent crystals*[250]*" that may not be named even with the name Emanation-*Ahtzeeloot).

*And the first world of the four that He (blessed be His name) emanated, that we are able to name, is called Emanation-*Ahtzeeloot. *And "Ahtzeeloot" has two meanings: as an expression of connection*[251] *as in "with Him"*[252]*, and as an expression of spiritual extension*[253]*, as in (B'midbar 11:25): "and He extended some of the spirit-*Ruakh, *(and as in (Y'khezkel 13:18): "his armpits", that are connected to the body at all times and also the place*

---

248 Rav Chayyim states that even though the mountains appear to already be in existence, in each moment they are being constantly renewed out of nothingness.

249 Heb.: *ah-va* (alt.: denser, thicker, more physical, more perceptible)

250 Heb.: *tzakh-tza-khote*, entities that exist in the perhaps infinite number of worlds that are beyond our perception here in the lowest of the four perceivable worlds.

251 Heb.: *l'shon chee-boor*

252 Heb.: *etz-lo*

253 Heb.: *l'shon hit-pash-toot roo-kha-nee*

*where the emanation of his arms begin). For the world of Emanation-*Ahtzeeloot *is [masc.] completely absolute Godliness*[254], *and as is stated in the introduction to the* Tikkoonim, *in* Ahtzeeloot*: "He and what He causes are one...", and in the* Etz Chayyim, Sha-ar Hishtal'sh'loot Ha-yood S'feerote *chapter 3, and in* Sha-ar Ha-tzellem *chapter 1, and in* Sha-ar Ha-shei-mote *chapter 1, and in* Sha-ar ABY"A *chapter 2 and the beginning of chapter 3, refer there. And it is called "Nothingness"*[255] *because no thought can grasp the true nature of the emanation and the connection, because He and His life force and His effect are one.*

*And the second world unfolded and descended a step lower than the first, and it can be perceived, from all perspectives, that a small part of its being can be called existent, and it [masc.] is the "existence from nothingness", and therefore it is called Creation-*B'reeya, *as I wrote above.*

*And the third world unfolded in the step-wise order from the second world, and became still denser, and its existence can be perceived still more, and it [masc.] is the forming using another thing that already exists, and therefore it is described with the name Formation-*Y'tzeera, *as one shapes clay [into an object], that is forming something from another thing that already exists.*

And the fourth world is the final stage of the construction of all the worlds that preceded it and their rectification for the good and truthful purpose that He (blessed be His name) intended in the matter of the general creation in toto. It is this the lowest world which is the residence

---

254 Heb.: *Eh-lo-koot ga-moor,* where there is absolutely not even a hint of physicality, and perhaps not even one of time or space.

255 Heb.: *Ayin*

of man who directs the worlds through the power of his actions. And as it is written in B'reisheet *(1:31): "And God-*Elohi"m *saw all that He made, and behold, it was very good". And they stated in* B'reisheet Rabba *(chapter 8): "'And behold, it was very good'—'And behold, it was good' means man". And similarly in chapter 9. And in chapter 3 there: "Rabbee Shmuel Bar Ami stated: 'From the beginning of the creation of the world, the Holy One (blessed be He) desired to enact a partnership with the lower ones'." And similarly in Tahn-khooma (parshat B'khoo-ko-tai and in parshat Nahso), refer there.*

*For that reason it is called Action-*Ahseeya, *teaching us about the rectification of the thing, as in the expression (*B'reisheet *18:7): "And he gave it to the youth [masc.] who hurried to prepare*[256] *it", and many others like it. And so too they stated in the* Zohar Chaddash *there: "Action-*Ahseeya *is the rectification of the thing in size and degree relative to how it was beforehand, as it's stated (Shmuel Bet 8:13): 'and Dovid gained renown*[257]*'," up to there.*

And as is written in *Sabbah* (100b): "Even the breath from the mouth has a place and a position, and the Holy One (blessed be He) does with it what He desires. And even one of man's words, and even a voiced sound, is not for naught—there is a place and a position for all of them." And in the section dealing with *M'tzora* (55:1): "Each and every word that man utters with his mouth rises above and splits the heavens and enters the place... ." And at the beginning of *parshat Nahso*: "The word that man utters with his mouth ascends and splits the heavens, and persists in the place... ."

---

256 Heb.: *la-ah-sote*

257 Heb.: *va-ya-ahs Dahveed sheim*

For every utterance has an effect above and arouses supernal energy, in one case with good speech that adds strength to the holy power—as is written in *Y'shaya* 51:17: "And I will put My words in your mouth... to plant the heavens... ."

And in *Zohar Ehmore* (105a): "For there isn't a single word... and one whose mouth utters a holy word, a word of Torah, it becomes a sound and ascends above and arouses the holy ones of the supernal King, and they become a crown for His head and then there is joy above and below." And refer at length to the section dealing with *Va-yahk-heil* (217a)—wondrous, awesome—regarding the utterance of holy words of Torah, that all the worlds are enlightened from the joy, and happiness and delight enter the holy supernal halls, and crown Him with holy crowns. And refer to the section on *K'doshim* (85a, end).

And that's how it's explained in many places in the *Tikkoonim*, that from each spoken word or sound or breath[258] of Torah or prayer are created a number of holy angels. And so too the opposite, with each bad utterance (heaven forefend) he constructs heavens and worlds of worthlessness for S"M[259] (heaven save us) and causes (may the Merciful save us) ruin and destruction of the worlds, the design of the holy Vehicle, that are pertinent to the root of speech.

Refer to *Zohar Tzav* (31b): "'There isn't any good and evil... [that doesn't have its roots above].' Woe to those creatures who observe but don't understand what they are

---

258 Rav Chayyim divides what is emitted from a person's mouth into three categories: word speech (*deeboor*), wordless sounds (*kol*), and the unvoiced breath (*heh-vel*).

259 S"M is an abbreviation for the name of the angel that is responsible for the world of impurity.

seeing, for there is no utterance that doesn't have a place, 'for the birds of the heavens carry the sound' [*Kohelet* 10:20]. And how many thousands of winged creatures grab onto it and elevate it to the masters of judgment, and they judge it," for good or, to the contrary, for evil (heaven forefend), as is written in *Zohar Lekh L'kha* (92a) and in the section on *K'doshim* (referred to above): "There isn't a single word... and how many angels of destruction attach themselves to that sound, until it ascends and the place of the great deep arouses... and how many are aroused over that man; woe to one from whose mouth issues evil speech... . " Refer there [for more details].

And it's written [*Kohelet* 5:5]: "Why should God be angry at your voice and destroy the work of your hands". And they said (*Talmud Ah-ra-khin* 15a): "Greater is the one who says with his mouth than the one who performs a physical action... ." And our sages stated (*Sanhedrin* 92a): "One who is inconsistent in his speech is as if he worships the constellations."

And this is what is written (*Ahmos* 4:13): "And He declares[260] to man what his speech is," as if to say that at the hour when man stands before Him (blessed be He) to give an accounting, then He (blessed be He) tells him the secret, the secret of words, what his conversations caused above in the supernal worlds. And we described above that the term "*ha-ga-da*" is defined as the secret of language.

CHAPTER 14

And too, regarding the arousal above via the aspect of thought, King Dovid (OBM) stated (*T'hillim* 33:16): "He who forms together their hearts/minds and understands the direction of all their actions... ." And it should have

260 Heb.: *oo-ma-geed*

said: "who understands all their actions..." And previously in chapter 12, we explained it in relation to action. And we can also explain it in relation to thought.

And thus, does it make sense that two people should perform the same sin, and being so, that their punishments are not equivalent? [It is so] because one's intelligence and grasp is greater than his peer, because the root of his soul is from a higher place and more elevated than his peer, and the punishment is related to the blemish that it caused above, and the blemish that each one causes reaches to the root of his soul-*Neshama*.

As we learned in the *Tikkoonim* (at the end of *Tikkoon* 43): "One who blemishes below also blemishes above to the place from where his soul-*Neshama* is quarried[261]." And also there (*Tikkoon* 70, 123:1): "And when man performs sins, relative to that person does his sin rise to the source from where his soul-*Neshama* is quarried... and his punishment is adjusted according to his level." And so also wrote the Ariza"l in *Sha-ar Ha-yikhoodim*[262], and the beginning of the section on rectifying sins[263], and in the *Pri Etz Chayyim* in the introduction to the chapter on *Shabbat* (chapter 11) and in *Gilgulim*. We can not compare one who sullies the courtyard of the king to one who sullies the palace; how

261 Quarrying is the process by which stone is mined from its source in a rock formation in the Earth. The *Tikkoonim* refers here to the Quarry of Souls (Heb.: *makh-tzahv ha-n'sha-mote*), the common source of all souls in Israel.

262 This reference can be found at the very beginning of third *ah-naf* of *Sha-ar Ha-yeekhoodim*. The most commonly available editions of *Sha-ar Ha-yeekhoodim* are comprised of the third and fourth *ah-nafim* of the *Pri Etz Chayyim*. The second *ah-naf* (referenced earlier) is not usually included there, but can be found as part of a manuscript in Yeshiva University's Gottesman Library.

263 Heb.: *tikkoon ah-vo-note*

much more so the throne, or the robes of splendor, and even more so the crown.

Even though, in a world that is more elevated and sublime, the sin has no power to cause within it as significant a blemish or impression, even so his punishment is still greater. For one who is appointed to polish and burnish the King's crown, if he left on it even a tiny speck of dust, there's no way to compare the extent of his punishment to the punishment of one who is appointed to clean the King's courtyard, even if he left or placed within it a large amount of mud or clay. And therefore God's judgments are many in the infinite different details of punishment, each one according to the level of the blemish at the root of his soul-*Neshama*, from which world it is quarried.

Also, two people's punishment won't be equal by reason that their thoughts weren't equivalent at the time they performed the sin, and the blemish drawn through the worlds is also according to the thought at the time it was performed. And if one attached his thoughts more to the sin, it is certain that he is worthy of a greater punishment, for then the blemish reaches (heaven forefend) to still higher worlds. And for this reason, one who unintentionally performs a sin receives a lesser punishment than one who does it purposely. And therefore they said (*Yoma* 29) that thoughts about sin are more severe than the sin itself[264].

And what is written (*T'hillim*, cited above): "He who forms together their hearts/minds..."—that is, that He envisions the thoughts of their hearts/minds as our sages explained in tractate *Rosh HaShanna* 18:1. "And understands the direction of all their actions"—as if to say that the lofty Former (blessed

---

264 As Rav Chayyim explained this is the case when the root of their soul came from a higher place, and they focused their intention.

be His name) envisions and understands the thoughts of their hearts/minds that joins in their actions, and judges each one according to the thought in his heart/mind at the moment he performed the sin.

And so said King Solomon (OBM) (*Kohelet* 12:14): "For each action [emphatic] will God-*Elohi"m* bring to judgment related to that which is hidden..."—intending to convey that in addition to the punishment for the physical action of the sin, God-*Elohi"m* (blessed be His name) will also bring to judgment the entire action, to repeat the judgment also on the hidden thought, how and in what manner it occurred at the moment of action.

And so he also said (*Mishlei* 3:19): "God-*YHV"H* founded the earth with wisdom, established the heavens with deep understanding; the depths of the oceans were cleaved with knowledge." He included in this generally all the worlds: "earth" is the middle world, "heavens" is the general category of the upper worlds, and "depths of the oceans" is the general category of the lower worlds.

And he said after this: "my son, may it not escape[265] your eyes". We've found the term "eye" a few places in TaNa"Kh in relation to topic of thought, as it says (*Kohelet* 1:16): "and my heart saw...," "the wise man, his eyes are in his head" (2:14). And the term "escape"[266] we found in the *Mishna* as a term of distortion (or crookedness), as in "crooked is he, and makes his Father in heaven depart from above him" (end of *Kil'ayim*). This is what is written: "My son, please spare and have compassion on the dear worlds that were created with wisdom, intelligence and knowledge, and take care that you shouldn't cause (heaven forefend) a distortion or

265 Heb.: *ya-looz-oo*
266 Heb.: *v'ya-lee-zoo*

corruption with one thought that isn't good (heaven forefend)."

And these three aspects: action, speech and thought, they are the three general inner aspects of man that are the three aspects: soul-*Neffesh*, soul-*Ruakh* and soul-*Neshama.*

For action, it is in the category of *Neffesh*, as is written (*B'midbar* 15:30): "and the *Neffesh* that you shall make," (*Va-yikra* 18:29) "the *Neffesh* [plural] who do..." and many others, such as (*D'varim* 12:23) "for the blood is the *Neffesh*", that the *Neffesh* inhabits and clothes itself in man's blood, and therefore the crux of attributing its abode to the liver is that it is full of blood. The circulation of blood in all the parts and divisions of the limbs, the implements of action, is what provides them with vital ability and arousal, so that they will be able to enact and to perform what is in their potential. If the circulation of blood should cease from a limb, that limb will wither and won't have the ability to do anything, and it is a dead limb.

And speech, it is in the category of *Ruakh*, as is written (*Shmuel Bet* 23:2): "God's spirit-*Ruakh* spoke within me," and (Y'shaya 11:4) "with the spirit-*Ruakh* of his lips," and as Onkeloos translated on the verse (*B'reisheet* 2:7): "and the man became a living soul-*Neffesh*": "a speaking spirit-*Ruakh*". And so it appears to the eye that with each speech action, a person's mouth emits a spirit [267]and vapor[268]. And the abode of the *Ruakh*, its essence and origin is in the heart, for speech's spirit and vapor, its essence and origin arises from the heart.

And thought, it is in the category of the *Neshama.* She teaches man knowledge and understanding via the

267 Heb.: *ruakh*
268 Heb.: *heh-vel*

holy Torah, and therefore the origin of its abode is in the brain, the tool of thought, and she is the highest category of them all. And so they said in *B'reisheet Rabba,* chapter 14: "She is called by five names...", "the *Neffesh* is the blood..., *Ruakh...*, *Neshama* is the nature of the creature"—["nature"] meaning his knowledge and thoughts, as was explained by the Arukh and RaSh"Y (OBM).

CHAPTER 15

And it might surprise you. After all the word "Soul-*Neshama*'s" meaning is "breath", and in this way it appears to the eye that a person's breath is a gaseous flow that arises from the heart, from below to above. And also in this way it is the characteristic of "returning light"[269]and not a feature of higher spirituality.

However, the matter that is referred to by the term "breath", the intention is not man's breath, rather [it is] as metaphor for His breath (blessed be His name), as is written (*B'reisheet* 2:7): "...and He blew into his nostrils the breath[270] of life".

And our rabbis (OBM) (*Sanhedrin* 91a, beginning of *Perek Cheilek*) have previously likened the context of the downward flow of the wind-*Ruakh* of life in Man to the making of a glass vessel in the context of the revival of the dead, and they said: "it can be deduced logically[271] from a glass vessel that is worked with the wind-*Ruakh* of flesh and blood... how much more so flesh and blood [worked] with

269 The term *ore chozeir* (returning light) implies that light originating above descended below, arrived at its destination and then returned to a point higher than its lowest point. Returning light has a lower quality than direct light.

270 Heb.: *nishmaht*

271 Heb.: *kal v'khomeir*

the wind-*Ruakh* of the Holy One (blessed be He)." And so it is in the *Shokhar Tov, T'hillim, mizmor* 2, refer there.

For what we are discussing resembles a supporting proof, for when we examine the craftsman's mouth's exhalation into the glass vessel during its fabrication we discover three phases. The first phase is when the breath's gaseous flow is still within his mouth prior to its entering the empty space within the hollow pipe; at this point it would be mistaken to refer to it as anything other than "breath". The second phase is when the gaseous flow enters and arrives within the pipe and is pulled along it as in a straight line; then it is referred to as wind-*Ruakh*. And the third, lowest phase is when the wind-*Ruakh* exits the pipe and enters the glass, and spreads within it until a vessel is formed according to the will of the glassmaker. Then he terminates his wind-*Ruakh*, and it is then referred to as soul-*Neffesh*, using a term used to denote completion and rest.

So according to this description the three qualities (*Neffesh, Ruakh* and *Neshama*) that flow metaphorically from His mouth's breath (blessed be His name), that the aspect of *Neffesh* is the lowest aspect [fem.], for she is completely within man's body.

And the aspect of *Ruakh* [male] arrives via an infusion from above, whose upper edge and part is attached to and gripped above in the lowest part of the *Neshama*, and flows and enters also within the body of man, and connects [fem.] there with the upper part of the *Neffesh*, as is written (*Y'shaya* 32:15): "until the spirit[272] be poured upon us from on high", "I will pour out my spirit[273]..." (*Yoel* 3:1), for it impresses its influence in man by way of pouring and infusion as we

272 Heb.: *ruakh*

273 Heb.: *ru-khee*

discussed above, and as will be explained further later[274] (God willing), the lengthy description of how they are connected.

However, the aspect of *Neshama* is the breath itself, whose innermost essence hides itself in concealment and its [fem.] blessed wellspring is (metaphorically) within the breath of His mouth (blessed be His name), for its essential aspect does not enter at all within the body of man. First Adam, before the sin, merited to its essence, and by reason of the sin it departed from within him and remained only hovering above him.

Except for Moses Our Teacher (peace be upon him), who merited to have its essence within his body, and therefore he was called "the man of God-*Elohi"m" (D'varim* 33:1), as is understood that all three worlds (Creation, Formation and Action), from the perspective of their *Neshama* and above, are absolute Godliness[275], as is written in the *Etz Chayyim, Sha-ar Ha-tzellem,* chapter 1, and at the beginning of the *Sha-ar Tzee-yoor O-la-mote ABY"A,* and in the introduction by Rav Chayyim Vittal (OBM), and in the *Sha-ar Ha-sheimote,* chapter 1.

And other than him, no other man earned her. Only the brightness of the sparks of lights, sparkling from within her, are over the head of the man that earned her—each according to his level and according to his measure.

And refer to the *Raa-ya M'hemna, Nahso* 123b: "And He exhaled into his nostrils the breath of life"—This is the image[276] that is above the man... . And in *Zohar Chaddash, Root* 64, *ahmood* 3: "If he is worthy... then an extra measure of greatness descends upon him from above..., from over him awakens an awakening of holiness, and it settles upon him and surrounds him on all sides. And that same

274 See chapter 17

275 Heb.: *eh-lo-koot ga-moor*

276 Aram.: *d'yoke-na*

awakening that settles upon him, it originates from a lofty place, and what is her name? *Neshama* is her name." Refer there [for more details].[277]

And she is what gives to man an extra measure of understanding[278] to intellectually grasp the inner intelligence hidden in our holy Torah. And as is written in the *Sitrei Torah* of *Zohar Lekh L'kha* 79b: "*Neshama* awakens in man understanding[279]. And in the *Zohar Chaddash, Root* 64a: "And I will awaken in you with lofty wisdom...[280]".

And refer in the *Etz Chayyim* (*Sha-ar Mokhin D'kahtnoot*, chapter 3), and this is what it says: "Surely not all men are worthy to earn it, and know that one who has the power in his actions... then he will have a wondrous memory in Torah, and will understand all the secrets of Torah... and all the secrets of Torah will be revealed to him correctly"- it ends here. And refer further on in the context of his root in the higher worlds and you will understand.

And this is what the text said (*Eeyove*, 32:8): "Indeed it is a spirit[281] in man, and the breath[282] of God-*Shadda"i* makes them understand", intending to convey that the aspect of *Ruakh* is what flows and impresses and enters within man. However the *Neshama* is "the breath of God-*Shadda"i*", meaning the breath of His mouth (blessed be He); its essence does not impress and reveal [itself] within man, for she dwells in the heavens, metaphorically within His mouth

---

277 Rav Chayyim emphasizes that the *Neshama* doesn't enter within man, but rather, if earned, appears to one who can perceive it as sparkling lights above and around him. The only exceptions were First Adam and Moshe Rabbeinu.

278 Heb.: *beena y'tei-ra*

279 Heb.: *beena*

280 Heb.: *chokh-ma-ta ee-la-ah*

281 Heb.: *ruakh*

282 Heb.: *nishmaht*

(blessed be He), only that she gives him understanding in the sparks of light above him, to make him understand the depths of the Holy Torah's hidden aspects.

And what is written in the *Zohar* and the Kabbalists (OBM) that the aspect of the *Neshama's* abode is in man's brain, they (OBM)) intended the sparks of brilliant light that impart intelligence to his mind and intellect, not her actual essence.

And the key part of their (OBM) intention about the three "heads" of the *Ruakh*, the secrets of the brains, is that sometimes they sparkle and sometimes depart, and they arrive via the secret of a temporary addition[283] to one who through merit earns it, as is known, and not as the essential aspect of the *Neshama*. And so our teacher, the great genius, the pious Rav Eliyahu[284] (OBM) wrote in his explanation on the *Heikhalote*, in the second *Heikhal*.

And they are identical: the lower aspect of the *Neshama* that sparkles in the parts of his mind called knowledge and intellect to impart intelligence, she [emphatic] is the three "heads" of the *Ruakh* in his brains, as will be explained next, God willing[285].

CHAPTER 16

And the intellectuals will understand that this situation also holds in his supernal root, that only the lowest part of the "mother of the children"[286]—the secret of the supernal *Neshama* of life[287]—she enters and spreads out within the

283 Heb.: *toe-seh-fet*

284 The Vilna Gaon

285 The lowest part of the upper aspect corresponds to the "heads" of the aspect below it.

286 Heb.: *eim ha-ba-nim*

287 Heb.: *nishmaht chayyim*

Supernal Man[288] via the secret of "temporary addition"[289], after being rectified by way of the desired actions of those in the lower worlds.[290]

And this is the secret of the holy brains[291], its three heads, whose essence is six parts (as is known), as is clear to one who understands the *Etz Chayyim, Sha-ar Abba V'eema*[292], chapter 1; and in the *Sha-ar P'ra-tei Ahteek Yomin*[293]; and in the *Sha-ar Ha-zeevoogim*[294] at the start of chapter 4; and at the end of the *Sha-ar Mokhin D'tzellem*[295]; and in the *Sha-ar D'rooshei D'tzellem*[296], second commentary (refer there carefully in each commentary); and in the eighth commentary there; and in the *Pri Etz Chayyim,* chapter 3 from the chapter of *T'fillin*; and in the *Sha-ar Ha-yikhoodim,* chapter 5, from *Tikkoon Ah-vo-note.*

And that they said that the *Neshama* settles in the brain, as is written there in the *Sha-ar O-rote, Neetzotzim, Keilim*[297], chapter 6; and in the *Sha-ar Ha-mokhin*[298] in all of chapter 7 and in chapter 8 and in chapter 12; and in the *Sha-ar D'rooshei D'tzellem* in the beginning of the second commentary. And the matter is explained further there in the Rabbi Chayyim Vittal's annotation

---

288 "Supernal Man" here refers to the *shiur koma ha-kollel,* the entirety of creation which has the form (so to speak) of an upright man.

289 Heb.: *toe-seh-fet*

290 Rav Chayyim refers to the process by which those in the lower worlds effect a temporary addition of the aspect of *Neshama* to specific parts of the upper worlds.

291 Heb.: *mo-khin ka-deesheen*

292 Gate of Father and Mother

293 Gate of the Details of the Ancient of Days

294 Gate of the Couplings

295 Gate of the Brains of the Tzellem

296 Gate of the Commentaries on the Tzellem

297 Gate of Lights, Sparks and Vessels

298 Gate of the Brains

(OBM), and in the *Sha-ar Ha-partzoofin*[299], beginning of chapter 1; and in the *Sha-ar P'neemeeyoot V'khee-tzo-nee-yoot*[300], the fourth and ninth commentaries; and the *Sha-ar Kleepaht Noga*[301], beginning of chapter 1. And it will be clear to the exceedingly fastidious in all the commentaries on the *tzellem.*

And its edge hovers and surrounds from above and shines upon his head by its proximity, it being the secret of the "crown with which his mother crowned him" (*Shir Ha-shirrim,* 3:11), by way of the secret of the breath[302] and the vapor that exits from the mother's mouth, to the light that approaches to surround him. As is written in the *Etz Chayyim, Sha-ar Ha-k'la-leem*[303], end of chapter 11; and in the *Likutei TaNa"Kh*[304], in *T'hillim,* in the verse: "*Ha-kol sog...,*" as was described above, that the aspect of the *Neshama* is the breath of the supernal mouth, but its essence is completely hidden above, and disappears in its source inside the mouth, and shines from a distance.

And by this will be understood their (OBM) intention in *Sh'mote Rabba,* section 41, on the verse: "For God-*YHV"H* will give wisdom from His mouth, knowledge and understanding" (*Mishlei* 2:6) where they said: "To what does it resemble? To a king who had a son. His son came from school and found a platter of food in front of his father. His father took one piece of it and gave it to him..., He said to him: 'I do not request anything other than a part of what is within your mouth'. What did he do? He gave it to him. ... ." That is, what the beloved son is requesting

---

299 Gate of the Aspects
300 Gate of Innerness and Outerness
301 Gate of the Husk of Nogah
302 Heb.: *n'sheema*
303 Gate of General Principles
304 Collection from TaNa"Kh

to attain is that He should impress upon him from the sparks of the light of the aspect of *Neshama,* whose source is deeply hidden in the breath of His mouth (blessed be His name).

And they provided further hints in their holy phrasing, that the metaphor they used was a young child who comes specifically from school. They reliably informed us that there is no worldly entrance to attain the aspect of the sparks of the light of the Soul-*Neshama* if not via the engagement and in-depth study and reflection in the holy Torah, from within a state of holiness, for the two of them originate from a single source[305], as is known to one who understands.

Annotation: *And based on this, one who looks into it will intellectually understand, according to the plain meaning regarding the matter mentioned in the* Zohar (parshat Ah-kha-rei *73a), that the Holy One blessed be He, the Torah and Israel are connected one to another. It's definite that his deep intention is toward profound secrets; even so it makes sense to also explain this matter in its plain meaning, based on this.*

*And the matter is, that the Holy One (blessed be He) is hidden and revealed (*Zohar parshat Ehmore *98b), for the essence of the Lord of All, the Infinite-*Ein Sof *is inconceivable, and thought can not grasp it at all. What we can grasp is a tiny part of a tiny part, that is only from the perspective of His*

---

305 The two being the Torah and the sparks of the Soul-*Neshama.* Here Rav Chaim sets the stage for presenting the nature of Torah and the necessity of and irreplaceable need for involvement with Torah. It's *only* via involvement with Torah that one can merit the connection to soul-*Neshama.*

relationship to the worlds[306]*, from the moment that He created them and renewed them, to vivify them and to sustain them each moment and to guide them, as is written (*N'khemya *9:6): "and You vivify them all".*

Therefore we praise Him (blessed be He) in our prayers that He is the "Life of the Worlds"[307]*, for the whole intention of our hearts in all of our prayers and supplications, are forbidden towards any but the Unity of the Universe, He being the Infinite-*Ein Sofe *(blessed be He). However, not only from the perspective of His essence (blessed be He), in the sense of His being separate from the worlds, but rather from the perspective of His attachment (blessed be He) via His simple will to the worlds and his concealment within them to vivify them. This is the general principle regarding worship and all of the commandments. This is all that we can grasp.*[308] *And refer further on in this work in Gate Two, chapters four and five for the topic at length.*

*The entire existence and sustenance of all the worlds are only the effect of the holy Torah when Israel is engaged with her, that she illuminates all the worlds and is their soul-*Neshama *and the vivifying force for all of them. And if the universe, from one end to the other, was empty even for one moment from engagement with and in-depth study of the holy Torah, all the worlds would return to chaos and emptiness, as they (OBM) said: "For the sake of Torah... ",*

---

306 Rav Chaim later explains (in Gate 3, chapter 11) the three aspects of God's relationship to creation, and how they are perceived.

307 Heb.: *chei oh-la-meem*

308 Rav Chayyim says that our prayers are directed only toward the Infinite-*Ein Sofe*—towards both the *essence* (so to speak) of *Ein Sofe* which is separate and apart from the worlds, and the *Chei Olahmim* which is the Ein Sofe connected to the worlds, hidden within them (so to speak) to sustain them.

> *and as they wrote: "and He planted eternal life within us", for the source of her heavenly root is above all of the worlds, therefore all of their existences depends on her*[309]*.*
>
> *And they also said: "for the sake of Israel...", as we will explain, for as a result of man's involvement with and his reasoning in the holy Torah, he attains the sparkling of the light of the aspect of soul-*Neshama *within him, to make him intelligent in the depths of her holy secrets, and then is given the name Israel, as is known in the* Zohar. *"...But by all that comes out of God-*YHV"H*'s mouth" (D'varim 8:3)—it is the aspect of man's soul-*Neshama, *His breath (blessed be He), they will also vivify and maintain all of the powers and worlds, for she is also the highest and the innermost of all the worlds, and this is 'the Holy One blessed be He and the Torah and Israel are all bound one to another', and that they said: " 'In the beginning...*[310]*' is for the sake of Torah, who [fem.] is called "first*[311]*", and for the sake of Israel who are called "first*[312]*".*

And this is what they stated there, that at the hour when Israel stood on Mount Sinai to receive the Torah, they requested to hear the spoken commandments from the mouth of the Holy One (blessed be He), and as is written (*Shir Ha-shirrim* 1:2): "He will kiss me with the kisses of His mouth".

---

309 The principle is that what is higher provides the sustenance for what is below. Torah is above all the worlds and so is the source of the sustenance for all the worlds below.

310 Heb.: *b'reisheet*

311 Heb.: *rei-sheet*

312 Heb.: *rei-sheet*

For during the time of the holy event, they all merited the brilliant sparks of clarity, for it (the aspect of Neshama) was hovering over them and shining upon them, metaphorically from the breath[313] of his (blessed be He) mouth, and it is the secret of the crowns that they merited at Sinai: "and the world's joy upon their heads" (*Y'shaya* 35, and refer to *Shabbat* 88a).

And in this way they merited to attain secrets of the inner Soul-*Neshama* of the holy Torah, as is written in the *Zohar* (*B'ha-ah-lo-t'kha* 152a): "The Torah has a body... the sages, servants of the highest King. They who stood at Mount Sinai are not gazing at anything other than its Soul-*Neshama,* that is the essence of the entire Torah, in actuality."

And this is what they stated in a number of places in *Midrash Rabba*: "They had armor at Sinai, and the ineffable Name was engraved upon it"—that is the high attainment in the *Neshama,* and the secret of the Torah is the ineffable Name. That's how it was then, above in its supernal root, as we mentioned in the last chapter, the secret of "the crown with which his mother crowned him" (*Shir Ha-shirrim* 3:11). And they expounded upon this in *Chazeeta*[314]: "'on the day he was wed' is Sinai, and 'the day his heart was joyous'—these are the words of Torah." And the phrase "with the crown"... these are the crowns we mentioned above that were at Sinai, the regal life force. And refer to the *Etz Chayyim, Sha-ar Ha-k'lalim,* end of chapter 5.

313 Heb.: *nishmaht*

314 *Chazeeta* is another name for *Midrash Shir Ha-Shirrim.*

CHAPTER 17

And we will explain the connection of the three aspects *Neffesh, Ruakh* and *Neshama* one to the other; it's the foundation and key principle of the subject of repentance. And the complete effect is to remove the sins from the sinner's *Neffesh*, and to purify it from the illness of its impurity.

A person should introspect how much he must monitor and contemplate the details of his service to his Creator (blessed be His name), so that his service will be perfect and whole, holy and pure. And he'll see to it that he closely examines and continuously inspects all of his actions, speech and thoughts (they being the three aspects mentioned above), to determine if perhaps he has not yet completed His (blessed be His name) desire and will, to attain it fully according to his soul's-*Neshama* root. Each day he should strive still more in Torah and mitzvote to perfect his *Neffesh, Ruakh* and *Neshama* to a state of absolute purity, as they were given to him, after perceiving in his mind's eye how He (blessed be His name) desires in His great goodness to do good for him in the end. He eagerly anticipates the rectification of the sinning *Neffesh*, for even if it is already drowning in the evil depths, even so each thing will return to its place and source—it will not be permanently pushed aside[315].

And the matter is, that it's known in the process of the unfolding of the worlds, that the uppermost part in each world is connected to the lowermost part of the world above it. And refer to *Zohar Va-yikra* 10b: "that all the worlds are connected, this one to that and that one to this, like the links of a chain are connected one to the

315 Heb.: *biltee yee-dakh mee-meh-noo nee-dakh*

other." And as is known from the writings of the Ariza"l, the outer aspect of *Mahl-khoot*[316] of each world and *partzoof*[317] becomes the innermost aspect of the *Ketter*[318] to the world or *partzoof* below it—that is, as a result of a person accepting the yoke of His (blessed be His name) kingship, raising all of his actions, speech and thoughts in Torah and mitzvote to a still higher level, from that is created an inner will[319] to subjugate his mind, words and actions to Torah and mitzvote in the secret of *Ketter Malkhut*[320].

And thusly is the matter of the three aspects *Neffesh, Ruakh* and *Neshama* for man: Each aspect of a holy thing is comprised of ten individual parts that are its ten *s'feerote.* And the highest aspect of the *Neffesh* holds onto and is connected with the tenth lowest aspect of the aspect of *Ruakh,* and the uppermost aspect of *Ruakh* connects with the lowest aspect of the *Neshama,* and the *Neshama* too connects and adheres in the *Shoresh ha-Neshama*[321], the secret of the *k'nesset yisrael*[322] she being the root of the general collective of all souls of Israel. And also according to this approach, the aspect of the *Shoresh ha-Neshama* also connects to higher above, from level to level, until the *Ahtzmoot Ein Sofe*[323] (blessed be He).

---

316 Sovereignty, or Kingship, the bottom-most of the ten *S'feerote*

317 Literally "face"

318 Crown, the highermost of the ten *S'feerote*

319 Heb.: *r'tzone p'neemee*

320 The *Ketter* of *Malkhut* is the higher-most part of the *s'feera* of *Malkhut.* It arises or activates as a result of one accepting the yoke of heaven. It is the "inner will" that controls and directs his thoughts, speech and actions.

321 Literally "root of the *Neshama*", also known as *Chayyah*

322 Congregation of Israel—the collective of all the souls of all Jews

323 The "essence" of the *Ein Sofe*

And this is what Avigayil said to Dovid (*Shmuel Aleph,* 25:29) "and may my lord's Soul-*Neffesh* be bound in the bundle of life[324] to God-*YHV"H* your lord", as if to say that the aspect his soul-*Neffesh* will adhere (so to speak) to Him (blessed be His name).

And as is written in the *Zohar* (*T'rooma* 142b): "When that *Ruakh* [fem.] ascends and becomes crowned… that specific *Neffesh* [fem.] connects with that specific *Ruakh* [fem.] and becomes enlightened from it [masc.] …, and the *Ruakh* connects with the specific *Neshama* [fem.], and that *Neshama* [fem.] connects within the extreme limit of thought that is called "secret[325]". And that specific *Neffesh* [fem.] connects with that lofty *Ruakh* [masc.], and that *Ruakh* [masc.] connects with that specific lofty *Neshama* [fem.], and that specific *Neshama* [fem.] connects in the *Ein Sofe,* and then she is great comfort to all[326] and a connection [is made] between all, above and below, all per the secret of "One"…, and that results in the *Neffesh*'s repose below. And about this is written "and may my lord's Soul-*Neffesh* be bound in the bundle of life to God-*YHV"H* your lord".

And in the chapter of *Ah-kha-rei* 71b: "We learned that it is written 'my lord's soul-*Neffesh* be bound..."—it should have said 'my lord's soul-*Neshama*'. However as we stated: meritorious is the portion of the righteous. Everything is connected one to the other, the *Neffesh* in the *Ruakh,* the *Ruakh* in the *Neshama,* and the *Neshama* in the Holy One (blessed be He); in that way the *Neffesh* is bound up in the "bundle of life". And refer further in *parshat Va-yikra* at the top of page 25.

---

324 Heb.: *tz'rohr ha-chayyim*

325 Heb.: *sode,* fem.

326 Heb.: *la-kol*

And this is the context of: "for a part of God-*YHV"H* is his nation, Yaakov is the rope of his inheritance", for they are part of God-*YHV"H*, adhering (so to speak) to Him (blessed be His name) via the connection of the three aspects discussed above, as a rope that is anchored above, and which unwinds and descends downward.

CHAPTER 18

And all of this [arises] from His overwhelming goodness and His (blessed be His name) great kindness, for He desires to exonerate us and to do good for us in the end. For this reason He created these wondrous designs, and made them permanent in this context, that each of these three should attach to the aspect above it [fem.], so that by way of this, man would be able to rise and connect from below to above, little by little, according to the degree of his involvement with His Torah and service of Him (blessed be His name), and the purity of his heart and his love and awe, until he shall ascend and attach (so to speak) to the "bundle of life" with God-*YHV"H* his Lord (blessed be His name), according to his root and level.

There's this and also more, for there are certain sins that if the soul-*Neffesh* commits one of them, it is liable for the punishment of being "cut off[327]" (heaven forefend). And the matter of "cutting off" is that the aspect of *Neffesh* is interrupted and cut off from its heavenly root, and the "rope[328]" that was connected and attached to it until now via the connection we discussed above is severed.

And as it is written in *Zohar T'rooma* that we mentioned above: "and there is a soul-*Neffesh*... in relation to it is

327 Heb.: *ka-reit*
328 Heb.: *cheh-vel*

written 'and that soul-*Neffesh* shall be cut off from before Me, I am God-*YHV"H*'. What is 'from before Me'? That the soul-*Ruakh* no longer rests upon him, and when the soul-*Ruakh* does not rest upon him, there is no connection at all with what is above... ." Refer there [for more details]. And refer to the *Likutei Torah, parshat Bo,* and in *Mekhilta, parshat Bo,* and at the end of *parshat Tee-sa,* and in *Sifri, parshat B'ha-ah-lote-kha,* and in *parshat Sh'lakh.* And "shall be cut off" is not complete cutting off but rather an interruption.

And that which is written (*Y'shaya* 59:2): "For your sins have separated between you and your God-*Elohi"m*", that is literally between you and your God-*Elohi"m* as we discussed above, and then it drowns in the depths of impurity and the husks (may the Merciful save us).

Refer to the *Etz Chayyim, Sha-ar K'la-loot ABY"A*[329], beginning of chapter 1, and in the *Sha-ar Ha-yikhoodim*[330], end of chapter 4, and there chapter 1 in the section addressing the rectification of sins, and in the *Likutei T'Na"Kh* in *Y'shaya* in the verse "for the soul-*Ruakh* that enwraps itself is from Me" (57:16), and in *Gilgoolim*[331], end of chapter 35. And so it is written in his holy writing from our great rabbi, our teacher Rabbi Eliyahu[332] (OBM), in his commentary on the *Hei-kha-lote,* in the second *Hei-khal.*

Lest he go completely astray, His (blessed be He) will issued a judgment that they shouldn't be cut off (heaven forefend) completely in all the ten aspects of the *Neffesh.* Only the nine lower aspects, from her Wisdom[333] and down they are cut off. However the uppermost aspect, the secret

329 Gate of Overall Description of ABY"A
330 Gate of Unifications
331 *Sha-ar Ha-gilgoolim*—Gate of Reincarnations
332 The Vilna Gaon
333 Heb.: *Chokhma*

of her crown[334] [*A] is not cut off; that from the perspective of her attachment and connection with the aspect of the *Ruakh* (as we described above) [*B] it [fem.] is judged to be aspect of *Ruakh* for which there is no cutting off, as we will learn later. And this comes from supernal compassion[335] (blessed is He), that via the aspect of *Ruakh*, that is via heart-felt verbal confession (which is the aspect of *Ruakh*, as we described above), the nine aspects of the *Neffesh* will rise to connect all of them with the aspect of *Ruakh* as before.

Annotation A: *That is to say, even if our souls-*Neffesh *are mired (heaven forefend) in evil desires (may the Merciful save us), even so His will (blessed be His name) established to elevate their soul-*Neffesh *via the aspect of His soul-*Ruakh *(blessed be His name), as in the context that is written (*Y'shayahu *59:21): "And as for Me, this is My covenant with them, says God-*YHV"H*: My spirit-*Ruakh *that is upon thee... shall not depart...", and as in the context of the Exodus from Egypt (*Sh'mote *20:2), and this is "and I am God-YHV"H your God-*Elohi"m *who took you out of the land of Egypt". And it's known in the* Zohar, *that I-*Ah-no-khee *is the aspect of the crown. This is the commentary of the sages (OBM) (*Shabbat *105a): "The word 'I-*Ah-no-khee' *is a* nootrikone[336] that *means 'I, Myself, wrote this and gave it to you[337] ...' [and another is] 'beautiful pronouncement'." And they are the two aspects of* Neffesh *and* Ruakh, *and the wise will understand.*

---

334 Heb.: *Ketter*

335 Heb.: *mei-khessed ha-el-yone*

336 A *nootreekone* is a word formed by appending the first letters of a sequence of words to form a new word. It can serve as a mnemonic device or to encode a deeper meaning.

337 Aram.: *Ahna nahfshee k'ta-veet y'ha-veet*

Annotation B: *That is to say that the inner will that crowns a* Neffesh *in Israel from the perspective of fear/awe-*yir'ah *is never, ever interrupted. And refer to the RaMBa"M at the end of chapter 2 relating to the ruling in a divorce issued under duress*[338]*: "...until he says 'I desire', for the divorce is deemed legal if the law allows that he can be forced to grant the divorce." And there they explained the reason that he is not considered "compelled": his true will is to perform all the commandments, but his evil inclination dominated him. Since he was beaten until his evil inclination weakened and he then said "I desire [to divorce her]", he divorced by his own will. Refer there for the holy one's*[339] *phrasing.*

And similarly, if he blemished and damaged (heaven forefend) his aspect of speech via sins that are dependent on speech—via evil speech and the like, or the other sins that are dependent in their root on the aspect of *Ruakh*—

338 The case here deals with divorce. A divorce must be issued by the man's own free will. If the divorce is issued under duress, the divorce is not legal. Maimonides ruled that a court may physically coerce a man to the point where he issues the divorce, and the divorce is considered legal. Isn't this a "divorce issued under duress"? The answer is "no" because the court considers a man who refuses to issue a divorce as one who is overcome by his evil inclination. Rav Chayyim seems to be saying that the court's physical coercion effects his repentence (i.e., the weakening of his evil inclination, which causes a disconnect in his *Neffesh*) and re-establishes the connection between the lower part of the *Neffesh* and the *Ruakh* above it. Therefore the divorce is considered valid.

339 RaMBa"M (Maimonides)

and the aspect of *Ruakh* is thereby damaged,[340]

(and even though the aspect of *Ruakh* is never cut off in any way—for we have never found in the Torah the context of cutting off except in relation to the aspect of *Neffesh* alone: "and that *Neffesh* shall be cut off" (*Va-yikra* 22:3), "and the souls-*Neffesh* who commited..." (there, 18:19) and many like that, and so is written in the *Likutei Torah, parshat Bo* there, and in chapter six in *Gilgoolim* at its end there—even so, via all sins that are dependent on their roots in the aspect of *Ruakh*, he damages and blemishes them, and the power of the impure *Ruakh* dominates (may the Merciful save us)),

from the perspective that the uppermost aspect (the secret of its *Ketter*) is connected and attached forever in the lower aspect of the *Neshama* as we described above, it[341] [male] is able to be rectified via the aspect of *Neshama*, with the stirrings of repentance in the thoughts of the heart/mind, it being the aspect of *Neshama*[342].

However the aspect of the *Neshama* is never blemished in any way, for the wellspring of her root is forever protected from foreign influence, and is forever attached in the *root of the Neshama*, as is known; for they are companions who are

340 The original structure of this paragraph is convoluted, and appears as a very long sentence with a lengthy embedded parenthetical. To make it clearer, I've broken out the parenthetical with an indentation. I suggest first reading the paragraph without the indented section, and then to include it in a second reading.

341 *Ruakh*

342 Rav Chayyim says that a blemish of the *Neffesh* is rectified via speech, which is an expression of *Ruakh*. A blemish of the *Ruakh* is rectified via thought, which is an expression of the *Neshama*.

never separated for all eternity[343], and the actions of man do not reach them in any way to damage them (heaven forefend). And if man should sin in a thought that is not good (heaven forefend), he causes evil to himself alone, that the sparks of the soul-*Neshama* should depart and be hidden from him, but not that it is blemished (heaven forefend).

CHAPTER 19

And this is the subject of the text (*Mishlei* 18:14): "The spirit-*Ruakh* of man will sustain his infirmity, but a beaten down spirit-*Ruakh*—who can bear her?"—meaning that the illness and sickness of the sin related to the aspect of *Neffesh*

> (Plainly, the majority of the sins are found in the quality of the *Neffesh*, for it [fem.] is the bottom-most, closest to the "other side[344]", "her legs descend [to] death" (*Mishlei* 5:5). And as is written (*Va-yikra* 5:1) "and if the soul-*Neffesh* shall sin...", "those who sinned in their soul-*Neffesh*" (*B'Midbar* 17:3) and many others like these. And refer to the *Etz Chayyim, Sha-ar Ha-ahkoodim*, end of chapter 5, and the *Pri Etz Chayyim, Sha-ar Kri-at Sh'ma Sheh-al Ha-meeta*, chapter 8.)

it is possible for it[345] to be rectified and even to rise to a higher level by the quality of *Ruakh*, as we described above. And if the *Ruakh* is beaten down, because he blemished and damaged his quality of *Ruakh* via sins that are depen-

343 The companions referred to here are *Abba* and *Eema*, the two *partzoofim* referred to by the first two letters of the Tetragrammaton. They also correspond to the s'feerote of *Chokhma* and *Beena*, and also to the *Neshama* and the *root of the Neshama*.

344 Heb.: *sitra ahkhra*

345 The *Neffesh*

dent on the aspect of *Ruakh*, then "who can bear her"[346]? His rectification is by way of the aspect of *Neshama* that is called "who[347]" as is known in the *Zohar*.

And an intelligent person will understand that the general principle is as we discussed above on the subject of the three qualities of man: *Neffesh*, *Ruakh* and *Neshama* of man. They also use the same process, in the supernal roots of these three qualities, who are the Holy One (blessed be He), the *Sh'kheena* and the Mother of the Children[348], that the sins of the lower beings cause the *Sh'kheena* of our Powerful One, the secret of the upper *Neffesh*, to wander from her heavenly relationship, according to the secret of exile[349] (this is when the souls-*Neffesh* of Israel are anchored in the depths of evil desires, heaven forefend).

Refer to the *Etz Chayyim*, *Sha-ar Mee-oot Ha-l'vahna*[350], chapter two, and in the *Sha-ar Seider ABY"A*[351], chapter two, and in the *Sha-ar Ha-kleepote*[352], all of chapter three, and in the introduction to the *Pri Etz Chayyim* in the general principles of *Z'eir Anpin* and *Nookva*, and in *Sha-ar Ha-yikhoodim*[353], chapter one of *Tikkoonei Ahvonote*[354].

---

346 Heb.: *mee yi-sa-ehna*

347 The Hebrew letters *mem* and *yud* together (pronounced *mee*), with a g'matria of fifty, signifying *Beena*.

348 "Mother of the Children" [Heb.: *eim ha-ba-neem*] refers to the *partzoof* of *Eema* (mother), or in the context of the *s'feerote*: *Beena*. The "Holy One Blessed Be He" refers to the *partzoof* of *Z'eir Anpeen*, or in the context of the *s'feerote*: *Tif-ehret*. The *Sh'kheena* refers to the *partzoof* of *Nookva d'Z'eir Anpeen*, or in the context of the *s'feerote*: *Malkhoot*.

349 Heb.: *ga-loot*

350 Gate of the Reduction of the Moon

351 Gate of the Structure of ABY"A

352 Gate of the Shells

353 Gate of the Unifications

354 Rectification of sins

However, [this applies to] not all ten of her components—only nine components, from *Chokhma* and below, as we described in the context of the person. But the uppermost component, the secret of her crown that is her root point, is forever connected and attached to the coronet[355] of the *Y'sode*, the component of *Ruakh*, and is never, ever separated from there (and therefore she is called "coronet", that is her crown).

And refer to the introduction to the *Pri Etz Chayyim* mentioned above, and in the *Sha-ar Ha-ahmeeda*[356] in the section on *Birkat Ha-minnim*[357], and similarly, wrote our great Rabbi[358] (OBM) in his commentary on the *Heikhalot*, there in the second *Heikhal*. (And refer to the *Etz Chayyim, Sha-ar Ha-m'lakhim*[359], chapter seven, and in the *Sha-ar Mee-oot Ha-l'vahna*, and in the *Sha-ar Ha-kleepote*, and you'll understand what is written in the *Pri Etz Chayyim* in the two references cited above. Also refer to the *Pri Etz Chayyim, Sha-ar Rosh Ha-shanna*, chapter two and you'll understand all that is mentioned above.)

But the component called upper *Ruakh* is never separated (heaven forefend) from its place as a result of the sins of those in the lower worlds; rather they cause within him blemish and damage (heaven forefend) in his six organs/limbs, as is known.

However, in the aspect of soul-*Neshama*, which is the secret of the brains—his three heads as we discussed in chapter 19—none of the results of the activities of those in the lower worlds arrive there at all to damage or blemish (heaven forefend). Rather, as a result of their activity

---

355 Heb.: *ahtahra*
356 Gate of the Ahmeeda
357 The blessing in the Ahmeeda that deals with apostates
358 The Vilna Gaon
359 Gate of the Kings

they can cause withdrawal from them (heaven forefend), as is known in the *Etz Chayyim*, for they come only as a [conditional] addition and are dependent on the actions of those in the lower worlds. For they result, as is known, from the unfolding downward of the lowest component of "the Mother of the Children[360]", and as the text states (*Kohelet* 3:19): "establishes heaven with intelligence"—and it [male][361] is a world that is guarded from contact with outsiders, as is known.

And this is relevant to the appearance of "the ladder in position earthward..." (*B'reisheet* 28:12), and it's not written "in position on the earth" but rather "earthward", whose meaning is "towards the earth". And its meaning is that its primary source is in the uppermost heavens and from there it unfolds downward until it reaches the earth. It [male] is the living soul-*Neshama* of the person who is emanated [fem.] (so to speak) from the breath of His mouth (blessed be His name). From there it unfolds like a ladder and chain, and connects with the soul-*Ruakh*, and the soul-*Ruakh* with the soul-*Neffesh*, until it descends to this world in a person's body.

And it is explained thusly in the *Raa-ya M'hemna* (*Nahso* 123:2 on *B'reisheet* 2:7: "And He blew into his nostrils the soul-*Neshama* of life...")—"Regarding this it commented (*B'reisheet* 28:12): 'and he dreamed and behold, there was a ladder...', that the ladder is certainly the soul-*Neshama* of life...", refer there [for more details]. "And behold, angels of God-*Elohi"m* ascend and descend on it"—as I wrote previously at length, that she, the living soul-*Neffesh* of the worlds and the powers and the heavenly angels, that

---

360 Heb.: *eim ha-ba-neem—Beena*, the lowest component of which is the *Malkhoot* of *T'voona*.

361 The world of *Abba*

all of their ascents and descents and all of their behaviors in every instant, are dependent only on the direction of the actions, speech and thoughts in man's body in each instant. (That it was written "ascending" first and after that "descending", is because the primary role of man is to first cause each world to ascend from lower to higher, and afterwards the energy is drawn from higher to lower.) Until finally we behold that God-*YHV"H* (blessed be He) is positioned above it, as mentioned previously.

And how pleasant are the words of our rabbis (OBM) who wrote in the *Talmud Yerushalmi* (*Ta'anit,* chapter 2): "Reish Lahkish, in the name of Rabbi Yokhanan, said: 'The Holy One (blessed be He) incorporated His name in Israel's name. This is similar to a king who had the key to a small palace. He said: "If I put it down somewhere simply as it is, it will be lost. I will make for it a chain, so that if it is lost, the chain will be attached to it." This is what the Holy One (blessed be He) said: "If I set Israel down as it is, they will be swallowed up among the nations of the world. Therefore, I include My great name in theirs".'" And they (OBM) discussed this in the context of the collective of the unique nation.

However, they (OBM), as they often do in relation to holiness, hinted also to [the context of] an individual person. And their discussions require in-depth study, for they made the simile of a key and chain, as I wrote above, that man is the one who makes the powers and the worlds accessible and inaccessible, the upper palace and the lower palace, because all of them are directed by the power of his actions, the aspect of soul-*Neffesh,* which is the primary source and root of the aspect of all worlds' soul-*Neffesh.*

And the Master of All (blessed be He), based on his enormous positive desire to bestow goodness on His creations, applied Himself assiduously to the process of our rectification, and said: "If I set them down simply as they are—if there weren't a link between the three aspects of soul-*Neffesh,* soul-*Ruakh* and soul-*Neshama*—firstly, if the quality of the lower soul-*Neffesh* should fall to the fathomless depths of evil (heaven forefend), there won't be another to raise it up, and it will be lost there forever (heaven forefend), similar to what it written: 'and I will destroy that soul-*Neffesh*' (*Va-yikra* 23-30), and then if there's a sinning soul-*Neffesh,* how will it atone?"

And therefore, He (blessed be His name) had wondrous inspiration, and made permanent the three levels of soul-*Neffesh,* soul-*Ruakh* and soul-*Neshama,* so that each one of them should have her first part, the uppermost part of that aspect connected to the lowermost of the level above her, like a chain, so that for each link in it [fem.], the uppermost edge is held by and passes through the lowermost edge of the link that's above it [fem.]. In that way, even if the soul-*Neffesh* should be cut off and fall to the depths of the powers of *toom'ah*[362] (heaven forefend), it [fem.] will be able to be rectified and to ascend via the connection of its [fem.] higher parts to the quality of soul-*Ruakh.* And it will happen in the same way in the situation where the aspect of soul-*Ruakh* is blemished, as we described above.

This is what was said there: "that I will include My great name within them", that the three levels *NR"N*[363] and the soul-*root-of-Neshama*—the wellspring of their source—are from the four letters of the great name (blessed be His name).

362 The phrase "depths of the powers of *toom'ah*" implies that there exists a realm of unholiness (or impurity), below (so to speak) the realm of holiness above.

363 *Neffesh, Ruakh* and *Neshama*

CHAPTER 20

(The explanation of the details of the process of their rectification and their connection to each other via repentance)

For when a person blemished the aspect of his soul-*Neffesh*, or even if he caused (heaven forefend) all [lower] nine of her *s'feerote* to be interrupted from or cut off from [the *s'feera* of] *Chokhma* and below, from her connection that was described previously, it then plummets to the fathomless depths of the *kleepote*[364] (heaven forefend). Then, as a result of sincere verbal confession originating in the depths of the heart, via the expression of his lips (the soul-*Neffesh* component of the soul-*Ruakh*[365]), [it] awakens via the sound of his words what is on high and even higher, and causes extra holiness to be emanated from Him (blessed be His name), first to the soul-*root-of-the-Neshama*, and from there to his soul-*Neshama* and soul-*Ruakh*. And the soul-*Ruakh* shines his great light that is being impressed upon him also upon the component of the soul-*Neffesh*, from the perspective of the connection that still remains between them (as we mentioned above), to obliterate and utterly consume[366] the powers of evil

---

364 The realm below of unholiness/impurity (mentioned in the last chapter), is referred to here as the realm of the *kleepote* (husks or shells).

365 Each component of the general overall soul is composed of the same components as the general overall soul. So the component that we refer to as soul-*Neffesh* consists of the *Neffesh*-of-the-*Neffesh*, the *Ruakh*-of-the-*Neffesh*, the *Neshama*-of-the-*Neffesh* and the *root-of-Neshama*-of-the-*Neffesh*. So it is too with *Ruakh* and the others components of the general overall soul.

366 Heb.: *u'le-ha-seim* (ref: Yekhezkel 24:10)

and the levels of unholiness/impurity[367], and to free from imprisonment all of her components, and to return them and to re-connect them as before with the component of soul-*Ruakh.*

And similarly, if he blemished and damaged the component of his soul-*Ruakh* (heaven forefend) with spoken words that are not good, or with other sins dependent on the component of soul-*Ruakh* (and outweighing them all is the wasting of time that could have been spent learning Torah[368]), and the power of the soul-*Ruakh* of the side of unholiness/impurity overcame it in this case (may the Merciful save us), then the component of his soul-*Neffesh* also isn't complete as it was before, for she receives the flow of life-sustaining energy and her light via the soul-*Ruakh,* as is known. In this case, via sincere regret in the heart/mind, and experiencing bitterness about the enormity of his sin (as in the context of "their heart screamed out to God-*ADN"Y* (*Eikha* 2:18)), and via pondering on stirrings of repentance in his thinking mind[369] (which is the dwelling place of the sparks[370] of the light of the soul-*Neshama*—and this is the *Malkhoot* of *T'voona*[371]), he similarly creates an arousal above to first cause to flow extra holiness and light on the soul-*root-of-Neshama,* and from there to the soul-*Neshama.* And she shines the brilliance of her light that is flowing upon her upon the component of soul-*Ruakh*

367 Just as the realm of holiness has levels upon levels (so to speak), the realm of unholiness/impurity also has levels upon levels.

368 Heb.: *vee-tool Torah*

369 Heb.: *makh-sha-va*

370 "Sparks" are glimmerings of light (so to speak), miniscule revelations of a larger light source.

371 The *Mal-khoot* of *T'voona* is the lowest *s'feera* of the bottom half of *Beena.*

also ("God-*Elohi"m* desires a broken spirit-*Ruakh* as a sacrifice"[372]), and it shatters the power of the soul-*Ruakh* of unholiness/impurity that previously dominated as a result of his sin, and purifies the component of his soul-*Ruakh* of holiness to re-connect with the component of the soul-*Neshama* as it was previously. From there, obviously it will influence also upon his soul-*Neffesh* to restore her to her initial state of perfection.

Similarly, if he sinned (heaven forefend) with an impure thought, and caused thereby that the sparks of his brilliant soul-*Neshama* (that until this moment were a shining lamp over his head[373]) should depart, then via involvement with Torah with an extra measure of rationality[374] with the depths of intellect[375], he stimulates that an extra measure of holiness will be emanated upon his soul-*root-of-Neshama.* From there it flows to his soul-*Neshama* so that her light is again shining upon him to enwisen him in the Torah with an extra measure of intellect[376] from the hidden recesses of her purity. And from that holiness and the light, it unfolds and flows also upon his soul-*Ruakh* and soul-*Neffesh* to perfectly complete them.

Therefore, they (OBM) said (*Shabbat* 119:2): "All who answer 'May the great Name be blessed'[377] with all his strength, the writ of judgment is torn up. And even if he has within him a scintilla of [the sin of] foreign worship, he is pardoned."

For the main intention of this praise is that an increase

---

372 *T'hillim* 51:19
373 See *Eeyove* 29:3
374 Heb.: *beena y'teira*
375 Heb.: *o-mek t'voo-na-toe*
376 Heb.: *beena y'teira*
377 This is the communal response to the *Kaddish.*

of blessing and an abundance of supernal energy/light will be emanated and influence all of the four worlds ABY"A [*]. This is "May the great Name be blessed". Namely, that blessing and an increase of holiness will be emanated from Him (blessed be His name) to "the world"[378] (the world of *Ahtzeeloot*), and from there to the "worlds"[379] (they being the two worlds of *B'reeya* [and] *Y'tzeera*), "world"[380] [fem.] is the world of *Ahseeya*, and they are the roots of the four levels of man, the soul-*root-of-Neshama* and N"RN.

When man intends, with the holiness of his thoughts, via the verbalization of this praise, to arouse and influence by his actions an increase in holiness and blessing upon his soul-*root-of-Neshama*, and from there upon his soul-*Neshama*, soul-*Ruakh* and soul-*Neffesh*, he creates the effect that all iniquity and sin that he sinned in any of these three components are utterly consumed and perish, and it is as if they never existed. This is the complete essence of the sincere repentance, as we described above, and therefore he is pardoned for all his sins.

Annotation: *And what they (OBM) stated "with all his power" bears two explanations: either (1) the full power of the one who answers, or (2) that the name Y"H should be blessed with all His powers, as in the context of "and now, please, may the power of God*-YHV"H *be enlarged"* [B'midbar *14:17*].[381]

However, these two explanations go together[382], *for the*

378 Aram.: *ah-lahm*

379 Aram.: *l'ahl-mei*

380 Aram.: *ahl-my-ya*

381 Here in the second explanation, R. Chayyim seems to be saying that the full powers of the *Ein Sofe* should descend on the name *Y"H.*

382 Heb.: *b'kha-da mahkh-ta*

root of the source of holy influence and blessings is part of the name Y"H[383], *and from it [the world of* Ahtzeeloot*] the world of* B'reeya *unfolds and is filled out; it being the world of thought, from the* meelui[384] *of* hei *of the name* Y"H *using* yud. *And from the world of* B'reeya *is filled out the world of* Y'tzeera, *it being the root of the beginnings of speech and the stirrings in the heart, from the* meelui *of* hei *using* alef. *And from the world of* Y'tzeera *is filled out the world of Ahseeya, it being the world of action, from the* meelui *of the letter* hei *that's in the name of Y"H using the letter* hei.

And they [fem., emphatic] are the root of the NR"N of man, them being all of the powers of the One -who-answers, and all the powers of the name Y"H *-namely all of its* meeluim*—and that is* "y'hei[385]" *the name [where "name"*

383 Namely, the Y in the name Y"H, which corresponds to the world of *Ahtzeeloot*

384 A *meelui* is a letter-wise expansion of a word, achieved by spelling out each of the individual letters in the word. For example, if a word started with the letter alef, the alef would be expanded to *alef-lamed-fei.* Some letters, like the letter *hei,* have alternate spellings: *hei-yud, hei-alef* or *hei-hei.* The first would be called *meelui yudin* because the *hei* is expanded with the letter *yud,* while the second would be called *meelui alfin* because it is expanded using the letter *alef;* similarly the third would be called *meelui hei-in.*

385 The Aramaic word *y'hei* (spelled *yud, hei, alef*) is the first word of the response to the first part of the *Kaddish* discussed here. Rav Chayyim seems to be saying that the three letters of this word refer to the three *meeluin* (using *yud, alef* and *hei*) taken together as one.

If we add up the three different *meeluim* of the name *Y"H* [1: *yud-vav-dalet* and *heh-yud* (35); 2: *yud-vav-dalet* and *heh-alef* (26); 3: *yud-vav-dalet* and *heh-heh* (30), we arrive at 91, the *yikhud* of the name *YHV"H* and *ADN"Y.*

is spelled shin-mem*]* Y"H[386] rabba m'vo-rakh… ". *Refer to the* Tosafote *in* Brakhote *3:1 that starts with "and they respond…".*

And this is also the context of what they (OBM) said (*Avoda Za-ra* 8:1): "The ox that First Adam sacrificed, it was that its horns preceded its hooves[387]"—that he intended via his sacrifice to correct what he had damaged, to build the demolished, to bring near that which he made farther away, and to unify that which he separated. He caused the purity of his holy thoughts and intentions to ascend, and to initially emanate the influence of the light and holiness upon the upper components and levels within him, "horns" being a metaphor for the soul-*root-of-Neshama* and soul-*Neshama.*

And from there, after that he drew [it] upon his soul-*Ruakh* and soul-*Neffesh,* to purify all of the limbs/organs of his body, from his head until his feet, per the context of "and it will be when *to the heel* you will attend"[388] (*D'varim* 7:12), commandments that a person repeatedly visits[389] with his heels, and those are the hooves of the animal soul-

386 Here Rav Chayyim breaks up the second word of the response—*sh'mei* (spelled *shin-mem-yud-hei*)—into two words: name (Heb.: *sheim,* spelled *shin-mem*) and one of God's names *Y"H* (not pronounced, spelled *yud-hei*). In so doing, he provides an alternate to the plain meaning of the response, changing it from "may His great name be blessed" to "may the great name *Y"H* be blessed".

387 This asserts that First Adam sacrificed an ox that was created during the seven days of creation, one that was created with its horns already grown, rather than growing them as it matured. RaSh"Y states that this first ox was drawn from the ground, and its horns emerged first, before its hooves. This ox was complete at its creation, just as Adam was.

388 Heb.; *v'haya eikev tish-m'oon*

389 Heb.: *dahsh*

Neffesh b'heimeet[390]. And this is what is stated (in *Va-yikra Rabba* 2 and in *Kohelet* 7) that the ball of his heel would eclipse [the sphere of the solar disc] [*].

Annotation: *And this is what King Dovid (OBM) stated (T'hillim 19), "God's-*YHV"H *Torah is perfect, restoring the soul-*Neffesh*"—that when he is involved with God's Torah, when he makes it [fem.] as perfect as it deserves to be, it [fem.] completely restores man's soul-*Neffesh *[connection] to its root. He closed there (*T'hillim *19) [with]: "also, when your servant is scrupulous in them, in observing them, there is great reward"*[391]*. The word "scrupulous*[392]*" is derived from the phrase for "they will shine"*[393]*; that is, in keeping all the commandments (each of which corresponds to a specific part of the first Adam's body), his soul-*Neffesh *and body were refined, until even in his heel there was great light and brilliance, per the context of "the ball of the First Adam's heel would eclipse... [the solar disc]" (*Va-yikra Rabba *2).*

And the inner meaning of the matter of "also, when your servant is scrupulous in them...great heel" [is]the purpose of the ascent of the aspect of King Dovid (OBM)[394] *in the root of*

390 *Neffesh b'heimeet* (lit.: animal soul-*Neffesh*) typically refers to the soul-*Neffesh* of the soul-*Neffesh*, essentially the lowest part of the soul-*Neffesh*. This part of the soul-*Neffesh* animates the physical body.

391 Lit.: "also, when your servant is scrupulous in them, in observing them a great heel"

392 Heb.: *nizhar*. The root *zayin-heh-reish* here is taken to mean taking care.

393 Heb.: *yazhiroo*. Rav Chayyim uses here the alternate meaning of the root *zayin-hei-reish*, which means shining.

394 Here Rav Chayyim mentions the "aspect of King Dovid" [Heb.: *meedaht Dovid ha-mellekh*], saying that its root in its supernal root is the root of the soul of First Adam, the *malkhoot* of *Ahdam Kadmone*.

its supernal root, in the Reisha D'lo It'ya-da[395] *that is the* Malkhut *of* Ahdam Kadmone, *the soul*-root-of-Neshama *of First Adam. And per the context of (*Divrei Ha-yameem *1, 17:16 and 17): "Who am I... that You should have brought me here[396]?" (and "*ha-lome*" is nothing other than sovereignty[397]). "And yet, this was insufficient in Your eyes, O God-*Elohi"m, *so you have spoken of your servant's household in the distant [future], and you have considered me as befits[398] a man of exalted stature, O God-*YHV"H-Elohi"m*", and in (*Shmuel Bet *7:19 and 20):* "v'zote toraht ha-ahdam",

---

395 The *Reisha D'lo It'ya-da* is the upper most of the three heads of the *s'feera* of *Keter* in the world of *Ahtzeeloot*, extending above into the lowest *s'feera* of *Ahdam Kadmone*. It is also known as *Nookva d'Ahtik Yomin*. (Refer to the *Etz Chayyim*: *Heikhal* 3, *Sha-ar* 1, *Perek* 1 and *Perek* 5, and *Sha-ar* 2 *Perek* 1 and 2 for further details.)

396 Heb.: *ha-lome*. As described in *Shabbat* 113b, this refers to sovereignty, per King Dovid's use of the word *ha-lome* in *Shmuel Bet* 7:18 and its use again in *Root* 2:14. See also *Tahna D'vei Eliyahu, Seder Eliyahu Rabba* 18: 6.

397 Heb.: *malkhoot*

398 Heb.: *k'tore*

and tore[399] *is a* giloofeen[400] *of God*-Adona"i—*the intelligent will understand. Therefore First Adam left over for Dovid his last seventy years*[401], *the lower seven [*s'feerote*] of Malkhut of* Ahdam kadmone. *And he was worthy to have lived another thirty years, to complete his three heads*[402], *per the context of* (Shmuel Bet, *23:1*): "n'oom ha-gevver hoo-kahm ol[403]",

---

399 "Spelled *tav-vav-reish.* These are the same letters used in the name *Root* (Ruth), King Dovid's ancestor.

400 The *g'matreeya* of a word represents its revealed (*nigleh*) meaning. The *giloofeen* represents its hidden (*nistar*) meaning.

A *g'matreeya* is the sum of the numerical-equivalents of the letters in a word, where *alef* is 1, *bet* is 2 and so on. For example, the *g'matreeya* of God's name *ADN"Y* comes to 65 (*alef* = 1, *dalet* = 4, *nun* = 50 and *yud* = 10).

A *giloofeen* is the *g'matreeya* of a *meelui* minus the value of the word's plain *g'matreeya.*

To get the *giloofeen* of *ADN"Y* we first create its *meelui*: *alef* spelled as *alef-lamed-fei, dalet* spelled as *dalet-lamed-tav, nun* spelled as *nun-vav-nun, yud* spelled as *yud-vav-dalet.* The *g'matreeya* of this *meelui* comes to 671. We then subtract the *g'matreeya* of the plain word: 65. The *giloofeen* comes to 606 (671 minus 65). The *g'matreeya* of *tore* (*tav* = 400, *vav* = 6 and *raish* = 200) also totals 606.

The *g'matreeya* of *Root* is also 606 (*reish* is 200, *vav* is 6 and *tav* is 400). *Root* was originally a non-Jew who was obligated only for the seven Noachide commandments. When she converted to Judaism, she obligated herself in an additional 606 commandments, for a total of 613.

(Thanks to Rav Meyer Twersky for his assistance in understanding this matter.)

401 A midrash (*Zohar B'reisheet* 91b) explains: First Adam was destined to live a full thousand years, while Dovid was destined to die at birth. First Adam donated seventy years of his life so that Dovid could live.

402 The "three heads" are the three upper *s'feerote*: *ketter, khokhma* and *beena,* or alternately (depending on context) *khokhma, beena* and *da'at.*

403 The word *ol* (spelled *ayin-lamed*) has a *g'matreeya* of one-hundred, hinting at Dovid's expected lifetime.

*and he is also the root of the soul-*Neshama *of the Messiah, about whom is written (*Y'shaya *52:13): "*ya-room v'neesa v'ga-va m'ode*", and they (OBM) commented on this*[404] *from* Avraham, *and from* Moshe *and from* First Adam *(meaning after the sin), and this is (*Shmuel Bet, *23:1): "*n'oom ha-gevver hoo-kahm ol, m'shee-akh Eh-lo-he"i Yaakov*", for then the honor of His (blessed be He) kingship will be enlarged and ascend to the original position of its root.*

CHAPTER 21

And this is the rule for a person, that while he is involved with Torah for its own sake[405], being scrupulous and fulfilling all that is written in it [fem.], it purifies his body from head to feet. This is per their (OBM) *midrash* (*B'rakhote* 16a): "Why were [the topics of] rivers and tents located near each other? Just as rivers raise man from impurity to purity[406], so too tents[407] raise a person from a state of obligation to a state of credit. And also per the context about which they (OBM) commented on (*Eiruvin* 4b) regarding the purification of the impure in the *mikveh*[408]: "all of his flesh in the water"—waters which by their effect cause his entire body to ascend, so it is with words of Torah, that it causes person's entire body to ascend by its effect. And the sages assigned value, cubit upon cubit, to a height of three

404 *Midrash Tahn-khooma*,on *Tole-dote*, which, in our version, refers to *Avraham, Moshe* and the *Mal-ah-chei ha-sha-reit*, rather than *Avraham, Moshe and Adam Ha-reeshone* (First Adam), as Rav Chayyim cites.

405 Involvement with Torah for its own sake is called *Torah lishma*—a central concept of the *Neffesh Ha-chayyim*.

406 Via ritual immersion

407 "Tents" refers to the places where Torah is learned.

408 A *mikveh* is a pool of water specifically used for immersion, so as to achieve a state of ritual purity (Heb. *ta-ha-ra*).

cubits—those are the three worlds and *NR"N*—action, speech and thought—relevant to Torah.

And just as a man's entire body ascends and is clarified via involvement with the Torah and the commandments, so too all the worlds, them having [emphatic] the stature of man as I wrote in chapter 6, they are also clarified, caused to be purified and to ascend.

And an upright person who is sincere in his service, will not redirect his mind[409] and thoughts during his service to Him (blessed be His name), even to cause his body and soul-*Neffesh* to ascend and to be purified. Rather he should improve the purity of his thoughts and intentions, and appeal upwards for the rectification and purification of the holy worlds.

And this was also the entire matter of the service of the Patriarchs, and all the early righteous ones who accomplished the Torah[410] before it was given, as our rabbis (OBM) commented on the verse (*B'reisheet* 7:8): "from the ritually permitted animals...". And they stated: "from here [we conclude that] Noakh learned Torah". And they stated (*Yoma* 28b):"Avraham the Patriarch upheld the entire Torah". And it's also stated in *B'reisheet Rabba* chapter 92, and in *B'midbar Rabba* chapter 14, and in *Tahnkhooma B'har*, and in *Midrash T'hillim* 1.

It's not that they were commanded and [thus] acting as they did from a legal perspective, for if it were so they would not have taken positions based on their own intellect and attainment, even if they had grasped that based on the context of the root of their soul-*Neshama* it would have been necessary to trespass and to change even a small part of one of all of God's-*YHV"H* commandments. *Yaakov* the Patriarch

409 Heb.: *da-ahtoe*

410 I.e., its prescriptions

(peace be upon him) would not have married two sisters, nor would have Amram married his aunt (heaven forefend).

[They operated] only from the perspective of what they could grasp, in the purity of their rationality, of the awesome rectifications that would be accomplished for each commandment, in the worlds and powers above and below, and the large blemishes, the holocaust and destruction (heaven forefend) that they would cause if they didn't perform them.

And therefore Noakh sacrificed specifically from the ritually pure animals, for he saw and grasped the power and the supernal root of each animal and beast, which of them drew its power from a root source on the side of holiness, and he sacrificed it. And those that drew the power of its soul-*Neffesh* from the side of ritual impurity and the "other side", he didn't select as a sacrifice before Him (blessed be He), for it would not have been acceptable.

And this is [the meaning of] (*B'reisheet* 5:24): "and Chanokh walked[411] with God-*Elohi"m"*, "*with* God-*Elohi"m* walked Noakh" (c.f. 6:9) and "the God-*Elohi"m* before whom my ancestors walked" (c.f. 48:15). For the definition of *Elohi"m* is "master of all powers", meaning that they grasped the matters of the upper and lower powers; the statutes of heaven and earth and those who enforce them; and the patterns of their behaviors, relationships and how they are assembled via all the contexts of human actions. According to this pattern and context, each one of them caused himself to act and behave in all his situations, because he saw and grasped the lofty rectifications according to the root of his soul-*Neshama*.

---

411 The form of the verb "walk" used in these examples is reflexive and also not literally the walking action, meaning something like "caused himself to follow in the ways of...", per *la-leh-khet b'draw-khav* (*D'varim* 30:16).

Therefore when our Patriarch Yaakov grasped according to the root of his soul-*Neshama* that he would cause great rectifications in the supernal powers and worlds if he would marry these two sisters (Rakheil and Lei-ah), and they (emphatically), the two of them, would construct the House of Israel, he labored many labors and tasks to attain them so that they would marry him. And likewise was the case with Amram (OBM), who married his aunt Yokheved, from whom issued Moshe, Aharon and Miryam.

And this is also one of the reasons that the Torah was not given to Noakh or the holy Patriarchs, for if it had been given to them, Yaakov would not have been permitted to marry two sisters, nor Amram his aunt, even if they had grasped that it was worthy for them to do so according to the root of their souls-*Neshama* . And in truth, [the effect of these later-forbidden actions was] the complete erection of the House of Israel, the Chosen Nation, and the rectification of all upper and lower worlds. And also in this context is what they (OBM) stated (*Sanhedrin* 58b): "and if you should assert that Kayin married his sister, [this is an example of how] 'the world is built on compassion' (*T'hillim* 89:3)".

CHAPTER 22

And from when Moshe came and brought it down to Earth, it is no longer in the heavens. And lest a great person whose attainments are vast becomes wise say: "I am one who sees the secret and hidden meaning of the commandments in the powers and upper worlds that are appropriate for me according to the root of my soul-*Neshama*", or for anyone else according to his root, to violate (heaven forefend) any commandment or to neglect any of the smallest of details of performance, to perform it with an omission of even one detail imposed by the *Sofrim*, or to change its appropriate time (heaven forefend)—for this reason the Torah concluded with (*D'varim* 34:10): "no other prophet like Moshe arose", and as they (OBM) taught [regarding] (*Va-yikra* 27:34): "these are the commandments". After that era ended, a prophet is not permitted to innovate anything (*Shabbat* 104a). And as the Torah spoke with authority (*D'varim* 13:1): "the entire word that I command…, do not add to it nor subtract from it." For even "if a prophet will arise in your midst…", that is, to add or subtract (heaven forefend), "do not listen to the words of that prophet. "Follow God-*YHV"H* your God-*Elohi"m.*"

And so it was that King Chizkiya who foresaw via *ruakh ha-kodesh*[412] that he would have wayward children, and for that reason he didn't marry (*B'rakhote* 10a), his intention was for the sake of heaven[413], not to increase the evil ones in the world. Even so Y'shaya came to him with God's-*YHV"H* word (*M'lakhim Bet,* 20:1): "for you shall die…", "and you shall not live" in the next world[414] because you didn't engage yourself with reproduction. All of his extreme and awesome righteousness didn't avail to bring him to the life of the next world, because he reasoned that he should free himself from one commandment from Moshe's Torah, even though he foresaw via his grasp of *Ruakh Ha-kodesh* that he would have wayward children, and also took into account that it was a [passive] not-doing of a positive commandment[415].

For the reasons behind the commandments and their final effects have not yet been revealed to any person in

---

412 *Ruakh Ha-kodesh* is the movement of the holy spirit, a level lower than prophecy.

413 Heb.: *l'sheim sha-my-eem*

414 The "next world" (Heb.: *o-lahm ha-ba*) is the "world-to-come".

415 He sought to restrain himself from performing a positive commandment, in contrast to actively doing something proscribed.

the world, not even to Moshe Rabbeinu (peace upon him), other than First Adam before the sin, and that is the "wine guarded in its grapes since the six days of creation" (*B'rakhote* 34b), along with the light of the first day with which First Adam "could visualize and examine the world from one end to the other" (*Chageega* 12a), and so on.

For the holy Torah is emanated from the above the head[416], beyond all conceptual grasp. How would it be possible for this matter to be placed within a human's grasp, to change its *halakhote* and the organization of its times according to the expanse of his knowledge[417]? And it's just as *Y'shaya* responded to *Chizkiya* (*B'rakhote* 10a): "Why are you concerning yourself with the secrets of the Merciful One? What He has commanded you, you should do, and what the Holy One (blessed be He) decides is satisfactory, that is what will happen."

And during the period that prophecy still existed in Israel, a prophet was permitted only to innovate a practice as a temporary affair, and also even to transgress one of God's commandments, for example Eliyahu on Mt. Carmel and other similar events.

However, this [permission] itself is derived from what we were commanded in *Moshe's* Torah (*D'varim* 18:15): "to him shall you hearken", it being a commandment and a warning to hearken to the words of the prophet, including when he prophecies in God's name (blessed be He) regarding transgressing a specific commandment when necessary, as our rabbis (OBM) commented (*Y'vamote* 90:b), with the exception of foreign worship.

---

416 Heb.: *l'ma'al-ah roshe*—essentially beyond the highest level accessible to us.

417 Heb.: *da-ah-toe*

But they may never (God forbid) innovate something and make it permanent for the generations. A case in point is Esther, who was one of the seven women prophets (*M'geela* 14a). Even so, when she instructed the sages to record her story "for the generations", they responded (*Mishlei* 22:20): "Surely I have written it for you as an adjutant,"[418] until they found an endorsement from the *TaNa"Kh* (*Mishlei* 7:1). And so it was with Chanuka candles, [that] it's certainly the case that they too found for themselves an endorsement from the *TaNa"Kh.* (Refer to the midrash that the RaMBa"N (OBM) cited in the *parshat B'ha'alote-kha* in the name of Rabbeinu Nissim Gaon (OBM).)

And from the moment that, because of our sins, prophecy ceased in Israel, even if all the sages of Israel to whom were passed the knowledge of the Creation Event and the Vehicle Event[419] would gather and apply their understanding and the purity of their intellect to change even one random detail of one random commandment, or to make the time of its fulfillment earlier or later, we would not accede to them[420] nor heed them. And even in the case of a heavenly voice they stated (*Bava M'tzeeya* 59b): "it is not in the heavens".

And once the holy Talmud was sealed, for us there's nothing to do but scrupulously guard and perform everything recorded in the holy Torah, written and oral,

---

418 They responded that they could endorse a temporary change but not a permanent one.

419 The Creation Event (Heb. *ma-ah-seh B'reisheet*) and the Vehicle Event (*ma-ahseh mer-ka-va*) are the two primary sources from which the hidden aspects of Torah (Kabbala) are derived. Rav Chayyim is referring to those to whom even the deepest secrets of Torah have been transmitted.

420 Heb.: *no-veh*—See *B'reisheet* 24:5 and 8, *D'varim* 13:9 and *M'lakhim Alef* 20:8

according to all their laws and mandates, and with their correct times, details and aspects of performance, without deviating from them even to the smallest degree.

And when the person of Israel fulfills them properly, even without intention, and even if he has no comprehension of the underlying reasons for and secrets of their intentions, even so, the commandments are fulfilled, and thereby the worlds are rectified, and holiness and light is increased, for each commandment according to its time, source and context[421]. And it provides strength to God-*Elohi"m* (blessed be His name). For the Creator (blessed be His Name) established the nature of all the worlds in this way, that they should be influenced by man's actions, and each commandment ascends on its own to cause the specific effect particular to it.

Those whom He (blessed be His name) privileged to attain the hidden aspects of our holy Torah that the great holy ones, the sages of the Talmud, transmitted to us,

> (for example: Rabbi Shim'on bar Yo-khai, his colleagues and students, and those from whom we drink their waters in these last generations, such as the holy rabbi, man of God-*Elohi"m*, the awesome Ariza"l, who enlightened us with a few of the reasons for and intention of the commandments),

it's only so that each one of us could contemplate, based on the limits of his intellect and ability, the effects of all the details of his actions, speech, thoughts and his entire situation on the upper and lower worlds and powers. And this will cause and awaken him to perform and fulfill each commandment, and the entire context of his service to his Creator (Blessed be his name), with ultimate scrupulousness, and with dread and awe and immense love and with holiness and purity of heart/mind, and via this cause

421 Heb.: *l'fee sha-ah-ta, u'm'koe-ra v'in-ya-na*

even greater rectifications in the worlds than if he was to fulfill the commandment without the holiness and purity of intention. However, even so, the essence of all the commandments are the details of the action associated with them.

Reb Itzele's Long Annotation

[Translator's note: In the 1824 first edition and all subsequent editions until roughly 1989, this Annotation is printed alongside the text of Gate 1. Only later was it broken out of the text and placed between Gates 1 and 2.]

(Regarding the matter of the *tzellem* that the Ariza"l split into three aspects *tzaddik, lamed* and *mem.*)

As is known, the primeval root of everything is the root of the four elements[422]: fire, wind, water and dust. And the essential active elements are the three elements: fire, water and wind[423], which in the *Sefer Y'tzeera* (3:1) are called the three "mothers": *aleph, mem* and *shin*[424], which are the "mothers"[425] of everything. And the actions of these three occur via the element of dust, which is passive and receives from them.

And they are the three letters *yud, heh* and *vav* of the Name (blessed be He), and the final *heh* is doubled. And they are the *mem* of the *tzellem*—each one of them

---

422 Heb.: *y'so-dote*

423 Rav Yitzkhak (whom we will henceforth refer to as Reb Itzele) changes the order of the three elements to correspond with the order stated in the *Sefer Y'tzeera.*

424 *Aleph* corresponding to air (*ah-veer*), *mem* corresponding to water (*ma-yim*), and *shin* corresponding to fire (*eish*)

425 Meaning the female ancestor

is multiplied by ten[426]. And the active ones are three, the *lamed*[427] of tzellem. And they are still the aspects of intellect[428] and brains[429] of the three[430]. And when they unfold/flow downward after this in the heart/mind[431] and in action[432], they are three times three[433], being the root of the *mee-dote*[434] *in the mahl-khoot*[435] of *t'voona*[436] that unfolds/flows in *Z'eir Ahnpin*[437]; the essential aspect of the *mee-dote*: *khessed, g'voora* and *tif-eh-ret*; and after that the

---

426 *Mem* has a numerical value of forty. Each of the four letters of the Name has a value of ten. Why? In the lowest world of *Ahseeya*, each letter has a value of one. In the next higher world of *Y'tzeera* they have a value of ten. In *B'reeya* they have a value of one hundred. And in the world of *Ah-tzeeloot* they have a value of one thousand. Based on this approach, Reb Itzele is stating that the Ariza"l attributes *tzellem* to the world of *Y'tzeera*.

427 *Lamed* has a numerical value of thirty, again assigning a numerical value of ten to each letter in the word *tzellem*.

428 Heb.: *sei-khel*

429 Heb.: *mo-khin*. The *mokhin* are the top three *s'feerote*: *ketter, khokhma* and *Beena*.

430 In the Ariza"l's formulation of the ten *s'feerote*, the top three (*ketter, chokhma and beena*, or alternately *chokhma, beena and da-aht)* are called the *mo-khin* (brains).

431 Heb.: *lev*—implying the lower seven *s'feerote*, which are referred to as the *mee-dote*

432 Heb.: *ma-ah-seh*

433 Three elements each at the three levels of *mo-khin, lev* and *ma-ah-seh*

434 *Mee-dote* refers to the bottom seven of the *s'feerote*.

435 *Mahl-khoot* is the bottom-most of the *s'feerote*.

436 *T'voona* is the lower part of *Beena*. *Beena* is the feminine half of the lower two *mo-khin*, with *Chokh-ma* being the male other half. The lower seven *mee-dote* receive their vitality from the *mahl-khoot* of *t'voona*.

437 *Z'eir Ahnpin* is the *partzoof* in the overall/general *shiur koma* that corresponds to the *vav* in the Tetragrammaton, and also to the world of *Y'tzeera*. It can also be described as the male aspect of Providence.

actual *mee-dote* of action: they being *neh-tzakh, hode, y'sode.* And this is the *tzaddik* of *tzellem*[438].

Refer to the *Zohar* (*Va-eira* 23b): "When the Holy One (blessed be He) created the world, He made man based on His *tzellem,* and rectified him with His rectifications... . Rabbee Shimon stated: 'Come and observe: Four primeval elements are part of the secret of *Ehmoona*[439], and they are the ancestors of all the worlds, and the secret of the supernal holy Vehicle, and they are: fire, wind, water and dust. They are the supernal secret, and they are the precursors of all the worlds...'." And in *Zohar Va-eira* 24a: "Come observe—Fire, wind, water, dust are the precursors and roots of the supernal, and both those below and above depend on them for their existence, and these four, corresponding to the four winds of the Earth... . Dust is cold and dry, and for that reason receives upon itself all the others, and all of them act through it, and it receives from all the others so as to express via their power."

And this is what was stated previously, that the essential active ones in the world and in the soul-*Neffesh* are the three elements: fire, wind and water. And via the element of dust the powers of the active elements are revealed in the world. And it is similar in the soul-*Neffesh,* that the powers of the three elements of fire, wind and water that are in the soul-*Neffesh* are revealed via the body of

---

438 The letter *tzaddik* has a numerical value of ninety, which corresponds to the nine *s'feerote* mentioned, multiplied by the ten that corresponds to the world of *Y'tzeera*—the world of *Z'eir Ahnpin.* By explaining in this manner, Reb Itzele situates the context of *tzellem* in the world of *Y'tzeera,* per the Ariza"l.

439 *Ehmoona* (literally"faith" or "reliability") is another name for the world of *Ah-tzeeloot.*

man (whose source is dust), as is explained in the *Zohar* (mentioned previously): "And all of them act through it... so as to express via their power".

And as we perceive with the senses, that the Earth puts forth vegetation, some of them are the effects of fire, as in the context of "and with the bounty of the sun's crops"[440]. And some of them are the effects of the waters, both moist and cold, as in the context of "and with the bounty of the moon's yield". And some of them are the effects of the wind, as in the context of "that it multiplies via the air"[441]—"wind after a rainfall is as rainfall itself, and sun after rain is like two rainfalls"[442]. As is known, it's the nature of fire and the wind to fly upwards, and water descends to low places, to the dust. And if the elements of wind and fire attach to the element of water, they too contribute their influence and are drawn to the earth. Then via the element of dust all of the varieties of vegetation are revealed when all three elements combine appropriately.

And every variation in the nature of everything in the world, from the depths of the earth to the skies above, everything is the effect of the variation in how the four elements combine, for they are the primeval roots, and their combination are the inner aspect of each thing. And based on the quality of their combination inside them are drawn the many different details in each thing: in the physical appearance and their color among the inanimate[443], and the variation among the vegetation[444] in their flavor, appearance and color. And so too among the

---

440 *D'varim* 33:14
441 *Eiruvin*
442 *Taanit* 3b
443 Heb.: *ba-doe-m'mim*
444 Heb.: *ha-tz'ma-khim*

natures of all animals[445], the appearance of their limbs/ organs, their appearance and shape and behavior change according to the combination of their soul-*Neffesh* and their blood from the four "humors"[446], they being the four elements.

And how the four elements are combined is derived from how they are managed by the stars which are fixed in their orbits in the heavens, as our sages (OBM) stated: "There isn't a single blade of grass on Earth that doesn't have a spiritual controller[447] in the heavens that strikes and says to it: 'grow'!" And the stars in their realm of control receive via angels acting as agents of the four living beings[448] of the Vehicle.

And everything is drawn from the name *YHV"H* (blessed be He)—as explained at length in the *Etz Chayyim*—it being that all four of the primeval roots are one single *YHV"H*, for it was God-*YHV"H*'s (blessed be His name) Will to create the entire world in the form of a *YHV"H* in this way, so that in all parts of existence would be found the powers of the four roots.

And in the same way all of man's natural powers, and the inclination of his intellect and the inclination of his will, vary based on the combination of his three roots. And as it's explained in the *Raa-ya M'hemna* (*Pinkhas* 234b): "There are natural living beings[449] appointed over bodies that are from the four elements and that are ritually pure. And corresponding to them are four living beings that are spiritually

---

445 Heb.: *ba-ah-lei chayyim*

446 The "humors" are the four liquids found in various balances in the human body: black bile, yellow bile, green phlegm and red blood, corresponding to earth, fire, water and air.

447 Heb.: *ma-zal*

448 Aram.: *chei-vahn tiv-ee-yote*

449 Aram.: *v'eet kheivahn tiv-ee-yote*

impure carnivores, founded upon the four humors: white humor, red humor, green humor, black humor. And there are living beings that surround the Throne. And there are those who are above them and higher over them."

And the four roots of the supernal man, they [emphatic] are the *tzellem* from which all the forms of powers in a person exist, as explained in the *Zohar Chaddash* (*Midrash Ha-neh-eh-lahm, Breisheet,* page 9a): "That the Creator (blessed be His name) created Man, and created him via the *tzellem,* and with form, and prepared him from four things independent one from the other: from fire, from wind, from water and from dust... ."

And as explained in the *Tikkoonei Zohar* (*Tikkoon* 38, page 34b): "Ascends via fire and wind, and descends via water and dust. And the secret of the phrase 'and lo, the angels of God-*Elohi"m* ascend and descend within it' (*B'reisheet* 28:12)—Two ascend and two descend..., dust being the vessel[450] for all of them."

And so, according to the internal combination of the fire and the wind that are in a person's soul-*Neffesh,* which by their nature ascend above, so too will a person's specific internal powers be drawn upwards. And according to the internal combination of the elements of water and dust that are in a person's soul-*Neffesh,* so too will his specific powers be drawn downwards.

And though how the internals of the elements in the person's soul-*Neffesh* combine is not perceptible by the senses in any way, however when the light of their combination shines upon their vessel—the element of dust (the root of the body)—then the body expresses outwardly the powers of the three "mothers"—*aleph, mem, shin*[451]—

450 Heb.: *klee*
451 See *Sefer Y'tzeera*

each according to its effects, as explained in *Zohar Va-eira* mentioned previously. And the power of the combination of the three elements—fire, wind and water—they [emphatic] are the roots from which are drawn all of the body's actions, but they are hidden and are not perceived.

And even when we see the body's actions that proceed from the combination of the four humors, lo, the elements are not revealed to us to perceive. It's only from the revealed actions can we deduce the extent of their combination in the spiritual, as explained in *Zohar Yitro* on the verse "and you shall discern" (*Sh'mote* 18:21)[452], and in *Tikkoonei Zohar* and in *Zohar Chaddash.*

And for that reason they stated in the *Zohar* and in the Ariza"l's writings that *tzellem* is from the aspect of hidden worlds, while *d'moot* is from the aspect of the revealed worlds. They also stated that the *tzellem* is male and *d'moot* is female, being the active and passive power.

And this is "with Our *tzellem,* per Our *d'moot*"—Just as the Holy One (blessed be He) is hidden from the perspective of His essence and no thought can grasp Him, and His goodness is revealed to us only via His good actions to the extent of their goodness, so too the person's soul-*Neffesh,* soul-*Ruakh,* soul-*Neshama* are not grasped in the mind except via its actions via the body. And even that can't be seen—it's only that its existence is grasped, as the sages stated (*B'rakhote* 10a): "These five verses of 'bless, my soul-*Neffesh*'...—Just as the Holy One (blessed be He) sees and is not seen, so too the soul-*Neshama* sees and is not seen ". And refer to the *Tomer D'vora,* that upon this is based all of the words of the holy one Rav Moshe Cordovero (OBM). And it's stated at the beginning of chapter one, and this is what it

---

452 This refers to the ability to perceive the effects of the combinations of the elements in a person's face and hands.

says: "A person is expected to resemble his Master, and then he will be per the secret of the supernal form[453], *tzellem* and *d'moot.* For if he should resemble in body but not in actions, lo, he counterfeits the form." (This completes the quote.)

And this is what is written in the *Etz Chayyim*, that the essential reason for the descent of the soul-*Neshama* to the body is to separate the bad from the good[454] in the aspect of the *tzellem.*

And the matter is that just as the definition of *tzellem* is "model"[455]—see RaSh"Y's commentary on the verse "with our *tzellem*, per our *d'moot*"—as for example, one who forms a mental image[456] of some specific form[457], to create an end result according to his mental image. First, he stimulates his mind to bring into existence a *tzellem* and model, in a manner that it will be able to be made—via the *tzellem*—the specific form that he desires. And he invents:

> An internal [aspects of the] model, so that by using it the internal aspects of the vessel could be made employing the media[458] that he desires; and also
>
> An external model that encompasses the external aspects[459] of the vessel, to delimit the external aspects in their thickness and dimensions according to his will. And the two of them are like one: a single *tzellem* and

453 Heb.: *ha-tzoora*

454 Heb.: *l'va-reir*

455 Heb.: Reb Itzele uses the term *d'foos*, perhaps relating to the classical process of printing using engraved or carved blocks of type, ink and paper. We translate it as "model", where a model is employed as a reference in creating something else that is just like the model.

456 Heb.: *sheh-m'tza-yeir b'makh-shahv-toe*—a mental visualization

457 Heb.: *ei-zeh d'moot pra-tee*

458 Heb.: *beit keebool*—literally "receptacle"

459 Heb.: *dahf-nei*

model. It's just that this enters into the interior of the vessel to make its interior space according to the correct dimensions; and the other encompasses and surrounds to set its exterior to the correct dimensions.[*] In this way (metaphorically) when the Creator (blessed be His name) desired to create man from dust, which is the vessel that is employed according to His (blessed be His name) will, He first involved *tzellem* and model, out of which that it would be possible to make the person's *d'moot* in body and limbs/organs, so that using them he could perform specific actions according to His (blessed be He) will. And He created four roots from which he brought into existence the spiritual internal and encompassing *tzellem.*

> **Annotation:** *And like "I am like a desert pelican" (*T'hillim *102:7) means that just as the pelican behaves so as to distance itself from settled areas and to cry out day and night with a wailing voice, so too he*[460] *distanced himself from his place and did scream and groan day and night. And the dominance of the component of the pelican's black humor causes her depression—to cry out, and lethargy—to remain in her place in the desert. And so too as a result of the large number of his afflictions, his black humor overwhelms him and causes him to flee from the company of people and to cry wailing, as it's stated (*T'hillim *102:10) "For I ate ashes like bread, and mixed my drink with tears"—it's the nature of those suffering black humor illness to have an appetite to eat charcoal and coals*[461]*, and to cry incessantly. And though from the behavior that's visible we observe only isolation and crying, and eating dust, the true nature of the internal domination by the black humor is not perceivable.*

460 Dovid Ha-mellekh
461 Both being black

> *Even so, it's understood by the intellect that the inner aspect of the black humor entered him as a result of worry, and the afflictions and worries that surround and encompass him too from without, they [emphatic] are the spiritual* tzellem *and the* model *that result in his behavior, in the specific form*[462]*, to cry and to wail and to isolate himself. (This completes the matter.)*

So now we understand the general aspects of *tzellem* and *d'moot* in relation to spirituality. For when the Creator (blessed be His name) desired with His simple will to create the world that would reveal the likeness of all the details of the world as they are, He emanated one power that the philosophers call *hyuli*[463], and we call it either "power" or "light" or "will". That is, that in that way He desired that His Will should be revealed via two powers: one that is drawn upwards (for example), and the second that would be drawn downwards (for example). And so that they shouldn't be separated, He brought into existence intermediaries between them, like the example of "fire" that ascends upwards, and "dust" that descends downwards. But here "air" is close to the nature of fire, to ascend upwards, and it can also descend downwards; and "water" that even though it is drawn to the "air"—as our rabbis stated (*Bava Batra* 75b): "the altitude of a cloud is three *parsa*"—even so, they leave their high place in the "air" and descend to a lower place, to the "dust".

And even though when it comes to the spiritual it makes no sense to refer to "above" [464] and "below"[465]—and even more so in the case of the supernal emanated

462 Heb.: *d'moot*
463 Primordial
464 Heb.: *ma-ah-la*
465 Heb.: *ma-ta*

power—however the context of "above" and "below" is not only used in relation to changes of physical position. [We see this] in "and you shall be only above and not below" (*D'varim* 28:13), whose meaning is that you will be superior in spiritual levels and not descend downwards from their levels, [*] as in the context of promoting an increase in holiness[466] and not a decrease (*Yoma* 12b). In the same way is the matter of powers that ascend "above", meaning that they are drawn to spirituality, to the level that's the highest of the high; and when they descend "below", meaning to the lower levels.

> **Annotation:** *It makes sense to state using the methods of homiletic interpretation that "and you shall be only above..." is a condition and a command, namely that He (blessed be His name) promises us all the blessings mentioned previously only when we will be "above" regarding holiness, and we will not descend below to the level of the nations of the world. And it explains afterwards what that level in holiness is: "If you hearken to God's-*YHV"H*, your God's-*ADoNa"Y *commandments... to observe and perform"* (D'varim *28:13). This is the uppermost of the high levels. "And do not turn away from any of the words..."—For in turning away from any of the things, even to the right side, you will descend (heaven forefend) to seek after other gods. [*]*

> **Annotation:** *It's also stated in the* Zohar*: "Torah without fear/awe and love doesn't ascend above"—meaning that one who doesn't have adequate passion and love for the words of Torah, and also isn't fearful of parting from it like parting from life itself, even if he learns sporadically, it's impossible for his learning to be accomplished at the highest level of his*

466 Heb.: *ma-ah-lin ba'kodesh v'lo mo-ree-deen*

potential.

*Again addressing the topic homiletically, they likened love and awe/fear to two wings, like a bird whose two wings are broken, even so it's essentially still kosher, as long as the lungs are not punctured, so that the sound of the Torah can be made to be heard, to fulfill (*Y'hoshua *1:8): "You should contemplate it day and night". (This completes the matter.)*

For it is only in the world of *Ahtzeeloot* and above[467] that each aspect adheres itself to the level above it, and also unfolds/flows down to impress a continued existence to the level that's below it. And just as, metaphorically, it's the nature of fire to convert all physicality to spirituality (as is known from the context of sacrifices), even so it results in a wind. And the nature of the motion of wind is to result in fire, but even so it enters into rain and maintains it. And the nature of water is to be drawn after wind with any of its movements, and even so it descends to the low place, to the dust, to cause it to sprout all forms of rain.

So it was the will of the Name (blessed be He) to bring into existence a power that would always yearn to attach to the root of its root, and that would also impress abundance to the continued existence of the levels below. And they [emphatic] are the "heavens and its legions, and the earth and its legions" (refer to the RaMBa"N's commentary on the Chumash on this matter) . For even though the yearning of the spiritual legions of the heaven is to attach to the higher levels—as per the context (*T'hillim* 19:2): "the heavens declare God's-*El* glory"—even so "their voice

467 Above the world of *Ahtzeeloot* are the worlds of *Ahdam Kadmone* (about which only a little is known) and the endless number of the "worlds of *Ein Sofe*" (about which nothing is known other than their existence)

goes out to the entire earth and their words reach to the furthest edges of the inhabited world" (*T'hillim* 19:5), namely their influence on the earth: "He made a tent for the sun among them" using language similar to "when His lamp would shine..." (*Eeyove* 29:3)—that via the Sun are gathered the spiritual lights of heaven, to enlighten towards the earth from level to level. And refer to the *Zohar* (*T'rooma* 136b and 137a).

And from that power or will, flows/unfolds and materializes in the word the powers of the elements, from level to level, until they finally impress their influence upon this entire lower existence. And they make their appearance according to the likeness of diverse details, based on the will of the Holy One's (blessed be He) that the creation of Man should be expressed in a body made of dust, and that via three elements (Fire, Water and Wind, being the *tzellem* and the spiritual model) all the vessels of the body are brought into existence in a manner that a person can use them to enact specific actions per His (blessed be His name) will.

And as a result of the details of how a person on this desolate Earth performs the commandments, his elements are caused to ascend to their primeval roots above, per His (blessed be His name) will. And the body is a vessel to actualize the power of those roots, that via his actions in Torah and commandments will be revealed the desire of the elements in his soul-*Neffesh* to ascend to the highest, as per the context about which Dovid Ha-mellekh (OBM) stated (*Divrei Ha-yamim Alef* 29:11): "To You[468], God-*YHV"H,* is the greatness... even everything in heaven and earth. To You, God-*YHV"H,* is the kingdom and sovereignty, above

468 Heb.: *l'kha*

the highest". It didn't state "From you[469], God-*YHV"H*, is the greatness" but rather "To You, God-*YHV"H*", namely, that all the powers found in the earth below, they are drawn to you, God-*YHV"H.* And even though among them are some that descend below to the earth, it being so that all of them, in the heaven and on the earth, it's that "To You, God-*YHV"H*, is the kingdom, and above the highest, even on the earth".

And thus, the Holy One's (blessed be He) will was to:

- Bring [everything] into existence via the three mothers: *alef*, *mem* and *shin*
- That vessels should be brought into existence level by level, and
- At each level the elements would combine in different ways, and
- That via each and every vessel according to its qualities, would be recognized via different qualities whose desire was to be drawn upwards, and
- Also to influence downwards to the vessel below it, so that even in the vessel at the lowest possible level would be brought into existence the original intention: to ascend to the highest.

For that reason their combination in people is in three vessels: the brain, the heart and the liver. And they [emphatic] are the vessels of the soul-*Neffesh*, soul-*Ruakh*, and soul-*Neshama* in a person. And in each of the three vessels the three mothers (*alef*, *mem* and *shin*) express physically to demonstrate their powers in a variety of observable ways. Namely, in the vessel of the brain the combination of elements is recognized via thought. And as is made known

469 Heb.: *mim-kha*

in the *Zohar*, that according to how the four elements are combined in the vessel of the brain, that's how the intellect will be revealed within it.

And the one who is better prepared to receive and grasp a deep intellect is one in whose nature the green humor dominates, and also the black humor, because the green humor is from the element of fire that ascends above to the depths of the intellect's spirituality. And via the air element in the brain it physically expresses to impress its form on the water element in the brain. And the intellectual forms take root in the position of the dust element in his brain, and becomes strongly fixed in his faculty of knowledge[470], as in the context of the faculty of knowledge that binds together all the powers from one extreme to the other, so that all the vessels of his mind will be completely filled with thoughts of Torah, to grasp all of God's (blessed be He) desires, and the thought of worshipping Him (blessed be He), and His greatness and love and fear/awe. And by this his intellect will be drawn to His (blessed be His name) will, so that all of his thoughts will be only toward God, in Torah and worship, until not a single, undesirable, wasted thought will arise.

And the combination of elements further unfolds/flows to the vessels of the heart/mind. And though in the heart/mind they are not as spiritual[471] as in the brain, for their motions in the heart/mind are felt more, because the brain is quiet and restful while in the heart/mind the elements act with a stronger energy. However, this is what the Name (blessed be He) desired:

---

470 Heb.: *b'da-ah-toe*

471 Heb.: *b'dah-koot*

- That their combination should be revealed more in the vessels of the heart/mind, for there is the source of life for all the limbs/organs, and
- So that the actions of the limbs/organs will reflect the plans of the heart/mind, the elements are combined with greater energy so that they will be to arouse with great energy the more physical limbs/organs per the spiritual plan.

And in the heart/mind the element of fire dominates, to elevate his heart/mind in the ways of God, to draw all the powers of the body away from the physicality of the world, to be employed for the sake of holiness, Torah , worship, love and awe/fear, per the nature of fire to transmute everything physical and to make it ascend.

And the power of the fire in his hearts/minds arouses the element of wind, to express his entire nature as a speaking being, in Torah and in prayer to the degree that he understands in his intellectual brain[472]. And that is "voice"[473] which is comprised of fire, wind and water, as is stated in the *Raa-ya M'hemna* (*Pinkhas* 227b): "'God's voice is over the waters' (*T'hillim* 29:3)—From the aspect of water (which is the intellectual brain) it exits to within the two sides of the lungs. 'The voice of God inscribes with torches of flame'—Considered from the aspect of the heart/mind, when it exits the mouth it's called speech." And thus we find that all of

472 Heb.: *b'mo-kho*

473 Aram.: *ka-la*—one the three ways that "wind" (*ruakh*) expresses: *hevvel* (vaporous breath), *kol* (non-speech voice) and *dibbur* (speech)

his speech is in Torah and prayer.[474]

And the vessels of the heart/mind and the five products of the mouth[475] are vessels to infuse its energy into the three mother letters *alef*, *mem* and *shin*, according to how they combine so that they will be directed to none other than God, and his speech will be about them and not about worthless things.

And from the heart/mind their combinations proceed to all of the vessels of action, to really actively accomplish all of God's commandments:

- In love and fear/awe from the perspective of water, and
- In the joy of the commandment from the perspective of fire, and
- With wondrous alacrity from the perspective of wind,

until all the movements of the limbs/organs of his body can be recognized as only proceeding from God, and all the vessels of the body, from the element of dust are vessels to express the power of their supernal roots, the three mother letters *alef*, *mem* and *shin*, in action.

And to the increasing extent that the three elemental letters *alef*, *mem* and *shin* connect to their roots (as previously mentioned), their light will increase, within them and surrounding them, and the entire body that comes from dust will be purified so that there won't be any

---

474 The *Raa-ya M'hemna* says that the element of water which expresses in a person's intellectual mind infuses the lungs and its element of wind. And then it travels from the lungs to the mouth and exits as speech, an expression of the element of fire which ascends as a transmutation of physicality to spirituality.

475 The five classes of sounds that the mouth produces: guttural, labial, palatal, lingual and sibilants

laziness nor heaviness in the limbs/organs of the body. And it will be able to run like the gazelle and be as light as the large bird of prey[476] to do the will of the Holy One (blessed be He), as it's written in *Zohar* (*Pinkhas* 225a): "The heart is more pure than all the others; from it comes all the good and the healthiness for all the limbs/organs, and all the strength, all the delight and the wholeness needed for all the limbs/organs". And in *Zohar* (*Va-yahk-heil* 198b): "Come and observe: When a person sets his will in accord with the Master's service, that will ascends first to the heart, which is the maintainer and the foundation of the entire body. And later that will ascends to all the limbs/organs of the body. The will of the heart and the will of all the limbs/organs of the body join together as one, and they draw upon themselves the splendor of the *Sh'kheena* to dwell among them. And that person becomes a part of the Holy One (blessed be He)."

And based on what was previously explained, the four supernal elements are [emphatic] the *tzellem* and the spiritual model by which will be brought into existence the details of a person's limbs/organ per the forms of the three vessels: brain, heart and liver, they being the soul-*Neffesh*, soul-*Ruakh*, and soul-*N'shama*. And they will cause in the observable world the activities of thought, speech and action, per the supernal Will. And they are drawn from the four letters *YHV"H* (blessed be He).

Being that the light of the supernal roots, at its root, is very great, for that reason they are fixed in place and surround the person from above, so that to the extent that he purifies the inner aspect of his body's vessels, the light will be able to extend and enter more fully into the inner aspect.

---

476 Heb.: *v'y'hee-yeh rahtz ka-tzvee v'kal ka-nehsher*

And it, the *mem* of the *tzellem*, is the four supernal elements. Each element is split into ten aspects (as is known). And the *lamed* of the *tzellem* surrounds the three "mothers" that cause their effects via their combinations in the brain. And the *tzaddik* is the internal brains based on the three "mothers" that enter into the body in the three vessels: brain, heart and liver. And this is what is explained in the *Etz Chayyim*, that the *tzaddik* flows into the entire body of *Z'eir Ahnpin*[477] in nine parts, and the *lamed* into half of *Z'eir Ahnpin*.

And that the *tzaddik* came first, and the *lamed* later, and finally the *mem*:—lo—if it were the will of the Holy One (blessed be He) that the supernal roots should perform their activities according to the plans designated for them, in the body of the person from the day he' was born, it would have been very simple for the person to merit to receive the brains of the *tzellem* (as previously described). However, the will of the Holy One (blessed be He) was that all activities of the supernal roots in the soul-*Neffesh*, soul-*Ruakh*, and soul-*Neshama*, are at first essentially hidden, and they are not immediately active from the day of birth until the child grows up. And what we perceive with our senses is that as the infant grows (in the vessel of the body), so too matures his intellect, speech and actions.

> **Annotation:** *As is known from the* Etz Chayyim (Sha'ar Mokhin D'kahtnoot,) *it's for that reason that He's called* Z'eir Ahnpin, *for even though he has all the brain's vessels, however the activities of the brains of the vessels of* tzellem *are not performing their functions and are essentially hidden. This is also per the context of how it is expressed in the* Zohar (Balak

477 *Z'eir Ahnpin* is the *pahrtzoof* corresponding to the *vav* of the Tetragrammaton., the Holy One (blessed be He), and the world of *Y'tzeera*.

185a): "He, the Holy and great and ascendant upon all the worlds, shrunk His light and hid[478] *His holiness relative to man". (Here ends the citation.)*

And during the time interval that his other good elements that are within him are hidden, and the supernal roots that surround him haven't transmitted their influence to the interior, there's the possibility that the powers of evil can dominate him (heaven forefend). (As we know from the *Etz Chayyim*, the place of the root of the domination of the side of evil is between the interior aspects and the surrounding ones.) "Let one who is a wild ass be reborn as a man" (*Eeyove* 11:12)—From the perspective of the four living beings[479] that trample, in impurity, the four humors—white humor, red humor, yellow humor, black humor—which correspond to the pure elements", as discussed previously in the *Ra'aya M'hemna* (*Pinkhas* 234b).

And even though "there are living beings of intellect[480] that encircle the throne, and there are those above them and even higher than them"[481], however the roots, at their root, exhibit the aspect of surrounding—they have not yet entered—and this is what is meant by "even higher than them".

And as a result of the dominance of the side of impurity, the evil qualities[482] are drawn from the four herd-animal[483] elements. From the element of fire is

478 Heb.: *v'tzim-tzeim*
479 Heb.: c*hayyot*
480 Aram.: *cheivan sikh-lee-yote*
481 This is a continuation of the preceding quote from the Raa-ya M'hemna 234b.
482 Heb.: *ha-mee-dote ra-ote*
483 Heb.: *y'so-dim d'v'eerin*

aroused pride and anger. [*]From the element of Wind: evil utterances. From the element of water sprout evil appetites. And from the element of dust: a vessel to express their energies in thought, speech and action via the body towards evil behaviors. And towards good behaviors the body is indolent, heavy and depressed, as Rav Chayyim Vittal explained at length in the *Sha'ar K'doosha.*

And when the Holy One (blessed be He) desired to impute merit to Israel, for that reason he heaped upon them [a vast] Torah and [many] commandments. For by their effect they will be able to subdue the evil inclination and to arouse the supernal roots that are drawn from the name *YHV"H* (blessed be He): to refine his entire body, so that all the vessels of his brain[484] are filled with thoughts of Torah; and with his entire hearts/minds[485] he'll contemplate words of Torah day and night; and with his entire body[486] he'll be involved with the commandments that are fulfilled by physical action. For Torah is the root of all supernal roots that pre-dated the creation of the world.

> **Annotation:** *And this is what is explained in the* Zohar*: we learn that the judgment of* Gehinnom *is to judge those who are guilty in this world. And* Gehinnom *is a flame that burns day and night*—just as *the guilty warm themselves in the evil inclination,* Gehinnom *burns in the same way, for it is written: "It is a fire; it consumes unto doom"* (Eeyove *31:12). For from the fire they were produced, and the fire will consume them.*

484 Heb.: *mo-kho*
485 Heb.: *l'va-vo*
486 Heb.: *goo-foe*

*For the primary abode of the evil inclination is in the heart/mind, and heart/mind is fire. And when the heart/mind burns a "foreign fire" that God did not command, the pride and haughtiness of the heart/mind becomes an abomination to God. Then, from the fire of pride he becomes thirsty for varieties of appetites (heaven save us!). And as is the manner of those who are thirsty to quench their thirst with water, in the same way he invents ways to quench his appetites' desires with the element of water that's in the brain, to invent thoughts how to actualize the appetites of his heart/mind, as in the context that's written (*Y'shaya *57:20*): "There is no peace for the wicked, and whose waters disgorge mire and mud"*. This refers to the foul, stinking waters that he brings down from his brain, his evil thoughts and reflections. And they arouse for him the element of Wind from the two "wings" of the lungs that sit over the heart, to emit words of evil speech, gossip, scoffing and others like that. The element of Dust is a vessel that expresses the powers of the three elements, and it serves to reveal the actions of the Fire, Wind and Water. Being that no one dies with even half of his desires fulfilled, for that reason he becomes depressed per the nature of the Dust.*

When a person strengthens his roots that are of holiness, then the element of Fire in his heart/mind raises up his heart/mind in the ways of God, to cause his root to cling. And in the flashes of fire burns Y"H'*s flame, and [he becomes] thirsty for Torah and worship per the context of (*T'hillim *63:2): "my soul-*Neffesh *thirsts for You" and as is written (*Y'shaya *55:1): "ho—everyone who is thirsty, go to the water". And it arouses the element of Water in his brain, which sprouts for him a fine intelligence in Torah and worship, and to rejoice over God in His commandments. And as is explained in the* Raa-ya M'hemna (Pinkhas *227b): "'God's voice is over the waters'—From the perspective of Water, which is the brain that arises in the "wings" of the lungs. 'God's voice quarries with shafts of fire'—This is from the perspective of the heart/mind." And it binds together the element* *of the Wind that are in the "wings" of the lungs that sit over the heart that pumps all kinds of fluids within the brain, and this is a sound comprised of Fire, Wind and Water to accomplish "And you shall contemplate it day and night". And the element of Dust is a vessel that expresses the powers of the three holy elements, in speech and action. And within it can be observed scoffing and lethargy not to transgress (heaven forefend) God's will (blessed be He), even regarding a minor prohibition, and depression over his iniquities.*

And for every incidence of depression of this sort there will be a further effect, for from the good fire that is in the heart/ mind is aroused the Beena *that is in the brain, from which is aroused judgment, to derive, by understanding of one thing from another, how many damages he caused with thought, speech and action; and how distant he is from God, and how greatly bereft he is. And to the extent that he enlarges his investigation of his ways and to research them, to that extent arises stern judgments, and he becomes embittered over his soul-*Neffesh *that he clothed it in thought, speech and actions that aren't good. And he arouses the Water within the brain to cry tears over this, and the judgments are sweetened with God's compassion. When the gates of tears are opened, which are [emphatic] the letter* yud *from the name* YHV"H *(blessed is He), the 119 judgments (which have the numerical value of "tear"*[487]*), of the 120 combinations of letters of the name* Elohi"m, *are sweetened. And his first root is sweetened at its root, with an open eye*[488]*, as is written (*Eikha *3:49): "my eye will flow and will not cease... until God looks down and takes notice from the Heavens". (This completes the citation.)*

487 Heb.: *dim'ah,* which has the *g'matria* (numerical value) of 119.

488 Aram.: *b'eina p'keekha*

And they [emphatic] are the essence of the Holy One's (blessed be He) desire to create the four supernal roots, as they (OBM) expounded: "'*B'reisheet*[489]—*F*or the sake of Torah which is called *reisheet*[490],and for the sake of Israel which is called *reisheet*'. And when he fulfills the Torah and the commandments with his thoughts, speech and actions, for the sake of the *YHV"H* (blessed be He), as a result he draws upon himself the name of God, for Israel connects to the Torah, and the Torah to the Holy One (blessed be He).

In *Zohar* (*parshat Shmini* 35b): "Rabbee Cheeya stated: 'The written Torah and the oral Torah provide the foundation for a person in the world[491]. For that reason it's written (*B'reisheet* 1:26): "Let us make man with our *tzellem* and *d'moot*"'." For lo, the Torah is called *tzellem* and *d'moot,* as we described: the matter of *tzellem* being the sealed away worlds, and *d'moot* being the revealed worlds.

In that way the Torah is fully integrated from beginning to end, this being what is stated in the *Zohar* (*Ehmor*98b): "The entire Torah is [both] sealed away and revealed[492], just as the holy name is [both] sealed away and revealed, because the entire Torah is God's holy name, and therefore it is [both] sealed away and revealed.

489 Translated as "in the beginning"

490 Translated as "beginning"

491 Heb.: *ma-ah-mee-deem lo la-ah-dahm ba-o-lahm*

492 Heb.: *sa-toom v'ga-lui*—Reb Itzele uses a number of words for different kinds and degrees of hiddenness. Here he uses *sa-toom,* implying being sealed away from observation and intellectual comprehension. In contrast he uses a single word for being revealed and accessible for observation & intellection: *ga-lui.*

This means that just as He (blessed be His name) is called "God-*Ei"l* who makes Himself hidden"[493] (*Y'shaya* 45:15), even though the worlds were created having many levels, relative to them He didn't change. It's only relative to them that He makes Himself hidden, so that it will appear to us that His actions have many levels, and so that we'll grasp His (blessed be His name) unity from within the hidden-ness of the lowest level.

His hiding Himself is entirely so that only in this way will be revealed to us the glory of His unity specifically in this manner, as will be seen in the coming Gates. And it's known that the hiding of the shining light has a purpose, so that it will be able to be revealed by its sheath, as is explained in the *Zohar* (*B'reisheet* 15a): "Being shielded within. this being its positive purpose, for the benefit of all." Refer there [for more details]. And this is "hidden", as a result of which it is revealed.

So too our holy Torah, even though the most supernal of supernal sparks are concealed within it, within it can also be found levels that are the roots of the vessels of action, speech and thought, corresponding to a person's *Neffesh*, *Ruakh* and *Neshama.* Hidden within them are the most hidden of the hidden, revealed to us via revealed aspects, the learning of which enables us to perform the commandments. Via the Torah and the commandments (written and oral Torah), we can draw upon and within ourselves *tzellem* from concealed worlds, and *d'moot* for the actions of our bodies from the revealed worlds. For that reason it also stated "sealed away", and it causes it

493 Heb.: *Ei"l mis-ta-teir- Mis-ta-teir* (hiding Himself) is the second term Reb Itzele used to denote a level of inaccessibility. "Hidden" is not as absolutely sealed away/inaccessible/not perceivable as "sealed away" (*sa-toom*).

to become "revealed", per His (blessed be His name) desire that we should grasp the hidden via the revealed. And this is only from our perspective, to shield it from the Other Side with regards to the performance of the commandments. And in any case, the light shining within it illuminates the supernal roots.

And this is how they (OBM) expounded in *Chageega* 12a and *Midrash Rabba* (*B'reisheet* chapter 11): "With the light that the Holy One (blessed be He) created on the first day, First Adam could view the world from one extreme end to the other..., and it was hidden away for the future use of righteous". They explained that "the world from one extreme end to the other" means all of existence, from the highest of the worlds to the extreme end of the World of Action [*]—it illuminated them all simultaneously as one.

This is similar to how they (OBM) expounded (*Chageega* 12a) about "First Adam's height extending from the ground unto the sky". And one stated that it meant from one extreme end of the world to the other. And also as they (OBM) stated (Ibid.) that both of those explanations are identical. (And as how in the *Etz Chayyim* it explains that *Ahdam Kadmone* has a presence in all the worlds[494]. And as it is explained in the *Zohar* (and in *Tahn-khooma Noakh* 58c) that the light is hidden within the Torah[495].

Annotation: *This is per the matter of saying "from the world and unto the world"[496] as they established (*B'rakhote *54a, and also refer to RaSh"Y there and on 63a in the comment*

494 Heb.: *o-veir b'chol ha-o-lahmote*

495 *Tahn-khooma* says this is specifically the oral Torah.

496 Heb.: *meen ha-o-lahm v'ahd ha-o-lahm*

*that starts with "*va-y'varkhoo*"). And they stated in the* Zohar *(*Va-yeitzei *158b): "All blessings mentioning the two worlds refer to the revealed and the hidden, and even so all are one...", for it's written: "Blessed are You, the God-*Elohi"m *of Israel from the world unto the world"—and this means from the extreme end of the spiritual world unto the extreme end of the physical world, because they are considered truly one.*

Therefore during First Temple times when the Sh'kheena's *presence was full and the hidden worlds would join with the revealed, and all saw that they were as one, they used to say only "unto the world". And during Second Temple times, where five things were missing, and the entire world did not grasp the one-ness, and the ones who damaged things did their work, they established that it should be said "from the world unto the world", to teach that in any case, this world is not primary, but rather secondary.*

And the specific language that the sages used conveyed more to those who can grasp it. The hidden world is unified with the revealed world. For that reason they didn't say "from world to world", but rather "from the world, to the world", because they are truly considered as one.[497]

And therefore the stature of First Adam was from the extreme end of the world unto the other extreme end. And based on the explanation, the hidden world—the tzellem*—and the revealed world—the* d'moot*—illuminate simultaneously as one, and with a very strong connection. And this is* (T'hillim 139:5) *"back and front you have restricted me"*[498]*, using the same word used in "and you shall wrap up the money"*[499]*, meaning that the internal brains were connected*

497 By using the phrase "the world", the sages were saying that even though we talk about two worlds—hidden and revealed—they are one and the same world.

498 Heb.: *ah-khor va-keddem trartahnee*

499 Heb.: *v'tzarta ha-kessef*

to the surrounding ones, and the surrounding ones with those that surround them above them. This is [what is meant by] "from the ground unto the sky", and we know the "sky" are those things that surround. Rabbee Elazar mentioned the surrounding things only in a general way. And Rav Y'hooda (in the name of Rav) mentioned the supernal surrounding things, that being the Mem[500] *of* tzellem, *the supernal roots, this being how he expounded "and connected from the edge*[501] *of the heavens and unto the edge of the heavens"* (D'varim *4:32). For Rabbee Elazar stated simply: "unto the sky"—the revealed surrounding thing. And then he added further that the edge of the sky too that will later be called heaven, unto the edge of the sky of the supernal skies. (And refer to the RaMBa"N's commentary on the* Choomash *on the verse* (B'reisheet *1:8):"and God-*Elohi"m *called the sky heavens". And what he wrote there [starting with] "but even more correct…"*[502]*, and regarding this they stated in the* G'mara*: "both of those explanations are identical". Refer to the* Tosafote *there [for more detail].*

And as a result of his having behaved corruptly and the surrounding part of the tzellem *were removed from him, his stature was reduced one hundred cubits. (Refer to the* Ein Yaakov *in* Chageega *there, and in the* Ma-har-sh"a's Cheedooshei Ahgadote *there [for more details].) This is in the context of the three vessels of the inner* tzellem, *each one being comprised of the three active elements, and his body completes in his* d'moot, *all of the aspects total up to ten. And as we know, that what is known as "groups of ten" really have no limit to their upper number, in that way each one that is comprised of ten is [really] a hundred, and it being*

500 The last letter of the word *tzellem*

501 Heb.: *oo-l'miktzei ha-sha-my-im v'ahd miktzei ha-sha-my-im*

502 Heb.: *ahvahl yoteir na-khone…*

that at the beginning the surrounding things were unified with the interior things, and according to the explanation the place where the evil inclination dominates is between the inner aspects and the surrounding ones, therefore he failed regarding the Tree of Good and Evil, and the descriptions of these are lengthy and there's no place here to explain them. (This completes [the annotation].)

Refer to the *Zohar 31b* that the light was hidden away for the righteous. And it closes there: "And it is hidden away for the righteous"—specifically for the righteous. The definition of "righteous" in all places is "righteous in behavior", because it's specifically via the actual physical performance of the commandments that the supernal lights that are hidden in Torah are aroused. And there are found the *tzellem*'s supernal roots. For that reason they (OBM) stated (*Ahvote* 3:12): "Anyone whose actions are greater in quantity than their wisdom, their wisdom is thereby preserved...". For the primary thing [*] is that first he must be victorious over his inclination, to subjugate it to the performance of the commandments, even if he does not yet have the brains of the *lamed* of the *tzellem.*

Annotation: *According to the above explanation, just as the* tzellem *comes from the hidden worlds, and* d'moot *comes from the revealed worlds, so too are a person's wisdom and intellect the* tzellem *hidden within him to express* d'moot, *the actual instruments of physical action*[503], *via the performance of the* mitzvote. *And just as at the start of the creation of the world the* d'moot *of the instruments of action are the* mitzvote—*them being what came to mind first: the arousal to actualize the instruments of the* tzellem—*so too now, the*

503 Heb.: *klei ha-ma-ah-she mahmahsh*

performance of the mitzvote *that a person actually accomplishes physically creates the arousal to draw upon himself the* tzellem *from its primeval roots.*

*And for that reason when man was created it's written (*B'reisheet *1:26) "Let us make man with our* tzellem *and per our* d'moot*". And when Adam birthed Shet it's written (*B'reisheet *5:3) "And he birthed with his* d'moot *and per his* tzellem*"—That when man was created, the Holy One (blessed be He) created the powers of the roots that are the* tzellem, *so that a person can perform the actions of the* mitzvote, *as is written (*B'reisheet *2:15): "to serve it and safeguard it"*[504]. *And our sages (OBM) expounded (*Zohar B'reisheet*): "these are the positive* mitzvote *and the negative* mitzvote*".*

But the choice was his, and the d'moot *was in potential and not yet active. For that reason it is written "Let us make man with our* tzellem *and per our* d'moot[505]*", using the* kaf-*of-similarity*[506]. *And for that reason, later it's written: "God-*Elohi"m *created the man with His* tzellem*; with the* tzellem *of God-*Elohi"m *He created him", and* d'moot *is not mentioned.*

Regarding Adam when he birthed Shet: "And he birthed with his d'moot *and per his* tzellem[507]*"—the* kaf-*of-similarity is used*[508]. *After the* tzellem *was taken away from him and he was reduced to a stature of one hundred cubits (as mentioned in the annotation), only the* d'moot *was left.*

---

504 Heb.: *l'avda oo-l'shamra*

505 Heb.: *ki'd'moo-teinoo*

506 Heb.: *kaf ha-dim-yone*—When the letter *kaf* with a cheereek vowel is added at the beginning of a word, it adds a sense that the word that follows is like something else. It's used that way here in relation to *d'moot.*

507 Heb.: *k'tzahlmo*

508 This time in relation to *tzellem.*

Using the d'moot, *his actions arouse to attract* tzellem. *And Shet too was able, via the* d'moot *of the details of his actions for good, to perfect his* tzellem *via his freedom of choice and acceptance of the sovereignty of heaven.*

And the acceptance of the sovereignty of heaven via action is the essential aspect of the original intention[509] *that caused Him (so to speak) to conceal all the worlds, so that man would be able to be created in the world of* Ahseeya. *And this is also stated in the* Zohar *regarding His (blessed be He) quality of Sovereignty*[510]*, that it is complete in all of its* s'feerote, *and is the completion of the nine aspects. And this is "ten and not nine"* (Sefer Y'tzeera *1:4). And it's explained in the* Etz Chayyim *that the key aspect of the characteristic of His (blessed be He) sovereignty is that it will become enlarged to be the "master of ten"*[511]*, in the context of becoming a* pahrtzoof. *This ends [the explanation].*

(And the teaching about the explanation of the letters[512] is: *tzadiq* is first, about action. After that *lamed* is the aspect of the surrounding intellect in the brains. And after that the *mem* is the aspect of the *nehtzakh/hod/y'sode* and *malkhoot* of *beena*—for "only if you call out to understanding[513]" (*Mishlei* 2:3). This is the context for "age of forty to understanding" and the forty days for the forma-

509 Heb.: *n'koodaht ha-p'neemeet*—literally "the inner point"

510 Heb.: *malkhootoe*

511 A complete *pahrtzoof* has ten component aspects. Until it has ten, it is not complete.

512 The three letters of the word *tzellem*—*tzadiq, lamed* and *mem*

513 Heb.: *kee eim la-beena tikra*—The *s'feera* of *beena* is also known as the *pahrtzoof* of *eema* ("Mother")

tion of the fetus[514]. And as is known, the closed form of the *mem* at the end of the word *eim*[515] is because that when she[516] is pregnant she is sealed.)

This is what they (OBM) stated (*Sota* 2a), that the assignment of a man's first mate is not based on his actions, while the assignment of his second mate is based on his actions. As is known from the *Zohar* (*Ehmore* 104), during the act of intercourse of male and female, a *tzellem* awaits over them. This is the matter of the three aspects of the *tzellem* mentioned previously, for the combination of the four elements and the primeval roots are not equal in each of the *NR"N*. The outer garment is from the four elements. The brains are from the four roots, which are drawn upon according to the degree of holiness of the father and mother during the act of mating; at that moment it is not yet dependent upon the actions of the future fetus.

And then the order of their being drawn and the way they couple in their combinations is: the *mem* first—the four supernal roots. And then the *lamed*—drawing their actions which are the three elements Fire, Wind and Water, excluding the element of Dust. Everything is still in the form of intellection[517] and what surrounds the brains alone. After that they unfold in *meedote* and in action, three-times-three, and that's *tzadiq* as we mentioned above. This is for the first mating which is dependent only on the degree of holiness of the father and mother.

---

514 The forty being the four *s'feerote.* Their being in the world of Y'tzeera supplies the multiplier of ten.

515 *Eim* (spelled *alef, mem*) is Hebrew for "mother". The form of the letter *mem sofeet (*the letter mem when used at the end of a word) is closed.

516 *Beena*

517 Heb.: *has-ka-la* (using the letters *sin* and *kaf,* as in the word *sei-khel*)

From that moment onward, all of the rectifications and the drawing [down] of the brains, to couple so as to express their actions in the world, that's the second mating, which is dependent on his actions. And their order is therefore *tzadiq, lamed, mem*[518]. And from this you'll understand the matter in its root in the supernal worlds.

Therefore, all of the rectifications of the worlds are referred to, both in the *Zohar* and in the writings of the *Ariza"l*, as "matings"[519]. From the outset we should consider that to be strange, because it's understood that it's only a metaphor about spiritual matters, as in the context of a person who first, in his mind, connects two theories in the mind. And from the joining of the two concepts are born for him a new theory, based on the precursors of the two initial theories. So what brought those holy supernals to metaphorize a spiritual matter using such a physical metaphor as this?

But the matter is to dam up the mouths of those who act as spokesmen and who expand the explanation of, and those whose mouths overflow with laughter regarding the state of the faithful of Israel, saying whenever a person [here] below performs the *mitzvote*, it results in great rectifications in the upper worlds.

And for that reason they created this model. Just as we are unable to intellectually grasp or understand how from a lowly act like the matter of mating is formed, from a stinking drop, a miraculous being and a complete stature, imbued with a spiritual mind that can grasp wondrous spiritual and holy matters, so too we can't understand the true root of the rectification of the supernal worlds and powers that interlace with spiritual lights via the perfor-

518 The opposite order of the first mating.
519 Heb.: *zeevoogim*

mance of the *mitzvote* that a person does below in this lowly world, just as He (blessed be His name) [*] commanded us. (And see the *Kuzari, ma-amar* 3, *siman* 23.)

Annotation: *And it's known that even the coupling of kissing, the connection of one spirit-*Ruakh *to another, only births the souls-*Neshama *of angels, intelligent and individual*[520]. *And from the coupling of Z'eir Ahnpin and Nookva are birthed the souls of people that are drawn down from the highest of the high to perform their actions on earth with their supernal powers. And it makes sense to see the matter as dependent on the scripture (*Kohelet 11:5*): "Just as you don't understand... are like the bones [formed] in the womb, so too you will not understand God's-*Elohi"m *actions by which He does everything." Meaning: God-*Elohi"m *actions are the actions that God-*Elohi"m *commands a person to perform so that he should live by their effect, that the action causes everything. And "He does" is the language of rectification of the thing, as in "and he hurried to do it" (*B'reisheet *18:7), and as in "and he didn't do his moustache' (*Shmuel Bet *19:25). (This completes the comment.)*

And the entire world agrees that the powers of the supernal zodiac are aroused to supply a part of the person, as our sages (OBM) wrote (*Shabbat* 156a): "One who is from Venus will be a person who remembers well and wise.... One who is from Libra will be a person of justice...". And even so, they contribute of their powers via the arousal resulting from the performance of the act of mating.

So too, the powers from the supernal worlds do not contribute their parts during a lifetime unless it's in response to the actual performance of a person's actions, in *mitzvote* and Torah scholarship that brings one to action.

520 Heb.: *sikhli-im nivdalim*

Then they are aroused to use their supernal light to also influence below via the combination of the four supernal roots in the soul-*Neshama* in the intellect, and also in the heart/mind as expressed in *meedote* and actions.

And being that the subject is lengthy regarding the details of the components of the *tzellem* per the the *Ariza"l*'s writings, indeed there's generally there's no need to discuss it further. "Give to a wise one and he'll grow wiser still"[521].

521 *Mishlei* 9:9

Gate 2

CHAPTER 1

It's written (*D'varim* 11:13): "to love God-*YHV"H* your [plural] God-*Elohi"m* and to serve Him with all your [plural] hearts/minds and all your [plural] souls-*Neffesh*[522]". And the rabbis (OBM) stated in the first chapter of *Ta'anit* (2a) and in *Sifri*: "What is 'service using the heart/mind'? You must admit, this is prayer."

Now the love mentioned, that must be with a complete heart/mind, is simple, for it's one of the commandments dependent on the heart/mind[523]. And so the matter of the love with all your soul-*Neffesh* that was mentioned, this is even to also give up your soul-*Neffesh*[524] for Him (blessed be His name) out of the immense, marvelous love of Him (blessed be He). And as was written in the first paragraph[525]: "And you [singular] shall love God-*YHV"H* your [singular] God-*Elohi"m* with all your [singular] hearts/minds and with all your [singular] soul-*Neffesh*...".

However, this [second] paragraph has something novel that it originated, that the service too (meaning prayer), must be with a complete heart/mind and a complete soul-*Neffesh*.

(And for that reason it wasn't written "and with all your resources[526]" in this paragraph as with the first paragraph in which it's written "and with all your

---

522 This verse appears in the second paragraph of the three paragraphs of the Sh'ma prayer.

523 There are commandments that are dependent on the body and others that are dependent on thought or intention. The latter are referred to as "commandments dependent on the heart" (Heb. *mitzvote ha-t'looyote ba-lev*..

524 I.e., to die for Him

525 Meaning the first paragraph of the three paragraphs of the Sh'ma prayer

526 Heb.: *oo-v'khol m'o-deh-kha*

resources". Because the first paragraph only teaches from the perspective of the commandment to love [and not regarding service], it's relevant to state that the love should be with all your resources too—meaning your monetary resources—as the sages (OBM) state (*B'rakhote* 61b): "If you have a person whose money is more beloved to him than his body, it's for this reason it states: 'with all your monetary resources'." However in this [second] paragraph in which it is also written "service" (meaning prayer), it's not so relevant to it [to mention] "and with all your resources".)

Now [the meaning of] what is stated regarding the context of prayer "with all your hearts/minds" is plain, and describes the intention of the text in two contexts.

The first, specifically, is to empty his heart/mind from the burden of thoughts[527], and to divert it to the direction of attending completely to the words of the prayer, wholeheartedly, and from the depths of the heart/mind, as they (OBM) stated in the *b'raita* at the start of *Perek Ein Ome-din* (*B'rakhote* 30b): "One who prays must adjust the direction of his heart/mind towards the heavens, for it says (*T'hillim* 10:17): 'prepare their heart/mind…'". And as it teaches there too in the story of *Channa* (*Shmuel Alef* 1:13): "…and *Channa*, she was speaking upon her heart/mind". From here we learn that the direction of the heart/mind of one who prays must be controlled. And as King Dovid (peace be upon him) stated (*T'hillim* 119:10): "with all my heart/mind I sought you."

And in *Zohar B'shahlakh* (63:2): "anyone who prays a prayer before the holy King must present his requests and pray from the depths of the heart/mind, so that his heart/mind should be considered perfect before the Holy One

527 Essentially, to still the mind.

(blessed be He), and he should control the direction of his heart/mind and will."

For that reason they (OBM) stated at the end *Perek T'feelaht Ha-shahkhar* (*B'rakhote* 30b), "that one who prays should settle down [the mind][528] ..." so that his mind should be stilled, and this is 'with all your hearts/minds', so that the entire heart/mind should be filled only with the intention of the words of the prayer, for if some other thought should arise, the heart/mind would be divided between two thoughts.

And the second is to eradicate from his heart/mind all worldly pleasures and their delights from all sources during the service of prayer, and to exclusively gaze heavenwards towards the majesty of the Creator (blessed be He). As was stated (*Y'va-mote* 105b): "One who prays must [...] transfer his heart/mind upwards[529]", until the entire power of his heart/mind is drawn only upwards, to delight in God-*H'* alone via the words of the prayer. And in the context of the early pious ones[530] who would settle down the mind for one hour, so that they could adjust the direction of their hearts/minds toward God-*Ma-kome* (*B'rakhote* 30a), and per what Rabbeinu Yonah (OBM) explained in that context (refer there and pay attention[531]), and as was stated in *Sh'mote Rabba* (parsha 22): "a person must purify his heart/mind before he prays".

(However, the entire essence of the matter of a pure heart/mind is only [to enhance the performance of] the commandment and not to obstruct its perfor-

528 Heb.: *sho-heh*
529 Heb.: *ha-mit-pa-leil tzareekh sheh-yee-tein leebo l'ma-ah-la*
530 Heb.: *ha-chassidim ha-reeshonim*
531 Heb.: *v'leeb-kha ta-sheet*

mance[532]. Also, in the context of prayer, even though it is called "service using the heart/mind", as was explained briefly above (the end of Gate 1), the essence of all commandments is the performance. Refer there [for more details].)

And to understand the matter of what the text stated: "...and with all your [plural] soul-*Neffesh*" regarding the service of the prayer, we must first explain the meaning and context of blessing Him (so to speak, blessed be His name) that we've noted a few times in the text: "and you shall bless God-*YHV"H,* your God-*Elohi"m*" (*D'varim* 8:10), "blessed is God forever" (*T'hillim* 89:53), "bless God-*YHV"H,* oh my soul-*Neffesh*" (*T'hillim* 103:1), and many others similarly. And also in the statements of our rabbis (OBM) we found (*B'rakhote* 7a) that He said (so to speak) to Rabbee Yishmael: "Yishmael, my child, bless Me", and so too the entire formulaic wording of all the prayers and blessings that the Notables of the Great Assembly[533] established, all of them begin and end with "blessed".

CHAPTER 2

And the matter of the word "blessed[534]" is not an expression of attributing glory and giving praise as is commonly accepted among the masses, for when He said to Rabbee Yishmael: "Yishmael, my child, bless me" (*B'rakhote* 7a), he didn't utter there any praise in his

532 So even if your heart is not yet completely pure or your mind not yet completely settled, you must still pray.

533 The Notables of the Great Assembly (Heb. *anshei k'nesset ha-g'dolah*) codified the prayer service. Among its members were the last of the prophets.

534 Heb.: *ba-rookh,* the first word of most blessings.

blessing, rather a prayer and a request for mercy [535]. And in the same context[536] in *Bava M'tzee-ah* (114a) they stated: "'and he will bless you' (*D'varim* 24:13)—this excludes *hekdeish* which doesn't require a blessing"[537]. And then the Talmud argues that this is not correct, and therefore it is written; "and you shall eat and be satisfied and bless God..." (*D'varim* 8:10).[538]

However, the truth is that *ba-rookh,* its meaning is an expression of increase and expansion, and consonant with the context of (*B'rakhote* 7a) "accept, please, my *b'rakha...*" (*B'reishit* 33:11), and "and He will bless your food" (*Sh'mote* 23:25), and "and He will bless the fruit of your womb..." (*D'varim* 7:13), and many others similar to these in the text, so that it's impossible to translate them as expres-

---

535 Implying that God wants and needs (so to speak) man's blessing, and that man effects something important via blessings.

536 Heb.: *v'khein*

537 Which would seem to imply that God does not need (so to speak) man's blessing.

538 Rav Chayyim brings this case from *Bava M'tzee-ah* to show that God needs (so to speak) blessing and that the purpose of blessing is not praise. The Talmud is discussing the case of a poor person who receives a loan and deposits a security article with the creditor. If the poor person needs the security article to survive, the creditor must return it, and as a result the poor person blesses the creditor. The Talmud then posits the case of a poor person who is a debtor to the Temple for a *hekdeish* contribution. The text states that in the context of this case, the debtor does not bless God. This might be taken as proof that God doesn't require blessing. To counter that argument, the Talmud then brings proof from a verse about *birkat ha-ma-zone* (grace after meals) that one must bless God. It then teaches that the Temple need not return a security article for a *hekdeish* contribution, as it doesn't fall in the category of charity, and that is the reason that no blessing of God occurs.

sions of attributing glory and giving praise; rather [it's] an expression of increase and expansion.

And in the *Zohar* it states in many places "*l'am-sheekha birkha'an...*[539]", "*l'a-ra-ka birkha'an*[540]", "*l'oh-soo-fei birkha'an*[541]", "*toseffet v'ribui birkha'an...*[542]". And refer to the *Raa-ya M'hemna* (beginning of *parshat Eikev* 71 and 72), that "*ba-rookh ah-tah YHV"H*[543]", its meaning is to draw forth and cause the flow of life [force] from the Source of Life to the name of the Holy One (blessed be He)[544].... And it's written (ibid): "and you shall eat and be satisfied and bless God your God-*Elohi"m*", and those are blessings that people cause to flow with those words...". Refer there at length [for more details].

And so it is written in the *Pri Etz Chayyim, Sha-ar Ha-kadishim,* chapter 1, and this is what it says: "The hidden meaning of *ba-rookh* is many kinds of expansion". And so it is too at the end of the *Sha-ar Ha-b'reeya,* and at the end of chapter two of the *Sha-ar Ha-ahmeeda*[545], and at the beginning of chapter three there, and in the *Sha-ar Ha-shabbat* in the beginning of chapter twelve, and in the *Sha-ar T'feelaht*

---

539 Aram.: to draw [down] blessings

540 Aram.: to cause to flow [down] blessings

541 Aram.: to expand blessings

542 Increase and expansion in blessings

543 Blessed are You God-*YHV"H*—the usual first three words of blessings

544 Rav Chayyim describes here a key part of the foundation of his understanding about God's relationship with the world. There is a Source of Life from which one can draw from and cause the flow of life to the name of the Holy One (blessed be He).

545 *Ahmeeda* (lit. *standing*) is an alternate name for the primary prayer service, recited thrice daily. It originally consisted of eighteen blessings, accounting for another of its names: *eighteen blessings* (Heb.: *shmo-neh es-rei*). It is also called, simply, *prayer* (Heb.: *t'fee-la*).

Rosh Ha-shanna, refer there. And so too wrote the *RaShb"A*[546] (OBM) in regard to the context of "Yishmael, my child, bless me". Refer there [for more details].

However the context of blessing Him (blessed be His name), the intention is not [aimed] towards the Essence[547] (so to speak) of the One Master (blessed is He), (never! never!), for He is far, far above any blessing. Rather the context is as is stated in the *Zohar* (*Ehmore* 98, and in other places), that the Holy One (blessed be He) is [both] revealed and hidden. For the Essence of the *Ein Sofe* (blessed is He) is the most hidden of the hiddens, and can't be assigned any name at all, not even the name *YHV"H* (blessed is He), nor even to the top thorn of its letter *Yud*[548].

And though the *Zohar* refers to Him (blessed be He) with the name *Ein Sofe*, it's not a descriptive name for Him (blessed be His name). Rather the intention is relative to how we perceive Him, from the perspective of the forces that are affected by Him via his purposeful relationship with the worlds. And for this reason He is referred to as "Without End" and not "Without Beginning[549]", for in truth from the perspective of His Essence (blessed be His name) He has no end and no beginning; [it's] only

---

546 Rabbi Shlomo ben Aderet (1235—1310), a Spanish Talmudist who was a student of the RaMBa"N and Rabbeinu Yona.

547 Heb.: *ahtzmoot.* By "the Essence", R. Chayyim is hinting at that which is beyond any descriptive name that is based on our perceptions of God's manifestations in the world.

548 The letter *Yud* (the first letter of the name YHV"H), has an upwards pointing apex in the shape of a thorn. If we consider that each letter of the name YHV"H refers to one of the four worlds, with the *Yud* referring to the world of Ahtzeeloot, then the thorn at the top of the *Yud* points to what is above (or before) *Ahtzeeloot.*

549 Heb.: *ein rei-sheet*

from our perspective of His powers (blessed be He). It's that all of our understanding is just a beginning, but there's no final destination at which we can arrive with an understanding of His powers (blessed be His name) that influence [the world].

And what we're able to grasp to some small degree, and [that] we [can] name and describe with a number of:

1. names that are physically descriptive,
2. names that are descriptive of relationship,
3. names that describe behavioral qualities, and
4. names that describe personality qualities[550], as we've encountered in the Torah and in the various expressions of prayer,

all of them are only from the perspective of His (blessed be He) relationship with the worlds and the powers from the moment of the creation, to set them up, to sustain them, and to control them according to His will (blessed be His name), and those are what are intended by the phrase: "unfolding of the *s'feerote*[551]".

And the names, appellations and descriptions [used to refer to God] vary according to the distinctions in the details of the control process that unfold and are drawn to this world (whether for judgment, compassion, or

---

550 Heb.: *t'arim, shei-mote, v'khi-noo-yim, u'mee-dote.* There are at least four different methods to developing names for things. We can assign a name related to how something appears, or one that's a description based on its relationship to us, or one that refers to a behavioral quality, or a personality quality.

551 The "unfolding of the *s'feerote*" describes how the worlds are connected and attached, and how "light" flows between and within them.

mercy), via the lofty powers and their combinations. Thus, each specific context in the control process has a unique appellation and a specific name, and this is what the definitions of all the descriptive names that are from the perspective of the created powers teach us. For example "Merciful and Graceful[552]" means "exhibiting mercy and grace toward the created beings".

And even the unique primary name *YHV"H* (blessed is He) is not applied in exclusivity to His Essence (blessed be He) that we uniquely attribute to Him; rather [it's applied] from the perspective of His (blessed be He) relationship with the worlds, per its definition as "existed, exists, will exist, and brings everything into existence", meaning that He (blessed be He) purposefully relates to the worlds to bring them into existence and to sustain them in each instant.[*] And this is what the *Ariza"l* stated in his holy explanation, brought in the introduction to the *Pri Etz Chayyim*, that all the appellations and names, they are names of the Essence that are distributed within the *s'feerote*. Refer there [for more details].

Annotation: *And what is stated in the* Pirkei d'Rabbee Eliezer, *that "Before the Holy One (blessed be He) created the world, He and his name alone existed[553]". He specifically used the words "Before He created-*Ba-rah*"—meaning the world of* B'reeya. *"He"—meaning His Essence (blessed be He). "And his name"—meaning the world of* Ahtzeeloot. *They alone existed. But if He (blessed be His name) had not emanated from within Him the world of* Ahtzeeloot,

552 Heb.: *ra-khoom v'kha-noon*

553 Heb.: *ko-dem sheh-ba-ra ha-Kadosh Ba-rookh Hu et ha-oh-lam, ha-ya hoo u'sh'mo l'vad*

there wouldn't have been any relevance of past, present or future existence to His Essence.

CHAPTER 3

And this is what those of blessed memory stated in *Sh'mote Rabba*, chapter 3: "'The God-*Elohi"m* of your ancestors sent me to you'(*Sh'mote* 3:13)—At that moment, the [the nature of] his task was clarified to Moshe.... At that moment Moshe was requesting that the Holy One (blessed be He) should tell him the great name.... Said the Holy One (blessed be He) to him (to Moshe): You desire to know My name? I am named according to My actions. At times I am called using the name *Ei"l Sha-d"ai*, *Tz'va"ot*, or *Elohi"m* or *YHV"H*. When I judge the creations, I am called *Elohi"m*. And when I wage war against the evil ones, I am called *Tz'va"ot*. And when I suspend the sins of Man, I am called *Ei"l Sha-d"ai*. And when I have mercy on my creation, I am called *YHV"H*... This is the [meaning of] 'I will be as I will be' (*Sh'mote* 3:14): I am named according to my actions."

And in the *Raa-ya M'hemna, parshat Bo* (42b): "For you have not seen any image...' (*D'varim* 4:15)—And isn't it written (*B'midbar* 12:8): 'And upon God's-*YHV"H* image does he gaze...'? And He doesn't have even that image in His place[554], rather when He descends to reign over them, and spreads over the created beings, and it appears to each one according to its image, vision, and likeness..., for before He created an image in the world and shaped a form He was One without form or image, and whomever perceives Him prior to the level of *B'reeya*, which is still exclusive of any form, he

554 In His place beyond the worlds of creation.

is forbidden to attribute any form or image..., even using the holy name and not even with any letter or a punctuation mark, and this is what the text says 'for you have not seen...'. But after He shaped the form of the Vehicle of the supernal man[555], He descended there and He, in that form, is called *YHV"H*, so that others could perceive Him there in His likenesses: *Ei"l, Elohi"m, Sha-d"ai, Ts'va"ot, EHY"H*, so that they will perceive Him according to each and every personality trait, how He directs the world with compassion and with judgment... . Woe to he who portrays Him according to one specific personality trait... . Rather His portrayal is according to His mastery over that specific trait, and even over all the created beings... and when He departs from it, He has no traits and no depiction." Refer there [for more details].

And in *parshat Pinkhas* (225a): "And He is not referred to as *YHV"H* or any other name until his light spreads over them. And when it departs from them, He doesn't have [associated with] his Essence any name at all... ." Refer there [for more details].

And in the *Tikkoonim* (*Tikkoon* 70, 121b), it dealt at length with the components of the organs/limbs of the Stature[556] (so to speak), [and] stated later that the entire matter is to express His sovereignty via each organ/limb, to inform man how the world is controlled and to know how to communicate with Him using each organ/limb correctly, and how His name changes according to that organ/limb, and that there's an organ/limb in which He is referred to as *Elohi"m*, and that there's an organ/limb in which he is referred to as... . *EHY"H* exhibits

---

555 Heb.: *merkava*

556 *Shiur koma*; see Gate 1, Chapter 6

and teaches about the essential nature of the Highest of the High..., that the Highest of the High is One in all the names and does not vary in any of them, that the variations are only in the names and not Him. Refer there [for more details]. And refer further to the *Raa-ya M'hemna Pinkhas* 257b and 258a. And refer to the *Etz Chayyim,* at the beginning of *Sha-ar Eegoolim V'yosher*[557], and also at the end of that *Sha-ar* in the beginning of the second edition[558], and you'll understand what is written there according to our exposition.

[*] And this is the entirety of what we can grasp about Him (blessed be He): all of it is from the perspective of His relationship with the worlds and his permeation of them. As is written in the *Raa-ya M'hemna,* (*parshat Bo*) that was mentioned above: "...and He doesn't have even that image in His place, rather when He descends to reign over them, and spreads over the created beings, and it appears to each one according to its image, vision, and likeness... . And this is [what is meant by] 'and I will be described via the capacities of the Prophets' (*Ho-shei-a* 12:11)[559]."

> **Annotation:** *And in this will be understood what those of blessed memory stated in* Chazit *on the verse (*Shir Ha-Shirrim *5:2): "My dove, My perfection". This is how they expressed it: "Rabbee Ya-nai stated: 'My twin' (so to speak). Not that I am greater than she, nor that she greater than Me." And this seems incredible, and according to our explanation it becomes clear, concluding that all of the inadequate frameworks that are used to discuss Him (blessed be He) are*

557 Gate of Sphere-ness and Straightness

558 Aram.: *ha-mahadoora tin-ya-na*

559 R. Chayyim offers an alternate reading of what could also be rendered as "and through the prophets I conveyed allegories".

> *only from the perspective of His (blessed be He) relationship with the worlds. And His (blessed be He) entire initial intention in creating the worlds and interacting with them was only for the sake of Israel... as they (OBM) stated: "'In the beginning'—for Israel's sake...". And what was stated: "'My perfection'—not that I am greater than she, nor that she...', meaning "in chronological age". Understand!*

And for that reason the Notables of the Great Assembly codified the formula of all blessings associated with commandments using second person (direct) and third-person (hidden[560]) expressions. They open with "Blessed are You"—a second-person (direct) expression, and close with "who sanctified us... and commanded us..."—a third person (hidden) expression.

From the perspective of His (blessed be He) purposeful relationship with the worlds, through which we attain some small degree of understanding, we state in the form of directness "blessed are You...", for the worlds require—for the matter of increase and expansion—blessings from His Essence (blessed be He), who interacts with them. And this is [the meaning of] "Sovereign of the Universe", as was stated in the *Raa-ya M'hemna* mentioned above: "when He descends to reign over them, and spreads over the created beings...".

And the One who commands us and sanctifies us, is exclusively His Essence (blessed be He), the *Ein Sofe* (blessed is He), the most hidden of all hiddens,[561], and therefore they codified it using an expression of hiddenness: "who sanctified us and commanded us".

---

560 Or indirect

561 Heb.: *sa-toom meekol s'teemeen.* This has the sense of "absolutely sealed in a way that precludes any access".

CHAPTER 4

And the reason that every blessing includes the two features mentioned above is because the fundamental cornerstone of our holy faith, [is] that the target of our hearts/minds' intentions in all of the blessings, prayers and supplications, is exclusively and only the One of the universe, singular Master, *Ein Sofe,* blessed is He.

However, it is not that we address Him (so to speak) as His Essence alone, in the aspect that is completely removed and separated from the worlds, similar to the situation that existed prior to creation, for if it were so how could we describe Him (heaven forefend) in all of our blessings and prayers with any name or appellation in the world at all?

And also, if He (blessed be He) hadn't demonstrated that His will was to interact with the worlds, and to reign over the created beings according to their accomplishments, we would not have had permission at all to pray to His Essence (blessed be He) that He should interact with the worlds and supervise the created beings. And therefore we begin with saying "you God-*YHV"H,* sovereign of the Universe", whose meaning is: after Your will was to create the worlds and to interact with them, to rule over them. For that reason our requests are that He (blessed be He), the source of will, rule thusly over the worlds.

And also, considering that the aspect of His Essence (blessed be He) does not interact with the worlds, there's no possibility of Torah or commandments at all. And regarding this was stated (*Eeyove* 35:6): "If you have sinned, how have you affected Him? ...If you were righteous, what have you done to Him, or what has He taken from your hand?" And likewise it is written (*Mishlei* 9:12): "If you have become wise, you have become wise for your own sake", for regarding the Essence of the Master of All (blessed is He), all of man's actions, whether for good or evil, do not in fact affect Him in any way (heaven forefend).

And this is what they (OBM) stated in *B'reisheet Rabba* (beginning of *parsha* 44: "'the promise of God-*YHV"H* is flawless[562] ...' (*T'hillim* 18:31)—Rav said, the commandments were not given for any reason other than to refine[563]... for what does the Holy One (blessed is He) care whether one slaughters at the front of the neck or the back?..." And so it is in *Tankhooma, parshat Sh'mini*, in the verse 'these are the creatures' (*Va-yikra* 11:2), and in *Midrash T'hillim, Mizmor* 18, refer there [for more details]. And in the *Tikkoonim*, (*Tikkoon* 70, 130 at end of first *ahmood*): 'The Highest of the High, is ascendant above all, He blesses them all and He has no need of blessings from others, for there is no one who affects him, as it says 'and exalted above all blessing and praise'."[*]

Annotation: *And what they wrote regarding the intentions of the prayers and blessings, to intend each blessing with a specific intention to a specific* s'feera, *it's not (heaven forefend) to the essence of that* s'feera, *for that would be uprooting the plantings*[564] *(heaven forefend).*

For just as in the context of the sacrificial service, our rabbis (OBM) stated in the b'raita *at the end of* M'na-khote *(110a), and it is taken from the* Sifri (parshat Pinkhas)*: "Come and see what is written in the chapter on sacrificial services, that*

562 Heb.: *tz'roo-fa*

563 Heb.: *l'tza-rafe*

564 The phrase "uprooting the plantings" is applied to someone who undoes all of the good he previously did. The phrase refers to the incident recounted in *Chageega* about the four who entered the *Pardes*, one of whom returned and became an apostate.

*the name that is mentioned in that context is not God-*Ei"l *and not God-*Elohi"m *but rather God-*YHV"H*, so that an opening should not be given to the accuser to argue." And as is written* (Sh'mote *22:19), one who brings an offering to* elohi"m[565] *shall be destroyed, other than to God-*YHV"H *alone." And refer ahead in Gate 3, chapter 9.*

It's the same in the prayer service: it's forbidden to intend to any specific power or one of the s'feerote*; rather [intention should be towards] the Essence of the Sole Master, in whom is inclusive all the powers in total, who wills to interact [with the worlds] (blessed be He) for hidden reasons known only to Him, to enact via that specific* s'feera *and that power, in the process of unfolding that He (blessed be He) fixed per His will, that each* s'feera *is specific to a particular context, and via its [fem.] capacity, actualizes that matter in the worlds.*

(And refer to the responsa of the RYVa"Sh[566], siman 157, in which Rabbi Yosef N. Shushan responded in this matter to the RiVa"Sh (OBM), and this will further settle what we said—understand!) And refer to the words of the Ariza"l that we mentioned before at the end of chapter 2. And refer further in the Tikkoon *22 (63a): "And that He is called by all the names… to exhibit to each one of Israel that from the place one calls out to Him… according to their needs," refer there [for more details]. And too, in* Tikkoon *70 mentioned herein, they stated: "to perceive with each body part…, to inform each person to call out to Him with each body part as appropriate."*

And this is what is written in Tikkoonei Zohar Chaddash *(81d): "And we might question why we pray to various levels of the Holy One (blessed be He), at times to a*

565 This *elohi"m* (with a lower case "e") is an entity other than God.

566 The RYVa"Sh is Rav Yitzkhak ben Sheshet Perfet (1326–1408), a Spanish Talmudic authority.

specific s'feera *and known quality; at times we pray to the 'right side'*[567]*..., at times to the 'left side...', at times to the 'central column'... each prayer has a destination of a specific level..., moreover, certainly God*-YHV"H *is in each and every* s'feera *..., when He desires to have mercy on the world its destination is to the right, and when He..., and all is intended to the name of*YHV"H *who is everywhere." And this is what our rabbis (OBM) stated in* Sifri *(on* D'varim *4:7): "...like our God*-Elohi"m *whenever we call to Him"—"To Him" and not to his qualities.*

What's more, all of our hearts/minds' intentions in all the blessings and prayers must be to the Essence of the *Ein Sofe* (blessed is He), from the perspective of His purposeful relationship (blessed be He) with the worlds. It's from their perspective that all of the changing descriptions and names exist, to activate and draw forth to them light and the influence of holiness from His Essence (blessed be He), according to the arousal to which they are entitled as a result of the human actions of each person from the treasured nation: whether from compassion, whether from judgment, whether from righteousness, whether from mercy, whether a little or a lot. And this is the way it is, in measure and proportion, in awesome precision, in quality and quantity, the matter of His (blessed be He) relationship with the powers and worlds, to vary how they connect

567 In the system of the Zohar as explained by the Ariza"l, from the perspective of the model that describes creation in vertical columns (Heb.: *yosher*), the left side is associated with judgment (Heb.: *din*), while the right side is associated with compassion (Heb.: *chessed*), and the center is associated with mercy (Heb.: *ra-kha-mim*, the balance of judgment and compassion).

to each other and how they draw forth the abundance of their light, and all the details of how they are controlled: whether for judgment and anger, whether for compassion and mercy—and also the amount of judgment and compassion: whether a little or a lot.

And this is what they stated in the statements mentioned above, that the commandments weren't given for any reason other than to refine the creations therewith. It is for a great purpose that they refine and purify, to separate the dross from all the powers, and the worlds and the creations will be purified and whitened. And also linguistically, "to refine[568]" is to weld together and to link all the powers, and the created worlds are corrected and organized according to the supernal intention and Will (blessed is He). And in any case, the entire house of Israel, the treasured nation, will be united in the special name (blessed be He) to [be] His portion and his patrimony, for it was only for this purpose that the commandments and the holy service in its entirety were given.

This is the context of blessing Him (blessed be He) in all the blessings and prayers, whose meaning is literally increase and expansion per the explanation mentioned above; that this, for His (blessed be He) hidden reasons, is His will (blessed be He)—that we should correct and unite the supernal powers and worlds via the blessings and prayers, so that they should be prepared and worthy to receive the abundant holiness of the supernal light, and to draw forth and add to them the holiness of the light and many blessings, from His Essence (blessed be He) who interacts with them and permeates them. And in any case this increase in blessing and holiness will influence also upon the treasured nation who caused and effected all this honor.

---

568 Heb.: *l'tza-rafe*

And this is what Rabbee Yishmael stated when He requested from him: "Yishmael, My child, bless Me". [He responded:] "May it be Your will that Your mercy will conquer Your anger, and Your mercy overcome your [other attributes]... and that You will behave towards your children with the quality of mercy, and that for their sake You will consider them [as obedient] beyond the minimum requirement of the law" (*B'rakhote* 7a).

And refer to the *Zohar Chaddash* on *Root* (67b): "Rabbee N. began: 'and you shall eat... and you shall bless God-*YHV"H* your God-*Elohi"m*...' (*D'varim* 8:6). And Rabbee Y. wrote: 'Great is the power of the blessing on food[569] for it increases the power of the heavenly entourage'. And therefore our rabbis (OBM) stated (*B'rakhote* 35, at the beginning of chapter *Kei-tzad M'vorkhin*) and also in *Zohar Chaddash* on that verse: "Anyone who eats and doesn't bless is called a robber, as is stated: 'He robs from his father and mother...'. And 'his father' is none other than the Holy One (blessed be He) ...", because he robs and withholds from the worlds the abundance of blessing and holiness that otherwise would have influenced them as a result of his blessing.

And so it is with all the verses: "Bless God-*YHV"H*, oh, my soul-*Neffesh*..." (*T'hillim* 103:1), "Blessed are you God-*YHV"H*, God-*Elohi"m* of Israel..." (*Divrei Ha-yamim Alef*, 29:10), and others like these. All are [stated] in this context and from the perspective of His will (blessed be He) to interact with the creation. And regarding this is stated: "Prayer [serves a] lofty purpose" (*M'na-khote* 64a, *Shabbat* 116b).

---

569 Heb.: *birkat ha-ma-zone*

CHAPTER 5

However, to understand the essence of the matter of increase and expansion in the worlds by way of man's actions, and the true nature of the matter of the worlds' need of it, we find that our Rabbis (OBM) stated (*B'rakhote* 10a): "There are five [statements of] 'Oh, my soul-*Neffesh* bless…'[570]". To what was Dovid referring? He was referring to none other than the Holy One (blessed be He) and the soul-*Neshama*. [*] Just as the Holy One (blessed be He) fills the entire universe, similarly, the soul-*Neshama* fills the entire body… ." And this is also what they stated in *Va-yikra Rabba* (*parsha* 4), and *D'varim Rabba* (end of *parsha* 2), and in *Midrash T'hillim* (*Mizmor* 103), and in the *Tikkoonim* (beginning of *tikkoon* 13), and as the *Raa-ya M'hemna* explained (*parshat Pinkhas*, 257b and 258a). And refer to the *Etz Chayyim*, (*Sha-ar P'nee-mee-yoot V'chee-tzo-nee-yoot*[571], at the end of *d'roosh* 11).

Annotation: *And considering that our rabbis (OBM) compared His (blessed be He) relationship with the worlds to the connection of the soul-*Neshama *with the body, one who sees their words shouldn't err (heaven forefend), that the two are similar (heaven forefend), for in truth, there is no equivalence or identity between them in any way, as is explained in the* Zohar *and in the* Raa-ya M'hemna *in many places. The Torah stated in unmistakable terms: "and to whom can you compare God-*Ei"l*". And also, anyone who sees with wisdom will understand that it is impossible to extend a description from created beings to the Creator (blessed be His name).*

*They (OBM) didn't liken the essence of the soul-*Neshama *to the Essence of the Creator (blessed be He); rather only to this*

570 Heb.: *bor-khee naf-shee*, a phrase used in *T'hillim*.
571 Gate of Interiority and Exteriority

> *[specific] comparison: just as the soul-*Neshama *is a power created from Him (blessed be He), even so, it is impossible to grasp its essence, to name it with a description or activity unless it's from the perspective of its relationship with the body. All the more so [concerning] the Creator (blessed be He), that it's impossible to grasp Him other than from the perspective of His relationship with the worlds.*
>
> *And also, it's a given that in the final analysis He can't be likened to any creation, for even the supernal crown*[572] *is darkness relative to the Highest of the High, or to any thing which you might compare—there's no equivalence—so they had to select a way of comparing it to a spiritual creation. And [it is] as with the context of the verse (*Mishlei *3:15): "she is more valuable than pearls", even though there is no comparison or equivalence between the holy Torah and pearls. For that reason the text itself concludes with "none of your possessions equal it".*

And what the rabbis (OBM) stated in tractate *Rosh Ha-Shanna* (24b) and in *Avoda Za-ra* (43b) in the *B'raita*, [that] depictions of all faces other than the human face are permitted, and the reason is explained (*Sh'mote* 20:20): "You shall not make [images of what is] with me[573]", [explained as] "you shall not make [images of] me[574]". And also what we found in the *Zohar* (*Yitro* 86, end of first folio). Refer there [for more details].

And in *B'reisheet Rabba* (beginning of *parsha* 27) they stated: "It is written (*Kohelet* 2:21): '...for there is a man who labored in wisdom...'—Rabbee Yudan stated: 'Great is the power of the prophets in that they ascribe form to

---

572 Heb.: *ketter el-yone*

573 Heb.: *lo ta-ah-soon ee-tee*

574 Heb. *lo ta-ah-soon oh-tee*

the Former, as is written (*Daniel* 8:16) "I heard a human voice in the midst of *Ulai*".' Stated Rabbee Y. ben S.: 'We have another text that is even more clear, for it is stated (*Yekhezkel*: 1:26): "...and upon what looked like a throne was what looked like the appearance of a man..."'." And in *B'midbar Rabba* (*parsha* 19): "'A man's wisdom lights up his face' (*Kohelet* 8:1)—Rabbee Y. stated: 'Great is the power of the prophets in that they ascribe similarity of the likeness of the heavenly Divine to the form of man...'."—refer there [for more details]. And so it is in *Kohelet Rabba* (*siman* 8, verse 1), and in *Tahn-khooma* (*parshat Choo-kaht*).

On the face of it this is amazing, for [it's written] "To whom can you liken..." (*Y'shaya* 40:18). However, the matter is as I wrote above (at the end of the third chapter), that our entire grasp (so to speak) of Him (blessed be He), is only from our perspective of His (blessed be He) relationship with the worlds, and the ordered structure of all the worlds and powers, the upper and lower taken altogether, organized (so to speak) in all their details in the physical likeness of an upright man, in an arrangement of all the components of its limbs/organs and sinews and all its internal details and their unification one with their neighbors, such that he integrates within him all of the powers and worlds, as was described above in the first Gate.

And this is the context of the *Shiur Komah* that they (OBM) mention in their statements in the *midrashim*. And refer to the *Etz Chayyim* (in *Sha-ar Eegoolim V'yosher*, *ahnaf* 2 and 3 and 4, and there at the end of the Gate at the beginning of the second edition). And he wrote there that this is hinted at by the text (*B'reisheet* 1:27):

"and God-*Elohi"m* created the man in his shape[575], in the shape of God-*Elohi"m*...". And refer further to the beginning of *Sha-ar Ha-tzellem* and in *Sha-ar Tzee-yoor O-la-mote ABY"A* there.

And His Essence permeates and is secreted within all of them, filling them, and He is their soul-*Neshama* (so to speak), like the matter of the soul-*Neshama* that permeates and is secreted in man's body. For that reason we are permitted to describe Him (blessed be He) in this manner. [*]

Annotation: *And this is the context of all the descriptive names in the Torah that are applied to Him—eye, arm, leg and others like them—all are from the perspective of His relationship (blessed be He) to the worlds, that they are organized according to this organization in all these limbs/organs, and they are names reflecting essential[576] characteristics of the powers and worlds, not metaphorical[577] characteristics.*

And so too in man, they are not names reflecting metaphorical characteristics, and also that in man they're not only to denote and hint at lofty, hidden matters (as with the context of man's name that denotes a specific form and physical shape that was agreeable to be called with this specific name), but rather that in man too they are names reflecting essential characteristics, for the reason that he is comprised of, integrates, and is organized in the image of the appearance of the physical form of the worlds.

And refer to the first part of the Moreh[578], *specifically*

---

575 Heb. *tzellem* is variously rendered as "image", "shape", "form" and otherwise.

576 Heb.: *ahtz-me-yim*

577 Heb.: *moosh-ah-lim*

578 RaMBaM's (Maimonides') *Mo-reh N'voo-kheem* ("Guide of the Perplexed").

> *there in chapter 26, and in the book* Ah-vo-dat Ha-ko-desh, *chapter 26 from section entitled* "Ha-takhleet", *and what he gleaned from the RaMBa"M in chapter 65 from this section, and the beginning of the book* Sha-ah-rei Orah[579] *and in the* Pardes[580], Sha-ar Ha-keenooyim *chapter 1, and in the* Sh'LaH[581], *in the preface to* Toldot Ahdam.

And the RaMBa"M too (OBM) wrote in the *Moreh* (chapter 72 from part 1), that this entire world is called *shiur koma,* and described at length the metaphor of the parts of the world corresponding to the components of the limbs/organs and all the matters included in it, and that He (blessed be He) is the soul-*Neshama* of the world, as in the context of the [relationship of the] soul-*Neshama* to the man's body—refer there [for more details]. And his words (OBM) are worthy of the one who stated them, for it is also explained thusly in the *Zohar* (*Tole-dote* 134c), refer there. And from his words (OBM) we can apply it to our current context, to the matter of the organization of all the worlds taken altogether.

And it's in common usage by the rabbis (OBM) that man has the physical and facial appearance of the Sovereign of the world (blessed be His name), as they stated in *Sanhedrin* (46a and b): "Do not hang his corpse... for a denigration of God-*Elohi"m* [is] hanging" (*D'varim* 21:23). We learn that Rabbee Meir stated: "They stated a simile. To what does it compare? To twin brothers..., one was

579 *Sha-ah-rei Orah* and the *Pardess Reemo-nim* were authored by Rabbi Moshe Cordovero (the RaMa"C), the noted kabbalist who lived in Tz'fat (Safed) and who preceded the Ariza"l.

580 *Pardess Reemo-nim*

581 The *Sh'nei Loo-khote Ha-breet* was authored by Rabbi Y'shayahoo Horovitz Ha-Leivee. He is often referred to using the acronym for the title of his book: the Sh'LaH.

appointed to be king and the other turned out to be a violent criminal. The king commanded and he was hung. Everyone who saw him stated: 'the king is hung…!'" And RaSh"Y explained: because man is made in the likeness of God-*Ma-kome.* And in *Sh'mote Rabba* (*parsha* 30 [:16]): "'One who strikes a person so that he dies…' (*Sh'mote* 21:12)—It's similar to one who struck an image of the King… . Said the King: 'You did not call… for anyone who touches my image is lost…'. So too, if a man murdered a soul-*Neffesh*… it's as if he stuck a pitchfork in the likeness of the King." Meaning, that's the reason the text closed with 'for in the likeness of God-*Elohi"m* was man made'."

CHAPTER 6

And just as the matter of the joining of the soul to the body and continued existence of the soul-*Neshama* in the body requires eating and drinking, and lacking them it would separate and depart from the body, in the same way, the joining of His essence (blessed be He) with the worlds, which is the secret of the "Great Man"[582], to erect them and sustain them. And so His soul-*Neffesh* won't reject them, His will decreed that it should be dependent on the treasured nation's involvement with Torah[583], [their] performing the commandments and the service of prayer. And lacking them, He (blessed be He) would remove his Essence (blessed be He) from them, and instantly all would return to void and nothingness.

---

582 "Great Man" (Heb.: *ha-ahdahm ha-ga-dole*) refers to *Ahdam Kahdmone* (Primeval Adam), the archetype of the human form whose creation preceded creation of the four worlds.

583 Heb.:*b'ei-sek ha-Torah*—See the footnote at the beginning of Gate 4 for a discussion of what "involvement with Torah" means to Rav Chayyim.

Therefore our rabbis (OBM) stated (*Ta'ahneet* 3b): "Why is it written (*Z'kharya* 3:7): 'for I have spread you out like the four winds[584]...'? For just as the world can't exist without the winds, [*] it's also impossible to have a world without Israel."

Annotation: *Refer to* Zohar *(*Va-eira *23:2): "The four elements (fire, wind, water and dust) come first and are the roots that are above, and lower and higher [creations] are sustained upon them, and they are the world's four sides. And refer to the* Raa-ya M'hemna *(*Pinkhas *227b) that over the four good human foundations rule the four angels of the Vehicle known as the four winds of the world, via their root of roots that is the four letters [of]* YHV"H, *(blessed is He). And about this the text stated (*Y'khezkel *37:9): "come from the four directions, oh soul-*Ruakh ... *".*

And this is what they stated in *Va-yikra Rabba* (end of *parsha* 4): "'May my soul-*Neffesh* bless God-*YHV"H...*' (*T'hillim* 104)—So what did Dovid perceive that prompted him to sing praises to the Holy One (blessed be He) with his soul-*Neffesh*? Indeed he stated: "this soul-*Neffesh...*"—This soul-*Neffesh*, when clothed in the body, does not eat; and before the Holy One (blessed be He) there is not eating... . And they used this theme in *Midrash T'hillim* (*Mizmor* 103): "Just as the soul-*Neffesh* neither eats nor drinks, so too the Holy One (blessed be He) does not eat nor drink."

In mentioning eating and drinking over other pleasures, it's telling us the matter discussed above: that even though the soul-*Neffesh* itself does not eat and does not drink, even so, the condition of the soul-*Neffesh* and

584 "Winds" can be rendered as "directions".

the body being bound together as one, and its existence for its limited number of days, depends on the body eating and drinking.

It's also the case that it is certain that the essence of the Sole Master, *Ein Sofe* (blessed be He), is not affected in any way (heaven forefend) by the performance of the commandments, Torah or prayer, and isn't concerned with them at all, as is written: "...so too the Holy One (blessed be He) does not eat nor drink". And it's as I wrote above regarding the texts cited in chapter 4.

However, the whole crux of the matter of His (blessed be He) relationship with the worlds that are organized as a unified system in the form of a man—including all the components and limbs/organs necessary for eating—His (blessed be He) will decreed that they should be dependent on the good deeds of his holy nation—

> they being [emphatically] the food and drink for the worlds [*1] [*2], to erect them and sustain them, and to increase the power of the holiness and light via His (blessed be He) relationship with them, as much as they deserve, according to the supernal will (may His name be blessed)—

everything according to the majority of the deeds of the treasured nation, for they [emphatically] rectify and unify the worlds so that they should be worthy to receive the abundance of light and increase from His holiness (blessed be He), [*3] as in the context of food that increases the body's strength and refines it.

Annotation 1: *And the same holds regarding man's soul-Neshama itself, as they (OBM) stated in* Kohelet Rabba (siman *2, verse 19): "'There is nothing better for a person than to eat and drink...'—All incidents of eating and drinking that are mentioned in this* m'geela, *refer to Torah and good deeds.*

And in siman *8, verse 12. And it's written* (Y'shaya *3:10): 'Tell the righteous man that it is good, for they will eat from the fruits of their deeds'. And so too the opposite (heaven forefend) is written* (Mishlei *1:31): "They will eat the fruit of their ways", and in the* Raa-ya M'hemna *(96:29b): "The food of the Torah is the food of the* NR"N*…", refer there [for more details]. And there in* parshat Pinkhas *(227, at the end of the first folio): "The soul-*Neshama *is maintained by words of Torah"*[585]*, that they are her food, per the relationship of food to the body, as used in the usual sense. And there 244, end of the second folio: "The soul-*Neffesh *that occupies itself with Torah 'from her Father's food she may eat…'"* (Va-yikra *22:13). And refer further there (252b) about this, this being in the context of the banquet in the world-to-come for the righteous, and as King Dovid (OBM) wrote* (T'hillim *23:5): "Prepare a table before me…". And this is* (Mishlei *9:5) : "Come and partake of my food".*

Annotation 2: *And just as:*

1. *in the varieties of foods there are foods whose power is only to restore the four elements to their initial strength, and*
2. *there are foods that have in their power to increase the strength of the four elements in quantity and quality, and*
3. *all of man's efforts are to increase the strength of his body beyond the baseline of wellness, and*
4. *he's not satisfied eating just a little, frugally, just enough to sustain life,*

*so too, the soul-*Neffesh *is not filled by consuming only a small serving of Torah and good deeds. And this is man's*

585 Compared to our editions of the Zohar, this appears to be a paraphrasing.

entire purpose: to expand Torah and to increase performance of the commandments until he can draw forth the increased expansion of holiness and blessing into the higher and lower [worlds], beyond the baseline that the Creator (blessed be His name) set at the moment of creation.

(The Etz Chayyim *explains that [the purpose of] all of our service is to draw forth the enveloping [energies] as a greatly expanded volume of great light, beyond the baseline of the line of light*[586] *that He (blessed be He) drew down at the moment of creation, for the crucial purpose of sustaining and maintaining the worlds.)*

Annotation 3: *And thus, based on the actual amount of how much the lower man consumes*[587]*—clean and pure, without a hint of anything indigestible—is based the amount of the worlds' nourishment [resulting from] his pure actions, whether few or many.*

*And for that reason, prior to First Adam's sin, his foods were processed and cleaned of any dross and impurity. And they stated (*Sanhedrin *59b) that the angels would roast his meat and filter his wine. The matter of this roasting and filtering is that the power of First Adam's soul-*Neffesh *was so great, per the secret of Ahdam Kadmone, of greater value than all of the powers of the highest of the high, to the point that the angels would roast his food for him so that it would be a supernal flame, a consuming fire, a fire that draws out any bit of coarseness from the food, [rendering it]*

---

586 Heb.: *Or yosher*, rendered as "linear light", the inner light that descends in a linear manner from the higher worlds to the lower. This is in contrast to *or eegoolim*, the encompassing light that descends in a spiraling/spherical manner.

587 Meaning how much he is involved with Torah study, performance of mitzvote and prayer

appropriate for one of his very high station. And the joyous supernal wine was filtered to remove any dregs, appropriate for one of his very high station, and per the context of the "wine that is being stored in its grapes" (B'rakhote *34b,* B'midbar Rabba *13). And after the sin that mixed evil into the good in the worlds' food it is written (*B'reisheet *3:18) "thorns and thistles…".*

And because of this, the generation of the desert, prior to the sin of the calf, was worthy in the matter of the manna that both replaced the other foodstuffs and was completely assimilated into their limbs/organs[588]*, as our rabbis (OBM) stated in chapter* Yom Ha-kippurim[589] *(75b): "Rather, what do I maintain? 'You should have a shovel…'"* (D'varim *23:14)—after they defecated*[590]*. And thus the rabbis (OBM) stated (*Shabbat *30b) that in the future, the land of Israel is destined to produce*[591]*…".*

And this is the context of the text (Mishlei 9:5): "Come and partake of my food", that our rabbis (OBM) explained (*Chageega* 14a), and in the *Raa-ya M'hemna* (*Tzav* 33b), and in *parshat Eikev* on the Torah (271b), refer there [for more detail]. This is actually [emphatically] "My food", as if to say His (blessed be He) food. And as they stated in *parshat Eikev* there: "Prepare a table for your Master". Refer there [for more detail].

---

588 Rav Chayyim makes the point that while in the desert, Israel was given the commandment to use a shovel to dig a pit outside the camp to bury its stinking excrement, even though at the time they were consuming manna which produced no such excrement.

589 *Talmud Bavli, Masekhet Yoma* 75b

590 They didn't need to defecate when they ate the manna, but only when they ate food that came from outside sources.

591 In the future the Land of Israel will produce fully prepared food and clothing.

And in *parshat Balak* (202, end of the first folio): "'From it you will eat' (*D'varim* 20:19)—That powerful Rock ..., that he who is worthy supports Her[592] (so to speak), and provides food for Her[593]... . Because of this it states 'from it you will eat', and there is no 'food' in the world other than what comes from him (from the Torah scholar[594])". Refer there [for more details]. And refer too to the *Raa-ya M'hemna* (*B'har* 110a), and in *parshat Pinkhas* there (224, top of second folio), and in the *Zohar* there (225, top of second folio) for this.

And the *Maggid*[595] also stated this to the *Beit Yosef* (*parshat B'sha-lakh*) regarding the manna: "...that all creations require sustenance... . And even *s'feerote*, because they are emanated, need (so to speak) sustenance... . And the sustenance of the *s'feerote* is the Torah and good deeds that are performed below." Refer there at length [for more details].

In the *Raa-ya M'hemna* (*Mishpahtim* 121a): "'Holy is Israel to God-*YHV"H*, His first crop' (*Yirmiya* 2:3)—Israel is called a 'great and strong tree', and 'sustenance', for

---

592 The manifestations of the *Ein Sof* in the world are perceived as having male qualities (e.g., the Holy One Blessed Be He) and female (e.g., the *Sh'kheena*, usually the most immediate source of heavenly providence in the world). Our rabbis (OBM) commonly use a word's gender to differentiate between the male and female manifestations. In this case the "Her" likely refers to the *Sh'kheena*.

593 How the actions, speech and thoughts of the worthy of Israel can (so to speak) provide sustenance for the *Sh'kheena* will be explained by Rav Chayyim in the next few paragraphs.

594 Literally "wise student" (Heb. *tal-meed cha-kham*)

595 Rav Yosef Caro (OBM), the author of the *Beit Yosef* and the *Shulkhan Ah-rookh*, was regularly visited by a heavenly, non-physical teacher. These teachers are referred to as *maggidim*. The record of the Maggid's teachings can be found in the book *Maggid Mei-sha-rim*.

everything comes from it. In it is Torah that is (fem.) the sustenance for what's above, and in it is prayer that is [fem.] the sustenance… . And even the angels do not have sustenance except through Israel, for if Israel refrained from involvement with Torah, sustenance would not descend for them from the perspective of Torah, which is likened to a tree—this being what is written: 'she is a tree of life…'—and to its fruit which is mitzva."

And the RaMa"C hinted at this in the book *Ei-leema*[596]. And what he said about this is also cited in the book *Shomeir Ehmoonim*[597] (refer there [for more details]), and in *To-la-aht Ya'akov*[598] and at the beginning of his book *Derrekh Emoona*[599]. And this is the context of their (OBM) statement: "Israel supports their Father in heaven[600]".

CHAPTER 7

And so too with the opposite: the actions that are not good (heaven forefend), they are to the worlds as the matter of unhealthy foods, as will (God willing) be explained.

And as was written in the *Raa-ya M'hemna* (*parshat*

596 *Ei-lee-ma Rabbatee,* authored by Rav Moshe Cordovero

597 *Shomeir Ehmoonim* (also known as *Shomeir Ehmoonim Ha-kahd-mone*) was authored by Rav Yosef Irgas (1685 -1730)

598 Authored by Meir ben Y'khezkeil ibn Gabai (1480—ca. 1540).

599 Also authored by Meir ben Y'khezkeil ibn Gabai (1480—ca. 1540).

600 Heb.: *Yisrael m'farn-sim l'ah-vee-hem sheh-ba-sha-ma-yeem.*

Ehmore, 99b and 71), this is what it says[601]: "On *Rosh Ha-shanna* Yitzkhak goes out by himself and calls to Eisav to offer a taste of all the world's food, for each person appropriately according to his way... and he reclines on the divan of judgment and calls to Eisav saying: 'Hunt game for me and prepare for me delicious food...' (*B'reisheet* 27:3), 'and as soon as he hurriedly left... and Eisav his brother returned from his hunting'—loaded down with burdens from all the world's actions. 'And he also made delicious food'—he sharpened his tongue to present [sharp legal] arguments... and he stated: 'arise my father', become aroused in [the function of] His judgment and 'eat' some of the evil deeds from all the world.'"

And in the *Tikkoonim* (*Tikkoon* 20, 47b): "'And prepare for me delicious food that I love'—from the positive commandments... . And the negative commandments provide sustenance for *S"M*[602] from the one who trespasses them, and that's what Eisav would bring to Yitzkhak, and he stated to him: 'arise my Father so that he may eat from his son's catch'. And on account of those [sins], *S"M* would approach the left[603] to offer a taste of his children's sins to the Holy One (blessed be He)—they are bitter foods... ."

---

601 The Raa-ya M'hemna uses the biblical episode of Yitzkhak and the blessing he intended to give to his son Eisav to describe part of the process of heavenly judgment on Rosh Ha-shanna. Yitzkhak is cast as the judge and Eisav as the accuser/prosecutor (the Satan) who goes out into the world and returns with evidence of Israel's crimes. The sins related to trespassing the negative commandments serve as sustenance for the Satan.

602 S"M is an acronym for "fatal poison" (Heb.: *sahm mah-vet*), referring to the accusing angel, also known as *Samael*, the Satan who also serves as the angel of death.

603 "Left" is symbolic of judgment (Heb.: *din*).

And in the *Raa-ya M'hemna* (*parshat Pinkhas,* 232, end of first folio): "And that heart/mind, it's not its way to desire… the foul parts of his nation's actions; rather [he] takes all the refined parts…, which are all the merits and all the good deeds. And all of the muddiness and the filthiness and the dirtiness (they being the evil deeds), he sets them aside for the liver[604], for it states about it: 'Eisav, a man of *Sa-ir…*'. And this is what is stated: 'and the he-goat[605] shall bear upon itself all of their sins' (*Va-yikra* 16:20)." And things similar to this can be found there at the end of the folio. Refer there [for more details].

And just as with the body's food, when it's not good and not accepted into the body, it does not feed and sustain the body; rather it is converted within it to waste and pollution and excrement, and it also saps [the strength] and weakens the entire body, for in this situation the soul-*Neffesh* is not distributed correctly within, and at times it will sicken from it. This is also the case that the actions that aren't good or desired (heaven forefend) are converted within the worlds into waste and filth (so to speak), and it is the dominance of the powers of impurity and the husks[606] [*] (may the Merciful save us) that are

---

604 The liver here considered to be the organ that filters the blood, passing along the refined blood to the heart, and keeping for itself the detritus that it has filtered out of the blood.

605 "Goat" (Heb.: sei-ir). The word *sa-ir* can be variously interpreted as the place Sa-ir, or as "hairy", or as "goat." The *Raa-ya M'hemna* observes that the meanings can be interchanged based on the two contexts of Eisav and the *sa-ir ha-mishta-lei-akh* (the scapegoat upon which is confessed the sins of Israel, and that is then sent away to Azazel in the context of the Yom Kippur service). The goat is seen as providing sustenance to the "other side" (the *Sitra Akhra*).

606 Heb.: *klee-pote*

called "vomitous excrement" (refer to the *Zohar* 1 190b, and 2 252a and 265b), per what the rabbis (OBM) stated on the verse "get out, you will say to him" (*Y'shaya* 30:22).

And it was also stated in the *Raa-ya M'hemna* (*Pinkhas* 32, mentioned above) and refer there [for more details], and there in *parshat Tei-tzei* 282a, that it's called foul trash and excrement, and that opinion is stated in the *Tikkoonim* (*Tikkoon* 70 229a) and in *Zohar Chaddash* in *Sitrei O-teeyote, parshat B'reishit,* 6c[607] on the verse "how can I soil them" (*Shir Ha-shirrim* 5:3), it being the repulsive *Sitra Akhra,* and there in *parshat B'har* (39d): "and excrement is none other than the evil inclination...", and refer in the *Ariza"l's Taamei Ha-mitzvote* (*parshat Yitro*) on this. And it is also where they nurse from in the supernal root—refer to the *Etz Chayyim, Sha-ar Heh-ah-raht Ha-mo-khin,* chapter 5.

Annotation: *And through this can be understood their (OBM) statements (*M'geela *25b): "All kinds of mockery are forbidden other than mockery of foreign worship*[608]*. That is permitted, for it is written (Y'shaya 46:1): 'Bel is kneeling, Nebo..., they could not rescue themselves from being carried off'*[609]*". On the face of it the ending of this matter is puzzling, for it ends "I will be patient and rescue", and I have puzzled over it.*

According to these our words, it would be understood by the wise per what I wrote above: that whenever we discuss Him (blessed be He), everything is only from the perspective of His (blessed be He) relationship with the worlds, that are organized in an integrated way as one, "in the appearance of the likeness of a man" (so to speak), in all of the limbs/organs

607 This shows up in the Bar Ilan responsa database as 9a

608 Heb.: *avoda za-ra*

609 Bel and Nebo were Babylonian deities, and the text is mocking them.

and contexts in him explicitly. And all the actions of a person of Israel, they [emphatically] affect the worlds, as with food for the body. And the actions that are not good (heaven forefend), they are converted within them into filth and foulness, and they are the powers of impurity.

This is what the text stated, that [the object of] foreign worship can't restrain itself, to be patient, to rescue itself and to properly extract the burden of the pollution with which they defile her. Rather "they have doubled over and fallen on their knees together...", that is, that they have no power of their own by which they could expel and remove, by themselves, the impurity from within them.

This is not the case with He (blessed be He) of awesome deeds, for His hand holds firmly to the Law, and He doesn't hasten to deliver all at once (heaven forefend) all of the powers of strict judgment and the husks that are the foulness and the filth that were manufactured, to the worlds that correspond to and relate to the digestive organs in man, for they would destroy (heaven forefend) the entire world[610]*. Rather, he holds onto them and exercises patience with them (so to speak), and rescues them properly from the worlds little by little over the course of time, to exercise judgment for the world via chastisements, little by little, as in the context of (*Ahmos *3:2): "You alone did I know... I will hold you accountable for all your iniquities", as is understood from their (OBM) statements on this (*Ahvoda Za-ra *4a), until in the fullness of days, all the filth and foulness will be scraped off completely, they being the powers of impurity, from*

610 Rav Chayyim explains how God chooses to restrain his quality of strict judgment, so that rather than requiring complete compensation for a sin immediately, possibly necessitating destruction of the entire world, He instead, with a balancing quality of compassion, stretches out the compensation over a significant time interval, so that the compensation occurs little by little, and only over time is completed in full.

> *the worlds, after man finishes receiving his punishment. So too is it within [the husks], that after finishing receiving their punishment, by their nature they perish, and then the worlds will return to their original state of perfect health and rectification. Understand!*

And this is also the case of the worship of *P'or*[611], and as was stated in the *Tikkoonim* cited above: "and the negative commandments provide sustenance for *S"M* from the one who trespasses them…". And this is the context of the text (*Y'shaya* 4:4): "when God-*Adona"i* washes the daughters of Zion's excrement…".

And what they stated in the *Zohar Chaddash* (*parshat Ah-kharei* 69a) in the context of Y'rav'am when he worshipped two calves (*M'lakhim Alef* 12:28), that the Holy One (blessed be He) said to the angels: 'Any abundance He would have been given you has turned for you into pollution'.

And this causes defect and illness and brokenness and weakening of strength (heaven forefend) in the worlds, according to the context and the manner of the deed, according to its level in its root in the worlds. For then, in those worlds up to the ones which the actions affect, the distribution and relationship of His (blessed be He) essence to them is not to the extent of fullness that they truly deserve, per His (blessed be He) intention. The location of that defect is not corrected while the illness is still within and the excrement has not been washed off. And ultimately, all the worlds are connected and integrated as one, and in any case all the worlds slightly experience partial effects of this defect.

And they do not return to the perfection of their original state of health and rectification until these powers

---

611 The worship of *P'or* was via defecation.

of impurity are disposed of[612] by way of a person receiving the punishment due him. And as it is written in the *Raa-ya M'hemna* (*Pinkhas* 234, end of the first folio and the top of second folio there), (refer there [for more details]), that in that way, in that case, as a result they are expelled, and in that moment they are finished and disappear. Refer above in Gate One (chapter 11). And then, in any case, the defect and the brokenness of the world is healed, and they are purified from the illness of their pollution, and they return to their original rectified state.

Or [it occurs] via the wholehearted and complete repentance that reaches its supernal root, that is called the World of Repentance, the world of total freedom and supernal shining, and from there arouses and draws forth holy supernal light, that is the wellspring of purity, to wash and purify all of the dirty waste products of the powers of impurity, and they are nullified and perish. And this is the context of the text (cited above): "when God-*Adona"i* washes the daughters of Zion's excrement...", and also (*Y'khezkel* 36:25): "and I will cast upon you pure water...".

CHAPTER 8

And this is what they (OBM) stated (*Bava Kamma* 50a): "All who say that the Holy One (blessed be He) makes concessions[613], his life will be conceded[614]", which on the face of it is amazing, and we already explained a little above in Gate 1, Chapter 12.

And in our current context, the matter is clarified further with a pleasing rationale, that it's not by way of

612 Heb.: *yit-roke-no*
613 Heb.: *vaht-rahn*
614 Heb.: *yee-va-troo chay-yahv*

revenge (heaven forefend), but rather just as it's in a person's nature that if he would eat a food that in its nature would damage and injure his body, that food would injure him or he might also sicken from it. And if it was a fatal poison, he would die from it, and he himself would be responsible for his death. It's the same regarding the sins of the soul-*Neffesh* that sins (heaven forefend), for this is what He (blessed be He) fixed with His will, the nature of how the worlds are organized and how they are, that man's good or bad deeds (heaven forefend) are like the matter of nourishment and food for them. Concessions are irrelevant to this, and he is required to dispose of [615] the filth of the impurity that was strengthened in the world as a result of his sins, via either one of the two [methods of] rectifications mentioned above[616].

And now you can envision and understand [emphatically] the matter of the increase and expansion of blessing, and how great the awesome need for our holy service, in totality, towards the very essence of maintaining the continued existence of the worlds, and to draw forth and distribute within them many blessings and an increase in holiness, from the perspective of His Essence's (blessed be He) link to them per His supernal will (blessed be He), as in the matter of eating and nourishment as mentioned above. And this is His will and His glory (blessed be He) for a reason that is hidden with Him (blessed be His name), that is beyond our ability to grasp.

And it's worthwhile for each person of the holy nation, whose heart/mind is anxious that his actions be acceptable before Him (blessed be He), to combine this thought and the purity of the desired intention in the involvement with

615 Heb.: *l'ha-reek*

616 Suffering and repentance

Torah[617] and the performance of all the commandments, to draw forth and to increase, by way of that nourishment, a holiness and new light in the worlds.

CHAPTER 9

And specifically when he stands before Him (blessed be He) to pray at the time designated for it [fem.], that [fem.] is the essence of nourishment for the worlds and the soul-*Neffesh* of the man himself [*]. And as is written in *Zohar B'reisheet* (24a): "His nourishment [is] prayer which is considered as a sacrificial offering.

And in the *Raa-ya M'hemna* (*parshat Eh-more*, mentioned above, in chapter 7[618]): "'And Rivka said to Yaakov...' (*B'reisheet* 27:6)—to be aroused by these tasty foods of his. And Yaakov was aroused from below, dons prayers and supplications..., and says: 'who—where—is the one who has hunted prey' (ibid 27:33)—using a number of prayers and supplications—'and I ate from all ...'." And in *parshat Pinkhas* 235a: "'and eat from his son's catch'—these are the prayers that leave and are expelled."

And in the *Zohar* there (226a and b) it explained the entire arrangement [referred to] in the text: "I ate my honeycomb..." (*Shir Ha-shirrim* 5:1), also the arrangement of the form of the prayer service in toto, from its beginning until its end, refer there. And too in the *Raa-ya M'hemna* (there 244a) they also explained a little about the arrangement of the prayer service in another way, refer there[619].

---

617 Heb.: *b'ei-sek ha-torah*—See the footnote at the beginning of Gate 4 for a discussion of what "involvement with Torah" means to Rav Chayyim.

618 100a

619 I couldn't find this topic on page 244a in the *Raa-ya M'hemna.*

And there (241b): "Rabbee Shim'on stated: 'Based on this secret, a person is forbidden to taste anything until the supernal King eats. And what is it [fem.]? Prayer… . 'Until the supernal King eats'- that's the first three [blessings[620]] and the last three. And once he's eaten… ." Refer there at length [for more details]. And all is per the intention discussed above, that is the drawing forth of an increase in holiness and blessing that radiates to all the worlds, and as is explained in the *Zohar Va-y'khee* that was mentioned above, refer there carefully [for more details]. And the sincere worshipper should intend this[621].

Annotation: *And the prayer services were designed to correspond to the continual sacrificial offerings*[622] *that were also, [when offered] in their proper time, the essence of the nourishment mentioned above, as in the context of (*B'midbar *28:2): "My sacrificial offering, My nourishment" ("the one lamb shall you prepare and offer in the morning and the second lamb shall you prepare and offer in the afternoon", as in the context of morning's breakfast and evening's dinner, that are the essence of nourishment). And it's written (*Va-yikra *21:8): "for he offers the food of your God-*Elohi"m*", and this what they (OBM) stated in* Chazeeta*: "'My friend'—'Friend' is none other than the one who maintains me, that they befriend me with the two continual sacrificial offerings… ." And refer to* Zohar Va-yei-tzei *164a: "began… 'My sacrificial offering, My nourishment…'", and in* parshat Va-y'khee *247b and 248a: "Binyamin is a predatory wolf…", and in* parshat

620 Of the *Ahmeeda* prayer

621 Rav Chayyim cites the *Zohar* that explains why we don't' eat before we complete prayer, and directs that a person who is sincere about praying should intend in his prayers to draw forth an increase of holiness and blessing so as to nourish all of creation.

622 Heb.: *t'meedim*

Bo *37b: "My beloved will come to His garden and dine…"* (Shir Ha-shirrim *5:1). Refer to all of these citations at length [for more details]. And in* parshat Va-yikra, *page 4a; and there on page 7, at the end of the first folio; and in* parshat Ba-lahk *202, end of the first folio; and in* parshat Pinkhas *241a; they expounded the entire matter of the text "I ate my honeycomb…" in the context of the hidden meaning of the sacrificial offerings, refer there [for more details]; and there in* parshat Pinkhas *252b, refer there in 240b [regarding] the wondrous context for this.*

And so in this way they broke down the details and explained all of the utensils used for cooking and digesting functions in the man, that they [emphatic] are identical in the order of the parts of the Vehicle[623]*, supernal worlds and powers called by the names of those actual limbs/organs, that they are the utensils that cook and clarify the sacrificial offering, refer there carefully on page 224a, and page 234 and 235 in* Zohar *and in* Raa-ya M'hemna *there, and in the hidden meaning of the four levels of the sacrificial offering: "a fire offering, a satisfying aroma to God-*YHV"H*"* (Va-yikrah *1:9). "Three levels: fire offering, aroma, satisfying—according to the order in the three key limb/organs of assimilation: liver, heart/mind, brain. 'Fire offering'- in the liver. "Aroma"—in the heart/mind. And "satisfying"—in the brain." (This is not the place to address at length the explanation of their context.) They are responsible for settling the three aspects of* NR"N[624]*, for the key places where they settle are in these three limbs/organs. And one other still higher level is hidden, the aspect of the soul-*Neshama-of-the-soul-Neshama *that is attached (so to speak) to Him (blessed be He), and this is "to God-*YHV"H*".*

*And for that reason our sages (OBM) stated (*B'rakhote *55a): "During the period when the Holy Temple existed, the altar atoned; now a person's dining table atones for him."*

623 Heb.: *merkava*

624 NR"N is an acronym for *Neffesh, Ruakh, Neshama.*

CHAPTER 10

And not just to this phrase "blessed are You[625]", whose definition is "increase and expansion", is this intention relevant, but rather for each and every word from the entire body of the prayer service is this holy intention also relevant. For each word from the prayer, or from any blessing, ascends upward and still further upward by those winged masters of lightness who transport it to perform its task in the supernal root unique to it. And he thereby becomes a partner (so to speak) of the Former of the Beginning, to construct and found a number of (and still more) worlds.

And as is written in the *Tikkoonim* (*Tikkoon* 18, 35b): "And when a person sends out vaporous breaths and words during his prayer, a number of winged creatures spread their wings and mouths to receive them; this is what is written: 'For a bird of the heavens will carry the sound and one who has wings...' (*Kohelet* 10:20). And the Holy One (blessed be He) accepts those words, and with them builds worlds, as is written in relation to them (*Y'shaya* 66:22): 'For just as the new heavens and the new earth...', and [in relation to] the secret of the word: 'and I have placed My words in your mouth... to plant the heavens...'" (*Y'shayah* 51:16). [And regarding the verse] "and to say unto Zion 'you are My people'", don't read it as "my people"[626] but rather as "with me"[627], my partner, and it's the same there in *Tikkoon* 69, 106b.

And the wise one will understand on his own that it wasn't for no reason that the one-hundred-and-

---

625 Heb.: *barukh ah-tah*

626 Heb.: *ah-mee*

627 Heb.: *ee-mee*

twenty elders (and among them a few prophets)[628] set the requirement for such a brief supplication and a short prayer such as this. Rather, that they [emphatic] discerned with their Holy Spirit and with the discernment of their supernal prophecy, and all the paths of the designs of the Creation and the parts of the Vehicle shone brightly for them, and because of this they set the foundation of and fixed the form of the blessings and the prayer service using these specific words, because of how they saw and discerned on which path the light of each specific word would rest, how [that word] is extremely necessary to rectify the multitude of worlds and the supernal powers and the assembly of the Vehicle. And as they (OBM) stated (refer to *Shabbat* 116b, *M'nakhote* 64a): "The service is a lofty necessity"[629].

And this is the context of what they (OBM) stated (*Y'vamote* 64a): "The Holy One (blessed be He) has a desirous passion for the prayers of the righteous". And in *Tahn-khooma, parshat Tole-dote* they stated: "And why were the Matriarchs childless? Rabbee Leivee stated: 'The Holy One (blessed be He) had a desirous passion for their[630] [masc.] prayers'." And in *Zohar Tole-dote* 137a: "Come and observe: twenty years Yitzkhak waited with his wife and she didn't give birth until he prayed his prayer, because the Holy One (blessed be He) desires the prayers of the righteous... . For what reason? So that the extra holiness will multiply and increase for anyone

628 These are the Notables of the Great Assembly (Heb.: *Anshei K'nesset Ha-g'dola*)

629 Heb.: *ha-ah-vo-da tzo-rekh ga-vo-ha.* Note that it doesn't state (as one might expect) *l'tzorekh ga-vo-ha* (serves a high purpose), but rather "*is* a lofty necessity".

630 The prayers of the Patriarchs

who required the prayers of the righteous." And it's stated explicitly (*Mishlei* 15:8): "but the upright's prayer is His desire[631]".

And for that reason the sages (OBM) called the matter of prayer (*B'rakhote* 6b): "words that stand at the pinnacle of the world"—it is [emphatic] the words themselves, they being the words of prayer, stand at the pinnacle of the worlds.

And in *Zohar Va-yahk-heil* (201a): "A man's prayer are the service of the soul-*Ruakh*, manifesting in the supernal secrets, and men don't know that a man's prayers splits the skies and splits the heavens, opens doors and ascends [fem.] upwards. And refer to the second folio there, and on page 202a, and the beginning of the second folio. Awesome and wonderful is the matter of how each and every word of the prayer ascends. And at the beginning of *parshat Va-et-kha-nahn* 260b: "and during the time of prayer, all of those words that come out of a man's mouth during that prayer, all of them ascend upward and split the heavens, until they arrive... and are crowned".

And with his voice of this lower world he arouses the supernal voice, the great voice mentioned in the *Zohar.* (And as is written in a few places in the *Zohar*, that prayer goes up in order to draw blessings from the depths of all, and that is the great voice.) And what is written (*B'reishit* 27:22): "the voice is Jacob's voice", that the voice of a man's prayer arouses the corresponding great voice. And therefore the sages (OBM) expounded (*Ta-ah-neet* 16b) on the verse (*Yirmiya* 12:8): "she raised her voice against Me; therefore I hated her"—and they stated: "this is an

631 This can be read both that He desires the prayers of the righteous, and also that the prayers of the righteous *are* God's desire.

improper leader of communal prayer", as if to say that only his voice is present, but his voice doesn't also cause the supernal voice to be aroused to join him. And when it says "she raised her voice against Me", it means just that voice alone, and it continues "therefore...". And this is what the text states (*Yoel* 2:11): "and God-YHV"H has emitted His voice before His army".

And for this reason, even though our sages (OBM) called the matter of prayer "service using the heart/ mind", even so, we learn from the text of Channah that one is required to enunciate with one's lips.

CHAPTER 11

And what is written "before his army" hints at the great fundamental principle of the matter of prayer, that the general principle of its purpose is for us to intend only to add power to holiness, for just as a soldier casts aside all of his concerns and personal needs, and devotes his life willingly only to the honor of the king, that he should capture the crown of that specific [enemy] nation and that his reign should be exalted, so too it's very fitting[632] for the righteous person to apply his entire attention/ intention[633] and clarity of thought[634] related to his prayers so as only to increase the strength given to the holy worlds, and to awaken the supernal voice with his voice , and to draw down from it blessings and light to

---

632 Heb.: *ra- ui m'ode*

633 Heb.: *ka-va-na-toe* (his *ka-va-na*). *Ka-va-na* refers to a focusing of awareness, either on incoming sensory/memory information, or on the outcome of a thought/speech/physical act. It can be translated, depending on context, variously as *intention* or *attention*. Sometimes it spans both meanings.

634 Heb.: *to-har makh-shav-toe*

all, and to cause the spirit of impurity to pass away from the world, and to rectify the world in His sovereignty (blessed be His name), and not in any way towards his own concerns or personal needs.

And we see when we examine the wording of the *Rosh Ha-shanna* prayer service, that it is organized from its start to its end so as to honor His sovereignty (blessed be His name), that it should be as exalted as it was in the beginning prior to the sin of First Adam. And also the wording of the daily prayer service, even though it superficially appears to mostly be organized relative to the matters of our personal needs, with certainty, it is clear to all who understand, as can be determined from its context[635], that the Notables of the Great Assembly did not intend the plain meaning of the words alone, and it's as I wrote above in chapter 10.

"And the prayer services were designed to correspond to the continual sacrificial offerings" (*B'rakhote* 26b)—that the sacrifices were wholly consumed by the fire. They departed completely to the supernal heights, and no part of them remained here in the mundane.

And even though it is clearly taught as a legal ruling in the Talmud (*Sanhedrin* 8a) that the individual is permitted to add statements in his prayers relating to his personal needs and suffering in each blessing according to its topic, again the primary intention should not be his own personal suffering; this is not the correct approach for those who are righteous in their hearts/minds[636].

For in truth, we would wonder how it could be appropriate to plead in any way from Him (blessed be His name) to relieve him of his suffering and torments. As with the

---

635 Heb.: *mim-komo hoo mookh-ra*

636 Heb.: *la-y'sha-rim b'lee-bo-tam*

healing of the body, if the physician administers powerful drugs, or if the physician must completely amputate a limb so that the toxins of the illness do not spread further, would the patient plead to him that he shouldn't administer the drugs or amputate the limb? Lo, the patient himself has hired him for that reason; thusly, how can he pour out his heart/mind[637] before Him (blessed be His name) to remove from upon him the torments, for aren't they [emphatic] the bandage and the life-preserving drug to atone for his sins? And the sages (OBM) stated (*Shabbat* 58a): "There are no torments without sin", for if it weren't so, how, using what method, could the sinning soul-*Neffesh* achieve atonement?

However, the purpose of the intention must only be as a lofty necessity[638], because in a place where there is a desecration of His name[639] (blessed be His name), as when the community of Israel is suffering—"when it is said of them: 'they are God's nation'" (*Yekhezkel* 36:21)—while they [emphatic] are stricken and tortured, it is incumbent upon them to supplicate and to pour out their hearts/minds before Him (blessed be His name) regarding the desecration of His name (blessed be His name), and to do it only for the sake of His name.

And so too the individual, regarding his own suffering, even if there is no desecration of the name in the matter, there is an opening[640] too [*A] to supplicate Him regarding the large amount of supernal suffering that occurs when a person merits suffering in the lower world, as the sages (OBM) stated in the *Mishna*, chapter six of *Sanhedrin* (46a): "Rabbee Meir stated: 'When a person regrets, what

637 Heb.: *yish-pokhe see-akh*

638 Heb.: *tzo-rekh ga-vo-ha*, meaning for the sake of heaven and not one's own needs

639 Heb.: *chee-lool ha-Shem* (lit. a voiding of the name)

640 Heb.: *ma-kome* (lit.: a space, or a place)

does the *Sh'kheena* say [fem.]? "I am disgraced by my head; I am disgraced by my arm"'." [*B]

Annotation A: *And the* Tanna[641] *hinted at these two perspectives in the* Mishna, *third chapter of* Rosh Ha-shanna*: "'And it would happen, that when Moshe raised his hand, Israel would dominate' (*Sh'mote *17:11)—Could it be that Moshe's hands do battle... rather it tells us...you can conclude that the result... ."*

The first perspective that's mentioned is the situation where there is a desecration of His name (blessed be His name), pointing out that the text hinted to us regarding the war with Amalek, *that it was a desecration of God's name (blessed be His name), as is known from what the sages (OBM) stated in* P'sikta[642]*: comparing it to a tub of exceedingly hot water*[643]*... . And truly, they stated there that they amputated their sexual organs and hurled them towards the heavens...*[644]*. What is written: "'"And it would happen, that when Moshe raised..."—Could it be that Moshe's arms...'—rather that while Israel were gazing only towards the heavens—for the cries of their prayers before Him (blessed be His name) were not to relieve their own suffering, but rather exclusively regarding the*

---

641 A *Tanna* is an author of a mishna.

642 *P'sikta* is a midrashic source

643 See RaSh"Y on *Devarim* 25:18, quoting *Midrash Tahn-khooma,* that Amalek cooled the fear of the non-Jewish nations' perception of Israel's invulnerability due to God's protection.

644 See RaSh"Y on *Devarim* 25:18, quoting *Midrash Tahn-khooma,* that Amalek attacked the stragglers who had difficulty keeping up with the main camp, amputated their sexual organs (referring to the covenant of circumcision), and hurled them upwards towards the heavens with impudent cries of "You chose these? Take these!"

desecration of the name of their Father in heaven, (blessed be His name)—then they would dominate [the battle]. And when not... ."

And they further stated, that in a situation where there isn't a desecration of God's name in the matter, the text hinted to us (in the matter of the copper snake) the form and the content of the supplication and prayer that is desired by Him (blessed be His name). "Does a snake execute capital judgment? Rather, when they would completely discard their own suffering and would gaze and pour out their pleas and supplications exclusively regarding the great heavenly suffering that they caused during the performance of the sin (may the Merciful save us!), and also the current suffering that is being caused above as a result that they [emphatic] are now mired in suffering from the torments of punishment because of their sins, then they were healed... ."

Annotation B: *And what the text states: "I am disgraced by my arm..." the context is the* t'fillin *of the head and the* t'fillin *of the arm. For our sages (OBM) stated (*B'rakhote *6a) that the Holy One (blessed be He) dons* t'fillin. *And the matter of His (blessed be His name)* t'fillin *is his bond (blessed be His name) to do good for us in everything, as they stated there: "What is written in the Master of the World's* t'fillin*? 'And who is like your people Israel, a singular nation'"* (Shmuel Bet *7:23), "For who is a great nation..."* (D'varim *4:7). And truly, all of the verses there are exclusively praises of Israel, and they're all written in the* t'fillin *of the arm. And this is per the context of (*D'varim *26:17 and 18): "You have distinguished God-YHV"H today...", and "God-YHV"H has distinguished you today", in that just as in our* t'fillin *are written praises of the Holy One (bless be He), so in His* t'fillin *(so to speak) are praises of us, and in that is the matter of being bound to each other. And this is the context of the* *text "Israel in whom I glory"* (Y'shaya *49:3), the secret of the* t'fillin *of the Master of the World, that* t'fillin *are called "glory"*[645] *as the sages (OBM) stated, refer to* Zohar B'shalakh *62, beginning of the second folio.*

Therefore, when a person regrets [his sins], and at that moment there isn't any connection or attachment (so to speak) between the person and Him (blessed be His name) in fullness as it should be, that's the context of "I am disgraced by my head, I am disgraced by my arm", that those are the places of the t'fillin, *that it would have been worthy for those places to have the holy bond.*

And they stated in *Sh'mote Rabba* (*parsha* 2), and in *Chazeeta* for the verse "I am sleeping": "'my twin...' (*Shir Ha-shirrim* 5:2)—What happens with these twins—that when one's head hurts, the other senses it—so too states the Holy One (blessed be He) (*T'hillim* 91:15): 'I am with him in [times of] distress'." And in *Tahn-khooma* (at the end of *parshat Ah-kha-rei*): "All salvation that comes to Israel is of the Holy One (blessed be He), for it states: 'I am with him in [times of] distress'"; that is to say that it concludes with "I will show him My salvation". It's Your salvation for it is stated (ibid 80:3): "it is for You to save us". And in *Shokheir Tov* (on *T'hillim* 13:6): "'My heart/mind will exult in your salvation'—Rabbi A. stated: 'This is one of the difficult texts, that the salvation of the Holy One (blessed be He) is the salvation of Israel. It doesn't say 'in our salvation' but rather 'in Your salvation'... Your salvation is our salvation." And refer to *Zohar Eh-more* (90, top of second folio) in the matter of the verse "salvation is God's-*YHV"H*".

And this is "I am with him in [times of] distress"—that

645 Heb.: *p'eir*

from the constricted places, he takes God (blessed be His name) as a partner; then "I will release him…"[646]. And when a person no longer feels his personal suffering from his torments because of his great bitterness over His suffering (so to speak), those bitters are [emphatic] the essence of the scouring of his sins, and in that he atones until his personal torments leave him. (And they [emphatic] are the holy judgments, for it is His (blessed be His name) way to sweeten bitter with bitter[647], and this is the rectification of the personality's features at their roots[648].)

CHAPTER 12

And for that reason the sages (OBM) stated (*B'rakhote* 63a): "Anyone who associates the name of heaven in their suffering, his livelihood is doubled." And the matter is that, besides the suffering caused above when he receives his punishment in the form of torments (may the Merciful save us), you can't compare nor conceive in any way this [current] suffering above relative to the enormous amount of suffering above that he caused at the moment he performed the sin (may the Merciful save us).

It's like the situation of the beloved son who, seduced by wine, fell to the ground and broke his neck and his body, and is in a critical state. He himself doesn't, at that moment, sense in any way the threat to his life, as is written (*Mishlei* 23:35): "They struck me, but I didn't become ill; they beat me, but I was unaware". However, his father's heart/mind is greatly embittered over this. When the physicians set the broken bones and prescribe poultices and dressings made

646 Heb.: *ah-khal-tzei-hoo*

647 Heb.: *l'hom-teek mar b'mar*

648 Heb.: *tee-koon ha-mee-dote b'shore-shon*

from searing compounds, the son bitterly cries out in pain from the searing compounds that devour his flesh. And though his father suffers at this moment from his screams and his many sighs, there's no way to compare the current suffering to the initial suffering and grief that his father experienced when he fell and broke his bones, almost to the point of despair over his life then.

So too in fact, in this way, is the matter of sin (may the Merciful save us). At the moment that a person does it, he causes great, enormous suffering above, without measure, and the person himself doesn't sense it at all, and doesn't realize that his life is in danger, for at that moment he is considered as if dead (heaven forefend), as the sages stated at the beginning of chapter *Mee Sheh-mei-toe* (*B'rakhote* chapter 3): "during their lives, evil ones are called 'dead'". And there are sins that cause his soul-*Neffesh* to be cut off (heaven forefend) from its connection to the holy portion, while He (blessed be His name), the compassionate Father, by suffering His suffering (so to speak) and out of His great compassion and benevolence (blessed be His name), sends him torments that are [emphatic] poultices and dressings to scour away his sin. And then the person experiences the pain of his torments, suffers, and thereby also awakens suffering above (as explained previously). However, this suffering does not compare in any way to the suffering that he caused above at the time he performed the sin (heaven forefend).

And therefore, when the entire point of a person's prayer before Him (blessed be His name) is to remove his suffering from upon him, doing so only because of the suffering above that participates in his suffering, and he repents and truly regrets his sin that caused (by his own fault) the suffering above, then the torments leave him.

And not only that, but he is evaluated according to the extent [of his effort], and his livelihood is doubled, corresponding to the two types of suffering he caused above and now regrets both of them—his willful transgressions, for him, convert themselves to merits[649].

And this is what the sages (OBM) expounded upon by [the story of] Channa (*B'rakhote* 31b): "'And she was bitter in her soul-*Neffesh*, and prayed to God-*YHV"H*[650]' (*Shmuel Alef* 1:10)—that she hurled words towards above, as if to say that even though she herself was bitter in her soul-*Neffesh*, even so, she cast her suffering away and didn't bother to pray about it at all. Rather, she hurled the words of her prayer before Him (blessed be His name) over the suffering above, caused on account of her now being steeped in suffering.

And therefore, they stated there (*B'rakhote* 32a): "that Moshe also hurled words towards above...—Don't read it as[651] 'towards God-*YHV"H*' but rather as 'upon God-*YHV"H*'." And according to its plain meaning, who forced them (the sages OBM), to expound it using the interpretive device of 'don't read it as' and to state that he hurled words upwards?[652] Indeed, they expounded this way so as to compliment him.

(And those who have the capacity will understand what they further state there, that Eliyahu also hurled words upwards, for it is stated (*M'la-khim Alef* 18:37): "thus will You turn their hearts/minds back". And this is like the

---

649 Heb.: *z'doe-note mit-hahp-khin lo l'z'khoo-yote*

650 Heb.: *hit-pa-leil al YHV"H* (lit. "prayed *on* God-*YHV"H*")

651 Heb.: *al tikri*

652 Rav Chayyim seems to imply here that *ChaZa"l* had the prerogative to interpret this verse as they saw fit, rather than as the result of a transmitted teaching (a *m'sora*). (Thanks to Rav Pahmer for this insight.)

context of "rock of my hearts/minds ..." (*T'hillim* 73:26). And refer to *Zohar T'rooma* 128, top of folio 2, and as was stated "because of your rebellious sins, your mother has been cast out" (*Y'shaya* 50:1), "retracted his right hand" (*Eikha* 2:3), and this is the same as "thus will You turn their hearts/minds back". And so it is explained in the *Pri Etz Chayyim, Sha-ar Ha-kree-at Sh'ma,* chapter 8, refer there [for more details].)

And if in the case of an individual's prayer regarding personal suffering, one's intention must be solely as a lofty necessity, how much more so in the formula of the blessings of the prayer service, made permanent and designed by the holy Notables of the Great Assembly. With certainty it is fitting not to intend in them for his own needs at all (per their plain meaning), rather only as a lofty necessity, to draw down the increased expansion of blessing and holiness to the worlds, from the perspective of His (blessed be His name) relationship with them, as we described previously at length.

And our sages (OBM) even also stated (*Eiruvin* 65a): "I could exempt the entire world from the requirement for prayer, for it says (*Y'shaya* 51:21): 'drunken, but not from wine'". And what can we say in these generations, when every person is as if laying at the end of a rope and in the middle of the oceans all their days, from the burden of earning livelihoods. And for that reason, no one pays attention to clearing his heart/mind and thoughts of the confusion caused by his overwhelming anxieties about the vanities of this lowly world, and to prepare himself to encounter his God-*Elohi"m* (blessed be His name).[653]

---

653 Rav Chayyim confirms the need to prepare for prayer by clearing the heart/mind of thoughts and anxieties about the world.

With all that, it's certain that each one, according to his intellect and ability, is required to devise schemes in his soul-*Neffesh* and to seek "holy war" strategies to escape from the confusion of impure thoughts, that his mind should be supportive of a proper prayer service, for the prayer service is, for us, in place of the sacrificial service that was completely dependent on the thoughts of the Cohein, for with his thoughts he could disqualify the acceptability of the sacrifice, and via the holiness of his thoughts the sacrifice would be elevated as a sweet savor before Him (blessed be His name).

CHAPTER 13

And the advice offered about this is as the *Maggid* stated to the *Beit Yosef* in the second warning at the beginning of the book *Maggid Meisharim*—this is what he said: "to be careful of thinking any thought during prayer, even related to Torah and mitzvote, other than the words of the prayer themselves."

Pay close attention to his words, that he didn't say to attend to the intention of the words, for in truth, none of us understand the slightest about the depths of the inner meaning of the prayer, for even what has been revealed to us about a few of the intentions of the prayer from our earliest sages (OBM, supernal holy ones), until the recent holy rabbi, man of God-*Elohi"m*, the awe-inspiring Ariza"l, who achieved wonders and greatness authoring incredible intentional-meditations[654], are not, in comparison, more than a drop in the ocean relative to the inner depths of the intentions of the Notables of the Great

654 Heb.: *ka-va-note,* intentional meditations executed during the recitation of the prayers.

Assembly codifiers of the prayer, who were one-hundred-and-twenty elders, among them a few prophets.

And those who are capable of understanding will understand that there's no one currently in the world who is capable of codifying such a wondrous and awesome rectification[655], to incorporate into and to hide in the formula of the prayer, permanently fixed and configured in a single formula, the rectifications for all the worlds, upper and lower, and the configurations of the components of the Vehicle[656]. And each occasion of praying causes new rectifications in the configuration of the worlds and the powers, and the drawing down of other new *mo-khin*[657]. From the moment that it was codified until the coming of the redeemer[658] (quickly, in our

---

655 Heb.: *l'tah-kein tee-koon nif-lah v'no-ra ka-zeh.* This phrase embodies a fundamental principle of Rav Chayyim's world-view, and of the other sages who subscribe to the Kabbalah of the Ariza"l. The world, as created, is broken, and it is Man's God-given purpose to heal the world, to repair what is broken, via the thought-acts, speech-acts and physical-acts defined in the Torah, to ultimately bring the world to wholeness and perfection—"wholeness and perfection" meaning the awareness of God's one-ness and adherence to and enactment of His will, as expressed in Torah. Each act of repairing is called a *tee-koon* (rectification). The same word is used for thought-acts (e.g., meditations, cognitions, intellections), speech-acts (e.g., prayers) or physical acts (e.g., physical mitzvote) that cause a rectification. To compose/author, design and codify a thought-act, speech-act or physical-act that achieves t*ee-koon* is *l'tah-kein tee-koon* (to codify a rectification).

656 Heb.: *mer-ka-va.* As previously described, the Vehicle is a model of Creation, describing the components of the creation, and how the worlds interconnect and interact.

657 *Mo-khin* are the uppermost aspects of each world, usually corresponding to minds and mind-states (e.g., awarenesses). For example, the three kinds of awarenesses known as *chokh-ma* (wisdom), *beena* (understanding) and *da'at* (knowledge) are referred to as *gimmel mo-khin* (three minds).

658 Heb.: *Bee-aht ha-go-eil*

day), there never was and never will be another prayer that, in its details, resembles others that came before and after in any way. "The garments worn in the morning are not worn in the evening, and those worn in the evening...", as is written in the *Tikkoonim* (*Tikkoon* 22), and so too each day relative to the ones that preceded and follow. And for that reason the sages (OBM) stated (*Chageega* 9b, and in *B'midbar Rabba*, chapter 9): "'what is distorted can not be corrected' (*Kohelet* 1:15)—one who missed the *k'ree-at sh'ma*[659]... or prayer"; and as is written at length in the *Pri Etz Chayyim*, chapter 7 of *Sha-ar Ha-t'feela*, refer there [for more details].

And it would have been impossible if not via the supernal level of prophecy and His holy spirit that manifested over them in an enormous manifestation during the codification of the wording of the formula of the prayer and the blessings. He (blessed be His name) placed in their mouths these numbered words, and hidden within them are all the rectifications. For that reason, who can understand God's hidden secrets to the depths of His (blessed be His name) intention, on which path will the light of each specific word settle[660]?

Rather, the essence of the prayer service is that, at the moment that the person pronounces each word of the prayer, he should visualize in his thoughts that word as its letters, as it [fem.] appears[661], [*] and to intend to increase thereby the power of holiness so that it will bear

659 *K'ree-at sh'ma* is the reading of the Sh'ma in its appointed time.

660 Rav Chayyim seems to imply that each word of the prayer potentially draws down "light" that illuminates or strengthens a specific "path" (perhaps referring to the connections between the various s'feerote).

661 Rav Chayyim emphasizes that the mental action during prayer should be a visualization of each word via the appearance of its individual letters, accompanied by an intention.

fruit above to multiply their holiness and light, as I wrote previously in chapter ten. For that reason prayer is called: "words that stand at the pinnacle of the world" (*B'rakhote* 6b): that each word, as it actually appears, it is what rises higher and higher, each one to its source and root, to perform wondrous actions and rectifications.

And this is a marvelous remedy, tried and tested, for those who get themselves used to practicing this, to annul and remove from upon them in this way any vain thoughts that cause anxiety and that obstruct purity of thought and attention, and anyone who increases the regularity of this practice will increase his purity of thought during prayer, and this is simple attention/intention.[662]

Annotation: *And even though there is a firm legal ruling in the* Sha"s (B'rakhote *13) that prayer can be recited in any language, that [ruling] is about the fulfillment of the minimal requirements of the mitzva of prayer. As was explained previously at the end of the first Gate, for all mitzvote, and even the mitzva of prayer that is called* (B'rakhote *31a) "service using the heart/mind", it is so that the key component to fulfill the minimal requirement is the physical action. However, to perform an especially desirable mitzva, he certainly must combine purity of thought and complete attention/intention. And the greater the purity of thought, that also improves the performance of the mitzva, and specifically the "service using the heart/mind" as in prayer. And though one who prays in any language fulfills his obligation, there is no comparison to one who prays in the holy language using those definite words that stand at the pinnacle of the world, and cleaves to them with all his strength.*

---

662 Rav Chayyim affirms that this mental practice (i.e., a meditation exercise) is effective at banning distracting thoughts and achieving focused attention.

CHAPTER 14

However, the explanation of the text discussed above at the beginning of our exposition: "...and to serve him... and with all your [plural] souls-*Neffesh*", [explaining] that perfect prayer must be performed with the soul-*Neffesh,* is a great matter to those who somewhat know and understand. And when a person is diligent in this spiritual level (that will be explained—with God's help), his purity [of focus and intention] will continuously grow[663].

For we found in a few places in the scripture and in the statements of our sages (OBM) that prayer is called by the name "soul-*Neffesh*", because some of the important rules regarding the fundamentals of prayer are those derived from the story of Channa, and about her is written (*Shmuel Alef* 1:15): "and I have poured out my soul-*Neffesh* before God-*YHV"H*". And it's written (*T'hillm* 103:1): "Bless God-*YHV"H,* O' my soul-*Neffesh*", (*T'hillim* 103:1), "Praise God-*YHV"H,* O' my soul-*Neffesh*" (*T'hillim* 146:1). And the sages (OBM) in the first chapter of *B'rakhote* (5b) stated: "Two who entered to pray, and one of them prayed earlier than the other and didn't wait for his companion, and left, [they] rip his prayers to shreds in front of him, as is stated (*Eeyove* 18:4): 'he who rips his soul-*Neffesh* apart in

663 Heb.: *yit-va-seif ta-ha-ra al ta-ha-ra-toe.* Purity (Heb.: *ta-ha-ra*) has two alternate meanings: ritual purity, in contrast to ritual impurity (Heb.: *toom-ah*), and unsullied physical purity (e.g., "pure gold"). In the current context, Rav Chayyim refers to the latter, implying that a person will progressively refine his spiritual practice of prayer.

anger…'"[664]. RaSh"Y explained: "It's speaking about you, because you yourself caused that your 'soul-*Neffesh*' should be ripped to shreds in front of you. And what is [fem.] 'soul-*Neffesh*? It is prayer, as was stated: 'and I have poured out my soul-*Neffesh*' (*Shmuel Alef* 1:15)."

And the context is that the service of prayer is in place of the sacrificial service.[*] And just as the matter of the sacrifice was to elevate the soul-*Neffesh* of the domesticated animal above, and for that reason the accomplishment of the atonement was dependent on the throwing of the blood (it being the soul-*Neffesh*)—and so too the consumption by flame of the inner organs[665], their main point being the intention of elevating the soul-*Neffesh*—so too, the main intent of the matter of prayer is to elevate and to deliver and to attach his soul-*Neffesh* above[666]. For a person's power of speech is called soul-*Neffesh*, as is written (*B'reisheet* 2:7): "and the man became a living soul-*Neffesh*", and Onkeloos translated it as "a speaking soul-*Ruakh*". And so it appears to the eye that with every word that a person speaks with his mouth, what comes out of his mouth are his heart/mind's moving air and vapor. And speech is the fundamental expression of a person's soul-*Neffesh*, it being the unique capacity that people have over animals. That being so, every word that comes out of a person's mouth is the power of and a part of his soul-*Neffesh*.

---

664 One explanation for this passage: Two people enter a synagogue together to pray. If one finishes praying and leaves before the other has finished, it's as if he expects that the Sh'kheena departed when he finished praying, when in fact the Sh'kheena is still present to the other's prayers. In response to this self-centered attitude his prayers are rejected.

665 Heb.: *hahk-ta-raht ha-ee-moo-rim*

666 Rav Chayyim states clearly that the purpose of prayer is to attach one's soul to its root above.

Annotation: *For via the sacrifices in the Temple—which was completely modeled on the heavens (its upper levels, rooms and all of its utensils that were used for service)—all the worlds and supernal powers and the pathways of the holy palaces would be interconnected and unified, all of them according to the design of the levels above and still higher, until the* Ein Sofe *(blessed be He), as explained in many places in the* Zohar, *in* parshat B'reisheet *45b,* Noakh *65a,* Lekh L'kha *89b,* Va-yee-gosh *206b,* Va-y'khee *244a,* P'koodei *259b,* Va-yikra *5b (top),* Tzav *26b,* Zohar Chaddash Tzav *38a, and there too in* Shir Ha-shirrim *51b—refer carefully there in all of these citations regarding this awesome matter. And refer to the* Pri Etz Chayyim *chapter 5 and chapter 7 from* Sha-ar Ha-t'feela, *[for] the detailed order of the elevation and connection.*

*And that's why it was called "*korban[667]*", as was stated in the* Bahir[668]*: "Why is it called '*korban*'? Because it draws the holy forms near...". And they stated "'for a satisfying aroma*[669]*...'* (Va-yikra *3:16)—The spirit-*Ruakh *would descend and unite with those holy forms, and draw near via the* korban, *and for that reason it was called* korban*"; this is what it states. And refer to the* Zohar Va-yikra, *top of page 5 and page 8a, and in the* Raa-ya M'hemna, Pinkhas *256b: "and it's called* korban *because they are drawn near by it...". And refer to the* Pri Etz Chayyim, *chapter 5 in* Sha-ar Ha-t'feela.

And from the moment, because of our sins, that the service of our Holy Home was interrupted, nothing remained other than the service of prayer to replace it, for it too, its special

---

667 The Hebrew word *korban* (commonly translated as "sacrifice") has as its root *K-R-B,* which means closeness, nearness or innerness.

668 See *Bahir* 109

669 Heb.: *rei-ahkh nee-kho-ahkh*

attribute is to connect and unify the worlds, up to the highest, with Ein Sofe *(blessed be He), as is explained in many places in the* Zohar. *And it's better explained in* parshat Va-yahk-heil *(213b): "When one serves his Master in prayer, his will is bound like the flame to the glowing coal, to unite those lower heavens that originate on the side of holiness, to crown them with one lower name, and then from there, continue on to unite those upper, inner heavens, to make all as one..., and while his mouth and lips are still murmuring, he should direct his heart/mind, and his desire will rise higher and higher, to unite everything per the deepest secrets, for there are settled all of the wills and thoughts that are found in the ongoing secret of* Ein Sofe.

And as is explained in the Pri Etz Chayyim, *that the entire fundamental purpose of the matter of prayer from it's start until after the completion of the* Ahmeeda, *is rectification of the worlds and their elevation from below to above, to bind and to incorporate each one of them into the one above it, higher and higher, until the* Ein Sofe *(blessed be He). And refer in that book to chapters four through seven from* Sha-ar Ha-t'feela *for the complete account.*

And refer to the Raa-ya M'hemna, *beginning of* parshat Eikev, *that this is the distinction between (1) the blessings associated with the mitzvote and benefits*[670] *and (2) the blessings that are part of the prayer service. The blessings associated with mitzvote and benefits are the drawing down of the abundance, to bring to earth the blessings from above to below, [while] the blessings of the prayer service are to rectify the worlds themselves and elevate them, and to bind each world to the world above it. Refer to the* Pri Etz Chayyim, *beginning of* Sha-ar Ha-b'ra-khote, *and the beginning of chapter three there. And what is further written there in*

670 Heb.: *birkhote ha-mitzvote v'ha-neh-heh-nim*

> Raa-ya M'hemna*: "..and from above to below"—that is the drawing down of the abundance from above to below after the* Ahmeeda, *and this is also from the perspective of returning and elevating the worlds, each one into the one above it, as he wrote in the* Pri Etz Chayyim, *at the end of chapter five of* Sha-ar Ha-t'feela, *and at the beginning of* Sha-ar Ha-ka-dee-sheem, *in the context of the forty-two [letter name of God] and in the alternate explanation there.*[671]

For that reason, when he stands to pray before his Possessor[672], he should slough his body off from his soul-*Neffesh*; that is, that he should remove all ideas of the vanities resulting from the body's functions, that have been engraved on and attached to his soul-*Neffesh*, so that his prayer service will be performed with only his soul-*Neffesh* and higher will.

And specifically, before he stands in prayer, he must annul and remove from upon him, in his mind, all of the pleasures of the body, everything that he enjoys, and all of his preoccupations, until he establishes solidly in his thoughts to despise the body, as if he has no body at all, and only his soul-*Neffesh* [fem.] is speaking her prayer.

And when he speaks each word [fem.], which is a power of and part of his soul-*Neffesh*, he should strongly attach his will[673] to her, to actually completely pour his

---

671 Rav Chayyim refers here to how the name of forty-two letters is used to elevate and connect one world to the next, as reflected in the *kadeeshim* that are used between the sections of the morning prayer service.

672 Heb.: *kono*. Rav Chayyim uses the term that describes the relationship between the possessor and the object (or person) of possession at the instant when possession takes place. This perhaps implies the relationship that comes into being each time prayer commences.

673 Alternately: desire

soul-*Neffesh* into her, and to attach her to the supernal root of the words of the prayer that exists at the pinnacle of the world. And as is written in the *Zohar Va-yahk-heil* mentioned in the annotation: "And while his mouth and lips are still murmuring, he should direct his heart/mind, and his will will rise higher and higher, to unite everything per the deepest secrets, for there are caught all of the wills and thoughts that are found in the ongoing secret of *Ein Sofe*."

And then it will be considered as if he doesn't exist in this world, and he is one of the residents of the abodes above, to such an extent so that even after prayer, it will be very difficult for him to turn his thoughts to the matters of this world, and it will appear to him as if he falls, and climbs [down], and descends from a great height into a deep pit, per the context of (*B'rakhote* 30a) the early pious ones who would still themselves[674] for an hour before and an hour after prayer. And this is what the Ariza"l also wrote about the reason for this: "to further still the minds...". And this is the context in which the sages (OBM) stated (*Y'vamote* 105b): "one who prays must position his heart/mind up high."

And so much will this expand and ignite his love of Him (blessed be He) via the power of his soul-*Neffesh*, resulting that he will sincerely yearn and desire, so that when he speaks at this moment the specific holy speech of any word from the formula of the prayer, his soul-*Neffesh* will completely leave [fem.] the body, and it [fem.] will be elevated to attach (so to speak) to Him (blessed be His name).

---

674 Heb.: *sho-heem*, pausing from their daily routine, perhaps similar to the practice of *hosh-ka-ta* (stilling the mind's internal dialogue), and *hi-bo-d'doot* (a meditative technique).

This is why it is stated here: "...and to serve... with all your souls-*Neffesh*", and also what Channa stated: "and I have poured out my soul-*Neffesh* before God-*YHV"H*", and it's clear. And so too we can explain what the sages (OBM) stated (*Ta-ah-neet* 8a): "a person's prayers aren't heard unless he places his soul-*Neffesh* in his high branches[675]", i.e., to elevate and to attach his soul-*Neffesh* up high with his prayers; and "his high branches" means his source, from the expression (*Eeyove* 15:32): "...and his canopy[676] will not flourish".

> **Annnotation:** *As Rabbeinu Yona (OBM) wrote (*perek Ein Ome-dim, B'rakhote 25b*) in the context of one who prays, that he should focus his eyes downward and his heart/mind upwards, these are his holy words there: "...as if stating that he should mentally visualize[677] as if he is in heaven, and he should clear his mind of all the delights of this world and all the pleasures of the body—as per the context that the early ones stated, that when you desire to perform an intentional/attentional act[678], slough your body off from your soul-*Neshama. *And after he arrives at this mental state, he should then simultaneously mentally visualize as-if he is in the earthly Holy*

675 Heb.: *ka-po.* In this context, it's similar to *ka-pote t'marim* (the branches of date plams) in Va-yikra 23:40.

676 Heb.: *chee-pa-toe*

677 Heb.: *yakh-shove b'leebo.* I've rendered this as "mentally visualize". "*Leebo*" literally means "heart", but also has the connotation of "mind". "*Yakh-shove*" implies cognitive activity. Rabbeinu Yona seems to say that one should mentally place oneself as-if in heaven, and as-if in the Beit Ha-mikdash. While one could do this with a mentally conjured attitude alone (without visualization), the Ariza"l's system of kavvanot uses visualizations, and so I've rendered the phrase as visualization.

678 Heb.: *l'kha-vein*

Temple[679]*, because the effect of this will be that his prayers will be more acceptable before the Omnipresent*[680]*. I received these words from my teacher the Rav (may he live and be well)." This completes Rabbeinu Yona's statement.*

It's well-known that Rabbeinu Yona was a student of God's holy one, the RaMBa"N[681] *(OBM), and his words are [emphatic] the RaMBa"N's (OBM) words in* parshat Ah-kha-rei *on the verse (*Va-yikra *18:4): "you shall observe my laws...". And this is what he said there: "And those who leave behind all the matters of this world, and pay no attention to it as if they have no body, and all of their intention/attention is on their Creator alone (as was the situation with* Cha-nokh *and* Eliyahu*), when they attach their soul-*Neffesh *to the honored name, they will live forever in their bodies and souls-*Neffesh*."*

*And this is also what Rabbeinu Yona cited in the name of the early ones: "'Slough your body off your soul-*Neshama*'— It is that he perceives that the body and all of its situations and delights are so degraded, despised, to the point that he has a huge desire to thrust his soul-*Neffesh *away from it, and that his soul-*Neffesh*'s entire desire would be for his Creator (blessed be He), as if he has no body; rather that he is as one of the hosts of the heights who serve in heaven, set apart and differentiated from all the matters of this world.*

*And this is Rabbeinu Yona's (OBM) intention, that he should think in his heart/mind as if he is in heaven; that is, he should feel of himself that all of the body's senses have been nullified, that he is the dirt of the ground, and all of his sensations should be regarding the soul-*Neffesh*, to bind it to its*

---

679 Rabbeinu Yona seems to say that during prayer, one's mental experience of place should be split, with heart/mind in the heavens while visualizing the earthly Holy Temple.

680 Heb.: *Ha-ma-kome*

681 Nachmanides

*heavenly root with great love, even so far that if they presented him with any delight among the pleasures of this world that a person's soul-*Neffesh *finds attractive, he would despise it with the ultimate disgust and hate. And this is (*T'hillim *97:10): "O lovers of God-*YHV"H, *despise evil". And this is (ibid 148:1): "Praise God-*YHV"H *from the heavens, praise Him in the heights".*

CHAPTER 15

And what is written: "and with all your [plural] souls-*Neffesh*[682]", it's known that our sages (OBM) had different opinions in several places in the Sha"s (*Sanhedrin* 78a). One opinion is that the word "*khall*" means "all of", while another opinion says it means "a part of" and "a very small part of". So too, in this context, both are accurate.

For there are a variety of qualities and levels related to this, with each person [achieving] based on his capacity to tightly focus his heart/mind and thoughts[683]. For a person who is strong in focusing his thought and attention/intention[684] is able to bind "all of his soul-*Neffesh*", based on his vast love and yearning for Him (blessed be His name). And each person [achieves] according to his strength—and also according to how well he prepared to tightly focus his heart/mind then, because, again, not every moment is

---

682 Heb.: *u-v'khall nahf-sh'khem*

683 Heb.: *ko-ahkh ta-ha-raht leebo u-mahkh-shahv-toe,* implying a clear, unsullied, and focused quality of heart/mind and attention/intention. I translate what would be literally translated as "according to the strength of the purity of heart and thought" as "based on his capacity to tightly focus his heart/mind and thoughts".

684 Heb.: *sheh-ha-ah-dahm sheh ko-khoe ya-feh b'ta-ha-raht ha-mahkh-sha-vah v'ha-ka-va-nah*

identical regarding a person's ability to focus his thought. This alone is worthwhile and correct: that in all cases, he should see to it that his attention/intention is sincere[685], to bind to Him (blessed be He), with his love and focused heart/mind, "a small part of his soul-*Neffesh*" in each word. For that reason the text stated "and with all your [plural] souls-*Neffesh*", for it can be understood from two perspectives, as discussed previously, each one according to his ability, level and preparation.

And the main preparation for this is based on his practice[686], all day and night, of Torah study and mitzvote[687].

And Channa was on the level that, in her prayer, she poured out before Him (blessed be His name) "all of her soul-*Neffesh*". Therefore she stated: "and I have poured out my soul-*Neffesh*...". And "pouring" means completely, as is known in the *Sha"s*. (And it's that she had no personal desire[688] remaining related to matters of this world, for "soul-*Neffesh*" means "personal desire", as is written (*Shmuel Alef* 20[:4]): "whatever your soul-*Neffesh* says, that I will do for you". And the overall quality of personal desire is included in the overall soul-*Neffesh*[689].

And so, all that we've discussed until now in the context of prayer—whose key feature is pouring out the soul-*Neffesh* to attach to Him (blessed be He) with each word—is the

---

685 Heb.: *r'tzoo-ya*

686 Heb.: *hahn-ha-ga-toe*, a construction of the word *na-hoog*.

687 Rav Chayyim asserts that the primary practice that should be used to prepare to achieve a focus of heart/mind, thoughts and intention is Torah study and mitzvote.

688 Heb.: *ra-tzone*—personal will; a quality of personally wanting something, that motivates effort towards acquiring or achieving it.

689 Rav Chayyim begins here to differentiate between the overall *Neffesh*, which is one part (the lowest part) of the overall soul, and the individual parts of the *Neffesh* itself.

pouring out of the overall soul-*Neffesh* to Him (blessed be He), without attention/intention to, nor distinction between, the parts that make up the soul-*Neffesh*.

However, there is another level[690], higher in this respect, and that is to attend/intend to the distinct components that make up the soul-*Neffesh* [*], but it takes training to get used to [being/functioning at] one level or the next. For after one is already used to praying for some time in the context of pouring out and attaching the overall soul-*Neffesh*, after that he can change direction to attend/intend to the distinct components that make up his soul-*Neffesh*.

Annotation: *And you need to know, that even when he prays at the level of connecting the distinct components of the soul-*Neffesh *to each other, he shouldn't abandon his practice of connecting the overall soul-*Neffesh, *for this is a specific context that requires the general[691], and a general context that requires the specific[692]. That is, that before praying[693], the key thing is to connect his overall soul-*Neffesh *and his personal desire, [both of] which*

690 Rav Chayyim refers to two aspects of the soul-*Neffesh*: that the soul-*Neffesh* itself is comprised of a soul-*Neffesh (Neffesh ha-Neffesh)*, soul-*Ruakh (Ruakh ha-Neffesh)* and soul-*Neshama (Neshama ha-Neffesh)*, and that simultaneously, it is the lowest part of a higher overall structure, consisting of the soul-*Neffesh*, a higher soul-*Ruakh*, and a still higher soul-*Neshama*.

691 Heb.: *praht ha-tza-reekh l'khlal*

692 Both are necessary.

693 Before praying one works on doing one thing; while praying one does something else—both are necessary. Here Rav Chayyim hints at what the Early Pious ones might have been doing when they "paused" for an hour prior to praying. Also see what Rav Azkari says about this in the *Sefer Chareidim* 254, end of chapter 65.

envelope/surround the totality of the components of his powers and personal desires, so as to be integrated into God's-YHV"H *light. And [during prayer,] to each and every word that he prays, he should bind the components of the powers of* NR"N, *and as a result of the strength of the overall connection, a stream of descending light*[694] *will be drawn down upon each component, so that each component of his personal-desire will have the ability to be integrated into the connection of the overall enveloping/ surrounding light's strength.*

Refer to the Etz Chayyim (D'roo-shei Ee-goo-lim V'yo-sheir*). And this is the matter that's explained there, that the stream of light that is drawn from the light of* Ein Sofe *(blessed be He) doesn't contact the lower edge of the enveloper/surrounder*[695]*. And refer to the* Ma-vo Sh'ah-rim *(chapter 2), and the matter of the surrounders/ envelopers being one within the other will be understood, created as a result of the drawing down of the stream of light. That is, each component's power at its own level, should be connected to the overall [structure], and also*

---

694 Heb.: *Or ya-shar*, in contrast to *or cho-zeir* (returning light)

695 Rav Chayyim refers to the Ariza"l's explanation that when the (metaphorical) stream of the Ein Sofe's (metaphorical) light is drawn down into the (metaphorical) spherical void created as a result of the (metaphorical) contraction (*tzim-tzum*), it descends a small distance as a straight line towards the bottom of the sphere, and then spreads out as a sphere inside the sphere, before it proceeds to descend once again as a line. This process repeats and repeats. The spheres-within-spheres eventually act as envelopers/surrounders (*orot mei-kee-feem*) while the line acts as an internal element (*orot p'nee-mee-eem*). The result is that the light of Ein Sofe both envelopes/surrounds the contents of the sphere, and inhabits it from within as well. The line never descends so far as to contact the bottom interior edge of the metaphorically spherical void.

that the overall [structure] depends on the relative value of the component. And the origin of this extra-fine quality stream of light is the drawing of the overall awareness/ thought[696] *to the heart/mind, the central focus of the body, for each word is drawn out from the vapor of the heart/ mind*[697]*, and this will be very clear to one who is capable of understanding based on his [experiential] knowledge.*

CHAPTER 16

For it's known that a person's soul-*Neffesh*, from an overall perspective, consists of three separate qualities, and they are *NR"N*, that themselves are the three qualities: action, speech and thought—together they comprise the entire person.

And each word also has within it three qualities: action, speech and thought, *NR"N*, and they are its letters, vowel points, and trup[698], as is written in the introduction to the *Tikkoonim* (7b): "The trup are its soul-*Neshama*, the vowel points its soul-*Ruakh*, and the letters its soul-*Neffesh*" [*]. And it's also found at the beginning of *Tikkoon* 67. Refer there [for more details].

Annotation: *And despite that in the Ariza"l's writings he splits them into four aspects:* T', N', T', A'[699] *(as is known),*

---

696 Heb.: *makh-sha-vah ha-k'la-leet*—this is accomplished before prayer begins

697 Heb.: *mei-hehvel ha-leiv*

698 Heb.: *oh-tee-yote, n'koo-dote, ta-ah-meem.* The trup (*ta-ah-meem*) are the symbols that denote how a word is to be sung, how it is connected to other words, where the emphasis of a word's pronunciation belongs, and where the middle and end of a sentence are to found.

699 The four initial letters of *ta-ah-meem* (trup), *n'koo-dote* (vowel points), *ta-geem* (crowns), *oh-tee-yote* (letters)

the two perspectives are saying the same thing, their main point being just the three fundamental qualities, for in the entire text of the Tikkoonim *they are split into only three qualities (trup, vowel points and letters) alone. And the matter of the crowns of the letters are not mentioned at all therein, with the exception of the three* zayins *used on the letters* ShATNe"Z G"Tz[700], *and they are a matter unto themselves.*

And the reason is explained concisely in the Etz Chayyim (Sha-ar TNT"A, *chapter 6). This is what it says there: "And from this also will be understood what is stated in the* Tikkoonim, *that one time he states that the letters are the body..., and in other places we found that the letters are the soul-*Neffesh.... *If so, the letters are called 'body'..., and the crowns... are the soul-*Neffesh *of the letters. And just as the soul-*Neffesh *is never separated from the body, so too, the crowns are never separated from the letters in the Torah scroll, unlike the vowel points and the trup..., for the crowns collaborate with and connect to the essence of the letters, for they are the body and the crowns are part of the letters..., and because of this the crowns are not hinted at or mentioned in the* Tikkoonim, *since they and the letters collaborate together... for whenever the body is mentioned, in any case, the soul-*Neffesh *is included, for they are collaborators, as mentioned before." This completes his words. Refer there at length [for more detail].*

The letters—they are the aspect of action[701], for if there are only letters lacking vowel points, it's impossible that they could be anything other than the aspect of action. It is specifically the act of writing, just as they are written in the Torah scroll without vowel points, for in the case of speech it's impossible to utter them without

700 The seven letters *shin, ayin, tet, nun, zayin, gimel* and *tza-deek*

701 The letters are associated with action. Action is associated with the world of *Ahseeya* and the soul-*Neffesh.*

linking the vowel points to them. For that reason, the letters alone without vowel points, are considered as the aspect of soul-*Neffesh* (specifically with the crowns, as we wrote in the annotation), for it is the aspect of action, as is known.

The vowel points—they are their[702] aspect of soul-*Ruakh*, as previously described. For the vowel points occur with the letters when a person uses speech, it being the aspect of soul-*Ruakh*[703]. And just as the key part of a person's life force is via the aspect of soul-*Ruakh* that is within him, and when it leaves him he dies, even though a part of his soul-*Neffesh* still remains within him (as is known), so too, the key part of the life force of the function of the letters is the vowel points, for without them it is impossible to utter the letters with the mouth, and as is written in a few places in the *Tikkoonim* that [the word]: "and the intelligent ones[704]", employs the vowel points of [the word] "shining[705]" that illuminate upon the letters.

And the word's trup—they are the aspect of thought and the attention/intention of the heart/mind, that is the aspect of soul-*Neshama*[706] as is known. For they are the melodies[707] of and behavior of the vowel points and letters, and their being inclined in any specific direction, a matter dependent upon thought in the intelligent mind.

---

702 "Their" means "the letters'".

703 The vowel points are associated with speech. Speech is associated with the world of *Y'tzeera* and the soul-*Ruakh.*

704 Heb.: *v'ha-mahs-kee-leem*

705 Heb.: *yahz-hee-roo*

706 The trup is associated with thought. Thought is associated with the world of *B'ree-ya* and the soul-*Neshama*

707 Heb.: *t'noo-ote*

And in *Zohar Chaddash* (*Shir Ha-shirrim* 57d[708]): "'golden turtle-doves' (*Shir Ha-Shirrim* 1:11)—they are the melodies of the trup..., because they originate in the head of the King, to impart knowledge and insight[709] to all the letters." And [for more details] refer further there in the context of the three aspects of *T'*, *N'* and *A'* at length.

And in the same cited source (58c)[710]: "The melodies of the trup, which are the rectification and perfection of the knowledge and insight to know knowledge..., all of their journeys are in wisdom and insight[711].... Their melodies which are the perfection of everything—where do they they manifest in man? Rather this secret... within him it's insight and knowing..., whether they are standing, whether walking..., all of it is knowledge and insight... ." Refer there [for more details].

And for that reason they are called *ta-ah-meem*[712], just as the reason[713] behind and the explanation of each matter is the intelligence hidden in the matter, from which a person is able to understand it in his thoughts.

And in *Tikkoon* 18 (35b): "and the letters relate to the vowel points as the body relates to the soul-*Ruakh*... . And the vessel that holds the vowel points is the soul-*Neffesh.* Soul-*Neshama* is the crown upon them all. And from it [comes] crowns that are the trup melodies of the vowel

---

708 This appears in the Bar Ilan responsa at 20b.

709 Aram.: *da-ah-ta oo-sookh-l'tahnoo,* as translated by Onkeloos from the Hebrew *da-aht oo-tvoonah (Sh'mote* 31:3)

710 This citation confirms that the trup are associated with the soul-*Neshama* and the intellect.

711 Aram.: *b'khokh-ma-ta oo-v'sookh-l'tahnoo*

712 *Ta-ah-meem* can be literally translated as "meanings" or "reasons".

713 Heb.: *ta-ahm*

points and letters. And it [fem.] is dependent on thought, and the vowel points are dependent on being spoken, and the letters on action."

For that reason, the sincere worshiper using the advised attention/intention should intend in his prayer to pour out completely and to connect together all three of the aspects (soul-*Neffesh*, soul-*Ruakh* and soul-*Neshama*) that comprise his soul-*Neffesh*. For at the moment when each word of the prayer leaves his mouth, having all three aspects *NR"N* in its letters, vowel points and trup, he should make a great effort with purity[714] of his heart/mind, with intense yearning, to connect and attach via that effort, from bottom to top according the order of levels, his soul-*Neffesh* with his soul-*Ruakh*, and his soul-*Ruakh* with his soul-*Neshama*, [*] and all will ascend to the root of that word in the supernal worlds.

And this is the context mentioned in the *Tikkoonei Zohar Chaddash* 76, top of first folio: "'And the intelligent ones...'—They are the ones who have the intelligence to know how the *t'feela* ascends... via the letters and vowel points and trup", refer there [for more detail]. And there on page 78, top of the third folio: "'And those who have the strength to stand[715] in the hall of the King" (*Daniel* 1:4)—In the *Ahmeeda* of prayer..., comprised of all the trups, vowel points and letters."

Annotation: *And in this manner will be rectified all of these three aspects, even if he blemished (heaven forefend) one of them, because of his no-good actions or speech or thoughts, and they caused (heaven forefend) to distance and separate the connections between them, as I wrote previously in Gate 1,*

---

714 With great clarity, single-mindedness and focus

715 Heb.: *la-ah-mode*

Chapter 18. Now in this manner they will be rectified to return and be connected each one to its upper neighbor as before. This is the root of the fundamental matter of repentance, as we wrote there at length, refer there [for more detail].

*And this is the context of the text (*Y'shaya *6:10): "Fatten the heart/mind of this nation, harden its ears, and seal its eyes, lest it see with its eyes, and hear with its ears and its heart/mind will understand, and it will repent and be healed"—that in the last part of the text, the order is reversed from the order of the first part*[716]*.*

For the heart/mind is the aspect of thought, as is known, and the ears are the vessels that hear speech, and the eyes are the vessels of sight, to see how actions play out, and they are the three aspects of NR"N.

*And as the result of man's sins, they depart slowly, in sequence. For from the moment that the notion arises in a person, exclusively in the aspect of soul-*Neffesh, *to perform any sin, the aspect of soul-*Neshama *departs, for she is the aspect that's highest and noblest. And if (heaven forefend) he sins more, the aspect of soul-*Ruakh *also completely departs from him, or is blemished or damaged (heaven forefend), and then he has no connection to the aspect of soul-*Neshama *in wholeness as should be. And if (heaven forefend) he continued to sin still more, then the aspect of his soul-*Neffesh *is blemished or cut-off (heaven forefend) completely from its connection to the aspect of soul-*Ruakh.

*And when he repents, he re-attains them in sequence from low to high, the opposite order of their prior departure. First he achieves the aspect of soul-*Neffesh, *and after that*

716 The order of departure during the ascent upwards is the opposite of the order of arrival during the descent downwards.

*the soul-*Ruakh *settles upon her*[717] *and connects within him. And after that the sparks of the light of the soul-*Neshama *come and hover over him. Then each one connects to its neighbor as intended. And this, by itself, explains the text.*

*And even though in Gate 1, chapter 2 was explained that if he blemished or cut off (heaven forefend) the aspect of his soul-*Neffesh, *and lowered all nine of its* s'feerote *into the depths of evil, his repentance emanates and directs holiness and supernal light from above, first upon the aspect of his soul-*Neshama, *and from her it is directed upon his soul-*Ruakh, *and then the soul-*Ruakh *shines, as a result of the brilliance of the great light that impresses upon him, also upon the soul-*Neffesh. *And as a result, it is raised from the depths of evil, to connect with the aspect of soul-*Ruakh *as before, And so too, in this manner, when the soul-*Ruakh *is blemished (heaven forefend), as is written there and as is known in the Ariza"l's writings, to rectify an aspect or component one must draw down the lights and new "brains"*[718] *from way on high, following the sequence of all the aspects and levels, until arriving at that specific aspect or component that must be corrected, for to it [male] are the brains directed.*

*Specifically, to raise the soul-*Neffesh *from the depths of impurity within which it is embedded, or to rectify her blemish, he must direct holiness and the supernal light "from above to below", to expel and to destroy—using the flames flashing from this torch—the powers of impurity that are embedded within them. Or to fill in her deficiencies, and to raise her up, purified and rectified, so that she will be able to connect with the soul-*Ruakh. *And likewise relative to the component of soul-*Ruakh *that was blemished, to return it and rectify it to as it was before.*

---

717 Upon the soul-*Neffesh*

718 Heb.: *mo-khin.* The three upper s'feerote are called *mo-khin.*

However, after they are rectified via repentance, the sequence of their entrance after that into the man's body is "from below to above", as we discussed before. And this is "and it returns[719]", meaning that when he returns each component to its place, then he is healed.

CHAPTER 17

However, God-*Elo"ha* has more to say to one who worships God-*Elohi"m* in holiness, in a more detailed perspective, that being:

1. the perspective of the soul-*root-of-the-Neshama*, it [fem.] being the "soul-*Neshama* of the soul-*Neshama*", mentioned in the Zohar (it being called soul-*Chayya*, and First Adam achieved it), and
2. to the component of soul-*Y'kheeda* that is included within it, it being the secret of the world of the *Ahdahm Kahdmone*[720].

And it is clear to one who understands the *Etz Chayyim* (end of *Sha-ar Ha-mo-khin*) that First Adam, through his merit, attained the genuine components of soul-*Chayya* and soul-*Y'kheeda* in their primary locations. Refer to the beginning of *Gilgoolim* and in chapter 17 there [for more detail].

And this was their (OBM) primary intent (refer to *B'reisheet Rabba* 7:5 and 8:1), when they expounded on the verse "let the earth bring forth living soul-*Neffesh*[721]"

719 Heb.: *va-shahv*

720 The world of Primeval Adam, a world about which only a very limited amount is known, and that pre-existed the four worlds.

721 Heb.: *neffesh chayya*

(*B'reisheet* 1:24): "Even the soul-*Neffesh* of First Adam, even the soul-*Neffesh* of the Messiah. For this component is the secret of the "Congregation of Israel"[722] , the "supernal land of the living"[723]. (Meaning the root of the foundation of Dust of the four foundations, primeval roots, precursors of all the worlds, mentioned in the *Zohar Va-eira* (23b), refer there [for more detail].)

And refer to *Zohar Sh'mote* 12a and in *parshat Sh'lakh* 174b [regarding] the secret of the verse "let the earth bring forth living soul-*Neffesh*"..., and in *parshat Sh'mini* 39b, "and all the living soul-*Neffesh*[724]"... . And refer to the end of *parshat Va-et-kha-nahn* in the *mishna*, and refer to the RaMBa"N (OBM) in the verse "let us make man" (*B'reisheet* 1:26), for God's-*YHV"H* spirit-*Ruakh* spoke within him.

And therefore, First Adam was capable of living forever, for "the wisdom enlivens its master" (*Kohelet* 7:12), and for that reason is called soul-*Chayya*. That is "let the earth bring forth *neffesh chayya*". Because of his sin it departed from him. [For more details] refer to what the Ariza"l (OBM) wrote in chapter 15, and at the beginning of chapter 21, and in chapter 31 of the *Gilgoolim*.

And since then, no other person merited achieving it [fem.] while he was still in this world. And *Chanokh*, when he arrived at this level and inherited First Adam's characteristic spiritual level (as is written in the *Zohar Chaddash, T'rooma* 35c; and there in *Shir Ha-shirrim* 54d, refer there; and in the *Raa-ya M'hemna, K'doshim*, chapter 83; and in the *mishna*, at the end of *parshat Va-etkhanahn*; as the Ariza"l explained them in *parshat B'reisheet* in *D'roosh Ahdam Ha-reeshone*; and in *Gilgoolim*, chapter 18, refer there; and as

722 Heb.: *k'nesset yisrael*
723 Heb.: *ehretz ha-chayyim ha-elyona*
724 Heb.: *Neffesh ha-khayya*

is written there in chapter 35: "the world could not endure him"), it was necessary for him to leave this world. And so too Eliyahu left this world when he achieved a small amount of that supernal brilliance, as is written chapter 19 of the *Gilgoolim*, and as is written in the *Zohar Va-yee-gosh* (209b, top): "The Holy One (blessed be He) said to him... the world can't endure that you should co-exist with other people." And we hope to achieve it after resurrection (if it be God's will), that spirit-*Ruakh* should pour down[725] upon us from the heavenly heights.

And it is the source of thought in man, for the aspect of thought is when his thoughts cohere to think some specific thing, (and this is the aspect of soul-*Neshama*, as is written: "and it is the soul-*Neshama* from God-*SHaDa"Y* that gives them understanding"—*Eeyove* 32:8), and then the thought is perceived, in all cases, to the person himself who is thinking. But the root of the source of the overall origin of the power of thought is wholly hidden and recondite, so that even the person himself can't grasp from where it arises. And that is the component of soul-*root-of-the-Neshama*[726].

And this, the recondite component, is the aspect of all the permutations of the letters in the word[727], it [male] being the root of the soul-*Neshama* of the letters, and their spiritual power in their supernal root.[728]

And we are currently unable to perceive the veracity of the true nature of the various permutations in their supernal root, being that we can't currently perceive the

725 Heb.: *yei-ah-reh* (c.f., *Y'shaya* 32:15)

726 *Chayya*

727 Heb.: *tzei-roo-fei ha-o-tee-yote*

728 Rav Chayyim seems to say that the taking-together of all the permutations of the letters that make up a word, are the root of the soul-*Neshama* (i.e., the *chayya*) that word springs from.

aspect of the soul-*root-of-the-Neshama.* And after the resurrection we will contemplate the understanding that is within the secret of the letter permutations in the root of their holiness. And that is what is mentioned in the *Zohar B'ha-ah-lote-kha* 152a: "Torah… and in the world-to-come, we will be invited to gaze at the soul-*Neshama* of the soul-*Neshama* that's in the Torah."

And this is the aspect of the souls-*root-of-the-Neshama* of the whole of Israel[729] taken together, the *Malkhoot* of *Ahtzeeloot*; for this reason it is called the Assembly of Israel[730]. [*]

Annotation: *And in our holy Torah (*B'midbar *16:22) it is called: "God-*Ei"l, *God-*Elohe"i *of the souls-*Ruakh *of all flesh". Refer to* Zohar Korakh *176b*: "'And they said: '*God-*Ei"l, *God-*Elohe"i *of the soul-*Ruakh *of all flesh…'— That this is the place of souls-*Neshama*—to there they go and from there they come. And our rabbis (OBM) expounded 'his father and mother…'—'his mother' is the Assembly of Israel. And refer to* Zohar B'midbar *119a, and at the beginning of* parshat Pinkhas, *and there 240b, and in* Raa-ya M'hemna Tei-tzei *277b, and at the end of the* Idra Zoota *296a, and in* Zohar Chaddash Root *59b. And refer to the* Etz Chayyim , Sha-ar Ha-m'la-khim, *beginning of chapter 7; and in the* Pri Etz Chayyim, Sha-ar Olam Ha-ahseeya, *chapter 2; and in* Sha-ar Ha-kree-aht Sh'ma, *chapter 5; and in* Sha-ar Ha-ahmeeda, *at the end of chapter 16. And that is the context of the text (*Y'shaya *46:3) "who are borne from birth…". And refer to the* Pri Etz Chayyim, Sha-ar Rosh Chodesh, *chapter 3. And therefore the whole of Israel taken together as one are called the "limbs of the* Sh'kheena*",*

729 Heb.: *k'lal Yisrael*
730 Heb.: *K'nesset Yisrael*

refer to Zohar Pinkhas *231b, and there 238 (top of second folio), and 252 (end of the second folio).*

*And this is the context of the verse (*Yirmiya *2:2) "Go and call out in the ears of Jerusalem..., I recall for you the kindness of your youth, your following me into the wilderness... ." The verse referred to the whole of Israel with the name "Jerusalem", for she was the assembly of the whole of Israel when they ascended to make an appearance before the Master God-*YHV"H *on the pilgrimage holiday. And there the whole of Israel received the flow of abundance, Torah, holiness and fear/awe, each one according to where the root of his soul-*Neshama *originates in the Assembly of Israel. And for this reason it is called "supernal Jerusalem"*[731]*; that is why the text says "the love of your [fem.] wedding"*[732]*, meaning wholeness*[733]*.*

*And this is the matter of "*Sh'kheena*" that is mentioned in many places. The simple definition of "*Sh'kheena*" is "permanent dwelling", as those (OBM) stated (*B'reisheet Rabba, parsha *4, and in* Tahn-khooma B'khoo-ko-tie*). From the day that the Holy One (blessed be He) created His world, He desired that He should have a dwelling place among the lowers, and the essence of His (blessed be His name) permanent dwelling was in Jerusalem, the revelation of His holiness without any concealing garments. And that is what they (OBM) stated (*Shabbat *145b): "It is said that in My city, [they honor me because of] My name; not in My city, [they honor me because of] My garments"; and their discussion requires significant scholarly effort*[734]*.*

---

731 Heb.: *Yerushalayim shel ma-ahlah*
732 Heb.: *ah-ha-vaht k'loo-lo-tie-ikh*
733 Heb.: *k'lee-loot*
734 Heb.: *talmood*

CHAPTER 18

And so we find, after one's prayer is well-practiced and structured in connecting the three aspects of *NR"N* that are in his overall soul-*Neffesh*, using the letters, vowel points, and trup in each word (as was explained above in chapter 16), he should make a great effort, with his single-minded thought and intention, to, after this, attach all three aspects of *NR"N* to the component of the soul-*Neshama*-of-the-soul-*Neshama* mentioned above (it being his soul-*root-of-Neshama*) [*], using the letter permutations of the words in their holy supernal root.[735]

And when he attaches in this level, then it is possible to be considered as if he is no longer in the world at all. In any case the world will be, from his perspective, nullified completely. For that level is far above the current level of the person, as I wrote previously, and he will integrate himself into his soul-*root of-Neshama*, in the overall supernal root of the souls-*Neshama* of the whole of Israel taken all together[736].

Annotation: *And for that reason they codified, that immediately after the* Ahmeeda, *he should completely dedicate his soul-*Neffesh, *soul-*Ruakh, *and soul-*Neshama *to be as if he is ready to die, as in the verse "I raise my soul-*Neffesh *to you, God-*YHV"H*", and to cause them to ascend with the* NR"N *of the three worlds, and to integrate them into the* Malkhut of Ahtzeeloot, *as is written in the* Pri Etz Chayyim, *at the end of chapter 7 in* Sha-ar Ha-t'feela. *And this is the crux*

735 In this final chapter Rav Chayyim explains a deeper level of prayer practice, the level of shedding the physical (Heb.: *hit-pahsh-toot ha-gahsh-meeyoot).*

736 Heb.: *k'lal nishmote Yisrael ya-khad*

of the intention of every "falling on the face[737]*" mentioned in the Torah, as is written in the* Zohar Korakh *176 that we mentioned previously in the context of: "Come observe that Moshe and Aharone prepared themselves for death. How do we know this? Because it's written 'they fell on their faces and they stated "God-*Ei"l, *the God-*Elohi"m *of the souls-*Ruakh[738]*... "'. And in all cases falling on the face is towards that place..., God-*Elohi"m *of the souls-*Ruakh*—that is the place to which the souls-*Neshama *of the world and all the souls-*Neshama *depart and from which they arrive. And therefore we require that the focus of the heart/mind must be as if one has expired completely from the world,"*[739] *as is written in the* Zohar *at the end of* parshat B'midbar *and the beginning of* parshat Va-et-kha-nahn. *And refer carefully to the* Pri Etz Chayyim *in all of Chapter 2 of* Sha-ar N'fee-laht Ah-pie-yeem, *and you will understand. And refer further there in Chapter 3 and Chapter 4 and in* Lee-koo-tei Torah, Parshat Sh'lakh. *Refer there [for more details].*

For that reason the Notables of the Great Assembly codified to say, before the beginning of the saying of the *Ahmeeda* prayer, the verse "God-*Adona"i,* open my lips", for whoever merits this level during the moment of prayer, as a result of this connection of the thinking mind, his body could be like an inanimate stone and like a mute who can't

---

737 Heb.: *n'fee-laht ah-pie-yeem*

738 Heb.: *Ei"l elohe"i ha-roo-khote*

739 Rav Chayyim's citation states that all of of Israel's souls descend at birth from the place called *K'nesset Yisrael* (alternately, *Elohe"i Ha-roo-khote*) and return there at death. During the part of the prayer service following the *Ahmeeda,* that we refer to as *n'fee-laht ah-pie-yeem* (falling on the face), one should be prepared to give up one's individual soul and return to that place.

say a word. It is only He (blessed be He) who will open his lips to recite before Him the words of the prayer. And for that reason it used the name *A-D-N-Y* specifically, for it is the secret of *K'nesset Yisrael* mentioned previously. And refer to the *Pri Etz Chayyim*, at the end of *Sha-ar Ha-bree-ya*, in the context of this verse before the prayer, about which the sages (OBM) stated that it is considered as one long prayer (*B'ra-khote* 4b)[740]. And this is why the sages (OBM) stated (*Y'va-mote* 105b): "One who prays must direct his heart/mind upwards", and per the way that Rabbeinu Yonah (OBM) explained it there. And so too the Early Pious Ones[741] would pause for an hour… to focus their heart/minds to God-*Ma-kome*, (*B'ra-khote* 4b), and it's clear[742].

Annotation: *For that reason the overall organization of the prayer service is in four parts, corresponding to the four components of* NR"N *and the soul*-root-of-the-Neshama. *The sacrifices correspond to the soul*-Neffesh, *and the world of* Ahseeya, *for they are brought as a result of sins relating to the soul*-Neffesh, *as it's written "and if a soul*-Neffesh *should sin"* (Va-yikra *5:1)… . And the Verses of Praise*[743] *correspond to the world of the soul*-Ruakh, *the world of the angels and the singers. And the* K'ree-aht Sh'ma *and its blessings correspond to the halls of* B'reeya, *acknowledged as the world of souls*-Neshama.

---

740 The sages stated that this verse, said just before the *Ahmeeda*, is not considered a separation between the preceding blessing of redemption (*g'oola*) and the *Ahmeeda*.

741 Heb.: *chassidim rishonim*

742 Rav Chayyim seems to be saying that it's clear that this is what they were doing during the hour before prayer: first, connecting the three lower worlds together, and finally, connecting them to the fourth world.

743 Heb.: *p'soo-kei d'zimra*

And while reciting the paragraphs of the sacrifices until Ba-rookh Sheh-ah-mar, *he should intend to cause the components of the souls-*Neffesh *of* Ahseeya *to ascend, which is the inner aspect of* Ahseeya, *to integrate them with the souls-*Ruakh *of* Y'tzeera. *And he should also integrate his soul-*Neffesh *with them, to connect them with his soul-*Ruakh. *And from* Ba-rookh Sheh-ah-mar *until the blessings of the* K'ree-aht Sh'ma, *he should integrate all of the souls-*Neffesh *of* Ahseeya *and the souls-*Ruakh *of* Y'tzeera, *and also the components of his own soul-*Neffesh *and soul-*Ruakh, *with the soul-*Neshama *of* B'reeya. *And from the blessings of the* K'ree-aht Sh'ma *until the* Ahmeeda, *he should integrate and cause to ascend all of the* NR"N *of* BY"A[744] (*and his own* NR"N *along with them*) *to integrate them together into the soul-*root-of-the-Neshama *and the root of the gathering of the overall souls of Israel all together.*

And for a partial reference for this topic, refer to the Pri Etz Chayyim, *Chapter 1 from* Sha-ar Ha-t'feela. *And this is what the Ariza"l hinted there when he stated: "and in this manner the* Sh'kheena *becomes comprised of all of them", refer there [for more details]. And this is [the meaning of] what the Ariza"l stated, that before prayer, one should accept upon himself the mitzva of "and you shall love your mate".*

---

744 *B'reeya, Y'tzeera* and *Ahseeya*

Gate 3

CHAPTER 1

And what is written here: *la Ma-kome*[745], and also too in *Ahvote* where they stated: "and when you pray, don't make your prayer static[746]; rather make it [an expression of] compassion and grace before the *Ma-kome* (blessed be He)", with the word "*Ma-kome*" they (OBM) hinted at a great matter. And the matter requires explication to understand the depths of their (OBM) intention by this, and to understand the verses that hint about this.

Previously they (OBM) stated in *Ahvote* (2:15): "that all of their words are like smoldering embers", that even though there is only the glimmer of flame, if you make an effort to turn it over and aerate it[747], as you aerate it more, the ember will flare and the glimmer will spread within it, until it's all ablaze and you can benefit from it to use its light and to warm oneself next to it. But only by being next to it, not to directly grasp it, for once it's ablaze one must be mindful not to be burned by it.

This same metaphor was applied to all of the sages' words. For even when their statements seem to be concise and have plain meanings, even so, they are like a shattering hammer blow, for the more a person turns them [male/plural] inside-out, and elaborates upon them and examines them meticulously, his eyes will be enlightened from the flame of their great light, for he will find within them deep matters, as they (OBM) stated (*Ahvote* 5:26): "Turn it [singular/fem.] inside-out and turn it [singular/fem.] inside-out again, for everything is within it [singular/fem.]".

---

745 Lit.: "to the place"

746 Heb.: *keh-va*

747 Aerate, as with a blacksmith's bellows

But one must be exceedingly mindful about their smoldering embers, not to introduce, contemplate and delve into texts for which one lacks permission to excessively contemplate their inner meanings, as they stated there: "and be warmed as-if next to the light of the sages", as-if to say "Do not distance yourself from ever contemplating them, for you'll not benefit from their light at all; but also do not approach them too closely, so that you won't get burned", as we stated above and as they concluded, following that with "and be mindful of their smoldering embers…".

And so too is it here, with the word *Ma-kome*, that even though its plain meaning is clear, when we examine it meticulously we'll find that another great matter is contained and hinted at within it.

For regarding the matter why He (blessed be He) is called *Ma-kome*, the sages (OBM) explained in *B'reisheet Rabba* (*parsha* 68) on the verse "and he encountered the place-*Ma-kome*" (*B'reisheet* 28:11): "Rav Hoona, in the name of Rav Ahmee, stated: 'For what reason do we assign a name to the Holy One (blessed be He) and call him *Ma-kome*? Because He is the universe's space, and the universe is not His space[748].'" And in *Sh'mote Rabba* (end of *parsha* 45), and in *Tahn-khooma* (*parsha Tee-sa*): "And God-*YHV"H* stated: 'Behold a place with me' (*Sh'mote* 33:21): Rav Yo-see bar Cha-lafta stated… : 'My space is subordinate to me; I am not subordinate to my space'", and so it states in *Sho-kheir Tove, T'hillim, mizmor* 90.

And according to its plain meaning it desired to express that just as a physical place tolerates and supports any thing or object that is rested upon it, so too, according to this metaphor, the Creator, Master of All (blessed be His

748 Meaning that He is the "space" (so to speak) within which the universe exists, rather than the other way around.

name), He is the true space that tolerates and preserves the existence of all the worlds and creations. For if (heaven forefend) His energy would depart from them for even one moment, the space where all the worlds persist and exist would be nullified, and as is stated (*N'khemya* 9:6): "and You enliven them all".

And this is a cornerstone of the Jewish faith, as the RaMBa"M (OBM) wrote in the beginning of his book.

For that reason, the *Zohar* calls the Master of All (blessed be His name) the "Soul-*Neshama* of All Souls-*Neshama*". For just as the soul-*Neshama* enlivens and preserves the existence of the body—and as is written (*Sanhedrin* 91b): "Is it possible for a piece of flesh three days..."—so too is He (blessed be His name) alone the life force of all the worlds, and as is [also] known from many citations in the *Tikkoonim* and the *Raa-ya M'hemna.* And refer to the beginning of the *Tikkoonim*'s second introduction, in the essay starting with "Eliyahu began...". And so too our sages (OBM) compared the preservation of the existence of the worlds via His (may He be blessed) energy, to the preservation of the existence of the body via the powers of the soul-*Neshama.* They stated (*B'rakhote* 10a): "Just as the soul-*Neshama* permeates and nourishes the entire body, so too the Holy One (blessed be He) permeates and nourishes...". This is the plain meaning of the matter of He (blessed be He) being called the universe's *Ma-kome.*

CHAPTER 2

However, the inner meaning of the matter of "the universe's *Ma-kome*" is a great matter indeed. For the reason why He (blessed be His name) is called "the universe's *Ma-kome*" is not comparable at all to the matter of a physical place that supports an object placed upon it, for the essence of a physical object's existence in this moment[749] and its persistence over time[750] is that it has an independent existence[751], and the physical place simply prevents it from falling and breaking. And similar to this is the matter of the body in relation to the soul-*Neshama,* regarding the body's current vitality[752] and persistence over time: the body has an independent existence and its existence doesn't disappear, even when the soul-*Neshama* leaves it.

But all of the worlds, the primary cause of their continued existence in each instant proceeds exclusively from Him (blessed be His name), and if He would remove His (blessed be He) Will from bringing them into existence anew in each instant, they would actually be a nil and nothingness[753].

And only because no created being, not even the highest of the high, has the power to grasp the true nature of the matter—how all the worlds and their legions are [emphatically] in actuality nothingness, and only that in each instant they are [emphatically] being brought into existence by Him (blessed be He)—for that reason they chose to use a metaphor to describe Him (blessed be He) and to explain to the "ear-that's-able-to-listen-in-the-company-of-wise-sages" using the word *Ma-kome.* [*A]

---

749 Heb.: *hit-ha-voot*

750 Heb.: *kee-yoom*

751 Heb.: *m'tzee-yoot bifnei ahtz-ma*

752 Heb.: *chee-yoot*

753 Rav Chayyim seems to be very careful here with his use of tenses. He seems to say that the continued maintenance of all of creation is happening *now,* in this very instant, and if He would remove the will for it to continue to exist, it would be a nil and nothingness.

Annotation A: *Using the method of homiletic interpretation*[754]*, we can derive from the series of verses starting with "And wisdom*[755]*, where can it be found"* (Ee-yove *28:12), that the greatest of all wisdoms that can be grasped from Him (blessed be He) is the marvelous wisdom that it's from nothingness that the existence of each instant originates. "And which is the place-*Ma-kome *of understanding*[756]*", implies that nowhere in existence is there a faculty of rational mind*[757] *to which we could point, where that is the place-*ma-kome *that has the capacity to accept upon it the quality of rational understanding to understand this marvelous power. And it concludes (28:23): "but He knows its place".*

For despite that:

1. His wisdom (blessed be He) decreed that this be so, to supply a being-ness to His universe in a manner that it is beyond all minds to grasp how the continuous bringing-into-existence proceeds from Him (blessed be He) each instant,
and
2. they are able to imagine, using their physical eyes, that the universe has an independent existence (heaven forefend),

our sages (OBM) were able to enlighten the rational intellect when they used the metaphor of place-*Ma-kome.* For

754 Heb.: *deh-rehkh d'rahsh*
755 Heb.: *chokh-ma*
756 Heb.: *bee-na*
757 Rav Chayyim seems to identify "understanding" (Heb. *bee-na*) with rational mind. *Chokh-ma* and *Bee-na* are two of the three s'feerote in the "head". *Bee-na* is incapable of grasping the marvelous wisdom of whence existence originates. *Sei-khel* is the Hebrew word that we translate as "rational mind".

just as an object exists in space and at the same time the object apparently has an independent existence, even so, if the object didn't have a space in which to exist, it would be as if it didn't exist. [*B]

Annotation B: *Another reason they described Him (blessed be He) using the term place-*Ma-kome*, is because space enables an object to exist, even if it*[758] *is not equal in value to the object. And also, space allows for many different objects to exist—by existing they don't cause any change in the space, and the space enables their existence and tolerates all of them equally. So too does He (blessed be He) enable the existence of all the worlds, even if there is no equivalence in value between Him (blessed be He) and them, for even the supernal crown*[759] *is like darkness in comparison to the* Ein Sofe. *Also, even though it appears to us that within creation there are tremendous variations, levels that differ one from another, and even if there are also powers of impurity and the "other side*[760]*" in all of their levels, and their continued existence proceeds only from Him (blessed be He), even so it does not change Him (blessed be His name), for He does not change. From His perspective He enables their existence in a manner similar to the metaphor of space.*

*And being that it is impossible for any rational mind to grasp how and what, and it being so incredible, for this reason the sages (OBM) intervened regarding "behold a place-*Ma-kome *with me*[761]*"* (Sh'mote *33:21): "My place is an incidental attribute to Me", meaning that no thought can capture how He exhibits the quality of immutable space. Only He alone can grasp His essential nature, grasp how He is the immutable space in which all the worlds exist, as in the*

---

758 The space

759 Heb.: *ketter el-yone*, referring to the highest world

760 Aram.: *sitra akhra*

761 Heb.: *hee-nei ma-kome ee-tee*

*context of "and He knows its [fem.] place" (*Ee-yove *28:23). And this is specifically what "with Me" means, as in the matter when the heart/mind does not reveal to the mouth*[762].

So too, even though the entire universe is normally perceived and described as having an independent existence, He (blessed be His name) is its space. But for the space in His Will to continuously bring the worlds into existence, how much more so would it be as if they never existed.

And what is stated in *Seifer Y'tzeera* (chapter 1, *mishna* 8): "'Ten *s'feerote* of non-existence'—Block your mouth from discussing it and your heart/mind from reflecting on it. And if your heart/mind runs off, return it to the place-*Ma-kome*, for it is stated for that reason: 'run off and return'[763] (*Yekhezkel* 1:14)." It uses the term "*la Ma-kome*" specifically, to point out that if the thoughts of a person's heart/mind should "run off" to attempt to grasp a rational explanation of how their continued existence proceeds from Him (blessed be His name) in each instant, "return to the place-*Ma-kome*" to grasp the value of the rational explanation from the similarity to what we normally perceive regarding space, as we discussed previously. And refer to the RaMBa"N's (OBM) explanation of this *mishna*.

And regarding this particular meaning did our holy sages (OBM) clear a trail, offering metaphors regarding His (blessed be He) relationship to the worlds, even though there is no comparison or resemblance between the metaphor and the reality, except to a very specific feature, and even this has only a very slight resemblance.

And as is written in the *Raa-ya M'hemna* (*parshaht Pinkhas,*

---

762 Aram.: *lee-ba l'fooma lo galya*—when a matter experienced by the heart/mind is beyond rational verbal description.

763 Heb.: *ra-tzo va-shove*

257b and 258a): "And one should know..., in this manner He created the soul-*Neshama*..., and just as the Master of the Worlds does not have a name that is known or a place that is known, rather His sovereignty is all-pervasive, so too the soul-*Neshama* does not have... rather her sovereignty is all-pervasive and there isn't a limb/organ vacant of it..., and in all these names and appellations referring to all the worlds..., to demonstrate that His sovereignty rules them, so too the soul-*Neshama*, she was likened to Him because of her sovereignty over all of the body's limbs/organs. It's not that the soul-*Neshama* resembles Him in an essential way, for He created her..., and moreover..., and for the reason that the soul-*Neshama* resembles Him in her sovereignty over all the body's limbs/organs, and not for any other reason." Refer there at length [for more detail].

And also like that are all the cases that the sages (OBM) listed there in the context of comparing Him (blessed be He) to the soul-*Neshama* in the body. All of them are only about the matter of His (blessed be His name) permeating the worlds, filling them, and His rule over them, as mentioned above, for only in that matter do they metaphorize Him in their expositions.

And they hinted at this in the *Tikkoonim* (end of *Tikkoon* 38), saying: "that His voice and speech will be heard from the throne, and angels, heaven and earth, that it should be made known to them completely, above and below, as a soul-*Neshama* that rules over the entire body, even in the smallest limb/organ, and no limb/organ is vacant of it [fem.]."

He precisely used the phrase "like a soul-*Neshama* that rules...". And in any case, it seems that in this case too where they (OBM) compared to Him, they didn't equate Him to her[764] in toto, for they said that just as the soul-*Neshama* perme-

764 To the soul-*Neshama*

ates the body, so too the Holy One (blessed be He) permeates the entire universe. And so too what they stated in the section of the *Tikkoonim* we mentioned above "like the soul-*Neshama*... and none of its limbs/organs", and also there in *Tikkoon* 70: "In each limb/organ there is a *YHV"H*..., there is no place vacant of Him, like a soul-*Neshama* that is present in each and every limb/organ of the body." The matter of the Holy One (blessed be He) filling the universe is not like the matter of the soul-*Neshama* filling the body, for after all, the body itself acts as a barrier between them, only that it permeates the interior of all the pieces of its components and sustains it[765], for when the soul-*Neshama* leaves the body, the body does not disappear as a result, but the Master of All (blessed be His name) fills all of the worlds and the creations, and they don't offer any barrier to Him (heaven forefend) in any way. And there is truly nothing other than He (blessed be He) at all in all the worlds, from the highest of the high to the depths of the deepest abyss in the earth, to the extent that you could say that there is nothing created here nor a universe at all, only that everything is full of the simple essence of His (blessed be He) unity.

Refer to the *Ro-kei-ahkh* at the end of *Shoresh K'doo-shaht Ha-yee-khood*: "The Creator doesn't require physical space or place, because He was before all existence, and no walls or columns[766] separate Him, for he would not create anything that would limit Him."

---

765 The body

766 The *Ro-kei-ahkh* (Rabbi Elozor ben Yehuda, circa 4920-4998/1160-1238 C.E., author of *Seifer Ha-Ro-kei-ahkh*, Worms) employs the unusual word *ha-ko-rote*. The singular of this word (*ha-ko-ra*) is used in 2 *M'lakhim Bet* 6:5, in the context of the prophet Elisha enabling the retrieval of a borrowed metal tool that was lost under water. The tool was being used to fell a tree trunk (*ha-ko-ra*). In the current text the word is used in an architectural context, hence I translate the word as "columns".

CHAPTER 3

And this is the matter of the verse (*Yirmiya* 23:24): "Do I not fill the heaven and the earth?" And it is explained even more clearly in the *Mishneh Torah* (*D'varim* 4:39): "You shall know this day... that God-*YHV"H* is the God-*Elohi"m* in the heaven above and on the earth below—there is none other". And also (*D'varim* 4:35): "You have been shown in order to know that God-*YHV"H* is the God-*Elohi"m*—there is none other than Him alone". This is literally true as written, that there is nothing at all other than Him (blessed be He), in any aspect or solitary detail in all the worlds, supernal and terrestrial, and all the creations—only the essence of His simple unity (blessed be His name) alone.

And that is the inner meaning of their (OBM) statements in *D'varim Rabba* (*parsha Bet*): "Another matter: 'for God-*YHV"H* is the God-*Elohi"m...*'—Yitro actually worshipped the heavenly bodies... . Rah-khav... . Moshe asserted His presence even in the voidness of the universe, as is stated (op. cit.): "that God-*YHV"H...* in the heaven above and on the earth below—there is none other"—even [emphatic] in the voidness of the universe.

And this is also included in their (OBM) statement that He (blessed be He) is the universe's place and the universe is not His place; that is, that all the places perceived by the senses as existing, are not the essential nature of "place". Rather, He (blessed be His name) is the space in which all places exist, that from His (blessed be He) perspective they are considered as if they don't exist at all—now is the same as before creation.

However, in our introduction at the beginning of our discourse, [we stated] that their (OBM) words were likened to fiery embers, that one should be exceedingly careful with their embers, not to engage in contemplating and researching them excessively, in matters for which permission is not granted to contemplate a lot, and be burned (heaven forefend). And so too is this awesome matter, the matter is intended only for one who is wise and capable of understanding based on his own knowledge[767] the inner dimensions of the matter, educating the heart/mind solely by momentarily considering it and then withdrawing[768], and in this way to enflame the purity of his heart/mind toward the service of prayer, while excessive contemplation of this matter is an enormous danger, and regarding this the *Seifer Y'tzeera* states: "If your heart/mind runs[769], return to the place[770]", as I previously wrote in chapter 2, and as I will write (God willing) further on in chapter 6.

And truthfully, I might have stopped myself from discussing this matter at all, for the early sages[771] (OBM) greatly hid this matter, as you'll see in the writings of the holy one of God, the *Ro-kei-ahkh* (OBM—quoted above), who addressed this topic using only hints, for their souls-*Ruakh* were faithful to God-*Ei"l*, and they hid it [772].

However, I reconsidered and noted that while this was proper for them in their generation, now a very long time has elapsed without a guide, and the ways of man are to follow the path that, led by his rational intellect, seems right. And the inclination of a person's heart/mind's

767 Heb.: *Cha-kham u-may-veen me-da-ah-toe*—Literally, a wise person who understands based on his own knowledge. This carefully chosen phrase uses the names of the three parts of the head: *chohkma*, *beena* and *da'aht*, implying a mature, refined, balanced and integrated personality.

768 Heb.: *b'rah-tzoe vah-shove*

769 Heb.: *eem rahtz leeb-kha*

770 Heb.: *la ma-kome*

771 Heb.: *ree-sho-neem*

772 Paraphrasing *Mishlei* 11:13

thoughts is exclusively to fly-off in fantasies to wherever his heart/mind leads him. And the most important reason is that this teaching has reached the general public, and is a metaphor espoused even by fools saying that every place and everything is absolute Godliness. And they aim constantly to deepen their understanding and to study it, to the point that it captures the heart/minds of the young and immature, and they determine their actions and behavior based on this rationale.

A person must exercise extreme caution in this matter and constantly guard his soul-*Neffesh.* For if (heaven forefend) our heart/mind would fixate on this idea[773], to permit ourselves to act based on this idea, it's possible for the effect of this (heaven forefend) to be the destruction of many of the holy Torah's basic principles (may the Merciful save us). And with ease he would be trapped (heaven forefend) in the snare of the [evil] inclination who will demonstrate to him that it is permitted based on this idea, for example, to ponder the words of Torah when in a state of disgust, even in filthy places, after he's first determined for himself that everything is absolute Godliness. And our sages (OBM) strongly opposed this, and employing their holy spirit[774], cut him off from having a share in the world-to-come (may the Merciful save us), as is written (*B'rakhote* 24b) that included in the category of "for he has denigrated God's word" is also one who ponders words of Torah in filthy alley ways. And in any case, the last part of that text says "he shall be cut off [emphatically][775]", and the sages (OBM) explained it to mean that he will be cut off

773 Heb.: *likbo-ah lah-noo makh-shah-va zoo*

774 Heb.: *roo-akh kode-shahm*

775 Heb.: *hee-kah-rate tee-kah-rate*

both from this world and the world-to-come. And many more errors could be caused (heaven forefend) if one determines active behavior in that way.

This is what brought me to initiate a discussion of this matter and to caution and distance others from errors that could be caused by this (heaven forefend), and to thoroughly understand what our sages (OBM) hinted at on this topic. And they are like all of God's righteous ways, this being an era with a pressing and urgent need[776].

CHAPTER 4

To start with a firm foundation, we'll explain the statement of the holy rabbis (OBM), as explained in the *Etz Chayyim* based on a few sections of the *Tikkoonim*, that He (blessed be His name) fills all worlds in a perfectly uniform manner. Yet we find that even in the supernal worlds that each world is divided from and different from the other worlds in various ways with regard to how He (blessed be He) relates to them. And as is stated in the introduction to the *Tikkoonim* (page 3b): "The ten *s'feerote* that have within them the emanation of the King[777], He and His essence are one in them, they and their life force are one in them, which is not the case for the ten *s'feerote* of *B'reeya* where they and He are not one. ..."

And refer to the *Etz Chayyim, Sha'ar Hish-tal-sh'loot Ha-Esser S'feerote*[778], at the beginning of the summary of the process of emanation, he wrote that the *Ein Sofe* (blessed is He), in the context of His being within and permeating all the worlds, only contacts and adheres to the world

776 Heb.: *v'eit la-ah-sote*

777 Meaning the ten *s'feerote* from the world of *Ahtzeeloot*

778 Gate of Unfolding of the Ten *S'feerote*

of *Ahtzeeloot,* and not to *B'reeya, Y'tzeera, Ahseeya*; for that reason, from there and below their essential nature will be different. And there in *Sha'ar D'rooshei ABY"A*[779] (chapter 7), in the explanation of the section in the *Tikkoonim* mentioned above, he wrote that the entire *Ahtzeeloot,* even the aspect of containers[780], is considered as absolute Godliness, which is not the case in *BY"A*[781], refer there [for more detail]. There it's also explained what the essential difference is between *Ahtzeeloot* and the three worlds *BY"A* in the matter of Godliness, refer there at the beginning of *Sha'ar Tzeeyoor O-la-mote ABY"A,*[782] in Rabbi Chayyim Vittal's introduction, and in *Sha'ar Hish-tal-sh'loot Ha-Esser S'feerote* (chapter 3), and in *Sha'ar Ha-tzellem*[783] (chapter 1), and in *Sha'ar Ha-shei-mote*[784] (chapter 1), and *Sha'ar Seder ABY"A*[785] (chapter 2 and beginning of chapter 3), and similarly many differences in qualities and various matters between the worlds, details upon details, that are explained in the entire *Zohar* and in the words of the Ariza"l.

And attend well to the end of the book *Arba Mei-ote Shekkel Kessef*[786] on the topic of His (blessed be His name) knowledge of man's actions before they occur, that the Ariza"l made distinctions between the worlds in this matter, for example (*B'reisheet* 14:19) "supernal God-*Ei"l*[787]" and (*T'hillim* 2:4) "*residing in the heavens*[788]", that if the text had

779 Gate of Expositions On The Four Worlds

780 Heb.: *kei-leem*

781 *B'reeya, Y'tzeera, Ahseeya*

782 Gate of the Description of the Worlds

783 Gate of the Image

784 Gate of the Names

785 Gate of the Order of the Four Worlds

786 The *Arba May-ote Shekkel Kessef* is one of the books of the Ariza"l's teachings.

787 Heb.: *Ei"l el-yone*

788 Heb.: *Yo-sheiv ba-sha-my-eem*

not written them, we would have been prohibited to state them. And in the same manner, the sages (OBM) listed ten levels of holiness[789] [of places within the land of Israel] and three levels of holiness [of the encampments in the desert], one above the other, but the truth of the matter, consider what you're hearing, and you'll apply your heart/ mind, and you'll proceed securely.

For it is explained in a few places in the *Zohar*, that the Sole Master, the *Ein Sofe* (blessed be He), permeates all worlds and surrounds all worlds, that is, from His (blessed be He) perspective He is called by the phrase "permeates all worlds", while from our perspective (as we are commanded in our holy Torah regarding how we behave relating to Torah and mitzvote and based on what we can perceive via the senses), He (blessed be He) is called by the phrase "surrounds all worlds", for the quality of permeating all worlds is, from our perspective, a recondite topic related to God's-*Elohi"m* glory[790].

And the situation is that it's definitely true that from His (may He be blessed) perspective, even now after He created and renewed the worlds with His intention, he permeates all the worlds and places and creations, all absolutely uniformly and with a simple unity. And [the verse] "there is nothing other than Him" is literally true, as I wrote previously from clearly expressed sources and in the name of the *Ro-kei-ahkh* (OBM). And those who preceded us (OBM) ruled that prior to praying we say "You existed before the universe's creation; You exist after the creation of the universe", implying that even

789 Heb.: *Esser k'doo-shote*

790 Heb.: *ka-vode.* The word is sometimes used to denote God's manifestation in the physical universe, as in (*Sh'mote* 33:18): "Show me now Your glory", and (*Sh'mote* 40:34): "...and the glory of God-*YHV"H* filled the tabernacle."

though the worlds have already been created employing His (may He be blessed) simple intention, even so there's no change or new aspect (heaven forefend), and no barrier as a result of them in His essence of His simple unity. And He [emphatic] is still now just as He was before the creation, when all was filled with the essence of the *Ein Sofe* (blessed be He), even in the space where the worlds currently exist.

Pay attention to the words of the holy one of Israel, Rabbeinu Shmuel, father of the holy Rabbee Yehudah Chaseed, in the poem of unification that he authored, in the unification for the second day of the week: "there's no edge... and there's no mediator separating between You and us[791]... ," us ...—refer there [for more details]. And in the poem of unification for the third day of the week: "surrounds everything and permeates everything, and being all, You are in everything"—refer there [for more details] regarding this matter.

And what the sages (OBM) stated in their words likening His (blessed be He) relationship to the worlds to the relationship of the soul-*Neshama* to the body—that the soul-*Neffesh* is pure in the body, and the Holy One (blessed be He) is pure in His world (Va-yikra Rabba, end of chapter 4)—they were conveying:

> That just as the matter of the soul-*Neshama* is that it permeates all the limbs/organs of a person's body—those that are clean and even those that are full of dirt, filth, and pollution—and even so they are not buffered from her regarding the matter of her purity, and she remains in her state of purity and holiness,

so too is the matter of He (blessed be He) permeating everything, including all the places, pure and holy places

791 Heb.: *Bay-no-tay-noo*

and also those that are not pure, even though they are not buffered at all, and they do not cause any change (heaven forefend) in the holy purity of His (blessed be He) essence and simple unity.

And this is what is written (*Malachi* 3:6) "I, God-*YHV"H*, have not changed."

And as is written in the *Tikkoonei Zohar Chaddash* (page 88, end of the fourth folio): "And all of Israel who received Torah from Him, with it they make Him one, and in all of His letters and holy names, and in all of the supernal and terrestrial abodes that were created employing them, and in all the supernal and terrestrial creatures, and above them—one. And below all of them and within all of them and outside of all of them, He is one... . So too He is within all of the worlds just as He is outside of all the worlds, and He is not changed... ."

Annotation: *And according to what will be explained (God willing) later regarding the distinctions between the two names* YHV"H *and* Elohi"m, *that the definition of name* Elohi"m *instructs about the aspect that is from our perspective, and the essential name* YHV"H *(blessed be He) instructs about the aspect that is from His (blessed be He) perspective, for that reason it is written: "I, God-*YHV"H, *have not changed."*

And refer to the Tikkoonim *(*Tikkoon *70), regarding the matter of the vessels*[792] *it stated: "and the four letters that are the* YHV"H, *they don't change in any place... , changes occur in the vessels of the body, but in Him there are no changes at all, for that reason it is written: 'I, God-*YHV"H, *have not changed'."*

792 Aram.: *Ood-neem*

CHAPTER 5

But even considering this[793], these [emphatic] are His (blessed be His name) heroic and awesome [works][794]: that even so, He hid (so to speak) His (blessed be He) glory so that it would be possible to actualize the matter of the existence of the worlds, and the powers, and created beings, both newly created and renewed, having different qualities and diverse situations, and distributed in different locations—places that are holy and pure, and the opposite: impure and filthy. And this is our perspective, namely, that our ability to perceive using our senses is limited to the realities as they appear, and on this perspective is built the system that mandates our behavior[795], as we were commanded directly[796] by Him (blessed be He), it being immutable law.

And from this perspective our sages (OBM) metaphorized Him (so to speak) per the matter of the soul's-*Neshama* relationship to the body. And as is stated in the *Zohar* that He (blessed be He) is the soul-*Neshama* of all the worlds, being that in people the senses only perceive a person's body, and:

- even though the soul-*Neshama* permeates the entire body, it is an aspect hidden to eyes of flesh but revealed to the mind's eyes,
- so too, based on our grasp of what can be perceived, so appears the reality of all the worlds and creations, and that He (blessed be His name) permeates and is hidden (so to speak) within them to enliven them and to sustain them,

---

793 That from His perspective nothing changes whether or not He creates the universe.

794 The creation of the worlds are His heroic and awesome acts.

795 Heb.: *sid-rei chee-yoov hahn-hah-gah-tei-noo*

796 Heb.: *mee-peev,* literally "from His mouth"

as in the matter of the soul-*Neshama* that permeates and is hidden within all the various parts of the body's limbs/ organs, to enliven it.

And all the names based on relationship, physical descriptions, behavioral qualities and personality characteristics applied to Him (blessed be He) that we found in our holy Torah, all of them express from this perspective that is our perspective and the system that mandates our behavior, that being the perspective of His (blessed be He) relationship to the worlds based on their perspective. And they effect all the variations in the details of the system of natural law, as was explained above in Gate 2[797].

And what is stated in the introduction to the *Tikkoonim* mentioned previously, that: "The ten *s'feerote* of *Ahtzeeloot* have the King within them, He and His essence are one in them, they and their life force are one in them, which is not the case for the ten *s'feerote* of *B'reeya* where they and He are not one, that He and they are not one and they and their essence are not one. And far above all of them He descends in the ten *s'feerote* of *Ahtzeeloot* and shines light upon the ten s'feerote of *B'reeya* and the ten categories of angels and the ten spheres of the heavens, and is not changed in any place."—this hints to the two qualities we discussed above, as explained.

And in *B'reisheet Rabba, parsha* 4 they stated: "When He desires, [then]'don't I entirely fill the heavens and the earth'. And when He desires he would converse with Moshe from between the two staves of the Ark. Rabbi Cheeya bar Abba stated: 'There are moments when the entire universe can't contain the glory of His godliness, and there are times when He converses with man from between the hairs of his

797 While God permeates all of creation equally and in simple unity, from our perspective we perceive great variation due to the natures of the different worlds.

head... .'" And so it is in *Sh'mote Rabba, parsha* 3, hinting also at these two qualities, as is clear to one who understands.

For that reason He (blessed be He) is referred to in all of our sages' (OBM) writings using the name "the Holy One (blessed be He)"; for they included in this honored name both of these two qualities. For the definition of "holy" is "separate" and "sublimely lofty", and this is from His perspective, that He is, in truth, apart from and separate and very sublime relative to any matter of variations and differences (absolutely not!); rather everything is completely filled with only a simple unity in absolute uniformity, and is far above any praise or blessing, and does not need to be blessed (heaven forefend). And refer to the *Tikkoonim, Tikkoon* 70, (130, end of first folio) [for more details]. And any consideration of increase and expansion in blessing is not relevant to this quality in any way, for the reason that everything is a simple unity alone, as it was before creation. And as is stated (*Y'shaya* 40:25): "'and to whom will you liken Me that I will be his equal' says the Holy One", that the text states this regarding His essential unity (blessed be He), as is known from the *Raa-ya M'hemna* and *Tikkoonim.*

And from the perspective of how we perceive the existence of the powers and worlds, He is called "blessed" (so to speak), from the perspective of His (blessed be He) relationship to them, for they require the matter of the increase and expansion of blessing and abundance via a person's desirable actions, as I wrote previously in Gate 2[798]. And this is "the Holy One, blessed be He"—namely, that from His perspective He is "Holy", and from our perspective He [emphatic] is called "blessed" so to speak, and both are one.

798 In the context of blessings and prayer

And regarding this specific quality that is from our perspective, that is what is mentioned in the texts: "Supernal God-*Ei"l*[799]", "Residing in the Heavens[800]" and many others like this.

CHAPTER 6

And so it is that all of the fundamental principles of the holy Torah, every one of the warnings and commandments, positive and negative, all operate within this context, that from our perspective there absolutely exist differences and variations between places. In clean/pure places we are permitted and also obligated to discuss and to reflect on the Torah's words. And in filthy places we are prohibited even to reflect on the Torah's words. And so it is with all the matters and the system of behavioral obligations that we are directly commanded in the holy Torah, and lacking this context of our perspective there wouldn't be any room for the Torah and commandments at all.

And even though, in truth, from His (blessed be He) perspective that has the capability of grasping His essential nature, he permeates everything with complete uniformity, without any barriers, and with no differences or variation between places at all; only that everything is a simple unity, exactly as before the creation. However, we are not able—and also not permitted—to engage in any way contemplating an understanding of this awesome matter, to intimately know and to grasp how the Sole Master (blessed be He) permeates every thing and all places with a simple unity and absolute uniformity—absolutely not [emphatic]!

---

799 Heb.: *Ei"l el-yone*

800 Heb.: *Yo-sheiv ba-sha-my-eem*

And it's as the *Ro-kei-ahkh* (OBM) wrote in the *Shoresh K'dooshaht Ha-yikhud*—these are his holy words: "'Into what is too wondrous for you do not delve...'—This is what is written in the beginning of *b'raita d'seifer y'tzeera*: 'return the Former onto His foundation, He is the Former of all...'. And in another *b'raita*: 'If your heart/mind runs, return to the place'. For that reason it was stated (*Yekhezkel* 1:14): 'The living beings[801] ran to and fro[802]', meaning that when you think with your heart/mind regarding the Creator of the universe, what is He and how He is present in every place, and about His actions, block your mouth from speaking and your heart/mind from pondering—remove the thought from your heart/mind. And if your heart/mind [persistently] runs to this thought, hurry quickly and do not ponder it, and return to the unity of the Place of the Universe to worship Him and be in awe/fear of Him... . And specifically regarding this matter a covenant was established, to not think about His godly qualities, for none of the wise ones can know it." This concludes his words. And refer there at length [for more details].

And all the hosts of the supernal multitudes ask: "Where is His place of glory?", for they can't grasp the true nature of the matter of the aspect of Him being the universe's place, mentioned above. And this is what the sages (OBM) stated in *Chageega*, in chapter *Ein Dorsheen* (13b): "but it is written: 'blessed is the glory of God-*YHV"H* from His place' (*Yekhezkel* 3:15). This indicates that no one can know His place." And Moshe Rabbeinu's (OBM) soul-*Neffesh* craved to grasp the matter when he stated (*Sh'mote* 33:18): "Show me, please, Your glory", namely the aspect of the place of His glory that we mentioned above, and he was not given permission.

---

801 Heb.: *cha-yote*

802 Heb.: *ra-tzo va-shove*

And only He (blessed be He) alone—the one who is able to grasp His essence—He knows the essential true nature of this wondrous and recondite matter—"the hidden are for God-*YHV"H* our God-*Elohi"m...*" (*D'varim* 29:28). We are permitted to contemplate only that for which we've been given permission—"but the revealed are for us"—according to our capacity to grasp, that being our perspective, that He (blessed be His name) is called by the name "surrounding all the worlds". In the end, even though it is so[803], He (blessed be He) constrained His glory with His simple will so that what appears to the perceiving eye is the reality of worlds and powers and creations continuously being renewed.

And for that reason, we are obligated to know and to fix in our heart/minds a firm and unshakable faith, that from our perspective there are definitely variations in place and different situations to which the legal system applies, as I stated above; for that is a cornerstone of the foundation of faith, and a central tenet of the Torah and all of the commandments.

And this is also one of the reasons that after the unification[804] in the first verse of the *kree-aht sh'ma*[805] we say "Blessed be the name of the glory of His sovereignty forever and ever". And this is (as we will discuss later in chapter 11) that the matter of the unification in the first verse is in the word "one"; namely to intend that the Sole Master (blessed be He), is one in each and all of the worlds and creations, a simple unity, just as it sounds. And all of them are considered as nothingness, and there is

---

803 That even though He permeates all of creation with perfect uniformity

804 A unification is an action (physical, speech or thought) that asserts God's unity.

805 The *kree-aht sh'ma* is the verse (*D'varim* 6:4) that translates as "Hear o' Israel, God-*YHV"H* is our God-*Elohi"m*, God-*YHV"H* is one".

absolutely nothing other than Him (blessed be He). And we shouldn't come to contemplate—(absolutely not!)—the true nature of this matter, how and what. And for that reason we say after it "Blessed be the name of the glory of His sovereignty forever and ever", so that it should be clear in saying that, that our intention is the matter as seen from our perspective: that it exhibits the existence of worlds and creations that are renewed by His Will (blessed be He), that need to be blessed from Him, and that He is sovereign over them—this being the "Blessed be the name of the glory of His sovereignty…". (And this is the context in which the Zohar calls the first verse the Supernal Unification[806], and the verse "Blessed be the name of the glory of His sovereignty forever and ever" is called the Lower Unification[807]. And now it's clear why.)

806 Aram.: *yee-khoo-da ee-la-ah,* literally Upper Unification
807 Aram.: *yee-khoo-da ta-ta-ah,* literally Lower Unification

CHAPTER 7

And these two contexts mentioned above, from His (blessed be He) perspective and from ours, they [emphatic] themselves are the matter of the *tzimtzoom*[808]

808 Heb.: *tzimtzoom*—The Torah speaks in terms that people can understand. In the parts of Torah we call Kabbalah (*Torat Che"N*), it employs a temporal/spatial metaphor to model the process of creation. This model is called *tzimtzoom*, which we translate hereafter as "the Constraining". We must keep in mind at all times that the Constraining is a model that necessarily has severe deficiencies. It serves only to give us a very minimal ability to think about and discuss what is fundamentally beyond thought and words.

Existence as we experience it implies an underlying structure of time and space. As Rav Chayyim has discussed so far in this Gate, *Ein Sofe* is emphatically not a being and not within time and space—the universe is not *Ein Sofe*'s place; rather, *Ein Sofe* is time and space's place. From the *Ein Sofe*'s perspective (so to speak) there is no creation, no time and no space; everything now is just as it was before creation. This is so at odds with our experience that it's exceedingly difficult for us to grasp how the infinite distance between the *Ein Sofe*'s perspective and ours could be bridged.

The Ariza"l, at the beginning of the *Etz Chayyim*, provides us with a description that can be considered a model of the process of creation, the process that bridges the infinite distance. With an exceedingly keen awareness of its deficiencies, he builds the model upon what he acknowledges is a fundamentally deficient temporal/spatial metaphor, describing the *Ein Sofe* as an infinite, uniformly distributed presence (so to speak). Speaking as-if from our perspective, he describes how at a certain moment (so to speak), a perfect sphere (so to speak) within that presence was modified (so to speak), creating a sphere within which the presence was no longer perceptible.

and the *kahv*[809] mentioned in the Ariza"l's writings. And it is explained there that from the perspective of the Constraining there's no justification for asserting any variation or difference in place, above and below, front and back[810], only an absolutely genuine uniformity. All the matters of the variations and differences between places, and all the names and appellations, are all applied solely from the perspective of the Channel[811]. Refer to the beginning of the book *O-tz'rote Chayyim*[812] [for more detail]. Know that everything that the Ariza"l wrote regarding these recondite topics are only metaphors, and the inner meaning of the matter of the Constraining and the Channel, the intention regarding these two contexts as

---

809 Heb.: *kahv*—literally *line.* In the context of the plumbing metaphor used by the Ariza"l it might be translated as *pipe,* while in the context of an electrical/electronic/optics metaphor it might be translated as *wire,* or *optical fiber* or *cable,* or *beam of directed energy.* In this era of information and communication theory, a better rendering might be *channel.* I chose to translate it hereafter as *Channel.*

(We continue with the description of the model.) A Channel was made to extend from the top outside surface of the sphere into the sphere, extending not quite to the bottom inner opposite surface of the sphere. As it enters the sphere, the Channel descends and spreads out in specifically defined ways.

The Channel provides a way for the light of *Ein Sofe* to enter (so to speak) the sphere in a very tightly controlled and constrained manner.

810 "Above and below" and "front and back" are prototypical examples of variations in place.

811 I.e., from our perspective.

812 The *O-tz'rote Chayyim* is an early part of Rabbi Chayyim Vittals' writings, compiled by Rav Yaakov Tzemakh, that were incorporated into the *Etz Chayyim* by Rav Moshe Papirsh. It is considerably shorter than the *Etz Chayyim,* which is a compilation of various versions and sources.

mentioned above, is that they are, in essence, completely one context and one matter.

For the definition of the word "Constraining" here, is not a way of referring to leaving a space, or transporting from place to place, to cause Himself to enter and to cause Himself to connect to Himself (so to speak), to actualize a vacant space (heaven forefend). Rather the matter is as stated in *B'reisheet Rabba*, at the end of *parsha* 45: "She constrained her presence[813] and she did not perceive the King". And in *Eikha Rabbatee* at the beginning of the alphabetic section "*ah-nee ha-gevver*": "She went and constrained her presence behind the column", whose explanation there is: using the language of being hidden and covered (refer to the *Ahrookh* in the entry for *Tz-M-Tz-M*[814]). So too here [is found] the word Constraining, namely, being hidden and covered.

And the intention is that His unity (blessed be His name), in the aspect of His essence that permeates all the worlds with absolute uniformity, is what we refer to as "Constraint" as a result of His unity that permeates all the worlds being constrained and hidden from our perception, per the context of: "Indeed, you are a God-*Ei"l* who conceals Himself" (*Y'shaya* 45:15).

And our conception of what we are able to grasp, of the extending/unfolding[815] of the worlds one above the other in various qualities, is what we refer to as "Channel",

---

813 Heb.: *pa-neh-ha*—literally "her face"

814 The four Hebrew letters *tzaddik, mem, tzaddik, mem.*

815 Heb.: *hish-tahl-sh'loot*—this word has the sense of something that is rooted above and then extends, unfolds, stretches, extrudes, unwinds, or radiates progressively only in one direction, in this case downward. An example would be an extension ladder based firmly on the ground that opens up progressively by extending upwards. Its root word implies relevance to the structure of a chain. We translate it as "extends/unfolds".

which is similar to a channel that extends/unfolds.

And this is what the Ariza"l stated, that from the perspective of the Constraint—namely from the perspective of His (blessed be He) essential unity in the worlds that permeates everything—from our perspective He appears to be constrained and concealed, while from the perspective of His essence it's incorrect to attribute "above and below". It's only from the perspective of the Channel—namely, from the perspective of our perception that we, from our perspective, grasp the structure of the worlds using the metaphor of an extending/unfolding like a channel—that our perspective [that there exist qualities of] above and below is correct.

> (And despite that being so, that from the perspective of the Constraint, namely, that even though He (blessed be His name) constrained and concealed from our perception the light of His essential unity that permeates everything, even so, we [still] couldn't attribute to Him "above and below" even from the perspective of our perception, if we were able to perceive an absolutely uniform degree of concealment in all places, like the matter of an encompassing sphere to which we couldn't attribute the matter of "above and below", or variations in place. [816]
> But from the perspective of the Channel, His Will (blessed be He) decreed that after the Constraint and the concealment we perceive the degree of conceal-

816 Rav Chayyim seems to be saying that, even within the universe of constraint, if His essential unity permeating all the worlds was uniformly distributed, then from our perspective we wouldn't be able to perceive it in any way. In reality we perceive, based on place, variations in the degree of revelation of God's presence; because of that we are able to perceive God's presence in our universe.

ment as not being uniform across all places equally. We perceive a range of perceptions based on variations in specific features, similar to the way a beam of light propagates, that it illuminates our perception to perceive the revelation of His (blessed be He) light in the worlds and diverse powers, so that the higher a world or power, the revelation of the godly light within it is greater.[817]

And also, our perception of the revelation of His (blessed be He) light in this world is also as a range of features and levels based on place, as the sages (OBM) enumerated (*Kei-lim* 1:6): "ten [levels] of holiness" and "three [levels of] holy camps", one higher than the other in degree of their holiness. So from the perspective of our perception of the revelation of the Channel of His (blessed be He) light, it is correct to attribute "above and below" and all variations in places and diverse features and their specifics that are explained in the words of the Ariza"l. And this is also the context for the phrases "supernal God-*Ei"l*" (*B'reisheet* 14:19) and "our God-*Elohi"m* is in heaven" (*T'hillim* 115:3), "residing in heaven" (*T'hillim* 2:4) and many others similar to them, that from our perspective it makes sense to say that in that place even we recognize a greater revelation of His (blessed be His name) godly light compared to another place, for the revelation of His (blessed be He) light has the quality of being concealed from our perception. And this is like the context of our Patriarch Yaakov (OBM) when he stood on the site of the Temple, as our teachers (OBM) interpreted "this is none other than God's residence" (*B'reisheet* 28:17),

---

817 From our perspective, we perceive more of God's light in the higher worlds than we do in the lower worlds.

intending to convey that in this place as perceived by human perception, that there is only a revelation of His (blessed be He) godly light alone.)

And this is the matter of the void and the vacant place that the sages (OBM) mentioned, and that the point of the matter of the Constraint was for the revelation of the containers. Namely, that His Will decreed, for reasons hidden with him, to conceal the light of oneness of His essence (blessed be He) within that space, the space where the worlds and creatures exist, to actualize in that way this wondrous situation, so that the existence of worlds and powers should appear and be perceived via a process of levels and extension/unfolding, and to illuminate them with revelation of His (blessed be He) light as a subtle light, with exquisite control and care, via an infinite number of attenuating partitions, until it is possible—thanks to the extension/unfolding and incredible attenuating partitions—that there should even be places that are not pure, and powers of impurity, and evil and husks, at the depths of the lowest levels, so that it appears and seems as if it is (heaven forefend) a void that is vacant of the light of oneness of His essence (blessed be His name). And we are unable to perceive anything but a very slight, subtle impression[818] and minimal amount of light like in the form of a Channel (as a metaphor), until when it finally arrives via the structure of levels and many attenuating dividers at the lowest of the lowest powers, the powers—the power of impurity and evil—we don't perceive the revelation of His light (blessed be He) at all. And this is what was stated that the Channel of light does not extend to the bottom inner surface [of

818 Heb.: *r'shee-ma.* This is an impression made (as if) by something that was once there and subsequently departed, leaving only a subtle impression of it having been there.

the sphere] and does not contact its bottom surface, and in this way are actualized qualities of "above and below", refer there. And it is now explained to one who can understand.

[819]The Constraint and the Channel are identical. And it's advisable to say that:

1. Even though it is certain that in the space where all the worlds and creations are, it's completely permeated, even now, only with His (blessed be His name) essence alone, just as it was before the creation,
2. It is, however, in the state of Constraint, namely, having the quality of concealment alone, wondrous and hidden from our perception,
3. So that because of this constraint and concealment our entire perception is of the worlds via the process of extension/unfolding.
4. And the drawing down of the revelation of His (blessed be He) light within them is via the process of levels alone, like the metaphor of a channel as we previously discussed.

And this is what is stated in *Sha-ar Eegoolim V'yosher*[820] (*ahnaf* 2), that the channel of the thread of light is not drawn all at once to the bottom, but rather little by little, intending to convey that it happens via very many levels, with exquisite control and care, according to what is needed for us to perceive the matter of the worlds and the structure of their levels. And one who is wise will understand according to what we've discussed—based on

---

819 The original paragraph was one long sentence that was very hard to parse, so I broke it up into numbered sections.

820 In the *Etz Chayyim*

what he knows—the complete foundations of this matter as discussed there, for it is impossible to accurately detail and explain his (OBM) entire exposition there.

CHAPTER 8

And for that reason research into and contemplation of the true nature of the matter of the Constraint was forbidden—as the Ariza"l stated, as I wrote above—that we are not permitted to contemplate it at all, to know and to grasp the true nature of the matter of the universe's place, how everything is completely permeated with His (blessed be He) simple unity only, and from His (blessed be He) perspective there is absolutely nothing other than Him. And the truth is that this question is included in the context of "what came before" that they (OBM) deduced (*Cha-gee-ga*, beginning of the chapter *Ein Dore-shin*) from an explicit verse (*D'varim* 4:32): "For inquire now regarding the early days that preceded you, from the day when God created man ...", "and you may not inquire...".

And the Ariza"l, who was permitted and amazingly revealed deep and lofty secrets, he (OBM) has already explained that the inner aspect of the intention of the verse "the early days that preceded you, from the day when God created man...", is about the world of Primeval Adam[821]. And also, in the matter of Primeval Adam he wrote that we are not permitted to discuss and research the matter

821 Heb.: *oh-lahm ah-dahm kahd-ma-ah*. The world called Primeval Adam (Heb.: *ah-dahm kahd-mone*), is the world from which the four worlds *ABY"A* were created. Only a very limited amount of information is available to us about this world and the process by which the lower four worlds were created. And about what is known there is some ambiguity.

of the essence of its inner aspect, but only the energies[822] that it emits; and of those, only from the energies of S"G[823] within it and below, but not the energies of A"B within it[824]. And also this: that we are not permitted to contemplate—absolutely not!—the nature of the matter of the Constraint as it is from His (blessed be He) perspective, but only the matter of the Channel, namely in the extension/unfolding of the worlds according to our ability to grasp. Regarding that he deeply expounded expansively, but regarding the matter of the Constraint, he addressed it in the manner of "running and returning"[825], and he did not discuss the nature of the matter in detail. And refer to the beginning of the *O-tz'rote Chayyim*, page 2, top of *ahmood* 3 [for more detail on this matter]. [826]And he did not reveal it, revealing only the facts in a general way to a wise person who could understand on his own, because it is definitely worthwhile for the righteous person who is of wise heart, who devotes all of his time to learning Torah and mitzvote, and whose soul-*Ruakh* is faithful to

---

822 Heb.: *o-rote,* literally "lights"

823 In Hebrew, the two letters *sa-mehkh* (S) and *gimmel* (G), taken together, have the numerical value of 63 (*sahmekh* is 60 and *gimmel* is 3). Pronounced *sahg,* S"G refers to the sum of the numerical values of the letters of the Tetragrammaton when the four individual letters are spelled out as: *yud-vav-daled* (20), *heh-yud* (15), *vav-aleph-vav* (13), *heh-yud* (15). This is referred to as *mee-lui yood-een v'ahl-feen,* and generally refers to the *s'feera* of *Beena.* Above S"G is A"B (pronounced *ahb,* with a numerical value of 72). Below it are M"H (pronounced *ma,* with a numerical value of 45) and B"N (pronounced *bahn,* with a numerical value of 52).

824 A"B is above and also within S"G.

825 "Running and returning" implies just touching upon the matter and then retreating from it.

826 Due to the length of this complex sentence, I broke it up into numbered sections.

God-*Ei"l*, to:

1. Know the facts of this awesome matter in a general way, that the Sole Master (blessed be His name) permeates everything and there is nothing other than He (blessed be He),
2. To ignite from this the clarity of his thoughts' holiness toward the service of prayer[827],
3. To direct his heart/mind into dread and awe and trembling towards the *Ma-kome,* He being the universe's place, (and being the place of the universe is [emphatic] the point of the matter of the Constraint, this having been explained above).

This is as the sages (OBM) stated (*Ahvote* 2:18) that one who prays must intend his heart/mind toward the *Ma-kome.* And so too they stated (*Ahvote* 2:18) "And when you pray, don't make...; rather make it [an expression of] compassion and grace before the *Ma-kome* (blessed is He)." And it's per the context when Rabbee Eliezer said to his students (*B'rakhote* 28b): "Know before Whom you [plural] are praying."

And so too with the unification of the first verse of the *Kree-aht Sh'ma* in the word "one", the sincere worshipper should intend, with purity of thought, that He (blessed be His name), from His perspective, is one (just as it sounds), and also in all of the creations a simple unity alone, just as before creation, and as we'll discuss (with God's help) later.

And he will also be very fearful and apprehensive about

827 Since he already spends all of his time learning Torah and doing mitzvote, the purpose of exposing him to this rarified knowledge is to provide him with a next step: a true understanding and practice of prayer.

trespassing (heaven forefend) one of His (blessed be He) commandments, for the universe is permeated with His glory, as the verse states (*Yirmiya* 23:24): "Can a man hide in concealed places and I will not see him... do I not fill the heaven and the earth?" And as King Dovid (OBM) stated (*T'hillim* 16:8): "I have set God-*YHV"H* before me at all times."

And this is the context of [the phrase] "hollowing out God-*YHV"H*'[828] that's mentioned in many places. For example as the Zohar explained on the verse "one who desecrates..." that it is a term for hollowing and vacating a space, vacant of Him (blessed be He). This is the situation here, that he displays behavior as if (heaven forefend) the place where he stands is hollow, vacant of Him (blessed be He), and he doesn't hesitate from transgressing His (blessed be He) commandments. And also for example their statement (OBM, end of the first chapter of *Kiddushin*): "Anyone who transgresses an offense while in concealment is as if he crushes the *Sh'kheena's* feet."

(And this settles the excellent question that puzzles everyone having a wise heart/mind: how did the Ariza"l permit himself to even discuss and mention the matter of the Constraint, since contemplation of it is prohibited? And how we described the matter of the Constraint, truthfully, that's the way it is treated in every place and time, and also in this world, for those remaining whom God calls upon to know the reality of this awesome matter for the reasons mentioned above[829]. And so too in the *Raa-ya*

828 Heb.: *chee-lool ha-shem*, literally "hollowing out God". The phrase is usually translated as "desecrating God's name" or "profaning God's name".

829 That is by just touching upon the matter, using hints that might aid one who is able and ready to proceed, and then leaving it.

M'hemna and *Tikkoonim*, and the holy-one-of-God Rabbeinu Sh'muel, author of the Poem of Unification mentioned above, and the *Ro-kei-ahkh* (OBM), who mentioned the matter in hints to one who could understand, all of them for the reasons we mentioned, and as is explained to one who understands in the *Ro-kei-ahkh*, there in the *Shoresh K'doo-shaht Ha-yee-khood*, refer there [for more detail].)

However, be exceedingly careful of your soul-*Neffesh*. Remember and don't forget what was explained above, that this topic is not mentioned except to understand the matter in your heart/mind in a general way, as a lesson for the heart/mind alone, but not to research deeply and contemplate (heaven forefend) the true nature of the matter. And also, be exceedingly careful that the tendencies of the heart/mind do not determine any of your practical behavior based on this awesome matter, for it would be so easy for it to result in many things that would oppose the statutes and the foundations of our holy Torah, and it states "and do not transgress". And as scripture states (*D'varim* 4:39): "And you shall know this day and take to your hearts/minds that God-*YHV"H*..., in the heavens above..., there is nothing else." It specifically states "to your hearts/minds", namely, only in the understanding of the hearts/minds. And, for example, what they stated with regard to prayer: "He should direct his heart/mind to the *Ma-kome*."

CHAPTER 9

And what is written (*D'varim* 4:39): "And you shall know this day... that God-*YHV"H* is God-*Elohi"m*", the difference between these two names is that the name *Elohi"m* is also applied to a subsidiary power[830] that derives[831] from Him (blessed be He), and the name *YHV"H* is applied to the source of all the powers that are derived from Him (blessed be He). And as they (OBM) stated in *B'reisheet Rabba* (13:3), after the entire Creation Event was completed, that it mentioned: "a complete name (namely *YHV"H Elohi"m*) on a complete universe". That the name *YHV"H* (blessed be He) is the source, for everything is within it, and during the creation, for each proclamation, a power (or subsidiary powers) was drawn from the source of all, to actualize and create that thing and its continued persistence, and for that reason no other name is mentioned during the entire Creation Event, only the name *Elohi"m* by itself. And after all the derivations of all the powers were completed according to His (blessed be He) will's decree to meet the universe's needs, then is stated (*B'reisheet* 2:4): "during the day when God-*YHV"H/Elohi"m* made..."—a complete name.

And this is (*D'varim*, ibid) "And you shall know this day and take to your hearts/minds that God-*YHV"H* is the God-*Elohi"m*." Namely, that one should not intend to become bound and to be attached via any worship service, to any power or subsidiary powers that are in the heavens above and that are on land below, [but rather] only to focus totally on the essential name that is unique, *YHV"H* (blessed be His name), the source and sum of the complete range of powers that are derived from Him.

And this was the whole context for the foreign worship[832] of the early generations, beginning in the age of the generation of Eh-noshe, that then they initiated

830 Heb.: *ko-ahkh p'ra-tee*

831 Heb.: *ha-nim-shakh*

832 Heb.: *ha-ah-vo-da za-ra*

in the world the matter of foreign worship, as is stated (*B'reisheet* 4:26): "then the name of God-*YHV"H* became profaned", that they would worship the powers of the stars and cosmological entities[833], each one to a specific star or a cosmological entity that he selected for himself. It's not that each one thought that specific star to be the deity who created everything, for from long ago it was generally accepted by the nations to call Him (blessed be His name) the "God-*Elohi"m* of gods-*elohim*" (*Daniel* 2:47), as the sages (OBM) stated. And Malachi the prophet said so too in his rebuke of Israel (*Malachi* 1:11): "For from the rising of the sun to its setting, My name is great among the nations..., for My name is great among the nations, says God-*YHV"H-Tz'va-ote*". But rather the start of the error of the generation of Eh-noshe was, using faulty reasoning, that God was elevated and His glory was far above the heavens and that it was not honorable for Him to monitor the creations in this lowly world. And for that reason they thought that He (blessed be He) cancelled his supervision of them, and transferred it to the powers and planets and cosmological entities, that they [emphatic] should manage the world as they willed. They considered it a mundane matter and that it is absolutely prohibited and a tremendous conceit against Him (blessed be He) to pray to His honored and awesome name, to request their lowly needs from Him, and for this reason they limited themselves, and focused all the aspects of their worship and their requests to the powers of the stars and cosmological entities. (And for a description of how they manufactured the object of foreign

833 Heb.: *ma-za-lote,* translated variously as constellations, fates, fortunes. Sometimes the singular form of his word—*ma-zahl*—refers variously to a physical cosmological entity, to a spiritual entity responsible for that cosmological entity, or to a person's prospects for success.

worship, and how they sacrificed and offered incense to it [fem.], refer to *Tikkoon* 66.)

And they also knew how to coerce[834] the angels appointed over the cosmological entities to know good and evil, and that they should in that way direct beneficial influences and the pleasures of this world to them, using their powers appointed to them from the Master of All (blessed be His name). And only a few of them, gifted individuals, recognized and honestly knew that He (blessed be His name), even though He is "enthroned on high", still "He descends to look upon the heavens and the earth" (*T'hillim* 113:5,6).

And some of them worshipped wild animals and birds, as is written (*M'lahkhim Bet*, 17:30). Their intention too was to attach themselves in this way to the supernal power and cosmological entity of that creature, that it should direct upon them from its power and authority appointed to it from the Creator (blessed be He), and this is what the cursed women said to Yirmiyahoo (*Yirmiya* 44:18): "From since we ceased offering incense to the queen of heaven and pouring her libations, we have lacked everything... ."

And some of them bound themselves and sacrificed and offered incense to whichever person they observed that the power of his cosmological entity was very great, thinking that by binding themselves and their worship of him, their fortune would ascend with his fortune.

And some didn't even intend their worship to the flow of pleasures of this world, but rather their intention was to achieve in that manner certain intellectual achievements that they desired, like the knowledge of charms and other similar achievements.

And there were some who attached themselves to the

---

834 Heb.: *l'hahsh-bee-ah*, literally "to bind with oaths".

worship of certain people, so as to draw upon the influence of the cult of Amon[835] and matters regarding predicting the future. And all of that is absolutely foreign worship, included in "you shall not have any other gods-*elohi"m*" (*Sh'mote* 20:3), as the RaMBa"N (OBM) exhaustively wrote in his commentary on the Torah there. And refer to *Likutei Torah*[836], end of *parshaht Noakh*, in the matter of the generation of the dispersion[837].

And even to devote oneself in service and to attach oneself in a kind of worship of the quality of the Holy Spirit-*Ruakh*[838] in a person who is a prophet or one who is the master of the Holy Spirit, this too is definitely considered foreign worship, as we found by Nebuchadnezzar, when he bowed to Daniel. Not because he considered him to be the creator of everything, but rather, by his bowing, he intended to bind himself and to attach himself to the Holy Spirit-*Ruakh* within him, as is written (*Daniel* 2:46): "Then King Nebuchadnezzar fell upon his face and prostrated himself to Daniel; and with offering and incense..., in truth I know that your God is the God over gods..., and Revealer of secrets, since you were able reveal this secret". And there (4:5) "finally there came before me Daniel ..., and in whom is the spirit of the Holy God...". And our sages (OBM) stated (*Sanhedrin* 93a) that the reason that why Daniel wasn't present when the commandment to bow to the statue was issued was because Daniel said "I will leave here so as to not fulfill through me 'you shall burn the physical representations of their gods'". And Nebuchadnezzar also said: "Daniel should leave here so

835 Amon is an Egyptian deity.

836 The *Likootei Torah* is one of the books containing the Ariza"ls teachings.

837 Heb.: *dore ha-hahf-la-ga*

838 Heb.: *ruakh ha-kodesh*

no one should say that he destroyed his own God in fire". And refer to the *Zohar Chaddash* (*Root* 60b, and in *B'reisheet Rabba* (*parsha* 96), and in *Tahn-khooma* (beginning of *parshaht Va'y'khee*). And you also find this in Daniel...[839], what is written: "then King Nebuchadnezzar... and with offering and incense he wished to exalt him", but Daniel didn't accept. Why? Just as one separates oneself from those involved with foreign worship, in the same way one separates oneself from the foreign worship itself. And so they cited this reason there in relation to our ancestor Yaakov (OBM), who didn't want to be buried in Egypt, for they (OBM) called this matter foreign worship, even though the intention was to the Holy Spirit of God-*Elohi"m* within him.

And it could be said, based on this verse (*Sh'mote* 20:3): "You shall have no other Gods-*Elohi"m* before my face[840]", intending to convey that one should not focus worship (heaven forefend) on any object, to any aspect or subsidiary power, even if that power is the aspect of "my face". Namely, even to the specific incidence of the Holy Spirit in any person, or a specific aspect of holiness that's in any supernal power occurring in the supernal realms, as over the matter of their (OBM) statement on (*Rosh Ha-shanna* 24b) on "thou shall not make beside me[841]" (*Sh'mote* 20:23), even the likeness of my servants who serve before me on high, for example the *ophanim* and *seraphim* and the holy

---

839 It's not clear to me why Rav Chayyim used a "*v'chu*" (an ellipsis) here.

840 Heb.: *ahl pa-nai*, literally, "before my face" or "in place of my face", and commonly translated as "before me".

841 Heb.: *lo ta-ah-soon ee-tee*

living beings[842].

And even though the essence of the text's warning regarding all the foreign worship mentioned above is specifically regarding the four proscribed categories of worship[843], these days however, since the service of prayer with devotion of the heart/mind replaces the sacrificial service, it's certain that the warning applies to it too.

And this is why the scripture says (*Sh'mote* 22:19): "One who sacrifices to gods, except to God-*YHV*"H alone, shall be excommunicated." Namely, that one shouldn't intend (heaven forefend) using any worship practice or context toward any specific subsidiary power from the powers that the Creator (blessed be He) established—(for God-*Elohi"m*'s name is the enabler for anything having a potential subsidiary power [844], as we discussed previously[845])—but rather to intend only to the essential name that is unique to Him (blessed be He) alone, the definition of which is that He makes everything exist in the present moment[846], namely the sum of and source of every one of all the powers, as we described previously.

(And this is "Hear Israel, God-*YHV"H* is our God-*Elohi"m*, God-*YHV"H* is One", intending to convey that all subsidiary powers that are derived from God-*YHV"H* (blessed be He), they [explicitly] are united and integrated in His

---

842 Heb.: *chayyote ha-kodesh.* The ophanim, seraphim and holy living beings are all what we commonly refer to as the angels of specific worlds.

843 The four categories of proscribed worship practices are bowing, sacrificial offerings, incense offerings and libation offerings. A fifth category includes any worship practices specific to that deity.

844 Heb.: *m'shoo-tahf l'khol ba'al ko-ahkh p'ra'tee*

845 In Gate 1, in the annotation at the end of the Chapter 2

846 Heb.: *m'ha'veh ha-kohl*

(blessed be He) power, His oneness being the source and sum.) All of this is from the perspective of His relationship with the worlds.

For that reason, every place that the Torah commands regarding the matter of sacrifices, it explicitly explains that it is to God-*YHV"H* specifically. And as they (OBM) stated (*M'na-khote* 110a): "Come and see what's written in the *parsha* of sacrifices, that regarding them it was not said God-*Ei"l* and not God-*Elohi"m*, but rather to God-*YHV"H*, so as not to create an opening for the prosecutor to take issue." And refer to *Zohar Chaddash, B'reisheet* 6d, 7a and 7b, where the matter is explained further.

CHAPTER 10

And in accordance with our approach to the matter of the two aspects we mentioned—from His (blessed be He) perspective and from ours, as was described—will be explained another distinction and difference between the two names God-*YHV"H* and God-*Elohi"m*. For the name God-*Elohi"m*'s definition is Master of All Powers. (For a part of the explanation of its context, refer to the beginning of Gate 1.) And continuing in the explanation of the matter of Master of All Powers, each power, from the lowest of the terrestrials until the highest of the supernals, its continued existence and vitality is derived from the power above it that is its soul-*Neshama*, which permeates within it. And as is known in the Ariza"l's statements, the light and the inner aspect of the soul-*Neshama* of each power and world is itself the exterior of the power and world that is above it. And so it goes according to this process, higher and higher, whether in the general context of the powers[847].

For the totality of all of the terrestrial creations and powers are an amalgamation of the four fundamental elements, and the root of the four fundamental elements are in the four angels that are called the four camps of the *Sh'kheena,* symbolized by A, R, G, MN[848]. And the four angels have their sources in the Vehicle's four living beings[849], who are, in turn, the totality of all the roots of the souls-*Neffesh* of all the terrestrial creations. For all the myriad varieties of wild animals, the root of their souls-*Neffesh* flows from the face of the lion in the Vehicle. And the souls-*Neffesh* of all varieties of domesticated animals flow from the face of the ox, and those of all varieties of birds from the face of the eagle. And as is stated in the *Zohar* (*Pinkhas* 240b): "The hidden aspect of the sacrifices..., the face of the ox extends soul-*Ruakh* to the domesticated animals from him"—refer there [for more details].

For that reason, each one is ruled by the same species whose form and name is like the form and name of a face from the Vehicle, as they (OBM) stated (*Chageega* 13b and *Sh'mote Rabba* chapter 23): Lion is king of the beasts..., and man's soul-*Neffesh* is from "face of man", for that reason humanity is exalted over all of them, for the essence and inclusive principle of the four faces of the Vehicle is the face of man, as written (*Yekhezkel* 1:5): "And in its midst was the likeness of four living beings. This was their appearance: they had the likeness of a man." And relating to this matter, refer to *Zohar Yitro* (chapter 72): "The man

847 The second part of the "whether" phrase seems to be missing. The complete phrase perhaps read: "whether in the general context of the powers *or the specific*".

848 The four symbols taken together spell out the word *ahr-ga-mahn,* which translates as "crimson".

849 Heb.: *ahr-ba chayyote ha-mehr-ka-va*

includes all of them...", and in *parshaht Tahzreeya* (48, the end of second folio) is written: "And the likeness of their faces...". And in *parshaht B'midbar* (118b): "And the likeness of their faces...". And refer to *Zohar Chaddash Yitro* in the section about the Vehicle Event (32c and 33, top of first folio). (The source of the man's source is from the Man on the throne, as discussed previously in Gate 1, chapter 6.) Their root and their sustenance come from the world above them, and so on, higher and higher.

Refer to *Zohar Yitro* (chapter 2, 2): "We learned in the supernal secret that the four living beings, it is that they are within... and they are the first, older than *Ahteeka Ka-deesha...* . We learned that just as is above, is below them, and so it is in all the worlds, each one is attached, this to that, and that to that." And in the *Raa-ya M'hemna*: "And there are living beings that surround the throne of *B'reeya...*, and there are living beings of the world of *Y'tzeera...*, and there are four living beings of the four foundations... ." And refer to the *Etz Chayyim, Sha-ar Keetzoor ABY"A* (end of chapter 8), and there too at the end of the Gate in the context of the powers of soul-*Neffesh* of man, refer there [for more details].

And the root of all of their roots is from the four letters of the name *YHV"H* (blessed be He), and they are the original roots, the secret of the reliable One, ancestor of all the worlds that are mentioned in *Zohar Va'eira* 23, end of second folio.

And so too, all the specific powers and species, each one has a source, and a source of the source, higher and higher, as those (OBM) stated (*B'reisheet Rabba* chapter 10): "There is no individual blade of grass that doesn't have a guiding power in the heaven[850] that strikes it and says to it: 'grow'", as

850 Heb.: *rah-kee-ah*

stated in *Eeyove* (38:33): 'Do you know the laws of heaven…'. And refer to *Zohar T'rooma* (151b) and in *parshaht K'doshim* (chapter 6a) for this matter somewhat at length.

For that star or guiding power is the inner aspect of its soul-*Neffesh* and its vitalizing force and the source of that plant—it receives from it the power to grow, that is its soul-*Neffesh*, as is known. And the source and the soul-*Neffesh* of that star or guiding power is the angel appointed over it; from it the star receives the power of growing to cause that plant to grow and mature, as is stated in the *Zohar T'rooma* mentioned above: "And over that star is appointed one…". And the source and soul-*Neffesh* of that angel is from the power and the world above it.

And for that reason, coercing of angels is done with names, for that name is that angel's soul-*Neffesh* and source of vitality and energizing light which the world and power that's above him radiates upon him to maintain him.

And refer to *Zohar Ba-lahk* (208a): "All of these holy angels above could not exist and could not survive without the supernal radiated light that shines upon them and sustains them. And if the supernal radiated light would be interrupted, it wouldn't be able to survive." Refer to the *Etz Chayyim, Sha-ar Tzeeyoor Oh-la-mote ABY"A*[851], in Rabbi Chayyim Vittal's introduction, and there at the end of chapter 1, and in the Gate of Names[852], chapter 7, that the angels are the aspect of containers, and the names are their essence and their inner soul-*Neshama*, and therefore it operates within him and leads him where ever it desires as a soul-*Neshama* controls the body, and so on in this way until the highest heights.

And it's the same in the matter of the souls-*Neshama* that are in each world. Each soul-*Neshama*, its source and the

851 Heb.: *Sha'ar Tzee-yoor Ha-o-lah-mote ABY"A*

852 Heb.: *Sha-ahr Ha-shei-mote*

wellspring of its vitality is from the aspect of the soul-*Neshama* of the world that is above it, that relative to it is called the soul-*Neshama* of the soul-*Neshama*, and so too for all of them.

And He (blessed be His name), He is the God-*Elohi"m*, Master of All Powers, for He is the soul-*Neshama* and the sustenance and the source of sources for all of the powers, as is stated (*N'khemya* 9:6): "and you give them all life", truly in each instant, and for that reason He (blessed be He) is called the soul-*Neshama* of all souls-*Neshama*, and the essential feature and source of all the worlds.

CHAPTER 11

And the matter is, as is known in the *Zohar*, that He (blessed be He) and His utterance are one. And every utterance and statement from the Holy One (blessed be He) in the Creation Event, that He pronounced and it came into existence, He is the soul-*Neffesh* and source of vitality of that thing that was created therewith and all of the myriad species included in it, including:

- the guiding powers appointed over them,
- and the angels appointed over those guiding powers,
- and their sources and the source of their sources, higher and higher, that are in each world.

And from that moment onward, for the duration of eternity, His utterance is positioned within them to radiate upon them and to sustain them in each instant, during all the details of their involvements and their individual interactions, and in structuring their situations.

Therefore, for all of the ten utterances, no name is mentioned other than God-*Elohi"m*, because that statement is the "Master of Powers" for that object, and all the species within it that were created using it[853], that it is their soul-*Neffesh* that permeates the interior of the pieces of its components. It is only that in this moment "our eyes are weakened, prevented from perceiving"[854] with physical eyes how and in what manner His utterance (blessed be He) extends/unfolds within them.

And regarding the future it is written (*Y'shaya* 40:5): "And all flesh together will see that the mouth of God-*YHV"H* has spoken", namely that our perception will be refined to the point that we'll merit to perceive and also see with physical eyes the matter of how His (blessed be He) utterance permeates everything in the universe, similar to how a perception of this kind already occurred at the time of the giving of the Torah. For it is written (*Sh'mote* 20:18): "and the entire nation sees the sounds"[*]. And this is also in the realm of their (OBM) statements at the end of the chapter *Eiloo Ovrim*: "The world-to-come is not like this world. In this world it is written as God-*Y"H* and pronounced as God-*ADN"Y*, but in the world-to-come, it's written as God-*Y"H* and pronounced as *Y"H*", and understand this.

Annotation: *And we could say, according to this statement of theirs (OBM) on this text (*M'khilta *on* RaSh"Y*'s interpretation in the* Chumash*), that they were hearing the visible and seeing the audible, intending to convey that the powers of the physical were nullified to such an extent, and their perceptions were refined so much, until the total experience of the matters associated with the physical senses that at first they experienced as a visual perception, at that moment no longer existed for them—not seeing with the visual sense nor contemplating it in any way—to the extent that, for example, if*

853 With that name

854 Heb.: *takh ei-nei-noo mir'ote* (Y'shaya 44:18)

someone wanted to understand a matter that would normally be perceived with the physical senses, they would have had to have it explained to them verbally, to tell them about what in fact exists; and the spiritual matters that, at first, they would have had to be explained verbally, at that moment they would see them with their physical visual sense and their perception would be wondrous.

This is the context of the text (*Y'shaya* 30:20): "Your Teacher will no longer be hidden behind His garment, and your eyes will behold your Teacher". And refer to *Zohar Chaddash Yitro* (34, end of first folio): "wings are coverings to hide their names…", pay attention well to the whole context there.

Therefore He (blessed be His name) began the ten utterances first with "I am God-*YHV"H* your God-*Elohi"m*", for this is the entire essential foundation of the faith, that each person of Israel should fix in his heart/mind that only He (blessed be His name) is the true "Master of Power", and its soul-*Neshama,* and its vitalizing force, and its essential source, and [so too] for all the created beings and powers and all the worlds. This is the context and definition of the name God-*Elohi"m*: Master of All Powers.

But even so, according to the definition and the context of this name, it appears that there are, in absolute fact, also worlds and powers that are constantly renewed via His (blessed be He) simple will; that He constrained his glory and left a place (so to speak) for the existence of powers and worlds. But He (blessed be He), He is their soul-*Neshama* and the source of the root of their vitalizing power that they receive from His (blessed be He) presence[855], that permeates and is concealed within them

---

855 Heb.: *mei-ee-toe*

(so to speak), like the matter of how the soul-*Neshama* permeates a person's body, that even though it permeates every part and distinct point within it, even so we couldn't say that the body becomes nullified in relation to it, as though it doesn't exist at all. So it is with every supernal power and world that permeates the entire essence of the power and the world below it, that even so, the lower power and the world remain in existence. And this is based on our perspective, in the context of our perceptions, as we discussed previously.

But the essential name God-*YHV"H* (blessed be He) informs us about the aspect and context as it is from His (blessed be He) perspective, that was explained above.

> (And this is so even though the name God-*YHV"H* is applied from the perspective of His (blessed be He) relationship per His Will to the worlds, for [relative to] the essence of the Sole Master, *Ein Sofe* (blessed be He), being bare of the worlds, there's no hint to any name whatsoever. Even so, the worlds are [emphatic] actually completely null and nullified relative to Him (blessed be He). From the perspective of this honored name, this resembles the situation according to how it is from His (blessed be He) perspective.)

And for that reason the essential name is called the

"Unique Name" (blessed be He).[856]

And this is what is stated in the text (*D'varim* 4:39): "For God-*YHV"H* is the God-*Elohi"m...*", wishing to convey that even if from the perspective of our perception He is called by the name God-*Elohi"m"*, and from His (blessed be He) perspective He is called by the aspect of God-*YHV"H* (blessed be He), in truth all is one, and God-*YHV"H* is God-*Elohi"m...*, as we learned previously in chapter 7, in the context of the Constraint and the Channel, that they are all one.

And this is also included in the matter of the unification of the first verse of the *Sh'ma*: "...God-*YHV"H* is our God-*Elohi"m* God-*YHV"H* is one", [*] desiring to convey that we should intend that He (blessed be He) is our God-*Elohi"m*, Master of the Powers, and the source of the root of our souls-*Neshama* and our vitalizing force, and for all the creations and worlds. And though He created and brought into reality the existence of powers and worlds and creations, even so from His (blessed be He) perspective:

1. He is in the aspect of God-*YHV"H* and is one,
2. All of the creations are not a barrier (heaven forefend) relative to His (blessed be He) simple oneness that permeates everything, and
3. He is called, now too, God-*YHV"H* and One.

856 This paragraph was unusually difficult to translate. It can be understood as saying that: (1) the name *YHV"H* is from God's perspective, as previously explained, and (2) although this name is from God's perspective, it is also from that perspective relative to the worlds that He created—it is *not* from *Ein Sofe*'s perspective, which has no name and relative to which everything is absolutely nullified, and (3) that this name therefore is unique and special because it serves to point to God's relationship to the worlds from a Godly perspective in which, somehow, the worlds are *not* rendered null. The nature of this unique perspective represented by this special name is not discussed here.

Annotation: *And based on this will be understood their (OBM) statements (*P'sakhim *56a) in the context of the praise "Blessed be the glorious name of His sovereignty forever and ever" in the unification of Sh'ma, in that they decreed that it be said in a covert manner, likening it to a king's daughter who smelled the aroma of spicy stew..., her servants began bringing it to her covertly." On the face of it we are surprised about their (OBM) metaphor, for isn't it great praise?*

And according to a plain explanation we can say that, in truth it is not praise at all. It's similar to this: would we consider it praise of a human king to say that he rules over a myriad of ants and gnats, and that they willingly accept the yoke of his sovereignty? All the more so, it's a simple deduction that this is not a worthy comparison for He (blessed be He) who has no limit to His holiness and the awesomeness of His simple unity, and for whom the entire universe taken together is insignificant in comparison. It's certain that truthfully it is not praise in any way that we praise Him (blessed be He) that He is blessed and magnificent in the glory of His sovereignty over the created worlds, for all of them are lowly and are not considered as anything significant in comparison. But it's only that He (blessed be He), "Where you find His greatness, you find His humility", that His Will decreed that He should accept our praise. For this reason they (OBM) likened it to a spicy stew, and regulated that even so, we should only say it covertly[857]*.*

And according to that opinion, we can explain the inner aspect of their (OBM) intentions, namely, that after we have designated Him one[858]*, with the verse* Sh'ma*—that He is unequivocally One, a simple unity and there is absolutely none other than Him—how, after that, could we praise Him that he is blessed via the glory of His sovereignty over worlds,*

857 Very quietly

858 Heb.: *yee-khahd-noo-hoo*

that the worlds too exist and that He (blessed be He) is sovereign over them? It can't be considered praise relative to the awesome unification of the Sh'ma *verse. Rather, His (blessed be He) will decreed that even so we should praise Him with this praise, for the reason that it is correct from the perspective of our perception and behavior, according to the foundations and precepts of our holy Torah, all of which were based on this aspect, as I wrote previously. For that reason we say it covertly.*

*(And on the face of it, we may find it difficult to understand what Rabbee Yirmiya said to Rabbee Cheeya bar Abba (*B'rakhote *13b): "that he would greatly stretch out the pronunciation of the word 'one'. And he said to him, 'once you've acknowledged Him as King above and below and towards the four directions of the heavens, you needn't do that again'." And according to our opinion it's a little difficult to learn that we acknowledge Him as King with the word "one". However this too is explained, as is known to those who are knowledgeable in the Ariza"l's (OBM) writings, that the entirety of the initiation of the start of His (OBM) conception in the matter of creation was according to the secret of the* Malkhoot *of the* Ein Sofe, *and understand.)*

CHAPTER 12

And this is the context within which they (OBM) expounded (*Chullin* 7b) on the verse "that God-*YHV"H* is the God-*Elohi"m*, there is none other than Him[859]" (*D'varim* 4:39): "Rabbee Chisda stated: even sorceries." For the entire context for acts of sorcery is drawn from

859 Later commentators might translate this as "there is nothing other than Him", as Rav Chayyim relates below.

the powers of impurity of the impure Vehicle[860], and that is the matter of the wisdom of sorcery about which the members of the *Sanhedrin*[861]were required to have

860 Heb.: *merkahva ha-t'mei-ah*—Rav Chayyim here again asserts the existence of a a spiritual structure of impurity that mirrors the spiritual structure of holiness. From the writings of the Ariza"l we learn that this mirroring only persists up to specific levels, and beyond that level there is only holiness.

861 The *Sanhedrin* was the highest judiciary court while the Temple was in existence.

intimate knowledge, namely:

1. the wisdom relating to the names of impurity, and
2. the knowledge of the contexts of the powers of the impure Vehicle, and
3. their names by which the masters of sorcery perform acts, and
4. other various contexts, as when they bind the powers of impurity using the aspect of good within it, to infuse within it a vitality to perform super-natural acts opposite to the order of the natural powers and guiding powers.

Refer to the *Etz Chayyim, Sha-ar Kleepaht Noga*, at the beginning of chapter 4 [for more detail].

As a result that the Creator, Master of All (blessed be He) determined that the context of their[862] powers be higher than the natural powers that are drawn from the astronomical entities and the guiding powers, because of that it is in their power to do actions even opposite to the natural powers of the "astronomical entities and guiding powers"[863] assigned to them at the time of creation. As is well known, the Creator (blessed be He) set within each power and world the power and ability to govern and direct the power and world below it, to anywhere it will have the spirit-*Ruakh*... .

And what they stated there—"that they contradict the heavenly retinue"—they intended to convey that the Creator permanently put into effect that the ability of the powers of impurity would be to subvert only the arrangement of powers of the retinue comprising the

862 The powers of impurity
863 Heb.: *ko-khahveem u'ma-za-lote*

"astronomical entities and guiding powers", but not that they should have the power to affect (heaven forefend) any of the holy actions of the powers of the holy Vehicle. And it's truly the opposite situation, that when they are coerced using the names of the powers of holiness, specifically in that moment all of their activities are completely nullified, as is written in *Tikkoon* 18: "Those who know about the *kleepote* perform a coercion using the names and essential names for the Holy One (blessed be He) aimed at those *kleepote* and nullify the decree." Refer to the *Etz Chayyim*, in the chapter mentioned above [for more details]. [This is so] because the power is not their own (heaven forefend), for there is no light other than His (blessed be He), Master of all the powers. And also that, truthfully, everything is permeated with just His simple essential unity (blessed be He), and nothing other than Him has any real power in any way, not the powers of impurity and not any power nor any world or creation in any way,. This is the meaning of what they stated: "There is none other than Him, even sorcery".

And this is what the Talmud relates there about this: "...how there was a certain woman who sought to collect the dirt [surreptitiously] from under Rabbee Chaneena's feet. He said to her: 'Collect—your effort will not succeed, for it is written "There is nothing but Him"'".

The text then makes an attempt to refute this assertion: "But Rabbee Yokhanan stated: 'Why are they called sorceries?[864] Because they contradict the heavenly retinue[865]'—Rabbee Chaneena was different [from the norm], for he had a great degree of merit."

---

864 Heb.: *k'sha-feem*

865 Heb.: *makh-khee-sheen pa-mahl-ya shel ma-a-la*—implying that Rabbee Yokhanan is not exempt from the effects of sorcery.

Certainly, he (Rabbee Chaneena) did not consider himself as having a great degree of merit by virtue of his Torah and his many good acts, with the result that because of them he was comfortable that acts of sorcery would have no effect on him. Rather the situation is as I described above, that in any case, in truth, the powers of the impure Vehicle don't have any power of their own (heaven forbid). It's rather that He (blessed be He) designated that their powers are above the natural powers of the astronomical entities and guiding powers, so that because of this it's within their abilities to act, even also to change the natural order of the guiding powers. But without Him they are nil and nothingness.

And for that reason even in the case of Rabbee Chaneena, it's not that he relied on the merit of the holiness of his Torah or his [long history of] positive behaviors, but only that he intimately knew and measured in his soul-*Neffesh*, that this reliability was established in his heart/mind as being true: that other than Him (blessed be He) there is absolutely no other power at all. And he attached himself via the purity of his thoughts to the Master of All Powers, unique Lord who fills all worlds, and no other power here has any control, nor real power at all. For that reason, that his heart/mind was rightly certain about this—that actions of sorcery that drew on the powers of the impure Vehicle would have no control over him—this is why he stated: "Your effort will not succeed, for it is written 'There is nothing but Him'".

And truthfully, this is a great matter and a wondrous treasure that takes him out of the realm of any other judgments and the desires of others, so that they can't control him, nor make any impression at all. When a person fixes it in his heart/mind to state, that after all:

- God-*YHV"H* is the true God-*Elohi"m* and there is no other power in the universe nor in all the worlds at all other than Him, and
- Everything is filled only with His (blessed be His name) simple unity, and
- He, in his heart/mind, completely nullifies all others, and does not attend to any power or will in the universe, and harnesses and adheres the purity of his thoughts only to the unique Lord (blessed is He),

then He will make it happen for him, that in any case all of the powers and desires that are in the universe will be nullified from upon him, so that they are not able to affect him in any way at all.

Annotation: *And this is the context of what they (OBM) stated in* Mishna Rosh Ha-shanna *(29:1): "'Make for yourself a fiery serpent...' (*B'midbar *21)—Does a serpent kill or a serpent cause to live? Rather, when Israel gazes upward and makes their hearts/minds subservient to their Father in Heaven...", intending to convey that when they gazed upward to the fiery serpent, and contemplated his evil power, and even so they nullified it in their heart/minds and did not attend to his awesome power, and made their heart/minds truly subservient only to their Father in Heaven alone, they were healed. This is the truth of the matter of how the powers of judgment can be sweetened at their root. This has now been clearly explained to one who understands.*

And this matter is also included in the intention of the *Zohar* (in the Introduction, page 12, end of the first folio): "The fourth commandment is to know that God-*YHV"H* is the God-*Elohi"m*, as it was stated: 'and you know today... that God-*YHV"H*, He is the God-*Elohi"m*'.

And also to integrate the name God-*Elohi"m* within the name God-*YHV"H*... . And when the person will have knowledge that all is one and doesn't impose any separation, even the Other Side will depart from the world." Understand!

And he will also be able to decree something and it will happen, to cause wondrous matters and miracles opposite to the natural order, because he harnesses and adheres the purity of his heart/mind's reliance with an unshakable truth only to Him (blessed be He) alone, and relative to Him it's all the same, each moment, whether to act in accordance with the decreed natural order or opposite to the natural order. This is as we found in the case of Rabbee Chaneena Ben Dosa who would decree something and it would be carried out per his will at all times, opposite to the natural order, as when he said (*Ta-ahneet* 25a): "The One who decreed to the oil that it should ignite, shall decree to the vinegar that it will ignite", intending to convey that relative to Him, this is the same as that, as mentioned above, and therefore He made it happen for him. And there are many others like this about him, as are brought in the Talmud about his wondrous situations.

CHAPTER 13

And this was the context of the Patriarchs' service all their days. For they [emphatic], in their awesome righteousness and purity of their holy heart/minds, would attach their thoughts to His Will (blessed be He) all their days without even a momentary interruption. And they nullified with their will all of the powers in the universe, and they were considered as nil and nothingness to them. And therefore they merited also to wondrous miracles that changed the system of nature and those associated with it[866], as described above. And therefore His (blessed be He) name was united with theirs to be called the God-*Elohi"m* of Avraham, the God-*Elohi"m* of Yitzkhak.... And as He (blessed be He) himself stated (*Sh'mote* 3:13): "the God-*Elohi"m* of your forefathers", and because of this they (OBM) stated (*B'reisheet Rabba* 47:22): "The Patriarchs, they [emphatic] are the Vehicle"[867].

However, Moshe Rabbeinu's (peace be upon him) level was still higher, as the Torah testified (*D'varim* 34:10): "Never again has there arisen a prophet...". And the essence of the difference between his level and theirs was as He (blessed be He) Himself explained, and He stated (*Sh'mote* 6:3): "I am God-*YHV"H,* and I appeared to Avraham... as God-*Ei"l Shadda"i,* but with My name God-*YHV"H* I did not make Myself known to them".

And this [specific] matter, it [emphatic] is the essence of the difference that was explained above between the name God-*Elohi"m* and the name God-*YHV"H* (blessed be He). For

866 Heb.: *b'shee-dood ha-ma-ah-ra-khote v'tzeev-ei-hem*

867 The Patriarchs are called "the Vehicle" in reference to the verses: *B'reisheet* 17:22 and 35:13, 28:13. In all of those verses God's presence is (so to speak) upon or permeates the Patriarch; God's presence settles upon/permeates them and then lifts off of them.

in the majority of cases, in the context of what the Patriarchs grasped, we found that the name used is God-*Elohi"m*: "O' God-*Elohi"m* before whom my forefathers Avraham and Yitzkhak walked" (*B'reisheet* 48:15); "the God-*Elohi"m* who shepherds me from my inception" (ibid). And so too we call Him (blessed be He) the "God-*Elohi"m* of Avraham...", as I described previously in the context of the holiness of their level, that they gave no credence to any other power or context in the universe at all. However, their achievement of prophecy was not by nullifying the powers from their existence in toto. And what the verse stated (*Sh'mote* 6:3): "and I appeared to Avraham... as God-*Ei"l Shadda"i*" (whose context is also the same as the context of the name G-d-*Elohi"m)*, intends to convey that I am the Master of All Powers, and if I so will it, each instant, I change the system of nature and the powers from how I fixed them at the time of creation—this is "God-*Ei"l Shadda"i*". But in the aspect of the context of "My name God-*YHV"H*," (whose context was described previously in chapter 11), "I did not make myself known to them" to be within their prophetic grasp.

But Moshe Rabbeinu (peace be upon him), his prophetic ability was in the context of the quality of the essential name, the unique God-*YHV"H* (blessed be He), and for that reason there was no power obstructing the light of his prophetic ability. Thus, via all the miracles of God-*YHV"H* that were performed by him, everyone observed a complete nullification of the existence of all the powers, and there is nothing other than Him (blessed be he) completely, just as it sounds. As the text stated: "You have been shown to know that God-*YHV"H* is...", and this is the context and explanation of the unified name God-*YHV"H,* as we described previously.

This is what is written (*Sh'mote* 6:2): "God-*Elohi"m* spoke to Moshe and said to him: "I am God-*YHV"H*". He informed him about the essence of the quality of his prophetic perception, that even the name God-*Elohi"m*, for him everything had the quality of God-*YHV"H*, as in the context of the verse (*D'varim* 4:35): "For God-*YHV"H* is the God-*Elohi"m*, there is nothing other than Him". And from that point on nothing else is mentioned in relation to him other than "and God-*YHV"H* spoke" and "and God-*YHV"H* said". And this is (*D'varim* 34:10): "And never again has there arisen a prophet... whom God-*YHV"H* had known face to face", and what is written in *Tikkoon* 26[868]: "Concerning the Patriarchs He did not appear to them except wearing shoes,[869], while concerning Moshe, it's without any garments at all. And this is the secret of the verse: 'and I appeared to Avraham'...". This concludes its words.

And this is also the context of their (OBM) statement at the end of chapter *kisui ha-dahm* (*Chullin* 89a): "What is said in relation to Moshe and Aharon is greater than what was said in relation to Avraham. For by Avraham it is written (*B'reisheet* 18:27): "although I am but dirt and ash[870]", and by Moshe and Aharon is written (*Sh'mote* 16:5): "for us, what are we?[871]".

For dirt and ash, from all perspectives, still appears to have the existence of dirt [*]. But Moshe Rabbeinu (peace be upon him) said "for us, what are we", as if they have no existence in the universe at all, totally. (And even though he also included Aharon with him in this context, and as per their great remark that was stated regarding Moshe and Aharon, that since Israel's complaint was about both of them, he responded in the plural; however the focus for this awesome level was him alone.)

---

868 In the context of a discussion of *yiboom* and *chaleetza*.

869 Heb.: *min-ah-leem*—the garments that cover the lowermost extremities of the body.

870 Heb.: *ah-far v'ei-fer*

871 Heb.: *v'nahkh-noo ma*

Annotation: *And the matter of dirt and ash is as per the context of the intention of the red heifer*[872]*, that the two hundred and eighty judgments should be re-integrated into their root in the* alef, *that being the plain power of all the letters. And the matter of the difference between* ah-far *and* ei-fer *is like the difference between* koot-note ore *and* or[873].

And what was written in *Sh'mote Rabba* (chapter 11): "Yitzkhak said to Moshe: 'I am greater than you in that I offered my neck... and I saw the face of the *Sh'kheena.*' Moshe responded: 'I was raised higher than you, because you saw the face of the *Sh'kheena* and your eyes were dimmed..., but I spoke with the *Sh'kheena* face to face and my eyes were not dimmed'." This is clear to one who understands. And refer to what Rav

---

872 Heb.: *ka-va-naht pa-ra ah-doo-ma.* The ashes of the red heifer (*pa-ra ah-doo-ma*—see *B'midbar* 19) are used to purify from the state of ritual impurity associated with death, caused by powers of judgment. The root of the Hebrew word for heifer is *par,* spelled *pei reish,* with a *g'matria* of two hundred and eighty, the number of powers of judgment. *Ei-fer* (ashes) is written *alef, pei, reish,* the same as *par* with the addition of an initial *alef,* which has a *g'matria* of one. The one is the root of the judgments. Rav Chayyim seems to be saying that the correct use of the ashes re-integrates the two hundred and eighty judgments into their root (the *alef*).

873 *Koot-note ore* is a reference to the garments that God made for Ah-dahm and Cha-va in the Garden of Eden (*B'reisheet* 3:21). *Ore,* written with an initial *ayin,* means skin or leather. Rabbee Mei-eer says (cited in *B'reisheet Rabba* 20:12) that it should be read, rather, that God made for them garments of light (rather than leather)—light is written as *or,* with an *alef* instead of an *ayin.* Rav Chayyim says here that the difference between dirt (*ah-far,* written with an *ayin*) and ashes (*ei-fer,* written with an *alef*) is like the difference between *ore* and *or.* For more details see *Etz Chayyim, sha-ar* 49 (*Sha-ar Kleepaht Noga),* chapters 3 and 4.

Chayyim Vittal (OBM) wrote in *Seifer Ha-gilgulim,* in the commentary on their (OBM) statement (*Sh'mote Rabba* 2): "'Avraham, Avraham' and 'Yaakov, Yaakov', have a *p'sik*[874] between them, and 'Moshe Moshe' does not have a *p'sik* between them", this being about the matter of the tiny separation and obstruction relating to the body, refer there [for more details].

CHAPTER 14

And for that reason Moshe our Teacher (peace be upon him) was prepared at all times for prophecy, as he stated (*B'midbar* 9:8): "Stand here and I will listen…", and as the sages (OBM) stated [*]. And so too he would perceive his prophecy in all places, in any place where he would be, with perfect uniformity, without any variation at all, as they (OBM) stated in *Sh'mote Rabba* (chapter 2) and in *B'midbar Rabba* (chapter 12), and in *Chazeeta* (*siman* 3) on the verse (*Shir Ha-shirrim* 3:10) "its columns He made silver". These are their words: "Why did the Holy One (blessed be He) speak with Moshe from within the bush…? To teach you that there is no unoccupied place in the universe that is not occupied by the *Sh'kheena,* that even within the bush He would speak with him." (This concludes their words.) And this is in accordance with his awesome level.

Annotation: *And this is also one of the reasons why Yaakov Ahveenu (peace be upon him) said "Blessed be the name of the glory of His sovereignty forever and ever"*[875]*, and Moshe*

874 A *p'sik* is one of the *ta-ah-meem* (the trup marks that are an integral part of the Torah's text that inform how to read the text). It denotes a break between words.

875 After hearing the *Sh'ma*

Rabbeinu didn't say that[876]*, as they (OBM) discussed (*P'sakhim 56a*). For the context of the praise "Blessed be the name of the glory of His sovereignty forever and ever" implies that there is a reality to the powers and the worlds, as I wrote previously in chapter 11. And for that reason Yaakov Ahveenu (peace be upon him) stated that, because it is in accordance with his level, as we mentioned previously. In contrast, Moshe Rabbeinu's (peace be upon him) level and grasp, as we explained, is also the core of the matter of the unification of the word "one" of the* Kree-aht Sh'ma, *as was explained there, and for that reason he did not say "Blessed be the name of the glory of His sovereignty forever and ever" when he unified Him (blessed be His name).*

And his soul-*Neffesh* only desired: "Show me, please, Your glory" (*Sh'mote* 33:18)—to comprehend the true nature of this awesome matter, and to visualize how it is that He (blessed be His name) fills the entire universe with His glory, and there is no place that is vacant of Him—this was not given him. And He (blessed be He) responded: "You will not be able to visualize me…, for a human can not visually perceive Me…".

And he continuously grew at this level, until it *was* possible for him[877]—and he merited to experience it prior to his departure from the world to the maximum degree possible for a person to merit while still being in this world—as we found in the *Mishneh Torah*[878] in the paragraph (*D'varim* 11:13) "And it will be so, if you hearken..", that first He stated

---

876 After Moshe Rabbeinu said the *Sh'ma*, he continued immediately into *v'ahavta*

877 Rav Chayyim is saying that Moshe Rabbeinu eventually did succeed in this quest

878 An alternate name for the book of *D'varim*

"to love God-*YHV"H* your God-*Elohi"m...*"[879], and immediately in the following verse he stated in the first person "and I will give you rain in your land...", where he is the giver and actor, for in his own eyes he had annulled himself from having any existence and just the *Sh'kheena* alone is speaking [fem.]. That is why he said "and *I* will give". And this is what they (OBM) stated (*Zohar Pinkhas* 232): "The *Sh'kheena* speaks from within Moshe's throat", and as the verse stated (*B'midbar* 12:8): "Mouth to mouth I speak in him[880]", and it's not written "to him", but rather "in him"—literally within him.

And to this level of perfection, no other person has merited it [fem.] other than he from the time of the First Adam. And also, no other will merit it [fem.], not any person on the earth, until the coming of the Redeemer (speedily in our day), as the holy Torah witnessed (*D'varim* 34:10): "And never has there arisen a prophet again in Israel like Moshe...". (And even though it was stated in past tense, the Torah is eternal and refers also to the time of the future generations, so that after each generation passes from the world we will still be able say that there did not arise in that generation a prophet like Moshe at that level.) And for that reason they stated in *Tahna D'vei Eliyahu* (chapter 25): "A person is required to state: 'when will my actions equal the actions of my ancestors Avraham, Yitzkhak and Yaakov'", and they did not state "to the actions of Moshe Rabbeinu (peace be upon him)"[881].

However, even so, it's worthy for every person who

879 Stated in the second person

880 Heb.: *ah-da-beir bo*

881 Because we are simply unable to reach the level of Moshe Rabbeinu

truly fears/stands-in-awe-of God-*YHV"H*, that in any event, when he prepares to pray, he should, in the purity of his hearts/minds [plu.], according to his ability and grasp, nullify all of the powers in the universe and all of his powers, as if they have no reality in the universe at all, and cause himself to adhere in heart/mind only within Him (may He be blessed), the Sole Master (blessed be He).

In any event, [he should accomplish this level] from time to time. For in truth not all moments are equal regarding the purity of the heart/mind. And specifically in these generations it's nearly impossible to always pray at this high level. And Rabbee Elazar[882] already stated[883]: "I have the ability to exempt the entire world from the judgment of prayer..."[884]. Even so, the worshipper-in-purity who visualizes and gazes always in the purity of his heart/mind regarding all of his matters, that they should be accepted before the Master of All (blessed be His name), can, in any event, from time to time, come to pray at this high level.

And now it's clear what their (OBM) intention was when they stated[885], that one who prays should intend his heart/mind to God-*Ma-kome*. And so too what they (OBM) stated in *Ahvote*[886]: "And when you pray, don't make..., but rather [beg for] compassion and [offer] supplications before the God-*Ma-kome* (blessed be He)." They intended to convey that he should be exceedingly careful about his soul-*Neffesh*; that he shouldn't focus nor aim his prayers (heaven forefend) towards any *s'feera*,

---

882 Rabbee Elazar ben Ah-zarya

883 *Eruvin* 65a

884 Our version of the *Talmud Bavli Eruvin* has a slightly different wording.

885 *Brakhote* 31a

886 *Ahvote* 2:18

even those that were emanated[887]. And not only that, he shouldn't intend towards any *s'feera* or supernal power by itself, for that is a worship to not-a-true-god and a heresy (heaven forefend). But also that it's worthy and correct that he should nullify with his will a complete nullification of all the powers, supernal and terrestrial, and also all his own power, as though they don't exist. (And not only with regards to prayer, but also that his involvement with Torah[888] should be fulfilled by him correctly, also that it should be according to this level, as the matter of their statement (OBM) (*Sota* 21b): "Words of Torah are not sustained except in one who consciously perceives himself as if he doesn't exist".) And he should intend and cause that the purity of his heart/mind in his prayer be adhered only to the God-*Ma-kome* of the Universe, He the universe's Unique One, *Ein Sofe* (blessed be He), who permeates the entire universe and all the worlds, and there is no place vacant of Him.

And refer to the *Ro-kei-ahkh* (OBM) towards the end of *Shoresh Z'kheeraht Ha-shem*, these are his words: "...and when he says 'Blessed are You, God-*YHV"H'*, don't think of the glory that appeared in the heart/mind of the prophets and the image on the throne, but rather about God-*YHV"H*, He being the God-*Elohi"m* in the heavens and in the earth, in the sky and in the sea and in all the universe—that He is the God-*Elohi"m* of the Patriarchs." (This concludes his words.) Understand!

---

887 In the highest world of *Ahtzeeloot*

888 Heb.: *ha-ei-sek ba-Torah*—See the footnote at the very beginning of Gate 4 for a discussion of what "involvement with Torah" means to Rav Chayyim.

Chapters

CHAPTER 1

You, agreeable reader, lo I have guided you (with G-d's assistance) along the paths of truth, to instruct you about the way which you should walk for security. And you'll be able to educate yourself slowly-but-surely about how the levels mentioned previously are arranged, how they are:

- dependent on the purity on your hearts/minds[889], and
- dependent on your ability to grasp more than what is set before you here, and also
- dependent on your current habits.[890]

With your own eyes you'll see that to the extent that you familiarize yourself with each of the levels mentioned previously, the purity in your heart/mind will increase beyond its current level of purity, whether in involvement with Torah, whether in fulfilling the mitzvote, and in fear/awe and love of Him (blessed be He).

However, be very wary and careful that your knowledge shouldn't make you arrogant so that your hearts/minds become haughty as a result of your serving your Creator with purity of thought[891]. At first examination you won't sense the haughtiness arising from this, and you should scrutinize and examine this very carefully.

---

889 Heb.: *tohar l'vavkha*

890 Rav Chayyim warns us here that, as we begin along this path that he has laid out for us, there is a danger of haughtiness, conceit or arrogance arising in our personalities. We must be exquisitely sensitive to the subtlety of their appearance.

891 Heb.: *ta-ha-raht ha-makh-sha-va*—Rav Chayyim here seems to equate purity of the heart/mind with purity of thought. Purity of thought is a state of clear focusing of thought, without distraction, per Rav Chayyim's earlier instructions.

And it's written explicitly: "Every haughty heart/mind is an abomination to G-d/*YHV"H*" (*Mishlei* 16:5), even if the haughtiness is not visible to other people, but only in the thoughts of his own heart/mind, in his own eyes, it is really an abomination before Him (blessed be He), as is known that it is the root and the source of fermentation[892] of all bad character traits.

And they stated (*Sota* 4b) that anyone who is haughty is as if he built a *ba-ma*[893] and the *Sh'kheena* wails over him, and it's as if he shoves away His legs (blessed be He), and complains about him stating: "He and I can't live together as one[894]" (*Sota* 5a) and the mattress will be too short to allow stretching out[895]. Woe to the child who elbows his father out from his father's palace. And they (OBM) went so far even to the extent that they stated there that it is as if he is worshiping idols and is a heretic, and as if he had all of the forbidden sexual relations. And they stated (*P'sakhim* 66b): "Anyone who is haughty, if he is wise, his wisdom departs him".

And anyone who's heart/mind has been sensitized by awe/fear of G-d, the hair on his head will stand on end and his eyes will fill with tears when he considers the source of this teaching that our sages (OBM) taught him, it being from Hillel the Elder, about whom, based their words (see *Shabbat* 31a), it is well known (even famous) the extent of his awesome humility and lowliness. Even so when one time—a happenstance, in a very small degree—he appeared to display something like conceit, based on his very high degree of lowliness of spirit he was immediately

---

892 Heb.: *s'or ba-eesa*

893 A platform used for idol worship

894 Our editions of *Sota* have "He and I can't live together in the world"

895 Isaiah 28:20

punished so that his memory of halakha was no longer accessible. What could we possibly say to emphasize to what degree we must scrutinize and be mindful about this at all times?

CHAPTER 2

Haughtiness can also cause a person, even though he is worshipping Him (blessed be He) with purity of heart/mind, to have a low opinion of another if he observes someone else who doesn't approach the matter of worshipping Him (blessed be He) with pure thought, and who fulfills all that is written in G-d's Torah but without a spiritual connection[896]. And all the more so when he observes some person involved with G-d's Torah, if he should contemplate it not being for its own sake[897]—in that case he would form a much denigrated opinion of him, and this would be a very grave sin—may the Merciful save us!

For the truth of the matter is that the entire matter of purity of heart/mind in the context of worshipping Him (blessed be He) is only an enhancement to the fulfillment of the commandment and not as a pre-requisite, as I wrote previously at the end of Gate 1, and as it will be further explained later (G-d willing). And anyone who fulfills G-d's commandment according to all that was commanded in the holy Torah (both written and oral), even without a spiritual connection[898], is still called a servant of G-d and is beloved by Him (blessed be He).

In the same way, one who is involved with G-d's Torah, even if not for its own sake, even though he is not yet at

896 Heb.: *d'veikoot*

897 Heb.: *lishma*

898 Heb.: *d'veikoot*

a genuinely high level, even so it is absolutely [emphatic] forbidden to denigrate him, even in the heart/mind. And the opposite is true, that all of Israel are required to behave respectfully toward him, as is written (*Mishlei* 3:16): "...at its left side, wealth and respect". And the sages (OBM, *Shabbat* 63a) explained it as "those who make it secondary"[899].

And in *Zohar Va-yeishev* (184b): "'G-d's Torah is perfect...'—How great is the requirement for people to involve themselves with Torah, for anyone who involves himself with Torah will have life.... And even one who involves himself with Torah and doesn't do it for its own sake as it deserves, merits a good reward in this world and they do not judge him in that world. And come and see, it's written: 'Length of days at its right side; at its left side wealth and respect'—he has a good reward and serenity in this world."

Lo, even if a person is involved with His (blessed be He) Torah not for its own sake, but rather for his personal benefit—but only if it does not cause vexation (heaven forefend), about which our sages (OBM) stated (*Yerushalmi B'rakhote* 11a): "it would have been better if the placenta had suffocated him", and they also stated (*Shabbat* 88b): "that it becomes like a fatal poison for him" (heaven forefend)—the Holy One (blessed be He) arranges a good reward for him, for he deserves to receive wealth, honor and peace of mind in this world, and he is not judged negatively in that world regarding the intention of his thought and inclination. And how much more so [this is true] if he didn't intend in any way towards personal benefit, even though his intention was not specifically for

---

899 Heb.: *la-mahs-m'eelim ba*—literally: those who use their left hands for it

its own sake (meaning for Torah's sake), as I will write later in the third chapter of Gate 4 in the name of the Ro"sh (OBM), but rather the main aspect of his involvement with Torah is straightforward, resembling doing it for its own sake. Lo, involvement with Torah is very dear in His (blessed be He) eyes, more so than all of the other commandments performed for their own sakes in holiness and purity of thought, as is fitting[900].

As explained and proven plainly from the *G'mara Ah-ra-khin* (16b): "Rabbee Yehuda the son of Rabbee Shim'on ben Pazi[901] inquired: 'Which of the two is preferable: rebuke for its own sake or humility not for its own sake?' And he said to him: 'Who would not agree that humility for its own sake is [most] preferable? For the master stated that humility is the greatest of them all. Then even when it's not for its own sake it is preferable, because Rabbee Yehuda stated in the name of Rav: "A person should always involve himself with Torah, even when not for its own sake, because from doing it not for its own sake, he will eventually come to doing it for its own sake".'" And thus it tells us that for the case of involvement with Torah, who wouldn't agree that Torah not for its own sake is definitely preferable to commandments performed for their own sake, for we learned an entire *mishna* (*Pei-ah* 1:1): "...and *talmud* Torah is equivalent to them all".

And in the same manner our sages (OBM) differed (*Sota* 21a) regarding the advantage of Torah's relative degree over the commandments, for the merit and

900 Rav Chayyim states clearly here that simple, straightforward involvement with Torah, even if not completely for its own sake, is more dear to G-d that all of the other mitzvote, even if they were performed in the choicest manner.

901 Our editions of *Ah-ra-khin* actually says: *Rabbee Yehuda the son of Rabbee Shim'on.* See the *Sheeta M'koo-beh-tzet* there.

light of the commandments persist both at the time of the involvement with them and when not involved with them; it [fem.] only shields from suffering but does not save a person from coming to sin. In contrast, the light of the Torah, even according to the final decision there, from all perspectives, while he is involved with it, it saves him from sin. And they stated in the Yerushalmi (*Pei-ah* chapter 1) that all the commandments taken together are not equivalent to even one word of the Torah, as will be explained later (G-d willing) in Gate 4 herein.

Thus, even involvement with Torah not for its own sake is still preferable to performing the commandments for their own sake, if only for this reason: that from doing it not for its own sake, he will eventually come to doing it for its own sake.

CHAPTER 3

And also, truthfully, when beginning to establish a study regimen, it's almost impossible to immediately arrive at the level of "for its own sake" as is fitting; "involved with Torah not for its own sake" is the level from which one can arrive at "for its own sake". For that reason it too is beloved of Him (blessed be He), because it is almost impossible to ascend from the ground to the heights if not via the steps of the ladder.

And for that reason they stated (*P'sakhim* 50b): "A person should forever[902] be involved with the Torah and the commandments, even if not for their own sake." They

902 Heb.: *l'olam*

stated "forever" intending to convey "a fixed regimen"[903], meaning that when he is just starting, he isn't required to do more than constantly learn with a fixed regimen[904], day and night.

And even though at times his thoughts will turn to his own benefit, to conceit and honor (or other things like it), even so he shouldn't pay any attention to it, to allow it to cause him to veer from his schedule or to lessen his effort as a result (heaven forefend). Rather, the opposite—he should greatly strengthen his effort towards involvement with the Torah, and he should be absolutely certain that as a result of his effort he will arrive at the level of "for its own sake". And that's also the case regarding the commandments, in this same way.

And one whose mind is filled with thoughts to denigrate and demean (heaven forefend) one who is involved with Torah and commandments even if not for its own sake, will not be cleansed of evil and will be held accountable in the future (heaven forefend). And not only that, but according to the words of our sages (OBM—*b'raita, Rosh Ha-shanna* 17a) he will be counted among those who have no share at

---

903 Heb." *b'kvee-oot.* The central question arises here what Rav Chayyim intended by "a fixed regimen" for someone who is starting on the path of "Torah for its own sake" . Did he intend by this phrase that one should have a study schedule of so-many-hours each day and each night from which one never deviates, or does he intend that one should study literally continuously, from the moment one arises in the morning until one retires to sleep at night? The *Ruakh Ha-chayyim* (2:2) (a compilation of Rav Chayyim's teachings on the *Mishna Ahvote* assembled by his students), describes "a fixed regimen" as being a fixed schedule of spending half of his time, both day and night, studying Torah in the *beit ha-midrash.*

904 Heb.: *b'kvee-oot ta-meed*

all in the world-to-come (heaven forefend), and *Gehinnom* will end but their punishment will not end even then, and they are considered as heretics, informers and apostates. And in the *Mishna* too, at the beginning of *Perek Cheilek*, they counted the apostates among those who don't have a share in the world-to-come. And they state in the *G'mara* there (*Sanhedrin* 99b): "Rav and Rabbee Chaneena both stated: 'This is one who denigrated a Torah scholar'. Rav Yokhanan and Rav Yehoshua Ben Levi stated… that this refers to one who denigrates his fellow in the presence of a Torah scholar…"—he is also "considered an apostate". And even if he says "Of what use are the rabbis? They study Scripture only for their own benefit. They study *Mishna* only for their own benefit", he is in the class of apostates who denigrate Torah scholars, and he is also called one who acts insolently toward the Torah (heaven forefend), and lo, he has lost his share in the world-to-come (may the Merciful save us).

And likewise Rabbeinu Yona (OBM), in *Sha-ar Ha-t'shoova*, listed the levels of severity of punishments. For the final level he listed the group about whom the sages (OBM) stated that they have no share in the world-to-come. And they included in that group those who denigrate a Torah scholar. And Rav Chayyim Vittal (OBM) listed him in the *Sha-ar Ha-k'doosha*, and also included him in that group. And the severity of his awful punishment is because he is among those who darken the light of the holy Torah's high degree, and profaned it (heaven forefend) as Rabbeinu Yona (OBM) described at length there—refer there to the words of the holy one of G-d. (And he (OBM) wrote there that the core of the punishment of all those listed among that group is also only because of the profaning of the holy Torah's honor, may the Merciful save us.)

For because he demeans and denigrates another who is involved with Torah for its own sake, he weakens the other's involvement with Torah, and the other won't ever be able to arrive at the level of "for its own sake", to be a consummate Torah scholar. And this is certainly called "denigrating a Torah scholar", and there is no desecration of Him (blessed be His name) and His holy Torah greater than this. And he demeaned and lowered its glorious splendor to the ground, down to the dirt, and also destroyed all of his own service to G-d (heaven forefend). For his own service to Him (blessed be His name) is not sustained as it should be among the congregation of Israel except via the actions of those Torah scholars who are involved with the Torah day and night. For the eyes of all of Israel are upon them to know what should be done in Israel, to instruct them regarding the path on which they should tread, and how they should behave. That being so, a person who causes Torah scholars to not be found among Israel, has totally destroyed his entire personal service of G-d (blessed be His name), for the congregation of Israel will (heaven forefend) be left without Torah and without an instructor, and they won't know what could make them stumble (heaven forefend). And Rabbeinu Yona (OBM) wrote much the same, refer there [for more details].

For that reason you must be careful in the opposite direction, to honor and to elevate with everything in your power anyone who is involved with and grasps onto God's Torah, even not for its own sake, so that a righteous person will stay his path without weakening from it (heaven forefend), so that he will be able to proceed along it to arrive at the level of "for its own sake".

And so too, even if we should observe that for his entire life—from his youth to old age and extreme old age—his involvement with her was not for its own sake, you are still required to behave with respect towards him, how much more so not to denigrate him (heaven forefend). For as a result of his being involved with G-d's Torah with fixedness, there's no doubt that many times his intention was for its own sake, as the sages (OBM) promised (*P'sakhim* 50a) that from the state of "not for its own sake" one comes to "for its own sake". The meaning of this is not specifically that by that he will come to "for its own sake", so that ever after he will be involved with it, all the rest of his life, only for its own sake. But rather, that any time he learns on a fixed schedule for several consecutive hours, even though, in general, his intention was not for its own sake, even so it's completely impossible that during his learning that it won't enter his heart, at least for a short time, the desired intention of "for its own sake". And at that point, whatever he learned until then "not for its own sake" is sanctified and purified via that short interval during which his intention was "for its own sake".

CHAPTER 4

And a person must exercise extra vigilance in these matters and others like them. And the sages already stated (*Sukka* 52a): "One who is greater than his fellow, his inclinations[905] are also greater", for the evil inclination schemes contrarily in all people, each according to his context and level regarding Torah and service[906]. So if it observes, relative to the high degree of a person's level, that if it attempts to lead him to ruin by getting him to leave his place and level, to go do some iniquity or sin,

905 Heb.: *yitzro*—urges both for good and for evil

906 Heb.: *torah v'ah-vodah*—both in his involvement with Torah, and his performance of mitzvote and prayer

serious or trivial, that he won't give in, then it searches for ways to appear to the person as the good inclination, to blind his intellect, to inject poison, to cause him to err in that exact characteristic and degree itself to which the person is attached, and seeks to show in some way that, at first glance, it is the recommendation of his good inclination, to guide him to an even higher path[*]. It displays in that recommendation aspects and features of purity. And the person quickly falls into its trap, as a bird hurries into a snare without any extended contemplation, and doesn't realize that its life is in danger and that it is descending towards death (heaven forefend).

> **Annotation:** *And the sages (OBM) might have also hinted at this when they stated (*Perek Ha-ro-eh [B'rakhote] *61a): "The evil inclination resembles a fly, and it sits between the two entrances to the heart/mind". For it's known that the abode of the good inclination is in the right cavity of the heart/mind, and the abode of the evil inclination is in the left cavity, as it is stated (*Kohelet *10:2): "A wise person's heart/mind is to the right, while a fool's heart/mind is to the left". And in this they state that the good inclination always remains and recognizes its place to the right; that it never, ever, advises a person other than toward the true good alone. But the evil inclination does not remain within its place that's set aside for it in the left cavity, to entice towards obvious iniquity and sin, but rather it skips away from its place also to the right cavity, to disguise itself as the good inclination leading him towards an increase in holiness, and he doesn't sense that within is hidden a situation of evil and bitterness (heaven forefend).*

For this reason, greatly safeguard your soul-*Neffesh* so that your inclination shouldn't lead you to ruin, saying:

1. "look, the essential thing is you should be involved all your days with purifying your thoughts as they should be; that the attachment of your thoughts to your Creator should be constant, without interruption; nothing should dissuade you to set aside the purity of your thoughts at any time at all"; and
2. that everything will be for heaven's sake when it says to you that the essential requirements of learning Torah and fulfilling commandments are specifically [emphatic] when they are with awesome intention and genuine attachment; and
3. that when a person's heart/mind is not wholeheartedly devoted to do them with holy intention, attachment and purity of thought, it's not considered as fulfilling a commandment nor service at all.

As we learned previously relative to the king who is aged and foolish[907], it aims to blind the eyes, bringing its proofs from scripture, *Mishna, Talmud, midrashim* and the book of *Zohar*, as in the context of "the Merciful One desires the heart/mind[908]" (*Zohar Tei-tzei* 281b), and many others like it—he brings sacks full of proofs.

However, if you should merit to discern the matter using your intelligence in accordance with the Torah, you'll understand and find that this is what it does all the time: presenting to a person that all is kosher[909] as if it is proceeding in holiness, while his legs descend into realms of death, may the Merciful save us!

And now, observe its ways and wise up in this matter too,

---

907 Paraphrasing Kohelet 4:13

908 Aram.: *rakhmana leeba ba-ee*

909 Heb.: *t'la-fahv b'seema-nei tahara*, literally "its hooves having the marks of purity"

how it knows how to obtain evil outcomes using the good. Today it will say to you that without attachment the entire Torah and commandments are nothing, and that you have to prepare your heart/mind, to raise your thoughts to the heights of the purest of the pure before performing any commandment or prayer. And your thoughts will be so burdened with preparing for the commandment before you perform it, that the time designated for the commandment or prayer will pass. And it will present arguments that every prayer or commandment that is performed with awesome intention is holy and pure even if it is not done in its designated time, and that it is valued even more than performing the commandment in its designated time but without intention.

And once your inclination gets you used to fixing in your heart/mind not to be concerned about changing the designated time of one or another commandment or prayer, drawing on your determined thoughts to first purify and empty your heart/mind, over time it will direct you, slowly but surely, with subtle instructions, step by step, and you won't perceive anything, until finally it will be like a permitted act to ignore the designated time for a prayer or commandments. And at the same time you'll empty your heart/mind in vain with worthless things, and it will seduce you completely. Nothing will remain for you—not the performance of a commandment in its designated time, nor even a good thought.

And also, this would result in the destruction of the entire Torah (may the Merciful save us) if (heaven forefend) we yield[910] to lend an ear to its smooth talk on this matter. And introspect on the matter, that if a person

---

910 Heb.: *no-veh*—See the footnote about this word in Gate 1, Chapter 22.

would expend serious effort on the first night of *Pesakh* regarding the intention of eating an olive-sized piece of matza, so that the eating should be in holiness, purity and attachment, and he stretches out the preparation the entire night, until the time of the eating stretches out to after sunrise, or after dawn, the result is that all of his purity of thought is an abomination, and rejected. And one who ate the olive-sized piece of matza in its designated time, even without extra holiness or purity, lo, he fulfilled the positive commandment that's written in the Torah, and a blessing will come upon him. And there are many other situations like this, that if we don't intend to be careful about all of the commandments in their proper periods and designated times, what would be the difference between one who blew the shofar with awesome intention on the first night of *Pesakh,* instead of the commandment of eating an olive-sized amount of matza? Or one who eats the olive-sized amount of matza on *Rosh Ha-shanna.* Or one who fasts on the eve of *Yom Kippur* while on *Yom Kippur* he takes the *lulav* instead of observing the commandment of fasting. And what will be Torah's place?

And not only that, if it doesn't make you fail by causing you to let the designated times pass, it will incline your heart/mind to work on clearing and purifying itself until you won't have enough time to be meticulous that the fulfillment of the commandment be, in all its aspects, according to the law in all of its details, and to be wary of trespassing laws that are well-defined in the *Talmud* and by our great sages (OBM). And don't let your inclination promise you that it can't cause you to ignore doing the details of performance because you involved yourself so much in purifying your thoughts. Know that as long as your thoughts are aligned with its perspective (i.e., that the core of what the Torah asks of a person is that any commandment or study be completely free of any dross or waste material until it's like the finest variety of flour, otherwise it's like trespassing the commandment of not seeing or finding any leaven in your domain on *Pesakh*), it bribes you and blinds your eyes, so that you won't be able to observe all the details of performance, the rules and laws, so that you'll transgress them (heaven forefend), and you won't even perceive doing so.

CHAPTER 5

And so that way, it's clear and understood, is like a fire that consumes all (heaven forefend), and destroys many of the foundations of the holy Torah and the words of our rabbis (OBM). We've already mentioned previously (at the end of Gate 1) that the essential part of all the commandments is the performance; purity of heart/mind is just a supplement to the performance of the commandment, and its lack is not a hindrance to the fulfillment of the commandment (refer there [for more details]). And so too it is understood by any intelligent person on the straight path that it's been established (*Z'vakhim* 2b) in the context of offering a sacrifice, that one offered without a specific intention is considered identical to one having a specific intention. And they plainly confirmed this (*Nazir* 23a) regarding one who eats the Passover sacrifice with the intention of gluttony, that even though his performance is not an especially fine one, he still fulfills the requirement of the Passover. But if, during the designated time for offering the Passover sacrifice and the designated time for eating it, a person should think awesome intentions regarding the matter of the Passover sacrifice via thoughts that are the loftiest of the loftiest and the purest of the pure, but didn't actually offer the Passover sacrifice, that person's soul-*Neffesh* is cut off, and similarly with all the other commandments.

And it's not only in the context of commandments that require a physical action where the essential part is the performance, but also in the case of the commandment of prayer (which is called "service of the heart/mind"). And they (OBM) learned this from the beginning of the first chapter of *Taanit*, from the verse "and to serve Him with all your hearts/minds" (*D'varim* 11:13). Even so[911], the essential part is that a person specifically must pronounce the words with his lips, each word of the prayer liturgy, as our rabbis (OBM) stated (*B'rakhote* 31a) at the beginning of chapter *Ein Ome-din* in the story of Channa where it's written about her (*Shmuel Alef* 1:13): "only her lips moved"—that one who prays should pronounce the words with his lips. And so it is in *Shokheir Tov* (*Shmuel, parsha* 2): "Could he just think them in his mind? It comes to teach us that 'only her lips moved'—How did she do it? She whispered with her lips."

And it's evident that it's not a matter of it teaching the best way to do it for the general case of commandments[912], but rather it's required even after the fact; for if he only thought the words of prayer in his heart/mind, he did not fulfill the obligation of prayer. And if the designated time for that prayer has not yet passed, he must pray a second time, pronouncing each word. And if the designated time has passed, the next time he prays twice[913], as per the rule of one who missed a prayer, as the *Magen Avraham* illumi-

911 Even though the commandment is one that we might think is fulfilled with thought only, it is not so.

912 But that if he didn't do it the best way, he still has fulfilled the commandment

913 He has to pray the *Ahmeeda* twice.

nated (*siman* 101, *s'if kattan* 2) with solid proofs that are adequate to rightly prove that via thoughts of prayer alone he has not fulfilled his obligation.

And it's known in the *Zohar* and the Ariza"l's writings that the context for prayer is the rectification of the worlds[914], and causing the ascension of their inner aspects, all of the qualities of their soul-*Neffesh*, soul-*Ruakh* and soul-*Neshama* that are within them, from below to above. And this is done by attaching and connecting a person's soul-*Neffesh* to his soul-*Ruakh*, and his soul-*Ruakh* to his soul-*Neshama*, as we learned at the end of Gate 2 (refer there). And they are connected by the bending and movement of his lips when he pronounces the words of prayer, which is speech's physical aspect[915], as our rabbis (OBM) stated (*Sanhedrin* 65b): "the bending of the lips[916] is the physical action". And in chapter *Kol Kitvei* (*Shabbat* 119b) they stated: "How do we know that speech is comparable to a physical action? For it's stated…". And this[917] is the aspect of soul-*Neffesh* in speech. And the motion of the air and the sound that is the speech itself is its aspect of soul-*Ruakh*. And the intention of the heart/mind in the words while saying them, that is the aspect of the soul-*Neshama* that's in speech.

For that reason, one doesn't fulfill the obligation of prayer via thinking and mental visualization of the words in the heart/mind alone. For how is it possible to connect to the aspect of soul-*Neshama* if he doesn't proceed according to the order of the levels from lower to upper, that speech's soul-*Neffesh* (which is the movement of the lips) should connect with speech's

---

914 Here Rav Chayyim summarizes the purpose of prayer.

915 Heb.: *b'kheenaht ha-ma-ah-seh b'deeboor*

916 Our editions of *Sanhedrin* use the word that translates as mouth (Heb. *peev*) rather than lips.

917 The physical movement of the mouth

soul-*Ruakh* (which is the breath and the sound of the voice), and afterwards those two would be connected to the soul-*Neshama* (which is the thought and intention in the heart/mind)? And if he should pray in his thoughts alone, his prayer is ineffective and he didn't rectify anything[918]. In contrast, when he prays verbally and pronounces the words alone, even if he didn't partner it with the heart/mind's thought and intention, even though it is certainly not at a high level of perfection, and can't ascend to the world of thought (the world of the soul-*Neshama,* being that it lacked the aspect of human thought), even so it is not for naught (heaven forefend). And done in that way he still fulfills his obligation, because in any event he has caused his soul-*Neffesh* to ascend, connecting his soul-*Neffesh* with his soul-*Ruakh,* and the world of the soul-*Neffesh* with the world of the soul-*Ruakh*[919].

Refer to *Zohar P'koodei* (262b): "...that prayer requires thought and the heart/mind's will, and vocalization, and words pronounced by the lips, to create a wholeness, connection and unification above, just as it is above... to connect the connection as it is supposed to be... . Thought, will, vocalization and speech are the four that create the connection. And after all of them are connected as one, they become one Vehicle[920] upon which the *Sh'kheena* can

---

918 Rav Khayyim again states that the purpose of prayer is to effect rectification.

919 Rav Khayyim states that connection of the worlds of *Neffesh* and *Ruakh* by simply verbalizing the prayers, even without thought or intention, though not ideal, still fulfills the basic requirements of prayer. And especially note that he states that by connecting our soul-*Neffesh* to our soul-*Ruakh* we cause the world of the soul-*Neffesh* to connect to the world of the soul-*Ruakh.*

920 Heb.: *mer-ka-va*

settle... . And the vocalization that is heard ascends to create connections from below to above... ." Refer there carefully [for more details].

And in *parshat B'midbar* (120b) they stated in a general way[921] that the primary aspect of prayer[922] depends initially on the actions that a person does, and then only afterwards on the specific words that he says (refer there as to the procedure).

And in *Idra Zoota* (294b): "Whatever a person thinks, and whatever a person contemplates in his heart/mind, has no effect until it is emitted from his lips..., and as a result any prayer or petition..., he must express them with his lips, because if he does not express them, his prayer is not considered a prayer, and his petition is not considered a petition. And once the words get expressed they split apart in the air and ascend..., and the one who takes them does so, and unifies them for the holy crown."

And as a general case they stated in *Zohar Emor* (105a): "Anyone who says that no action is required, nor to express words vocally, may their soul-*Ruakh* explode[923]" (may the Merciful save us). And our sages (OBM) didn't require intention in order to fulfill the obligation[924] other than for *Birkaht Ahvote*[925].

And in *parshat Va-y'khee* (243b, near the end): "One whose heart/mind is pre-occupied and wants to pray his prayer, or who is afflicted and can't properly arrange praises for his Master, say to him that even though he can't

---

921 Rav Chayyim here paraphrases *Zohar B'midbar* 120b.

922 The primary aspect being the process of *tikkoon ha-o-lamote* (rectification of the worlds)

923 Aram.: *teepahkh rookhei*

924 Of prayer

925 The opening blessing of the *Ahmeeda*.

summon intention for his heart/mind and will, why should he diminish the procedure of praising his Master? Rather he should follow the procedure of praising his Master even though he is unable to summon intention... ."

CHAPTER 6

And though it's certain that a person's thought is what ascends way above to the heights of heaven in the supernal worlds, and that if a person should include purity of thought and intention during the performance of the commandments then his actions will effect greater rectifications in the more supernal of the worlds, even so we do not consider the thought as central, as was explained.

Refer to *Zohar Yitro* (93b, top): "If he should have the opportunity to do an action, and has intention regarding it, he is considered worthy. But even if he didn't have intention he is considered worthy because he fulfills his Master's commandment, but he is not considered as one who performs His Will for its own sake and has the intention of will..., he is as one who is unaware..., for it is dependent on will[926]... . And along with this, if there is no will of the heart/mind[927]..., regarding this Dovid prayed and said 'our handiwork, may He establish for us... .' What is 'may He establish for us'? Establish and rectify rectifications above as should be. 'For us'—even though we are unaware of how to employ will, rather [we are aware of our] actions alone. 'Our handiwork, may he establish'—for whom? For the specific level for which rectification is necessary... ." Refer there [for more details].

And similarly in the matter that was explained above in Gate 3 regarding prayer, we should intend it to the world's

926 Intention
927 Intention

Ma-kome (blessed be His name), as was explained there regarding the matter of the world's place[928], refer there [for more details].

And similarly, the matter of the intention of "one[929]" in the first verse of the reading of the *Sh'ma* that was explained in chapter 11—refer there carefully—it's all for enhancement of the commandment and its lack doesn't block the fulfillment. For even in the case of someone who is:

1. completely unaware of this, because he's not used to it, or
2. for one whose mind can't tolerate it because he didn't get to the bottom of it, or
3. who fears for his life that he shouldn't endanger himself (heaven forefend) by destroying some of the fundamentals of Torah (as could happen if he—heaven forefend—is someone who's mind is inadequately prepared), as is stated there (refer there [for more details]),

but rather he:

1. worships Him (blessed be He),
2. and fulfills all that is written in G-d's Torah, written and oral, and according to our great sages, and
3. believes and intends in a general way during the first verse of the *Sh'ma* that He (blessed be He) is one, even if he doesn't understand the matter of His (blessed be He) oneness, and
4. intends toward Him during his prayer in a general way, without extensive research,

928 Heb.: *m'komo shel o-lahm*

929 Heb.: *eh-khahd*

he too is called a worshipper of G-d (as is stated in the *Pardes*[930], *Sha-ar* 1, *Perek* 9, in the matter of belief in the existence of the *S'feerote*, refer there). For none of these things[931] are mentioned except in regards to one who's mind is prepared, and moreover to those who stand in fear/awe of G-d and who contemplate His name, for they have the power to engage in this way.

For this reason, be it far from us to reject any part of the details of performance, even one minute detail from the teachings of the Scribes[932], and similarly to change the time of its performance (heaven forefend) due to absence of pure thought. And anyone who increases the precision of his performance is worthy of praise.

CHAPTER 7

Furthermore, your [evil] inclination could camouflage itself by saying to you that the essential aspect of worship is that it should be only for heaven's sake, and also that a transgression and a sin will be considered a commandment if it is done for heaven's sake, for the rectification of some matter—citing "the Merciful desires the heart/mind"[933] (*Sanhedrin* 106b), and "a sin for its own sake is greater" (*Nazir* 23b, *Ho-ra-yote* 10b), and many other proofs like that. It will also try to convince you by saying that you were commanded thusly, to walk in the footsteps of your holy ancestors and all the early pious ones who lived before the Torah was given, all of whose actions, speech and thoughts, and all their interactions in the world were with attachment, and the purity of their thoughts

930 Rabbi Moshe Cordovero's *Pardes Rimonim*

931 Regarding the benefit of having intention

932 Heb.: *deek-dook eh-khahd mi-deevrei sofe-rim*

933 Our editions of *Sanhedrin* have "the Holy One (blessed be He) desires the heart/mind" (*ha-KB"H leeba ba-ee*)

was for the sake of Heaven. And they faced upwards to cause the worlds and supernal power to be rectified, to ascend and be unified, in every situation that occurred, and in every way and in every moment, and not via actions and commandments that are permanent and designed to be immutable law, as exhibited in the case of our patriarch Yaakov (OBM) in the situation of Lavan and the sticks[934]. And so said the Maggid[935] to the Beit Yosef[936] regarding Cha-nokh, that he was stitching shoes, and with every stitch of the needle he praised the Holy One (blessed be He)—refer to the *Ma-geed Meisharim, parshat Meekeitz*.

And though our sages (OBM) stated that the Patriarchs fulfilled the entire Torah[937], and similarly they stated in *Va-yikra Rabba* (chapter 2[938]) deriving that Noakh learned Torah, it's not that they were commanded and then responded, and that they had the specific Halakha and the prescribed law[939]. Rather it's as I wrote previously at the end of Gate 1 (chapter 21), that they fulfilled the Torah as a result of their grasping via their wondrous understanding of how the worlds are rectified, and [also] the arrangement of the supernal powers that are rectified with each and every commandment. However they were also given permission to worship Him even using other actions and situations beside the commandments. And they could even transgress a specific commandment, not doing per the Torah's prescribed actions, according to

934 *B'reisheet* 30:25—43

935 The spiritual being who taught Rav Yosef Karo, and whose teachings are recorded in the book *Ma-geed Meisharim.*

936 Rav Yosef Karo was the author of both the *Beit Yosef* commentary on the *Toor,* and the *Shoolkhan Ahrookh.*

937 See RaSh"Y on *B'reisheet* 26:5, Yuma 28b and *Kiddushin* 82a

938 See *Va-yikra Rabba, parsha* 2, *siman* 10

939 Heb.: *ha-halakha v'ha-din*

their own perception and grasp that this situation and specific behavior was necessary then to rectify the worlds. (And on this matter refer to the book *Sefer Ha-eh-moonote* by Rav Sheim Tov, and similarly he cited there in the name of Rabbeinu Chooshiel Gaon (OBM), only that he greatly condensed his account in accordance with the Rishonim's (OBM) manner in matters of holiness, that they greatly concealed and hid these matters.

And if your senses are intelligent, you'll perceive neither a proof nor a supporting source here in any way, not even the amount of support that a slender reed could provide. For the clear truth is as was explained previously at the end of Gate 1, that worship in this way was allowed only before the giving of the Torah. However, from the moment that Moshe came and brought it down to the Earth, "it is not in the heavens". And we provided proof there (with G-d's help) from the context of Chizkiyahu with Yeshayahu, that it is forbidden for us to change (heaven forefend) anything of one of G-d's commandments, even if the intention is for heaven's sake. And even if a person should grasp that destruction will result if he should fulfill one of the commandments that is incumbent upon him, even in the case of passively not acting, even so, it is not within his range of choice to desist from it (heaven forefend), because the reasons for the commandments have not been revealed; refer there at length [for more details].

CHAPTER 8

And it can also seduce you with sacks full of proofs that:

- the essential aspect of a person's service is to attain awe/fear of the majesty; and
- that his eyes and heart/mind should focus exclusively upon this during his entire life; and
- that fear of both punishment and shame before

other people is a characteristic that is the worst of the worst; and

- that it's worthwhile to uproot it from your heart/mind.

Your inclination will encourage[940] you to heap fear/awe upon fear/awe relative to the majesty, until you'll fix in your heart/mind that fear of both punishment and shame before other *people* is a transgression, and you'll flee from it as one who flees from a transgression, until it could happen that you will be trapped in its net and not keep away from what is prohibited so long as you don't have adequate fear/awe of the majesty.

And you'll make light of everything, because it will show you perspectives among the many perspectives relating to this. And you might end up in the situation that if a person reproves you and shows you that you are transgressing a specific law, your heart/mind will lead you to not stop doing it as long as you're vividly experiencing the fear of the one who reproved you, for you'll say that there's no fear/awe of G-d in it but only fear of a person, an extraneous fear.

And our sages (OBM) already taught us in the case of Rabbee Yokhanan's blessing of his students (*B'rakhote* 28b): "...that the fear/awe of heaven should be upon you similar to the fear of flesh and blood...". And who among us is as great and as pious as Rav Amram Chasida, and even so when the opportunity to sin sprang upon him (may the Merciful save us), as recounted towards the end of *Kidooshin* (81a), he battled strategically so as to be saved from his inclination's traps, even at the expense of shame before others, only that he not transgress (heaven forefend) his Creator's (blessed be His name) commandments. And it also appears that even though the Holy

940 Heb.: *ya-nee-akh l'kha yitz-r'kha*

One (blessed be He) is careful about not dishonoring the pious, even so, this account was included in the *Talmud* to teach us G-d's straight paths.

So now I've shown you a few of the ways that the inclination camouflages itself strategically, as the sages (OBM) stated (*Kiddushin* 30b): "A person's inclination is renewed each day, for it's stated (*B'reisheet* 6:5) 'exclusively evil all day long'." It's not enough that it dominated the person by plotting strategically the day before yesterday; rather, it continues to plot anew each day. And it's seems as if it is not seducing him towards evil in any way. Rather, the opposite—it shows the person that whatever he learned in Torah or fulfilled commandments, not a bit of good was in them yet, and he's been exclusively evil all day long. In this way it dominates the person, as the sages (OBM) stated (*Sukka* 52b) on the verse "The wicked one waits for the righteous and seeks to kill him..." (*T'hillim* 37:32)—"he" being the evil inclination; he is the angel of death, full of eyes, and he waits to see what will be the result, how to cause him to fail, (for the context of "waiting" is about something that will come to be in the future), until a person will no longer know to be careful.

And you, the reader, don't imagine that I am making this up, for I have examined and tested all of this, as I focused my heart/mind to explain and research. And my eyes have observed many who desire G-d's nearness, and they fail in these very matters we just mentioned, as they sincerely expressed to me in their own words. With my own eyes I observed in one place some people who over a long period of time so habituated until they all but forgot the correct time that our sages (OBM) set for praying *Minkha*. Rather, the opposite became the practice, that out of long habit they fixed in their heart/minds as a statute and law—that the essential requirement of the *Minkha* prayer is to do it after the stars appear. And when a person says to his associate "let's pray *Minkha*", he responds "let's observe and carefully confirm if the stars are already visible in the sky". And may G-d forgive them, and provide atonement for the mistaken and the simpleton.

You should attend to the knowledge of the wise, masters of Torah, as our sages (OBM) have previously taught us, that the essential part is the performance of the commandment in its correct time with all of its specifics and details, as immutable law. Join the purity of proper thought to the action, and then you'll proceed securely, and you will use your ability to fulfill both. And they taught a plainly understood teaching (*Ahvote* 3:9) that anyone whose actions are more numerous than their wisdom[941], even their wisdom will exist in a state of holiness, purity and attachment. And is it an insignificant matter that that our sages (OBM) stated that one whose actions are more numerous than his wisdom is likened to a tree whose branches are few but whose roots are numerous, that all the winds in the world are unable to dislodge it from its place? And the one who hears will hear.

941 Presumably referring to those who fulfill the commandments, even if they lack a deep understanding of their rationale and their role in the framework of rectification

GATE 4

CHAPTER 1

Additionally, I desired to include the following in the range of the book's contents:

1. the tremendous obligation of involvement with Torah[942] that's incumbent upon each person of Israel day and night, and
2. to expand a bit in words about the greatness of:
   a. the Torah's splendorous honor and high degree[943]; and of
   b. the righteous person who is involved with and attends deeply[944] to it [fem.][945], the Torah of compassion being on his tongue so as to gratify his Former and Creator (blessed be His name); and of
   c. the person of knowledge who expends effort to support it [fem.], and nourish it [fem.] and to reinforce its [fem.] condition, even after so long for Israel, during which the involvement with the holy Torah was denigrated in each successive generation.

And lo, now, in these generations, due to our many sins, it has fallen very far. It is cast in the hidden recesses of the lowest levels (may the Merciful save us), as we see

942 Heb.: *ei-sek ha-Torah.* I translate this as "involvement with Torah", implying that there is an active and intentional element, rather than it being incidental. Rav Chayyim, as it will be seen in this Gate, understands "involvement with Torah" to be constant active engagement with the Torah's actual words and ideas, and not the performance of *mitzvote,* peripheral involvement with Torah, Jewish life in general, or other activities that promote Jewish life.

943 Heb.: *g'doolaht y'kar tif-ahr-ta u-ma-ah-la-ta shel Torah*

944 Heb.: *v'ho-geh*

945 With "her" being the Torah

now for the majority of our nation, as a result of the great difficulty of bearing the burden of earning a living, may God-*YHV"H* have mercy.

And also some of those who desire to come close to God-*Elohi"m*[946], they [emphatic] chose for themselves to make their steady practice, the core of their studies, books that cultivate awe/fear and teach ethical guidance[947] all their days, without making a steady practice—the core of their involvement—with our holy Torah, in scripture and myriad laws[948]. And in their entire lives they have not yet

---

946 Heb.: *kirvaht elohi"m yakh-p'tzoon* (*Y'shaya* 58:2). This verse is used in the context of people who may be sincere about growing close to God but who take the wrong path. By using this verse, Rav Chayyim may be establishing a context in which a desire to approach and grow close to a just God requires truly understanding and integrating into ourselves the foundations of justice, which are the written Torah and the laws that are derived from it.

947 Heb.: *sifrei yir-ah u-moo-sar*

948 Heb.: *b'mikra-ote va-ha-la-khote m'roo-bote.* Rav Chayyim begins here to define what he considers to be the key features of involvement with Torah (*ei-sek ha-Torah*). He seems to take as a given that involvement with Torah primarily means the learning of texts, and then putting what's learned into practice.

His central focus here is the definition of what constitutes Torah. He specifically uses two words: *mikra-ote* and *ha-la-khote. Mikra* usually refers to the *Choomahsh* (the five books of Moses), but often includes the entire written Torah. *Ha-la-kha* usually refers to the texts that derive the Torah's laws from the *Mikra* or other sources; this is usually taken to be the oral Torah, which is *Sha"s* (*Mishna* and *G'mara*) and *Po-skim* (rabbinic responsa).

Also refer to *N'khemya* 8:8, where *mikra* means reading from a book (there specifically the *Choomahsh*) and *Bava Batra, perek* 1 (*yikh-n'soo*) and *perek* 8 (*kahtahn b'koolahm rabban yokhanan ben zakai, amroo ahlahv…*).

seen the sources of light in the heavens[949], and the light of Torah[950] has not touched upon them (may God forgive them, for their intention is towards heaven), but this is not the path by which the light of Torah will dwell within them.

And the truth is that books that cultivate awe/fear are like all the righteous ways of God, for the earlier generations had made a steady practice, all their days, of involvement with and rational consideration of our holy Torah, engrossed in the study tents of *G'mara*, RaSh"Y's commentary and *Tosafote*. The flame of the love of our holy Torah burned in their heart/minds like a burning fire, in a pure love and awe/fear of God-*YHV"H*. Their whole desire was to increase its [fem.] honor and make it mighty. And they expanded their range via many proper students so that the earth would be filled with knowledge.

And as the ages passed, it being the manner of the [evil] inclination, from of old, to be envious of God's nation when they [emphatic] are treading on the path of God in the way it deserves, it injected poison into them, causing some of the students to focus all of their regular practice and involvement only in hair-splitting intellectualism[951] and nothing else but that[952]. And we learned in our *Mishna*[953]: "If there's no awe/fear, there's no wisdom", and there are many other statements of our sages (OBM) like this, as we'll bring in chapter 4, G-d willing. For that reason, some of their great ones, the eyes of the commu-

---

949 Heb.: *m'oh-rote*, this being the word that is used for the Sun and the Moon and the stars in the sky. Literally, "the illuminators".

950 The light of Torah is mentioned many times in this Gate. See footnote 91 in Gate 1, Chapter 2.

951 Heb.: *pil-pool*

952 Lacking the quality of awe/fear (*yir-ah*).

953 *Mishna Ahvote* 3:21

nity—those whose path in holiness was to be assiduous in correcting the collective of our siblings, the house of Israel—awakened themselves to remove the obstacles and seal the breeches, to lift the barrier from the path of God's nation. They occupied themselves with rebukes and ethical guidance and character traits, and they authored books of awe/fear to straighten out the nation's heart/mind so that they would be involved in the holy Torah and in worship with a pure awe/fear of God.

However every intelligent person whose intellect operates honestly will understand on his own that they didn't intend therewith to cause the involvement with the main body of Torah to be abandoned (heaven forefend), and to be involved solely, all the time, with their books of ethical guidance. Rather their intention was that the holy nation's primary steady practice of learning would be only the holy Torah, written and oral, and myriad laws, them [emphatic] being the essentials of Torah, but accompanied by a pure awe/fear of God.

And so it came to be in these generations, because of our many sins, it became inverted. What was high was caused to fall, and some put the primary steady practice of their learning for most of their days only in books of fear/awe and ethical guidance, asserting that the whole purpose of man in his world is to always be involved with them, because they ignite the heart/minds, that then his heart/mind will submit and cause the [evil] inclination to surrender and subdue its desires, and become righteous via good character traits. And the Torah's crown was set down in the corner. And with my own eyes I've seen in one province, that so much has this spread for them, until in most of their study halls there's nothing in them but a vast number of books of ethical guidance, and it doesn't have even one complete set of *Sha"s*. And their eyes are prevented from seeing[954], their heart/minds from understanding and intellectually knowing, that this is not the path that God chose, that it will not be accepted. And in a little while, as time passes, it could happen (heaven forefend) that they will be without a teacher[955]. And Torah—what will become of it?

And so, for this reason, whoever is capable with words should stop others, and tell the loyal tribes of Israel, those who awe/fear God-*YHV"H* and who contemplate His name, about the path on which they can walk towards the light of Torah. Woe is us on the Day of Judgment. Woe is us on the day of rebuke because of the transgression of disruption of Torah[956], when He (blessed be His name) becomes zealous for it [fem.] to demand satisfaction for its [fem.] insult.

And first, I'll focus my words[957] on the matter of involvement with Torah for its own sake[958]—what "for its own sake" means—for this too is connected to a horrible misunderstanding[959], for there are some who halt themselves from involvement with the holy Torah because they think that the definition of the matter of "for its own sake" is "with a great attachment[960], without interruption".

And there's an evil even more pathological than this: in their thoughts they hypothesize that involvement with

---

954 Ref: *Y'shaya* 44:18

955 Heb.: *l'lo ko-hein mo-reh,* literally: "without a priest teacher"

956 Heb.: *bee-too-la shel Torah*

957 Heb.: *ah-seem divrahtee.* Ref.: *Eeyove* 5:8.

958 Heb.: *Torah lishma.* Literally "Torah for the name [fem.]" or "Torah for its name [fem.]". We translate it as "Torah for its own sake". *Torah lishma* is the primary theme of Gate 4.

959 Heb.: *pree cha-taht,* ref: *Meekha* 6:7: *pree vitnee, cha-taht nahfshee,* denoting the horribly mistaken idea that the sacrifice of a child could atone for a transgression

960 Heb.: *b'd'veikoot ga-dole*

Torah without attachment amounts to nothing, and has no benefit (heaven forefend). And for that reason, when they observe that their heart/mind doesn't arrive at the level where their learning would be with a constant attachment, they don't even start to learn, and the result of this would be that the Torah will fade away (heaven forefend).

And as the matter progresses, it will be explained (G-d willing) therefore, the high degree of the holy Torah and of the person who is involved with it [fem.] as it deserves.

To this end, there is a necessity to cite a few of our rabbi's (OBM) statements in the *Sha"s* and *midrashim* and *Zohar*, for in them are discussed the wonders of the holy Torah's high degree and of he who is involved with it, and the magnitude of its reward and punishment (may the Merciful save us). Even though all of those statements are well known and famous, even so I gathered them together to impassion the heart/minds of those who desire to motivate themselves to be attached[961] to the love of His (blessed be He) Torah, and to motivate themselves to rest[962] in her awesomely supernal shadow.

CHAPTER 2

The matter of involvement with Torah for its own sake—The clear truth, is that "for its own sake" does not mean "attachment" as most of the world today hypothesizes. For our rabbis (OBM) stated in the *midrash* (*Shokheir Tov*) that King Dovid requested of Him (may He be blessed) that one who is involved with *T'hillim* should be considered by Him as if he was involved in [the laws of] skin lesions and

961 Heb.: *l'hit-da-beik*
962 Heb.: *l'hit-lo-nein*

habitations[963], because the involvement in the legal discussions of the *Sha"s* with depth and effort is a matter much more sublime and beloved before Him (blessed be He) than the recitation of *T'hillim.*

And if we should say that the definition of "for its own sake" is specifically "attachment", and on this only hangs the entire matter of involvement with Torah, surely there is no more wonderful attachment than the recitation of *T'hillim* all day long.

And also, who knows whether the Holy One (blessed be He) agreed with him regarding this, for we haven't found in their (OBM) words what response He (blessed be He) gave him to his request (as we found in *Bava Batra* 17a: "the other explains this to mean that he is praying for mercy").

And also, for the matter of attachment it should be sufficient with one tractate or chapter, or one *mishna*—that he should be involved just with it for his entire life, with attachment. And we didn't find that our rabbis (OBM) agreed, for they stated (*Sukka* 28a) about Rabbee Yokhanan ben Za-kai that "he never stopped learning scripture, *mishna*..., discussions of oral law and midrashic sources...[964]", and this is specifically because he constantly kept them from leaving his heart/mind, for even at that point he hadn't completed his obligation of involvement with Torah for its own sake via what he learned until then, and for that reason he was diligent all his days to add lessons constantly, from day to day and from hour to hour.

And in *Mishlei Rabbta,* chapter 10: "Rabbee Yishmael stated: 'Observe how trying the Day of Judgment is, for in the future the Holy One (blessed be He) will judge the

---

963 Heb.: *n'ga-im v'aw-haw-lote*

964 Heb.: *mikra, mishna, ha-la-khote v'ah-ga-dote*

entire world..., one who comes and who has *mikra* at hand but doesn't have *mishna* at hand, the Holy One (blessed be He) turns His face away from him and the jailers of *Gehinnom* overcome him..., and they take him and cast him into *Gehinnom*. One who comes and has at hand two or three *sidras*[965], the Holy One (blessed be He) says to him: 'My child, why didn't you learn all the legal discussions?' One who has the legal discussions at hand comes before Him, He says to him: 'The law of the *Kohanim*, why didn't you learn that, for there is within it...'. One who has the law of the *Kohanim* at hand, the Holy One (blessed be He) says to him: 'My child, why didn't you learn the five books of Torah, for within them are the reading of the *Sh'ma*, *t'fillin* and *m'zooza*?' One who has the five books of Torah at hand comes, the Holy One (blessed be He) says to him: 'Why didn't you learn the midrashic stories[966]...?' One who has the midrashic stories at hand comes, the Holy One (blessed be He) says to him: 'Why didn't you learn the derivations of the oral law[967]...? One who has the derivations of the oral law at hand comes, the Holy One (blessed be He) says to him: 'You availed and involved yourself with the derivations of the oral law; did you delve into the Vehicle[968]...? My throne of glory—describe its structure..., *khashmal*—describe its structure, and in how many directions does it turn itself..."—refer there at length [for more details].

And we can hypothesize also in this way, that after all, how many myriad of legal requirements are in the *Sha"s*, that during the moment that a person is involved with them,

965 A *sidra* is one of the six parts of the *Mishna*.

966 Heb.: *ha-ga-da*

967 Heb.: *talmood*

968 Heb.: *tzee-pee-ta ba-mehr-ka-va*

he must concentrate and delve his thoughts and rational mind into their physical aspects, for example details of specific sacrificial offerings and the timing details of the menstrual cycle[969], for they [emphatic] are the main body of law. Or the negotiation process to determine the law in the *Sha"s*, and the principle of awarding a judgment when a cheater could have presented a patently winning claim and didn't[970]. And it's almost impossible that he would also have, then, perfect attachment as it deserves.

CHAPTER 3

But the truth is that the matter of "for its own sake" means for the sake of the Torah. And the matter is as the Ro"sh[971] (OBM) explained on the statement by Rabbee Elazar b'rebbee Tza-doke (*N'darim* 62a): "'Do things for the sake of their Maker'—For the Holy One's (blessed be He) name, who did all of it for His own sake. 'And discuss them for their own sake'—All of your discussions and give and take about the words of Torah should be for the Torah's sake, for example to know and to understand, to increase even more the lessons learned, and to make the effort to have an even deeper understanding, and not to provoke others, nor for egotistical reasons." This concludes his words.

He carefully explained Rabbee Elazar b'rebbee Tza-doke's variation in language—that regarding action he said "for the sake of their Maker", while for speech he said "for their own sake". For that reason in the context of action he explained "for the sake of the Holy One's

969 Heb.: *kee-neen oo-pit-khei needa*

970 Heb.: *meego shel ra-ma-oot*

971 The Ro"sh is Rabbi Asher ben Y'khiel, the author of the *Toor*.

(blessed be He) name, who did it all for His own sake"; while in the context of study[972] he explained "for the sake of the Torah...".

And his (OBM) intention is clear, specifically, that the performance of the commandment must certainly be as fulfillment of the commandment to the highest possible degree of perfection, with attachment and the purest of the pure of thought, according to his intellect and ability, so that the praise ascends to cause the rectification of the worlds and the powers and the supernal structures. This is what "for the sake of their Maker" means, for "all of God's-*YHV"H* actions are for His sake" (*Mishlei* 16:4). And the sages (OBM) stated: "as praise for Him[973]".[974]

And even if it's certain that regarding commandments too, the primary requirement for them is the act of doing, and the additional intention and purity of thought is not required for fulfilling [the commandment] in any way, as was explained above at the end of Gate 1 with certainty (with God's help), even so, he should join holiness and purity of thought to the primary act of doing, to arouse and cause even greater rectifications in the worlds than there would have been if the commandment was performed without attachment and holiness of thought.

But regarding a person's behavior at the moment of his involvement with Torah addressing the laws of the

972 He interprets "discussion" as the context of study

973 Heb.: *l'kee-loo-so*

974 The performance of the *mitzvote* should be done with the highest possible perfection and attachment (*d'veikoot*). The effect is to cause the greatest possible rectification of the worlds. Involvement with Torah perhaps has another purpose.

commandments and their associated rules, he stated: "and discuss them", meaning to teach us that the discussion of the matters of the commandments and their associated rules should be for their sake, meaning for the sake of the words of Torah—specifically to know and understand and to increase even more the lessons learned and to make the effort to have an even deeper understanding[975].

(And RaSh"Y (OBM) had another interpretation there: "and discuss them for the sake of heaven". For that reason he explained that your entire intention should be toward heaven. However, the context and explanation of "for its own sake" that the sages (OBM) stated in many places, certainly RaSh"Y (OBM) too would explain per the Ro"sh's (OBM) explanation here, according to his interpretation. And RaSh"Y (OBM) too here, his intention is not attachment, rather it comes to exclude [specific purposes]: that his learning shouldn't be to provoke [others] or for egotistical reasons, as the Ro"sh (OBM) wrote, and as is confirmed by the conclusion of the words of Rabbee Elazar b'rebbee Tzadoke: "Do not make them a crown to glorify yourself therewith".)

And what the *Sha"s* concludes regarding Rabbee Yokhanan ben Zakkai, that he never set it down... was to fulfill what is stated (*Mishlei* 8:21): "I have what to bequeath to those who love Me...", that the matter is explained there in that entire section, which is the holy Torah's own statement that should be sung out publicly[976]: that it has within its ability to bequeath and to offer a goodly reward

975 And not with any special attention to attachment. At this point in Rav Chayyim's discussion, it's not clear whether involvement with Torah for its own sake does or does not cause rectification of the worlds.

976 Ref.: *Mishlei* 1:20

to all who think about it and involve themselves with it [fem.] based on their actual love for it [fem.], namely to increase even more the lessons learned, and specifically to make the effort to have an even deeper understanding. And that is what "to those who love Me" means.

CHAPTER 4

However, it's certain that it's impossible to say that the matter of involvement with Torah does not require any purity of thought and fear/awe of God (heaven forbid), for after all, we learned an entire *mishna*: "If there's no fear/awe, there's no wisdom". And they stated (*Yoma* 72b): "Why is it written (*Mishlei* 17:16): 'Why is there money in the hands of a fool to purchase wisdom, though he lacks a heart'? Woe to them, Torah scholars[977], who involve themselves with Torah but don't have within them fear/awe of heaven." And in *Sh'mote Rabba* (chapter 40): "Anyone who knows but hasn't achieved fear of sin hasn't achieved anything, for the integration of Torah occurs by way of fear of sin."

And in the introduction to the *Zohar* (11b), Rabbee Shim'on bar Yo-khai stated that fear/awe is the gateway to enter faith, and the entire world is preserved by this commandment..., and this is the essence of and the foundation for all the rest of the commandments in the Torah: one who keeps fear/awe is as if he keeps everything, and if he does not keep fear/awe, he doesn't keep the Torah's commandments..."—refer there [for more details].

And in *parshat B'har* (108a): "What is the 'yoke of heaven' other than being like the ox... . So too must a

977 Heb.: *tal-mee-dei cha-kha-meem,* lit.: "students of the wise" (students of the sages)

person first accept upon himself a yoke and afterwards employ it as much as he needs. And if he doesn't first accept the yoke upon him, he can't work. And this is what they stated: 'Serve God in fear/awe.' What is 'in fear/awe'? It's as is written: 'The beginning of wisdom is fear/awe of God...', and for that reason it is the beginning of everything..., because with this he can enter into the rest of holiness, and if this is not present with him, the supernal holiness does not settle within him... ."

And furthermore they stated (*Ahvote* 3:11): "Anyone whose fear/awe precedes his wisdom, his wisdom is preserved", for fear/awe of God comes first; it is the essence of the preservation of the wisdom of Torah. And as our rabbis (OBM) stated (*Shabbat* 31a): "Reish La-keesh stated: Why is it written (*Y'shaya* 33:6): 'faithfulness to your charge...'? 'Faithfulness'—this is *Seder Z'ra-im*...[978]." In this verse is the entire *Sha"s*, and even so it concludes "fear/awe is his storehouse." The text likened the Torah to a vast amount of grain, and fear/awe to the storehouse that holds within it a massive amount of grain that are guarded within it. For fear/awe of God is the storehouse for the wisdom of the holy Torah, that by its agency it is preserved in that person's domain. And if he didn't first prepare for himself a storehouse of fear/awe, then the vast amounts of the grain of Torah are as if left in the field to be trampled by the legs of the ox and the donkey (heaven forefend), so that is not preserved in his domain at all.

And in the same vein they stated about this text (in *Sh'mote Rabba* 30): "You find a person learning *midrash ha-la-khote* and *ah-ga-dote*, and if he doesn't have within him fear/awe of sin, he has achieved nothing. This is likened

978 This verse ends "fear/awe of God is her storehouse". This verse is read as referring to the six *s'darim* of the *Mishna*.

to a person..., 'I have a thousand measures of grain'. Someone said to him: 'Do you have secure places to store them in?', as is stated: 'faithfulness to your charge...'." Refer there [for more details].

CHAPTER 5

And based on the size of the storehouse of fear/awe that a person has prepared for himself, so too according to that measure will be able to enter inside of him, and to be safeguarded within him, and to be preserved within him, the grain of the Torah, based on how much his storehouse can hold.

For the father who gives out shares of grain to his children, he gives each one a measure of grain based on the capacity of the storehouse the child has prepared beforehand for this purpose. For even if the father should desire and is ready to give him a lot, if however the child isn't able to receive any more as a result of his storehouse not being large enough to hold more, right now the father also isn't able to give him more. And if the child didn't prepare for himself even a small storehouse, so too the father will not give him anything, because he doesn't have a secure place in his domain where it will be preserved.

So is it with Him (blessed be His name): His hand (so to speak) is open to always impress upon each person of his treasured nation much wisdom and boundless understanding, so that they should preserve it in their domains, and bind it to the most accessible part of their heart/mind[979], for them to enjoy when they arrive in the world of repose[980], having what they learned available to them.

However, the matter depends on the storehouse of fear/awe that a person prepares. For if he prepared for himself a great storehouse of pure fear/awe of God, so too God will give him wisdom and understanding in great abundance based on what his storehouse can hold—[*] it completely depends on the capacity of his storehouse.

And if a person didn't prepare even a small storehouse, that he doesn't have within him any fear/awe of God (heaven forefend), then too He (blessed be His name) won't impress upon him any wisdom at all, for it will not be preserved in his domain, for his Torah is repulsive (heaven forefend), as our sages (OBM) stated.

And regarding this the text (*T'hillim* 111:10) stated: "The beginning of wisdom is fear/awe of God-*YHV"H*". And as it's written in the introduction to the *Zohar* (7b): "Rabbee Cheeya began: 'The beginning of wisdom is fear/awe of God-*YHV"H*...'—This text should have stated 'the end result of wisdom is...'[981]. Rather, it [fem.] is the first to enter within the level of supernal wisdom..., the first gate

---

979 Heb.: *v-yik-sh'reim al loo-ahkh lee-bahm*—Literally: "upon the tablets of their heart/minds". *Loo-ahkh* is the same word used in "two tablets of the covenant", where "tablet" means a surface that can be seen and read. I interpret this phrase to refer to the most accessible part of the heart/mind.

980 Heb.: *l'o-lahm ha-m'noo-kha*

981 Rabbee Cheeya suggests that perhaps fear/awe of God arises only after wisdom is acquired.

to the supernal wisdom is fear/awe of God-*YHV"H*[982]." Refer there [for more details].

So it's clear that even though fear/awe is one commandment, and they stated in the *Yerushalmi* (beginning of *Pei-ah*) that the sum total of all the commandments are not equal in worth to one word from the Torah, however the commandment of acquiring fear/awe from Him is very, very great from the perspective that it is a prerequisite for the primary purpose of preserving and safeguarding the holy Torah. And without it it's even considered repulsive in the eyes of others. For that reason it's required to be in a person's domain first, before involvement with Torah.

Annotation: *And in this way is explained their (OBM) statement at the beginning of* Perek Ha-ro-eh[983]*: "The Holy One (blessed be He) does not award wisdom except to one who [already] has wisdom within him, for it's stated (*Sh'mote *31:6): 'and in the heart/mind of everyone who has a wise heart/mind I have placed wisdom', 'He gives wisdom to the wise' (*Daniel *2:21)". And on the face of it this is surprising, for if it is so, how could the initial wisdom be found in a person's domain?*

*However the matter is that it's written explicitly that fear/awe is also called wisdom, as it is written (*Eeyove *28:28): "Yes, fear/awe of God-ADN"Y, she is wisdom". And it's for the reason mentioned above, that it [fem.] is the good storehouse for*

---

982 Rabbee Cheeya asserts that fear/awe of God is the first manifestation of, and the initial entry way into supernal wisdom. We can interpret the verse such that awe/fear of God refers to the *s'feera* of *Malkhoot*, the lowest *s'feera*. We get this from the verse (*Mishlei* 31:30): "*ee-sha yir-aht YHV"H, hee tit-ha-lahl*" (a woman who fears/is-in-awe of God-*YHV"H*, she shall be praised), which refers to *Malkhoot*. When we begin to approach *Chokhma* from below to draw spiritual energy from it, the first *s'feera* we encounter is *Malkhoot*.

983 *B'rakhote* 55a

wisdom, within which it will be safeguarded and preserved. And this is what they stated, that the Holy One (blessed be He) does not award nor impress the supernal wisdom of Torah so that it should be preserved in his domain and that this learning should be available to him, except to one who [already] has wisdom within him, namely a storehouse of fear/awe that is a necessary prerequisite in a person's domain, as described above.

(And a person of deep understanding will understand the inner meaning of their (OBM) statement in consonance with our approach, according to the secrets of the Zohar *and the writings of the Ariza"l, who stated that the supernal wisdom is revealed only via the aspect of His (blessed be He) sovereignty*[984]*, specifically accepting the yoke of the sovereignty of heaven*[985]*.)*

*And in this way will also be understood that we found that the rabbis (OBM) stated: "The Holy One (blessed be He) doesn't have for Himself in His world other than only four cubits of law" (*B'rakhote *8a). And in* perek Ein Ome-deen *(33b) they stated: "The Holy One (blessed be He) doesn't have for Himself in his treasury anything other than only a supply of fear/awe of heaven". And according to our thesis, in truth all of them are identical, and for that reason they stated a supply of fear/awe of heaven". This completes [their words].*

CHAPTER 6

Because of this truth that is the correct way, that was chosen by Him (blessed be He), whenever a person prepares himself to learn, it's worthwhile for him to settle himself down before he begins[986], at least for a small amount of

984 Heb.: *mal-khoo-toe*

985 Heb.: *ol malkhoot sha-ma-yim*

986 Heb.: *l'hit-ya-shev kodem sheh-yaht-kheel*

time, in pure fear/awe of God with a pure heart/mind, to cause himself to confess his sins from the depths of his heart/mind, so that his Torah should be holy and pure. And he should intend to attach himself to the Holy One (blessed be He) via his learning the Torah, specifically to cause himself to attach with all of his powers to the word of God (this being the halakha), and in this way actually be attached to Him (blessed be He) so to speak, for He and His will are one, as is written in the *Zohar*. And every judgment and halakha from the holy Torah is His (blessed be He) Will, for that is what His will decreed, that such is the judgment, kosher or disqualified, impure and pure, forbidden and unrestricted, guilty and innocent.

And furthermore, if he is occupied with stories[987] that have no bearing on any judgment, he is also attached to the speech of the Holy One (blessed be He). For the entire Torah, in her generalities, specifics and details, and even what a young student asks of his teacher, all of it was emitted from His (blessed be He) mouth to Moshe at Sinai, as the rabbis (OBM) stated at the end of chapter two of *M'geela*; and in the first chapter of *B'rakhote* 5a; and in *Kohelet Rabba* 61, chapter 11 and there in *Siman* 5, chapter 6; and in the *Yerushalmi* in chapter two of *Pei-ah*; and in *Va-yikra Rabba* chapter 22, refer there [for more details]. And in *Sh'mote Rabba* chapter 43: "'Write for yourself these words' (*Sh'mote 34:27*)—When the revelation of the Holy One (blessed be He) occurred at Sinai to give the Torah to Israel, He told Moshe regarding the order of the *mikra, mishna,* laws and stories, for it stated (*Sh'mote* 20:1): 'And God-*Elohi"m* spoke all of these words', even what a student asks his teacher." This completes [their words].

And not only that, but even when a person is involved

987 Heb.: *ahsook b'divrei aggada*

with Torah [here] below, each word that he utters from his mouth, they [emphatic] are the words that are being emitted (so to speak) also from His (blessed be He) mouth at the same actual moment, as is found in the first chapter of *Gittin*, regarding the story of the concubine in Giv'ah: "'And his concubine strayed from him'—Rabbee Evyatar stated: 'He found a fly from her', Rabbee Yonatan stated: 'He found a hair from her'. And Rabbee Evyatar encountered Eliyahu and he said to him: 'What is the Holy One (blessed be He) doing?' He responded: 'He is involved with the "concubine in Giv'ah".' 'And what is He saying?' He responded: 'Evyatar my child says such and such. Yonatan my child says such and such.'" And specifically, because Rabbee Evyatar and Rabbee Yonatan were involved together in the matter of the concubine in Giv'ah, then at the same moment He (blessed be He) too was learning their actual words.

And He (blessed be His name) and His words are identical, as is explained in the holy Torah in the *Mishneh Torah* (*D'varim* 30:6): "to love God-*YHV"H* your God-*Elohi"m*". And our rabbis (OBM) explained it in *N'darim*, in the *b'raita* (62a) that deals with involvement with Torah, refer there [for more details], and the end of the verse "and to attach to Him".

For that reason King Dovid (OBM) stated (*T'hillim* 119:72): "The Torah of Your mouth is better to me than..."—He said that my heart/mind rejoices in my labors in the holy Torah with great courage when I realize that she is the Torah from Your mouth, that each actual word from the Torah that I am currently involved with, all of it was emitted, and even now it is being emitted from Your (blessed be He) mouth.

And for that reason, the entire Torah, her holiness is uniform without any variation or division whatsoever (heaven forefend), for it's all the actual speech of His (blessed be He) mouth. And if a single letter from the verse "the Timna clan" was left out of a Torah scroll, it is considered as disqualified for use as if it were missing one letter from the ten commandments, or the verse "*sh'ma yisrael*", and as the RaMBa"M (OBM) wrote, and that's sourced from *Tahna D'vei Eliyahu, Sefer Eliyahu Zoota, perek* 3.

CHAPTER 7

And this being so, it's worthwhile for a person to prepare himself each time, before starting to learn, to consider his Owner (blessed be His name) for a while in purity of heart, in fear/awe of God, and to become purified from his sins by reflecting upon repentance, so that he will be able to connect and attach during his involvement with the holy Torah, to His (blessed be His name) words and will, and will also accept upon himself to perform and to fulfill according to all that is written in the written and oral Torah, and what he will perceive and understand of His way from our holy Torah. And in the same way, when he wants to focus on words of law, it's worthwhile to pray that He (blessed be He) should grant him the merit to bring the matter to a proper halakhic conclusion[988], to intend towards the Torah's truth.[989]

And in the same way, in the middle of learning a person is permitted to stop for a short time, before his fear/awe of Him (blessed be He) that he accepted upon him before starting learning is extinguished from his heart/mind, and to contemplate anew a bit more about fear/awe of God, as our rabbis (OBM) stated further

988 Aram.: *l'ah-so-kei sh'mahta ahleeba d'hilkha-ta* (ref.: Yoma 26a)

989 Rav Chayyim here differentiates between the general learning of Torah and the specific learning of halakha.

(*Shabbat* 31a)[990]: "this is likened to a person who said to his agent: 'Bring a measure of wheat for me to the upper storehouse…". He said to him: 'Did you mix salty minerals into it?' He responded 'No'. He said: 'It would have been better if you hadn't brought it up!' And the wisdom of the Torah stands on this example of grain, that it's worthwhile also to mix his fear/awe into it, to preserve his learning ability.

And for that reason he brought in support of it the *b'raita*: "The academy of Rabbee Yishmael taught: 'A person may mix up to a *kav* of salty minerals[991] into a *koor* of wheat and not be concerned about it'", this being a law in the context of the laws of theft and fraud whose place is in *Seder N'zikin*[992]. What relevance does it have here? However, we are taught by this that just as in business, that even though it might be thought of as theft and fraud, however being that the *kav* of minerals acts as a safeguard and preservative for the *koor* of grain, there's no concern about it being considered as theft, so too a person is allowed to take a break and waste a small amount of time from learning, to contemplate fear/awe of God for a short while, and he shouldn't worry about this as disruption of the Torah[993], because its result is the preservation of the wisdom of Torah in his domain.

---

990 This story is brought to make the point that without having a measure of fear/awe, one's learning of Torah is not effective and doesn't persist.

991 Heb.: *kav chome-teen*—The salty mineral acts as a preservative.

992 *Seder N'zeekeen*, one of the six major divisions of the Talmud, includes the laws governing damages and recompense.

993 Heb.: *beetool Torah*

CHAPTER 8

However, also deduce from it, from the matter of the two metaphors[994] to which our sages (OBM) likened it too in the matter of the Torah and fear/awe, the opposite of how some of the majority of the members of our nation erred, who make their regular practice, the entirety of their involvement with learning, with books of fear/awe and ethical guidance alone.

Just as in the matter of having the [availability of a] storehouse precede the grain that's stored within it, would it enter a person's mind that, because the central focus of the safeguarding and preservation of the grain is the storehouse, that he should involve himself full-time or most of his time, only with building the storehouse and never ever store grain in it? In the same way how could it enter a person's mind to say that this is a person from Israel's central purpose, that he should place his entire regular practice of learning in the building of the storehouse of fear/awe of heaven alone? It's an empty storehouse, and he didn't accomplish anything by his labor other than observing one commandment (*D'varim* 6:13): "Only God-*YHV"H* your God-*Elohi"m* shall you fear/awe", and also, it doesn't even deserve the name "storehouse" at all.

Our sages (OBM) didn't intend by the statement mentioned above ("The Holy One (blessed be He) doesn't have for himself… anything other than only a supply of fear/awe of heaven") anything other than the specific fear/awe that within it is placed huge quantities of grains: *mikra, mishna* and *halakhote* and the rest of the Torah's matters, for which fear/awe is their excellent storehouse. It ensures that they will be preserved in his domain, in

994 As a storehouse and as a preservative

good order and readily available, and engraved on the most accessible part of his heart/mind[995], as is proven and necessarily derived from what is written: "The Holy One (blessed be He) doesn't have for Himself in His world other than only four cubits of law".

(And as is known at the root of the issue, the matter of the two qualities of Torah and fear/awe of God are among the supernal virtues[996]. The aspect of fear/awe has nothing of its [fem.] own, for it [fem.] appears on the scene unencumbered[997]. It [fem.] is only the storehouse, the receiving place, for the supernal abundance from the quality of Torah. And as is written (*Chabakook* 2:20): "and God-*YHV"H* is in His holy abode", and refer to the *Tikkoonim, Tikkoon* 2 and 3[998].)

And this is what the text (*Mishlei* 15:16) stated: "Better a little with fear/awe of God-*YHV"H* than a great storehouse filled with confusion".

CHAPTER 9

And it's the same situation in the matter of the permissibility to take a break during learning, to contemplate fear/awe of God a bit more, which our sages (OBM) likened to the permissibility of mixing a *kav* of salty minerals into a *koor* of grain. This is the same situation, that just like if we mixed into a *koor* of grain more than a *kav* of salty

995 Heb.: *va-kha-roo-tim ahl loo-ahkh leebo*; literally "engraved on the tablet of his heart/mind"

996 Heb.: *ba-mee-dote ha-el-yo-neem*, referring to the *partzufim* of *Ze'er Anpin* and *Malkhut*.

997 Heb.: *n'kee-ya*, which we render as "unencumbered" but could also be rendered as "poor", "bare" or "clean".

998 Rav Chayyim draws on the Vilna Gaon's commentary on *Tikkoonim* 2 and 3.

minerals—which wasn't necessary to preserve the grain—it's considered theft and fraud, so too in the matter of fear/awe, that if a person devotes more time than what is necessary to preserve and safeguard the bulk of grain of Torah, it's considered that he is stealing that extra time from the Torah that he would have learned then. For he was not permitted to be involved in the contemplation and acquisition of fear/awe except to the extent considered necessary by his intellect according to his nature and the context, for this time is needed and required for him to be involved with acquiring fear/awe and ethical guidance for the purpose of the safeguarding and preservation of the grain of Torah.

And truthfully, a person who has a steady practice of involvement with Torah for its own sake (as we explained in chapter 3 the matter of "for its own sake") doesn't need as much effort and toil and a lengthy period of involvement with books of fear/awe—so that fear/awe of Him should be fixed in his heart/mind—as a person who doesn't have a steady practice of involvement with Torah.

For the holy Torah will itself clothe him in fear/awe of God that's apparent, in little time and with little effort to achieve that effect, for this is her way and the special quality of the holy Torah, as they stated (*Ahvote* 6:1): "Anyone who involves himself with Torah for its own sake..., and it clothes him with humility and fear/awe."

And in *Mishlei Rabbatta, parsha* 1: "'The fools despised wisdom and ethical guidance'—If ethical guidance, why wisdom? And if wisdom...? Rather, if a person learned Torah and sits and involves himself in it [fem.] according to his need, then he has both wisdom and ethical guidance available to him, and if not... ."

And in *Tahna D'vei Eliyahu, Seder Eliyahu Rabba, perek* 18:12: "'And by the stream, on its banks, on both sides will grow all types of trees that produce food...' (*Yekhezkel* 47:12)—And what is the tree that will grow in this stream? They are the Torah scholars who have Torah within them, *mikra* and *mishna*, *halakhote* and *aggadote*, and good deeds and service to the Torah scholars.... They offered a metaphor: 'To what is this similar...? This is how the Torah scholars are in this world relative to the Torah's words. Because they read the scripture and learned..., and the words of Torah are sweet upon them, the Holy One (blessed be He) has compassion upon them and places within them wisdom and understanding and knowledge and rational intellection to perform good deeds and the learning of Torah, and all of it is complete before them...'."

CHAPTER 10

And during the involvement with and concentrated study of Torah, it's certain that there's no need then for the matter of attachment at all, as discussed previously. For via the involvement and concentrated study themselves is he attached to His (blessed be He) will and words, and He (blessed be He) and His will are identical.[999]

And this is the matter of their (OBM) statement in *Sh'mote Rabba (parsha* 33:6): "A person removes a purchase... [from the marketplace], out of concern that its original owner will reclaim it; in contrast, the Holy One (blessed be He) gave the Torah to Israel and says to them: 'It's as if it is Me you are taking...'." And this is what is written in a few places in the *Zohar*, that the Holy

---

999 This is the difference between the involvement with Torah and the performance of other *mitzvote*. The involvement with *mitzvote* ideally requires attachment (*d'veikoot*), while involvement with Torah is itself attachment—no special intention or attention is necessary to achieve attachment.

One (blessed be He) and the Torah are identical[1000]. And even greater than this is found in *parshat B'sha-lakh* 60a: "And we learned that the Holy One (blessed be He) is called Torah..., and Torah is none other than the Holy One (blessed be He)."

And also that the supernal root of the holy Torah is the most supernal of the worlds that are called the "worlds of *Ein Sofe*"[1001], the secret of the concealed garment[1002] that is mentioned in the recondite wonders of wisdom from the Torah of our rabbi the Ariza"l, that is "beginning"[1003], the secret of the letters of the holy Torah. And as is written (*Mishlei* 8:22): "God-*YHV"H* made me, the beginning of His path, before any of His works from of old". And this is what those (OBM) stated, that it pre-existed the world, namely even before all of the worlds in totality. For after all, they stated in *B'reisheet Rabba parsha* 1, that it pre-existed the throne of glory[1004]. And the truth is that it's as if it pre-existed even the world of *Ahtzeeloot*[1005] (blessed be) as mentioned previously, but the *Ahtzeeloot* is called Nothingness[1006]. From the secret of the throne begins the secret of, so to speak, the Stature[1007]. For that reason they stated that

---

1000 Here Rav Chayyim introduces a primary theme, based on the Zohar, that the Holy One (blessed be He) and the Torah are to be considered as identical—that God and the Torah are one.

1001 Heb.: *o-la-mote Ein Sofe*

1002 Heb.: *ha-mahl-boosh ha-neh-eh-lahm*

1003 Heb.: *reisheet*

1004 The world of *B'reeya* is called the "world of the throne". Rav Chayyim is saying here that Torah pre-existed the world of *B'reeya.*

1005 Rav Chayyim seems to say that in some sense, the Torah even pre-existed the world of *Ahtzeeloot.*

1006 Heb.: *ayin*

1007 Heb.: *shee-oor ko-ma*

it pre-existed the throne of glory[1008].

And for that reason, using it [fem.] were emanated and created all of the worlds, upper and lower, as is written (*Mishlei* 8:30): "And I was with Him as a nursling[1009]". And they (OBM) stated (*B'reisheet Rabba* 1:2): "Don't read it as 'nursling', but rather as 'craftsman'[1010]...". And in *Mishlei Rabbatta*, beginning of *parsha* 9: "'With all forms of wisdom did it [fem.] build its [fem.] house' (*Mishlei* 9:1)—This is Torah, for it [fem.] built all the worlds."

And the context is that the holy Torah is His (blessed be He) speech, and by the utterances of His (blessed be He) mouth during the creation event, were all the worlds created; that by sequencing the metamorphoses of the

---

1008 Rav Chayyim seems to be saying the sages said that the Torah pre-existed the world of *B'reeya*, which is the world of the throne of glory, which is the starting point for the Stature (the *shee-oor ko-ma*). And also, that in some way, it even pre-existed the world of *Ahtzeeloot*, which is known as Nothingness (*ayin*). We would think that if *Ahtzeeloot* is called Nothingness, then it is essentially beyond language to assert that anything (even Torah) pre-existed it, for Nothingness can not be said to exist.

Even so, Rav Chayyim states at the beginning of this paragraph that the supernal root of Torah is in the "most supernal of the worlds that are called the worlds of Ein *Sofe*." What are the "worlds of *Ein Sofe*"?

In the Etz Chayyim, *hei-khal ah-dahm kahd-mone, sha-ar bet, ah-nahf bet*, Rav Chayyim Vittal states that there are a countless number of worlds between the *Ein Sofe* and the highest of the supernal worlds that are accessible to man. The highest accessible world that we can discuss only with great trepidation and with vastly incomplete knowledge is the "world" of Primeval Adam (*o-lahm ah-dahm kahd-mone*). Presumably, the source of Torah is even above that. Language and thought fail to be adequate for the task of addressing this topic.

1009 Heb.: *o-mahn*

1010 Heb.: *oo-mahn*

combination of letters according to the sequence of the two hundred and thirty-one gates, front and back, that are in the statement "In the beginning created…" [*B'reisheet* 1:1], were the worlds emanated and created, the highest of the high, myriad, in their every arrangement of how they are situated, and the details of their contexts, and everything integrated within them. And so too with each and every utterance in it, according to the method discussed previously, all the details of the species and the contexts in that variety were created, about which that utterance was mentioned.

As is written in *Zohar T'rooma* 161a: "That when the Holy One (blessed be He) created the world, He gazed into it [fem.], into Torah, and created the world. And with the Torah was the world created, as we established, for it is written 'And I will be a craftsperson in His domain…'. The Torah screams: 'And I will be a craftsperson in His domain'—Using me did the Holy One (blessed be He) create the world, for before the world was created, the Torah existed prior... . And when the Holy One (blessed be He) desired to create the world, He gazed within it [fem.], the Torah, into each and every word, and acted based upon it [fem.] to craft the world, because all of the words and actions of all the worlds are in the Torah… , for it is written in the Torah: 'In the beginning created…'. He gazed on that word and created the heavens. In the Torah is written: 'And God-*Elohi"m* stated: let there be light'—He gazed at that word and created light. And that's the way it was for each and every word that's written in the Torah: the Holy One (blessed be He) gazed and did that word. And regarding this it's written: 'And I will be a craftsperson in His domain'. In this way the entire world was created." This completes the quote.

And for that reason the entire Torah, and all of the worlds, taken as wholes and in all their details and structures and all of their contexts, are all incorporated and hinted at in the ten statements of the creation event. And this is as our great rabbi, the genius, the pious, our teacher Rabbi Eliyahu[1011] (may the memory of the righteous and holy be for blessing) wrote in his commentary on the *Sifra D'tzniuta* in chapter five. And [for more details] refer to *Zohar B'reisheet* 47a.

And for that reason they stated in the *Zohar*: "The Torah illuminates all the worlds, is their sustenance, maintains them and is the root of them all."

And the matter is, that the worlds proceed according to the order in which they unfolded and gradually descended, that each world that is above and higher, it alone is the soul-*Neshama*, and the life-force, and the maintaining force, and the light of the world below it. However, the world of *Ahtzeeloot* has an additional quality over the three worlds *B'reeya, Y'tzeera, Ahseeya*, in that it extends and illuminates to all three of the worlds *B'reeya, Y'tzeera, Ahseeya* that are below it[1012]. Refer to the *Etz Chayyim, Sha'ar P'nee-mee-yoot V'khee-tzo-nee-yoot, d'roosh bet*; and there at the beginning of *d'roosh chet* and the beginning of *d'roosh yud*; and in *Sha'ar D'rooshei ABY"A*, chapter 7; and in *Sha'ar Ha-shei-mote*, chapter 1; and in *Sha'ar Klee-paht Noga*, chapter 1. It is godliness in its entirety, as is written in the introduction to the *Tikkoonim*, that the King is within the ten *s'feerote* of *Ahtzeeloot*—He and His essence are identical in it, He and His sustenance are identical in it—which is not the case in the ten *s'feerote* of *B'reeya*, where they and He are not identical, He and their essence are not identical.

1011 The Vilna Gaon

1012 The *Etz Chayyim* explains that while each world is nourished and maintained by the world immediately above it, the world of *Ahtzeeloot* is exceptional, and performs those functions for all three worlds below it.

For that reason, the holy Torah, whose supernal hidden root is exceedingly high above even the emanation of His holiness[1013] (blessed be He) as mentioned above, and the Holy One (blessed be He) and the Torah are completely identical—it [fem.] is the soul-*Neffesh* and the sustenance and the illumination and the root of all the worlds.

It being that just as at the time of the creation, within it [fem.] were emanated and created all of them, so too since then it [fem.] is their soul-*Neshama*, sustenance, maintaining force according to how they are situated. And lacking the influence of its [fem.] light within them, literally in every instant, to illuminate them, sustain them and maintain them, they would all return to literal nothingness and chaos.

CHAPTER 11

And consequently, the primary component of their sustenance and illumination and maintenance of all the worlds certainly is only when we are involved with it correctly[1014], for the Holy One (blessed be He) and the Torah and Israel are all identical (refer to *Zohar parshat Ah-kha-rei* 73a), that every individual of Israel, the root of his supernal soul-*Neshama* is adhered and clutches to one letter of the

---

1013 Heb.: *mei-ah-tzee-loot kahd-sho*—Since the Torah's origin is above even the world of *Ahtzeeloot, it* is the source of sustenance and illumination for all of the worlds below it, including Ahtzeeloot.

1014 Here Rav Chayyim states his primary thesis about the nature of involvement with Torah. Since Torah is the source of creation's existence, it is our involvement with Torah that sustains, illuminates and maintains all of creation. This is in contrast to attachment during the performance of *mitzvote,* which only rectifies the worlds to a degree that's dependent on level of attachment.

Torah, and they become a literal unity.[1015]

And relative to this they stated in *B'reisheet Rabba* (chapter 1) that the thoughts of Israel[1016] preceded everything, and it doesn't come to argue about what they stated that the Torah preceded everything, because they are all one in their roots, one is the other.[1017] And this is why it is written "the thoughts of Israel"[1018].

And just as they stated "Israel arose in the thought", intending to convey the beginning of thought, [that is] the secret of the supernal will, as is written in the *Zohar Va-yeira* 118b, "for Israel arose in the Holy One's (blessed be He) will before the world was created."

And the will is the beginning of everything, absolute godliness (so to speak), from the worlds of *Ein Sofe*[1019], as mentioned there in *parshat Noakh* (65a) and *P'koodei* (268b): "Rabbee Shim'on stated: 'I raised my..., when the supernal will..., all of these illuminations from the hidden aspect of the supernal and terrestrial thought are all called *Ein Sofe*'." Refer there carefully [for more details]. And in Rav Chayyim Vittal's (OBM) annotation there, and in the *Etz Chayyim, Sha'ar Ee-goolim V'yosher,*

1015 Again drawing on *Zohar*, the Ariza"l and midrashic sources, Rav Chayyim continues to develop his primary theme, extending the one-ness of God and Torah to include Israel. The root of each Jewish person's supernal soul-*Neshama* is inherently connected to one letter of the Torah; they are joined to each other and become a unity. Since the Torah is the root of all creation, it is the collective of Israel which is ultimately responsible for sustaining all of creation via involvement with Torah.

1016 Heb.: *sheh-mahkh-shahv-tahn shel yisrael*

1017 I.e., that Israel and Torah are one.

1018 Heb.: *mahkh-shahv-tahn*

1019 Heb.: *mei-o-lah-mote ein sofe.* Rav Chayyim again refers to the worlds of *Ein Sofe*, as he did in chapter 10.

ah-nahf daled, and in *Sha'ar Hish-tal-sh'loot Ha-yood S'feerote,* beginning of *ah-nahf bet.*

And it is for that reason they stated: "'*B'reisheet*'[1020]—For the sake of the Torah that is called *reisheet*[1021] and for the sake of Israel who are called *reisheet.*"

(And for that reason the sages stated (*Mo-ed Ka-tahn* 25a): "'One who is standing by a dead person at the time the soul departs is obligated to rend his garment'—To what is this analogous? To one who sees a Torah scroll being burned, for the holiness of any individual-in-Israel's soul is [emphatic] literally the holiness of the Torah scroll."[1022])

And for that reason, from the moment of creation, when the Torah was still concealed in the wellspring of its source that is hidden from all the upper worlds, and only from afar did it illuminate all the worlds to vivify and sustain them, and its [fem.] essence did not literally unfold downwards to this world so that the gathering of those below could be involved with it, the worlds were still weak and unstable and were not settled on their real foundations, and our sages (OBM) called them (*Avoda Za-ra* 9a) "two thousand[1023] of chaos", and their existence was conditional until the moment of the giving of the Torah[1024], as is known from their (OBM) statement (*Shabbat* 88a): "that the Holy One (blessed be He) made a conditional agreement with all of creation. If Israel accepts..., and if not...". And so too in *Sh'mote Rabba* chapter 47, and *D'varim Rabba* at the end of chapter 8 and at the beginning of *Tahn-khooma.* And in *Rabba Shir*

1020 "In the beginning..."

1021 "beginning"

1022 Here Rav Chayyim uses a Talmudic source to again differentiate between the quality of the soul of a Jew and a non-Jew.

1023 Two thousand years

1024 Heb.: *ma-tahn torah*

Ha-shirrim (1:50): "'I likened thee, my beloved' (1:9)—The rabbis stated: the beloved of my world because they accepted my Torah, for if they had not accepted it I would have returned My world to chaos and emptiness, for Rabbee Chaneena stated in the name of Rabbee Ah-kha: it is written (*T'hillim* 75:4): 'the Earth melts away...', 'I have firmly established its pillars—Selah'—If it had not been the case that when Israel stood at Mount Sinai that they stated (*Sh'mote* 24:7): 'Everything that God-*YHV"H* has said, we will do and we will obey', the world would have melted away and returned to chaos and emptiness. And who laid the foundations of the world? I..., in the merit of 'I am God-*YHV"H* your God-*Elohi"m*' (*Sh'mote* 20:2) did I firmly fix its pillars, selah."

And from the time when it unfolded and descended (so to speak) from the wellspring of its concealed source into this world—as they (OBM) stated[1025]: "Moshe came and brought it down to the earth"—the entire life force and sustenance of all the worlds is the result only of the vapors from our mouths[1026] and our intellectual efforts[1027] relative to it [fem.].

And the truth, without any doubt at all, is that if the entire world, from one end to the other, would be empty (heaven forefend) literally for even one moment from our involvement with and contemplation of the Torah, immediately all of the worlds would be destroyed, supernal

---

1025 In early editions there is no record of Rav Chayyim supplying a citation for this quotation. Later editions add a citation for *B'reisheet Rabba* 19:7, which refers to the *Sh'kheena* rather than the Torah, and states: "Moshe came and brought it down below". The phrase "brought it down to the earth" (Heb.: "*la-ah-retz*") is not used.

1026 Heb.: *heh-vel peenoo*

1027 Heb.: *v'hehg-yo-nei-noo ba*

and terrestrial, and would become emptiness and chaos (heaven forefend). And so too, the abundance of the light they receive, or its lack (heaven forefend), is totally only according to the context of and the degree of our involvement with it [fem.].

For that reason, we make the blessing upon it [fem.]: "and the life of the world did You plant among us"[1028], per the matter of planting, that its planting is to make fruit so as to increase good. So too, if we hold fast onto the holy Torah with all of our power properly, we inherit everlasting lives, and draw from its concealed source above all the worlds expansions of holiness and blessing and great light in all the worlds. This is what is written in *Mishlei Rabbata, parsha* 2: "More than you guard any thing, safeguard your heart" (*Mishlei* 4:23), so that it should not flee from words of Torah. Why? "Because from it [come] the results of life", to teach you that from words of Torah result life for the world.

And also to build the demolished with great rectifications[1029], to connect and unify and to perfect the supernals with the terrestrials, and all the worlds are balanced[1030] and illuminate as one, as they (OBM) stated in *Perek Cheilek* (99b): "Rabbee Alexandri stated: 'Anyone who involves himself with Torah for its own sake, it is as if he makes

1028 Heb.: *v'kha-yei o-lahm nah-tah b'toe-khei-noo*—This would usually be translated as 'and everlasting life did You instill in us". Rav Chayyim interprets this verse to convey that the Torah is literally the force that sustains the life of the worlds.

1029 Involvement with Torah also accomplishes great rectifications—like the performance of *mitzvote*—and also binds the worlds together and unifies them.

1030 Heb.: *sh'kee-lin*

peace[1031] among the hosts above and among the hosts below, for it's stated (*Y'shaya* 27:5) "or let him take hold of My strength, that he may make peace with me..."[1032]'. Rav stated: 'It is as if he built a palace above and a palace below, for it is written: (*Y'shaya* 51:16): "And I will place My words in your mouth... to plant the heavens and to lay the foundations of the earth"'."

And in *Chazeeta*: "'His legs are like marble pillars' (*Shir Ha-shirrim* 5:15)—These are the Torah scholars[1033]. Why are they likened to pillars? Because they support the world, as is stated (*Yirmiya* 33:25): 'As surely as I have established my covenant with the day and the night...'." And in *Mishlei Rabbata*: "'With wisdoms did she build her house...' (*Mishlei* 9:1)—The Holy One (blessed be He) said: 'If a person merits and learns Torah and wisdom, it's as important to Me as though he created the heavens and as if he fixed in place the entire world in its totality. And there, regarding chapter *Eishet Chayil* (*Mishlei* 31: 10-31) they stated: "The Holy One (blessed be He) said to Israel: 'My children, be involved with Torah day and night and I will consider you as if you are supporting the entire world'."

And in *Zohar B'reisheet* (47a): "Anyone who labors in Torah each day merits that he will have a portion in the world-to-come, and it will be considered for him as

---

1031 Heb.: *k'eeloo o-seh sha-lome*—In our current versions of *Sanhedrin*, chapter 11 (which is entitled *Cheilek*), we find an alternate reading: instead of "it is as if he makes peace" (*k'eeloo o-seh sha-lome*) is written "promotes peace" (Heb.: *mei-sim sha-lome*).

1032 The verse continues: "yea, let him make peace with Me", repeating the phrase. Rav Chayyim interprets the repeating of the phrase as referring to the hosts above and the hosts below.

1033 Heb.: *tal-mee-dei cha-kha-meem*

if he constructed worlds, for it was with the Torah that worlds were constructed and perfected. And this is what is written: 'God-*YHV"H* with wisdom laid the foundations of the world…', and it's written: 'And I will be a craftsperson in His domain…', and anyone who makes an effort with her, perfects worlds and preserves them. Observe that with a spirit-*Ruakh* did the Holy One (blessed be He) make the world, and with the spirit-*Ruakh* is it preserved; this is the spirit-*Ruakh* of those who engage in the Torah."

And there in *parshat Va-yei-shev*, after it first lengthily described the awesome meritorious level of the person who involves himself with Torah in this world and in the world-to-come, and his great punishment in the two worlds when he desists from her (heaven forefend), it concluded and stated: "As a result, everything depends on carrying out the Torah, and the world is not preserved in existence except via Torah, for she preserves the worlds, supernal and terrestrial, for it is written: 'As surely as I have established my covenant with the day and the night…'."

And in *parshat T'rooma* (161a), after it dealt at length with the matter, to explain how all the worlds were created using the Torah, it stated after that: "Because when the world was created, each and every thing did not come into being until it arose in will to create man who could labor in Torah, and for him the world was brought into existence. Now anyone who gazes into the Torah and labors in her, it is as if he preserves the entire world. The Holy One (blessed be He) gazed into the Torah and created the world. A person gazes into the Torah and preserves the world. We find that the creation and the preservation of the entire world is Torah, and as a result of this, fortunate is the person who involves himself with Torah, because he preserves the world."

And in *parshat Va-yikra* (11, end of the second folio): "Because the world was not created except for the sake of the Torah, any time that Israel is involved with the Torah, the world exists. And any time that Israel disrupts their involvement with Torah, what is written? 'As surely as I have established my covenant with the day and the night…'."

And for that reason they stated in *perek Ma-a-lote Ha-Torah*[1034] that anyone who involves himself with Torah is called "beloved", for it is as if he is made a partner to the Former of the Beginning (blessed be He), because it is he who now preserves all the worlds via his involvement with Torah. And lacking this they would all return to chaos and emptiness. As is written in the *Midrash* mentioned before: "'I likened thee, my beloved'—beloved of my world, that they accepted my Torah… ."

CHAPTER 12

And even more so, regarding true Torah innovations that are newly developed by people, there's no limit to the value of the greatness of their awesome, wondrous and amazing contexts, and what they effect above. For each and every specific word that is innovated from a person's mouth, the Holy One (blessed be He) kisses it [fem.] and crowns it [fem.], and from it is built a new, independent world, and they [emphatic] are "the new heavens and the new earth" that the scripture mentioned.

As is written in the introduction to the *Zohar* (4b): "Rabbee Shimon began: 'And I placed My words in your mouth' (*Y'shaya* 51:16)—How valuable is it for a person to labor in the Torah day and night, for the Holy One (blessed be He) pays attention to the voices[1035] of those

---

1034 Ahvote chapter 6

1035 Aram.: *le-kaw-lei-hoon*

who involve themselves with Torah, and from every word that they innovate in Torah by laboring in the Torah is made a single heaven. We learned that at the moment that words of Torah are innovated from a person's mouth, that utterance ascends and is crowned before the Holy One (blessed be He), and the Holy One (blessed be He) takes that utterance and kisses it and crowns it with seventy[1036] carved and engraved crowns, and the wise utterance that was innovated ascends and alights upon the head... , and from there it flies and glides in seventy-thousand[1037] worlds and ascends to the Ancient of Days[1038]... . And that same sealed wise utterance that was innovated here, when it ascends, is connected to the utterances of the Ancient of Days, and then it ascends and descends with them, and enters into the eighteen worlds that have been hidden, that no eye has ever seen... , and they leave there and roam and arrive whole and complete, and testify before the Ancient of Days. Then the Ancient of Days hosts that word and it is welcomed before Him in all aspects. He takes that word and crowns it with three-hundred and seventy thousand[1039] crowns. And that word roams and ascends and descends and becomes one heaven. And so it is that each and every wise word becomes heavens that exist in complete fulfillment before the Ancient of

---

1036 The *Ma-toke Me-d'vash* explains that the seventy crowns come from the bottom seven *s'feerote*, each of which consists of ten *s'feerote*.

1037 The seventy thousand comes from the lower seven *s'feerote* of the *partzoof* of *Arikh Anpin*, in whose world (Ahtzeeloot) each *s'feera* is counted as a thousand.

1038 Heb.: *Ah-teek Yo-min*

1039 The *Ma-toke Me-d'vash* explains that the three-hundred come from the top three of the ten *s'feerote*, while the seventy comes from the bottom seven. And in the world of *Ah-tik Yo-min* (Ahtzeeloot) each *s'feera* counts as a thousand.

Days. And He calls them "the new heavens"..., recondite secrets of the supernal wisdom, and all the rest of the words of Torah that are innovated stand before the Holy One (blessed be He) and ascend and become the Lands of Life[1040], and descend and are crowned..., and they are renewed and all of it becomes a new land from that specific utterance that was innovated in the Torah. And about this is written (*Y'shaya* 66:22): 'For just as the new heavens and the new earth that I am making will endure before me...'—It does not say 'I made' but rather 'am making', that He makes it now from those innovations and secrets of the Torah. And about this it is written: 'I will place my words in your mouth... to plant the heavens and place the foundations of the earth...'. Rabbee Elazar stated: 'What does "and with the shade of My hand I covered you" mean?' He answered him... , and right now when that word ascends and is crowned and stands before the Holy One (blessed be He), He drapes over that word and covers that person... until from that word is made new heavens and a new earth... . 'And to state to Zion: you are My nation...'—Don't read it as "My nation"[1041] but rather as "with me"[1042], to make you my partner, that just as I made the heavens and the earth with my words..., you do so too. Fortunate are those who labor in the Torah."

And in *parshat V-y'khee* (243, top of first folio) is written: "'The mandrakes yield their fragrance...' (*Shir Ha-shirrim* 7:14)—These are those that Reuven found... . 'And at our doors are all kinds of delicacies'—They caused that there should be at the doors of the synagogues and study

1040 Heb.: *ar-tzote ha-khayyim*

1041 Heb.: *ah-mee*

1042 Heb.: *ee-mee*

halls all kinds of delicacies, 'new ones and old ones'. How many new and old words of Torah that are revealed via... . 'My beloved I have hidden away for you'—From this we learn that anyone who makes an effort in Torah correctly, and knows how to explain words and to innovate words, those words ascend all the way to the throne of the King, and *K'nesset Yisrael* opens gates for them and stores them in the treasury. And when the Holy One (blessed be He) enters the Garden of Eden to amuse Himself with the pious ones, He brings them out before Him, and the Holy One (blessed be He) gazes upon them and is happy. Then the Holy One (blessed be He) crowns Himself with the supernal crowns and is happy..., and from that moment His words are written in a book... . Fortunate is the lot of one who is involved with Torah correctly. Fortunate is he in this world, and fortunate is he in the world-to-come."

And in *Tahna D'vei Eliyahu* (*Seder Eliyahu Rabba*, chapter 18, page 84a[1043]): "'Along the banks of the stream will grow every type of food tree' (*Yekhezkel* 47:12)—And the text explains fully there that this refers to words of Torah. And it states there: 'What is "and those who innovate/renew, He treats as a first-born"[1044]? It refers to those who innovate/renew Torah, who innovate/renew the Torah each day

---

1043 The page number is for the Lewin-Epstein edition (Jerusalem, 1978), corresponding to page 93 of the Meir Friedmann edition that is based on manuscript Vatican MS 31.

1044 Heb.: *la-kha-da-shahv y'va-keir.* While *la-kha-da-shav* is often translated as "every new month", *Tahna D'vei Eliyahu* interprets it as "to those who innovate/renew". And while *y'va-keir* is related to the word *b'khore* (first-born), and in its usage here is usually translated as "it offers new fruit", *Tahna D'vei Eliyahu* renders it as "treats as a first-born". So according to this understanding, the phrase translates as "and those who innovate/renew, He treats as a first-born".

continuously, to a son who is first born..., who innovates/renews words of Torah that gladden everyone therewith..., a gladness that he renews for his Father each day..., ...and to any place that they innovate/renew Torah, for when learning in the synagogue and when learning in the study hall, a joy is renewed for the Holy One (blessed be He), each day, continuously...'." Refer there [for more details].

CHAPTER 13

And via involvement with the holy Torah His intention for creation is fulfilled, for it was only for the sake of the Torah, that Israel should be involved with it, per their (OBM) statements: "'*B'reisheet*'—For the sake of the Torah..., and for the sake of Israel..., and for the sake of Moshe...", for he is the procuring agent for the receiving of the Torah, and, so to speak, He rejoices in His actions, in His world and creations, that they inspire favor[1045] before Him (blessed be He) as during the first hour of creation, as He (blessed be He) Himself intended (so to speak).

It is as written in *Rabba B'reisheet* (chapter 9:4): "This is likened to a king who built a palace. He looked at it and it appeared exceedingly pleasant to him. He said: 'Palace, palace! Would that you should always inspire favor in me...'. So too did the Holy One (blessed be He) say to His world: 'My world, My world! Would that you should always inspire favor in me, as you inspire favor in me right now'." And therefore it is stated (*Mishlei* 5:19) in praise of the Torah: "a beloved doe, inspiring favor".

And in *Zohar Tzav* (35a): "Rabbee Elazar began and stated: 'and I have placed my words in your mouth...' (*Y'shaya* 51:16)—We have learned that any person who

---

1045 Heb.: *sheh-ma-ah-leen chen*

makes an effort with Torah and his lips speak words of Torah..., and not only that but he maintains the world's existence, and the Holy One (blessed be He) is pleased as on the day when He planted the heavens and the earth. And this is what is written: 'to plant the heavens and to place the foundations of the earth'."

And in *parshat T'rooma* (151b): "Rabbee Cheeya began and stated: 'For it is a time to act for God-*YHV"H*, they have violated your Torah' (*T'hillim* 119:126)—At any time that Torah is maintained in the world and people make an effort with it, it's as if the Holy One (blessed be He) is pleased with His hands' labors, and pleased with all the worlds, and the heavens and the earth are maintained in their existence. And not only that but the Holy One (blessed be He) gathers all the heavenly hosts and says to them: 'Observe the holy nation that I have upon the earth, that the Torah is crowned because of them...'. And when they observe their Master's pleasure in His nation, immediately they begin to say 'And who is like Your nation, like Israel...' (*Shmuel Bet* 7:23)."

And at the beginning of *parshat Shmini*: "How fortunate are Israel, that the Holy One (blessed be He) gave them the holy Torah, the delight of all, delight of the Holy One (blessed be He) and His enjoyment, for it is written: 'And I become a source of delight each and every day'[1046] (*Mishlei* 8:30)."

CHAPTER 14

And also, all the worlds and the creations are then in a state of extraordinary joy, and are illuminated by the splendor of the supernal light that flows abundantly upon them from the place that's the supernal source of the Torah,

1046 The Torah itself states this.

as is stated in the chapter of the levels of Torah (*Ahvote*, chapter 6): "brings joy to God-*Ma-kome*, brings joy to the creations". And Torah also said the same (*Mishlei* 8:30): "And I become a source of delight each and every day".

And in *Zohar Va-yahk-heil* (217a): "...began and said: 'then those who fear God-*YHV"H* were spoken[1047] to one another...' (*Malachi* 3:16). It should have said 'then they spoke[1048]'. Why does it say 'were spoken'? It's that those holy vehicles[1049] were spoken above, all of those holy hosts, as an effect of the holy words that ascend heavenward. And how many of them proceed before them and carry them before the holy King, and are crowned in a number of crowns via those supernal lights, and all are spoken before the supernal King. Who has seen the joy? Who has seen the praises that ascend to all those heavens before the holy King. And the holy King gazes at them and crowns them, and they ascend upon His head and become a crown, and then descend and rest in His bosom inside His power, and from there they ascend upon His head. And regarding this the Torah stated: 'And I become[1050] a source of delight each and every day'." And it doesn't state 'and I became'[1051] but rather 'and I become', at every moment and in every instant that supernal words ascend before Him." (This completes the quote.)

And whenever a person involves himself and attaches himself to it [fem.][1052] as is deserving, the words are as joyous

---

1047 Heb.: *nid-b'roo*

1048 Heb.: *dibroo*

1049 Aram.: *ra-ti-khin*—a vehicle moves something from one place to another. In this case, the words of Torah are moved from the lower worlds into the upper ones.

1050 Heb.: *va-eh-heh-yeh*—in the present tense

1051 Heb.: *v'ha-yee-tee*—in the past tense

1052 Torah

as they were when given at Sinai, as is written in *Zohar*, beginning of *parshat Chu-kaht*: "Rabbee Yosee began: 'And this is the Torah…' (*D'varim* 4:44)—Observe, the words of Torah—holy they are, supernal they are, sweet they are, as is written (*T'hillim* 19:11): 'They are more desirable than gold…'. One who labors in Torah is as if he stands each day on Mount Sinai to receive the Torah, this being what is written (*D'varim* 27:9): 'This day you have become a nation'."

And in *parshat Ah-kha-rei* (69a): "We learned that anyone who listens to words of Torah, he is fortunate in this world as if he received the Torah from Sinai. And one must listen to words of Torah from all people, and one who inclines his ear to receive them gives honor to the holy King, and gives honor to the Torah. About him is written 'this day you have become a nation…'."

And the reason for it is, that just as at the moment of the sanctified occasion[1053] they were attached to His (blessed be He) words, so too now, at literally every instant that a person is involved with and meditates upon/studies[1054] it [fem.][1055], he is literally attached by it [fem.] to His (blessed be He) words as a result that all of it are the utterances of His (blessed be He) mouth to Moshe on Sinai. And that even includes what a young student asks of his teacher, as mentioned previously in chapter six. Now too, when a person is involved with it [fem.], for each word, that specific word is literally quarried at that moment as a fiery flame from His (blessed be His name) mouth (so to speak) as we learned. And it is considered as if we are now receiving it at Sinai from His (blessed be His name) mouth, and for that reason our sages stated a few times: "and the words were as joyous as when they were given at Sinai".

1053 The giving of the Torah at Sinai
1054 Heb.: *ho-geh*
1055 The Torah

And then the abundance of light and blessing flows downwards and is drawn from the source of its supernal root upon all the worlds, and even the earth is illuminated from its glory and is blessed, and it brings much goodness and the abundance of blessing to the world.

And in *Tahna D'vei Eliyahu, Seder Eliyahu Rabba*, chapter 18 it states: "Because he studies the Torah, lo—this brings goodness to the world, and he's able to request mercy and to pray before the Holy One (blessed be He), and it will shake the sky and bring rain to the world…".

And it says more there: "Whenever Israel are involved with Torah and perform the will of their Father in heaven, the Holy One (blessed be He) Himself is caused to turn toward them for blessing, for it is stated (*T'hillim* 85:12): 'Truth will sprout from the earth and justice will peer[1056] from heaven', and there is no 'peering' except for the purpose of blessing, for it is stated (*D'varim* 26:15): 'peer… and bless Your people Israel…'."

CHAPTER 15

And it is so, that the one who blesses is blessed. And as a result of the blessings of the worlds, the person will also be blessed, the one who involves himself with it [fem.] as she in fact deserves, the one who is the cause of all this. And God's glory protects him from above[1057] all day and he attains a soul-*Neshama* that is emanated from a holy place, relative to the great value of his involvement with and attachment to it [fem.], as they stated (*Yoma*

1056 Heb.: *nish-kaf*

1057 Heb.: *cho-feif ah-lahv kol ha-yome*—This reference is found in *D'varim* 33:12, the blessing that Moshe gave to Binyamin.

39a): "[When] a person sanctifies himself from below, they sanctify him from above; a small amount, they sanctify him greatly".

And in the introduction to the *Zohar* (12b): "'The fifth *mitzva...*'—In this text there are three *mitzvote...*, and one is to be involved with Torah and to labor in it each day to rectify his soul-*Neffesh* and soul-*Ruakh*, for the reason that the person who is involved with Torah is rectified with a different holy soul-*Neshama*, for it's written 'teeming living creatures'[1058], a soul-*Neffesh* from the holy soul-*Chai-ya*[1059].... And when he is involved with Torah, via the sounds that he makes during Torah study[1060] he merits the soul-*Neffesh Chai-ya*[1061] and to become like the holy angels.... This is the Torah that is called 'water'. They[1062] will multiply and produce the sound of the 'soul-*Neffesh Chai-ya*' in the *Chai-ya*'s place, and draw it downward, as we learned. And about this Dovid said: 'A pure heart did God-*Elohi"m* create for me'—to be involved with Torah. And then: 'and an upright soul-*Ruakh* renew within me'."[1063]

And he subjugates and rules over everything, and all of the negative judgments upon him leave, and they have no

---

1058 Heb.: *sheh-retz neffesh chai-ya.* Onkeloos translates *sheh-retz* as *rah-khash* (making sounds).

1059 The soul-*Chai-ya* is the fourth aspect of the human soul, above the soul-*Neshama*, the *root-of-the Neshama*, and corresponds to the part related to the world of *Ahtzeeloot.*

1060 Aram.: *r'khee-shoo d'ra-kheesh ba*

1061 The *Ma-toke M'dvash* explains the *Neffesh Chai-ya* as being the soul-*Neshama* of *Ahtzeeloot*, which is the *par-tzoof* of *Beena.*

1062 The insights of Torah study

1063 This section of the *Zohar* can be summarized as: via involvement with the Torah and development of new insights from its study, a new soul is drawn down from the *Chai-ya* which is in *Beena*, the world of *Ahtzeeloot*, rectifying the original soul-*Neffesh* and soul-*Chai-ya.*

command over him (heaven forefend), even though he is still in this world, as is written in the first chapter of *B'rakhote* (5a): "Rabbee Shimon ben Lahkish stated: 'Anyone who is involved with Torah, things that cause suffering stay away from him'." And in perek *Kei-tzad M'ahb-rin* (*Eruvin* 54a): "One who feels pain in his head should involve himself in Torah, for it stated...; one who feels pain in his throat should involve himself in Torah, for it stated...; one who feels pain in his stomach should involve himself in Torah, for it stated...; one who feels pain in his entire body should involve himself in Torah, for it stated (*Mishlei* 4:22): 'and a healing for all his flesh'." And similarly in this manner they stated in *Va-yikra Rabba* (*parsha* 12), and in *Tahn-khooma* (*parshat Yitro*), and in *Midrash T'hillim* (*Mizmor* 109), refer there.

And in *Tahna D'vei Eliyahu, Seder Eliyahu Rabba* (chapter 5): "'He raises the needy from the dirt'—A person who transgressed many transgressions, and a sentence of death was declared upon him..., and he regretted it and did repentance, and reads Torah, Prophets and Writings, and learned *midrash*, laws and narratives, and served Torah scholars, even if a hundred penalties were decreed upon him, the Holy One (blessed be He) will rescind them... ."

And there at the beginning of chapter 6: "'The King brought me to His chambers (*Shir Ha-shirrim* 1:3)'—Just as the Holy One (blessed be He) has an innermost chamber of the many chambers in His Torah, so too do the Torah scholars have for themselves, each and every one of them, an innermost chamber among the chambers in His Torah. And if you should observe that afflictions are materializing[1064] and coming upon you, run to the Torah's chambers and immediately the afflictions flee you, as it is stated (*Y'shaya* 26:20): 'Go My nation, enter into your chambers'—For that reason

1064 Heb.: *m'ma-sh'shin*

is it stated: 'the King brought me to His chambers'. 'Let us rejoice and be glad in it [fem.]' (*Shir Ha-shirrim* 1:4)—In how You made us great and ascendant, and rewarded us[1065] greatly with the words of Torah, from one end of the world and all the way to the other."

And there in chapter 5: "'And as they [emphatic] were walking and conversing[1066]' (*M'lakhim Bet* 2:11)—And 'conversing' is none other than words of Torah..., and when an angel was sent..., he arrived and found that they were involved with the words of Torah, and wasn't able to exert control over them... . From here they stated that when two people are walking along the way and are involved with the Torah, nothing bad can control them... ." Refer there [for more details].

And in *Zohar Va-y'khee* (245a): "'Yissa-khar is a strong-boned donkey'—He began and stated: 'Of Dovid: God-*YHV"H* is my light...'—How pleasant are the words of Torah, how pleasant are those who involve themselves with Torah before the Holy One (blessed be He), for anyone who involves himself with Torah has no fear of the scourges of the world; he is protected above and he is protected below. And not only that, but he ties up the world's scourges and forces them to descend to the depths of a great abyss. Observe: when night comes..., when the north wind awakens and splits the night[1067], an arousal of holiness awakens in the world... . Fortunate is the lot of that man who arises at that hour and involves himself with Torah. As a result of his starting with Torah, all of these varieties of harmful entities, he makes them enter the portals of the great abyss..., as a result of Yissa-khar who

---

1065 Heb.: *ka-shar-ta la-noo keh-tehr ga-dole*

1066 Heb.: *ha-lokhe v'da-beir*

1067 At midnight

was involved with Torah, he ties up the donkey and forces it to descend...—for it would have ascended to cause damage to the world—and causes it take up residence in the piles of garbage...'."[1068]

And so too did the sages (OBM) state in chapter 3 of *Sota* (21a), that the Torah shields from suffering both while he is involved with it and when not involved with it, refer there [for more details]. For it [fem.] "She bestows only goodness upon him, never evil, all the days of her life" (*Mishlei* 31:12)[1069], namely, even when he is not involved with her, whenever he is attached and not separated (heaven forefend) from the way of life of her world, and his awareness is always upon her to return and think about her.[*]

> **Annotation:** *And what is written "She bestows upon him..."—For the definition of "bestows" is repayment to one who did good for him previously. This is what was stated that the Torah repays a good reward to the person who does a favor for it [fem.], namely when he is involved with it [fem.] for its [fem.] own sake. And also if they were involved with it [fem.] not for her own sake, for their own benefit, and didn't do a favor for it [fem.], it would have been expected that the Torah would repay him with evil (heaven forefend). Even so it [fem.] does not repay him with evil (heaven forefend). Rather the opposite, even with "her left hand", namely to those who are offhandedly involved with it [fem.], not for its [fem.] own sake, it [fem.] still gives him "wealth and honor" in this world". This concludes this annotation.*

1068 Rav Chayyim quotes the *Zohar* here, which asserts that by learning Torah one causes the forces of evil to descend out of the world.

1069 Rav Chayyim here likens Torah to a wife who bestows only good upon her husband.

CHAPTER 16

And also he is pardoned from and relieved of all worries and matters relating to the burden of earning a living..., and all other matters of this world that are barriers to continuous involvement with the holy Torah, as they stated (*Ahvote* 3:6): "Everyone who accepts upon himself the yoke of Torah is relieved of the burden of serving the temporal government and the burden of earning a living." And they stated in *B'midbar Rabba* and in *Tahn-khooma parshat Choo-kaht* that it was for this reason that the Torah was given in the desert, because a desert is neither sown nor developed. In this way one who accepts upon himself the yoke of Torah is relieved of the yoke..., and just as a desert does not have government taxes levied upon it, so too are students of Torah[1070] free people.

And in *Zohar Va-y'khee* (242b): "Anyone who knows how to be involved with Torah and does not involve himself is considered guilty of a capital offense. Not only that, but he is assigned the yoke of earning a living and evil servitude, for it's written regarding Yissa-khar 'he bent his shoulder to the burden' (B'reisheet 49:15). One who inclines himself and his direction to not bear the burden of the yoke of Torah, immediately 'and he became an indentured serf'. And vice versa... ."

And this is the judgment recorded in *halakha* in the *Sha"s*, that Torah scholars are exempt from taxes, as they stated (*N'darim* 62b and in the first chapter of *Batra* 8a): "A Torah scholar is permitted to say 'I will not pay the head tax, for it is written (*Ezra* 7:24) 'None shall have the authority to impose upon them [three kinds of taxes]'.

1070 Heb.: *b'nei Torah*

And also cited there: "Rav Huna bar Rav Chisda[1071] levied a head tax on the rabbis. Rav Nakhman bar Yitzkhak said: 'You have transgressed a precept of the Torah, or the Prophets and of the Writings, for it is written…'." As they stated there, the rabbis do not need human protection.

And in *Tahna D'vei Eliyahu* (*Eliyahu Rabba*, chapter 4): "Any Torah scholar who is involved with Torah each and every day so as to increase heaven's honor, has no need of a sword or a spear, nor any other object that could protect him. Rather, the Holy One (blessed be He) protects him personally… ." And there in chapter 18: "If a person has within himself only a profession and *mikra*[1072], he is supplied with one angel to protect him, for it is written… . If a person read Torah, Prophets and Writings, he is supplied with two angels, for it is written (*T'hillim* 91:11): 'He will charge His angels[1073] for you, to protect you…'. But if he read Torah, Prophets and Writings, and learned *Mishna* and *midrash halakhote* and *agadote*, and served Torah scholars, the Holy One (blessed be He) protects him personally…, for it stated (*T'hillim* 121:5): 'God-*YHV"H* is your protector…'."

And according to the degree to which he accepts upon himself the yoke of Torah earnestly and with all of his power, so too, to that degree he will be relieved of and pardoned of the burdens of worldly matters, and the supernal protection covers him, and he is like the son who exerts an effort to make himself acceptable to his father[1074], and his father does what he wants and fulfills his every desire. As the sages (OBM) stated (*Avoda Za-ra* 19a): "Anyone who is involved with Torah,

---

1071 Our version of the Talmud on *Bava Batra* 8a has a slightly different text: "*Rav Nakhman bar Rav Chisda rah-ma karga ah-ra-ba-nan…*".

1072 Heb.: *deh-rekh eh-retz u-mikra l'vahd*

1073 Stated in the plural, implying two angels

1074 Heb.: *k'vein ha-mit-kha-tei ahtzmo al ah-veev*

the Holy One (blessed be He) does for him what he wants". And so it is also found in the *Midrash T'hillim* (*Mizmor* 1). And there they also stated that it's written in the Torah, and repeated a second time in the Prophets, and repeated a third time in the Writings that anyone who involves himself with Torah has his assets prosper.

And in *Mishlei Rabbta* (end of *parsha* 8): "'...and who draws favor[1075] from God-*YHV"H*' (*Mishlei* 8:35)—Anyone who derives conclusions from words of Torah and teaches them in public, so too I, at times of favor, make favorable conclusions about him..., and his meals are always available for him, without any toil and with minimal labor for them. For they stated there in the chapter "a valorous woman" (*Shir Ha-Shirrim* 31:10-31): 'Whenever a Torah scholar sits and involves himself with Torah...'. And not only that, but the Holy One (blessed be He) provides his meals for him each and every day, for it stated 'and she provides nourishment to the members of her household' (*Mishlei* 31:15)."

And in *Tahna D'vei Eliyahu, Seder Eliyahu Rabba* (chapter 18): "Blessed is God-*Ma-kome* who selected the sages and their students... . Just as they sit in the synagogues and study halls and anywhere that is made available for them[1076], and read[1077], and learn[1078] for the sake of heaven, and fear/awe is in their hearts/minds, and they strengthen words of Torah with their pronouncements, and fulfill in themselves the verse 'It is good for a man that he be burdened with a yoke during his youth' (*Ei-kha* 3:27) in this manner (so to speak), even if they should request the entire world in

1075 Heb.: *va-ya-fek ra-tzone*

1076 Heb.: *u-v'khahl mah-kome sheh-hoo pah-nui la-hem*

1077 Read scripture

1078 Learn *Mishna*

one hour He gives it to them immediately... ."

And beyond that, even though he absolutely flees from honor and greatness -

> for lacking that characteristic it's almost impossible, in this world, to be involved with Torah for its own sake, and it will not thrive in his domain at all, as they (OBM) stated in the chapter of the Levels of Torah (*Ahvote*, chapter 6): "Do not seek greatness for yourself, and do not covet honor", for a person is forbidden to turn his attention there at all -

even so, He in His (blessed be His name) great council, awards him joy and greatness against his will, as it is written in *Tahna D'vei Eliyahu* there: "Blessed is God-*YHV"H*, blessed is He, who selected the sages and their students... . Just as they sit in the synagogues and study halls each day, and read and learn for the sake of heaven, and fear/awe of heaven is in their hearts/minds, and they strengthen words of Torah with their pronouncements, and who joyfully accept upon themselves the yoke of heaven, in this manner (so to speak) the Holy One (blessed be He) awards them (to the righteous ones) joy against their will and not for their benefit... ." (This ends the citation.)

And as the verse states (*T'hillim* 23:6): "May only goodness and kindness pursue me all the days of my life", meaning that even though I flee from them, they [emphatic] pursue me against my will.

CHAPTER 17

[This holds too] after his expiration from this world. The sages stated (*Chageega* 27a): "Torah scholars, the fires of Gehinnom[1079] exert no control over them...". And they also stated there that if a Torah scholar became corrupt, what he previously learned of Torah is not loathed. And in *Mishlei Rabbta*, on the verse "to understand parable and epigram..."[1080] (*Mishlei* 1:6): "...this is Torah itself. And why is Torah's name called 'epigram'? Because it [fem.] saves[1081] those who are involved with it [fem.] from the judgment of Gehinnom." And there at the beginning of *parsha* 2: "'My child, if you will accept my words' (*Mishlei* 2:1)—The Holy One (blessed be He) said to Israel on Mount Sinai: 'If you merited to conceal[1082] and to accept my Torah and to perform it, I will save you from three punishments: from the war of Gog and Magog, from the pangs of the Messiah and from the judgment of Gehinnom'. '... And my commandments you shall conceal with you'—If you merit to conceal my Torah, I will satisfy you with the good that is concealed for the future that is coming, as it is stated 'how abundant is Your goodness that You have concealed...'."

And there in *parsha* 10: "Rabbee Chaneena ben Dosa stated: 'There is no act of righteousness[1083] that saves a person from the judgment of Gehinnom other than Torah..., for it has the power to save him from that day of judgment. And even if a person was convicted in the matter of a transgression, it [fem.] can save him from the

---

1079 Hell
1080 Heb.: *l'ha-veen ma-shahl oo-m'lee-tza*
1081 Heb.: *ma-tzeh-let*
1082 Alt.: to go north—Heb.: *l'hatzpin*
1083 Heb.: *tz'da-ka*

day of judgment… . So we can conclude from this that a Torah scholar who transgressed some transgression, that it [fem.] saves him.'"

And in *Midrash T'hillim* (*Mizmor* 19:7): "and its season..., and nothing escapes its scorching heat"—Rabbee Yanai and Rabbee Shimon ben Lakish both said: 'In the future there will be no Gehinnom other than this sun, and it will incinerate the evil ones, for it stated (*Malachi* 3:19): "Lo, the day comes burning like a furnace, and all the scoundrels… and incinerate them… ." But in the future, who will be hidden from its heat? One who is involved with Torah. What is written subsequently? 'God's-*YHV"H* Torah is perfect… .' And he also states there: 'There is no darkness, nor shadow of death where evildoers can be concealed' (*Ee-yove* 34:22). And who is concealed? One who is involved in Torah… ." Refer there [for more details]. And it's a simple deduction from *Elisha Ahkheir*[1084], where they stated (*Chageega* 15b): "We cannot execute a judgment of Gehinnom against him because he is learned in Torah."[1085]

And so too they stated in *Yerushalmi* there, and in *Kohelet Rabba* (*siman* 7) on the verse "The end of a matter is better than its beginning…" (*Kohelet* 7:8)—"But did we not learn that a book's cover is saved along with the book…? Elisha is saved by the merit of his Torah[1086]."

1084 Rabbee Elisha ben Abuya, after his heresy, was referred to as Elisha Ah-kheir (Elisha the Other).

1085 Heb.: *law meidan nee-dahn-ya mee-shoom d'gawmeer o-rai-ta*—Our version of Chageega has a slightly different wording: *law meidan lee-dai-nei mee-shoom d'ah-sahk b'o-rai-ta*—"We can't execute a judgment against him because he was involved in Torah". No mention of Gehinnom is made but it is implicit as indicated by the following phrase. And rather than "learned in Torah" we have "involved in Torah."

1086 The Torah within Elisha, for which Elisha is the container, serves to save him.

And in *Zohar Yitro* (83b), Rabbee Yitzkhak stated: "Why was the Torah given in the midst of fire and darkness...? Because anyone who involves himself with Torah will be saved from the other fire of Gehinnom, and from the darkness that all of the other nations create for Israel... ." Refer there [for more details].

And in the *Raa-ya M'hemna T'rooma* (134b): It's a *mitzva* to learn Torah every day, it being the secret of the supernal faith/reliability[1087] to know the Holy One's (blessed be He) ways, such that anyone who involves himself with Torah merits in this world and merits in that world, and is saved from all negative accusations, because the Torah is the secret of faith/reliability, and anyone who involves himself with it [fem.] is involved with the supernal faith/reliability. His *Sh'kheena* settles within him in a way that it will never leave him."

And [it's also] per their (OBM) statement (*Shabbat* 63a) on the verse "long life on her right side..." (*Mishlei* 3:16): "Long life to those who act skillfully towards her[1088], and all the more so wealth and honor." And this is in two worlds: wealth and honor in this world and long life in the next world. For the key feature of "long life", its intention is to the world that is everlasting, as the sages (OBM) stated in various places, and in *Zohar Va-yeishev* (190, top of first folio), refer there [for more details].

And there in *parshat Cha-yei* (131b): "Rabbee Elazar began: 'Unveil my eyes and I will perceive wonders from your Torah' (*T'hillim* 119:18)—How many people are

---

1087 Aram.: *d'm'heim-noota ee-la-ah*

1088 Heb.: *la-mai-mee-neem ba,* literally to those who act right-handedly towards her, perhaps referring to those who involve themselves with Torah for its sake and not their own (per RaSh"Y).

fools, for they don't know enough to, and don't set a fixed gaze on, involving themselves with Torah. For the Torah is the totality of life, and the totality of freedom, and the totality of goodness, in this world and the world-to-come. It is the freedom in this world and freedom in the world-to-come, life in this world—so that they will merit perfection of days in this world, as is written...—and to long life in the world-to-come, because they are a perfect life, they are a life of freedom, a life without sadness, a life that is truly life. Freedom in this life, freedom from all, for anyone who involves himself with Torah, all of the nations of the world are not able to assert sovereignty over him.... And for that reason, anyone who involves himself with Torah has freedom from everything: in this world from servitude to the nations of the world, and freedom in the next world, for they will not demand any judgment of him in the world-to-come." Refer there [for more details].

And in *Tahna D'vei Eliyahu, Seder Eliyahu Rabba* (chapter 18), on the verse (*Yekhezkel* 47:12): "'And along the banks of stream will grow, on this side and the other, every variety of tree bearing edible fruit...'—What does 'and they will not experience the coming of heat' (*Yirmiya* 17:8)[1089] mean? It comes to tell you that anyone who involves himself with the Torah never encounters the quality of calamity, whether it's in this world, in the days of the descendant of Dovid, or in the world-to-come. And as the sages (OBM) explained (*Sota* 21a): "'When you go forth, it will guide you...' (*Mishlei* 6:22)—in this world. 'When you lie down, it will safeguard you'—in the grave. 'And when you awake, it will converse with you'—for the world-to-come."

1089 The verse in *Yirmiya* refers to a tree that is planted near water, which continues to produce fruit even in times of heat and drought.

And in *Zohar, parshat Va-yei-shev* (184b and 185a)—"Rabbee Yehuda began and stated: 'God's-YHV"H Torah is perfect, restoring the soul-*Neffesh*...' (*T'hillim* 19:8)—How great an effort must a person make in Torah, for whomever involves himself with Torah will have life in this world and in the world-to-come, and merits both worlds. And even if he involves himself with Torah but doesn't involve himself for its sake correctly, he merits a good reward in this world and is not subject to judgment in that world. And observe that it's written 'length of days in her right, and in her left: wealth and honor'—'Length of days' for one who involved himself with Torah for its own sake, that he has length of days in that world that has length of days.... 'In her left: wealth and honor'—A good reward and tranquility (which are wealth and honor) will he have in this world. And anyone who involves himself with Torah for its own sake, when he exits this world, the Torah proceeds before him and announces before him, and guards him so that the masters of judgment can't approach him. And when his body lies in the grave, it [fem.] stands guard over him. And when the soul-*Neshama* leaves to depart to its place, it [fem.] proceeds before that soul-*Neshama*, and many sealed gates are broken open before the Torah until it ascends to its place, and it stands over the person until it awakens in the time when the dead of the world arise, and it declares its merits. This is what is written (*Mishlei* 6:22): 'When you go forth it will guide you. As you recline it will guard you. And when you awaken it will converse with you', as it stated. 'When you recline it will guard you'—At the time when the body lies in the grave, for at that time the body is judged in the grave, and then the Torah shields it from the judgment of the grave. 'And when you awaken it will converse with you'—When the dead of the world awaken from the dust, then the Torah will be a defense spokesman for you, to declare your merits."

And so too did our sages (OBM) state in *Perek Cheilek* (99b) on the verse (*Mishlei* 16:26): "'The soul-*Neffesh* works, works for him...'—He labors in this place and the Torah labors for him in another place." And in *Mishlei Rabbta, parsha* 14: "'The wisest among women builds her house'—Anyone who earned his wisdom in this world, can be certain that it [fem.][1090] built him a home in the world-to-come. 'But the foolish one tears it down with her hands'—Anyone that hasn't earned wisdom for himself can be certain that he's earned Gehinnom for himself in the future."

And in *Sitrei Torah*[1091] *Lekh L'kha* (88a): "'After these events'—These are the words of Torah... . And what is written in the text: 'Do not fear Abraham—I will shield you'—from all the evil tribulations of Gehinnom. 'Your reward is very great' because anyone who involves himself with Torah in this world merits and inherits an inheritance of partrimony in the world-to-come... ." Refer there [for more details].

And in *Zohar Va-yahk-heil* (200a): "Because when a person is involved with Torah, the Holy One (blessed be He) stands there..., and saves the person from three judgments: from judgment in this world, from judgment of the angel of death who isn't able to have any control over him, and from judgment of Gehinnom." And as the sages (OBM) stated in *Perek Ma-ah-laht Ha-Torah* (*Ahvote* chapter 6), and in *B'midbar Rabba* (chapter 16), and in *Chazeeta* on the verse "Who is she who ascends...". And in *Tahn-khooma parshat Eikev*: "Don't read it as 'engraved', but rather as 'free'"—For no one is a free person other than one who is involved with learning Torah. And the sages explained: "'freedom'—from the angel

1090 "It" being Torah.
1091 Part of the *Zohar*

of death."[1092] And they also said this in chapter four[1093] of *Ma-kote* (10a) that words of Torah provide refuge from the angel of death. And in *Zohar parshat Cha-yei* (on the page mentioned previously[1094]): "Freedom in this world, freedom from all… . Freedom from the angel of death, so that he has no ability to rule over him. And so it is clear that if First Adam would have attached himself to the tree of life, that is Torah, he would not have caused death for himself and for the entire world. And for that reason, when the Holy One (blessed be He) gave the Torah to Israel, what's written there? 'Engraved on the tablets…'. And the Holy One (blessed be He) Himself stated (*T'hillim* 82:6): 'I had taken you for divine beings and descendants of the Most High, all of you… .' And therefore, anyone who involves himself with Torah, that evil serpent who darkens the world has no ability to rule over him."

CHAPTER 18

And for that reason, the person who accepts upon himself the yoke of the holy Torah for its own sake, to express its truth, (as described previously regarding the meaning of "for its own sake"), he is elevated above all the matters of this world, and is personally supervised[1095] directly by Him (blessed be He), superseding the entire system of the laws of nature and of fate [1096]. [This is] because he is literally attached to the Torah and to the Holy One (blessed be He), so to speak, and is sanctified with the supernal holiness of the holy Torah which is inconceivably

1092 *Sh'mote Rabba* (*Kee Teesa* 41), *Va-yikra Rabba* (*M'tzora* 18) and others.

1093 This is likely a printer error, as folio10a of *Ma-kote* is found in chapter two.

1094 131b

1095 Heb.: *hahsh-ga-kha pra-teet*

1096 Heb.: *mei-ho-ra-aht ko-khote ha-tiv-im v'ha-ma-za-lote koolam*

higher than all the worlds. And Torah is the one that provides sustenance and maintenance to all of the worlds and to all the laws of nature. The result is that a person who is involved with Torah sustains and maintains all the worlds, and is higher than all of them. So how could it be that His administration of him would be via the powers of nature?

And this is what our sages (OBM) state (*P'sakhim* 50b): "It is written: 'for great *until* heavens is Your compassion' (*T'hillim* 57:11). And it is [also] written: 'for great *above* heavens is Your compassion' (*T'hillim* 108:5)." It's not a question[1097]. Here it's regarding those who are involved[1098] in it for its own sake, and here it's regarding those who are involved in it not for its own sake."

That is, that one who is involved with Torah not for its own sake, even though it is certain that he is considered satisfactorily before Him (blessed be He), even if his intention is to get some other result, with the provision that the result isn't something that would be held against him (heaven forefend)—

> and even more so if he doesn't have the intention to get some other result but rather, that he does it in a habitual way, because from within that context he'll arrive at the level of doing it for its own sake, as is known from their (OBM) statements—

even so he is not yet sanctified and exalted so that His (blessed be He) administration of him will be above the powers of nature. For that reason it's written only "until heavens", namely within the context of the powers of nature that are decreed in the heavens, but not beyond them.

1097 Heb.: *lo kahsh-ya*—This phrase is not found in our editions. Instead we have *ha kei-tzad* (*when is this?*).

1098 Heb.: *ba-oh-skim*—Our editions have *ba-oh-sin* (do it).

In contrast, regarding one who is involved with Torah for its own sake, it states "above heavens", meaning that the totality of His (Blessed be He) administration of him will exclusively be beyond the system of the laws of nature.

And what is written in the *Raa-ya M'hemna* (*Pinkhas* 216b): "Observe: all of the world's creations, before the Torah was given to Israel, were dependent on fate..., but after Torah was given to Israel, it removed them from being obligated to stars and constellations..., and because of this, anyone who involves himself with Torah has his obligation to stars and constellations disrupted if he learns the Torah in order to fulfill its commandments. And if not, he's as if he didn't involve himself with Torah and does not have the obligation to stars and constellations disrupted."

And it's the opposite situation: that the powers of nature are handed him to do with what he will, and to bend them to whatever he desires. And the dread of him falls upon all, as is written in *parshat ha-Torah* (*Ahvote*, 6:1): "...and awards him majesty and sovereignty", because the crown of his God-*Elohi"m*, the light of Torah, illuminates and glistens upon his head, and he is sheltered in the shade of the *Sh'kheena*'s wings, as is written in the *Zohar* (*Tzav* 35a): "Rabbee Elazar began and stated: 'And I will place my words in your mouth and with the shade of my hand I will cover you'—We learned that any person who is involved with words of Torah, and his lips utter Torah, the Holy One (blessed be He) shelters him from above and the *Sh'kheena* spreads her wings over him. This is what is stated: 'And I will place my words in your mouth and with the shade of my hand I will cover you...'."

And in the introduction to the *Zohar* (11a) and so too in identical language in *parshat V'et-kha-nahn* (260a): "Observe how powerful is the power of the Torah and how elevated it is over everything else, for anyone who involves himself with the Torah does not fear those who are higher or lower, and does not fear the world's evil disqualifiers, because he is held fast by the tree of life and consumes from it each day, for the Torah teaches a person to walk in the path of truth, counsels him... ."

And in *parshat B'sha-lakh* 46a: "Rabbee Yosee began: 'How highly esteemed is the Torah before the Holy One (blessed be He), for anyone who involves himself with Torah is loved above, loved below, the Holy One (blessed be He) pays attention to his words, does not abandon him in this world and does not abandon him in the world-to-come... ." Refer there [for more details].

And in *parshat M'tzora* (52b): "And when he's involved with the Master's service and delves into Torah, how many guardian angels are ready to receive him and guard him, and the *Sh'kheena* settles upon him, and all of them proclaim ahead of him and state: 'Give honor to the [one who] resembles the King.' He is safeguarded in this world and in the world-to-come; how happy is his portion."

CHAPTER 19

And God's name is called upon him, for the entire Torah is the Holy One's (blessed be He) names, as they (OBM) stated (*B'rakhote* 21a): "How do we know the requirement for a blessing on the Torah, before the act[1099], is from the Torah? For it states (*D'varim* 32:3): 'When I call out the name of God-*YHV"H...*'." And furthermore they learned that one who is involved with Torah, he is steeped in the presence of the *Sh'kheena*, as it is written (*Sh'mote* 20:21): "Wherever I permit My name ... ." And in *Zohar B'midbar* (118a): "How well-loved is the Torah by the Holy One

1099 Before reading or learning Torah

(blessed be He), for wherever the words of Torah are heard, the Holy One (blessed be He) and all of His hosts all pay attention to his words, and the Holy One (blessed be He) comes to dwell with him, this being what is written: 'Wherever I permit My name …'."

And in *parshat Mishpatim* (124a): "Any one who guards the ways of Torah and who is involved with them is considered as one who is involved with the holy name, for we learned that the entire Torah is the name of the Holy One (blessed be He). And one who is involved with it is as one who is involved with the holy name, because the entire Torah is one holy name, a supernal name, a name that includes all names. And one who omits one letter from it is as if he created a blemish in the holy name." And in *parshat Va-yikra* (13b): "Rabbee Abba stated: 'All this came upon us, yet we have not forgotten You…' (*T'hillim* 44:18)—We have not forgotten the words of Your Torah. From this we learned that anyone who forgot words of Torah and is not willing to be involved with them, is as if he forgot the Holy One (blessed be He), for the entire Torah is the Holy One's (blessed be He) name." And there (19a, end of folio): "For the Torah, one who is involved with it is crowned with the crown of the holy name, for the Torah is a holy name, and one who is involved with it is impressed with and is crowned with the holy name, and then he knows the sealed pathways and deep secrets." And it is also found at the beginning of *parshat Shmini,* and in *parshat Ah-kha-rei* 71b, 72a at the end of the folio, 73a, and 75a, and in *parshat Eh-more* 89b, and at the beginning of *parshat Korahkh.* Refer there [for more details].

And for that reason too they stated that the Holy One and the Torah are one, for He and His name are one, as is stated in the *Zohar Yitro* 90b: "And the entire Torah is one name, literally a holy name of the Holy One (blessed be He). Fortunate is he who merits it, for one who merits the Torah merits to His holy name literally. Rabbe Yosee stated: 'He merits literally to the Holy One (blessed be He), for He and His name are one'."

And for that reason is stated in *Tahna D'vei Eliyahu* (*Rabba*, chapter 18) that anyone who quarrels with a Torah scholar is as if he quarrels with the One who spoke and the world came into being, for it is stated (*B'midbar* 26:9): "He is Da-tahn and Aviram..., when they contended against God-*YHV"H*". For that reason, when a person comes in the name of God, all are in awe/fear and are shocked by him, as is written (*D'varim* 28:10): "And all the nations of the land will see that the name of God-*YHV"H* is called upon you, and they will be in awe of/fear you". And as is written (*T'hillim* 91:14): "For he has yearned for me and I will deliver him; I will elevate him because he knows My name"—"For he yearned for me"—literally for Him (blessed be He), so to speak, as mentioned above.

And in *parshat Ba-lahk* (202a): "Observe how well-appreciated are those who involve themselves with Torah before the Holy One (blessed be He), for even when judgment is hanging over the world and permission is granted the destroyer to destroy, the Holy One (blessed be He) commands them regarding those who are involved with Torah and thus said the Holy One (blessed be He) (*D'varim* 20:19): 'When you besiege a city...', because of their many sins..., come and I'll command you regarding the members of my household. 'Do not cut down its trees'—This is the Torah scholar in that city, the tree of life that brings forth fruits. 'Its trees'[1100] are those who advise[1101] the inhabitants of the city..., and who teach them

1100 Heb.: *ei-tza*, its [fem.] trees
1101 Heb.: also *ei-tza*, advice (a homonym)

the path upon which they should walk, and for that reason [it is written] 'do not cut down its trees, by wielding an axe against them', to wield judgment upon him and not to extend a flaming sword over him… . 'For is a tree of the field the man?'—This one is called 'man' who is known above and below… . And all these commands of the Holy One (blessed be He) regarding those who are involved with Torah… ." Refer there at length [for more details].

CHAPTER 20

And he is the precious child among the residents of the King's palace, among those in the King's hall, in that only he is given permission at all times to search in the holy King's treasury. And all of the supernal gates are open before him, per their (OBM) statement (*Sota* 49a): "Anyone[1102] who involves himself with Torah, while being situated in adversity[1103]… . Rabbee Ah-kha bar Cha-neena says: Even the barrier[1104] is not locked before him, for it states (*Y'shaya* 30:20): 'Your Teacher will no longer be cloaked'."

And he enters within the gates of the holy Torah, to grasp and to gaze at the inner light, into the depths of her supernal secrets, as is stated in the chapter on Torah (*Ahvote* 6:1): "...and they reveal to him the secrets of Torah". And so too they stated (*Avoda Za-ra* 35b): "...and not only that, but things that are hidden from people are revealed to him".

And in *Midrash T'hillim* (*Mizmor* 19) they stated about

1102 Our editions of *Sota* say: "any Torah scholar who...".

1103 The quote continues: "...his prayer is heeded".

1104 Heb.: *par-gode,* which is a curtain. This refers to the barrier that is perceived to separate us from the heavenly court.

Shmuel who stated: "I am familiar with the streets of heaven…", (and in the *Sha"s* it's stated as "the paths of heaven are clear to me). Did Shmuel ascend to heaven? Rather, that by laboring in the Torah's wisdom, he learned from within it what is in the heavens[1105].

And in *Mishlei Rabbati* (*parsha* 8): "'and what opens my lips are righteous words' (*Mishlei* 8:6)—Words that make accessible for you the innermost rooms in heaven[1106]." And in *Tahna D'vei Eliyahu, Seder Eliya Rabba* (chapter 27): "'Blessed be the *Ma-kome* who selected the words of the sages and their students…'—Just as they sit in the synagogues and study halls in every place that is available for them, and they read and study for the sake of heaven [1107], with fear/awe in their hearts/minds, and they maintain the words of Torah in their mouths, in the same way the Holy One (blessed be He) sits opposite them and reveals to them the secrets of the Torah in their mouths and in their hearts/minds… ."

And His (blessed be He) holy spirit will dwell upon him continuously, as is stated in *Zohar Sh'mote* (6b): "Sages are superior to prophets in every way, for with prophets, the holy spirit settles upon them at some times and at other times not, while sages never have the holy spirit removed from them even one tiny instant, and they know what is above and what is below and do not desire to reveal."

And in *Tahna D'vei Eliyahu, Seder Eliyahu Zoota* (chapter 1): "…and as a result of a person having read[1108] Torah, Prophets and Writing, and studied[1109] *Mishna, Midrash Halakhote* and *Ha-ga-dote*, and studied *G'mara*, and studied

---

1105 Heb.: *sh'kha-kim*
1106 Heb.: *ba-ma-rome*
1107 Heb.: *v'ko-rin v-sho-nin l'sheim sha-my-im*
1108 Heb.: *sheh-ka-ra*
1109 Heb.: *sha-na*

intellectual analysis for its own sake, immediately *Ruakh Ha-kodesh* settles upon him, for it is stated (*Shmuel* 2 23:2): 'God-*YHV"H* spoke within me...'." And in general they stated in the chapter on Torah (*Ahvote* 6) and anyone who is involved with learning Torah, that person elevates himself...". And so we learn (end of *Perek Ha-ro-eh*[1110]): "If you have been shamed in raising yourself up..." (*Mishlei* 30:32)—Anyone who willingly shames himself over words of Torah[1111] exalts himself, to the extent that the sages (OBM) stated that their level is above the level of the prophets, as is written (*Bava Batra* 12a): "A sage is superior to a prophet[1112]", and as is written in *Zohar Sh'mote* mentioned above.

And the matter is further explained in [*Zohar*] *parshat Tzav* (35a): "Come observe: What's the difference between those who involve themselves with Torah and the faithful prophets? Those who involve themselves with Torah are superior to prophets at all times. What's the reason? They function at a much higher level than prophets. Those who involve themselves with Torah function above, in the place called Torah[1113] which is what maintains all reliability/faith. And prophets function below in a place called *Neh-tzakh* and *Hode*[1114]. For that reason those who are involved with Torah are superior to prophets and are far above them, for they function above while they function below... . And for that reason those who involve themselves with Torah are meritorious, for they are at a level above everyone else."

1110 *B'rakhote* 63b

1111 This refers to a student who admits to his teacher what he does not yet understand.

1112 Heb.: *cha-khahm ah-deef me-na-vee*

1113 Referring to the level of *Tif-eh-ret*

1114 As the Ariza"l explains in the first section of *Sha-ar Ha-gilgoolim*

CHAPTER 21

And if the level of those who labor in Torah is so marvelous even while they are still in this dark world, being able with their *Ruakh Ha-kodesh* to grasp and to gaze upon the supernal light, the righteous are immeasurably greater after their deaths than they were while alive (*Chulin* 7a), after his pure soul-*Neshama* greatly satiated itself [fem.] with Torah and *mitzvote*, and it[1115] [fem.] returns to its [fem.] Father's home sanctified and purified as when it [fem.] left. And with the additional light of the learning of holy Torah in his hand, all of the gates are opened before him, and he departs and the heavens are split..., and he is bound in the bundle of life[1116] with God-*YHV"H* his God-*Elohi"m* (blessed be His name).

And in *Tahna D'vei Eliyahu, Seder Eliyahu Rabba* (chapter 4) he stated: "Lest you say that as a result of Moses' entering his eternal abode, his crown of having an illuminating countenance expired, the text comes to teach us (*D'varim* 33:10) 'No prophet has arisen... face to face'. Just as the illuminated face that is above exists for ever and ever, so too did Moses' illuminating face enter with him into his eternal abode. ... And not only Moses, but rather any student of the sages who involves himself with Torah from his youth through his old age and then dies, in truth he does not die, but rather he is still living, forever and ever, for it is stated (*Shmuel Alef* 25:29): '... and my master's soul-*Neffesh* will be bound in the bundle of life with God-*YHV"H* your God-*Elohi"m*', comparing

1115 The *neshama*

1116 Heb.: *v'tza-roor b'tz'rore ha-khayyim*

the righteous wise student to God-*Elohi"m*[1117], that just as God-*Elohi"m* (may His name be blessed) is alive and continuing..., so too the wise student who involved himself with Torah all his days and then died, we conclude that he is alive and has not yet died, and he lives forever... . And where is his soul-*Neshama*? Beneath the throne of Glory." (This concludes the quote.)

And his soul-*Neffesh* is satiated by the brightness of the supernal hidden light, per the sages' statement (*Sota* 49a): "Any wise student who involves himself with Torah, being greatly driven..., Rabbee Ah-va-hu states: "They even satiate him from the glow of the *Sh'kheena*, for it is stated (*Y'shaya* 30:20): 'and your eyes will see your teacher'." And in the first chapter of *Batra* (10a): "What is the meaning of (*T'hillim* 17:15): 'I will be satiated by your image while still awake'? These are the students of the wise who shake off sleepiness in this world. The Holy One (blessed be He) satiates them with the glow of the *Sh'kheena* in the world-to-come." And in *Perek Cheilek*[1118] (100a): "Rabbee Yehuda the son of Rabbee See-mone expounded: 'Anyone who darkens his face[1119] over words of Torah in this world, the Holy One (blessed be He) makes him glow in the world-to-come'."

And it's all according to the degree of the majority of his involvement and his wondrous attachment to the holy Torah, as is stated in *Tahna D'vei Eliyahu, Seder Eliyahu Zoota* (chapter 12): "In relation to the righteous, what is said about them? 'And those who love him are like the sun revealing itself in its great power' (*Shofe-tim* 5:31), which is not the case with the servant angels. How beautiful is

---

1117 The words "comparing the righteous wise student to God-*Elohi"m"* are not found in our editions.

1118 Sanhedrin

1119 Who, in his zeal to learn Torah, neglects his physical health

the power of the Master of the House, that He makes His servants' crown beautiful, just like His own crown. And if you say that one who read and learned much, and one who read and learned only a little, that the illumination of their faces will be equal regarding the degree of their facial illumination in the world-to-come, it is not so! Blessed is God-*Ma-kome* (blessed be He), that there is no undeserved reward[1120].... ...It is stated in another place (*Mishlei* 12:26): 'a righteous one is greater than his acquaintance.' ... Rather, each one receives a reward according to his path... ."[1121]

And this [emphatic] is the secret of the light that was created on the first day of creation, that the Holy One (blessed be He) hid away for the righteous. And thus it is written in the *Zohar* (*B'reisheet* 47a): "Rabbee Eliezer began: 'How great is the goodness that You have hidden away...[1122]'—Come observe: the Holy One (blessed be He) created man in this world and designed him so that he should be perfected via his service, and that he should refine his ways so that he should merit the supernal light that the Holy One (blessed be He) hid away for the righteous, as is written: 'no eye has beheld it... . He will do it for the one who awaits Him'. And how will a person merit this light? Via Torah."

And our sages (OBM) stated (*Chageega* 14a): "'...for those who did not spare effort, and the time has not come for a river[1123] to cast their foundations' (*Ee-yove* 2:16)—These are the students of the wise who restrain their eyes from sleep in this world. The Holy One (blessed be He) reveals a secret to

1120 Heb.: *ma-so pa-neem*

1121 The quotation is not ordered per our current editions.

1122 *T'hillim* 31:20

1123 Heb.: *na-har*, a cognate for the Aramaic *n'heera*, which means light.

them in the world-to-come, for it is stated: 'a river to cast their foundations', and these are the hidden reasons underlying Torah, they being the hidden supernal light."

And for that reason it is stated in *Perek Ha-Torah* (*Ahvote*): "Anyone who involves himself with Torah for its own sake merits many things." It was concealed and not explained what those [many] things are. And it's impossible to state that it is those things that it lists there afterwards, for it explicitly states: 'and not only these…' to inform us that they are other things.

However, it hinted to the soul-*Neffesh*'s pleasure and refinement via the hidden light, that none of the supernal angels, nor *Chayyote* nor holy *Seraphim*, nor any prophet nor seer has ever perceived its essential nature, as the sages (OBM) stated (at the end of *Perek Ein Ome-deen* (34b): "None of the sum total of prophets prophesied... . Other than the students of the wise, no eye has beheld it… ." And this is the garden and the "wine that is still being stored in its grapes." For they stated there: "What is 'no eye has beheld it…'"? These all refer to the same thing, the secret of the reasoning underlying Torah that has not been revealed yet. For that reason it is states plainly "many things", that it's not something that is already grasped, that can be stated and explained.

And in *Tahna D'vei Eliyahu, Seder Eliyahu Rabba* (chapter 27) it says: "Fortunate is the person who has within him words of Torah, and he sits and reads and learns in a place that's modest and hidden. Next to whom is he placed? Let it be stated: near the Holy One (blessed be He), for it was stated (*T'hillim* 91a): 'He dwells in supernal concealment, in God-*Shadd"ai*'s shade will he dwell'. Just as they make themselves unique in this world and no outsider is among them, so too in the world-to-come they sit near only the Holy One (blessed be He) … ."

CHAPTER 22

And if (heaven forefend) we make only a weak effort to involve ourselves with it, the influence of the supernal light in all the worlds lessens (so to speak), each one [world] according to its relative position. And in the hidden places His soul-*Neffesh* cries (so to speak), as the sages (OBM) stated (*Chageega* 5b): "There are three over whom the Holy One (blessed be He) cries", and one of them is "one who could involve himself with Torah but doesn't." And they also said there: "These three expressions of tears, to what do they refer? ...And there are some who say that one is for the neglect of Torah study[1124]." Woe to the child who causes his Father to weep each day. And the matter of this crying is the intensification of judgment, when the supernal light (which is the great compassion in the hidden worlds) is reduced.

And the person who has not yet perceived the light of Torah during his lifetime and never involved himself with it, does not in any way merit the supernal holiness to settle upon[1125] him, and does not merit the acquisition of a pure/undefiled soul-*Neffesh*. As is written in the introduction to the *Zohar* (12b): "The fifth *mitzva*... . In this verse there are three *mitzvote*. The first is to exert oneself with the Torah..., for when a person does not involve himself with Torah, he doesn't have a holy soul-*Neffesh*, and the supernal holiness does not settle upon[1126] him... ."

And also, he is cast off and left to the judgmental powers of the Other Side [1127], so that they are able to have power over him, as the sages (OBM) stated in the first chapter of

---

1124 Heb.: *beetool Torah*

1125 Heb.: *sheh-tishreh ah-lahv k'doosha el-yo-na*

1126 Aram.: *sharya ahloy*

1127 Aram.: s*itra ahkhra*

B'rakhote (5a): "That anyone who has the opportunity to be involved with Torah and does not, the Holy One (blessed be He) visits upon him ugly afflictions, and he becomes fouled, as is stated (*T'hillim* 39:3): 'I was silent in the face of good, and my pains made me ugly'." And he causes the loss of a great good from himself and the entire world, for he tipped the scales of justice (heaven forefend) to the side of owing a debt for himself and the entire world. As the sages (OBM) stated in the *D'vraim Rabba,* at the beginning of *parsha* 4:2: "'Hear... and don't be haughty' (*Yirmiyahu* 13:15)—Hear the words of Torah.... 'And don't be haughty'—Don't prevent the good[1128] from entering the world." And as they stated in the first chapter in *Batra* (8a): "That calamities only happen because of the ignorant. And if (heaven forefend) a calamity should befall an individual or a nation, even at the farthest reaches of the world, he caused it himself[1129]"—may the Merciful (blessed be His name) save us!

And if he had previously been involved with it [fem.] and then separated from it [fem.] (heaven forefend), he lessens (heaven forefend) the power of the heavenly retinue, and the structures of the worlds and the holy vehicle are damaged and disordered, and the efforts of the other side are victorious (may the Merciful save us). And it's as if the power of the supernal holiness, the imminent presence of the our fierce One, the Faithful one of Israel, is weakened and darkened, whose imminent presence is always among us as a result of involvement with Torah correctly.

As is written in *Zohar T'rooma* (155b): "Rabbee Cheeya began and stated: 'For it is a time to act for God-*YHV"H*—they have breached your Torah' (*T'hillim* 119:126)—Whenever

1128 The phrase *al tig-b'hoo* in this context translates as "do not hold it aloft so that it can't enter".

1129 Aram.: *dein g'ra-ma dee-lei*

the Torah is preserved in the world and people involve themselves with it [fem.], it's as if the Holy One (blessed be He) is pleased with His handiwork, and pleased with the entire world, and both the heavens and earth are maintained in their existence.... But when Israel disrupts its relationship with Torah, it's as if it lessens His power..., and then it is 'a time to act for God-*YHV"H*'. And those in the world who are the remaining righteous ones must gird themselves to perform good deeds so that the Holy One (blessed be He) will be strengthened through them, the righteous.... For what reason? Because they "breached your Torah" and the people of the world do not involve themselves with it correctly.... And when Israel involves itself with Torah..., at that moment the reliable One[1130] is rectified in Her rectifications[1131], and is ornamented in Her perfection[1132] correctly. And when Israel disrupts its involvement with Torah, at that moment She is not in a rectified state and is not in a state of perfection, and not in the light. Then, about that is written: "It is a time to act for God-*YHV"H*". What is "to act..."? Here too it is "a time to act", [because] She remains unrectified and imperfect. Why? It's because "they have breached your Torah", because Israel below[1133] disrupted their relationship with the words of Torah. Because in each moment She is in the middle, and is either elevated by or descends based on Israel's behavior."[1134]

1130 I.e., the *Sh'kheena*

1131 From the actions of those below in this world

1132 From above.

1133 Aram.: *Yisrael l'ta-ta*, the Israel that is in this lowest, physical world. This contrasts with the Israel that manifests in the upper worlds.

1134 This Zohar seems to state that the *Sh'kheena*'s relationship to the world depends on the character of Israel's involvement with Torah.

And it's as if he distances himself from Him (blessed be He), as is written in *Zohar Va-yikra* (21a) : "When a person distances himself from the Torah, he is distant from the Holy One (blessed be He)...", because the Holy One (blessed be He) and the Torah are one, as explained previously.

And the supernal shield of holiness leaves him, and he becomes available to and recognized by the powers of judgment that he himself caused to become dominant, and now they can rule over him, both during his lifetime[1135], as our sages (OBM) stated in the first chapter of *B'rakhote* cited above. And it's also found there (63a), and in *Mishlei Rabta* at the beginning of chapter 24: "Rabbee Tovia[1136] stated: 'Anyone who applies himself weakly to words of Torah is unable to withstand the day of misfortune, because it says (*Mishlei* 24:10): "If you were weak in a day of affliction, your strength will become limited"'." And in *Perek Shtei Ha-leh-khem* (*M'na-khote* 99b): "Anyone who safeguards the Torah[1137], his soul-*Neshama* is safeguarded. And anyone who does not safeguard the Torah...". And in *Midrash T'hillim* (*Mizmor* 57[1138]): "The Holy One (blessed be He) said to Israel: 'If you safeguard the Torah, I will safeguard you, for it states (*D'varim* 11:22): "...if you will safeguard [emphatic]..."'."

1135 It seems as if this phrase is a fragment and should read "both during this lifetime and after his expiration from this world". Rav Chayyim addresses "in this lifetime" immediately here. He deals with "after his expiration from this world" in the next chapter.

1136 See [Visotzy 1983, Ph.D. thesis, JTS] for variations in this text.

1137 Our editions have "his Torah".

1138 I could not find this quote in our editions of the *Midrash Shokheir Tov.*

And as is well known from their (OBM) statement in *B'reisheet Rabba* (*parsha* 65): "When the voice[1139] is the voice of Yaakov in the synagogues and study halls, the hands of Eisav do not dominate. When the voice of Yaakov weakens[1140], then his hands dominate"—may the Merciful save us.

And they stated in *Va-yikra Rabba* (*parsha* 35:6) and in *D'varim Rabba* (at the beginning of *parsha* 4:2): "The sword and the book were given interleaved with each other… . The Holy One (blessed be He) stated: 'If you safeguard what is written in the book, you'll be saved from the sword. But if not…'."

[1141]And in the *P'teekh-ta Eikha*[1142] and in *Tahna D'vei Eliyahu* (*Seder Eliyahu Rabba*, chapter 18): "Under what circumstances can the hostile government[1143] issue a decree[1144] and it succeeds? It's when Israel casts the words of Torah to the ground. And this is what's written (*Daniel* 8:12): 'An army[1145] will be assigned over the discontinuation of the daily offering, because of sin'—'An army' is a hostile government… . 'Because of sin' is the sin related to Torah. Whenever Israel casts the words of Torah to the ground, the government issues decrees and they succeed, for it is written: 'It will throw truth to the ground…'. 'Truth' is none other than Torah… . If you throw the words of Torah to the ground, immediately the hostile government succeeds, and this is what is written: '…and it will achieve and prosper'."

1139 Heb.: *ha-kol*

1140 Heb.: *hei-keil*

1141 This paragraph is not found in many editions, including 1837 and 1873, but is in the 1824 first edition.

1142 *Midrash Rabba, Eikha P'teekha-ta* 2

1143 Heb.: *ha-mahl-khoot*

1144 A decree against Judaism

1145 Heb.: *tza-va*

And furthermore they stated there that the Holy One (blessed be He) is [relatively] lenient regarding [punishment for the sins of] idol worship, illicit sexual relationships and murder, but never lenient regarding the rejection of Torah, for it stated (*Yirmiya* 9:11): "For what reason did the land perish?" It isn't written [that it will perish] because of idol worship, illicit sexual relationships or murder. Rather (*Yirmiya* 9:12): "and God-*YHV"H* said: it is because they rejected my Torah".

Continuing in the *Tahna D'vei Eliyahu*: "Observe how great is the power of sinning against the Torah, for Jerusalem and the Temple were not destroyed for any reason other than sinning against the Torah, for it stated...".

And in *Tahn-khooma B'sha-lahkh*: "Just as it's impossible..., so too it's impossible for Israel to survive unless they involve themselves with words of Torah. And to the degree that Israel separates itself from Torah, to the same degree their enemy comes to oppose them.... And so you will find that the enemy comes only as a result of a lax effort with regards to Torah... ." Refer there [for more details].

CHAPTER 23

And so too, after his expiration from this world, they stated (*Bava Batra* 79a): "Anyone who slackens his effort towards words of Torah, falls into *Gehinnom*..."[1146]. And they furthermore continued there: "Anyone who separates himself from words of Torah, and involves himself with words of conversation, fire consumes him..."[1147].

1146 Our edition of *Bava Batra* (79a) has "Anyone who separates himself from words of Torah, falls into *Gehinnom*".

1147 Our edition of *Bava Batra* (79a) has "Anyone who separates himself from words of Torah, fire consumes him".

And in *Mishlei Rabbati* (*parsha* 10): "'One who abandons reproof goes astray' (*Mishlei* 10:17)—Rav Alexandri stated: 'A scholar who abandons the words of Torah is like one who deceives the One who spoke and brought the world into existence. And furthermore, as a result of his abandoning the Torah in this world, the Holy One (blessed be He) abandons him regarding the world-to-come…'."

And in *Zohar Va-yikra* (25b): "Rabbee Shimon stated: 'Fortunate are those who are masters of the soul-*Neshama*[1148], masters of the Torah, in the service of the holy King. Woe to those guilty ones who don't merit to cleave to their Master, and don't merit Torah, for anyone who doesn't merit Torah doesn't merit to receive a soul-*Ruakh*[1149], nor a soul-*Neshama*, and his cleaving is to that aspect of the evil kinds, and he has no portion in holiness. Woe to him when he leaves this world, for he becomes available and known to those evil aspects, masters of overwhelming insolence like a dog, messengers of the fires of *Gehinnom*, who will have no mercy upon him'."

And in *parshat Va-yei-shev* (185a), after expounding at length about the great praiseworthiness and the high level of one who is involved with Torah, in both this world and the next, it stated after that: "Come and observe: the person who doesn't merit to be involved with Torah in this world, and who goes around in darkness, when he leaves this world they take him and force him to enter *Gehinnom*, the place below where they will not have mercy on him, that is called the 'raging water pit, the slimy mud', as it is

---

1148 The portion of the soul that corresponds to the world of *B'reeya*.

1149 The part of the soul that corresponds to the world of *Y'tzeera*. According to the Zohar, one who doesn't involve himself with Torah is limited to having a soul-*Neffesh*, and can't achieve the level of soul-*Ruakh*, nor soul-*Neshama*.

stated in *T'hillim* (40:3): 'He raised me from the raging water pit, from the slimy mud...'. And because of this, what is written about one who doesn't involve himself with Torah in this world and who defiles himself with the defilements of the world? 'And they took him and cast him into the pit' (*B'reisheet* 37:24)—This is *Gehinnom*, the place where those who don't involve themselves with Torah are judged. 'And the pit was bare'—just as he is empty. Why? Because it has no water[1150] within it. And come and observe: how great is the punishment of Torah, for Israel were not exiled from the Holy land for any reason other than they separated themselves from the Torah and abandoned it, this being what is written (*Yirmiya* 9:11): 'Who is the wise person who will understand...?'—Why did the land perish? God-*YHV"H* stated: 'because they abandoned my Torah'."

And furthermore, the first thing he is judged upon when he arrives to be judged before Him (blessed be He) is about words of Torah, as is written at the end of the first chapter of *Kiddushin* (40b) and in the first chapter of *Sanhedrin* (7a): "Rav Hahmnoona stated: 'The initial judgment is regarding words of Torah, for it's stated (*Mishlei* 17:14): 'Exempting oneself from water[1151] is the commencement of judgment[1152]'."

And they stated in *Ahvote* (6:2): "Each day an echo issues from Mount Chorev and announces... that anyone who does not involve himself with Torah is labeled 'rebuked'...". For this is indeed his legal sentence: he

---

1150 Water being a metaphor for Torah, per *Y'shaya* 55:1: "Ho, everyone who is thirsty, go to the water...".

1151 Heb.: *po-teir ma-yim*, interpreting *po-teir* as "exempting oneself", and again using water as a metaphor for Torah

1152 Heb.: *rei-sheet ma-doan*, interpreting *ma-doan* as being derived from *din* (judgment)

reaps the fruits of his actions. Because he didn't desire to choose life and the true good, for himself and for all the creatures and the world in toto, and didn't cause himself to cleave to Him (blessed be He), and reduced the flow of the worlds' light, and he damaged and mixed up the structures of the holy vehicle and darkened them, and caused evil to befall himself by removing garments of holiness[1153], and instead he donned fouled and filthy garments made from involvement with the lusts of this world and the pleasures of its matters, and he becomes defiled and filthy as a result. Certainly they will not depart from him and he will not be able to enter, and all the holy guardians who safeguard him distance themselves from him because they can't make contact with his filthy outer garments[1154]. And he leaves and wanders about in the world, and he cries "defiled, defiled" as he cleaves to his like kind, to the defiled forces of the powers of defilements that he allowed to overcome him.

As it's written in the *Zohar* (beginning of *parshat M'tzora*): "How much effort must a person make to guard their path and to be in awe/fear before the Holy One (blessed be He), so that they shouldn't veer off the correct path and won't transgress the words of Torah, so that they shouldn't come to forget it. For anyone who doesn't study Torah and doesn't make an effort is reprimanded by the Holy One (blessed be He). He is distant from Him. The *Sh'kheena* doesn't hover upon him. And the guardians who travel with him depart. And not only that, they announce before him and say: 'Stay away from being around so-and-so because he's insufficiently concerned with the honor of his Master'.

1153 Heb.: *bigdei ha-kodesh*

1154 Heb.: *b'l'vu-shahv*

Woe to him whom those above and those below have abandoned. He has no share in the path of life. But when he makes an effort... and involves himself with Torah, many guardians are readied to greet him and to safeguard him, and the *Sh'kheena* hovers upon him and all announce before him and say: 'Give honor to the image of the King; give honor to the King's son". He is safeguarded in this world and in the next world, fortunate is his lot."

And they stated in the *Mishna*, first chapter of *Chageega* (9a): "'A twisted thing can not be made straight' (*Kohelet* 1:15)—Rabbee Shimon bar Yokhai states: Someone is not called 'twisted' unless he was originally straight and then became twisted. To whom does this refer? To a scholar who separates himself from the Torah. And woe to them, those creatures who see but don't understand what they are seeing. Woe to us on account of the insult to Torah."

And how much must a person contemplate this always, and focus his attention and make tremendous effort lest he proceed in darkness all his vain days, the number of days that are allotted to him in His mercy and compassion (blessed be He), in the crookedness of his soul-*Neffesh* [that's] cast free of Torah, for it is in his soul-*Neffesh.* For when his decreed time arrives and the dust settles upon the ground, and the soul-*Ruakh* will not return to the God-*Elohi"m* to be bound up in the supernal bundle of life[1155], because his share will be cursed to be flung away. And he won't be soothed because it will be called "cast out", reprimanded above and reprimanded below. Woe to her because of that embarrassment..., may the Merciful (blessed be He) save us.

1155 Heb.: *l'hee-tza-reir b'tzrore ha-khayyim ha-el-yo-neem*

CHAPTER 24

And our rabbis (OBM) so emphasized this via the severity of punishment meted out to someone who has the opportunity to involve himself with Torah and does not, or who once learned and then separated himself (heaven forefend), to the point that, perceived via their power of the holy spirit, they cut him off completely from the world-to-come (may the Merciful save us). As is written in *Perek Cheilek* (*Sanhedrin* 99a): "'For he held the word of God-*YHV"H* in contempt'—Rabbee Natan stated: 'This is one who doesn't heed the *Mishna*'. Rabbee Nehorai stated: 'This is one for whom it is possible to be involved with Torah and doesn't do so'." And the ending of that verse is "that soul-*Neffesh* is cut off and will be cut off[1156]". And they (OBM) explained "is cut off" refers to this world, and "will be cut off" refers to the world-to-come.

The verse comes to teach us the seriousness of this specific case of being cut off, that it's not like the other cases of being cut off mentioned in the Torah as a result of other sins. In those cases, even though the judgment is finalized—that he is cut off (heaven forefend)—even so he hasn't forfeited his share of the world-to-come; it's only that tiny spark of his soul-*Neffesh* with which he performed the transgression that is cut off from the connection and attachment to the energized cable, that was until now connected and attached to the root of his soul in the Holy One (blessed be He), as was explained above at length in the first Gate. Here, in contrast, it states "now and in the future", meaning that the *entire* soul-*Neffesh* totally loses its share in the world (heaven forefend), and it [fem.] has no share in the world-to-come at all.

1156 Heb.: *hee-ka-reit tee-ka-reit*

And the RaMBa"M (OBM) ruled accordingly in the laws of learning/teaching Torah[1157] (chapter 3, law 13), and the Beit Yosef in the *Shoolkhan Arookh* confirms this to be law. And so too Rabbeinu Yona (OBM) in *Sha-ar Ha-t'shoova* listed ten levels of increasing severity regarding the punishments for sins, and in the final level he lists the group that our sages (OBM) ruled have no share in the world-to-come. And he mentioned there (*Sha-ar* 3:153) that included in that group are those who have the opportunity to be involved with Torah and don't. And so too wrote Rabbi Chayyim Vittal (OBM) in *Sha-ah-rei K'doosha* (section 2, *sha-ar* 8, section 2)—he also listed them among the group that has no share in the world-to-come. And they are considered as one group, that the judgment he received is equal to those about whom the sages (OBM) stated in the first chapter of *Rosh Ha-shanna* (17a): "The normal twelve month term of punishment in *Gehinnom* will complete, but their term there will continue forever[1158]", may the Merciful save us.

And the RaMBa"M (OBM) wrote, and the Beit Yosef (OBM) too on that matter, that one who learned *TaNa"Ch* and *Mishna/Talmud* and then left them for the vanities of the world, and who set down his learning/teaching and abandoned it, his sentence is identical to one who had the opportunity to be involved with Torah and didn't.

And so too in relation to judgment[1159], his no-good actions will distance him, and his sins will prevent the good from reaching him, after he had the opportunity and was given the potential to be involved with Torah, and with malicious intent and disgust chose evil for himself and others and all the worlds, and rejected the eternal

1157 Heb.: *talmud torah*

1158 Heb.: *g'hinnom ka-leh v'heim einam ka-leem*

1159 After death

life of the holy Torah, the vitality and the light of all the worlds, which via it [fem.] he could have attached himself (so to speak) to the Holy One (blessed be He, blessed be His name), who enlivens all of them. And he acts to destroy the King's palace, and he lessens and darkens and extinguishes the flow of light to the worlds, and also to his own soul-*Neffesh.* Why would he be granted true life[1160]? For after all, his eyes are darkened from seeing and beholding the eternal light of life, and he could not bear the awesome greatness of the supernal light, for he never attempted to experience it while he was in this world. And he expels himself and cuts himself off from Eden, God-*Elohi"m's* (blessed be He) garden, from being bound to the bundle of life[1161] with God-*YHV"H* his God-*Elohi"m* (blessed be His name). And he proceeds from evil to evil (heaven forefend), woe to him for that embarrassment... .

And this is how they (OBM) ruled and specified his sentence. They ruled that his hope is lost forever (heaven forefend), that eternally he will not see the light, so that he will not live eternally at the end of days, when those who sleep in the ground will awaken to eternal life. As they (OBM) stated (at the end of *K'toobote*): "'For the dew of lights will be your dew' (*Y'shaya* 26:19)—Anyone who makes use of the light of Torah, the Torah enlivens him. And anyone who doesn't make use of the light of Torah, the light of Torah does not enliven him."

And our teachers (OBM) did not define a rectification for the unlearned people[1162] so that they will revive at the time of the resurrection other than their grasping onto and depending in every way on the Tree of Life, depending

1160 Again after death, in the world-to-come

1161 Heb.: *m'l'hee-tza-reir b'tzrore ha-khayyim*

1162 Heb.: *l'ah-mei ha-ahretz*

on the Torah, to benefit scholars with their property, as they stated there: "He said to him: 'My teacher: I found a medication for them, that is mentioned in the Torah: "And those of you who cling to God-*YHV"H* your God-*Elohi"m*, you are all alive today" (*D'varim* 4:4)—Is it possible to cling to the *Sh'kheena*? Rather, anyone who marries off his daughter to a Torah scholar, or who provides a stipend[1163] for a Torah scholar, or who lets a Torah scholar benefit from his property, it is considered as if he clings to the *Sh'kheena*'."

And in *Tahna D'vei Eliyahu* (*Seder Eliyahu Rabba*, chapter 5): "'Awaken and shout for joy those who dwell in the ground' (*Y'shaya* 26:19)—About this King Dovid (OBM) stated: 'May my portion be among those who exert mortal effort over words of Torah…'. 'Awaken and shout for joy those who dwell in the ground'—About this they stated: "Anyone who becomes familiar with the ground[1164] during his life, his dust[1165] is stirred[1166] during the resurrection. And anyone who does not become familiar with the ground during his life, his dust is not stirred during the resurrection… ." This refers to people who settle themselves on the ground to learn Torah. The Holy One (blessed be He) brings upon them the dew of the lights of Torah…, and brings them to the life of the world-to-come, for it is stated (*Y'shaya* 26:19): "For the dew of lights will be your dew".

And for that reason they (OBM) applied the verse: "A twisted thing can not be made straight" (*Kohelet* 1:15) to a Torah scholar who separates himself from the Torah

---

1163 Aram.: *prahk-maht-ya*
1164 One who lives a spare life, without luxuries, dedicated to learning Torah
1165 The remains of his corpse
1166 Is resurrected

(*Mishna Chageega* 9a), that (heaven forefend) he has no possibility of rectification for all of eternity—may the Merciful (blessed be His name) save us from that and anything like it.

CHAPTER 25

And this holds only when there are those of Israel who cleave to Him (blessed be He) and to His Torah in depth, with diligence and great painstaking effort for its own sake, and their only desire is Torah all their days. And then those people who completely disrupt their involvement with Torah because of the evilness of their choices, will descend to *Sh'ol* while they are yet alive, and be excluded from joining the heritage of God's servants who cleave to Him (blessed be He) and His Torah, and they will be cut off from the land of the living (heaven forefend). And in any case, [they will be cut off from] the world—even all the worlds—being that they[1167] were caused to have their holiness reduced and light lessened as a result of those sins that are affecting their soul-*Neffesh*, and being that they were almost caused to be deflected into destruction (heaven forefend), as is written in *Tahna D'vei Eliyahu Rabba* (chapter 2): "The sages stated: 'Whenever people disrupt their involvement with Torah, the Holy One (blessed be He) seeks to destroy the world...'."

And there in *Seder Eliyahu Zoota* (chapter 5): "'For the pillars of the Earth are God-YHV"H's, and He set the world upon them'—And 'pillars' are Torah scholars... . Each day angels of demolition go out from before the Holy One (blessed be He) to demolish the entire world, and if there didn't exist synagogues and study halls where Torah

---

1167 The worlds

scholars sit and involve themselves with the Torah's words, they would immediately demolish the entire world...". Refer there [for more details].

Even so, they[1168] could still be maintained in existence via the survivors whom God-*YHV"H* calls upon, those who are involved with the Torah day and night[1169], so that the world won't be disrupted completely to return to emptiness and chaos.

But if (heaven forefend) the world was completely empty, even one moment, from the Holy nation's involvement with and contemplation of the holy Torah, immediately and instantly all of the worlds would be totally destroyed and disrupted from existence (heaven forefend). But even just one person from Israel, he has great strength, for he has the ability to sustain and maintain all the worlds and all of creation in its totality via his involvement with and contemplation of the holy Torah for its own sake, as is written in *Cheilek* (99b): "'Anyone who involves himself with Torah for its own sake...'—Rabbee Yokhanan states: 'he even safeguards the entire world'." And so too it is written in the *Perek Ha-Torah* (*Ahvote* chapter 6): "Anyone who involves himself with Torah for its own sake... . And not only that, but that the continued existence of the entire world in toto would be justified to sustain just him."

And how could a person's heart/mind not be enflamed when he considers and contemplates this awesome matter, and fear and trembling will come upon him lest he weaken (heaven forefend) his constant involvement with the holy Torah, that he think in his hearts/minds (heaven

---

1168 The worlds

1169 Involved for the Torah's sake, as Rav Chayyim states at the beginning of the chapter.

forefend) that at this moment the entire world, from one end to the other, is totally empty from involvement with the holy Torah, and without his involvement and his heart/mind's intellection with the Torah at this moment, all of the worlds would be destroyed, and instantly end and disappear (heaven forefend). This is Torah and this is its very great reward, it being impossible to place a limit on it, that he receives the entire reward of all of them after he fulfills and sustains with his great strength all of the worlds now. And it is for this situation that the sages (OBM) stated in the *Mishna* (*Sanhedrin* 37a): "That everyone in Israel is required to state: 'The world was created for my benefit'."

And even though:

1. relative to the other sins there are tens of thousands of holy supernal worlds that no sin or transgression of those in this lower world can affect them at all to blemish them (heaven forefend), and
2. their glorious place of existence is continuously one of boldness and delight, and
3. about them is stated (*T'hillim* 5:5): "No evil sojourns with You",

in contrast, the sin of disrupting Torah is superior to all of them, for it affects the maintenance of *all* the worlds.

CHAPTER 26

And the reason for this, as was explained above, is because the source of the hidden supernal root of the holy Torah is far above all of the worlds, in the very beginning and root of the emanation[1170] of His (blessed be He) holiness,

1170 Heb.: *ahtzeeloot*

the secret of the supernal garment[1171], as our teacher the godly, awesome Ariza"l wrote. It's only that it unfolded downward and descended, so to speak, to the Earth upon which it shines with its glory, and He (blessed be He) transmitted it and planted it among us, so that we can be the holders and the supporters of the tree of life.

For that reason, since then, all of what enlivens and sustains all of the worlds depends on and remains in place only according to the degree of our involvement with and intellectual relationship to it [fem.]. For if we are involved with it, and hold onto it and support it as it deserves, without any weakening at all, we awaken the source of its supernal root, the source of the holinesses and the blessings, to draw down and effectively drain the [reservoir of] increased blessing and everlasting life and awesome holiness upon all the worlds, each world according to its requirements for holiness, what it is able to receive and tolerate.

But if (heaven forefend), our involvement with it is weak, the holiness and the supernal light of Torah becomes distorted and lessened[1172] to all the worlds, each one goes on lacking what it needs, shivering[1173] and weakened (heaven forefend). And if (heaven forefend) every one of us would neglect it [fem.] and abandon involving ourselves with it [fem.] in any way, the worlds too would in an instant be disrupted in every way (heaven forefend).

This is different than all the other *mitzvote*, even the *mitzva* of prayer. For even if (heaven forefend) all of Israel neglected and turned their backs on praying to Him

---

1171 Heb.: *mahl-boosh*

1172 Heb.: *mit-ka-meit oo-mit-ma-eit*

1173 Heb.: *ro-t'tim*, written with two *tavs*, rather than *tets* as is common usage

(blessed be He), the worlds would not, because of that, revert to nothingness and chaos. And it's for that reason that prayer is referred to in the words of our sages (OBM) as "transitory life"[1174], while Torah is called "everlasting life"[1175], as they (OBM) stated in the first chapter of *Shabbat* (10a): "Ravva observed Rav Hahmnoona, that he prayed for a long time. He said: 'One neglects everlasting life to be involved with transitory life'." This is because the matter of prayer is about increasing the world's rectification by increasing holiness and blessing in that specific time interval that's dedicated to [assisting] them. And therefore if that moment passed, he won't ever again be able to effectively give the worlds that additional holiness and blessing.

In contrast, the matter of involvement with the holy Torah touches upon the core of what enlivens and sustains the support of the worlds so that they will not be totally destroyed. Therefore a person is required to be involved with it and contemplate it at each and every moment, to support and sustain all of the worlds each instant.

And not only that, but also that the entire matter of prayer is dependent entirely on involvement with the holy Torah, and lacking that it is not heeded (heaven forefend), as the verse stated (*Mishlei* 28:9): "One who turns a deaf ear to Torah, his prayer is also an abomination". And as the sages (OBM) stated in *Shabbat* (cited above), and in *Mishlei Rabbata* (*parsha* 28), and they stated at the end of *Sota*, (49a): "Anyone who involves himself with Torah despite adversity, his prayers are heeded...", and "...the heavenly partition is not locked before him". And in *Zohar* (*Meekeitz* 202b): "'But desire realized is a tree of life'—We

1174 Heb.: *cha-yei sha-ah*
1175 Heb.: *cha-yei o-lam*

learn that one who desires that the Holy One (blessed be He) will accept his prayers should involve himself with Torah, for it is the tree of life…".

For that reason we have the ruling in the *Talmud* (*M'geela* 27a): "It is permitted to convert a synagogue into a study hall"[1176], for it raises it to a higher level of holiness, because it is only Torah that provides the flow of vitality and holiness and light to all the worlds, because it is higher than all of them.

CHAPTER 27

And it[1177] [fem.] also has an additional measure of awesome holiness as compared to the worlds, because even though the supernal worlds have a great degree of holiness, however when they unfold downward and descend via an immense downward flowing and lowering by levels, even though each world integrates a copy and impression of all the structures of the world that's immediately above it (of its actual likeness and image)—

> as we know and as is written in the *Zohar* (*Yitro* 82b): "We learned that as it is above, so too it is below them, and so too in all the worlds, each of them connected, this one to that one, and this one to that one"; and as it is written in the *Etz Chayyim* in the matter of the four worlds *ABY"A*, refer there in *Sha'ar Drooshei ABY"A*, chapter 1 and in chapter 4 there, and in *Sha'ar Ha-shei-mote* at the beginning of chapter 1—

even so, the degree of its holiness and light is neither identical to, nor at all similar, to the world above it, because they become so much coarser, and they are reduced in holiness

1176 Heb.: *beit ha-k'nesset mootar la-ah-soto beit midrash*
1177 Referring to the Torah

and light as a result of the immense downward flowing and lowering by levels, until in this world they become so profane that we can relate to them with profane behavior.

However the holy Torah, even though it also flowed downward and descended from the supernal root of its source in the holy, uncountable levels, from world to world and level to level, even so its initial holiness, as it is in the root of its initial source, remains the same also in this world, that it is all holiness and it is forbidden to behave relative to it in a profane manner (heaven forefend)—even thinking about it in filthy places is forbidden. For that reason our sages (OBM) were strict about and broadened its punishment, and they stated (in *Perek Cheilek* 99a) that it too[1178] is included in the class of "for he has scorned God's word" (*B'midbar* 15:31). And the end of that verse is "he is cut off, he will be cut off[1179]"—"is cut off" refers to this world; "will be cut off" refers to the world-to-come.

And they stated (*M'geela* 32a) that one who holds a Torah scroll bare-handed is buried bare of that *mitzva*[1180]. They even prohibited carrying it from place to place. And the *Zohar* (*Ah-kharei* 73b) even prohibited carrying it from one synagogue to another synagogue, (refer there [for more details]), based on the reason that it remains forever in its initial holiness.

(And even if the root of a person's soul-*Neshama* is from a supernal world that's very high, from the highest of the worlds, and he adopts in his mind a fine thought to bind himself to the purity of some fine character trait, he is permitted to continue thinking this thought in filthy places.

1178 Thinking about Torah in a filthy place

1179 Heb.: *hee-ka-reit tee-ka-reit*

1180 Bare of the *mitzva* he was doing when he held the Torah bare-handed

But if he thought about Torah—e.g., the laws regarding the impurity of wounds and dwelling places, or other laws, or any words of Torah—it's prohibited in filthy places.)

And this is also the context of their (OBM) statement in the *Zohar* that "The Holy One (blessed be He) and the Torah are one". This means that even though all the worlds follow the process of lowering of level and flowing downward and many differences regarding their degree of holiness, all of this is only from our perspective. However, from His perspective there is no difference between one place and another in any way (heaven forefend). And as is written (*Malachi* 3:6): "I, God-*YHV"H*, have not changed", and the holiness has not changed, as I wrote above at length in Gate 3. Refer there [for more details].

So too the holy Torah, even though it unfolded downward via many immense lowerings of levels, even so its holiness was not changed in any way, and it still remains in its original holiness in this lowest of worlds, as it when it nursed with Him[1181] (blessed be He) at the source of its root, without any variation or change of place in any way.

However, even though from His (blessed be He) perspective all places are equal, without any differences at all, for filthy places do not partition off His oneness nor His (blessed be He) immense holiness—and it's the same in the matter of the holiness of the holy Torah—even so we are prohibited to discuss or even to think about it in filthy alleys, because from our perspective there is definitely a difference between places, as was explained there at length.

But the holy Torah in its essence, its holiness and light, is not changed as a result of its descent. It's only that our eyes are obstructed from seeing the immensity

1181 Heb.: *b'omna eetoe*

of its holiness and internal light. It's for that reason that King Dovid (OBM) stated (*T'hillim* 119:18): "Open my eyes that I may perceive the wonders of your Torah"[1182]. For in truth, the holy Torah's holiness and light—being its concealed inner aspects—they [emphatically] are explicit and revealing[1183], illuminating via the holiness of its supernal light in its actual state[1184]. It's only that our eyes are unable to withstand the immensity of its holiness and light in its actual state.

CHAPTER 28

And to that end, in the process of lowering its level and unfolding downward from level to level and from world to world, it hid itself, clothed itself in each world to address the matters of that world according that world's contexts and values, so that the world should be able to withstand the Torah's holiness and light. When it finally descended to arrive in this world, it also clothed itself to address the values and contexts of this world using stories about this world, so that this world should be able to withstand its holiness and light. However, even though it seems to address matters of these lower worlds, with the stories it hints at the primary matters[1185] of Torah, and interior matters, and those that are even deeper within the interior, higher and higher without end.[1186]

1182 King Dovid prays that the obstructions should be removed from his eyes.

1183 Heb.: *m'fo-ra-sheem, v'neegleem*

1184 The Torah remains at its original exceedingly supernal level.

1185 Heb.: *goofei Torah*

1186 Rav Chayyim states that the seemingly mundane stories of the Torah hide deeper meaning, as the stories, words and letters are the outer "clothing" that hides/shields the aspects of the Torah's inner supernal holiness and light. These include the many aspects of *PRD"S* (*p'shat, remmez, droosh, sode*).

Refer to *Zohar B'ha-a-lote-kha* (162a): "Rabbee Shimon stated...", and in *parshat Toldote* (145b): "Rabbee Yosee stated: 'Everything that the Holy One (blessed be He) does in the world, all is based in the secret of wisdom...'." And in *parshat Ba-lahk* 202a: "He furthermore began and stated: 'How goodly are the paths and roads of the Torah...'." And in *parshat B'sha-lakh* (end of 55b): "Rabbee Abba began...: 'How very important is it for us to delve deeply into the Torah...'." And in *parshat Toldote* (end of 134b): "In the Torah are sealed all of the supernal secrets...", they being the details of the matters of the tens of thousands of worlds and levels with which it clothed itself during the process of its descent.

And for that reason it's often stated in the *Zohar* that the Torah is both "hidden and revealed", which is clear to everyone who understands that the phrase means that the holy Torah's hidden path is not written explicitly and well-explained, but rather these matters are hidden and concealed within clues in its words; and the revealed path within it is the plain reading of the text, that is written explicitly and well-explained within it.

(And it's not as I saw written in a book by one who researched the matter, about why the wisdom of the *Kabbala* is called "concealed"[1187]. Isn't it the case that for one who understands them they're revealed? And for people who do not know and understand it's also the case that they can't explain even the plain meaning of the text, and for them even the plain meaning of the text is hidden from them. And there he took the position that he took.[1188])

1187 Heb.: *nistar*

1188 Rav Chayyim seems to say that the wisdom of the Kabbala is called *nistar* (concealed) because its knowledge is concealed within the plain text of the Torah. Refer to the *Lehshem Sh'vo V'ahkh-la-ma, droosh 5, siman 7, ote 8*

Refer to *Zohar B'ha-a-lote-kha* (149a and 149b): "How precious are the words of Torah, for in each and every word there are supernal secrets...". Refer there [for more details].

And each person gazes into the secrets of the depth of their[1189] inner aspects based on how much wisdom and clarity of mind he has, and the holiness of the purity of his hearts/minds, and how much he involves himself with it and ponders it.

However, the core of the Torah's underlying reasoning[1190]—the secret of the soul-*Neshama*-of-its-soul-*Neshama*[1191], the most hidden of the hidden—those are things that the Ancient of Days concealed and diverted away[1192] from his creations. And to this day no person has knowledge of them. It was only our original ancestor[1193], the one who accomplished the acquisition of his soul-*Neshama*-of-the-soul-*Neshama*, who was able use it[1194] to contemplate the supernal splendor, the soul-*Neshama*-of-the-soul-*Neshama* of the holy Torah, and the supernal wisdoms were revealed to him at the root of their supernal roots.

And from the moment he sinned and the supernal splendor departed from him, and the supernal processes became confused and mixed up, the supernal paths and trails of the Torah's wisdom were also sealed up, being the secret of the soul-*Neshama*-of-its-soul-*Neshama*.

And again at the time of the holy event, the time when the holy Torah was received, even though the whole world was made pleasant to the point that they (OBM)

1189 The inner aspects of the Torah's words

1190 Heb.: *eekar ha-taamei torah*

1191 Heb. *nish-ma-ta d'nish-ma-ta deela*

1192 Heb.: *v'heh-eh-tee-kan mi'b'ree-yo-tav*

1193 The first Adam

1194 The core of the Torah's underlying reasoning—the *taamei torah*

stated (*Shabbat* 146a): "When Israel stood at Mount Sinai, their contamination ceased", even so they only merited to receive the depths of the inner aspect of the Torah's soul-*Neshama* but not the aspect of the soul-*Neshama*-of-the-soul-*Neshama*. That won't occur until He (blessed be He) pours His spirit upon all flesh[1195]. Then the causeways of wisdom will be revealed, the wondrous paths of the supernal wisdom, its soul-*Neshama*-of-the-soul-*Neshama*.

As is written in *Zohar B'ha-a-lote-kha* (152a): "The Torah has a body..., the world's fools only gaze upon that clothing..., those who know more don't gaze upon the clothes but rather upon the body which is under the clothes. The wise, servants of the supernal King, those who stood at Mount Sinai gaze only upon the soul-*Neshama* which is the actual core of the entire Torah, and in the future they will come to gaze upon the soul-*Neshama*-of-the-soul-*Neshama* that is within the Torah." And as is written (*Y'shaya* 30:20): "And your own eyes will behold your Teacher" and "and your Teacher will no longer be hidden behind His garment"[1196].

And this is the matter of the light of the first day that was stored away for the use of the righteous in the future to come (*Chageega* 12a). And it is about this that the sages (OBM) stated (*N'darim* 8b): "In the future to come, the Holy One (blessed be He) will take the sun out of its sheath...", and this is the secret of the Eden, as is known, which is the soul-*Neshama*-of the-soul-*Neshama*.

And the first Adam, before his sin, lived in the Garden of Eden. From within it he would gaze upon the Eden mentioned above. And from when he sinned and after,

1195 Ref.: *Yoel* 3:1, in the end of days

1196 Rav Chayyim reverses the order of these two phrases relative to their order in *Y'shaya*.

this supernal aspect departed from him, and for that reason he was then cast out of the Garden of Eden. And this is the secret of its letter combinations, in the manner that it's written in heaven, as was explained above at the end of Gate 2.

And regarding this they stated in *Midrash T'hillim* (at the beginning of *Mizmor* 3): "'Mankind doesn't know its order...' (*Eeyove* 28:13)—The sections of Torah were not transmitted in their proper order, for had they been transmitted in their proper order, anyone who read them would be able to create a world and to resurrect the dead...".

Let us now return to explain a bit about the difference in quality and relative greatness that the light of the holy Torah has relative to the *mitzvote.*

CHAPTER 29

We find that the sages (OBM) stated (*Sota* 21a): "Rabbee M'nakhem expounded on: 'For a *mitzva* is a lamp and Torah is light' (*Mishlei* 6:23)—The verse linked the *mitzva* to a lamp and the Torah to light to teach you that just as a lamp only protects temporarily, so too a *mitzva* only protects temporarily. And just as light illuminates forever, so too Torah shields forever." And it concludes that Torah "protects[1197] and saves[1198] during the time that one is involved with it; and when one is not involved with it, it protects him and does not save him. While a *mitzva,* whether at the time one is involved with it or not, protects him and does not save him". And they also said there "a transgression extinguishes a *mitzva,* but a transgression doesn't extinguish Torah".

1197 From punishment
1198 From sinning

And similarly, it is known from the *Zohar*, that the six-hundred-and-thirteen *mitzvote* correspond to the six-hundred-and-thirteen limbs/organs and sinews in the human body, and when a person performs one of God's *mitzvote* correctly, that specific corresponding limb/organ is sanctified by it and is enlivened by it. Or, if he comes to have the opportunity to control and separate himself[1199] so as to not do one of God's negative *mitzvote*, about which our rabbis (OBM) stated (*Talmud Yerushalmi*, first chapter of *Kiddushin*): "If a person did not act and did not transgress a transgression, he is rewarded as if he performed a [positive] *mitzva*", that specific corresponding sinew is purified and sanctified also, and it is enlivened by it. As the verse states (*Va-yikra* 18:5), that these are the *mitzvote* "that a person shall carry out that he should live by them", for then he is called a "living person[1200]".

However, when a person is involved with Torah, it's written (*Mishlei* 4:22): "and it heals his entire flesh". And as they stated (*Eiruvin* 54a): "one who feels pain in his head should involve himself with Torah, for it states: 'for they are a gracious adornment for your head' (*Mishlei* 1:9). One who feels pain in his throat should involve himself with Torah, for it says.... One who feels pain in his stomach should involve himself with Torah.... One who feels pain in his entire body should involve himself with Torah, for it says 'and it heals his entire flesh'." And so it is in *Va-yikra Rabba* (*parsha* 12), and in *Tahn-khooma Yitro*, and in *Midrash T'hillim* (*Mizmor* 19), that via involvement with Torah, *all* of his limbs/organs

---

1199 Rav Chayyim seems to be saying that by actively controlling himself and not allowing himself to transgress one of the negative *mitzvote*, he rectifies the corresponding sinew.

1200 Heb.: *ish chai*

and sinews and powers are sanctified and clarified, and for that reason they stated (*Pei-ah* 1): "and the study of Torah corresponds to them all"[1201].

And so too the opposite (heaven forefend): the sin of ignoring Torah[1202] also corresponds to all of them, for when one transgresses one of God's *mitzvote*, only the limb/organ that corresponds to it is blemished, that the life force of holiness and the supernal light, the secret of the name YHV"H (blessed be He) that settles upon each limb/organ leaves him (heaven forefend), and the death of the Other Side settles within him (may the Merciful save us), and he becomes blemished, missing that limb/organ. But as the result of ignoring Torah (heaven forefend), he blemishes all of his limbs/organs and sinews, and all of his powers, and his body's holy life force departs, and immediately becomes as an actual corpse that has no life force (heaven forefend), as it states (*D'varim* 30:20): "For He is your life...".

And as the sages (OBM) stated (*Avoda Za-ra* 3b)[1203]: "Why is it written (*Chabakook* 1:14) 'You have made man like the fish of the sea...'? Why are people likened to the fish of the sea? To state that just as the fish of the sea

---

1201 Heb.: *v'talmood torah k'negged koolam*—This quote from *Pei-ah* is normally translated as meaning that the study of Torah is equivalent to the performance of all the other *mitzvote*. Here Rav Chayyim seems to understand the phrase to mean that while each *mitzva* corresponds to a single limb/organ or sinew, the study of Torah corresponds to them all.

1202 Heb.: *bittul torah*. This is a critical term. As with the term *ei-sek ba-Torah* which I translate it as "involvement with Torah", I translate *bittul torah* as "ignoring Torah", an active, conscious act. It implies that a person is actively *not* involved with the words and ideas of Torah. It's not an incidental or an unconscious act, and it applies only to the context of "involvement with Torah".

1203 Our editions of the *Talmud Avoda Za-ra* have a slightly different wording.

immediately die when they are separated from water, so too people, when they separate from the Torah, immediately die." (This is the interpretation of the *Yalkoot Chabakook*[1204], allusion 562 on the above mentioned verse.) And in the *Raa-ya M'hemna*, near the end of *parshat Shmini*: "Just as the fish of the sea must live in water, and if they are separated from it they immediately die, so too scholars, masters of the *Mishna*, their lives are in Torah, and if they are separated from the Torah, they immediately die".

And this is what the sages (OBM) stated (*B'rakhote* 5a): "If a person observes that tribulations are coming upon him, he should scrutinize his actions[1205]. If he scrutinizes them and doesn't find cause, he should consider them as caused by ignoring Torah[1206]." And this should surprise us, because if he's ignored Torah (heaven forefend), isn't it the case that there is no "doesn't find" greater than this, and how could he say "and doesn't find cause"[1207]? Indeed, RaSh"Y (OBM) has already given us a clue in relation to this, in what he explained there, that he didn't find a sin worthy of bringing those specific tribulations upon him.

And it's His (blessed be He) way that a person's actions are repaid measure for measure—the specific limb/organ that he damaged and blemished via his sin, he brings suffering upon that specific limb/organ. And the point of His (blessed be He) intention by this is that by identifying the site of the suffering, the person will understand which sin caused it, and he'll set his heart/mind to confess, stop doing it and repent, and then he will be healed.

1204 *Yalkoot Shim-o-nee, Cha-ba-kook*, chapter 1

1205 For mis-deeds. Heb.: *y'fahsh-peish b'ma-ah-sahv*

1206 Heb.: *yitleh b'vittul torah*

1207 If he searched his actions for sins, he should have discovered his episodes of neglecting Torah.

And this is what they stated, that if a person observes that he is experiencing suffering, he should scrutinize his actions and he'll understand how he's misbehaved based on the nature of punishment. And if he scrutinizes and doesn't uncover a sin that he did with that specific limb/organ and in the manner that would be worthy of those specific punishments, measure for measure, he should consider them as caused by ignoring Torah, because regarding the sin of ignoring Torah the paradigm of "measure for measure" doesn't apply, for its neglect (heaven forefend) touches upon his entire body, all places and all limbs/organs, as mentioned above.

And the reason for this is as I wrote above in Gate 1, chapter 6. The source of the supernal roots of the *mitzvote* are dependent upon and connected to the secret of the Stature and the parts of the Vehicle, being the secret of the supernal man (so to speak). Each individual *mitzva*'s supernal root is connected to and integral to one of the Stature's worlds and powers. And every person is like this, that he too, all of his limbs/organs and sinews and detailed parts, and all the details of his powers, achieve rectification and are set in order based on the plan of the form of the Vehicle and Stature [1208]. And for that reason, each *mitzva* corresponds to one of a person's specific limbs/organs or sinews, while the holy Torah includes *all* of the worlds, as mentioned above. For that reason it is the equal of all of the *mitzvote* taken together, and for that reason it "heals his entire flesh".

1208 Heb.: *b'tahvneet d'moot ha-mehr-ka-va v'shee-oor koma*

CHAPTER 30

And furthermore, the holy Torah has an advantage of greater amount of light and additional holiness over all of the *mitzvote* taken together. For even if a person accomplished all of the six-hundred-and-thirteen *mitzvote* in toto, with true perfection (as appropriate), in all of their details and precision and with pure and holy intention, so that the person then becomes a complete Vehicle in all his limbs/organs, parts, and all of his powers, so that the supernal holiness of all the *mitzvote* should settle upon them, even so there's no comparison nor likening in any way of the holiness and light of the *mitzvote* to the huge awesomeness of the holiness and light of the holy Torah, whose light manifests over the person who is involved with it and contemplates it appropriately.

For the origin of its holy path, is far, far above the root of the holiness and the supernal lights of all the *mitzvote* taken together, as mentioned previously. And this is what they stated in *parshat ha-Torah* (*Ahvote* 6:1): "…and makes him great and ascendant over all activities", this being the activities of all the *mitzvote.* And they also stated this in the *Yerushalmi* (chapter 1 of *Pei-ah*), that all of the *mitzvote* taken together aren't equivalent to one word from the Torah.

And it's also that the holiness and light of the *mitzva* whose light will dwell on that thing or object with which or by which the *mitzva* will be performed, settles upon them only temporarily, at the moment that they are used to perform the *mitzva.* But after the *mitzva* is performed with it, the holiness and the light ascends and departs from them immediately, and it is left as it was beforehand.

In contrast, the holy Torah, any place that its light and holiness shines or appears once, it has eternal holiness and remains continuously in its state of holiness, as we learned in the *B'raita* (*M'geela* 26b) that the objects used for performing a *mitzva* may be discarded after their *mitzva* is performed, while objects of holiness must be stored away. And for that reason they included the objects of *t'fillin* and *m'zooza* in the class of holy objects, by virtue of the paragraphs of Torah that were once placed within them.

And you will never find anything among their (OBM) words that is not hinted at in scripture. And we can apply the verse (*Mishlei* 6:23): "for a *mitzva* is a lamp and Torah is light" also upon this matter that we mentioned, according to their (OBM) explanation mentioned above in *Sota*: that a lamp illuminates only temporarily, while light illuminates forever. And they (OBM) made a distinction between them with regards to being a shield and protection for a person. And it's possible to also explain it in this way too, that the text also hints to the difference and distinction between the holy Torah and the *mitzvote* that is explained in the *B'raita* in *M'geela* mentioned above.

And not only that, but even that holiness and the enlivening forces and lights of the *mitzvote* that make a person holy and enliven the person who performs them, is taken from and has influence based only on the holiness and light of the holy Torah, for a *mitzva* has no inherent life force or holiness or light of its own at all. It's only from the perspective of the holiness of the letters of the Torah that are written in relation to the context of that *mitzva*. And we can also apply the matter in the verse: "for a *mitzva* is a lamp and Torah is light", to the context of the lamp that has no light of its own—it only has the light that illuminates within it.

It's also certain that one who is involved with Torah alone, without performing any *mitzvote* at all (heaven forefend), also has nothing, as our rabbis (OBM) stated (*Y'va-mote* 109b): "Anyone who asserts that he has nothing but Torah[1209], he does not even have Torah[1210]". And in chapter 2 of *B'rakhote* (17a): "Rava often repeated: 'The purpose of wisdom is repentance and good deeds, so that a person does not read[1211] and learn[1212] and [then] kick his father and teacher ...[1213], ...it doesn't state 'to those who learn it' but rather 'to their practitioners'."[1214]

And in *Sh'mote Rabba* (chapter 40): "If someone knows Torah and doesn't behave in accordance with it, it would have been better for him if he'd never come into the world, that the placenta smothered him." And so it is in *Va-yikra Rabba* (*parsha* 35), and in *Tahn-khooma parshat Eikev.*

And in *Zohar Sh'mote* (5b, top of page): "Rabbee Yehuda stated: 'Anyone who involves himself with Torah in this world, and who considers good works to be a highly valued treasure[1215], inherits a complete world. And one who involves himself with Torah in this world but does not do good works, does not inherit, neither this[1216] nor that[1217]...'. Rabbee Yitzkhak stated: 'We learned this applies only for someone who has no good works at all'."

[This is true] even to the point that they stated in

1209 There should be an ellipsis added here, as Rav Chayyim deleted a few words from his quote.

1210 For the word "even" our editions of *Y'vamote* have the word *ah-feeloo* rather than *ahf.*

1211 Torah

1212 *Mishna*

1213 Our editions of *B'rakhote* have "his father and his mother and his teacher"

1214 Our editions of *B'rakhote* have "it doesn't state 'to practitioners' but rather 'to their practitioners'."

1215 Aram,: *m'sa-geil o-va-din ta-vin*

1216 This world

1217 That world (i.e., the world-to-come)

the first chapter of *Avoda Za-ra* (17b): "'Anyone who only involves himself with Torah could be compared to someone who has no God-*Elo"ha*', for without fulfilling the *mitzvote* (heaven forefend), there is nothing to which the light of Torah can attach nor connect, to settle upon, nor in which it can be manifested. It can be compared to an illuminating flame not having a wick; indeed the *mitzva* receives the essence of the light from the letters in the Torah that are written about it.

And this is what they stated in *parshhat Ha-Torah* (*Ahvote* 6:7): "Torah is great in that it gives life to those who put it into practice", and it didn't say "to those who learn it" or "to those who are involved with it"—it says "to those who put it into practice". It intends to convey that it's the Torah that also gives eternal life and holiness to those who perform the *mitzvote* written within it, and for that reason they stated in *Tahn-khooma B'khoo-ko-tai,* that even if he is righteous[1218] but doesn't involve himself with Torah, he hasn't accomplished anything[1219] (heaven forefend).

And the reason for this is also as was explained previously[1220], that the *mitzvote,* in the source of their root, are connected and dependent upon the design of the components of the Vehicle: the worlds and the supernal powers. And the supernal source of the root of the holy Torah is very lofty, above the totality of all the worlds and the powers. And it unfolds downward within them all, and they receive from it the essence of their life force and the overflowing abundance of their holiness. For that reason it is the provider of, and what impresses, life force, holiness and light upon all of the *mitzvote.*

1218 Heb.: *tzaddik*

1219 Heb.: *ein b'ya-do kloom*

1220 In Gate 1, Chapter 6

CHAPTER 31

And also for this reason, involvement with Torah atones for all of a sinning soul-*Neffesh*'s sins, as they (OBM) stated (at the end of *M'na-khote* 110a): "Why is it written (*Va-yikra* 7:37) 'This is the Torah of the burnt-offering, of the meal-offering and the sin-offering…', and they deduce that anyone who is involved with Torah has no need for a burnt-offering, nor a meal-offering, nor a sin-offering, nor a guilt-offering. And so it's written in *Tahn-khooma parshat Tzav*, and in *Sh'mote Rabba parsha* 38: "'Take words with you, and return to God-*YHV"H*' (*Hoshei-ah* 14:3)—…because Israel says… we are destitute and we have nothing from which we can bring sacrifices. The Holy One (blessed be He) said to them: 'It is words I ask of you… and I forgive all your sins'. And 'words' are none other than words of Torah… ." And in *Tahn-khooma Va-yahk-heil*[1221] in the context of the Ark[1222] they stated that it bears the sins of Israel—that the Torah within it bears the sins of Israel.

And in *Tahna D'vei Eliyahu, Seder Eliyahu Rabba*, chapter 5: "A person who transgressed many sins and the court imposed a death sentence…, and he returned and repented, and reads Torah, Prophets and Writings, and learned *Mishna* and *Midrash Ha-la-khote* and *Ha-ga-dote*, and served scholars, even if a hundred decrees were pronounced upon him, the Holy One (blessed be He) removes them from him…".

And in *Zohar Sh'lahkh* (159a): "Rabbee Yehuda began… 'It is important for people to deeply contemplate the Holy One's (blessed be He) work. It's important for people to deeply contemplate the words of the Torah, for anyone who

1221 In Siman 7
1222 The Ark of the Covenant

is involved with Torah is as if he offers all of the sacrifices in the world before the Holy One (blessed be He). And not only that, but the Holy One (blessed be He) awards atonement for all of his obligations, and they prepare for him a number of thrones in the world-to-come'."

And also those serious sins for which sacrifices do not atone, involvement with Torah atones, as our sages (OBM) stated in regards to the sons of Eli (*Rosh Ha-sha-na* 18a): "The sin can't be atoned for by a sacrifice or a meal offering, but it can be atoned for by Torah study". And so too they stated (*M'geela* 3b): "The study of Torah is even greater than the daily sacrifices."

And in *Zohar Tzav* (35a): "Come and observe..., because of that, one who labors in Torah doesn't need sacrifices nor offerings, for the Torah is better than all of them and connects all the parts of *ehmoona*[1223]. And regarding this it is written (*Mishlei* 3:7): '...and her paths are all paths of pleasantness'. And it's written (*T'hillim* 119:165): 'Great peace will come to those who love your Torah, and they will have no obstacles'."

And in *parshat K'doshim* (80b): "'With sacrifice and offering...'—but he is atoned for with words of Torah. Why? Because the words of the Torah rise above all the sacrifices in the world, as they asserted, for it is written (*Va-yikra* 7:36): 'This is the Torah for the burnt-offering, the meal-offering and the sin-offering...'—Torah is considered equal to all the sacrifices in the world. He[1224] said to him: it's exactly as you explain, that anyone who involves himself with Torah, even though punishments have been decreed upon him from above, he provides

---

1223 The *partzufim* of *Ah-tzeeloot* are called *ehmoona* (lit.: reliable, faithful).

1224 Rebbee Yosee

greater pleasure than all the sacrifices and offerings, and that punishment is torn up. And come and observe: a person is never refined of his sins except via words of Torah… . And the Torah is called 'holy', for it is written (*Va-yikra* 20:26): 'For I God-*YHV"H* am holy'—this is the Torah because it is the holy supernal name. And regarding this [is written that] one who involves himself with it is refined, and later is made holy… . This teaches us that the holiness of the Torah is a holiness that rises above all other kinds of holiness."

And in *Midrash Ha-neh-eh-lam Va-yeira*[1225] (100a) they stated: "The sacrifices were annulled; Torah was not annulled. Therefore, one who is unable to be involved with sacrifices should involve himself with Torah, and this will yield even better results…, for Rabbee Yokhanan stated: 'When the Holy One (blessed be He) explained the sacrifices Moshe said: "Master of the World—this will suffice when Israel dwells in their land. What will they do when they are exiled from their land?" He said to him: "Moshe, they should involve themselves with Torah and I will forgive them on its [fem.] account, even more than all the sacrifices in the world, for it is written: 'This is the Torah for the burnt-offering, the meal-offering and the sin-offering…'—this Torah is in place of the burnt-offering; this Torah is in place of the meal-offering...".' Rav Kros-p'da-ee stated: 'One who verbally recalls the matter of the sacrifices in the synagogues and study halls… a covenant was established that the angels who are appointed to mention his obligations to cause evil to befall him can't do evil to him, only good'."

And that stated furthermore in the second chapter of *B'rakhote* (16a) and in *Tahna D'vei Eliyahu, Seder Eliya*

1225 Part of the *Zohar*

Rabba (chapter 25[1226]): "Why are brooks[1227] mentioned in close proximity to tents[1228], as is written (*B'midbar* 24:6): 'stretching out like brooks..., like tents pitched by God-*YHV"H'*? To tell you that just as streams raise a person from a state of spiritual impurity to spiritual purity, so too tents raise a person from a state of obligation to a state of merit." And there[1229] in chapter 18: "'Pour your heart out like water'—Just as those waters are a pure immersion pool for Israel and to everything created in the world..., so too the words of Torah are a pure immersion pool for Israel wherever they settle. Come and observe how great is Torah's power, that it spiritually purifies the sinners of Israel when they repent, even from their acts of idol worship, for it states (*Y'khezkel* 37:25): 'And I will sprinkle pure water upon you, and you shall be purified...'." Refer there [for more details]."

For the essence of true complete repentance that arises out of love is only via involvement with Torah to the level it deserves[1230], as is written in the chapter of the levels of Torah (*Ahvote*, chapter 6): "...loves the *Ma-kome*", and as is written "Return us, our Father, to your Torah... and restore us before you with a complete repentance".

And in *Zohar Va-yikra* (21a): "When a person distances himself from the Torah, he is far from the

1226 I'm unable to find this reference in the *Tahna D'vei Eliyahu.*

1227 Heb.: *n'kha-lim*

1228 Heb.: *k'o-haw-lim.* Tents are used here as a metaphor for Torah study halls. This verse in *B'midbar* actually uses the word *k'ah-haw-lim*, which translates as "like aloes", while the *G'mara* comments on it as if it were written as *k'o-haw-lim* which translates as "like tents". Perhaps, the *G'mara*'s reference to tents is to the previous verse (24:5) in *B'midbar* (see *Torah T'mima, Tosafote RA"Sh*).

1229 In *Tahna D'vei Eliyahu, Seder Eliya Rabba*

1230 Heb.: *ka-ra-ooi*

Holy One (blessed be He). And one who comes closer to the Torah, the Holy One (blessed be He) brings him closer to Him."

For the love of Torah will cover up all sins[1231], as is written in *Tahna D'vei Eliyahu, Seder Eliyahu Rabba* (chapter 3) on this verse (*Mishlei* 10:12)[1232]. And so too they wrote in *P'tee-kha-ta Eikha* (2): "The lamp with which he is returned to good condition". And in *Perek Heh-kha-leel* (*Sukka* 52b): "If that revolting one[1233] engages you, drag him to the study hall; if he is a stone, he will dissolve... ." And they said something similar to this in *Tahn-khooma, parshat Ha-ah-zeenu,* refer there [for more details]. And in *B'reisheet Rabba* (*parsha* 22): "If your inclination comes to wear you down, entertain him with words of Torah". And in *Midrash T'hillim* (end of *Mizmor* 34): "If the evil inclination waits for you, feed him the bread of Torah."

And in *Zohar Va-yeishev* (190a): "Rabbee Yosee stated: 'When a person observes that bad thoughts come to him, he should involve himself with Torah, and they will then leave him'. Rabbee Elazar stated: 'When that evil side comes to seduce a person, lead him to the Torah and he will leave'."

This is what is stated in *Parshat Ha-Torah* (*Ahvote,* chapter 6): "and he will become as a spring that overcomes and goes on its way". And there's room to also explain it relative to this matter mentioned above, that just as a spring gushes and splits anything in its path, even though at times it's mired and clogged by large

---

1231 This phrase ("for the love of Torah covers all sins") is Rav Chayyim's variation on *Mishlei* 10:12: "and love covers all sins" (*v-al- kawl p'sha-in t'kha-she ah-ha-va*)

1232 That love is none other than Torah

1233 Referring to the evil inclination

amounts of mud and clay, even so it gushes and unblocks its path, and overcomes and flows slowly but surely, until after many days it overcomes and is fully and completely revealed, and flows as before. So too one who is involved with Torah for its own sake, even if he is at first soiled with awesome transgressions and sins, and is very mired in the depths of the mud and clay (may the Merciful save us), even so, via involvement with the Torah, his heart/mind will be surely set aright, for the lamp within it will certainly return him to good condition, and the good will overcome the evil within him little by little, until finally, without a doubt, the good will overcome and flow in every part of him completely, and he will be sanctified from his spiritual impurity, and spiritual purity will flower in every part of him.

And so it stated there: "'...and koshers[1234] him to become a righteous, pious person...', employing the specific language of koshering—scouring via immersion in water[1235] and scouring via fire[1236] from the loathsome, evil, abhorred things that were within him beforehand. And as is written (*Yirmeeya* 23:29): 'Are not my words like fire...'—that scours it like fire and koshers it...". And it's written likewise in *Tahn-khooma Va-yahk-heil* that the Torah spiritually purifies the heart/minds and kidneys/emotional center of Torah scholars.

1234 Heb.: *oo-mahkh-shahr-toe*
1235 Heb.: *hahg-ah-la*
1236 Heb.: *lee-boon*

CHAPTER 32

And everything stems from the reason mentioned previously: that the holy Torah's supernal root is above all of the worlds.

And the matter is as I wrote previously (in Gate 1, chapter 20) regarding the reason why they (OBM) stated (*Shabbat* 119b) that anyone who answers "May the great Name be blessed"[1237] with all his strength is pardoned for all his sins—refer there [for more details]. In the same manner serious involvement with Torah awakens its supernal root to emanate and influence the abundant overflowing of its supernal light and holiness on all the worlds. Its sparks are sparks of fire, an awesome flame that expels and disintegrates all of the spiritual impurities and filths that he caused by his actions in all the worlds, so that they become holy and are able to be more illuminated by the supernal holiness, to connect one to the others. And all the blemishes/gaps are filled in, and all that were damaged are repaired, and all that was destroyed is rebuilt, and the joy and the great delight and the supernal light expands in all the worlds.

And also though it's known that nothing is repaired except via its supernal root, and the supernal root of each person-in-Israel's soul-*neshama* is based in one letter in the holy Torah, for that reason *all* of the blemishes of the sinning soul-*Neffesh* are repaired and sweetened in their root via the holy Torah, via serious involvement with it.

And as the scripture stated (*T'hillim* 19:8): "God's-*YHV"H* Torah is perfect, restoring the soul-*Neffesh*"—That even if the soul-*Neffesh* was already cut off from its root (heaven forefend), and it descended debased to the

1237 Aram.: *y'hei shmei rabba m'vawrakh...*—part of the kaddish bottom-most depths of evil (heaven forefend), the holy Torah with which he is involved elevates it and releases it from imprisonment, and re-connects it as it was before and with the additional light of the holy Torah. And this is what they stated in the first chapter of *Ta-ah-neet* (7a): "Rabbee B'na-ah stated: 'Anyone who involves himself with Torah for its own sake, his Torah becomes for him as a medication that saves his life, for it stated (*Mishlei* 3:18): "It is a tree of life...", and it states *Mishlei* 8:35): "For the one who finds me finds life..."'." And they stated in *M'khilta*: "What does the verse 'for I am God-*YHV"H* your healer' (*Sh'mote* 15:26) mean? The Holy One (blessed be He) said to Moshe: 'Tell Israel that the Torah that I've given you is life for you, for it's stated (*Mishlei* 4:22): "for they are life to he who find them"'."

And for that reason the early ones (OBM) formulated the formal confession[1238] using the order of the twenty-two letters, so as to awaken the supernal root of his soul-*Neffesh*, with which it is connected and linked with the holy Torah, to spiritually purify it and to make it holy.

And to the degree that a person is connected to and attached to His (blessed be He) Torah, and in its love he continuously thrives, so too will it shine in his direction and safeguard him in everything he does so that he shouldn't stumble into the trap of the evil inclination (heaven forefend), as it's stated in *Sh'mote Rabba, parsha* 36—refer there [for more details].

And in *Midrash T'hillim*, in *Mizmor* 119[1239]: "In my heart I stored your word, so that I might not sin unto you"—The

---

1238 Which begins: *ah-shahmnoo, ba-gahdnoo...*

1239 Literally "*Mizmor* eight times", called thusly because in that psalm each letter of the alphabet is used to start a verse eight times.

evil inclination does not dominate relative to the Torah, and one who has the Torah in his heart, the evil inclination can't dominate him and can't touch him.

And in *Tahna D'vei Eliyahu, Seder Eliyahu Zoota* (beginning of chapter 16) and in *Ahvote D'rabbee Nattan*: "Rabbee Shimon bar Yokhai stated: 'Anyone who keeps words of Torah in mind,[1240] he is relieved of ten intensely difficult[1241] things: anxiety about his transgression[1242], anxiety about violent threat to his life[1243], anxiety about oppression from government[1244], anxiety about foolish things[1245], anxiety about succumbing to the evil impulse[1246], anxiety about wrong sexual behavior[1247], anxiety about an evil wife[1248], anxiety about idolatry, anxiety about mortality[1249], anxiety about wasting time[1250]... '."

And modesty clothes him, and fear/awe of God is apparent on his face, and all of his personality characteristics are upright, and he doesn't fear being seduced by his inclination in matters of the pleasures of the world and their enjoyment, because he has control of his inclination. He leads it in whichever direction he desires, and based on its advice he will guide it, and it will place him in a beam of its lights, and on everything he does the Torah's light glows, until everything in this world for him is also in a good situation, in proper measure and balanced, as

---

1240 Heb.: *kol ha-no-tein divrei torah al leebo*

1241 Heb.: *d'varim ka-shim*

1242 Heb.: *hir-hoo-rei ah-vei-ra*

1243 Heb.: *hir-hoo-rei cheh-rev*, literally "sword"

1244 Heb.: *hir-hoo-rei mal-khoot*

1245 Heb.: *hir-hoo-rei shtoot*

1246 Heb.: *hir-hoo-rei yeitzer ha-ra*

1247 Heb.: *hir-hoo-rei z'noot*

1248 Heb.: *hir-hoo-rei eesha ra-ah*

1249 Heb.: *hir-hoo-rei ba-sar va-dahm*

1250 Heb.: *hir-hoo-rei d'varim b'tei-lim*

it should be. As they (OBM) stated (*Kidooshin* 30b): "'And you shall place...'[1251] (*D'varim* 11)—perfect medicine[1252]. Torah is likened to a life-preserving medication. A parable is brought about a man who struck his son, wounding him greatly. He put a dressing on his wound and said to him: 'My son—for as long as this dressing is on your wound, eat whatever pleases you and drink whatever pleases you, and you needn't worry. But if you remove it, lo—infections will arise[1253].' Thus said the Holy One (blessed be He): 'My children—I created the evil inclination. I created the Torah as an antidote. If you involve yourselves with the Torah, you are not handed into its power, for it is stated: "If you improve yourself, you will be uplifted". But if you do not involve yourselves with the Torah, you are handed into its power, for it is stated: "Sin crouches at the door"."

> **Annotation:** *And interpreted homiletically, we could address the verse "and the tablets were God-*Elohi"m*'s handiwork, and the writing upon them were God-*Elohi"m*'s writing, engraved..."* (Sh'mote *32:16)—They stated as a homily "Don't read it as 'engraved...'." And the matter is like the pious one Luzzatto*[1254] *(may the memory of the righteous and holy one be a blessing) in his book* M'seelaht Y'sharim *(chapter 5) regarding the statement of the sages (OBM) mentioned above: "I created the evil inclination. I created the Torah as an antidote." Just as in the context of curing the body, that the physician gives the sick person a medication comprised of a variety of spices and herbs, each one in the proper amount,*

1251 Heb.: *v'sahm-tem*- The *Talmud* explains that the word *sahm-tahn* can be explained as the combination of two words: *sahm*—meaning "medication", and *tahm*—meaning "perfect".

1252 Heb.: *sahm-tahm*

1253 Heb.: *ma-ah-lah noomi*

1254 Rabbi Moshe Chayyim Luzzatto (known as the RaMKha"L

with great accuracy, as required by the illness, as known to the physician. Would it arise in the mind of the sick person that to cure his illness he should compound another antidote comprised of other spices and herbs that he happens to be able to gather? Would he be such a fool and not understand that the physician is the one who has knowledge of his illness, and understands the natures of the spices and herbs. He knows which spices and herbs are required by the nature of his illness, and the amounts to be used and how they balance each other.

He (blessed be His name) says the same: Don't imagine that you can escape from seduction by the inclination and its situations using your own strategies and methods that you'll choose based on your own imagination. After all, it was I who created the evil inclination and know how it works. And to oppose it I created the Torah as an antidote and a life-saving medication, to cure the illness it causes. And know that other than the involvement with Torah learning, there is no other strategy.

*That's why they stated: "and the tablets were God-*Elohi"m*'s handiwork". They being the tablets of the coveting heart/mind (similar to the matter of "write them on the tablets of your heart/mind"—*Mishlei *3:30). He (blessed be His name) made them, and He knows the matter of your inclination that is planted in your heart/mind. "And the writing is God-*Elohi"m*'s writing"—That to oppose it He gives you the method of being involved with Torah, to write them and to engrave them on the tablets of your heart/mind, to use it to escape from the situations of the inclination. And for that reason you'll know that there is no one who is free from the situations of the inclination other than one who is involved with Torah learning, and there is absolutely no strategy other than it.*

And as the sages (OBM) explained regarding "'As you go forth, it will guide you' (*Mishlei* 6:22)—In this world." And in *Mishlei Rabbta*: "Fortunate is the person who acquires Torah for himself. Why? Because it safeguards him from an evil path, as is written (*Mishlei* 6:22) 'As you go forth…'." And it's also as discussed in *Va-yikra Rabba* (chapter 35), because it straightens and directs his heart/mind until his hearts/minds are fully in harmony with his God-*Elohi"m*, and reliable with God-*Ei"l Roo-kho*, to worship Him (bless be He) with the totality of his hearts/minds—both of his inclinations[1255]. It's as they stated in the first chapter of *Chageega* (3b): "'The words of the wise are like goads' (*Kohelet* 12:11)—Why are the words of Torah likened to a goad? Just as a goad directs a cow along the furrow to bring life to the world, so the words of Torah direct the heart/mind of those who learn it away from paths of deaths to paths of life." And they stated so also in *B'midbar Rabba* (*parsha* 14) and in *Tahn-khooma* (*parshat B'ha-ah-lote-kha*) and at the beginning of *parshat Va-yelekh* there.

For there is no other remedy nor rectification of any kind in the world that will allow him to be saved from his inclination's net, forever spread before his feet to trap him and to cause him to fall to the nethermost depths of *Sh'ol*, to cause him to die an everlasting death (heaven forefend), other than by involvement with the holy Torah, which thereby he is called a "living person", for he is adhered by it to his portion in the life of the true world, as is written "for it is your life" (*Mishlei* 4:13).

And the sages (OBM) stated (*Avoda Za-ra* 3b): "What is the meaning of what is written 'You have made man like the fish of the sea…' (*Chabakook* 1:14)?" Just as the fish in the sea immediately die when separated from the sea, so too people, when they separate themselves from Torah, immedi-

---

1255 *B'rakhote* 54a

ately die[1256]. And Rabbee Ahkeeva responded to Pappus in the same manner: "If in the climate where we thrive" it is so… (*B'rakhote* 61b). And in the *Raa-ya M'hemna* at the end of *parshat Shmini*: "Just as the fish of the sea thrive in water, so too Torah scholars, masters of the *Mishna*, thrive in the Torah, and if they are separated from it they immediately die." And in *Tahn-khooma, parshat Eikev* (5): "'For they are life to he who finds them' (*Mishlei* 4:22)—Anyone who finds words of Torah, finds life... ." For that reason it is stated: "For they are life to he who finds them."

And in *Zohar Lekh L'kha* (92a): "Fortunate is Israel's portion, that the Torah teaches them the paths of the Holy One (blessed be He)… with certainty. It's written 'God-*YHV"H*'s Torah is perfect…' (*T'hillim* 19: 8)—Fortunate is the portion of one who involves himself with Torah and does not separate from it, for anyone who separates from Torah even one hour is like one who separates from the world's source of life, for it is written 'for it is your life…', and it is written 'for they add to you length of days and years of life and peace'."

And at the beginning of *parshat B'ha-ah-lote-kha*: "Fortunate is Israel's portion, that the Holy One (blessed be He) desired them and gave them the true Torah, the tree of life, by which man can grasp and inherit life in this world and in the world-to-come. Anyone who involves himself with Torah and grasps it, he has life and grasps life. And anyone who leaves the words of Torah and is separated from Torah is as if he separates from life, because it is life and all of its words are life, this being what is written: 'For they are life …' (*Mishlei* 34:22), and as it is written: 'It is health to your navel…' (*Mishlei* 3:8)."

1256 This is not a direct quote of the Talmud.

CHAPTER 33

And for that reason we were commanded via a fearsome warning from Him (blessed be He): "This book of the Torah shall not cease from your mouth, and you shall contemplate it day and night" (*Y'hoshua* 1:8). And as it's written in the introduction to the *Zohar*: "Come and observe how powerful is the Torah and how ascendant it is over everything..., and because of this a person must be involved with it day and night, and should not depart from it. This is what is written: 'Contemplate it day and night'. And if he should depart or separate from it, it's as if he separated himself from the tree of life."

And in *Tahna D'vei Eliyahu, Seder Eliyahu Zoota* (chapter 13) he said[1257] that a person should personally make an effort in words of Torah, because words of Torah are likened to food and water..., to teach you that just as a person can't survive without food and water, so too it's impossible for a person to survive without Torah, for it is stated: "This book of the Torah shall not cease from your mouth... ." And so too they stated in *Tahn-khooma, parshat Ta-vo,* on the verse: "and it will come to pass if you hearken..." (*Sh'mote* 11:13), and in *parshat Ha-ah-zeenu,* and in *Midrash T'hillim* (*Mizmor* 1).

And scripture stated (*Mishlei* 3:18): "It is a tree of life for those who hold fast to it", because a person has to fix in his heart/mind, and visualize using his power of imagination, that if he were drowning in a rushing river and he saw before him in the river a strong tree, it is certain that he would make a great effort to hold fast and attach himself to it with all of his strength, and he will not weaken his grip

1257 This is a paraphrasing with slight wording changes from the text in the *Tahna D'vei Eliyahu.*

from it even for a single moment, being that his entire life is now dependent on it. Who could be a fool and not understand that if he should get lazy (heaven forefend) for even one moment, and weaken his grip from holding fast to it, he would immediately drown.

In that same way, the holy Torah is called *Etz Chayyim—ee-la-na d'khai-yei*[1258]—for it's only in those moments when a person is held fast in its love, and is involved with and contemplates it fixedly, it is then that he is living a truly supernal life, connected to and attached to (so to speak) the Eternally Living (blessed be He), for the Holy One (blessed be He) and the Torah are one. And if (heaven forefend) he should abandon his learning, and separate from constancy of involvement with it, to get involved with the world's vanities and pleasures, he's interrupted from and cut off from the supernal life, and drowns himself in the malicious waters (may the Merciful save us).

And in *Zohar Va-yei-tzei* (152a): Fortunate are Israel, for the Holy One (blessed be He) gave them the Torah of truth with which to involve themselves day and night. For anyone who involves himself with Torah is freed from all things: free from death, which is unable to rule over him..., for anyone who involves himself with Torah and as a result holds to it, he holds to the tree of life. And if he slackens himself from the tree of life, lo, the tree of death rules over him and grabs onto him, and this is what is written: "If you were weak..." (*Mishlei* 24:10).

For that reason the Torah itself states (and you can see for yourself): "...but one who sins against me does violence to his soul-*Neffesh*" (*Mishlei* 8:36). And as it is written (*D'varim* 4:9): "Only guard yourself and guard your soul-*Neffesh* lest you forget the things... ." And as the sages (OBM) wrote

1258 The "Tree of Life" in Hebrew and Aramaic respectively.

regarding this (*M'nakhote* 99b): "This is likened to a person who gave a swallow[1259] to his servant. He told him: 'Don't think that if it dies in your care that I will claim a monetary value from you; your soul-*Neffesh* I will claim from you'." And as is well known, their (OBM) statement about this in *D'varim Rabba*, at the beginning of *parsha* 4, that the Holy One (blessed be He) said to Adam: "My lamp is in your hands, and your lamp is in my hands. If you safeguard my lamp I will safeguard your lamp. But if you don't safeguard my lamp..."—refer there [for more details]. And similarly it is written *Tahn-khooma, parshat Teesa*, and in *Midrash T'hillim* (*Mizmor* 7)—refer there [for more details].

CHAPTER 34

And from the time when our holy Temple was destroyed and the children were exiled from their Father's table, the Presence of His Glory[1260] (blessed be He) departed, was sent away (so to speak) and can't be soothed, and nothing is left other than this Torah. When Israel, the holy nation, chirp[1261] about it and contemplate it as it deserves, they [emphatic] become for her a miniature Temple[1262], to groom her and to nourish her, and she dwells with them and spreads her wings over them (so to speak); in any event there is some rest... . As they (OBM) stated in the first chapter of *B'rakhote* (8a): "From the day that the Temple was destroyed, the Holy

---

1259 Heb.: *tzee-por d'ror* - Rav Chayyim cites a *G'mara* that likens the Torah to a captured bird, normally free, that is given to a servant to tend, and which if he neglects, may cost him his life.

1260 Heb.: *Sh'kheenaht k'vodo*

1261 Heb.: *m'tzahf-tzeif*

1262 Heb.: *mikdahsh m'aht*

One (blessed be He) has no place in the world other than only the four cubits of *Halakha*".

And they further stated there: "How do we know that when even one person sits and involves himself with the Torah, that the *Sh'kheena* is present with him? Because it states 'in every place where I mention…'." And in *Mishlei Rabbta,* at the end of *parsha* 8: "'For the one who finds Me finds life'—the Holy One (blessed be He) stated: 'Anyone who can be found in the company of words of Torah, so too I am found by him in every place'. For that reason it is stated 'For the one who finds Me find life'."

And in *Zohar Ba-lahk* (202a): "He began and stated: 'When you lay siege to a city…, do not destroy its trees' (*D'varim* 20:19)—This is a Torah scholar, for he is the tree of life… . '…For from it you shall eat'—Is the one who would destroy it the [same] one who eats from it?[1263] No, rather 'for from it you shall eat' refers to the hard stone[1264] from which all the powerful, holy souls-*Ruakh* originate, for the Holy Spirit[1265] has no pleasure nor desire in this world other than from the Torah of that righteous one. He (so to speak) supports her and gives her nourishment in this world, more than all the sacrifices in the world. And from the day that the Holy Temple was destroyed and the sacrifices ceased, the Holy One (blessed be He) has nothing other than the words of Torah, and the Torah that

---

1263 The *Zohar* asks if the one who lays siege to the city and would cut down the trees is the same one who would eat of and benefit from those trees.

1264 The phrase "hard stone" (Aram.: *teenra takeefa,* Heb.: *tzoor chazak*) refers to the source of the holy souls. That source is called Stone, for the souls are (so to speak) quarried from it. It is also called the Quarry of Souls (*mahkh-tzav ha-n'sha-mote*). [*Matoke Mi'd'vash*]

1265 The *Sh'kheena*

is renewed in his mouth. As a result of this 'for from it you shall eat', and He has no other nourishment in this world other than from him and others like him.... 'For man is the tree of the field'—The man we are discussing is known above and below as 'tree of the field', a great and strong tree of that 'field that was blessed by God-*YHV"H*'[1266], attributing to him that he is the tree that is always known to that field."

And this is also the inner intention when they (OBM) stated in the first chapter of *Ta-ah-neet* (7a): "Why was it written 'for a person is the tree of the field..., for from it you shall eat'? If he is a proper Torah scholar, then 'from it/him[1267] you may eat'. And if not... ."

And in *Zohar Va-yishlakh* (174b): "How does someone strengthen the Holy One (blessed be He)? He strengthens via the Torah, for anyone who strengthens via the Torah strengthens the tree of life, and he (so to speak) strengthens the *K'nesset Yisrael*[1268] to be stronger. And what if he weakens his effort? That's what is written (*Mishlei* 24:10): 'If you were weak...', that's if he weakened his effort related to Torah, then 'in the day of tribulation your strength will be constrained'—on the day that tribulation comes, it will be (so to speak) that he pushes the *Sh'kheena* away, she who is the source of strength in the world."

And by being involved with Torah he (so to speak)

1266 The field again being the *Sh'kheena*. The Torah scholar is the one who supports and maintains the *Sh'kheena* in this world, and is therefore known to the *Sh'kheena*. [*Matoke Mi'd'vash*]

1267 The Hebrew word *mee-mehnu* can apply to both an object and a person.

1268 The *K'nesset Yisrael* is the sum total of all the souls of Israel, again the Quarry of Souls, the *Sh'kheena*, who is also called *ko* (the Hebrew letters *kaf* and *heh*) the last two letters of the word we translated as "your strength" (Heb. *ko-kheh-kha)* [*Matoke Mi-d'vash*]

makes a home for Him (blessed be He) among those in the lower world, in which His (blessed be He) glory rests in the land. It is as they (OBM) stated in *Sh'mote Rabba*, (*parsha* 33): "Before the Torah was given to Israel: 'and Moses ascended to the God-*Elohi"m*'. And after the Torah was given: 'and they shall make me a Temple and I shall dwell among/within them'."

And these, our words, are adequate for the wise, that from within them he will see and understand his path of holiness, and will hold fast to the righteousness of his path, to persist in the task of safeguarding his involvement with the holy Torah all the days that he lives, and to be disgusted by evil and to choose the good, for himself and for the totality of all the creations and the worlds, to gratify his Former and Creator (blessed be He).

And may it be His Will (blessed be His name) that our hearts shall be opened to His Torah, and may He place within our hearts His love and awe/fear, and may His intention in creating His world be fulfilled that the world should be rectified in the sovereignty of God-*Sha-Da"Y*, and all those who are the effects of His actions[1269] will know..., and they will accept upon themselves the yoke of His (blessed be He) sovereignty, in accord with the supernal Will (blessed be He), and God-*YHV"H* will be one and His name one. Amen, may it be His will.

Perfect and Complete

Third day of the week, *Parshat Korakh*, 26 Sivan 5584.
Blessed be the One who gives the weary strength.
Blessed are You God-*YHV"H*, teach me your statutes.
Direct my eyes and I shall observe the wonders of your Torah.

1269 Heb.: *pa-ool*

NOTES

NOTES

Notes

NOTES

שער ד

ובטלתו יתב׳ : ויה״ר מלפניו ית״ש שיפתח לבנו בתורתו וישם בלבנו אהבתו ויראתו · ויושלם סוכתו בבריאת שלמה שיתוקן עולם במלכות שדי · וידע כל פעול כי ויקבלו כולם עול מלכותו ית׳ כפי הרצון העליון יתב׳ · ויהיה ה׳ אחד ושמו אחד :· אכי״ר :

תם ונשלם

בנל״ך : בא״י למדני חקיך : גל עיני ואביטה נפלאות מתורתך :

תיקונים

שער א	דף ה׳ ע״ד בסוף הג״ה	ומתגלה · צ״ל כתגלה :
	דף ו׳ ע״א בסופו .	וכל · צ״ל וכן :
	דף ז׳ ע״א שורה י׳ ·	טוב · צ״ל רוב :
	דף ח׳ ע״ד שורה י״א ·	עמי · עמו :
שער ב	דף י׳ ע״ב שורה ל״א ·	רוחנית · צ״ל רוחניותיהם :
שער ג	דף א׳ ע״ג שורה י״ד ·	אן · צ״ל כן :
	דף ט׳ ע״ד שורה ט״ז	פ״ב · צ״ל ס״ב :
שער ד	דף ג׳ ע״ד שורה כ״א ·	הוראה · צ״ל היראה :
	דף ג׳ ע״ד שורה ג׳ ·	להתיר · צ״ל להיתר :
	דף י״ב ע״א שורה ו׳ ·	ירננו · צ״ל ורננו :
	דף י״ד ע״ב שורה כ׳ ·	ופרטיו · צ״ל ופרקיו :

ולמה לו חיים · כי כבר נטבע במים הזדונים ר"ל ונשקע בעמקי מצולות הרע ונחשב כמת ממש גם בעודו בזה העולם · הולך מדחי אל דחי ללמות ולא סורים ולא ידע כי בנפשו היא · ולזאת התורה שלמה אמריה תאמר ותועלתי חומס נפשו · וכמ"ש השמר לך ושמור נפשך מאד פן תשכח את הדברים כו' וכמאמרם ז"ל ע"ז (מנחות ל"ט ב') משל לאדם שמסר צפור דרור לעבדו א"ל כמדומה אתה שאם אתה מאבדה איסר אני נוטל ממך נשמתך אני נוטל ממך · וכידוע מאמרם ז"ל ע"ז בדברים רבה רפ"ד שאמר הקב"ה לאדם נרי בידך ונרך בידי אם שמרת את נרי אני משמר את נרך ואם לא שמרת את נרי כו' ע"ש · וכ"ה בתנחומא פ' תצא ובמדרש תהלים מזמור ו' ע"ש :

פרק לד ומעת

חורבן בית קדשינו וגלו הבני' מעל שלחן אביהם · שכינת כבודו יתב' אזלא ומתרכא כביכול ולא תרגיע · ואין שיור רק התורה הזאת כשישראל עם הקדש מלפלפים ועוסקים בה כראוי · כן המה לה למקדש מעט להכין אותה ולסעדה ותורה עמהם ופורשת כנפיה עליהם כביכול · ובין כך אית נייחא מעט כו' · כמאמרם ז"ל בפ"ק דברכות (ח' ע"א) מיום שחרב בהמ"ק אין לו להקב"ה בעולמו אלא ד"א של הלכה בלבד · ואמרו שם עוד מנין שאפי' א' שיושב ועוסק בתורה ששכינה שרויה עמו שנאמ' בכל המקום אשר אזכיר וכו' · ובמשלי רבתא ספ"ח כי מוצאי מצא חיים אמר הקב"ה כל מי שהוא מצוי בד"ת אף אני מצוי לו בכל מקום לכך נאמ' כי מוצאי מצא חיים · ובזוהר בלק ר"ב א' פתח ואמר כי תצור אל עיר כו' לא תשחית את עצה דא ת"ח דאיהו אילנא דחיי כו' · כי ממנו תאכל וכי בהוא מחבלא אכילמני' · לא אלא כי ממנו תאכל ההוא מיכלא תקיפא קדישא דכל רוחין תקיפין קדישין נפקין מנה דלית הנאה ותיאובתא לרוח קודשא בהאי עלמא אלא אורייתא · דההוא זכאה כביכול איהו מפרנס לה ויהיב לה מזונא בהאי עלמא יתיר מכל קרבנין דעלמא כו' · ומיומא דאתחריב בי' מקדשא ובטלו קרבנין לית לי' לקב"ה אלא אינון מלין דאורייתא ואורייתא דאתחדשת בפומי' · בג"כ כי ממנו תאכל ולית מזונא בהאי עלמא אלא ממנו ואינון דכוותי' כו' · כי האדם עץ השדה דא אקרי אדם דאשתמודע עילא ותתא · עץ השדה אלנא רברבא ותקיף דההיא שדה אשר ברכו ה' דכתיב עלי' · אילן דאשתמודע לההוא שדה תדיר : וזהו ג"כ המכוון הפנימי במאמרם ז"ל בפ"ק דתענית (ז' ע"א) מ"ד כי האדם עץ השדה כו' כי ממנו תאכל כו' אם ת"ח הגון הוא ממנו תאכל כו' ואם לאו כו' · ובזוהר וישלח קע"ד ב' והיך יתתקף ב"נ בי' בקב"ה יתקיף באורייתא · דכל מאן דאתתקף באורייתא אתתקף באילנא דחיי · וכביכול יהיב תוקפא לכ"י לאתתקפא · ואי הוא יתרפי מה כתיב התרפית אי איהו אתרפי מן אוריי' ביום צרה צר כחכה ביומא דייתי לי' עקו כביכול דחיק לה לשכינתא דאיהי חילא דעלמא · ובעסק התורה הוא עושה כביכול דירה לו יתב' בתחתונים לשכון כבוד בארץ ית"ש · כמאמרם ז"ל בשמות רבה פל"ג עדן שלא ניתנה תורה לישראל ומשה עלה אל האלקים · משניתנה תורה אמר הקב"ה ועשו לי מקדש ושכנתי בתוכם : ודי בדברינו אלה למשכיל אשר מתוכם יראה ויבין דרכו בקדש · ויאחז לדק דרכו לעמוד על משמרת העסק בתו"הק כל הימים אשר הוא חי ולהיות מאום ברע' ובחור בטוב לו ולכל הבריות והעולמות כולם לעשות נחת רוח ליוצרו

שער ד

והמכתב מכתב אלקים הוא. שכנגד זה הוא הנותן לך ענין עסק התורה לכתבם ולחקקם על לוחות לבך להמלט על ידה מעניני היצר. ולזאת תדע שאין לך בן חורין מעניני היצר. אלא מי שעוסק בתלמוד תורה. ולא שום תחבולה אחרת זולתה:

שבים כיון שפירשים מן המים מיד מתי' אף ב"א כיון שפורשי' מן התורה מיד מתים. וכן השיבו ר"ע לפפוס ומה במקום חיותינו כך כו' (ברכות ס"א ב'). וברע"מ ס"פ שמיני מה נוני ימא חיותן במיא אוף ת"ח מארי מתני' חיותייהו באורייתא ואי אתפרשן מנה מיד מתים. ובתנחומא פ' עקב כי חיים הם למוצאיה' כל מי שמוצא ד"ת חיים הוא מוצא כו' לכן נאמר כי חיים הם למוצאיהם. ובזוהר לך לך כ"ב א' זכאה חולקיהון דישראל דאורייתא אוליף להו אורחוי דקב"ה כו' ודאי כתיב תורת ה' תמימה וגו' זכאה חולקיה מאן דאשתדל באורייתא ולא יתפרש מנה דכל מאן דיתפרש מאורייתא אפילו שעתא חדא כמה דאתפרש מחיי דעלמא דכתי' כי היא חייך וגו' וכתיב אורך ימים ושנות חיים ושלום יוסיפו לך. ובר"פ בהעלותך זכאה חולקיהון דישראל דקב"ה אתרעי בהון ויהב להון אורייתא דקשוט אילנא דחיי דביה אחיד בר נש וירית חיין להאי עלמא וחיין לעלמא דאתי דכל מאן דאשתדל באורייתא' ואחיד בה אית ליה חיין ואחיד בחיין. וכל מאן דשביק מלי דאורייתא ואתפרש מאורייתא כאלו מתפרש מחיין בגין דהיא חיין וכל מלה חיין הה"ד כי חיים הם וגו' וכתיב רפאות תהי לשרך וגו':

פרק לג ולזאת נצטוינו בתורה מראה מפיו יתברך לא ימוש

ספר התורה הזה מפיך והגית בו יומם ולילה. וכמ"ש בהקדמת הזוהר ת"ח כמה הוא חילא תקיפא דאורייתא וכמה הוא עלאה על כולא כו'. ובג"כ בעי ליה לב"נ לאשתדלא באורייתא יממא ולילייא ולא יתעדי מנה הה"ד והגית בו יומם ולילה ואי אתעדי או אתפרש מנה כאלו אתפרש מאילנא דחיי. ובתד"א סא"ז פי"ג אמר וישתדל אדם בעצמו כד"ת שד"ת הן משולים בלחם ובמים כו'. ללמדך שכשם שא"א לו לאדם לעמוד בלא לחם ובלא מים כך א"א לו לאדם לעמוד בלא תורה שנאמר לא ימוש ספר התורה הזה מפיך וגו'. וכן אמרו בתנחומא פ' תבא בפ' והיה אם שמוע ובפ' האזינו ובמדרש תהלים מזמור א'. ואמר הכתוב עץ חיים היא למחזיקים בה וגו'. כי צריך האדם לקבוע בלבו וידמה בדעתו. כי אלו היה טובע בנהר שוטף ורואה לפניו בנהר אילן חזק. ודאי יאמץ כח להתאחז ולהתדבק עצמו בו בכל כחו ולא ירפה ידיו הימנו אפילו רגע אחד. אחר שרק בזה תלוי עתה כל חיותו מי פתי ולא יבין שאם יתעלל ח"ו אף רגע א' וירפה ידיו מהתאחז בו יטבע תיכף. כן התו"הק נק' עץ חיים אילנא דחיי. שרק אותו העת שהאדם אחוז באהבתה ועוסק ומהגה בה בקביעות. אז הוא חי בחיים האמתים העליונים קשור ודבוק כביכול בחי העולמים ית"ש שהוא וקב"ה ואורייתא חד. ואם ח"ו יניח תלמודו ופורש מקביעות העסק בה לעסוק בהבלי העולם והנאותיו. הוא נפסק ונכרת מהחיים העליונים וטובע עצמו במים הזדונים ר"ל. ובזוהר ויצא קנ"ב א' זכאין אינון ישראל דקב"ה יהב לון אורייתא דקשוט לאשתדלא בה יממא ולילי'. דהא כל מאן דאשתדל באורייתא אית ליה חירו מכלא חירו מן מותא דלא יכלא לשלטאה עליה כו' בגין דכל מאן דאשתדל באורייתא ואתאחיד בה אתאחיד באילנא דחיי. ואי ארפי גרמי' מאילנא דחיי הא אילנא דמותא שריא עלוי ואתאחיד ביה הה"ד התרפית כו' ע"ש. וכמה צריך האדם לתקוע ולקבוע זה הענין הגורא במחשבות לבו בל תמוט. שכל האדם וחייו הוא רק אותו העת שהוא דבוק בתו"הק. וכשמסלק ופורש עצמו הימנה לפסוק בעניני זה העולם החשוך ה"ה מסור ביד יצרו

ותמה

שער ד

היא לכם חיים היא לכם שנא' כי חיים הם למוצאיהם ולכן תקנו הראשונים ז"ל נוסח הוידוי ע"פי סדר הכ"ב אותיות · כדי לעורר שרש העליון של נפשו אשר היא מקושרת ונאחזת בתו"הק לטהרה ולקדשה:

וכל עוד שהאדם קשור ודבוק בתורתו יתברך ובאהבתה ישגה תמיד · אף היא תאיר אליו ומשמרתו בכל דרכיו ועניניו שלא יפול ברשת היצ"ר ח"ו · כמ"ש בשמות רבה פל"ו ע"ש · ובמדרש ..ס במזמור תמניא אפי בלבי צפנתי אמרתך למען לא אחטא לך אין יצ"הר שולט אל התורה ומי שהתורה בלבו אין יצר הרע שולט בו ולא נוגע בו · ובתדב"א סא"ז רפט"ז ובאבות דר"נ אמר רשב"י כל הנותן ד"ת על לבו מעבירין ממנו עשרה דברים קשים · הרהורי עבירה · הרהורי חרב · הרהורי שטות · הרהורי יצר הרע · הרהורי זנות · הרהורי אשה רעה · הרהורי עבודת כוכבים · הרהורי עול בשר ודם · הרהורי דברים בטלים · ומלבשתו ענוה ויראת ה' על פניו וכל מדה נכונה · ואינו מתיירא מפתויי יצרו בעניני הנאות העולם ותענוגותיו · כי יצרו מסור בידו לכל אשר יחפוץ יטנו · ובעלתה תנחהו ותעמידהו בקרן אורה ועל כל דרכיו נגה אור התורה עד שגם כל עניני זה העולם הם אצלו בענין טוב במדה ובמשקל כראוי · כמאמרם ז"ל (קדושין ל' ע"ב) ושמתם סם תם נמשלה תורה כסם חיים · משל לאדם שהכה את בנו מכה גדולה והניח לו רטיה על מכתו ואמר לו בני כל זמן שרטי'ז על מכתך אכול מה שהנאך ושתה מה שהנאך ואין אתה מתייר' ואם אתה מעביר'ה מעלה נימא · כך אמר הקב"ה בני בראתי יצ"הר בראתי לו תורה תבלין (*) אם אתם עוסקין בתורה אין אתם נמסרים בידו שנאמ' הלא אם תטיב שאת ואם אין אתם עוסקין בתורה אתם נמסרים בידו שנא' לפתח חטאת רובץ · וכמו שפירשו ז"ל בהתהלכך תנחה אותך בעוה"ז · ובמשלי רבתא אשרי אדם שקנה לו תורה למה שהיא משמרה אותו מדרך רעה דכתיב בהתהלכך כו' · וכ"ה בויקרא רבה פל"ה · כי היא מיישרת ומכוונת את לבו עד אשר ישא לבבו שלם עם אלקיו ונאמנה את אל רוחו לעבדו ית' בכל לבבו בשני יצריו · כמ"ש בפ"ק דחגיגה (ג' ב') דברי חכמים כדרבונות למה נמשלו ד"ת לדרבן מה דרבן זה מכוין את הפרה לתלמיה להביא חיים לעולם אף ד"ת מכוונין לב לומדיהן מדרכי מיתה לדרכי חיים · וכן אמרו בבמדבר רבה פי"ד ובתנחומא פ' בהעלותך ובר"פ וילך שם · כי אין תרופה ותקנה אחרת בעולם כלל להנצל מרשת יצרו אשר פורש לרגליו תמיד ללכדו ולהפילו עד שאול תחתית להמיתו מיתת עולם ח"ו · אלא ע"י העסק בתו"הק · אשר אז נקרא איש חי שהוא דבוק על ידה בחלקו בחיי עול' האמתים כמ"ש כי היא חייך כו' · ואחז"ל (עכ"ומז ג' ע"ב) מ"ד ותעשה אדם כדגי הים כו' מה דגים

שבים

הגה"ה

(*) וי"ל ע"ד דרש הכתו' והלוחו' מעשה אלהים המה והמכתב מכתב אלהים הוא חרות וכו' ודרשו א"ת וכו' והענין כענין שכתב החסיד הלוצאטו זצוק"ל בס' מסילת ישרים במאמרם ז"ל הנ"ל בראתי יצ"הר בראתי לו תורה תבלין · שכמו כענין רפואה הגיף שהרופא נותן להחולה תבלין ממוזג מכמ' מיני סמנים ועשבים · והכל במדה ומשקל בדקדוק עצום כפי הנצרך לענין החולי הידועה להרופא· האם יעלה ע"ד החולה שהוא יעשה לו לרפאות חוליו· תבלין אחר ממוזג מסמנים ועשבים אחרים כפי שתעלה בידו· מי פתי ולא יבין · הלא הרופא הוא היודע ענין חוליו ויודע טבעי הסמנים והעשבים· הוא היודע איזה סמנים ועשבים הנצרכים לטבע חוליו · ושיעור מדתם ומשקלם· כן אומר הוא ית"ש· אל תדמו בנפשכם להמלט מפתויי היצר ועניניו בתחבולות וענינים אשר תבחרו לעצמכם· כי דמיוניכם הלא אנכי שבראתי היצ"הר ויודע ענינו· ואנכי בראתי נגד זה תורה תבלין וסמא דחיי לרפאות חלאת עניניו ותדעו שלבד העסק בתלמוד תורה · אין שום תחבולה אחרת לזה · ז"ש והלחו' מעשה אלקי' המה הם להות הלב החומד · (כענין כתבם על לוח לבך)· הוא ית"ש פעלם· והוא היודע ענין יצרך הנטוע בלבך

והמכתב

שער ד

שבידם שנאמר וזרקתי עליכם מים טהורים וטהרתם כו' ע"ש · כי עיקר התשובה שלימה האמתית שהיא מאהבה · הוא רק ע"י עסק התורה כראוי כמ"ש במעלות התורה אוהב את המקום · וכמ"ש השיבנו אבינו לתורתך כו' והחזירנו בתשובה שלימה לפניך · ובזוהר ויקרא כ"א א' כד ב"נ אתרחיק מאורייתא רחיק הוא מקב"ה · ומאן דקריב לאורייתא קריב לי' קב"ה בהדי' . כי על כל פשעים תכסה אהבת התורה כמ"ש בתד"א סא"ר פי"ג ע"ז הפסוק · וכן אמרו (פתית' איכה) המאור שבה מחזירו למוטב · ובפ' החליל (נ"ב ב') אם פגע בך מנוול זה משכהו לבה"מד חם אבן הוא נימוח וכו' · וכעין זה אמרו בתנחומא פ' האזינו ע"ש · ובב"ר פכ"ב אם בא יצרך להשחיקך שמחהו בד"ת · ובמדרש תהלים סוף מזמור ל"ד אם עמד עליך יצה"ר האכילהו לחמה של תורה כו' · ובזוהר וישב ק"ל ע"א א"ר"י כד חמי ב"נ דהרהורין בישין אתיין לגבי' יתעסק באורייתא וכדין יתעברון מני' א"ר"א כד ההוא סטרא בישא אתי למפתי לי' לב"נ יהא משיך ליה לגבי אורייתא ויתפרש מני' :

וז"ש בפ' התורה ונעשה כמעין המתגבר והולך · ויש מקום לפרשו גם ע"ז הענין הנ"ל · שכמו המעין הנובע אף שלפעמים נרפש ונשחת בהרבה רפש וטיט · עכ"ז הוא נובע ובוקע ומתגבר והולך מעט מעט · עד שברבות הימים יתגבר ויתגלה לגמרי ויתפשט כמאז · כן העוסק בתורה לשמה אף אם נתלכלך תחלה בעוונו' וחטאי' עצומים ונטבע מאד ברפש וטיט מגולות הרע ח"ו · עכ"ז ע"י עסק התורה יהא נכון לבו בטוח שודאי שמאור שבה יחזירו למוטב · והטוב מתגבר והולך על הרע שבו מעט מעט · עד שלסוף בהכרח יתגבר הטוב ויתפשט בכולו לגמרי·והוא מתקדש מטומאתו ופרחה עבירה בכולו · וכן אמר שם ומכשרתו להיות צדיק חסיד כו' לשון הכשר והגעלה וליבון מפיגול גיעולי הרע שהיה בו תחלה · וכמ"ש (ירמי' כ"ג) הלא כה דברי כאש כו' שהיא מלבנתו ומכשרתו כו' · וכ"א בתנחומא ויקהל שהתורה מטהרת לבן וכליותן של ת"ח :

פרק לב והכל מטעם הנ"ל ששורשה העליון של התוה"ק היא מעל כל העולמות כולם · והענין הוא כמש"ל (בשער א' פ"כ) טעם מאמר' ז"ל שכל העונה אמן יש"ר בכל כחו מוחלין לו על כל עונותיו ע"ש · כן הענין שע"י עסק התורה כראוי · הוא מעורר שרשה העליון · להאציל ולהשפיע שפעת אור עליון וקדושה על העולמות כולם · ורשפיה רשפי אש שלהבת נורא לגרש ולכלות כל הטומאות והזוהמות שגרם במעשיו בכל העולמות להתקדש ולהאיר עוד בקדושה העליונה להתקשר יחד א' בחבירו · וכל הפגמים מתמלאים וכל הקלקולים נתקנים וכל ההריסות מתבנים · והשמחה וחדותא יתירתא ואור העליון מתרבה בכל העולמות · וגם כי ידוע שכל דבר אינו נתקן אלא בשרשו העליון · וכל א' מישראל שורש העליון של נשמתו הוא מאות א' מהתורה הקדושה · לכן כל פגמי הנפש החוטאת נתקנים ונמתקים בשרשם בתוה"ק ע"י העסק בה כראוי · וכמש"ה תורת ה' תמימה משיבת נפש · שאף אם כבר נכרתה הנפש משורשה ה"ו ותרד פלאים בעמקי מצולות הרע ח"ו · התוה"ק שעוסק בה היא מקימה ומוליאה ממסגרים ומשיבה אותה להתקשר כבתחילה וביהרון אור התוה"ק·וז"ש בפ"ק דתענית (ז' א') תניא ר' בנאה אומר כל העוסק בתורה לשמה תורתו נעשית לו סם חיים שנאמר עץ חיים היא כו' ואומר כי מוצאי מצא חיים כו' · ואמרו במכילתא מה ת"ל כי אני ה' רופאך א"ל הקב"ה למשה אמור להם לישראל תורה שנתתי לכם רפואה

היא

ומקבלים ממנה עלם חיותם ושפעת קדושתם · לכן היא הנותנת ומשפעת החיות והקדושה והאור להמלות כולן :

פרק לא ומזה הטעם ג"כ · עסק התור' היא מכפר' על כל העונו'

של הנפש החוטאת· כמאמרם ז"ל (סוף מנחות) מ"ד זאת התורה לעולה למנחה ולחטאת כו' · ומסיק שכל שעוסק בתורה א"צ לא עולה ולא מנחה ולא חטאת ולא אשם · וכ"ה בתנחומא פ' צו · ובשמות רבה פל"ח קחו עמכם דברים ושובו אל ה' לפי שישראל אומרים ט' · עניים אנו ואין לנו להביא קרבנות א"ל הקב"ה דברים אני מבקש כו' · ואני מוחל לכם על כל עונותיכם·ואין דברי' אלא ד"ת כו'·ובתנחומא ויקהל בענין הארון אמרו שהוא נושא עונותיהם של ישראל שהתורה שבו נשא עונותיהם של ישראל · ובתד"א סא"ר פי"ח אדם שעבר עבירו' הרבה ונקנסו עליו מיתה ט' · וחזר ועשה תשובה וקורא תורה נביאים וכתובים ושנה משנה מדרש הלכות והגדות ושימש חכמים אפי' נגזרו עליו מאה גזירות הקב"ה מעבירן ממנו כו' · ובזוהר של"ח קנ"ט א' ר"י פתח כו' · כמה אית להו לבני נשא לאסתכלא בפולחנא דקב"ה · כמה אית להו לאסתכלא במלי דאורייתא · דכל מאן דאשתדל באורייתא כאלו מקריב כל קורבנין דעלמא לקמי' קב"ה ולא עוד אלא דקב"ה מכפר לי' על כל חובוי ומתקנין לי' כמה כורסיין לעלמא דאתי · וגם על אותן הטועים האומרים שאין הקרבנות מכפרים עסק התורה מכפרת · כמא"ר ז"ל בבני עלי (ר"ה י"ח א') בזבח ובמנחה הוא דאינו מתכפר אבל מתכפר הוא בד"ת · וכן אמרו (מגילה ג' ע"ב) גדול ת"ת יותר מהקרבת תמידין · ובזוהר צו ל"ה א' ת"ח כו' וע"ד מאן דלעי באורייתא לא אצטריך לא לקרבנין ולא לעלוון דהא אורייתא עדיף מכלא וקשורא דמהימנותא דכלא · וע"ד כתיב דרכיה דרכי נועם וכו' וכתיב שלום רב לאוהבי תורתך ואין למו מכשול · ובפ' קדושים פ' ע"ב בזבח ובמנחה כו' אבל מתכפר הוא בד"ת אמאי בגין דד"ת סלקין על כל קרבנין דעלמא כמה דאוקמוה דכתיב זאת התורה לעולה למנחה ולחטאת כו' שקיל אורייתא לקביל כל קרבנין דעלמא · א"ל הכי הוא ודאי דכל מאן דאשתדל באורייתא אע"ג דאתגזר עלי' עונשא מלעילא ניחא לי' מכל קרבנין ועלוון והההוא עונשא אתקרע · ות"ח לא אתדכי ב"נ לעלמין אלא במלין דאורייתא כו' · ואורייתא קדושה אתקרי דכתיב כי קדוש אני ה' ודא אורייתא דהיא שמא קדישא עלאה · וע"ד מאן דאשתדל בה אתדכי ולבתר אתקדש כו' · תאנא קדושה דאורייתא קדושה דסליקת על כל קדושין כו' ע"ש · ובמד"הנ ויקרא ק' ע"א אמרו בטלו הקרבנות לא בטלה התורה האי דלא איעסק בקרבנות ליעסק בתורה ויהני לי' יתיר דאר"י כו' א"ל יעסקו בתורה ואני מוחל להם בשבילה יותר מכל הקרבנות שבעולם · שנאמר זאת התורה לעולה למנחה כו' זאת התורה בשביל עולה בשביל מנחה כו' · א"ר כרוספדאי האי מאן דמדכר בפומי' בב"כ ובב"מד עניינא דקרבני' כו' ברית כרותה הוא דאינון מלאכיא דמדכרן חובי' להבאשא לי' דלא יכלין למעבד לי' אלא טיבו · ואמרו עוד בפ"ב דברכות (י"ו א') ובתד"א סא"ר פכ"ה למה נסמכו אהלים לנחלים דכתיב כנחלים נטיו וכו' כאהלים נטע ה' כו' לומר לך מה נחלים מעלין את האדם מטומאה לטהרה אף אהלים מעלים את האדם מכף חובה לכף זכות . ובפ"יח שם שפכי כמים לבך כו' מה מים הללו מקוה טהרה הן לישראל ולכל אשר נברא בעולם כו' כך ד"ת מקוה טהרה הן לישראל בכל מקומות מושבותיהם · בא וראה כמה גדולה כחה של התורה שמטהרת את פושעי ישראל בזמן שעושין תשוב' אפי' מעבוד' כוכבי'

שער ד

תופיע נהרה על האדם העוסק והוגה בה כראוי. כי ראשית דרכה בקדש הוא הגבה למעלה מעלה משורש הקדושה ואור העליון של המצות כולן יחד כנ"ל. וז"ש בפ' התורה ומגדלתו ומרוממתו על כל המעשים היינו על כל מעשי המצות כולן. וכן אמרו בירושלמי פ"א דפאה שכל המצות כולן אינן שוות לדבר א' מן התורה:

וגם כי קדושת ואור המצוה אשר תשכין אורה על אותו הדבר והחפץ אשר בו וע"י תעשה המצוה. אינו שורה עליהם רק לפי שעתו בעת שהמצוה נעשית בהם. אבל אחר שנעשה בהן מצותן הקדושה והאור מתעלה ומסתלק מהם תיכף ונשאר כבראשונה. אבל התוה"ק כל מקום שחוזרת ותופיע אורה וקדושתה פעם א'. קדושת עולם תהיה לו ונשאר תמיד בקדושתו. כמו ששנינו בברייתא (מגילה כ"ו ב') תשמישי מצוה נזרקין לאחר שנעשה מצותן ותשמישי קדושה נגנזין. ולכן מנו שם תשמישי תפילין ומזוזות בכלל תשמישי קדושה. מחמת פרשיות התורה שהיו מונחים בתוכם פעם א'. ואית לך מידי בדבריהם ז"ל דלא רמיזא בקרא. ויש לכוין הכתוב כי נר מצוה ותורה אור גם ע"ז הענין הנזכר ע"פי פירושם ז"ל הנ"ל בסוטה שם מה נר אינו מאיר אלא לפי שעה. ומה אור מאיר לעולם. והם ז"ל עשו ההפרש ביניהם לענין ההגנה וההצלה להאדם. ואפשר לפרשו ג"כ שירמוז הכתוב גם לענין ההפרש וההבדל בין התוה"ק והמצות המבואר בברייתא דמגילה הנ"ל:

ולא עוד אלא שגם אותה הקדושה וחיותן ואורן של המצוה שמקדשים ומחיים להאדם המקיימם. הוא נלקח ונשפע רק מקדושתה ואורה של התוה"ק. כי המצוה לית לה מגרמה שום חיות וקדושה ואור כלל רק מצד קדושת אותיות התורה הכתובות בענין אותה המצוה: ויש לכוין גם זה הענין בכתוב כי נר מצוה ותורה אור. כענין הנר שאין לה בעצמה שום אור כלל רק מהאור המאיר בה. ודאי שגם העסק בתורה לבד בלי קיום המצות כלל ח"ו. ג"כ אין כלום כמרז"ל (יבמות ק"ט) כל האומר אין לו אלא תורה אף תורה אין לו. ובפ"ב דברכות (י"ז א') מרגלא בפומיה דרבא תכלית חכמה תשובה ומע"ט שלא יהא אדם קורא ושונה ובועט באביו וברבו כו' ללומדיהם לא נאמר אלא לעושיהם. ובשמות רבה פ"מ. כל מי שהוא יודע תורה ואינו עושה מוטב לו שלא יצא לעולם אלא נהפכה השליא על פניו. וכ"ה בויקרא רבה פל"ה. ובתנחומא פ' עקב. ובזהר שמות ה' ריש ע"ב דאר"י כל מאן דאשתדל באורייתא בהאי עלמא ומסגל עובדין טבין ירית עלמא שלימא וכל מאן דאשתדל באורייתא בהאי עלמא ולא עבדין עובדין טבין לא ירית לא האי ולא האי כו'. אר"י לא תנן אלא מאן דלית ליה עובדין טבין כלל. עד שאמרו בפ"ק דעבו"ז (י"ז ב') כל העוסק בתורה לבד דומה כמי שאין לו אלוה. כי בלתי קיום המצות ח"ו אין דבר במה להאחז ולהתקשר בו אור התורה לשרות עליו ולהתקיים בו. כדמיון האור בלא פתילה. אמנם עצמות האור מקבלת המצוה מאותיות התורה הכתובות בענינה ח"ש בפ' התורה גדולה תורה שהיא נותנת חיים לעושיה. ולא אמר ללומדיה או לעוסקיה אלא לעושיה ור"ל שהתורה היא הנותנת חיי עד וקדושה גם לעושי המצות הכתובות בתוכה. ולכן אמרו בתנחומא בחקתי שאף אם היה צדיק ואינו עוסק בתורה אין בידו כלום או:

והטעם בזה ג"כ כמש"ל. שהמצות במקור שרשן קשורות ותלויות בסידור פרקי המרכבה העולמות וכחות העליונים. ומקור שרש העליון של התוה"ק היא מאד נעלה מעל כל העולמו' והכחות כולם והיא המתפשטת בפנימיות כולם ומקבלים

עבירה נותנין לו שכר כעושה מצוה · נטהר ונתקדש ג"כ אותו הגיד הפרטי המכוון נגדה ותחיה אותו כמש"ה אלה המצות אשר יעשה אותם האדם וחי בהם שאז הוא נקרא איש חי · אמנם כשהאדם עוסק בתורה כתיב בה ולכל בשרו מרפא · וכמ"ש (עירובין נ"ד א') חש בראשו יעסוק בתורה · שנא' כי לוית חן הם לראשך חש בגרונו עסוק בתורה שנאמר כו' · חש בבני מעיו יעסוק בתורה כו' · חש בכל גופו יעסוק בתורה שנא' ולכל בשרו מרפא · וכ"ה בויקרא רבה פי"ב ובתנחומא יתרו ובמדרש תהלים מזמור י"ט · שע"י עסק התורה מתקדשים ומזדככים כל אבריו וגידיו וכחותיו כולם · ולכן אמרו ות"ת כנגד כולם · וכן להיפוך ח"ו עון ביטול תורה הוא ג"כ כנגד כולם · כי בעברו על אחת ממצות ה' · נפגם רק אותו האבר או הגיד לבד המכוון נגדה · שהחיות של הקדושה ואור העליון סוד שם הוי"ה ית' השורה על כל אבר מסתלקת ממנו ח"ו · ומותא דס"א שריא בי' ר"ל · ונעשה בעל מום חסר מאותו אבר · אבל בעון ביטול תורה ח"ו הוא פוגם את כל אבריו וגידיו וכל כחותיו כולם · וחיות הקדושה של כל גופו מסתלקת והוא נעשה פגר כמת ממש שאין לו שום חיות ח"ו · כמ"ש כי הוא חייך וכו' · וכמאחז"ל (עכו"ם ג' ע"ב) מ"ד ותעשה אדם כדגי הים למה נמשלו ב"א לדגי הים לומר לך מה דגים שבים כיון שפורשין מן המים מיד מתים כך ב"א כיון שפורשין מן התורה מיד מתים (כך היא גרסת הילקו' חבקוק רמז תקס"ב על פסוק הנ"ל) · ובר"מ ס"פ שמיני מה נוני ימא תיותן במיא אוף ה"נ אורייתא מתני תיותייהו באורייתא ואי אתפרשו מנה מיד מתים · ואמרז"ל (ברכות ה' א') אם רואה אדם שיסורים באים עליו · יפשפש במעשיו פשפש ולא מצא יתלה בביטול תורה · ולכאורה יפלא כיון שיש בידו עון ביטול תורה ח"ו הלא אין לך מצא יותר מזה ואיך אמר ולא מצא · אמנם כבר נזהר רש"י ז"ל מזה במה שפירש שם שלא מצא עון שיהיו ראוין היסורין הללו לבא עליו · וזהו כי מדתו ית' שפועל אדם ישלם מדה כנגד מדה · שאותו האבר שקלקל ופגם בחטאו. על אותו האבר עצמו מביא עליו יסורין · ותכלית כוונתו ית' בזה כדי שמתוך היסורין יבין האדם וידע על איזה חטא באו · וישיב אל לבו להיות מודה ועוזב ושב ורפא לו · וז"ש שאם רואה אדם שיסורין באים עליו יפשפש במעשיו ויבין דרכיו מתוך היסורין · ואם פשפש ולא מצא בידו עון אשר חטא באותו אבר ובאותו אופן שיהיו ראוין היסורין הללו דוקא לבא עליו מדה כנגד מדה · יתלה בביטול תורה כי בעון ביטול תורה לא שייך מדה כנגד מדה · כי ביטולה ח"ו היא נוגע לכל נושא איזה מקום ואיזה אבר שיהיה כנ"ל:

וטעמו של דבר · הוא כמש"ל בשער א' פ"ו · שמקור שרשם העליון של המצות תלויות וקשורות בסוד השיעור קומה ופרקי המרכבה סוד האדם העליון כביכול · שכל מצוה פרטית שורשה העליון קשור ואחוז בעולם וכח א' מהשיעור קומה וכן זה כל האדם שהוא ג"כ מתוקן ומסודר בכל אבריו וגידיו ופרטיו וכל פרטי כחותיו בתבנית דמות המרכבה ושיעור קומה · ולזאת כל מצוה מכוונת נגד אבר או גיד א' פרטי שבאדם · אמנם התורה"ק היא כוללת העולמות כולן כנ"ל · לכן היא שקולה נגד כל המצות · ולכן היא ג"כ לכל בשרו מרפא:

פרק ל

ועוד זאת יתירה התורה"ק ביתרון אור ותוספות קדושה גם על כל המצות כולן ביחד · שגם אם קיים האדם כל התרי"ג מצות כולן בשלימות האמיתי כראוי · בכל פרטיהם ודקדוקיהם ובכוונה וטהרה וקדושה · אשר אז נעשה האדם כולו בכל אבריו ופרקיו וכל כחותיו מרכבה גמורה שתשרה עליהם הקדושה עליונה של המצות כולן · עכ"ז אין ערוך ודמיון כלל קדושת ואור המצות לגודל עוצם קדושת ואור התורה"ק אשר

תוסיף

שער ד

אחד שחקר על הענין מפני מה קוראים לחכמת הקבלה בשם נסתר · הלא מי שמבין בהם אלו הם גלוים · ולאנשים שאינם יודעים ומבינים · הלא יש שגם פשוטו של מקרא אינם יודעים לפרש ואללם גם הפשוטו של מקרא דרכו נסתרה מהם · ותירץ מה שתירץ)· ועיין זוהר בהעלותך קמ״ט א׳ וב׳ כמה חביבין מלי דאורייתא דבכל מלה ומלה אית רזין עלאין כו׳ · ע״ש: וכל א׳ מסתכל בסתרי עומק פנימיות׳ כפי רוב חכמתו וזך שכלו וקדושת טהרת לבבו · ורוב עסקו והגיונו בה · אמנם עיקר הטעמי תורה סוד נשמתא לנשמתא דילה סתרי סתריה · המה דברים שכיסה עתיק יומין והעתיקן מבריותיו ואיש לא ידעם עדיין רק אבינו הראשון הוא אשר השיג בחי׳ נשמתא לנשמתא דילי׳ · שכה היה מסתכל בזיהרא עלאה נשמתא לנשמתא של התורה והחכמות העליונות היו גלויות לפניו בשורש שרשם העליון · ומעת אשר חטא ואסתלק מני׳ הזיהרא עלאה ונתבלבלו ונתערבבו הסדרים העליונים · נסתמו גם הנתיבות ושבילין עליונים דחכמתא דאורייתא סוד הנשמתא לנשמתא דילה · וגם במעמד הקדוש בעת קבלת התורה אף דאתבסם עלמא · עד שאמרו ז״ל ישראל שעמדו על הר סיני פסקה זוהמתן · עכ״ז לא זכו להשיג רק עומק פנימיות הנשמתא דאורייתא אבל לא בחי׳ הנשמתא לנשמתא · עד אשר יערה רוח ממרום וישפוך הוא ית׳ את רוחו על כל בשר · אז יתגלו מבועין דחכמתא נתיבות פליאות החכמה העליונה נשמתא לנשמתא דילה . כמ״ש בזוהר בהעלותך קנ״ב א׳ אורייתא אית לה גופא כו׳ טפשין דעלמא לא מסתכלי אלא בההוא לבושא כו׳ · אינון דידעין יתיר לא מסתכלן בלבושא אלא בגופא דאיהו תחות ההוא לבושא · חכימין עבדי דמלכא עלאה אינון דקיימו בטורא דסיני לא מסתכלי אלא בנשמתא דאיהי עקרא דכלא אורייתא ממש · ולעלמא דאתי זמינין לאסתכלא בנשמתא דנשמתא דאורייתא· וכמ״ש והיו עיניך רואות את מוריך ולא יכנף עוד מוריך · והוא ענין האור של יום ראשון שגנזו לצדיקים לע״ל ושארז״ל לע״ל הקב״ה מוציא חמה מנרתיקה כו׳ (נדרים ח׳ ע״ב)· והוא סוד העדן כידוע שהוא הבחי׳ נשמתא דנשמתא · ואדה״ר קודם חטאו היה דר בגן ומתוכו היה מסתכל בעדן הנ״ל · ובחטאו אשר מאז נסתלקה ממנו זאת הבחי׳ העליונה · לכן גורש אז מג״ע · והוא סוד הצרופי אותיות דילה כאשר היא כתובה במרום כמש״ל סוף שער ב׳ · וע״ז אמרו במדרש תהלים ריש מזמור ג׳ לא ידע אנוש ערכה כו׳ לא ניתנו פרשיותיה של תורה על הסדר שאלמלא ניתנו על הסדר כל מי שהוא קורא בהן מיד היה יכול לברא׳ עולם ולהחיות מתים כו׳ : ונשוב לבאר קצת ענין ההפרש ויתרון אור קדושת התורה הקדוש׳ על המצות :

פרק כט

הנה רז״ל אמרו (סוטה כ״א א׳) דרש רמב״י כי נר מצוה ותורה אור· תלה הכתוב את המצוה בנר ואת התורה באור · לומר לך מה נר אינו מאיר אלא לפי שעה אף מצוה אינה מגינה אלא לפי שעה · ומה אור מאיר לעולם אף תורה מגינה לעולם · ומסיק דתורה בעידנא דעסיק בה מגינה ומצלא בעידנא דלא עסיק בה אגוני מגני אצולי לא מצלה · מצוה בין בעידנא דעסיק בה בין בעידנא דלא עסיק בה אגוני מגני אצולי לא מצלה · וכן אמרו שם עבירה מכבה מצוה ואין עבירה מכבה תורה · גם ידוע בזוהר שהתרי״ג מצות הם מכוונים נגד התרי״ג איברים וגידים שבאדם · ובעשות האדם אחת ממצות ה׳ כראוי מתקדש על ידה אותו האבר המכוון נגדה ומחיה אותו · או אם בא ויזדמן לידו אחת ממצות ה׳ אשר לא תעשינה ונמנע ופירש ולא עשאה · אשר עליו ארז״ל (בירושלמי פ״ק דקדושין) ישב אדם ולא עבר

עבירה

ההרהור בד"ת אסור במקומות המטונפים · ולזאת החמירו והפליגו רז"ל בעונשו ואמרו (בפ' חלק צ"ט א') שנס הוא בכלל כי דבר ה' בזה · ושיפי' דהאי קרא הכרת תכרת ופי' רז"ל הכרת בעה"ז תכרת לעה"ב · ואמרו האומו ש"ת ערום נקבר ערום מאותה מצוה · גם אסרו לטלטלה ממקום למקום · ואף מבי כנישתא לבי כנישתא אסרו בזוהר פ' אחרי ע"ג ב' לטלטלה ע"ש · מטעם שהיא לעולם בקדושתה הראשונה עומדת · (וכן אפי' האדם שטורש כשמתו היא מעולם עליון וגבוה מאד · מהעולמות העליונים · ויקח לו בשכלו מחשבה נכונה להתדבק לטהרת איזה מדה נכונה · הוא רשאי לילך בזאת המחשבה גם במקומות המטונפים · ואלו ההרהור ד"ת בדיני טעמים ואהלות · או שארי דינים ואיזה ד"ת שתהיה אסור במקומות המטונפים) :

והוא ג"כ ענין מאמרם ז"ל בזוהר דקב"ה ואורייתא חד · והוא שאע"פי שהעולמות הולכי' כולם דרך הדרגה והשתלשלות ושינויים רבים בערך קדושתם · כ"ז הוא רק מצדינו · אבל מצדו ית' אין שום חילוק ושינוי מקומות כלל ח"ו · וכמ"ש אני ה' לא שניתי ולא נשתנה הקדושה · כמ"ש באורך למעלה בשער ג' ע"ש · כן התוה"ק אף כי ירדה ונשתלשלה דרך הדרגות רבות עצומות · עכ"ז היא לא נשתנתה מקדושת' כלל · ובקדושתה הראשונ' עומדת גם בזה העולם התחתון · כאשר היתה באמנ' אצו ית' במקור שרשה · בלא שום חילוק ושינוי מקום כלל · אמנם אע"פי שמצדו ית' כל המקומות שוים בלי שום שינוי כלל · שאין מקומות המטונפים מוללים לאחדותו ועולם קדושתו יתב' · וכן הוא בענין טולם קדושת התו"הק . עכ"ז אנחנו נאסרנו לדבר גם להרהר בה במבואות המטונפות · כי מצדינו ודאי יש חילוק ושינוי מקומות כמו שנתבאר שם באורך · אבל התו"הק בעצמותה לא נשתנתה

בסבת ירידתה מקדושתה ואורה העליון · רק שסח עינינו מראות בעילם קדושתה ואורה הפנימי ולכן אמר דוד המע"ה גל עיני ואביטה נפלאות מתורתך · כי באמת קדושת ואור התו"הק סם פנימיות סתריה המה מפורשים ונגלים ומאירים בקדושת אורם העליון כאשר הוא · רק שעינינו אין יכולות לסבול עוצם קדושתה ואורה כאשר הוא :

פרק כח

ולזאת אף היא דרך ירידתה והשתלשלותה ממדרג' למדרגה ומעולם לעולם · למלאה עצמה להתלבש בכל עולם לדבר מעניני אותו העולם · כפי ענין וערך אותו העול' כדי שיוכל לסבול קדושתה ואורה · עד שבררדתה לבא לזה העולם · נתלבשה ג"כ לדבר בערכי ועניני זה העולם וספורין דהאי עלמא כדי שיוכל זה העולם לסבול קדושת אורה · אמנם אם שהיא מדברת בתחתונים · רומזת היא בהם גופי תורה ועניניס פנימים ופנימים לפנימים · גבוה מעל גבוה עד אין תכלית · ועיין בזוהר בהעלתך קנ"ב א' רש"א כו' · ובפ' תולדות קמ"ה ב' אר"י ירחי כל מה דעביד קב"ה בארעא כלא הוה ברזא דחכמתא כו' · ובפ' בלק ר"ב א' תו פתח ואמר כו' כמה עדין איטון ארחין ושבילין דאורייתא כו · ובפ' בשלח נ"ה סוף ע"ב ר"א פתח כו' כמה אית לן לאסתכלא בפתגמי אורייתא כו' · ובפ' תולדות קל"ד סוף ע"ב באורייתא אינון כל רזין עלאין חתימין כו' · והם פרטות עניני כל הרבי רבואות העולמו' והמדרגו' שנתלבשה בהם דרך ירידתה : ולכן שגורה בפי הזוהר דאורייתא' כולה איהי סתים וגליא שהוא מבואר לכל מבין בפי' הוא שהוא הדרך הנסת' מהתורה הק' · שאינו כתוב מפורש ומבואר בה · אלא שנסתר ונטמן הענינים אלו ברמז בדבריה · ודרך הנגלה שבה הוא הפשוטו של מקרא שהוא כתוב מפורש ומבואר בה · (ולא כמו שראיתי בספר כתוב

מאחד

שער ד

של התוה"ק אחד נעלה מעל כל העולמות. ראשית זכרם אצילות קדשו יתברך. סוד המלבוש העליון כמ"ש רבינו איש האלקים נורא האריז"ל. רק שנשתלשלה וירדה כביכול עד לארץ אשר אורה מכבודה. ומסרה ונטעה הוא ית' בתוככו שנהיה אנחנו המחזיקים ותומכים בעץ החיים. לזאת מאז כל חיותם וקיומם של העולמות כולם. תלוי ועומד רק כפי ענין ורוב עסקנו והגיונינו בה. שאם אנחנו עוסקים בה ומחזיקים ותומכים אותה כראוי בלי רפיון כלל. אנו מעוררים מקור שרשה העליון מקור הקדושות והברכות. להמשיך ולהריק תוספת ברכה וחיי עולם וקדושה נוראה על כל העולמות. כל עולם לפי ערך קדושתו שיוכל לקבל ולסבול. ואם ח"ו עסקנו בה ברפיון. מתקמט ומתמעט הקדושה ואור העליון של התורה מכל העולמות. כל אחד לפי ערכו הולך וחסר רותתים ורפויים ח"ו. ואם ח"ו היינו כולנו מניחים ומזניחים אותה מלהתעסק בה מכל וכל. גם העולמות כולם כרגע היו מתבטלים מכל וכל ח"ו. משא"כ בכל המצות ואפילו מצות התפלה. שגם אם היו ח"ו כל ישראל מניחים ועוזבים מלהתפלל לו ית'. לא היו חוזרים העולמות עבור זה לתהו ובהו. ולכן התפלה נקראת בדברי רז"ל חיי שעה. והתורה נק' חיי עולם כמאמרם ז"ל בפ"ק דשבת (י' ע"א) רבא חזי' לר"ה דקא מאריך בצלותא אמר מניחין חיי עולם ועוסקין בחיי שעה. שענין התפלה הוא הוספת תיקון בהעולמות בתוספות קדושה וברכה באותו עת הקבוע להם. ולכן אם עברה השעה שוב לא תועיל כלל להוסיף את בהעולמות התוספת קדושה וברכה. אמנם ענין העסק בתוה"ק הוא נוגע לעצם החיות וקיום עמידת העולמות בל יהרסו לגמרי. לכן האדם חייב לעסוק ולהגות בה בכל עת תמיד. כדי להעמיד ולקיים כל העולמות כל רגע: ולא עוד

אלא שגם כל עיקר ענין התפלה אינה תלויה רק בעסק התוה"ק ובלאו אינה נשמעת ח"ו. כמש"ה (משלי כ"ח) מסיר אזנו משמוע תורה גם תפלתו תועבה. וכמשרז"ל בשבת שם ובמשלי רבתא פכ"ח. ואמרו (בסוף סוטה) כל העוסק בתורה מתוך דוחק תפלתו נשמעת ואין הפרגוד ננעל בפניו. ובזוהר מקץ ר"ב ב' ועץ חיים אהוא באה הכינן מאן דבעי דקב"ה יקבל צלותיה ישתדל באורייתא דאיהי עץ חיים כו'. לכן הדין פסוק בש"ס (מגילה כ"ז א') ביהכ"נ מותר לעשותו בה"מ. משום דעלויי קא מעלי ליה לקדושה יותר חמורה. שרק היא הנותנת השפע חיות וקדושה ואור לכל העולמות מטעם שהיא למעלה מכולם:

פרק כז ועוד זאת יתירה ערך ויתרון קדושתה הגדול' מהעולמו'.

כי העליונים אף שקדושתם רבה מאד. אמנם כאשר השתלשלו וירדו דרך השתלשלות והדרגות עצומות. שגם שבכל עולם נצטייר ונאחז כל סדרי העולם שמעליו בדמותו כצלמו ממש כידוע. וכמ"ש בזוהר יתרו פ"ב ב' תאנא כגוונא דלעילא אית לתתא מנייהו וכן בכלהו עלמין כלהו אחידן דא בדא ודא בדא. וכמ"ש בע"ח בענין הד' עולמות אבי"ע ע"ש בשער דרושי אבי"ע פ"א ובפ"ד שם ובשער השמות רפ"א. עכ"ז אינו שוה ודומה כלל ערך קדושתו ואורו להעולם שמעליו. עד שכ"כ נתעבו ונתמעטו מקדושתם ואורם דרך השתלשלות והדרגות עצומות עד שבזה העולם נעשו חולין שאנו נוהגין בהן מנהג חול. אמנם התורה הקדושה אף שגם היא נשתלשלה וירדה ממקור שורשה העליון בקדש מדרגות אין שיעור מעולם לעולם וממדרגה למדרגה. עכ"ז קדושתה הראשונה כמו שהוא במקור שרשה ראשית דרכה בקדש כדקאי קאי גם בזה העולם. שכולה קודש ואסור לנהוג בה מנהג חול ח"ו. שגם

ההדיוט

שער ד

להנות ת"ח מנכסיה' · כמ"ש א"ל רבי מלאתי להם תרופ' מן התור' ואתם הדבקי' בה' אלקיכ' חיים כלכ' היום · וכי אפשר לדביקי בשכינה כו' · אלא כל המשיא בתו לת"ח והעושה פרקמטי' לת"ח והמהנה ת"ח מנכסיו· מעלה עליו הכתו' כאלו מדבק בשכינה ובחד"א סא"ר פ"ה הקיצו ורננו שוכני עפר מכאן אמר דוד המע"ה יהא חלקי עם אלו שהם ממיתין את עצמן על ד"ת כו' · הקיצו ורננו שוכני עפר מכאן אמרו כל הנעשה שכן לעפר בחייו עפרו ננער לתחיית המתים וכל שאין נעשה שכן לעפר בחייו אין עפרו ננער לתה"מ כו' · אלו בני אדם שמשכימים עצמם על העפר ללמוד תורה הקב"ה מביא עליהם טל אורות של תורה כו' · ומביאן לחיי עה"ב שנא' כי טל אורות טלך · ולזאת קראו ז"ל המקרא מעוות לא יוכל לתקן על ת"ח הפורש מן התור' (משנה חגיג' פ' א') · שח"ו אין לו תקנה עולמית · הרחמן ית"ש יצילנו מזה וכל כיוצא בו :

פרק כה וכ"ז

כשעדיין יש אנשים מישראל שדבקים בו ית' ובתורתו בעיון ושקידה ויגיעה גדולה לשמה · ורק בתורת ה' חפצם כל הימים · ואז האנשים שבטלים לגמרי מעסק התורה מרוע בחירתם · המה ירדו שאול חיים ומגורשים מהסתפח בנחלת עבדי ה' הדבוקים בו ית' ובתורתו · ומארץ חיים יכרתו ח"ו · ועכ"פ העולם גם כל העולמות · הגם כי נתמעטו וירדו מקדושתם ואורם · בסבת החטאים האלה בנפשותם · וכמעט שנטיו רגלם ליחרב ח"ו כמ"ש בתד"א סא"ר פ"ב אמרו חכמים כיון שבני אדם מבטלין מן התורה מבקש הקב"ה להחריב את העולם כו' · וכם בסא"ז פ"ט כי לה' מצוקי ארץ וישת עליהם תבל ואין מציקין אלא ת"ח כו' · בכל יום יוצאים מלאכי חבלה מלפני הקב"ה לחבל את כל העולם כולו ואלמלא ב"כ וב"מד שת"ח יושבין בהם ועוסקים בד"ת היו מחבלין את כל העולם כולו מיד כו' ע"ש · עכ"ז עדיין יוכלו להתקיים ע"י השרידים אשר ה' קורא · העוסקים בתוה"ק יומם ולילה · שלא יתבטלו לגמרי לחזור לתהו ובהו ח"ו · אבל אם היה ח"ו העולם פנוי לגמרי אפילו רגע אחת ממש מעסק והתבוננות עם סגולה' בתו"הק · תיכף כרגע היו כל העולמות נחרבים ונבטלים ממציאות לגמרי ח"ו · ואף גם איש א' מישראל לבד · רב כחו · שבידו להעמיד ולקיים את כל העולמות והבריאה בכללה ע"י עסקו והתבוננותו בתו"הק לשמה · כמ"ש בחלק (צ"ט ב') כל העוסק בתורה לשמה כו' · רי"א אף מגין על כל העולם כולו · וכ"א בפ' התורה כל העוסק בתורה לשמה כו' · ולא עוד אלא שכל העולם כולו כדאי הוא לו · ואיך לא יתלהב לב האדם בהעלותו על לבו ומתבונן בזה הענין הנורא · ותפול עליו אימתה ופחד לבל יתרפה ח"ו מעסק התו"הק תמיד · כאשר יחשוב בלבבו אולי ח"ו לעת כזאת העולם כולו מקלה ועד קצהו פנוי לגמרי מעסק התו"הק · ובלתי עסקו והגיון לבו עתה בזה העת בתורה · היו נחרבים כל העולמות וכרגע ספו תמו ח"ו · זו תורה וזו שכרה מרובה מאד אין להעריך · שהוא הנוטל שכר כולם · אחר שהוא אשר קיים והעמיד ברב כחו את כל העולמות עתה · ועל כגון זה אחז"ל במשנה (סנהדרין ל"ז א') שכל א' מישראל חייב לומר בשבילי נברא העולם · ואף שבעלה עונות יש אלפי רבואות עולמות קדושים עליונים שאין שום חטא ועון התחתונים מגיע עדיהם כלל לפוגמם ח"ו · ותמיד עז וחדוה במקום כבודם ועליה' נאמר לא יגורך רע · אמנם עון ביטול תורה היא העולה על כולם שהוא נוגע לקיום כל העולמות :

פרק כו וטעמו

של דבר · כמשל שמקור שורשה העליון העולם של

אוי לנו מעלבונה של תורה · וכמה צריך האדם להתבונן ע"ז תמיד ולשית דעתו וכליותיו ישתונן · בל ילך חשך ח"ו כל ימי הבלו מספר ימיו אשר נקצבו לו ברחמיו וחסדיו ית"ש באות נפשו משולח חפשי מן התורה · כי בנפשו הוא · כי יגיע עת פקודתו וישוב העפר על הארץ והרוח לא תשוב אל האלקים להצרר בצרור החיים העליונים · כי תקולל חלקתו להתקלע ולא תרגיע כי נדחה קראו לה · נזיף לעילא נזיף לתתא · אוי לה לאותה בושה כו' · הרחמן ית"ש יצילנו :

פרק כד וכ"ב

הפליגו רז"ל בחומר עונשו של האדם שאפש' לו לעסו' בתורה ואינו עוסק · או שנה ופירש ח"ו · עד שכרתוהו ברוח קדשם מעה"ב לגמרי ר"ל · כמ"ש בפ' חלק (צ"ט א') כי דבר ה' בזה כו' · ר' נתן אומר כל שאינו משגיח על המשנה · ר' נהוראי אמר כל שאפשר לו לעסוק בתורה ואינו עוסק · וסיפי' דהאי קרא הכרת תכרת הנפש ההיא ופירשו ז"ל שם לעיל מינה הכרת בעה"ז תכרת לעה"ב · השמיענו הכתוב חומר זה הכרת שאינו כשאר הכריתות האמורות בתורה על שאר עונות · אשר אף אם דינו חרון שהוא נכרת ח"ו · עכ"ז לא איבד חלקו בחיי עולם הבא · שרק אותו הניצוץ הקטן של הנפש שעשה בו את העון הוא הנכרת מקישור ודיבוק החלק הנשרש שהיה מקושר ודבוק עד עתה עד שורש נשמתו בקב"ה כמש"ל בשער א' באורך · אמנם כאן אמר הכרת תכרת היינו שכל חלק בחי' נפשו איבדה חלקה בחיי עולם לגמרי ח"ו ואין לה חלק לעה"ב כלל · וכן פסק הרמב"ם ז"ל להלכה בהלכות ת"ת פ"ג הלכה י"ג · וקבע כן הב"י בש"ע שם סי' רמ"ו סעיף כ"ה להלכה · וכן ה"ר יונה ז"ל בספר התשובה מנה עשר מדרגות בחומר עונשי העונות · והמדרגה האחרונה מונה אותם הכת שארז"ל עליהם שאין להם חלק לעה"ב ומנה שם בכלל זה גם מי שאפשר לו לעסוק בתורה ואינו עוסק · וכן הר"או ז"ל בשערי קדושה ש"א ח"ב מנה אותו ג"כ בכלל אותם שאין להם חלק לעה"ב · ובאחדא מחתא מחתינהו שם שדינו שוה עם אותן שאמרו ז"ל עליהם בפ"ק דר"ה (י"ג א') שגיהנם כלה והם אינם כלים ר"ל · וכתב הרמב"ם ז"ל והב"י ז"ל שם שמי שקרא ושנה ופירש להבלי עולם והניח תלמודו וזנחו ג"כ דינו אחד עם מי שאפשר לו לעסוק בתור' ואינו עוסק · וכן בדין · מעשיו אשר לא טובים המה ירחקוהו · וחטאתו מנעו הטוב מאתו · אחר שהיה אפשר לו וסיפק בידו לעסוק בתורה · ובזדון לב ושאט נפש בחר ולקח מקח רע לעצמו ולאחרים והעולמות כולם · ומאס בחיי עולם של התוה"ק חיותא ונהירו דכל עלמין אשר על ידה היה מתדבק כביכול בקב"ה ית"ש המחיה את כולם · ושלח ידו להרוס פלטין של מלך והמעיט והחשיך וכבה שפעת אורם של העולמות · וגם של נפשו · למה לו חיים אמיתים · כי הלא החשכה עיניו מראות והבט באור החיים הנצחים ולא יוכל לסבול גודל עולם האור עליון · כי לא נשה בזה מעודו בזה העולם · והוא מגורש ונכרת מאליו מעדן גן אלקים ית"ש מלהצרר בצרור החיים את ה' אלקיו ית"ש · ומרעה אל רעה הוא יוצא ח"ו · אוי לאותה בושה כו' :

וכן פסקו וחתכו ז"ל דינו שגזרה אבדה תקותו לדור דורים ח"ו · שגם עד נצח לא יראה אור · בל יחי עוד לנצח בעת קץ הימין · אשר ישני אדמת עפר יקיצו לחיי עולם · כמאמרם ז"ל בסוף כתובות כי טל אורות טלך כו' · כל המשתמש באור תורה אור תורה מחייהו וכל שאין משתמש באור תורה אין אור תורה מחייהו · ולא מצאו שם רז"ל תקנה לע"ה שיקומו לעת התחי' · אלא בהחזיקם ותומכים עכ"פ בעץ החיים תמכי דאורייי'

לכנית

שער ד

אוכלתו כו׳ · ובמשלי רבתי פ״י ועוזב תוכחת מתעה אר״א כל ת״ח שהוא עוזב ד״ת כאלו מתעתע במי שאמר והיה העולם ולא עוד אלא כיון שעוזב ד״ת בעה״ז הקב״ה עוזבו לעה״ב כו׳ · ובזוהר ויקרא כ״ה ב׳ אר״ש זכאין אינון מארי דנשמתא מארי דאורייתא בני פולחנא דמלכא קדישא · ווי לאינון חייבין דלא זכאן לאתדבקא במאריהון ולא זכאן באורייתא · דכל מאן דלא זכי באורייתא לא זכי לא ברוח ולא בנשמה · ואתדבקותא דלהון בההוא סטרא דזינין בישין · והאי ליה לי׳ חולקא דקדושה · ווי לי׳ כד יפיק מהאי עלמא דהא אשתמודע הוא לגבי אינון זינין בישין מארי חציפותא תקיפי ככלבי שלוחי דנורא דגיהנם דלא מרחמא עלייהו כו׳ · ובפ׳ וישב קפ״ה א׳ אתר שהאריך שם בגודל שבחו ומדרגתו של העוסק בתורה בעה״ז ועה״ב · אמר אח״ז ת״ש ההוא ב״נ דלא זכי לאשתדלא בהאי עלמא באורייתא ואיהו אזיל בחשוכא · כד נפק מהאי עלמא נטלין לי׳ ואעלין לי׳ לגיהנם אתר תתאה דלא יהא מרחם עלי׳ דאקרי בור שאון טיט היון כד״א ויעלני מבור שאון מטיט היון כו׳ · ובג״כ ההוא דלא אשתדל באורייתא בהאי עלמא ואתטנף בטנופי עלמא מה כתיב ויקחהו וישלכו אתו הבורה · דא הוא גיהנם אתר דדיינין להו לאינון דלא אשתדלו באורייתא · והבור ריק כמה דאיהו הוה ריק מ״ט בגין דלא הוה בי׳ מים · ות״ח כמה הוא עונשא דאורייתא דהא לא אתגלו ישראל מארעא קדישא אלא בגין דאסתלקו מאורייתא ואשתבקו מינה הה״ד מי האיש החכם ויבן כו׳ על מה אבדה הארץ ויאמר ה׳ על עזבם את תורתי כו׳ · ולא עוד אלא שתחילת דינו של אדם בבאו למשפט לפניו ית׳ הוא על ד״ת · כמ״ש בספ״ק דקדושין ובפ״ק דסנהדרין (ז׳ א׳) א״ר המנונ׳ אין תחלת דינו של אדם אלא על ד״ת שנאמר פוטר מים ראשית מדון כו׳ :

ואמרו בכל יום ויום בת קול יוצאת מהר חורב ומכרזת כו׳ שכל מי שאינו עוסק בתור׳ נקרא נזוף כו׳ · כי כן משפטו מפרי מעלליו ישביעהו · כיון שלא רצה לבחור בחיים ובטוב האמיתי לו ולכל הבריות והעולמות כולם ולהתדבק עצמו בו ית׳ · והמעיט שפעת אור של העולמות וקלקל ובלבל סדרי המרכבה הקדושה · והחשיכם · וגרם רעה לעצמו בפשט בגדי הקדש ולבש תחתם בגדים צואים ומטונפים הנעשים מעסקי תאות זה העולם ותענוגו׳ עניניו והוא מטומא ומטונף מהם · ודאי שלא יניחוהו ולא יוכל ליכנס · וכל החיילין קדישין השומרים אותו נתרחקים מאתו בלא יוכלו יגעו בלבושיו המטונפים · ואזיל ומשוטט בעולם וטמא טמא יקרא שמתדבק במינו בחיילין טמאים של כחות הטומאה אשר הגבירם על עצמו · כמ״ש בזוהר ר״פ מצורע ר״א פתח כו׳ כמה אית לון לב״נ לאסתמרא ארחייהו ולדחלא מקמי קב״ה דלא יסטי מארחא דכשרא ולא יעבור על פתגמי אורייתא ולא יתנשי מינה · דכל מאן דלא לעי באורייתא ולא ישתדל בה נזיפא איהו מקב״ה רחיקא הוא מניה · לא שרי׳ שכינתא עמי׳ · ואינון נטורין דאזלין עמי׳ אסתלקו מניה · ולא עוד אלא דמכרזי קמיה ואמרי אסתלקו מסוחרניה דפלניא דלא חש על יקרא דמארי׳ ווי לי׳ דהא שבקוהו עלאין ותתאין · לית לי׳ חולקא בארחא דחיי · וכד איהו אשתדל כו׳ · ולעי באורייי׳ כמה נטורין זמינין לקבלי׳ לנטרא לי׳ ושכינת׳ שרי׳ עלי׳ · וכולהו מכרזי קמיה ואמרי הבו יקרא לדיוקנא דמלכא · הבו יקרא לברי׳ דמלכא אתנטיר הוא בעלמא דין ובעלמא דאתי זכאה חולקי׳ · ואמרו במשנה פ״ק דחגיגה (ט׳ א׳) מעוות לא יוכל לתקן רשב״י אומר אין קורין מעוות אלא למי שהיה מתוקן בתחלה ונתעוות ואי זה זה ת״ח הפורש מן התורה · ואוי להם לבריות שרואות ואינן יודעות מה רואות

כו · ואל תגבהו אל תגביהו את הטובה מלבא לעולם . וכן אמרו בפ״ק דבתרא (ח׳ ע״א) שאין פורענות באה לעולם אלא בשביל עמי הארץ · ואם ח״ו יבא פורענות על איזה אדם או מדינה אפילו בקצה העולם דין גרמא דילי׳ ח״ו · הרחמן ית״ש יצילנו ·

ואם כבר עסק בה ופירש הימנה ח״ו · הוא מהים ח״ו כח פמליא של מעלה ומהקלקלים ומתבלבלים סדרי העולמות והמרכבה הקדוש׳ וגברה יד הס״א ר״ל · וכביכול מחלים ומחשיך כח הקדושה העליונה שכינת עוזנו אמונת ישראל השוכנת בתוכנו תמיד על ידי עסק התורה כראוי · כמ״ש בזוהר תרומה קנ״ה ב׳ פתח ר״ח ואמר עת לעשות לה׳ הפרו תורתך בכל זמנא דאורייתא מתקיימ׳ בעלמא וב״נ משתדלין בה· כביכול קב״ה חדי בעובדי ידוי וחדי בעלמין כולהו ושמיא וארעא קיימי בקיומייא כו׳ · ובשעתא דישראל מתבטלין מאוריי׳ כביכול תשש חיליה וכדין עת לעשות לה׳ איכון בני עלמא לדיקיא דאשתארון אית לון לתגרא חרצין ולמעבד עובדין דכשרן בגין דקב״ה יתתקף בהו בצדיקייא כו׳ · מ״ט בגין דהפרו תורתך ולא משתדלי בה בני עלמא כדקא יאות כו׳ . והכי בזמנא דישראל משתדלו באורייתא ההוא עת מהימנותא מתתקנא בתקונהא ומתקשטא בשלימותא כדקא יאות · ובזמנא דישראל מתבטלי מאורייתא ההוא עת לאו איהו בתקונהא ולא אשתכחת בשלימו ולא בנהורא · הה״ד עת לעשות לה׳ מאי לעשות כו׳ · אוף הכי עת לעשות אשתאר בלא תקונא ובלא שלימו · מ״ט משום דהפרו תורתך בגין דאתבטלו ישראל לתתא מפתגמי אורייתא · בגין דההוא עת הכי קיימא או סלקא או נחתא בגיניהון דישראל · וכביכול הוא מתרחק ממט יהב׳ כמ״ש בזוהר ויקרא ה״א א׳ כד בר נש אתרחיק מאורייתא רחיק הוא מקב״ה · כי קוב״ה ואורייתא חד כנ״ל · והשמירה העליונה של הקדושה סר מעליו ואשתמודע וניכר לכחות הדין אשר הגביר בעצמו שיוכלו לשלוט עליו בין בחייו כמשרז״ל בפ״ק דברכות המובא לעיל · וכ״א שם (ס״ג א׳) ובמשלי רבתא ר״פ כ״ד א״ר טוביה א״ש כל המרפה עצמו מד״ת אינו יכול לעמוד ביום צרה שנאמר התרפית ביום צרה צר כחכה · ובפ׳ שתי הלחם (צ״ע ב׳) כל המשמר את התורה נשמתו משתמרת וכל שאינו משמר את התורה כו׳ · ואמרו במדרש תהלים מזמור כ״ז אמר הקב״ה לישראל אם שמרת את התורה אני אשמור אותך שנאמר אם שמור תשמרון כו׳ · וכידוע ג״כ מאמרם ז״ל בב״ר פס״ה בזמן שהקול קול יעקב בב״כ ובב״מד אין ידי עשו שולטות הקל קול יעקב או ידיו שולטות ר״ל · ואמרו בויקרא רבה פל״ה ודברים רבה רפ״ד הסייף והספר ניתנו מכורכין כו׳ אמר הקב״ה אם שמרתם מה שכתוב בספר הזה ניצולים מן הסייף ואם לאו כו׳ · ואמרו שם עוד מצינו שויתר הקב״ה על עכומ״ז וג״ע וש״ד ולא ויתר על מאסה של תורה שנאמר על מה אבדה הארץ על עבודת כוכבים וג״ע וש״ד אין כתיב כאן אלא ויאמר ה׳ על עזבם את תורתי · ובתד״א שם בא וראה כמה גדול כח פשעה של תורה שלא חרבה ירושלים ולא חרב בית המקדש אלא בפשעה של תורה שנאמר כו׳ · ובתנחומא בשלח כשם שא״א כו׳ כך א״א לישראל לחיות אלא א״כ מתעסקין בד״ת ולפי שפירשו ישראל מד״ת לפיכך השונא בא עליהם כו׳ · וכן את מילא שאין השונא בא אלא ע״י רפיון ידים מן התורה כו׳ ע״ש :

פרק כג ובן

אחר פטירתו מזה העולם · אמרו (כ״ב ע״ש א׳) כל המרפה עצמו מד״ת נוכל בגיהנם כו׳ · ואמרו בס עוד כל הפורש עצמו מד״ת ועוסק בדברי שיחה אש אוכלתו

שער ד

והודביו כלאת השמש בגבורתו משא"כ במ"כש. מה יפה כחו של בע"הב שהוא מיפה כתר עבדיו כמו כתרו. וא"ת מי שקרא הרבה ושנה הרבה יתי שקרא ושנה קימעא יהיה מאור פניהם שוין כאחד במאור פנים לע"הב. אינו כן. ברוך המקום ברוך הוא שאין לפניו משא פנים כו' נאמר במקו' אחר יתר מרעהו צדיק כו'. אלא כל א' וא' לפי דרכו כו'. והוא הוא סוד האור. שנברא ביום ראשון שגנזו הקב"ה לצדיקים. וכ"א בזוהר בראשית מ"ז א' ר"א פתח מה רב טובך אשר צפנת כו'. ת"ח קוב"ה ברא נה"ג בעלמא ואתקין ליה למהוי שלים בפולחנא ולאתתקנא ארחוי בגין דיזכי לנהורא עלאה דגניז קוב"ה לצדיקייא כד"א עין לא ראתה כו'. יעשה למחכה לו ובמה זכה בר נש להוא נהורא באורייתא כו'. ואחז"ל (חגיגה י"ד א') אשר קמטו ולא עת נהר יוצק יסודם אלו ת"ח שמקמטין שינה מעיניהם בעו"הז הקב"ה מגלה להם סוד לע"הב שנאמר נהר יוצק יסודם: והם הטעמי תורה הגנוזים שהם האור העליון הגנוז:

ולכן אמר בפ' התורה כל העוסק בתורה לשמה זוכה לדברים הרבה. סתם ולא פירש מה הם אותן הדברים. וא"א לומר שהם הדברים שפרש שם אח"ז. שהרי אמר אח"ז ולא עוד כו'. משמע שהוא מלתא באפי נפשא. אמנם רמז להעדון ותענוג הנפש באור הגנוז. אשר גם כל מלאכי מעלה וחיות ושרפי קודש ושום נביא וחוזה לא השיגוהו כלל עלם עניו. וכמאמרם ז"ל (ס"פ אין עומדין) כל הנביאים כולן לא נתנבאו אלא כו'. אבל ת"ח פלמן עין לא ראתה כו'. והוא העדן והיין המשומר בענביו שאמרו שם מאי עין לא ראתה וכו'. והכל א'. סוד הטעמי תורה הגנוזים שלא נתגלו עדיין. לכן אמר סתם לדברים הרבה שאינו דבר המושג לאומרו ולבארו. ובא"דא סא"ר פכ"ו אמר אשרי אדם שיש בו ד"ת והוא יושב וקורא ושונה במקום צנוע וסתר אצל מי מלינין אותו הוי אומר אצל הקב"ה שנאמר יושב בסתר עליון בצל שדי יתלונן. כשם שהם מטימין עצמן יחידים בעו"הז ואין עמהם זר כמו כן הם בע"הב הם יושבין אצל הקב"ה לבדו כו':

פרק כב

ואם חס ושלום אנחנו עוסקים בה נרפין כביכול מתמעט שפע האור עליון בכל העולמות כל אחד לפי ערכו. ובמספיקים תכלה נפשו יתברך כביכול. כמרז"ל (חגיגה ה' ב') ג' הקב"ה בוכה עליהם ואחד מהן על מי שאפשר לו לעסוק בתורה ואינו עוסק. וכן אמרו שם ג' דמעות הללו למה כו' וא"ד אחת על ביטול תורה. ואוי לו לבן המוריד דמעות אביו בכל יום. וענין זאת הבכיה הוא התגברות הדין בהתמעטות האור עליון שהם הרחמים הגדולים בעולמות הנסתרים. והאדם אשר עדן לא ראה אור התורה מימיו ולא עסק בה מעולם אינו זוכה כלל שתשרה עליו קדושה העליונה. ואינו זוכה לנפש טהורה. כמ"ש בהקדמת הזוהר י"ב ב' פקודא תמינאה כו' בהאי קרא אית ביה תלת פקודין חד למלעי באורייתא כו' דכד ב"נ לא אתעסק באורייתא לית ליה נפשא קדישא. קדושה דלעילא לא שריא עלוי כו'. וגם הוא משולח ונעזב חו לכחות הדין של הס"א שיהיו יכולין לשלוט עליו. כמארז"ל בפ"ק דברכות (ה' א') שכל מי שאפשר לו לעסוק בתורה ואינו עוסק הקב"ה מביא עליו יסורין מכוערין ועוכרין אותו שנאמר החשיתי מטוב וכאבי נעכר. ומאבד טובה הרבה ממנו ומגל העולם כי הכריע חיו את עצמו ואת כל העולם לכף חוב. כמאמרם ז"ל בדברי קבלה רפ"ד שמעו ואל תגבהו שמעו לדיה כו'

שער ד

לי שבילי דרקיעא ס') וכי שמואל עלה לרקיע אלא ע"י שיגע בחכמתה של תורה למד מתוכה מה שיש בשחקים. ובמשלי רבתא פי"ח ומפתח שפתי מישרים דברים שהם פותחין לכם חדרי חדרים שבמרום. ובתדב"א סא"ר פכ"ז ברוך המקום שבחר בדברי חכמים ובתלמידיהם כו' כשם שהם יושבים בבה"כנ ובבהמ"ד ובכל מקום שפנוי להם וקורין ושונין לשם שמים ויראה בלבבם ומחזיקין ד"ת על פיהם כמו כן הקב"ה יושב כנגד' ומגלה להם סודות התור' בפיהם ובלבבם כו'. ורוח קדשו יתב' ישכון לבטח עליו תמיד כמ"ש בזהר שמות ו' ב' חכימי עדיפי מנביאי בכלא דהא לנביאי לזמנין שראת עליהון רוח קודש' ולזמנין לא וחכימין לא אעדי מנהון רוח קודשא אפי' רגעא חדא זמי' דידעין מה די לעיל' ותתא ולא בעו לגלא'. ובתד"א סא"ז פ"א וכיון שקרא אדם תורה נביאים וכתובים ושנה משנה מדרש הלכות והגדות ושנה הגמרא ושנה הפלפול לשמה מיד רוח הקודש שורה עליו שנאמר רוח ה' דבר בי כו'. ודרך כלל אמרו בפ' התורה שכל העוסק בת"ת ה"ז מתעלה כו'. וכ"א (בס"פ הראה) אם נבלת בהתנשא כל המנבל עצמו על ד"ת מתנשא. עד שאמרו ז"ל שמדרגתם למעלה ממדרגת הנביאים. כמ"ש חכם עדיף מנביא וכמ"ש בזהר שמות הנ"ל ויותר מבואר הענין בפ' לו ל"ה א' ת"ח מה בין אינון דמשתדלי באורייתא לנביאי מהימני דאינון דמשתדלי באורייתא עדיפי מנביאי בכל זמנא. מ"ט דאינון קיימי בדרגא עלאה יתיר מנביאי. אינון דמשתדלי באורייתא קיימי לעילא באתרא דאקרי תורה דהוא קיומא דכל מהימנותא ונביאי קיימי לתתא באתר דאקרי נ"וה. ע"ד אינון דמשתדלי באורייתא עדיפי מנביאי ועלאין מנהון יתיר. דאלין קיימין לעילא ואלין קיימין לתתא כו'. וע"ד זכאין אינון דמשתדלי באורייתא דאינון בדרגא עלאה יתיר על כולא כו':

פרק כא ואם

כ"כ נפלאה מדרגתם של עומלי תורה גם בעודם בזה העולם החשוך. להשיג ולהסתכל ברוח קדשם באור העליון. גדולים צדיקים במיתתן יותר מבחייה' לאין ערוך. אחר אשר נשמתו הטהור' רבת שבעה לה תורה ומצות. וכ"א שבה אל בית אביה מקודשת ומטוהרה כאשר נתנה וביתרון אור התורה תלמודו בידו. כל השערים נפתחים לפניו וסליק ובקע רקיעין כו'. ולדור בצרור החיים את ה' אלקיו ית"ש. ובתדב"א סא"ר פי"ד אמר ושמא תאמר הואיל ונכנס משה לבית עולמו שמא בטל ממנו תואר הכתר של מאור פנים. ת"ל ולא קם נביא כו'. פנים אל פנים מה אור פנים שלמעלה קיים לעולם ולעולמי עולמים כך מאור פניו של משה נכנס עמו לבית עולמו כו'. ולא משה בלבד אלא כל תלמיד חכם שעוסק בתורה מקטנותו ועד זקנותו ומת. באמת לא מת אלא הוא עדיין בחיים לעולם ולעולמי עולמים שנאמר והיתה נפש אדני צרורה בצרור החיים את ה' אלקיך. מקיש הת"ח הצדיק אל אלקים מה אלקים יהא שמו הגדול מבורך חי וקים כו'. כך ת"ח שעסק בתורה כל ימיו ומת הרי הוא בחיים ועדיין לא מת והוא חי לעולם כו'. והיכן הוא נשמתו תחת כסא הכבוד ע"כ. ונפשו תשבע בצחצחות האור עליון הגנוז. כמאמרם ז"ל (סוטה מ"ט א') כל ת"ח העוסק בתורה מתוך הדחק כו' ר' אבהו אומר אף משביעין אותו מזיו שכינה שנאמר והיו עיניך רואות את מוריך. ובפ"ק דבתרא (י' ע"א) מאי אשבעה בהקיץ תמונתך אלו ת"ח שמנדדין שינה מעיניהם בעוה"ז הקב"ה משביען מזיו השכינה לעוה"ב. ובפ' חלק (ק' ע"א) דרש ר"י בר"ש כל המשחיר פניו על ד"ת בעוה"ז הקב"ה מבהיק זיוו לעוה"ב. והכל לפי ערך רוב עסקו ונפלאות דביקותו בתורה"ק. כמ"ש בתד"א סא"ז פי"ב אצל הצדיקים מה נאמר בהם ואוהביו

פרק יט ושם ה' נקרא עליו • כי התורה כולה שמותיו של הקב"ה •

כמאמרם ז"ל (ברכות כ"א א') מנין לברכת התורה לפניה מן התורה שנאמ' כי שם ה' אקרא וגו' • וכן למדו שהעוסק בתורה שכינה שרוי' עמו דכתיב בכל המקום אשר אזכיר את שמי כו' • ובזוהר במדבר קי"ח א' כמה חביבא אורייתא קמי' קב"ה דהא בכל אתר דמלי דאורייתא אשתמעו קב"ה וכל חיילין דילי' כלהו צייתין למלולי' וקב"ה אתי לדיירא עמי' הה"ד בכל המקום אשר אזכיר את שמי וגו' • ובפ' משפטים קכ"ד א' דכל מאן דינטר ארחי דאורייתא ואשתדל בה כמאן דאשתדל' בשמא קדיש' דתנינן אורייי' כלא שמא דקב"ה ומאן דמשתדל בה כמאן דמשתדל בשמא קדיש' בגין דאורייי' כלא שמא חד קדישא איהי• שמא עלאה • שמא דכליל כל שמהן • ומאן דגרע את חד מינה כאלו עביד פגימותא בשמא קדישא • ובפ' ויקרא י"ג ב' ר"א פתח כל זאת באתנו ולא שכחנוך כו' • ולא אנשינן מלולי אורייתך • מכאן אוליפנא כל מאן דאנשי מלולי אורייתא ולא בעי למלעי בה כאלו אנשי לקב"ה דהא אורייתא כלא שמא דקב"ה הוי • ושם דף י"ט סוף ע"א דהא אורייתא מאן דישתדל בה מתעטר בעטרוי דשמא קדישא דהא אורייתא שמא קדישא הוא ומאן דישתדל בה אתרשים ואתעטר בשמא קדישא• וכדין ידע ארחין סתימין ורזין עמיקין כו • וכ"א בר"פ במדבר ובפ' אחרי ע"א ב' וע"ב סוף ע"א וצ"ג א' וצ"ה א' ובפ' אמור פ"ט ב' ובר"פ ק"ח ע"ש • ולכן גם מזה הטעם אמרו דקב"ה ואורייתא חד • כי הוא ושמו' חד הוא • כמ"ש בזוהר יתרו צ' ע"ב ואורייתא כלא שמא חד הוי שמא קדישא דקב"ה ממש וזכאה חולקיה דמאן דזכי בה מאן דזכי באורייתא זכי בשמא קדישא דקב"ה ממש ריא בקב"ה ממש זכי דהא הוא ושמי' חד הוא • ולכן אמר בתד"א שכל מי שעושה מריבה על ת"ח כאלו עושה מריבה על מי שאמר והיה העולם שנאמ' הוא דתן ואבירם כו' • בהצותם על ה' • לכן כאשר האדם בא בשם ה' • הכל יראים ומזדעזעים ממנו כמ"ש וראו כל עמי הארץ כי שם ה' נקרא עליך ויראו ממך • וכמ"ש כי בי חשק ואפלטהו אשגבהו כי ידע שמי • כי בי חשק בו ית' ממש כביכול כנ"ל • ובפ' בלק ר"ב א' ת"ח כמה חביבין אינון דמשתדלי באורייי' קמי' קב"ה • דאפי' בזמנא דדינא תלי' בעלמא ואתיהיב רשו למחבלא לחבלא • קב"ה פקיד לי' עלוייהו על אינון דקא משתדלי באורייתא • והכי ה"ל קב"ה כי תצור אל עיר בגין חוביהון שגיאין כו' תא ואפקיד לך על בני ביתי • לא תשחית את עצה דא ת"ח דאיהו במתא דאיהו אילנא דחיי אילנא דיהיב איבין • את עצה ההוא דיהיב עיטא למתא כו' ואוליף לון אורחא דיהכון בה • וע"ד לא תשחית את עצה • לנדוח עליו גרזן לנדחא עלי' דינא ולא לאושטא עלי' חרבא מלהטא כו' • כי האדם עץ השדה דא אקרי אדם דאשתמודע עילא ותתא כו' • וכל דא פקיד קב"ה על אינון דמשתדלי באורייתא כו' ע"ש באורך :

פ"ק כ והוא הבן יקיר מבני פלטרין דמלכא • מבני היכלא דמלכא

אשר לו לבדו הרשות נתונה בכל עת לאשם בגנזי דמלכא קדישא • וכל השערים עליונים פתוחים לפניו • כמאמרם ז"ל (סוטה מ"ט א') כל העוסק בתורה מתוך דוחק כו' ר' אחא ב"ח אומר אף אין הפרגוד ננעל בפניו שנא' ולא יכנף עוד מוריך • ונכנס בשערי התו"הק להשיג ולהסתכל באור הפנימי בעמקי רזין עלאין דילה • כמ"ש בפ' התורה ומגלין לו רזי תורה • וכן אמרו (עכומ"ז ל"ה ב') ולא עוד אלא שדברים המכוסין מבני אדם מתגלין לו • ובמדרש תהלים מזמור י"ט אמרו על שמואל שאמר מכיר אני חוצות הרקיע כו' (ובש"ם הגרסא נהירין

לשלטאה עלוי · והכי הוא ודאי דאי אדם הוה אתדביק באילנא דחיי דאיהו אורייתא׳ לא גרים מותא לי׳ ולכל עלמא · ובג״כ כד יהיב קב״ה אורייתא לישראל מה כתיב בה חרות על הלחות כו׳ · וקב״ה אמר אני אמרתי אלקים אתם כו׳ · ועי״ד כל מאן דאשתדל באורייתא לא יכיל לשלטאה עלוי ההוא חויא בישא דאחשיך עלמא :

פרק יח

ולזאת האדם המקבל ע״ע על התורה הקדושה לשמה לאמיתה כמו שהתבאר לעיל פי׳ לשמה · הוא נעלה מעל כל עניני זה העולם · ומושגח מאתו יתב׳ השגחה פרטית למעלה מהוראת כחות הטבעים והמזלות כולם · כיון שהוא דבוק בתורה ובהקב״ה ממש כביכול · ומתקדש בקדושה העליונה של התו״הק שהיא למעלה לאין ערוך מכל העולמו׳ והיא הנותנת החיות והקיום לכולם ולכל הכחות הטבעים . הרי האדם העוסק בה מחיה ומקיים את כולם ולמעלה מכולם · ואיך אפשר שתהא הנהגתו מאתו יתב׳ ע״י הכחות הטבעים · ואמרז״ל (פסחים נ׳ ע״ב) כתיב עד שמים חסדך · וכתיב מעל שמים חסדך · ל״ק כאן בעוסקים לשמה כאן בעוסקים שלא לשמה · היינו שהעוסק בתורה שלא לשמה אם כי ודאי שגם הוא מרוצה לפניו יתב׳ · אף אם כוונתו לשם איזה פניה שתהיה · רק אם אינו לקנטור ח״ו וכ״ש אם אינו מכוין לשום פניה · רק לפי שהורגל בכך · כי מתוכה יבא למדרגת לשמה כידוע מאמרם ז״ל · עכ״ז עדן לא נתקדש ונתעלה שיהיה הנהגתו יתב׳ אתו בכל עניניו למעלה מכחות הטבעים · לכן כתיב בי׳ רק עד שמים היינו עד הכחות הטבעים הקבועי׳ בשמים · ולא למעלה מהם · אבל על העוסק בה לשמה · אמר מעל שמים · ר״ל שכל הנהגותיו יתב׳ עמו רק למעלה מהוראת כחות הטבעים · וז״ש ברע״מ פנחס רי״ו ב׳ ת״ח כל בריין דעלמא קודם דאתיהיבת אורייתא לישראל הוו תליין במזלא כו׳ · אבל בתר דאתיהיבת אורייתא לישראל אפיק לון מחיובא דככבי ומזלי כו׳ . ובג״ד כל המשתדל באוריי׳ בטיל מיני׳ חיובא דככביא ומזלי אי אוליף לה כדי לקיימא פקודהא · ואי לאו כאלו לא אשתדל בה ולא בטיל מיני׳ חיובא דככביא ומזלי :

ואדרבה הכחות הטבעים מסורים אליו כאשר יגזור אומר עליהם · ולכל אשר יחפוץ יטם · ואימתו מוטלת על כלם · כמ״ש בפ׳ התורה ונותנת לו מלכות וממשלה · כי נזר אלקיו אור התורה מאירה ומבהקת על ראשו · וחופה כביכול בצל כנפי השכינה · כמ״ש בזוהר לו ליה א׳ פתח ר״א ואמר ואשים דברי בפיך ובצל ידי כסיתיך כו׳ · תנינן כל ב״נ דאשתדל במלי דאורייתא ושפוותי׳ מרחשן אורייתא · קב״ה חפי עלי׳ ושכינתא פרשא עליה גדפהא הה״ד ואשים דברי בפיך ובצל ידי כסיתיך כו׳ · ובהקדמת הזוהר י״א א׳ וכ״ה באותו הלשון בפ׳ ואתחנן ר״ס ע״א ת״ח כמה הוא חילא תקיפא דאורייתא · וכמה הוא עלאה על כולא · דכל מאן דאשתדל באורייתא לא דחיל מעלאי ותתאי ולא דחיל מערעורין בישין דעלמא · בגין דאיהו אחיד באילנא דחיי ואכיל מיני׳ בכל יומא · דהא אורייתא אוליף לי׳ לב״נ בארח קשוט אוליף לי׳ עיטא כו׳ · ובפ׳ בשלח מ״ו א׳ ר״י פתח כו׳ · כמה חביבא אורייתא קמי׳ דקב״ה · דכל מאן דישתדל באורייתא רחים הוא לעילא רחים הוא לתתא קב״ה אציה לי׳ למלולי׳ לא שביק לי׳ בהאי עלמא ולא שביק לי׳ בעלמא דאתי כו׳ ע״ש · ובפ׳ מצורע נ״ב ב׳ וכד איהו אשתדל בפולחנא דמארי׳ ולעי באורייתא כמה נטורין זמינין לקבלי׳ לנטרא לי׳ ושכינתא שריא עלוי׳ וכלא מכרזי קמי׳ ואמרי הבו יקרא לדיוקנא דמלכא אתנטיר הוא בעלמא דין ובעלמא דאתי זכאה חולקיה :

שער ד

פתח גל עיני ואביטה נפלאות מתורתך כמה אינון ב"נ טפשין דלא ידעין ולא מסתכלין לאשתדלא באורייתא · בגין דאורייתא כל חיין וכל חירו וכל טוב בעלמא דין ובעלמא דאתי איהו חירו דעלמא דין ודעלמא דאתי איהי · חיין אינון בעלמא דין דיזכון ליומין שלימין בהאי עלמא כד"א כו' וליומין אריכין בעלמא דאתי . בגין דאינון חיין שלימין אינון חיין דחירו חיין בלא עציבו חיין דאינון חיין חירו בעלמא דין חירו דכלא · דכל מאן דאשתדל באורייתא לא יכלין לשלטאה עלוי כל עמין דעלמא כו' וע"ד כל מאן דישתדל באורייתא חירו אית ליה מכלא בעלמא דין משעבודא דשא' עמין חירו בעלמ' דאתי בגין דלא יתבעון מיני' דינא בההוא עלמא כלל כו' ע"ש · ובמ"דא סא"ר פי"א בפסוק ועל הנחל יעלה על שפתו מזה ומזה כל עץ מאכל כו' · מאי ולא יראה כי יבא חס לומר לך כל העוסק בתורה אינו רואה מדת פורעניות בין בעוה"ז בין לימות בן דוד ובין לעה"ב · וכמו שפי' ז"ל בהתהלכך תנחה אותך בעוה"ז · בשכבך תשמור עליך בקבר · והקיצות היא תשיחך לעוה"ב · ובזוהר פ' וישב קפ"ד ב' וקפ"ה א' ר"י פתח ואמר תורת ה' תמימה כו' כמה אית לון לב"נ לאשתדלא באורייתא · דכל מאן דאשתדל באורייתא להוי לי' חיים בעלמ' דין ובעלמא דאתי וזכי בתרין עלמין · ואפי' מאן דאשתדל באורייתא ולא אשתדל בה לשמה כדקא יאות זכי לאגר טב בעלמא דין ולא דיינין לי' בההוא עלמא · ות"ח כתיב אורך ימים בימינה כו' · אורך ימים בההוא דאשתדל באורייתא לשמה דאית לי' אורך ימים בההוא עלמא דבי' אורכא דיומין כו' · בשמאלה עשר וכבוד אגר טב ושלוה אית לי' בהאי עלמא · וכל מאן דישתדל באורייתא לשמה כד נפיק מהאי עלמא אורייתא אזלא קמי' ואכרזת קמי' ואגינת עלוי' דלא יקרבון בהדי' מאריהון דדינא · כד שכיב גופא בקברא היא נטרת לי' · כד נשמתא אזלת לאסתלקא למיתב לאתרה איהי אזלת קמא דההיא נשמתא וכמה תרעין אתברו מקמא דאורייתא עד דעאלת לדוכתא · וקיימא עלוי' דב"נ עד דיתער בזמנא דיקומון מתייא דעלמא ואיהי סניגורא עלוי' · הה"ד בהתהלכך תנחה אותך בשכבך תשמור עליך כו' · בהתהלכך תנחה אותך כמה דאתמר · בשכבך תשמור עליך בשעתא דשכיב גופא בקברא דהא כדין בההוא זמנא אתדן גופא בקברא וכדין אורייתא אגינת עלוי' · והקיצות היא תשיחך כמה דאתמר בזמנא דיתערון מתי עלמא מן עפרא היא תשיחך למהוי סניגורא עלך כו' · וכן אחז"ל בפ' חלק (נ"ט ב') בפסוק נפש עמל עמלה לו כו' · הוא עמל במקום זה והתורה עומלת לו במקום אחר · ובמשלי רבתא פי"ד חכמות נשים בנתה ביתה · כל מי שקנה לו חכמה בעוה"ז יהא מובטח שהיא בונה לו בית לעוה"ב · ואולת בידיה תהרסנו כל מי שלא קנה לו חכמה יהא מובטח שקנה לו גיהנם לעת"ל · ובס"ת לך לך אחר הדברים האלה דא פתגמי אורייתא כו' · הה"ד אל תירא אברם אנכי מגן לך מכל זייני גיהנם · שכרך הרבה מאד בגין דכל מאן דאשתדל באורייתא בהאי עלמא זכי ואחסין ירותא אחסנתי' לעלמא דאתי כו' ע"ש · ובזוהר ויקהל ר' ע"א בגין דכד ב"נ עסיק באורייתא קב"ה קאים תמן כו' · ואשהזיב ב"נ מתלת דינין · מדינא דהאי עלמא · ומדינא דמ"המ דלא יכיל לשלטאה עלוי' · ומדינא דגיהנם · וכשרז"ל בפ' מעלת התורה · ובבמדבר רבה פס"ז · ובאזי"א בפסוק מי זאת עולה כו' · ובהנחומא פ' עקב א"ת חרות אלא חירות שאין לך בן חורין אלא מי שעוסק בתלמוד תורה ופי' ז"ל חירו' ממלאך המות · וכן אמרו בפ"ד דמכות (י' ע"א) שדברי תורה קולטין ממ"המ · ובזוהר פ' חיי בד' כנ"ל חירו בעלמא דין חירו דכלא כו' חירו דמה"מ דלא יכול

לבטלה

שער ד

לשם שמים ויראה בלבבם ומחזיקים ד"ת בפיהם ומקיימין עליהם הפסוק טוב לגבר כי ישא עול בנעוריו כך כביכול אפילו הם ישאלו את כל העולם כולו בשעה אחת הוא נותן להם מיד כו' · ויתר על כן · אלא הגם שהוא עצמו ודאי בורח מהכבוד וגדולה · כי בלא זה בלתי אפשר בעולם כלל להיות עוסק בתורה לשמה · ולא תתקיים אצלו כלל · כמאז"ל כפ' מעלות התורה אל תבקש גדולה לעצמך ואל תחמוד כבוד · כי האדם אסור לו לפנות דעתו לזה כלל · אמנם גדול העצה ית"ש נותן לו שמחה וגדולה בע"כ · כמ"ש בתד"א שם ברוך המקום ברוך הוא שבחר בחכמים ובתלמידיה' כו' כמו שהם יושבין בב"כ ובבי"מד בכל יום וקורין ושונין לשם שמים ויראת שמים בלבבם ומחזיקים דברי תורה על פיהם ומקבלין עליהם בשמחה עול מ"ש כך כביכול הקב"ה נותן להם שמחה לצדיקים בעל כרחם שלא בטובתם כו' ע"כ · וכמאמר הכתוב אך טוב וחסד ירדפוני כל ימי חיי ר"ל הגם שאני בורח מהם המה רודפים אחרי בע"כ :

פרק יז בין

אחר פטירתו מזה העולם · ארז"ל (חגיגה כ"ז ב') ת"ח אין אור של גיהנם שולט בהם כו' · וכן אמרו שם ת"ח שסרח אין תורתו נמאסת · ובמשלי רבתא בפ' להבין משל ומליצה כו' ומליצה זו התורה עצמה למה נקראת שמה מליצה שהיא מצלת עוסקיה מדינה של גיהנם · ושם רפ"ב בני אם תקח אמרי כו' אמר הקב"ה לישראל על הר סיני אם זכיתם להצפין ולקבל תורתי ולעשותה אני מציל אתכם משלש פורעניות · ממלחמת גוג ומגוג · מחבלו של משיח · מדינה של גיהנם · ומצותי תצפן אתך אם איתם להצפין תורתי אני משביע אתכם מטוב הצפון לע"ל שנא' מה רב טובך אשר צפנת כו' · ושם בפ"י ארחב"ד אין לך צדקה שמצלת את האדם מדינה של גיהנם אלא תורה בלבד כו' · שיש בה כח להציל אותו מיום הדין · ואפילו נתחייב אדם בדבר עבירה יכולה להציל אותו מיום הדין כו' · הרי מכאן לת"ח שעבר בדבר עבירה שהיא מצלת אותו · ובמדרש תהלים מזמור י"ט ותקופתו כו' ואין נסתר מחמתו כו' ר"י ורשב"ל אמרי תרוייהו אין גיהנם לעה"ל אלא השמש הזו היא מלהטת את הרשעים שנאמר הנה היום בא בוער כתנור והיו כל זדים כו' ולהט אותם כו' אבל לעתיד לבא מי נסתר מחמתו מי שהוא עוסק בתורה מה כתיב אחריו תורת ה' תמימה כו' וכן הוא אומר אין חשך ואין צלמות להסתר שם פועלי און ומי נסתר מי שהוא עוסק בתורה כו' ע"ש · וק"ו מאלישע אחר · שאמרו (חגיגה ט"ו ב') לא מידן נדייני' משום דגמיר אורייתא · וכן אמרו בירושלמי שם ובקהלת רבה סימן ז' בפסוק טוב אחרית דבר כו' ולא כן תנינן מצילין תיק הספר עם הספר כו' מצילין לאלישע בזכות תורתו · ובזוהר יתרו פ"ג ב' אר"י אמאי אתייהב אורייתא באשא וחשוכא כו' דכל מאן דישתדל באורייתא אשתזיב מאשא אחרא בגיהנם ומחשוכא דמחשכין כל שאר עמין לישראל כו' ע"ש : וברע"מ תרומה קל"ד ב' פקודא ללמוד תורה בכל יומא דאיהו רזא דמהימנותא עלאה למנדע ארחי' דקב"ה · דכל מאן דאשתדל באורייתא זכי בהאי עלמא וזכי בעלמא דאתי ואשתזיב מכל קטרוגין בישין · בגין דאורייתא רזא דמהימנותא איהי דמאן דיתעסק בה אתעסק במהימנותא עלאה אשרי שכינתא בגוי' דלא תעדי מיני' כו' ע"ש · וכמאמרם ז"ל ע"פ ארך ימים בימינה כו' למיימינים בה ארך ימים וכ"ש עושר וכבוד · והוא בשני העולמים · עושר וכבוד בעה"ז וארך ימים לעוה"ב · שעיקר האורך ימים הכוונה לעולם שכולו ארוך כמ"ש רז"ל בכמה דוכתי ובזוהר וישב ק"ל ריש ע"א ע"ש : ושם בפ' חיי קל"א ב' ר"א

פתח

דאשתדלותיה באורייתא כפית ליה לחמור ונחית ליה כו' דאיהו סליק לנזקא עלמא ושוי מדורי' בין המשפתים כו' · וכן אמרו ז"ל בפ"ג דסוטה (כ"א א') דהתורה אגוני מגני מן היסורין בין בעדנא דעסיק בה בין בעדנא דלא עסיק בה ע"ש · כי היא גמלתהו רק טוב ולא רע כל ימי חייה · הייט אפי' בעדנא דלא עסיק בה · כ"ז שהוא דביק ולא פירש ח"ו מחיי עולם שלה ודעתו עליה תמיד לחשר ולהגות בה (*):

הגה"ה

(*) ומ"ש גמלתהו וכו' · כי גמול פירוש תשלום גמול למי שהטיב אתו מקודם · ז"ש שהתורה משלמת גמול טוב להאדם שעושה טובה עמה היינו כשעוסק בה לשמה · וגם אם עסקו בה שלא לשמה לגרמיה ולא להטיב אתה · שמהראוי היה שהתורה תגמלנו רעה ח"ו · עכ"ז אינה גומלת לו רעה ח"ו · ואדרבה גם בשמאלה הייט למשמאילים בה שלא לשמה · היא נותנת לו עושר וכבוד בעולם הזה · ע"כ :

פרק טז וגם מעבירין ומסלקין מעליו כל הטרדות והעניים

מעול ד"א וכו' · וכל שאר עניני זה העולם המונעות תמידות העסק בהו"הק · כמ"ש כל המקבל עליו עול תורה מעבירין ממנו עול מלכות ועול דרך ארץ · ואמרו בבמדבר רבה ובתנחומא פ' חקת שמזה הטעם ניתנה התורה במדבר כשם שמדבר אינו נזרע ואינו נעבד כך המקבל עליו עול תורה פורקין ממנו עול כו' וכשם שמדבר אינו מעלה ארנון (ר"ל מס) כך בני תורה בני חורין כו' · ובזוהר ויחי רמ"ב ב' דכל מאן דידע לאשתדלא באורייתא ולא אשתדל אתחייב בנפשיה · ולא עוד אלא דיהבין עליה עולא דארעא ושעבודא בישא דכתיב בישככר ויט שכמו לסבול כו' מאן דסטא ארחיה וגרמיה דלא למסבל עולא דאורייתא מיד ויהי למס עובד · וכן להיפך כו' · וכך הדין הלכה פסוקה בש"ס שת"ח פטורין ממסים · כמ"ש (נדרים כ"ב ב' ובפ"ק דבתרא ח' א') שארי לי' לצורבא מרבנן למימר לא יהיבנא כרגא דכתיב מנדה בלו והלך לא שליט למרמא עליהום · ושם ר"ה בר"ח שדא כרגא ארבנן · א"ל רנב"י עברת אדאורייתא אדנביאים אדכתובים דכתיב כו' · כמש"ש דרבנן לא צריכי נטירותא · ובתד"א בא"ר פ"ד כל ת"ח שעוסק בתורה בכל יום תמיד בשביל להרבות כבוד שמים · אינו צריך לא חרב ולא חנית ולא כל דבר שיהיה לו שומר אלא הקב"ה משמרו בעצמו כו' · ושם בפי"ח אם יש בו באדם ד"א ומקרא לבד מוסרין לו מלאך א' לשומרו שנאמר כו' · קרא אדם תורה נביאים וכתובים מוסרים לו שני מלאכים שנאמר כי מלאכיו יצוה לך לשמרך כו' · אבל קרא אדם תורה נביאים וכתובים ושנה משנה ומדרש הלכות ואגדות ושמש ת"ח הקדוש ב"ה משמרו בעצמו כו' שנאמר ה' שומרך כו' · וכפי ערך הקיבול אשר יקבל עליו עול תורה באמת ובכל כחו · כן לפי זה הערך יסירו ויעבירו ממנו טרדות עניני זה העולם · והשמירה עליונה חופפת עליו · והוא כבן המתחטא על אביו · ואביו עושה לו רצונו ומשלים לו כל חפצו · כמ"ש רז"ל (עכומ"ז י"ט א') כל העוסק בתורה הקב"ה עושה לו חפצו · וכ"א במדרש תהלים מזמור א' · ואמרו עוד שם שכתוב בתורה ושנוי בנביאים ומשולש בכתובים שכל העוסק בתורה נכסיו מצליחין · ובמשלי רבתא ספ"ח ויפק רצון מה' כל מי שהוא מפיק בד"ת ומלמדו ברבים · אף אני בעת רצון מפיק לו רצון כו' · ומזונותיו מוכנים לו תמיד בלא שום עמל ויגיעה מוטעת עליהם · כמ"ש שם בפ' אשת חיל כ"ז שת"ח יושב ועוסק בתורה כו' ולא עוד אלא שהקב"ה ממציא לו מזונותיו בכל יום ויום שנאמר ותתן טרף לביתה · ובתד"א סא"ר פי"ת ברוך המקום ברוך הוא שבחר בחכמים ובתלמידיהם כו' כשם שהם יושבין בבה"כ ובבה"מד ובכל מקום שהוא פנוי להם וקורין ושונין

 לשם

שער ד

פ"ח אמר. כיון שלומד את התורה הרי זה מביא טובה לעולם ויכול הוא לבקש רחמים ולהתפלל לפני הקב"ה ויפקפק את הרקיע ויביא מטר לעולם כו'. ואמר שם עוד כ"ז שישראל עוסקין בתורה ועושין רצון אביהם שבשמים הקב"ה בעצמו נפנה אליהם לברכה שנאמר אמת מארץ תצמח וצדק משמים נשקף ואין השקפה אלא לברכה שנאמר השקיפה כו' וברך את עמך כו':

פרק טו

והנה המברך מתברך. ומברכתם של העולמות יבורך גם האדם העוסק בה כראוי לאמיתה הגורם לכ"ז. וכבוד ה' תוסף עליו כל היום ומשיג לנשמה אצולה ממקום קדוש. לפי ערך גודל עסקו ודיבוקו בה כמ"ש אדם מקדש עצמו מלמטה מקדשין אותו מלמעלה. מעט מקדשין אותו הרבה. ובהקדמת הזוהר י"ב ב' פקודא חמישאה כו' בהאי קרא אית תלת פקודין וכ'. וחד למלעי באורייתא לאשתדלא בה ולאפשא לה בכל יומא לתקנא נפשי' ורוחי'. דכיון דב"נ אתעסק באורייתא אתתקן בנשמתא אחרא קדישא דכתיב שרץ נפש חיה נפש דההיא חיה קדישא כו' וכד אשתדל באורייתא בההוא רחשו דרחיש בה זכי לההיא נפש חיה ולמהדר כמלאכין קדישין כו'. דא אורייתא דאקרי מים ישרצון ויפקון ריחשא דנפש חיה מאתר דההיא חיה ומשכין לה לתתא כמ"דא. וע"ד אמר דוד לב טהור ברא לי אלקים למלעי באורייתא ובדין ורוח נכון חדש בקרבי:

והוא הרודה ומושל בכל. וכל הדינין בישין מסתלקין מעליו ואין להם עליו שום שליטה ח"ו. בין בעודו בזה העולם. כמ"ש בפ"ק דברכות (ה' א') אר"ש בל כל העוסק בתורה יסורין בדלין הימנו. ובפ' כילד מעברין (נ"ד א') חש בראשו יעסוק בתורה שנאמר כו'. חש בגרונו יעסוק בתורה שנאמר כו'. חש במעיו כו'. חש בכל גופו יעסוק בתורה שנאמר ולכל בשרו מרפא. וכעין סגנון זה אמרו בויקרא רבה פי"ב ובתנחומא פ' יתרו ובמדרש תהלים מזמור ק"ט ע"ש. ובת"דא סא"ר פי"ח מקימי מעפר דל כו'. אדם שעבר עבירות הרבה ונקנס עליו מיתה כו'. וחזר ועשה תשובה וקורא תורה נביאים וכתובים ושנה משנה מדרש הלכות והגדות ושימש חכמים. אפילו נגזרו עליו מאה גזירות הקב"ה מעבירן ממנו כו'. ושם רפ"ו הביאני המלך חדריו כשם שיש להקב"ה חדרי חדרים בתורתו. כך יש להם לת"ח לכל אחד ואחד חדרי חדרים בתורתו. ואם ראית שהיסורין ממשמשין ובאין עליך רוץ לחדרי תורה ומיד היסורין בורחין ממך שנאמר לך עמי בא בחדריך וגו'. לכך נאמר הביאני המלך חדריו. נגילה ונשמחה בך במה שגדלתנו ורוממתנו וקשרת לנו כתר גדול בד"ת מסוף העולם ועד סופו. ושם בפי"ה ויהי המה הולכים הלוך ודבר ואין דבר אלא ד"ת כו'. וכשנשתלח מלאך כו'. ובא ומצאן שהיו עוסקין בד"ת ולא היה יכול לשלוט בהם כו'. מכאן אמרו שני ב"א שהולכין בדרך ועוסקין בתורה אין דבר רע יכול לשלוט בהן כו' ע"ש. ובזוהר ויחי רמ"ב סוף ע"א יששכר חמור גרם כו' פתח ואמר לדוד ה' אורי כו' כמה חביבין אינון מלין דאורייתא. כמה חביבין אינון דמשתדלי באורייתא קמי קב"ה. דכל מאן דאשתדל באורייתא לא דחיל מפגעי עלמא. נטיר הוא לעילא' נטיר הוא לתתא. ולא עוד אלא דכפיית לכל פגעי דעלמא ואחית לון לעומקא דתהום רבה. ת"ח בשעתא דעאל ליליא כו' כד אתער רוח צפון ואתפליג ליליא אתערותא קדישא אתער בעלמא כו'. זכאה חולקיה דההוא בר נש דאיהו קאים בההיא שעתא ואשתדל באורייתא. כיון דאיהו פתח באורייתא כל אינון זינין בישין אעיל לון בנוקבא דתהום רבה כו'. בג"כ יששכר דאשתדלותי'

שער ד

אותה ועכ"ל. ואמר פלטין הלואי תהא מעלה חן כו · כך אמר הקב"ה לעולמו · עולמי עולמי הלואי הלא מעלת חן לפני בכל עת כשם שהעלית חן לפני בשעה זו · וכן נאמר בשבח התורה אילת אהבים ויעלת חן · ובזוהר נו ל"ה א' פתח ר"א ואמר ואשים דברי בפיך כו' תנינן כל בר נש דאשתדל במלי דאורייתא ושפוותיה מרחשן אורייתא כו' · ולא עוד אלא דהוא מקיים עלמא וקב"ה חדי עמיה כאלו בהוא יומא נטע שמיא וארעא הה"ד לנטוע שמים וליסוד ארץ · ובפ' תרומה קנ"ה ב' פתח ר"א ואמר עת לעשות לה' הפרו תורתך ט' בכל זמנא דאורייתא מתקיימא בעלמא ובני נשא משתדלין בה · כביכול קב"ה חדי בעובדוי ידוי וחדי בעלמין כולהו · ושמיא וארעא קיימי בקיומייהו · ולא עוד אלא קב"ה כניש כל פמליא דיליה ואמר לון חמו עמא קדישא דאית לי בארעא דאורייתא מתעטרא בגיניהון כו · ואינון כד חמו חדוה דמאריהון בעמי' מיד פתחי ואמרי ומי כעמך ישראל גוי אחד בארץ · ובר"פ שמיני זכאין אינון ישראל דקוב"ה יהב לון אורייתא קדישא חדוותא דכלא חדוותא דקוב"ה ואטיילותא דיליה דכתיב ואהיה שעשועים יום יום כו':

פרק יד

וגם העולמות והבריות כלם הם אז בחדוותא יתירתא ונהירין מזיו האור העליון השופע עליהם ממקום שורש עליון של התורה · כמ"ש בפ' מעלות התורה משמחת את המקום משמחת את הבריות · וכן אמרה התורה ואהיה שעשועים יום יום · ובזוהר ויקהל רי"ז א' פתח ואמר אז נדברו יראי ה' כו' אז דברו מבעי ליה מאי נדברו · אלא נדברו לעילא מכל אינון רתיכין קדישין וכל אינון חילין קדישין · בגין דאינון מלין קדישין סלקין לעילא וכמה אינון דמקדמי ונטלי לון קמי מלכא קדישא ומתעטרין בכמה עטרין באינון נהורין עלאין וכולהו נדברו מקמי מלכא עלאה · מאן חמי הדוון מאן חמי תושבחן דסלקין בכל אינון רקיעין קמי מלכא קדישא · ומלכא קדישא מסתכל בהו ואתעטר בהו ואינון סלקין על רישיה והוו עטרא ונחתין ויתבין על חיקי' לגו בתוקפיה ומתמן סלקין על רישי' · וע"ד אמרה אורייתא ואהיה שעשועים יום יום והייתי לא כתיב אלא ואהיה בכל זמן ובכל עידן דמלין עלאין סלקין קמיה ע"כ · ובכל עת שהאדם עוסק ומתדבק בה כראוי · הדברים שמחים כנתינתן מסיני · כמ"ש בזוהר ר"פ חקת ר"י פתח וזאת התורה ט' ת"ח מלין דאורייתא קדישין אינון עלאין אינון מתיקין כמה דכתיב הנחמדים מזהב כו' · מאן דאשתדל באורייתא כאלו קאים כל יומא על טורא דסיני לקבל אורייתא הה"ד היום הזה נהיית לעם · ובפ' אח"י ס"ט א' דתאנא כל מאן דאצית למלוי דאורייתא זכאה הוא בהאי עלמא וכאלו קביל תורה מסיני · ואפילו מכל ב"נ נמי בעי למשמע מלוי דאורייתא · ומאן דארכין אודניה לקבלי' יהיב יקרא למלכא קדישא ויהיב יקרא לאורייתא עליה כתיב היום הזה נהיית לעם כו' · והטעם שכמו שבעת המעמד המקודש נתדבקו כביטול בדבורו ית' · כן גם עתה בכל עת ממש שהאדם עוסק והוגה בה · הנה דבוק על ידה בדבורו ית' ממש · מחמת שהכל מאמר פיו ית' למשה בסיני ואפילו מה שתלמיד קטן שואל מרבו כנ"ל פ"ו · וגם עתה בעת שהאדם עוסק בה בכל תיבה · אותה התיבה ממש נחצבת אז להבת אש מפיו ית' כביכול כמ"ש · ונחשב כאלו עתה מקבלה בסיני מפיו ית"ש · לכן ארז"ל כמה פעמים והיו הדברים שמחים כנתינתן מסיני: ואז משתלשל ונמשך שפעת אור וברכה ממקור שרשה העליון · על כל העולמות · וגם · הארץ האירה מכבודה ומתברכת · ומביא הרבה טובה ושפעת ברכה לעולם · ובתד"א סא"ר

פי"ח

שער ד

וכל מלה דאתחדש באורייתא על ידא דההוא דאשתדל באורייתא עביד רקיעא חדא · תנן בההוא שעתא דמלה דאורייתא אתחדש מפומיה דב"נ ההיא מלה סלקא ואתעתדת קמיה דקב"ה וקב"ה נטיל לההיא מלה ונשיק לה ועטר לה בשבעין עטרין גליפין ומחקקן · ומלה דחכמתא דאתחדשא סלקא ויתבא על רישא כו' וטסא מתמן ושטאת בשבעין אלף עלמין וסליקת לגבי עתיק יומין כו' · וההיא מלה סתימאה דחכמתא דאתחדשת הכא כד סלקא אתחברת באינון מלין דעתיק יומין וסלקא ונחתא בהדייהו ועאלת בתמניסר עלמין גניזין דעין לא ראתה כו' נפקין מתמן שאטן ואתיין מליאן ושלימן ואתעתדו קמיה ע"י · בההיא שעתא ארח עתיק יומין בההיא מלה וניחא קמיה מכלא · נטיל לההיא מלה ואעטר לה בש"ע אלף עטרין · ההיא מלה טסת וסלקא ונחתא ואתעבידת רקיעא חדא · וכן כל מלה ומלה דחכמתא אתעבדין רקיעין קיימין בקיומא שלים קמי ע"י והוא קרי לון שמים חדשים כו' סתימין דרזין דחכמתא עלאה · וכל אלין שאר מילין דאורייתא דמתחדשין · קיימין קמי קב"ה וסלקין ואתעבידו ארצות החיים ונחתין ומתעטרין כו' ואתחדש ואתעביד כלא ארץ חדשה מההיא מלה דאתחדש באורייתא · וע"ד כתיב כי כאשר השמים החדשים כו' אשר אני עושה כו' עשיתי לא כתיב אלא עושה דעביד תדיר ואינון חידושין ורזין דאורייתא · וע"ד כתיב ואשים דברי בפיך כו' לנטוע שמים וליסוד ארץ כו'· אר"א מהו ובצל ידי כסיתיך א"ל כו' ובשעתא דהאי מלה סלקא ואתעטרא וקיימא קמי קב"ה · איהו חפי על ההיא מלה וכסי על ההוא בר נש כו' עד דאתעביד מההיא מלה שמים חדשים וארץ חדשה כו' · ולאמר לציון עמי אתה כו' אל תקרא עמי אלא עמי למהוי שותפא עמי מה אנא במלולא דילי עבדים שמים וארץ כו' אוף הכי את · זכאין אינון דמשתדלין באורייתא · ובפ' ויחי רמ"ג ריש ע"א כתיב הדודאים נתנו ריח כו' אלין אינון דאשכח ראובן כו' ועל פתחינו כל מגדים אינון גרמו למהוי על פתחי ב"כ וב"מד כל מגדים · חדשים גם ישנים כמה מלי חדתאן ועתיקין דאורייתא דאתגלייא על ידייהו כו' · דודי צפנתי לך מהכא אליפנא כל מאן דאשתדל באורייתא כדקא יאות וידע למחדי מלין ולחדתותי מלין כדקא יאות אינון מלין סלקין עד כרסייא דמלכא וכ"י פתח לון תרעין וגניז לון · ובשעתא דעאל קב"ה לאשתעשע עם צדיקייא בגנתא דעדן אפיקת לון קמי' ומסתכל בהו וחדי · כדין קב"ה מתעטר בעטרין עלאין וחדי כו' · ומההיא שעתא מלוי כתיבין בספרא כו' זכאה חולקיה מאן דאשתדל באורייתא כדקא יאות · זכאה הוא בהאי עלמא וזכאה הוא בעלמא דאתי · ובת"דא סא"ר פי"ח ועל הנחל יעלה על שפתו מזה ומזה כל עץ מאכל ופי' שם כל זה הכתוב על ד"ת ואומר שם מהו לחדשיו יבכר למחדשי תורה שמחדשין את התורה בכל יום תמיד · לכן שהוא בשר כו' שמחדש ד"ת שהכל שמחין בו כו' שמחה מתחדש לו לאביו בכל יום כו' · ובכל מקום שמחדשין תורה שבכנסיות ב"הכ ובישיבות ביהמד שמחה מתחדש להקב"ה בכל יום תמיד כו' ע"ש :

פרק יג ועל ידי עסק התו"הק · נשלם טונתו ·יתב' בבריאה

שהיה רק בשביל התורה שיעסקו בה ישראל · כמאמרם ז"ל בראשית בשביל התורה כו' · ובשביל ישראל כו' · ובשביל משה כו' שהוא הסרסור בקבלת התורה · וכביכול הוא ית' שמח במעשיו בעולמו ובריותיו שמעלים חן לפניו ית' כשעה ראשונה בעת הבריאה · כמו שקודם הוא ית' בעצמו כביכול · כמ"ש ברבה בראשית פ"ט למלך שבנה פלטרין ראה אותה

שער ד

ואור גדול בכל העולמות · ז"ש במשלי רבתא פ"ב מכל משמר נצור לבך שלא תברח מד"ת למה כי ממנו תוצאות חיים ללמדך שמד"ת יוצאין חיים לעולם · וגם לבנות הנהרסות בתיקונים גדולים · לקשר ולייחד ולהשלים העליונים עם התחתונים · וכל העלמין שקילין ובהירין כחדא · כמאמרם ז"ל בפ' חלק (צ"ט ב') א"ר כל העוסק בתורה לשמה כאלו עושה שלום בפמליא של מעלה ובפמליא של מטה שנא' או יחזק במעוזי יעשה שלום לי כו' רב אמר כאלו בנה פלטרין של מעלה ופלטרין של מטה שנא' ואשים דברי בפיך וכו' לנטוע שמים וליסוד ארץ · ובחזית · שוקיו עמודי שש אלו ת"ח למה נמשלו לעמודים שהם עמודי עולם שנא' אם לא בריתי יומם ולילה כו' · ובמשלי רבתא חכמות בנתה ביתה כו' · אמר הקב"ה אם זכה אדם ולמד תורה וחכמה חשוב לפני כמו שברא שמים וכאלו העמיד כל העולם כולו · וגם בפ' אשת חיל אמרו · אמר הקב"ה לישראל בני היו מתעסקין בתורה ביום ובלילה ומעלה אני עליכם כאלו אתם מעמידים את כל העולם ובזוהר בראשית מ"ז א' כל מאן דאשתדל באורייתא בכל יומא יזכי למהוי ליה חולקא בעלמא דאתי · ויתחשיב ליה כאלו בני עלמין · דהא באורייתא אתבני עלמין ואשתכלל דכתיב ה' בחכמה יסד ארץ וגו' · וכתיב ואהיה אצלו אמון כו' וכל דאשתדל בה שכלל עלמין וקיים ליה · נה"ח ברוח עביד קב"ה עלמא וברוחא מתקיימא דא רוחא דאינון דלעאן באורייתא כו' · וגם בפ' וישב · אחר שהאריך שם:ה במעלתו הנוראה של האדם העוסק בתורה בעה"ז ובעה"ב · ועונשו הגדול בשני העולמים כשמתרפה ממנה ח"ו · סיים ואמר בג"כ לא קיימא על קיומא דאורייתא ועלמא לא אתקיים בקיומיה אלא באורייתא דאיהו קיומא דעלמין עילא ותתא דכתיב אם לא בריתי יומם ולילה כו' · ובפ' תרומה קס"א א' אחר שהאריך בענין לבאר איך שבהתורה נבראו כל העולמות · אמר אח"ז כיון דאתברי עלמא כל מלה ומלה לא הוה מתקיים עד דסליק ברעותא למברי אדם דיהוי משתדל באורייתא ובגיני' אתקיים עלמא · השתא כל מאן דאסתכל בה באורייתא ואשתדל בה כביכול הוא מקיים כל עלמא · קב"ה אסתכל באורייתא וברא עלמא · ב"נ אסתכל בה באורייתא ומקיים עלמא · אשתכח דעובדא וקיומא דכל עלמא אורייתא איהי · בג"כ זכאה איהו ב"נ דאשתדל באורייתא דהאי איהו מקיים עלמא · ובפ' ויקרא י"א סוף ע"ב בגין דעלמא לא אתברי אלא בגין אורייתא וכל זמנא דישראל מתעסקי באורייתא עלמא מתקיימא · וכל זמנא דישראל מתבטלי מאורייתא מה כתי' אם לא בריתי יומם ולילה כו' · ולכן אמרו בפ' מעלות התורה שכל העוסק בתורה לשמה נק' ריע · כי כביכול נעשה שותף ליוצר בראשית ית"ש · כיון שהוא המקיים עתה את כל העולמות בעסק תורתו · ובלתי זה היו חוזרים כלם לתוהו ובוהו · וכמ"ש במדרש הנ"ל דמיתיך רעיתי רעיתי דעולמי שקבלו תורתי כו':

פרק י"ב וכ"ש חידושין אמיתים דאורייתא המתחדשין ע"י האדם ·

אין ערוך לגודל נוראות נפלאות ענינם ופעולתם למעלה · שכל מלה ומלה פרטית המתחדשת מפי האדם · קב"ה נשיק לה ומעטר לה · ונבנה ממנה עולם חדש בפ"ע · והן הן השמים החדשים והארץ החדשה שאמר הכתוב · כמ"ש בהקדמת הזוהר ד"ד ע"ב ר"ש פתח ואשים דברי בפיך כמה אית ליה לב"נ לאשתדלא באורייתא יממא ולילא · בגין דקב"ה ציית לקליהון דאינון דמתעסקי באורייתא ·

דבריאה דלאו אינון ואיהו חד לאו אינון וגרמיהון חד. ולכן התורה הק׳ ששורשה העליון הנעלם הוא למעלה מעלה גם מאצילות קדשו ית׳ כנ״ל וקב״ה ואורייתא כלא חד. היא הנפש והחיות ונהירו ושרשא דעלמין כלהו. שכמו שבעת הבריאה בה נאצלו ונבראו כולם. כן מאז היא נשמתם וחיותם וקיומם על סדר מצבם. ובלתי שפעת אורם בהם כל רגע ממש להאירם להחיותם ולקיימם. היו חוזרים כולם לתהו ובהו ממש:

פרק יא ולזאת עיקר חיותם ואורם וקיומם של העולמות

כולם על נכון. הוא רק כשאנחנו עוסקים בה כראוי. כי קב״ה ואורייתא וישראל כולא חד. שכ״א מישראל שרש נשמתו העליונה מדובק ונאחז באות א׳ מהתורה והיו לאחדים ממש. ולכן אמרו בב״ר פ״א שמחשבתן של ישראל קדמה לכ״ד. ולא בא לחלוק על מ״ש שהתורה קדמה לכ״ד כי הכל א׳ בשרשן. והיא היא. וז״ש מחש״בתן של ישראל. וכמ״ש ישראל עלה במחשבה ר״ל ראשית המחשבה סוד הרעותא עלאה כמ״ש בזוהר וירא קי״ח ב׳ דהא ישראל סליק ברעותא דקוב״ה עד לא יברא עלמא. והרעותא היא ראשית הכל אלקות גמור כביכול. מעולמות א״ס. כנז׳ שם בפ׳ נח ס״ה א׳ ופקודי רס״ח ב׳ אר״ש ארימית כו׳ דכד רעותא עלאה כו׳ וכל אינון נהורין מרזא דמחשבה עלאה ולתתא כלהו אקרון א״ס. ע״ש היטב ובהגהת הרח״ו ז״ל שם ובע״ח שער עיגולים ויושר ריש ענף ד׳ ובשער השתלשלות הי״ס ריש ענף ב׳. ולכ״א בראשית בשביל התורה שנקראת ראשית ובשביל ישראל שנקראו ראשית. (ולכן אמרו ז״ל (מ״ק כ״ה א׳) העומד על המת בשעת יציאת נשמה חייב לקרוע הא למ״הד לרואה ס״ת שנשרף. שקדושה נשמת כל א׳ מישראל היא היא קדושת ס״ת ממש). ולכן מעת הבריאה שהיתה התורה גנוזה עדיין במקור שרשה הנעלם מכל העולמות עליונים. ומרחוק לבד האירה לכל העולמות להחיותם ולקיימם. ולא נשתלשלה עצמותה ממש למטה לזה העולם שיעסקו בה קרוצי מטה. עדיין היו העולמות רופפים ורותתים ולא היו על מכונם האמתי. וקראום רז״ל שני אלפים תהו. והיו תלוים ועומדים עד עת מ״ת. כידוע מאמרם ז״ל (שבת פ״ח א׳) שהתנה הקב״ה עם מע״ב אם מקבלין ישראל וכו׳ ואם לאו וכו׳. וכ״ה בשמות רבה פמ״ז ודברים רבה ספ״ח ובריש התנחומא. וברבה שה״ש דמיתיך רעיתי רבנן אמרי רעיתי דעולמי שקבלו תורתי שאלו לא קבלו הייתי מחזיר את עולמי לתו״ב דאר״ח בשם ר״א כתיב נמוגים ארץ כו׳ אנכי תכנתי עמודיה סלה אלולי ישראל שעמדו על הר סיני כו׳ ומי בסס העולם אנכי כו׳ בזכות אנכי ה׳ אלהיך תכנתי עמודיה סלה. ומאז שנשתלשלה וירדה כביכול ממקור שרשה הנעלם לזה העולם כמאמרם ז״ל בא משה והורידה לארץ. כל חיותם וקיומם של כל העולמות הוא רק ע״י הבל פינו והגיוננו בה. והאמת בלתי שום ספק כלל. שאם היה העולם כולו מקצה עד קצהו פנוי ח״ו אף רגע אחת ממש מהעסק והתבוננות שלנו בתורה. כרגע היו נחרבים כל העולמות עליונים ותחתונים והיו לאפס ותהו חס ושלום. וכן שפעת אורם או מיעוטו ח״ו הכל רק כפי ענין ורוב עסקנו בה. לכן אנו מברכים עליה וחיי עולם נטע בתוכנו. כענין הנטיעה שנטיעתה כדי לעשות פרי להרבות טובה. כן אם אנו מחזיקים בתוה״ק בכל כחנו כראוי. אנו מנחילין חיי עד וממשיכים משרשה הנעלם למעלה מכל העולמות. תוספות קדושה וברכה

ואור

שער ד

פרק י

ובשעת העסק והעיון בתורה. ודאי שא״צ אז לענין הדביקות כלל. כנ״ל שבהעסק ועיון לבד הוא דבוק ברצונו ודבורו ית״ש והוא ית״ש ורצונו ודבורו חד. והוא ענין מאמרם ז״ל בשמות רבה פל״ג אדם לוקח חפץ שמא יכול לקנות בעליו. אבל הקב״ה נתן תורה לישראל ואומר להם כביכול לי אתם לוקחים כו׳. וז״ש בכ״מ בזוהר דקב״ה ואורייתא חד. וגדולה מזו בפ׳ בשלח ס׳ ע״א ואוליפנא דקב״ה תורה איקרי כו׳ ואין תורה אלא קב״ה. וגם כי שרשה העליון של התורה הקדושה הוא בעליון שבהעולמות הנקראים עולמות הא״ס. סוד המלבוש הנעלם הנזכר בסתרי פליאות חכמה מתורת רבינו האריז״ל. שהוא ראשית סוד אותיות התורה הקדוש׳. וכמ״ש ה׳ קנני ראשית דרכו קדם מפעליו מאז. וא״ם ז״ל שקדמה לעולם היינו גם מכל העולמות כולם. שהרי אמרו בב״ר פ״א שקדמה לכסא הכבוד. והאמת שקדמה כביכול גם לעולם האצילות יתברך כנ״ל. אלא שהאצילות נקר׳ אין ומסוד הכסא מתחיל סוד השיעור קומה כביכול לכן אמרו שקדמה לכסא הכבוד. ולכן בה נאצלו ונבראו כל העולמות עליונים ותחתונים. כמ״ש (משלי ח) ואהיה אצלו אמון ואמרו ז״ל א״ת אמון אלא אומן וכו׳. ובמשלי רבתא רפ״ט חכמות בנתה ביתה זו התורה שבנתה כל העולמות:

והענין כי התורה הקדושה היא דבורו ית״ש. ובמאמר פיו ית״ש במע״ב נבראו העולמות כולם. שע״י סידור גלגול צרופי האותיות עפ״י סדר הרל״א שערים פנים ואחור שבמאמר בראשית ברא וכו׳. נאצלו ונבראו העולמות עליונים עליונים רבי רבוון בכל סדר מצבם ופרטי עניניהם וכל הנכלל בהם. וכן בכל מאמר ומאמר שבו ע״ד הנ״ל נבראו כל פרטי המינים והענינים שבאותו הסוג שעליו נאמר אותו המאמר. כמ״ש בזוהר תרומה קס״א א׳ דכד ברא קוב״ה עלמא אסתכל בה באורייתא וברא עלמא ובאורייתא אתברי עלמא כמה דאוקמוה דכתיב ואהיה אצלו אמון כו׳ אורייתא לוותה ואסיה אצלו אמון כד ברא קוב״ה עלמא דעד לא אתברי עלמא אקדימת אורייתא כו׳. וכד בעא קוב״ה למברי עלמא הוה מסתכל בה באורייתא בכל מלה ומלה ועביד לקבלה אומנותא דעלמא בגין דכל מלין ועובדין דכל עלמין באורייתא אינון כו׳. באורייתא כתיב בה בראשית ברא וכו׳ אסתכל בהאי מלה וברא את השמים. כתיב בה ויאמר אלקים יהי אור אסתכל בהאי מלה וברא את האור. וכן בכל מלה ומלה דכתיב בה באורייתא אסתכל קוב״ה ועביד ההוא מלה. וע״ד כ׳ ואהיה אצלו אמון כגיד כל עלמא אתברי׳ ע״כ. ולכן כל התורה בכלל וכל העולמות כלליהם ופרטיהם וסדורם וכל עניניהם כולם כלולים ורמוזים בעשר המאמרות דמע״ב. וכמ״ש רבינו הגדול הגאון החסיד מוהר״א זלוק״ל בפי׳ על הספ״ד בפ״ה. ועיין בזה בזוהר בראשית מ״ז א:

ולכן אמרו בזוהר דאורייתא היא נשמתא דכל עלמין וחיותא וקיומא ושרשא דכלהון:

והענין כי העולמות הולכים על סדר ההשתלשלות וההדרגה. שכל עולם היותר עליון וגבוה הוא נשמתו וחיותו וקיומו ואורו של העולם שתחתיו לבד. אמנם יתרון עולם האצילות על הג׳ עולמות בי״ע. שהוא מתפשט ומאיר לכל הג׳ עולמות בי״ע שתחתיו. ע׳ בע״ח שער פנימיות וחיצונות דרוש ב׳ ושם ריש דרוש ח׳ וליש דרוש י׳ ובשער דרושי אבי״ע פ״ז ובשער השמות פ״א ובשער קליפת נגה פ״א. שכולו אלקות גמור. כמ״ש בהקדמת התיקונים דע״ס דאצילות מלכא בהון איהו וגרמיה חד בהון איהו וחיוהי חד בהון מה דלאו הכי בע״ס דבריאה

שער ד

אמנם מורות בזה. שכמו במ"ות הנס שנראה כגזל ואונאה. אמנם כיון שהקב עפר הוא השימור והקיום של כל הכור תבואה אינו חושש משום גזל. כן רשאי האדם להפסיק ולבטל זמן מועט מהלימוד. להתבונן מעט ביראת ה'. ואינו חושש בזה משום ביטול תורה כיון שהוא הגורם שתתקיים אצלו חכמת התורה:

פרק ח אמנם דון מינה כמו מענין ב' המשלים שהמשילו ז"ל

בענין התורה והיראה. היפך מאשר שגו בזה כמה מרבית בני עמנו. שקובעים כל עסק לימודם בספרי יראה ומוסר לבד. שכמו בענין קדימת האוצר לתבואה שבתוכו. וכי יעלה כלל על לב אדם כיון שכל קיום ושימור התבואה הוא האוצר יעסוק כל זמנו או רובו בבנין האוצר לבד. ולא יכנים בו תבואה מעולם. כן איך יעלה על לב איש לומר שזה תכלית האדם מישראל. שישים כל קביעת לימודו בבנין האוצר של י"ש לבד. והוא אוצר ריק. ולא עלתה בידו מכל עמלו רק מצוה א' של ה' אלקיך תירא. וגם אין עליה שם אוצר כלל. ולא כיוונו רז"ל במאמרם הנ"ל אין לו להקב"ה כו' אלא אוצר של י"ש בלבד. אלא על אותה היראה שבתוכה מונחים המון תבואות. מקרא משנה והלכות ושארי עניני התורה. שהיראה היא אוצרם הטוב ומשמר' שיתקיימו אצלו. ערוכים ושמורים בפיו וחרותים על לוח לבו. כמו שמוכח ומוכרח ממ"ש עוד אין לו להקב"ה בעולמו אלא ד"א של הלכה בלבד. (וכידוע בשרש דבר ענין ב' הבחי' של תורה ויראת ה' במדות העליונים. שבחי' היראה לא"ל מגרמה כלום. כי היא נקי' בשה רק שהיא אוצר בית קיבול השפע עליון מבחי' התורה. וכמ"ש וה' בהיכל קדשו. ועי' בתיקונים ת"ב וג'). וזש"ה (משלי ט"ו) טוב מעט ביראת ה' מאוצר רב ומהומה בו:

פרק ט וכן בענין ההיתר להפסיק באמצע הלימוד להתבונן עוד מעט

ביראת ה'. שהמשילוהו ז"ל להתיר עירוב הקב חומטין בכור תבואה. מינה כמי. שכמו שאם עירב בכור תבואה יותר מקב חומטין אשר אינו צריך לקיום התבואה. הרי זה גזל ואונאה. כן בענין היראה. אם יאריך בה האדם זמן יותר מכדי מדתה הנצרך לקיום ושימור רב תבואות התורה. הרי זה גוזל אותו הזמן הפנוי מהתורה שהיה צריך ללמוד באותו העת. כי לא הורשה לעסוק בהתבוננות וקניית היראה. אלא כפי אשר ישקול בשכלו לפי טבעו ועניינו. שזה העת הוא צורך והכרחי לו לעסוק בקניית היראה ומוסר. לצורך השימור והקיום של תבואת התורה: **ובאמת** כי האדם הקבוע בעסק התורה לשמה כמו שפירשתי בפ"ג ענין לשמה. אינו צריך לרוב עמל ויגיעה ואורך זמן העסק בספרי יראה עד שיוקבע בלבו יראתו ית'. כאותו האדם אשר אינו קבוע בעסק התורה. כי התורה הקדושה מעצמה תלבישהו יראת ה' על פניו במעט זמן ויגיעה מועטת ע"ז. כי כך דרכה וסגולתה של התורה הקדושה כמ"ש כל העוסק בתורה לשמה כו' ומלבשתו ענוה ויראה. ודמשלי רבה פ"א חכמה ומוסר אוילים בזו אם מוסר למה חכמה ואם חכמה כו' אלא אם למד אדם תורה וישב ונתעסק בה כדי צרכו הרי בידו חכמה ומוסר ואם לאו כו'. ובת"דא סא"ר פי"ח ועל הנחל יעלה על שפתו מזה ומזה כל עץ מאכל כו' (יחזקאל מ"ז) ומהו העץ אשר יעלה בנחל זה אלו ת"ח שיש בהם תורה מקרא ומשנ' הלכות ואגדות ומעשים ושימוש ת"ח כו'. משלו משל למה"ד כו'. כך ת"ח בעוה"ז בד"א כיון שקראו את המקרא ושנו כו' וד"ת מתוק עליהם. הקב"ה מרחם עליהם ונותן בהם חכמה ובינה ודעה והשכל לעשות מע"ט ותיה והבל מתוקן לפניהם כו':

פרק

שבכל עת שיכין האדם עצמו ללמוד ראוי לו להתיישב קודם שיתחיל · עכ"פ זמן מועט ביראת ה' טהורה בטהרת הלב להתודות על חטאתו מעומקא דלבא · כדי שתהא תורתו קודש וטהורה · ויכוין להתדבק בלימודו בו בתורה בו בהקב"ה · היינו להתדבק בכל כחותיו לדבר ה' זו הלכה · ובזה הוא דבוק בו ית' ממש כביכול · כי הוא יתב' ורצונו חד כמ"ש בזוהר · וכל דין והלכה מתורה הקדושה הוא רצונו ית' שכן גזרה רצונו שיהא כך הדין כשר או פסול טמא וטהור אסור ומותר חייב וזכאי · וגם אם הוא עסיק בדברי אגדה שאין בהם נפקותא לשום דין ג"כ הוא דבוק בדבורו של הקב"ה · כי התור' כולה בכלליה ופרטיה ודקדוקיה · ואפי' מה שהתלמיד קטן שואל מרבו הכל יצא מפיו ית' למשה בסיני · כמ"ש רז"ל סוף פ"ב דמגילה · ובפ"ק דברכו' ה' א' ובקהל' רבה ס"א פי"א ושם בסי' ה' פ"ו ובירושלמי פ"ב דפאה ובויקרא רבה פ"כב ע"ש · ובשמות רבה פ"מג כתב לך את הדברים האלה בשעה שנגלה הקב"ה בסיני ליתן תורה לישראל אמר למשה על הסדר · מקרא ומשנה הלכות ואגדות שנא' וידבר אלקים את כל הדברים האלה · אפילו מה שהתלמיד שואל לרב ע"כ · ולא עוד אלא כי גם באותו העת שהאדם עוסק בתורה למטה · כל תיבה שמוציא מפיו הן הן הדברים יוצאים כביכול גם מפיו ית' באותו העת ממש · כדאשכחן בפ"ק דגיטין גבי פלגש בגבעה' והנה עליו פלגשו ר' אביתר אמר זבוב מצא לה רי"א נימא כו · ואשכחי' ר"א לאלי' א"ל מאי קעביד קב"ה א"ל עסיק בפלגש בגבעה ומאי קאמר אביתר בני כך הוא אומר יונתן בני כך הוא אומר · והיינו מפני שר"א ור"י עסקו ביניהם בענין פלגש בגבעה או באותו עת · גם הוא ית' שנה דבריהם ממש · והוא ית"ש ודבורו חד · וכמפורש בתו"הק במשנה תורה לאהבה את ה' אלהיך כו' ופירשוהו רז"ל בנדרים בברייתא (ס"ב א') דקאי על עסק התורה ע"ש וסיפי' דקרא ולדבקה בו · ולכן אמר דוד המ"ע טוב לי תורת פיך כו' · אמר כי לבי שמח בעמלי בתורה הקדושה ברוב עוז בהעלותי על לבי שהיא תורת פיך שכל תיבה ממש מהתורה שאני עוסק בה כעת הכל יצא · וגם עתה היא יוצאת מפיך יתב' · ולכן כל התורה קדושתה שוה בלי שום חילוק ושינוי כלל ח"ו · כי הכל דבור פיו ית"ש ממש · ואם חסר בס"ת אות א' מפסוק אלוף תמנע היא נפסלת · כמו אם היה נחסר אות א' מעשרת הדברות · או מפסוק שמע ישראל · וכמ"ש גם הרמב"ם ז"ל והוא מתד"א סא"ז פ"ג :

פרק ז ולזאת ראוי להאדם להכין עצמו כל עת קודם שיתחיל ללמוד · להתחשב מעט עם קונו ית"ש בטהרת הלב ביראת ה' · ולהטהר מטומאתו בהרהורי תשובה · כדי שיוכל להתקשר ולהתדבק בעת עסקו בתוה"ק בדבורו ורצונו ית"ש · וגם יקבל ע"ע לעשות ולקיים ככל הכתוב בתורה שבכתב ובע"פ · ואשר יראה ויבין דרכו והנהגתו מתוה"ק · וכן כשרוצה לעיין בדבר הלכה · ראוי להתפלל שיזכהו ית' לאשוקי שמעתא אליבא דהלכתא · לכוין לאמיתה של תורה :

וכן באמצע הלימוד · הרשות נתונה להאדם להפסיק זמן מועט · טרם יכבה מלבו יראתו ית"ש שקיבל עליו קודם התחלת הלימוד . להתבונן · מחדש עוד מעט ביראת ה' · כשרז"ל עוד (שבת לא) משל לאדם שאמר לשלוחו העלה לי כור של חטים לעליה כו' א"ל עירבת לי בהן קב חומטין א"ל לא · א"ל מוטב שלא העלית · וקאי על אמצע העסק בתבואות תבונות התורה שראוי ג"כ לערב בתוכו יראתו יתב' · כדי שתתקיים תלמודו בידו · ולכן סמך אללו הברייתא תני דבי ר"י מערב אדם קב חומטין בכור של תבואה ואינו חושש · והוא דין מדיני גזל והונאה אחר מקומו בס' נזיקין ומאי שייטי' הכא ·

שער ד

מ"ד והיה אמונת עתיך כו' אמונת זה סדר זרעים כו' · חשיב שם בזה הפסוק כל הש"ס ומסיים ואפ"ה יראת ה' היא אוצרו · דמה הכתוב את התורה לרב תבואות· והיראה לאוצר המחזיק בו המון תבואות ומשתמרים בתוכו · שיראת ה' היא האוצר לחכמת התו"הק שעל ידה תתקיים אצל האדם . ואם לא הכין לו האדם תחלה אוצר היראה·הרי רב תבואות התורה כמונח ע"פ השדה למרמס רגל השור והחמור ח"ו שאינה מתקיימת אצלו כלל · וכן אמרו ע"ז הכתוב בשמות רבה פ"ל אתה מוצא אדם שונה מדרש הלכות ואגדות ואם אין בו יראת חטא אין בידו כלום משל לאדם כו' יש לי אלף מדות של תבואה · א"ל יש לך אפותיקאות ליתן אותם בהם כו' · שנאמר והיה אמונת עתך כו' ע"ש · :

פרק ה

ולפי ערך גודל אוצר היראה אשר הכין לו האדם· כן ע"ז הערך יוכל ליכנס ולהשמר ולהתקיים בתוכו תבואות התורה כפי אשר יחזיק אוצרו · כי האב המחלק התבואה לבניו · הוא מחלק ונותן לכל א' מדת התבואה כפי אשר יחזיק אוצרו של הבן אשר הכין ע"ז מקודם· שאף אם ירצה האב וידו פתוחה ליתן לו הרבה· אמנם כיון שהבן אינו יכול לקבל יותר מחמת שאין אוצרו גדול כ"כ שיוכל להחזיק יותר · גם האב א"א לו ליתן לו עתה יותר · ואם לא הכין לו הבן אף אוצר קטן · גם האב לא יתן לו כלל · כיון שאין לו מקום מבורר שתתקיים אצלו · כן הוא ית"ש ידו פתוחה כביכול להשפיע תמיד לכל איש מטוב סגולתו רב חכמה ובינה יתירה ושתתקיים אצלם ויקשרם על לוח לבם להשתעשע אתם בבואם לעולם המנוחה ותלמודם בידם · אמנם הדבר תלוי לפי אוצר היראה שתקדם אל האדם · שאם הכין לו האדם אוצר גדול של יראת ה' טהורה · כן ה' יתן לו חכמה ותבונה ברוב שפע כפי שמחזיק אוצרו · *) הכל לפי גודל אוצרו · ואם לא הכין האדם אף אוצר קטן שאין בו יראתו ית' כלל ח"ו · גם הוא ית' לא ישפיע לו שום חכמה כלל· אחר שלא תתקיים אצלו · כי תורתו נמאסת ח"ו כמש"רזל · וע"ז אמר הכתוב (תהלים קי"א) ראשית חכמה יראת ה' · וכמבואר בהקדמת הזוהר ז' ב' ר"ח פתח ראשית חכמה יראת ה' כו' האי קרא הכי מבעי לי' סוף חכמה כו' · אלא איהי ראשית לאעלא לגו דרגא דחכמתא עלאה כו' · תרעא קדמאה לחכמה עלאה · יראת ה' איהי כו' ע"ש :

הרי מבואר · הגם שהיראה היא מצוה א' ואמרו בירושלמי ריש פאה שכל המצו' אינן שוות לדבר א' מן התורה אמנם מצות קניית היראה ממנו ית' רבה היא מאד · מצד שהיא מוכרחת לעיקר הקיום ושימור התו"הק ובלאה גם נמאסת ח"ו בעיני הבריות · לכן צריכה שתקדם אצל האדם קודם עסק התורה :

הגה"ה

*) **ובזה** יבואר מאמרם ז"ל ריש פרק הרואה אין הקב"ה נותן חכמה אלא למי שיש בו חכמה שנאמר ובלב כל חכם לב נתתי חכמה · יהיב חכמתא לחכימין (דניאל ב) · ולכאורה יפלא· דא"כ חכמה הראשונה מאין תמצא אצל האד' אמנם הענין· כי כתוב מפורש שגם היראה נקראת חכמה כמ"ש (איוב כ"ח) ויאמר לאדם הן יראת ה' היא חכמה· והוא מטעם הנ"ל · שהיא אוצרו הטוב של החכמה שתשתמר ותתקיים בה ז"ש שאין הקב"ה נותן ומשפיע חכמה העליונה של התורה · שתתקיים אצלו ויהא תלמודו בידו· אלא למי שיש בו חכמה היינו אוצר היראה· שהיא מוכרחת שתקדם אצל האדם כנ"ל · (ואיש תבונות · יבין פנימיות מאמרם ז"ל זה לדרכנו ע"פ סתרי הזוהר וכתבי הא"ריז"ל · אשר אמרו שהחכמה העליונה מתגלית רק ע"י מדת מלכותו יתברך היינו קבלת עול מ"ש כנ"ל : **ובזה** יובן ג"כ שתלים לרז"ל שאמרו אין לו להקב"ה בעולמו אלא ד' אמות של הלכה בלבד (ברכות ח' ע"א) ובפ' אין עומדין (ל"ג ב) אמרו אין לו להקב"ה בבית גנזיו אלא אוצר של יראת שמים בלבד · ולדבריהם באמת הכל א'· ולכן אמרו אוצר של יראת שמים· ע"כ :

פרק ו

לזאת האמת שזו היא הדרך האמתי אשר בזה בחר הוא ית"ש ·

שבכל

שער ד

פרק ג אבל האמת · כי ענין לשמה פירש לשם התורה · והענין כמו שפירש הרא"ש ז"ל על מאמר ר"א בר' צדוק (נדרים ס"ב א') עשה דברים לשם פעלן ודבר בהן לשמן · ז"ל עשה דברים לשם פעלן · לשמו של הקב"ה שפעל הכל למענהו · ודבר בהן לשמן · כל דבורך ומשאך בד"ת יהיה לשם התורה כגון לידע ולהבין ולהוסיף לקח ופלפול ולא לקנטר ולהתגאות עכ"ל דקדק לבאר שינוי לשונו דר"א ב"צ שבעשיה אמר לשם פעלן · ובדבור אמר לשמן · לכן בענין העשיה פירש לשמו של הקב"ה שפעל הכל למענהו · ובענין הלמוד פירש לשם התורה כו' · וכוונתו ז"ל מבואר היינו כי עשיית המצוה ודאי שצריכה להיות למצוה מן המובחר בדביקות ומחשבה טהורה שבטהורות כפי שכלו והשגתו · כדי שיתקלס עילאה לגרום תיקוני העולמות וכחות וסדרים העליונים · וזהו לשם פעלן כי כל פעל ה' למענהו ואז"ל לקילוסו · ואם כי ודאי שגם במצות העיקר בהם לעכובא הוא העשיה בפועל · והכוונה היתירה וטוהר המחשבה אינה מעכבת כלל כמו שנתבאר לעיל סוף שער א' על נכון בע"ה · עכ"ז מצטרף קדושת וטוהר מחשבתו לעיקר העשי' בפועל לעורר ולפעול תקונים יותר גדולים בהעולמות מאם היתה המצוה נעשית בלא דביקות וקדושת המחשבה · אבל על הנהגת האדם בשעת עסק התורה בדיני המצות והלכותיהן אמר ודבר בהן ר"ל הדבור בעניני המצו' והלכותיהן · יהיה לשמן · פי' לשם הד"ת היינו לידע ולהבין ולהוסיף לקח ופלפול · (ורש"י ז"ל גי' אחרת היתה לו שם ודבר בהן לשם שמים · לכן פירש שתהא כל כונתך לשמים · אמנם ענין ופי' לשמה שארז"ל בכ"מ ודאי שגם רש"י ז"ל יפרש כפי' הרא"ש ז"ל כאן לפי גרסתו · וגם רש"י ז"ל כאן אין כונתו דביקות · אלא דאתי לאפוקי שלא יהא לימודו לשם קינטור וגיאות כמ"ש הרא"ש ז"ל · כדמוכח מסיום דברי רא"בצ אל תעשם עטרה להתגדל בהם כו') · וזהו שמסיים הש"ס גבי ריב"ז שלא תאמר כו' לקיים מה שנאמר להנחיל אוהבי יש כו' · שמבואר הענין שם בכל אותה הפרשה שהוא מאמר התורה הקדושה עצמה אשר בחוץ תרונה · שיש לאל ידה להנחיל וליתן שכר טוב לכל ההוגה ועוסק בה מחמת אהבתה עצמה ממש · היינו להוסיף בה לקח ופלפול · וזהו אוהבי:

פרק ד אמנם ודאי דא"א לומר שח"ו לענין עסק התורה שום טוהר המחשבה ויראת ה' חלילה · שהרי משנה שלימה שנינו אם אין יראה אין חכמה · ואמרו (יומא ע"ב ב') מ"ד למה זה מחיר ביד כסיל לקנות חכמה ולב אין אוי להם לת"ח שעוסקים בתורה ואין בהם י"ש כו' · ובשמות רבה פ"מ כל מי שהוא יודע ואין בידו יראת חטא אין בידו כלום שקפליות של תורה ביראת חטא · ובהקדמת הזוהר י"א ב' אמר רשב"י שיראה איהי תרעא לאעלא לגו מהימנותא ועל פקודא דא אתקיים כל עלמא כו' ודא עקרא ויסודא לכל שאר פקודין דאורייתא מאן דנטיר יראה נטיר כולא לא נטיר יראה לא נטיר פקודי אורייתא כו' ע"ש: ובפ' בהר ק"ח א' מאי עול מ"ש אלא כהאי תורא כו' ה"נ אצטריך לי' לבר נש לקבלא עלי' עול בקדמיתא ולבתר דיפלח לי' בכל מה דאצטריך · ואי לא קביל עליה האי בקדמיתא לא ייכול למפלח · הה"ד עבדו את ה' ביראה נוהו ביראה כד"א ראשית חכמה יראת ה' כו' · וע"ד האי בקדמייתא הוא דכלא כו' בגין דבהאי עייל לשאר קדושה ואי האי לא אשתכח לגביה לא שריא ביה קדושה דלעילא כו': ואמרו עוד כל שיראת חטאו קודמת לחכמתו חכמתו מתקיימת · כי יראת ה' תחלה היא עיקר הקיום של חכמת התורה · ובמשרז"ל (שבת ל' ע"א) אר"ל

מ"ד

שער ד

הן לזאת עיר במלין מי יוכל · להודיע בשבטי ישראל נאמנה ליראי ה' וחושבי שמו את הדרך ילכו בה לאורה של תורה · אוי לנו מיום הדין · אוי לנו מיום התוכחה על עון ביטולה של תורה כאשר הוא ית"ש יקנא לה לתבוע עלבונה: ותחלה אשים דברתי בענין עסק התורה לשמה מהו ענין לשמה · כי גם זה פרי תאות לכמה המונעים עצמן מעסק התורה הקדוש'. בחשבם כי ענין לשמה פי' בדביקות גדול בלי הפסק · וגם רעה חולה יותר מזה · שסוברים בטעות שעסק התורה בלא דביקות אין כלום וללא שום תועלת ח"ו · לזאת כשרואין עצמן שאין לבם הולך לזאת המדרגה שיהא לימודם בדביקות תמידי · לא יתחילו כלל ללמוד · ועי"כ תשתכח תורה ח"ו · ומהמשך הענינים יתבאר אי"ה ממילא מעלתה של התורה הקדושה והאדם העוסק בה כראוי · לזאת הוכרחתי להביא קצת ממאמרי רז"ל בש"ס ומדרשים וזוהר אשר בם ידובר נפלאות מעלת התור' הקדוש' והעוסק בה וגודל שכרה ועונשה ר"ל · הגם שכל אלו המאמרים ידועים ומפורסמים · עכ"ז קבצתים לשלהב לבות התמימים להתדבק באהבת תורתו ית' · ולהתלונן בצל העליון נורא:

פרק ב ענין עסק התורה לשמה · האמת הברור · כי לשמה אין פירושו

דביקות כמו שסוברים עתה רוב העולם · שהרי אחז"ל במדרש שבקש דוד המע"ה מלפניו ית' שהעוסק בתהלים יחשב אצלו ית' כאלו היה עוסק בנגעים ואהלות · הרי שהעסק בהלכות הש"ס בעיון ויגיעה הוא ענין יותר נעלה ואהוב לפניו ית' מאמיר' תהלים · ואם נאמר שלשמה פי' דביקות דוקא ורק בזה תלוי כל עיקר ענין עסק התורה · הלא אין דביקות יותר נפלא מאמירת תהלים כראוי כל היום · וגם מי יודע אם הסכים הקב"ה ע"ז בזה · כי לא מצינו בדבריהם ז"ל אם תשובה השיבו הוא יתברך על שאלתו (כמו שמצינו ב"ב יז א ואידךהוא רחמי' הוא דקא בעי) · וגם כי היה די לענין הדביקות · במסכת אחת או פרק או משנה א' שיעסיק בה כל ימיו בדביקות · ולא כן מצינו לרז"ל שאמרו על ריב"ז שלא הניח מקרא משנה הלכות ואגדות כו' · והיינו כי מהעלותו על לבו תמיד כי עדן לא יצא י"ח עסק התורה לשמה במה שלמד עד עתה · לזאת היה שוקד כל ימיו להוסיף לקח תמיד מיום ליום ומשעה לשעה · ובמשלי רבתא פ"י א"ר י' בא וראה כמה קשה יום הדין שעתיד הקב"ה לדון את כל העולם כולו כו' · בא מי שיש בידו מקרא ואין בידו משנה הקב"ה הופך את פניו ממנו ומצירי גיהנם מתגברין בו כו' · והם נוטלין אותו ומשליכין אותו לגיהנם · בא מי שיש בידו שני סדרים או שלשה הקב"ה א"ל בני כל ההלכות למה לא שנית אותם כו' · בא מי שיש בידו הלכות א"ל בני תורת כהנים למה לא שנית שיש בו כו' · בא מי שיש בידו ת"כ הקב"ה א"ל בני חמשה חומשי תורה למה לא שנית שיש בהם ק"ש תפילין ומזוזה · בא מי שיש בידו חמשה חומשי תורה א"ל הקב"ה למה לא למדת הגדה כו' · בא מי שיש בידו הגדה הקב"ה א"ל בני תלמוד למה לא למדת כו' · בא מי שיש בידו תלמוד הקב"ה א"ל בני הואיל ונתעסקת בתלמוד צפית במרכבה כו' · כסא כבודי האיך הוא עומד כו' · חשמל האיך הוא עומד · ובכמה פנים הוא מתהפך כו' ע"ש באורך: ומסתברא נמי הכי · שהרי כמה הלכות מרובות יש בש"ס שבעת אשר האדם עוסק בהם · הוא צריך לעיין ולהעמיק מחשבתו ושכלו בעניני הגשמיות שבהם · כגון קינין ופתחי נדה שהן הן גופי הלכות · או המשא ומתן בש"ס וכללי דיני מיגו של רמאות שהיה הרמאי יכול לטעון · וכמעט בלתי אפשר שיהא אצלו אז גם הדביקו' כשלימו כראוי ·

פרק

שער ד

פרק א

עוד זאת

אמרתי לבא במגלת ספר כתוב בגודל החיוב של עסק התורה · על כל איש ישראל יום ולילה · ולהרחיב מעט הדבור בלשון מדברת גדולת יקר תפארתה ומעלתה של התורה · והאדם הישר העוסק והוגה בה בתורת השם על לשמו לעשות נחת רוח ליוצרו ובוראו ית"ש · ואיש דעת המאמץ כח לתומכה ולסעדה ולהחזיק בדקיה · אחרי אשר זה ימים רבים לישראל שהושפל עסק תורה הקדושה בכל דור ודור · והן עתה בדורות הללו בעו"ה נגלה מאד מאד · נתונה בשפל המדרגה התחתונה ר"ל · כאשר עינינו הרואות עתה ברבת בני עמנו מגודל שפל משא עול הפרנסה ה' ירחם · וגם כמה מאותן אשר קרבת אלקים יחפצון . המה בחרו לעצמם לקביע כל עיקר לימודם בספרי יראה ומוסר כל הימים · בלא קביעות עיקר העסק בתוה"ק במקראות והלכות מרובות · ועדן לא ראו מאורות מימיהם ולא נגה עליהם אור התורה · ה' יסלח להם · כי כוונתם לשמי' · אבל לא זו הדרך ישכון בם אור התור': **והאמת** כי ספרי יראה שגם בכל דרכי ה' הישרים · כי דורות הראשונים היו קבועים כל ימיהם בעסק והגיון תוה"ק תקועים באהלי המדרשות בנ"פת · ושלהבת אהבת תוה"ק שיה בוער בלבם כאש בוערת · באהבת ויראת ה' טהורה · וכל חפצם להגדיל כבודה ולהאדירה · והרביצו גבולם בתלמידים רבים הגונים למען תמלא הארץ דעה · וכאשר ארכו הימים · הנה כן דרש של היצר מעולם להתקנא בעם ה' אלה · כאשר המה דורכים בדרך ה' כראוי · להטיל בהם ארס · עד שכמה מהתלמידים שמו כל קביעותם ועסקם רק בפלפולה של תורה לבד ולא זולת כלל · ושנינו במשנתינו אם אין יראה אין חכמה · ועוד הרבה מאמרי רז"ל מזה כמו שיובא להלן פ"ד אי"ה · לזאת התעוררו עצמם כמה מגדוליהם עיני העדה אשר דרכם בקדש לשקוד על תקנם כלל אחינו בית ישראל · ליישר ההדורים ולגדור פרצותם . להרים המכשול מדרך עם ה' · ומלאו את ידם לבוא בתוכחות במוסרים ומדות · וחברו ספרי יראה להישיר לב העם · להיותם עוסקים בתורה הקדוש' ובעבוד' ביראת ה' טהורה · אמנם כל איש תבונות אשר שכלו ישר הולך . יבין מדעתו כי לא כיונו בהם להזניח ח"ו העסק בגופי התורה · ולהיות אך עסוק כל הימים בספרי מוסרם · אלא כוונתם רצויה היתה שכל עיקר קביעת לימוד עם הקדש · יהיה רק בתורה הקדושה שבכתב ובעל פה והלכות מרובות · הן הן גופי תורה · וגם ביראה ה' טהורה :

והן עתה בדורות הללו · בעוה"ר נהפוך הוא · הגבוה השפל · שכמה וכמה שמו כל עיקר קביעת לימודם רוב הימים רק בספרי יראה ומוסר · באמרם כי זה כל האדם בעולמו לעסוק בהם תמיד · כי המה מלהיבים הלבבות אשר אז יכנע לבבו להכניע ולשבר היצר מתאוותיו · ולהתיישר במדות טובות · וכתר תורה מונח בקרן זוית · ובעיני ראיתי בפלך א' שרוב התפשט אלגם זאת · עד שברוב בתי מדרשם אין בהם רק ספרי מוסר לרוב · ואפי' ש"ס א' פלס אין בו · וטח עיניהם מראות מהבין והשכיל לבותם · אשר לא זו הדרך בחר בו ה' כי לא ירצה · ועוד מעט בהמשך הזמן יוכלו להיות ח"ו ללא כהן מורה ותורה מה תהא עליה :

כא   אן

הכוכבים · וכשאדם אומר לחבירו נתפלל תפלת מנחה · הוא משיבו נראה ונעיין אם כבר נראו הכוכבים ברקיע · וה' יסלח להם · ויכפר לשוגה ופתי :

פרק ח

אבל לבך תשית לדעת חכמים בעלי תורה אשר כבר הורונו חז"ל שהעיק' היא עשיית המצוה בזמנה בכל פרטיה ודקדוקיה אך ולא יעבור · וטהרת המחשבה טובה תצרף למעשה · אז תלך לבטח · וזה וזה יתקיימו בידיך · ומשנה מפורשת שנו כל שמעשיו מרובים מחכמתו · אף גם חכמתו מתקיימת בקדושה וטהרה ודביקות · ומי זוטר הוא מה שהמשילו חז"ל כל שמעשיו מרובים מחכמתו לאילן שענפיו מועטין ושרשיו מרובין שכל הרוחות שבעולם אין מזיזין אותו ממקומו · והשומע ישמע :

גם במעשים ועניינים אחרים לבד המצות · ואף גם לעבור על איזה מצוה שלא כתורה· כפי שראו והשינו שזה הענין והמעשה הפרטית הוא נצרך או לתיקון העולמות· (וע' מזה בסו' ס' האמונו' לרס"ט· וכן הביא שם כן בשם רבינו חושיאל גאון ז"ל · רק שקיצר מאד בעמן· כדרכם בקדש של כל הראשונים ז"ל שהעלימו והסתירו מאד כל הענינים) · ואתה תחזה אם עיני שכל לך · שאין כאן לא ראיה ולא סמך כלל · אף לא משענת קנה רצוץ · כי האמת הברור כמו שנתבאר לעיל סוף שער א' · שהעבודה על זה הדרך לא היתה נוהגת אלא קודם מתן תורה לבד · אבל מעת שבא משה והורידה לארץ · לא בשמים היא · והוכחנו שם בע"ה מענין חזקיהו עם ישעיהו · שאסור לנו לשנות ח"ו משום אחת נוהגה ממצות ה' · אף אם תהיה הכונה לשם שמים · ואף אם ישיג האדם שאם יקיים מצותו המוטלת עליו יוכל למיפק מיניה חורבא באיזה ענין · ואף גם בשב ואל תעשה · עכ"ז אין הדבר מסור ביד האדם להמנע ממנה ח"ו · כי טעמי מצות לא נתגלו · וע"ש באורך :

פרק ח עוד אחה יוכל לפתותך בחבילות ראיות · שתכלית-עבודת

האדם הוא רק להשיג יראת הרוממות · ורק על זה יהיו עיניו ולבו כל הימים · ושיראת העונש ובושה מבני אדם · היא מדה גרועה שבגרועות · והראוי לשרש אותה מלבך · ויניח לך יצרך להוסיף יראה על יראה ביראת הרוממות עד שיקבע בלבך שיראת העונש והבושה מבני אדם היא עבירה · ותהיה בורח ממנה כבורח מן העבירה · עד שיוכל להיות שתלכד ברשתו שלא לאפרושי מאיסורא בזמן שאין לך יראת הרוממות כראוי · ויקל לך כל דבר באשר יראה לך פגים מפנים שונים בזה·ויוכל להולד מזה· שאם יוכיחך אדם ויראה לך שאתה עובר על איזה דין · ישיאך לבך ·שלא לאפרושי מזה כל זמן שיראת המוכיח עלי פניך · באמרך שרק אין יראת אלקים בזה רק יראת אדם · ויראה חצונית · וכבר הורונו חז"ל בברכת ריב"ז לתלמידיו (ברכות) שתהא מורא שמים עליכם כמורא ב"וד וכו' · ומי לנו גדול וחסיד מדב עמרם חסידא · ועכ"ז כשנזדמן לידו פעם א' דבר עבירה פתאום ר"ל כמובא שלהי קדושין · נלחם בתחבולות להנצל מרשת יצרו אף מחמת הבושה מהבריות · רק שלא לעבור ח"ו על מצות בוראו ית"ש · ונראה הגם שהקב"ה חס על כבודן של צדיקים · עכ"ז קבעוה להאי עובדא בתלמוד· להורות לנו דרכי ה' הישרים :

ועתה הראיתיך קצות דרכי היצר המתחפש בכל מיני תחבולות · כמשרז"ל (קדושין למ"ד ע"ב) א"ר יצחק יצרו של אדם מתחדש עליו בכל יום שנא' רק רע כל היום · שלא די לו שמתגבר בתחבולותיו שהתנכל על האדם מתמול שלשום · אלא שעוד מחדש כל יום בחדשות · וכאלו אינו מסיתו לרע כלל · ואדרבה מראה לאדם שכל מה שלמד תורה או פעל מצות · עדן לא היה בהם שום טוב · והוא רק רע כל היום · ובזה הוא מתגבר על האדם כמ"ש ז"ל ע"פ צופה רשע לצדיק ומבקש להמיתו וכו'· והוא היצ"הר הוא המ"הת מלא עינים וצופה לראות הנולד במה להכשיל (כי ענין צפיה הוא על דבר שעתיד להיות אח"כ) · עד אשר האדם לא ידע להזהר עוד : **ואתה הקורא** · אל תדמה שמלבי הוצאתי הדברים · כי את כל זאת בחנתי ונסיתי כאשר נתתי לבי לדרוש ולתור · ועיני ראו רבים אשר יחפצו קרבת אלקים · ונכשלים במו אלה הדברים הנ"ל אשר מפיהם אלי נאמרו מלבם · ובעיני ראיתי במקום א' איזה אנשים שהורגלו בזה זמן כביר עד שכמעט נשכח מהם זמן תפלת המנחה שקבעו לנו רז"ל · ואדרבה נקבע בלבם מרוב ההרגל כמו דין והלכה שתפלת המנחה עיקרה אחר צאת הכוכבים ·

פרק הוז

אע"ג דלא יכיל לכוונא לבא ורעותא · סדורא ושבחא דמארי' אמאי גרע · אלא יסדר שבחא דמארי' אע"ג דלא יכיל לכוונא כו' :

פרק ו והנה שודאי שמחשבת האדם היא העולה למעלה ראש בשמי רום בעולמות העליונים · ואם יצרף האדם גם טוהר המחשבה והכוונה בעת עשיית המצות · יגיעו מעשיו לפעול תקונים יותר גדולים בעולמות היותר עליוני' · אמנם לא המחשבה היא העיקר אצלינו כמו שנתבא' ועיין בזוהר יתרו צ"ג ריש ע"ב ואי אזדמן לי' עובדא ויכוין בי' זכאה איהו · ואע"ג דלא מכוין בי' זכאה איהו דעביד פקודא דמארי' · אבל לא אתחשב מאן דעביד רעותא לשמה ויכוין בי' ברעותא כו' כמאן דלא ידע כו' דהא ברעותא תליא כו' ואפי' הכי אי לאו תמן רעותא דלבא כו'·עכ"ד לגי דוד ואמר ומעש' ידינו כוננה עלינו כו' · מאי כוננה עלינו כוננה ואתקין תקונין לעילא כדקא יאות · עלינו אע"ג דלית אנן ידעין לשואה רעותא אלא עובדא בלחודוי · מעשה ידינו כוננהו למאן דההוא דרגא דאצטריך לאתתקנא כו' ע"ש · וכן בענין שנתבאר למעלה בשער ג' בענין התפלה לכוין אותה למקומו של עולם ית"ש · כפי שנתבאר שם ענין מקומו של עולם ע"ש · וכן ענין כוונת אחד דפסוק ראשון דק"ש שנתבאר שם בפ"א עש"ה · הכל הוא רק למצוה ולא לעכובא · שגם מי שלא ידע בזה כלל כי לא הורגל בזה · או שמוחי' לא סביל דא שלא ירד לעומקו · או שירא לנפשו שלא יסתכן ח"ו בהריסת כמה יסודי התורה שיכול לבא מזה ח"ו למי שאין דעתו יפה בזה כראוי כמ"ש שם ע"ש · אלא שהוא עובד אותו יתב' ומקיים ככל הכתוב בתורת ה' שבכתב ובע"פ ורבותינו הגדולים · ומאמין ומכוין דרך כלל בפסוק ראשון דק"ש שהוא יתב' הוא אחד גם שאינו יודע ענין אחדותו יתב' · ומכוין תפלתו דרך כלל לו יתב' בלא חקירה · ג"כ נקרא עובד ה' · (כענין מ"ש בפרדס שער א' פ"ט בענין האמונה במציאות הספירות ע"ש) · כי אין כל הדברים האלו אמורים אלא למי שדעתו יפה · וכ"ש ליראי ה' וחושבי שמו אשר להם כח לעמוד בזה :

לזאת חלילה וחלילה לנו · לדחות שום פרט מפרטי המעשה אף דקדוק א' מד"ס · וכ"ש לשנות זמנה ח"ו · בשביל מניעת טהרת המחשב' וכל המרבה לדקדק במעשיו ה"ז משובח :

פרק ז עוד זאת יוכל יצרך להתחפש · באמור לך שכל עיקר העבודה הוא · שיהיה רק לשם שמים · וגם עון וחטא למצוה יחשב אם הוא לשם שמים לתיקון איזה ענין · ורחמנא לבא בעי · וגדולה עבירה לשמה . וכהנה רבות ראיות · גם יראה לך פנים לאמר · כי כן צויה לילך בעקבי אבותיך הקדושים וכל הצדיקים הראשונים שהיו קודם שניתנה התורה · שעיקר דרך עבודתם לו ית' היתה · שכל מעשיהם ודבורם ומחשבתם וכל ענייניה' בעולם היה הכל בדביקו' וטהרת מחשבתם לשם שמים · ופנו למעלה לתיקון והעלאת ויחוד העולמות וכחות העליונים · באיזה מעשה שתהיה ובאיזה אופן ובאיזה זמן שיהיה · ולא במעשים ומצות קבועים ומדורים שיהיו חק ולא יעבור · כמו יעקב אבינו ע"ה בענין צאן לבן והמקלות · וכן אמר המגיד להב"י בענין חנוך שהיה תופר מנעלים ובכל זמנא דמעייל מחטא בסנדלא הוה משבח לקב"ה · ע' מגיד מישרים פ' מקץ · ואף שארז"ל האבות קיימו כל התורה · וכן אמרו בויקרא רבה פ"ב מלמד שלמד נח תורה · לא שהיו מצווים ועושים והי' להם חטלכה והדין כך · אלא כמש"ל סוף שער א' שהמה קיימו את התורה מחמת שהשיגו בנפלאות השגתם תקוני העולמות וסדרי הכחות העליונים אשר יתקנו בכל מצוה ומצוה · אבל היה ג"כ הרשות נתונה להם לעבדו

גם

פרק יה

ולא זו בלבד שבמצות מעשיות · העיקר בהם
הוא חלק המעשי· אלא שגם במצות התפלה
שנקראת עבודה שבלב·ולמדוהו ז"ל בר"פ ק דתענית
מכתוב ולעבדו בכל לבבכ׳ · עכ"ז העיק׳ שצריך האד׳
לחתך בשפתיו דוקא כל תיבה מתטבע התפלה ·
כמשרז"ל בר"פ אין עומדי׳ מקראי דחנה דכתי׳ בה
רק שפתיה נעות מכאן למתפלל צרי׳ שיחתוך בשפתיו·
וכ"א בשו"ע שמואל פ"ב יכול יהא מהרהר בלב ת"ל
רק שפתיה נעות כו׳ הא כיצד מרחיש בשפתיו·וברור
הוא · דלאו לענין לכתחלה ולמצוה בעלמא הוא
דאגמרוהו · אלא גם לעכובא דיעבד · שאם הרהר
תיבות התפלה בלב לבד לא יצא י"ח תפלה כלל · ואם
עדיין לא עבר הזמן צריך להתפלל פעם אחרת
בחתוך שפתים כל תיבה · ואם עברה זמנה צריך
להתפלל שתים תפלה שאחריה · כדין מי שלא התפלל
כל עיקר · כמו שהעיר ע"ז המ"א בסי׳ ק"א ס"ק ב׳
בראיות נכונות·שהמה כדאי להכריע בלדק דבהרהור
התפלה לבד לא יצא י"ח· וידוע בזוהר וכתבי האריז"ל
שענין התפלה הוא תיקון העולמות והעלאות
פנימיותם כל בחי׳ נרנ"ן שבהם מתטה למעלה · והוא
ע"י התדבקות והתקשרות נפש האדם ברוחו ורוחו
בנשמתו כמ"ש בע"ה לעיל סוף שער ב׳ ע"ש · והם
נקשרים ע"י עקימת ותנועת שפתיו בחתוך תיבות
התפלה שהוא בחי׳ המעש׳ שבדבור כמשרז"ל עקימת
שפתיו הוי מעשה · ובפ׳ כל כתבי (קי"ט ב׳) אמרו
מנין שהדבור כמעשה שנאמר כו׳ · והוא בחי׳ הנפש
שבדבור · וההבל והקול שהוא הדבור עצמו הוא
בחי׳ רוח שבה · וכוונת הלב בהתיבות בעת אמירתם
הוא בחי׳ הנשמה שבדבור · לזאת לא יצא י"ח ענין
התפלה במחשבה והרהור התיבות בלב לבד כי
איך אפשר להגיע להתקשר בבחי׳ הנשמה אם לא
ילך בסדר המדרגות מתטה למעלה שיתקשר הנפש
של הדבור שהוא תנועת השפתים · ברוח של הדבור
שהוא ההבל והקול·ואח"כ יתקשרו גם שניהם בנשמה
שהוא המחשבה והכוונה שבלב · וכשהתפלל רק
במחשבה לבד · לא הועילה תפלתו ולא תיקן כלום ·
אמנם כשהתפלל בקול ובחתוך אותיות הדבור לבד
אע"פי שלא צירף המחשבה וכוונת הלב אליה · הנה
שודאי אינה במדריגה שלימה וגבוה כראוי · ואינה
יכולה לעלות לעולם המחשבה עולם הנשמה · כיון
שחסר ממנה בחי׳ מחשבת האדם · עכ"ז אינה לריק
ח"ו ויולא בה י"ח · כי עכ"פ הרי העלה וקישר נפשו
ברוחו · ועולם הנפש בעולם הרוח · ועיין זוהר
פקודי רכ"ב ב׳ דאצטריך צלותא תגו מחשב׳ ורעותא
דלבא וקלא ומלה דשפוון למעבד שלימו וקישורא
ויחודא לעילא כגוונא דאיהו לעילא כו׳ לקשרא
קשרא כדקא יאות כו׳ מחשבה ורעותא קלא ומלה
אלין ד׳ מקשרין קשרין לבתר דקשירו קשרין כלא
כחדא אתעבידו כלהו רתיכא חדא לאשראה עלייהו
שכינתא כו׳ · קלא דאשתמע סליק לקשרא קשרין
מתתא לעילא כו׳ עש"ה · ובפ׳ במדבר קי"ב ע"ב
אמרו דרך כלל דעקרא דצלותא תליא בעובדא
בקדמיתא ולבתר במילולא דפומא דוקא ע"ש סדרן
וכא"ז רל"ד ב׳ כל מה דחשיב ב"נ וכל מה דיסתכל
בלבי׳ · לא עביד מלה עד דאפיק לי׳ בשפוותי׳ כו׳ ·
ובג"כ כל צלותא ובעותא כו׳ בעי לאפקא מלין
בשפוותי׳ · דאי לא אפיק לון לאו צלותי׳ צלותא ולאו
בעותי׳ בעותא· וכיון דמלין נפקין מתבקעין באוירא
וסלקין כו׳ ונטיל לון מאן דנטיל ואחיד לון לכתרא
קדישא כו׳ ודרך כלל אמרו בזוהר אמור ק"ה
א׳ מאן דאמר דלא בעיא עובדא בכולא או מלי
לאפקא לין ולמעבד קלא בהו תיפח רוחי׳ ר"ל · ולא
הצריכו רז"ל ענין הכוונה לעכובא אלא בברכת
אבות לבד · ובפ׳ ויחי רמ"ג סוף ע"ב מאן דלבי׳
סריד ובעי לצלאה צליתי׳ ואיבו בעקו ולא יכיל
לסדרא שבחא דמארי׳ כדקא יאות מאי הוא · א"ל

אע"ג
כף

פרק ד

לשמות עינים ולהביא ראיותיו ממקרא ומשנ' ותלמוד ומדרשים וספר הזוהר · כענין רחמנא לבא בעי וכהנה רבות עמו חבילות ראיות · אמנם אם תזכה להבחין בעיני שכל ע"פי התורה · תבין ותמצא שזה כל ענינו להראות להאדם עלפיו בסימני טהרה שדרכי בקודש ורגליו יורדות מות ר"ל : ועתה ראה דרכיו וחכם גם בזה · איך שהוא חכם להרע מענין טוב · היום יאמר לך · שכל תורה ומצוה שבלא דביקות איננה כלום · וצריך אתה להכין לב ולהגביה עוף מחשבתך קודם עשיית כל מצוה או תפלה למחשבה טהורה שבטהורות · וכ"כ תהא מחשבתך טרודה בהכנת המצוה טרם עשותה · עד שיעבור זמן המצוה · או התפלה · ויראה לך פנים · שכל תפלה או מצוה שנעשית בכונה שלמה בקדושה ובטהרה אף שלא בזמנה · הרי היא יקרה מקיום המצוה בזמנה · ושלא בכונה · וכשירגילך יצרך שיוקבע בלבך שלא לחוש כ"כ לשינוי קביעות זמן של איזה מצוה או תפלה · מחמת קביעות מחשבתך להטהר ולפנות הלב תחלה · בהמשך הזמן ידריכך לאט לאט בחלק שפתיו ממדרגה למדרגה ולא תרגיש כלל עד שממילא יהא לך כהיתר להעביר מועד התפלה או המצות · אף גם שתפנה לבך לבטלה בדברים בטלים · וידיחך מכל ולא ישאר לך לא מעשה מצוה בזמנה ולא מחשבה טובה · וגם הרי הוא הריסת כל התורה בכללה ר"ל · אם ח"ו נאבה לו להטות אזן לחלק שפתיו בדרכו זה · והגע עצמך כגון אם יטריד אדם עצמו לילה הראשונה של פסח בכונת אכילת כזית מצה · שתהא האכילה בקדושה וטהרה ודביקות · וימשיך ההכנה כל הלילה עד שיומשך זמן האכילה עד לאחר שעלה השחר או לאחר כ"ה · הרי כל טהרת מחשבתו פיגול הוא לא ירצה · ומי שאכל הכזית מצה בזמנה אף בלא קדושה וטהרה יתירה · הרי קיים מצות עשה המפורשת בתורה ותבא עליו ברכה · וכהנה רבות אשר אם לא נכוין לבנו לחוש לעשות כל המצות במועדם ובזמנם · וכי מאי נפקותא בין זה למי שהיה תוקע שופר בכוונה שלמה בליל ראשון של פסח במקום מצות אכילת כזית מצה · ואוכל הכזית מצה בר"ה · ומתענה בעי"הכ · וביו"הכ נוטל לולב במקום מצות עינוי · ואיה מקום לתורה · ואף גם זאת אם לא יכשילך בהעברת הזמן · יטה לבך לפנות' ולטהרה עד שיביאך שלא יהא לך פנאי לדקדק שתהא עשיית המצוה באופניה כדין בכל פרטיה וליזהר מלעבור על דינים מפורשי' בתלמוד ורבותינו הגדולים ז"ל : ואל יבטיחך יצרך שלא יוכל להיות שמרוב עסק טהרת המחשבה יוגרם ביטול פרטי המעשה · כי תדע שכל זמן שלבך יהא משוך לדעתו לאמר שכל עיקר תורת האדם הוא · שכל מצוה או לימוד שאינה נקיה מכל סיג ופסולת כסלת נקיה · הרי היא בבל יראה ובל ימצא · הרי הוא משחדך בזה ומעור עיניך · שלא תוכל להשגיח על כל הפרטי מעשים והלכות ודינים שתעבור עליהם ח"ו · ולא תרגיש בהם כלל :

פרק ה

והנה גלוי ומבואר · שזאת הדרך אם היא עד אבדון תאכל ח"ו · והורם כמה יסודות התוה"ק ודרז"ל · וכבר הזכרנו לעיל סוף שער א' · שהעיקר בכל המצות הוא חלק המעשה · וטהרת המחשבה איננה אלא מצטרפת למעשה · ולמצוה ולא לעכובא ע"ש · וכן מבואר לכל משכיל ישר הולך · שהרי קי"ל בענין הקרבת הקרבנות דסתמן כלשמן דמי · וכן אמרו להדיא (נזיר כ"ג א') באוכל את הפסח לשם אכילה גסה נהי דלא קא עביד מצוה מן המובחר פסח מיהו קעביד · ואם יחשוב האדם בשעת חיוב הקרבת הפסח ועת חיוב אכילתו כונות נוראות של ענין הפסח במחשבה גבוה שבגבוהות וטהורה שבטהורות וחדל מעשות הפסח ונכרת' הנפש ההיא · וכ"ה בכל המצות

ואל

כי כיון שהוא משפיל ומבזה את העוסק בתורה שלא לשמה הרי הוא מרפה את ידיו מעסק התורה ולא יוכל לבוא לעולם למדרגת לשמה להיות ת"ח גמור · והרי ודאי מקרי בזה מבזה ת"ח · ואין לך חילול שמו ית' ותורתו הק' יותר מזה · וכבר השפיל והוריד את יקר תפארתה של התוה"ק לארץ יניענה עד עפר · והרס גם את כל העבודה בכללה ח"ו · כי אין עבודתו יתברך מתקיימת כראוי בעדת ישראל · בלתי ע"י הת"ח עוסקי התוה"ק יומם ולילה · כי עיני כל ישראל עליהם לדעת מה יעשה ישראל · להורות להם הדרך ילכו בה ואת המעשה אשר יעשון · א"כ האיש אשר יבא לגלום שלא יהיו ת"ח מצויים בישראל · הרי כבר הרס גם כלל עבודתו יתברך לגמרי · כי ישארו עדת ישראל ח"ו בלא תורה ובלא מורה ולא ידעו במה יכשלו ח"ו · וכענין זה כתב ג"כ רבינו יונה ז"ל שם פ"ט: לזאת אתה צריך ליזהר אדרבה לכבד ולהגביה ככל אשר בכחך · את כל העוסק ומחזיק בתורת ה' אפילו שלא לשמה · כדי שיאחז צדיק דרכו בל יתרפה ממנה ח"ו · כדי שיוכל לבא ממנה למדרגת לשמה: וגם אם נראה שכל ימי חייו מנעוריו ועד זקנה ושיבה היה עסקו בה שלא לשמה · ג"כ אתה חייב לנהוג בו כבוד וכ"ש שלא לבזותו ח"ו · שכיון שעסק בתורת ה' בתמידות בלתי ספק שהיה כונתו פעמים רבות גם לשמה · כמו שהבטיחו רז"ל שמתוך שלא לשמה בא לשמה · כי אין הפי' דוקא שיבא מזה ללשמ' עד שאח"כ יעסוק בה תמיד כל ימיו רק לשמה · אלא הייט שבכל פעם שהוא לומד בקביעות זמן כמה שעות רצופים · אף שדרך כלל היתה כונתו שלא לשמה · עכ"ז בלתי אפשר כלל שלא יכנס בלבו באמצע הלימוד עכ"פ זמן מועט כונה רצויה לשמה · ומעתה כל מה שלמד עד הנה שלא לשמה נתקדש ונטהר ע"י אותו העת קטן שכיון בו לשמה:

פרק ד וכמה זהירות יתירה צריך האדם

להזהר בעניני' כאלו וכיוצא בהם · וכבר אחז"ל (סוכ' נ"ב א') כל הגדול מחבירו יצרו גדול הימנו · כי היצר מתהפך בתחבולותיו לכל אדם כפי ענינו ומדרגתו בתורה ועבודה · שאם הוא רואה שכפי גובה מדרגתו של האדם · לא ישיאהו שיניח מקומו ומדרגתו לעשות בפועל איזה עון וחטא חמור או קל · שלא יאבה לו · הוא מתחפש להתדמות אל האדם כיצר טוב · לסמות שכלו להטיל ארס ולהטעותו באותו האופן והמדרגה עצמה שהאדם דבוק בה · שמראה לו בה איזה דרך הנראה להאדם בהשקפה ראשונה שהוא עצת יצרו הטוב להדריכו בדרך יותר גבוה (*) · כפי שמראה לו בה פנים וסימני טהרה · והאדם נופל ברשתו כמהר לפור אל פח בלי התבוננות רב ולא ידע כי בנפשו הוא ורגליו יורדות מות ח"ו:

הגה"ה

ואולי גם לזה רמזו רז"ל באמרם (ס' הרואה ס"א א') יצה"ר דומה לזבו' ויושב בין שני מפתחי הלב · כי ידוע שמשכן היצ"ט בחלל הימיני של הלב · ומשכן היצה"ר בחלל השמאלי · כמ"ש (קהלת י') לב חכם לימינו ולב כסיל לשמאלו · וזה אמרם · שהיצ"ט שומר ומכיר את מקומו לימין תמיד · שאינו מייעץ לאדם לעולם רק לטוב אמיתי לבד · אבל היצה"ר אינו שומר את מקומו המיוחד לו בחלל השמאלי להסית לעון וחטא נגלה · אלא הוא מדלג ממקומו לפעמים גם לחלל הימין · להתדמות להאדם כיצר טוב להנהיגו בתוספת קדושה · ואינו מרגיש שתוכה ענין רע ומר ח"ו:

לזאת הזהר בנפשך מאד · שאל ישיאך יצרך לאמר · שעיקר הכל הראה שתהא אך עסוק כל ימיך לטהר מחשבת' כראוי · שתהא דביקות מחשבתך בבוראך בתמידות בל תמוט · ולא תשוב מפני כל להניח מוכר מחשבתך בשום עת כלל · והכל לשם שמים · באמרו לך שכל עיקר תורה ומצות המה דווקא כשהם בכוונה עצומה ובדביקות אמיתי · וכל זמן שאין לב האדם מלא לעשותם בכונה קדושה ובדביקות וטהרת המחשבה · אינה נחשבת למצוה ועבודה כלל · כאשר כבר לומד המלך זקן וכסיל לסתום

עלמא על אודה המחשבה והפני' שכיון בה. וכ"ש אם אינו מכוון כלל לשום פני' לגרמי'. הגם שאין כוונתו לשמה דוקא היינו לשם התורה כמש"ל בפ"ג משע"ד בשם הרא"ש ז"ל. אלא עיקר עסקו בה בשמחה אשר כלשמה דמי. הרי עסק תורתו יקר נאה בעיניו ית' יותר מכל המצות לשמה בקדושת וטהרת המחשבה כראוי. כמבואר ומוכח להדיא מגמ' דערכין (י"ו ב') בעי מני' ר"י ברי' דרשב"פ הוכחה לשמה וענוה שלא לשמה הי מנייהו עדיפא. וא"ל מי לא מודית דענוה לשמה עדיפא דאמר מר ענוה גדולה מכולן. שלא לשמה נמי עדיפא דאר"י א"ר לעולם יעסוק אדם בתורה ובמצות אפי' שלא לשמה שמתוך שלא לשמה בא לשמה. וממילא נשמע דקותה נמי בעסק התורה מי לא מודית דתורה לשמה ודאי דעדיפא ממצות לשמה. שהרי משנה שלימה שנינו ות"ת כנגד כולם. וכן חילקו רז"ל (סוטה כ"א א') ביתרון ערך מעלת התורה על המצו' שזכות ואור המצו' בין בעדנא דעסיק בה ובין בעדנא דלא עסיק בה היא רק מגינה מהיסורין ואינ' מצלת את האדם שלא יבא לידי חטא. אבל אור התורה גם לפי המסקנא שם עכ"פ בעידנא דעסיק בה היא גם מצלת אותו מחטא. ואמרו בירושלמי פ"א דפאה שכל המצות אינן שוין לדבר אחד מן התורה. וכמו שיתבאר להלן אי"ה בש"ד בזה. א"כ גם עסק התורה שלא לשמה נמי עדיפא ממצות לשמה מזה הטעם עצמו שמתוך שלא לשמה בא לשמה :

פרק ג **וגם** כי באמת כמעט דלא אפשר לבא היכף לתחל' קביעת לימודו למדרגת לשמה כראוי. כי העסק בתורה שלא לשמה הוא המדרגה שמתוך כך יוכל לבא למדרגת לשמה ולכן גם הוא אהוב לפניו ית'. כמו שבלתי אפשר לעלות מהארץ לעליה אם לא דרך מדרגות הסלם. וזה אמרו (פסחים ג' ע"ב) לעולם יעסוק אדם בתורה ובמצות אפי' שלא לשמה. אמרם לעולם ר"ל בקביעות היינו שבתחלת לימודו אינו מחוייב רק שילמוד בקביעות תמיד יומם ולילה. ואף אם לפעמים ודאי יפול במחשבתו איזה פניה לגרמי' לשום גיאות וכבוד וכיוצא. עכ"ז אל ישים לב לפרוש או להתרפות ממנה בעבור זה ח"ו אלא אדרבה יתחזק מאד בעסק התורה ויהא נכון לבו בטוח שודאי יבוא מתוך כך למדרגת לשמה. וכן הוא ג"כ בענין המצות עד"ז. ומי שימלאו לבו לבזות ולהשפיל ח"ו את העוסק בתורה ומצות אף שלא לשמה. לא ינקה רע ועתיד ליתן את הדין ח"ו :

ולא עוד אלא שנמנה בדברי רז"ל (בברייתא ר"ה י"ז א') בין אותם שאין להם חלק לעה"ב לגמרי ח"ו וגיהנם כלה והם אינם כלין והם האפיקורסין. וכן במשנה ר"פ חלק מנו את האפיקורס בכלל אותן שאין להם חלק לעה"ב. ואמרי' בגמ' שם (צ"ט ב') רב ור"ח דאמרי תרוייהו זה המבזה ת"ח ור"י וריב"ל אמרי שאפי' המבזה חבירו בפני ת"ח נמי אפיקורס הוי. ואף אם אומר מאי אהנו לן רבנן לדידהו קרו לדידהו תנו ה"ז בכלל אפיקורס מבז' ת"ח וגם מגלה פנים בתורה נמי מקרי ח"ו. וה"ז איבד חלקו בחיי עולם הרחמן יצילנו. וכן הר' יונה ז"ל בשער התשובה שמנה סדר מדרגות חומ' העונשים ומדרגה האחרונה-מנה את הכת שארז"ל עליהם שאין להם חלק לעה"ב ומנה ג"כ שם המבזה ת"ח בכלל זאת הכת. וכן מנה אותו הרה"ו ז"ל בשער הקדושה בכלל אותה הכת. וכל חומר עונשו הנורא הזה הוא מטעם על שהוא במורידי אור מעלת התוה"ק וחיללה ח"ו. כמו שהאריך בזה הרבינו יונה ז"ל שם ע"ש דברי קדוש ה'. (וכתב הוא ז"ל שם שגם עיקר העונש של כל המנויים שם באותה הכת הוא ג"כ רק מפני חילול כבוד התוה"ק רח"ל).

כי

פרק א ב

פרק א אתה הקורא נעים · הנה הדרכתיך בע"ה בנתיבות האמת · להורות לפניך הדרך אלך בה לבטח · ותוכל לחנך עצמך לאט לאט בסדר המדרגות הנ"ל · לפי טוהר לבבך · ולפי השגתך · יותר ממה שערוך לפניך כאן · וגם לפי רוב הרגל · ובעיניך תראה שכל אשר תרגיל עצמך יותר בכל מדרגה מאלו הנ"ל · יתוסף בלבך טהרה על טהרתך · הן בעסק התורה והן בקיום המצות ויראתו ואהבתו יתב' :

אמנם השמר והזהר מאד שלא תזוח דעתך עליך ותתגאה לבבך מאשר אתה עובד את בוראך בטהרת המחשבה · ובהשקפה ראשונה לא תרגיש כ"כ בהתגאות לבבך מזה · וצריך אתה לפשפש ולמשמש בזה מאד · וכתוב מפורש תועבת ה' כל גבה לב (משלי ט"ז) · שאף אם לא יתראה ההתגאות לעיני ב"א רק במחשבת הלב לבד בעיני עצמו היא תועבה ממש לפניו יתב' · כידוע שהיא השרש והשאור שבעיסה לכל המדות רעות . ואמרו (סוטה דף ד' ע"ב) שכל המתייהר כאלו בנה במה · ושכינה מיללת עליו וכאלו דוחק רגליו יה"ש שקובל עליו ואומר אין אני והוא יכולין לדור כאחד (שם ה' ע"א) וקצר המצע מהשתרע · ואוי לו לבן המגרש את אביו בזרוע מבית פלטין של אביו · והפליגו בה ז"ל מאד עד שאמרו שם שהוא כאלו עובד ע"ז וכפר בעקר וכאלו בא על כל העריות · ואמרו (פסחים ר"פ אלו דברים) כל המתייהר אם חכם הוא חכמתו מסתלקת הימנו · וכל אשר יראת ה' נגע בלבו תסמר שערות ראשו ותדמע עינו בהעלותו על לבו ממי למדוהו רז"ל זאת · מהלל הזקן אשר ידוע ומפורסם בדבריה' ז"ל הפלגת ענותנותו ושפלותו הנוראה · עכ"ז כאשר נזדמן לידו פעם א' קצת ענין שהיה נראה בהשקפה כהתגאות לפי מדרגת גודל נמיכת רוחו תיכף נענש ע"ז שנתעלמה הימנו הלכה · מה נאמר ונדבר אנחנו איך אנו צריכים לפשפש ולמשמש ע"ז בכל עת ·

פרק ב גם תוכל לגרום לאדם ההתגאות בלב מאשר הוא עובד אותו יתב' בטהרת הלב · שיקל בעיניו ח"ו אם יראה מי ומי שאין עניני עבודתו לו יתב' במחשבה טהורה ומקיים ככל הכתוב בתורת ה' בלא דביקות · וכ"ש כשיראה איזה איש עוסק בתורת ה' ויתבונן עליו שהוא שלא לשמה יתבזה בעיניו מאד ח"ו · והוא עון פלילי הרחמן יצילנו · כי באמת כל ענין הטהרת הלב בעבודתו יתב' הוא למצוה ולא לעכובא כמש"ל סוף שער א' ויתבאר עוד להלן אי"ה · וכל המקיים מצות ה' ככל אשר צונו בתוה"ק שבכתב ובע"פ אף בלא דביקות כ"כ ג"כ עובד אלקים ואהוב לפניו ית' :

וכן האדם העוסק בתורת ה' אפילו שלא לשמה · אם כי ודאי שעדן אינו במדרגה הגבוה האמתית · אמנם חלילה וחלילה לבזותו אפי' בלב ואדרבה כל איש ישראל מחויב גם לנהוג בו כבוד · כמ"ש בשמאלה עושר וכבוד ודרז"ל (שבת ס"ג) למשמאילים בה כו' · ובזוהר וישב קפ"ד ב' תורת ה' תמימה כו' כמה אית לון לב"נ לאשתדלא באורייתא דכל מאן דאשתדל באורייתא להוי לי' חייב כו' · ואפי' מאן דאשתדל באורייתא ולא אשתדל בה לשמה כדקא יאות זכי לאגר טב בעלמא דין ולא דיינין לי' בההוא עלמא · ות"ח כתיב אורך ימים בימינה בשמאלה עושר וכבוד כו' בשמאלה עושר וכבוד אגר טב ושלוה אית לי' בהאי עלמא · הרי שאפי' האדם אשר עסקו בתורתו יתב' שלא לשמה כראוי · אלא בשביל איזה פניה לגרמי' רק אם אינו לקנטור ח"ו אשר עליו אמרז"ל נוח לו שנהפך שלייתו על פניו וכן אמרו (שם פ"ח ב') שנעשית לו סם המות ח"ו · הקב"ה קובע לו שכר טוב שמגיע לו עושר וכבוד ושלוה בהאי עלמא · וגם לא דיינין לי' בההוא

שלא להוציא הנייר חלק בכדי, אחרתי להעמיד איזה חידושים שעלו על רעיוני

פסחים כ״ט ב׳ תוס׳ ד״ה ר״א אמר · בסופו מכאן מוכיח ר״י וכו׳ וטעמא משום דלא ירא׳ ניתק לעשה · ונראה לומר דלפי שיטת התוס׳ דהשביתו אינו ביטול רק שריפה או ביעור אחר · גם לדידן דאסרינן חמץ בהנאה בפסח מ״מ הוי לאו הניתק לעשה · אבל לשיטת רש״י דהשביתו היינו גם ביטול · לא מוכח דהוי ניתק לעשה רק לרי״הג המתיר בהנאה ויכול לקיים העשה דהשביתו גם בביטול אף לאחר זמן איסורו · מאחר דברשותו קיימא להנאה כמו קודם זמן איסורו · אבל לדידן דאסור בהנאה לאחר זמן איסורו ואינו יכול לקיים השביתו רק בביעור · אין סברא שיקרא לאו הניתק לעשה · אלא לאו שקדמה עשה · וברייתא דלקמן נ״ה ע״א נוקמי אליבא דרי״הג · ולפי סברא זו יתורץ הרמב״ם פ״א מה׳ ח״ומ׳ דין ג׳ שפסק דלוקה עיין שם במ״ל · ועיין פ״ב שם שכתב דהשבתה שבתורה הוא בטול :

סוכה ד׳ ע״ב · ורב נחמן אמר באמצע הגג מחלוקת וכו׳ · עיי׳ רש״י שם שפירש שר״י דמכשיר אף באמצע דוקא בקונדיסין רחבים טפח · ואף כי לדברי ר״ה איירי הברייתא אף בקונדיסין כ״ש · וגם לדברי ר״כ על שפת הגג איירי אף בקונדיסין כ״ש · הוכחת רש״י מדקמדמי הגמרא נעץ ד׳ קונדסין בארץ וסיכך על גבן לאמצע הגג · ובארץ אינו מכשיר רק ברחבים · וכברייתא השניי׳ שר״י אומר רואין וכו׳ ויש בהן טפח וכו׳ : ואף שמה אנחנו להרים ראש · אך לא באנו ח״ו לסתור דבריו · רק לשום חלקנו בתורתו הנראה לענ״ד . שאולי גם באמצע היינו מלד הכתלים מכשיר ר״י אף בקונדסים כ״ש · יחכמי׳ אינם מכשירים בקונדסים כ״ש אלא דוקא כשעומדים מכוון על הכתלים שתחת הגג אבל כשעומדים בלד הכתלים לא אמרי׳ גוד אסיק · והברייתא דמותיב מינה איירי בנעץ ד׳ קונדסין בארץ בלד הכתלים . ודמי ממש לנעץ על גבי הגג בלד הכתלים · ולכך לא אמר ר״מ כאן רואין כמו בברייתא השני׳ דמיירי בנעץ בארץ ואין ביניהם כתלים :

ב״ב דף קי״ב ע״א תוס׳ ד״ה מנין ליאיר שלא היה לשגוב · תימה לרשב״א וכו׳ · אם נפרש תמיהתם כפשוטה קשה טובא · דאף אם לבאי הארץ נתחלקה הארץ · הלא לא הי׳ לו ליאיר שהי׳ משבט יהודה · לירש ירושת אבות בגלעד שהוא חלק שבט מנשה · כמבואר בקרא (ד״ה א׳ ב׳ כ״ב) · ונראה לפרש שלא באו לסתור דיוקא דגמרא באמת · רק כוונתם שלפי האמת הי׳ לו להש״ס לדייק וכי מה לו ליאיר לחלק מנשה אם לא עיי ירושת הבעל ומתמיהים על ליסנא דכי מנין ליאיר שלא הי׳ לשגוב · ונראה לתרץ · דלכך לא מדייק מה ליאיר לחלק מנשה · כי אבי אביו חלרון לקח את בת מכיר בן מנשה (שם פ׳ כ״א) · רק הדיוק הוא וכי מנין לו ליאיר שלא היה לשגוב · פי׳ מאבי אביו חלרון לא הי׳ לו לירש רק מן שגוב אביו שירשו תחלה · אלא דנסיב אתתא וכו׳ :

וכו׳ · ותיכף לו בפסוק שאחריו אמר בלשון מדבר בעדו ונתתי מטר ארצכם כו׳ שהוא הנותן והפועל · כי התבטל בעיני עצמו מתציאות כלל ורק השכינה לבד המדברת לכן אמר ונתתי · וז״ש ז״ל שכינה מדברת מתוך גרונו של משה · וכמש״ה פה אל פה אדבר בו ולא כ׳ אליו אלא בו בתוכו ממש ולזאת המדרגה בשלימות עדיין לא זכה אליה שום אדם זולתו מעת חטא אדה״ר וגם לא יזכה אליה, שום אנש על יבשתא עד ביאת הגואל ב״ב · כמו שהעידה התו״הק ולא קם נביא עוד בישראל כמשה כו׳ (ואף שנאמר בלשון עבר · התורה היא נצחית וקאי גם על זמן דורות הבאים · שאחר עבור כל דור מהעולם יכול לומר שלא קם כזה הדור נביא כמשה בזאת המדרג׳)· ולכן אמרו בתד״א חייב אדם לומר מתי יגיעו מעשי למעשי אבותי אברהם יצחק ויעקב · ולא אמרו למעשי משרע״ה · אמנם עכ״ז ראוי לכל ירא ה׳ אמיתי·שעכ״פ בעת עמדו להתפלל יבטל בטוהר לבבו כפי יכולתו והשגתו כל הכחות שבעולם וכל כחותיו כאלו אין שום מציאות בעולם כלל · ולהתדבק בלבו רק בו יתב׳ אדון יחיד ב״ה · ועכ״פ לפרקים · כי באמת לא כל העתים שוות בענין טהרת הלב · ובפרט בדורות הללו כמעט בלתי אפשר להתפלל בתמידות ,בזאת המדרגה הגבוה · וכבר אמר ר״א יכולני לפטור כל העולם מדין תפלה · אעפ״כ העובד הטהור הרואה ומסתכל תמיד בטהרת לבבו על כל עניניו שיהיו לרצון לפני אדון כל יח״ש · יוכל להגיע שיתפלל עכ״פ לפרקים בזאת המדרגה :

ועתה מבואר כונתם ז״ל במאמרם שהמתפלל צריך שיכוין את לבו למקום·וכן מאמרם ז״ל בא׳בות וכשאתה מתפלל אל תעש וכו׳ אלא רחמי׳ ותחנונים לפני המקום ב״ה · ר״ל שצריך ליזהר בנפשו מאד שלא לכוון ולשום מגמת לבו בתפלתו חיו לשום ספי׳ אפי׳ מהנאצלים · ולא זו בלבד שלא לכוון לשום ספי׳ וכח עליון לבד כי הוא עבודה זרה אלקי אמת וקיצוץ נטיעות ח״ו אלא שגם ראוי ונכון שיבטל ברצונו ביטול גמור כל הכחות עליונים ותחתונים וגם כל כחותיו כאלו אינם במציאות · (ולא זו בלבד בענין התפלה · אלא שגם העסק בתורה שתתקיי׳ אצלו כראוי·ג״כ צריכה שתהיה ע״פ זאת המדרגה ·כענין מאמרם ז״ל (סוטה כ״א ע״ב) אין ד״ת מתקיימין אלא במי שמשים עצמו כמי שאינו) ולכוון ולהדביק טהרת לבו בתפלתו רק למקומו של עולם הוא יחידו של עולם א״ס ב״ה הממלא כל העולם והעולמות כולם ולית אתר פנוי מני׳ · וע׳ רוקח ז״ל סוף שורש זכירת השם ז״ל · וכשיאמר ברוך אתה ה׳ אל יחשוב על הכבוד הנראה בלב הנביאים ומראה על הכסא · כי אם על ה׳ הוא האלקים בשמים ובארץ באויר ובים ובכל העולם שהוא אלקי האבות עכ״ל · והבן :

סליק שער ג

שער ג

שמי הוי"ה (כמו שנתבאר פי' ענינו לעיל פי"א) לא נודעתי להם בהשגת נבואתם: אבל משרע"ה היתה השגת נבואתו בענין בחי' השם העצם המיוחד הוי"ה ב"ה ולכן לא היה שום כח חוצץ בפני אור השגת נבואתו. וכן ע"י כל נסי ה' שנעשו על ידו ראו כולם ביטול מציאות כל הכחות לגמרי ואין עוד מלבדו יתב' לגמרי כמשמעו. כמש"ה אתה הראת לדעת כי ה' הוא וכו'. והוא ענין ופי' השם המיוחד הוי"ה ב"ה כנ"ל: ז"ש וידבר אלקים אל משה ויאמר אליו אני הוי"ה. הודיעו עצם בחי' השגת נבואתו שגם השם אלהים אצלו הכל בחי' הוי"ה. כענין הכתוב כי ה' הוא האלהים אין עוד מלבדו: ומאז ואילך לא נזכר אצלו אלא וידבר ה' ויאמר ה'. וזהו ולא קם נביא וכו' אשר ידעו הוי"ה פא פ. וז"ש בתיקון כ"ו, ולגבי אבהן לא אתחזיא אלא במנעלים כו' אבל לגבי משה בלא כסויא כלל ורזא דמלה וארא אל אברהם וכו' עכ"ל:

והוא ג"כ ענין מאמרם ז"ל בש"פ כסוי הדם גדול שנא' במשה ואהרן יותר ממה שנאמר באברהם. דאלו באברהם כתיב ואנכי עפר ואפר ואלו במשה ואהרן כתיב ונחנו מה. כי עפר ואפר עכ"פ מתראה עדיין למציאות עפר. (*) אבל משרע"ה אמר ונחנו מה כאלו אין שום מציאות בעולם כלל לגמרי. (ועם כי גם את אהרן כלל אתו בזאת הבחי' וכמאמרם גדול שנאמ' במשה ואהרן. לפי שתלונת ישראל היתה על שניהם השיבם בלשון רבים אבל העיקר בזאת המדרגה שנוראה היה הוא לבד). וז"ש בשמות רבה פ"א יצחק אמר למשה אני גדול ממך שפשטתי צוארי כו' וראיתי את פני השכינה. א"ל משה אני נתעליתי יותר ממך שאתה ראית פני השכינה וכהו עיניך כו' אבל אני הייתי מדבר עם השכינה פנים בפנים ולא כהו עיני. ומבואר למבין. וע' מ"ש הרא"ו ז"ל בס' הגלגולים בפי' מאמרם ז"ל אברהם אברהם יעקב יעקב פסיק טעמא. ומשה משה לא פסיק טעמא. שהוא על ענין הפסק וחלילה מועטת מענין הגוף ע"ש:

הגה"ה

וענין עפר ואפר היא כענין כוונת פרה אדומה שיכללו הפ"ר דינין במקור שרשם באלף שהוא כח הפשוט של כל האותיות. וענין החילוק בין עפר לאפר כענין החילוק בין כתנות עור לאור:

פרק יד

ולזאת היה משרע"ה מוכן כל רגע לנבואה כמ"ש עמדו ואשמעה וכו'. וכמ"ש רז"ל (*). וכן היה משיג נבואתו בכל המקומות באיזה מקום שיהיה בהשואה גמורה בלא שום חילוק כלל. כמאמרם ז"ל בשמות רבה פ"ב ובבמד' רבה פ"ב ובחזית סי' נ' בפסוק עמודיו עשה כסף ז"ל למה דיבר הקב"ה עם משה מתוך הסנה וכו' ללמדך שאין מקום פנוי בארץ פנוי מהשכי' שאפי' בתוך הסנה היה מדבר עמו עכ"ל. והוא כפי בחי' מדרגתו הנוראה. ורק אשר בקשה נפשו הראני נא את כבודך לעמוד על מהות זה הענין הנורא ולראות איך הוא ית"ש מלא כל הארץ כבודו ולית אתר פנוי מני' זה לא ניתן לו והשיבו הוא יתב' לא תוכל לראות וכו' כי לא יראני וכו'.

הגה"ה

והוא ג"כ אחד מהטעמים מה שיעקב אבינו ע"ה אמר בשכמל"ו ומשרע"ה לא אמרו כמאמרם ז"ל (פסחים נ"ו א') כי ענין שבח בשכמל"ו משמע שיש ג"כ מציאות כחות ועולמות וכמש"ל פי"א ע"ש. ולכן אמרו יעקב אבינו ע"ה שהוא כפי מדרגתו כנ"ל. אמנם מדרגת והשגת משרע"ה כפי' שביארנו הוא ג"כ עצם ענין היחוד דאיהו אחד דק"ש כפי שנתבא' שם לכן הוא לא אמר בשכמל"ו ביחודו ית"ש:

והיה הולך וגדול בזאת המדרגה כל עת עד שעלה בידו וזכה אליה קודם סלוקו מן העולם. בשלימות היותר אפשרי בכח האדם לזכות בעודו בזה העולם כמו שמצינו במשנה תורה בפ' והיה אם שמוע שתחלה אמר לאהבה את ה' אלקיכם וכו'

שער ג

עולם אדון יחיד המלא כל עלמין ואין כאן שום שליטה ומציאות כח אחר כלל. לכן היה נכון לבו בטוח בזה שלא ישלטו עליו פעולות הכשפים הנמשכים מכחות המרכבה טמאה. וז"ש לא מסתייע מלתך אין עוד מלבדו כתיב:

ובאמת הוא ענין גדול וסגולה נפלאה להסר ולבטל מעליו כל דינין ורצונות אחרים שלא יוכלו לשלוט בו ולא יעשו שום רושם כלל. כשהאדם קובע בלבו לאמר הלא ה' הוא האלקים האמתי ואין עוד מלבדו יתברך שום כח בעולם וכל העולמות כלל והכל מלא רק אחדותו הפשוט ית"ש. ומבטל בלבו ביטול גמור ואינו משגיח כלל על שום כח ורצון בעולם. ומשעבד ומדבק טוהר מחשבתו רק לאדון יחיד ב"ה. כן יספיק הוא יתב' בידו שממילא יתבטלו מעליו כל הכחות והרצונות שבעולם שלא יוכלו לפעול לו שום דבר כלל.* וזה הענין הוא גם כן בכלל כוונת הזוהר בהקדמה דף י"ב סוף ע"א פקודא רביעאה למנדע דה' הוא האלקי' כד"א וידעת היום וגו' כי ה' הוא האלקים ולאתכללא שמא דאלקים בשמא דהוי"ה וכד ינדע ב"כ דכלא חד ולא ישוי פרודא אפי' ההוא ס"א יסתלק מעל עלמא כו' והבן. וגם יגזור אומר ויקם לו לפעול ענינים ונסים נפלאים היפוך סדור כחות הטבעים. כיון שמשעבד ומדב' טוהר אמונת לבנו באמת בל תמוט רק לו יתב' לבד. ואללו יתב' פכל שום כל רגע. לפעול בסידור הטבע שקבע או היפוך סידור הטבע. כמו שמצינו בר' חנינא בן דוסא שהיה גוזר אומר ופועל כפי רצונו כל עת היפוך סידור הטבע כאמרו מי שאמר לשמן וידליק יאמר לחומץ וידליק ר"ל הלא אצלו יתב' שוה זה כמו זה כנ"ל. וכן הספיק הבורא ב"ה בידו. וכהנה רבות אתו כמובא בש"ס מנפלאות עניניו:

הגה"ה

וזהו ענין מאמרם ז"ל במשנ' ר"ה (כ"ט א') עשה לך שרף וכו' וכי נחש ממית או נחש מחיה. אלא בזמן שישראל מסתכלין כלפי מעלה ומשעבדין את לבם לאביהם שבשמים וכו'. ר"ל כשהסתכלו כלפי מעל' להבח' השרף והתבוננו בכחו הרע ועכ"ז בטלוהו מלבם ולא השגיחו על כחו הנורא ושעבדו את לבם באמת רק לאביהם שבשמים לבד היו מתרפאין. והוא אמיתת ענין המתקת כחות הדינים בשרשם. והוא מבואר למבין:

פרק יג וזה היה ענין עבודת האבות כל ימיהם. כי המה בנוראות לדקתם וטהרת קדושת לבם היו מדבקים מחשבתם לרצונו יתברך כל ימיהם בלי הפסק רגע. ובטלו ברצונם כל הכחות שבעול' ולאפס ותהו נחשבו אצלם ולכן זכו גם לנסים נפלאים בשדוד המערכות ולבאיהם כנ"ל. ולכן נתיחד שמו יתברך עליהם להקרא אלהי אברהם אלהי יצחק וכו'. וכאמרו יתב' בעצמו אלקי אבותיכם. ולזה אמרו ז"ל האבות הן הן המרכבה:

אמנם מדרגת משרע"ה היתה עוד יותר גבוה. כמו שהעידה התורה ולא קם נביא וכו'. ועצם חילוק מדרגתו ממדרגתם ביאר הוא יתב' בעצמו ואמר אני הוי"ה. וארא אל אברהם וכו' באל שדי ושמי הוי"ה לא נודעתי להם. והענין הוא עצם החילוק שנתבאר למעלה בין השם אלקים לשם הוי"ה ב"ה. כי על הרוב בענין השגת האבות מצינו נאמר השם אלקים. האלקים אשר התהלכו אבותי לפניו. האלקים הרועה אותי מעודי. וכן אנחנו קוראים אותו יתב' אלהי אברהם וכו'. כמש"ל בענין קדושת מדרגתם שלא השגיחו על שום כח וענין בעולם כלל. אמנם השגת נבואתם לא היתה בביטול הכחות ממציאותם לגמרי. וזש"ה וארא אל אברהם וכו' באל שדי שענינו ג"כ כענין השם אלקים ור"ל שאני בעל הכחות כולם וברצותי כל רגע אני משדד מערכת כל הכחות אשר קבעתי בהם בעת הבריאה. זהו אל שדי. אבל בבחי' ענין

באמת אינו שבח כלל שנשבחהו יתב' שהוא ברוך ומפואר בכבוד מלכותו על עולמות נבראים שכולם שפלים ולא חשיבין קמי' כלל · רק שהוא יתב' במקום גדולתו תמצא ענותנותו שגזרה רצונו לקבלו מאתנו לשבח · לזאת המשילוהו ז"ל לציקי קדרה · והתקינו שעכ"פ לא נאמרהו אלא בחשאי :

ועפ"ד הנ"ל י"ל פנימיות כוונתם ז"ל היינו שאחר שיחדנוהו בפסוק שמע שהוא רק אחד אחדות פשוט ואין עוד מלבדו כלל וכל העולמות הם כאלו אינם במציאות כלל · איך נשבחהו אח"ז שהוא מבורך בכבוד מלכותו על עולמות · שגם העולמות ישנם במציאות והוא יתב' המולך עליהם · ואינו נחשב לשבח נגד עוצם יחוד פסוק שמע · אלא שגזרה רצונו יתב' שאעפ"כ נשבחהו בזה השבח · מחמת שכן הוא הענין מצד השגתנו והנהגתנו ע"פי יסודות וחקי תוה"ק שבננו כולם ע"ס זה הבחי' כמש"ל · לזאת נאמרהו בחשאי : (ולכאורה יקשה ממאי דאמר לי' רבי ירמיה לרחב"א (כר"ס היה קורא) דהיה מאריך טובא בתי' אחד · וא"ל כיון דאמליכתי' למעלה ולמטה ולארבע רוחות השמים תו לא צריכת · ולפ"ד קשה קצת ליסגי דאמליכתי' על תיבת אחד · אמנם גם זה לא תברה · כידוע ליודעים בדברי האר"י ז"ל שכל תחלת ראשית מחשבתו ית' בענין הבריאה היתה בסוד מלכות דא"ס והבן) :

פרק יב

וזהו הענין שדרשו ז"ל (חולין ז' ב') על פסוק כי ה' הוא האלקים אין עוד מלבדו א"ר חנינא אפילו כשפים · כי כל ענייני פעולות הכשפים נמשך מהכחות הטומאה של המרכבה טמאה · והוא ענין חכמת הכשוף שהיו הסנהדרין צריכין לידע · היינו חכמת שמות הטומאה וידיעת ענייני כחות המרכבה טמאה בשמותיהם . שע"י יפעלו בעלי הכשופים פעולות ועניינים משונים כשמשביעין כחות הטומאה בבחי' הטוב שבו שישפיע בהוכו חיות לעשות נפלאות היפך סדר כחות הטבעי' והמזלות · ועיין ע"ח שער קליפת נגה ריש פ"ד · מחמת שכן קבע הבורא אדון כל ית' ענייני כחותיה' למעלה מכחות הטבעי' הנמשכים מהכוכבי' והמזלות שעי"ז יהא בכחם לעשות פעולות גם היפוך טבעי כחות הכוכבים ומזלות שהוקבע בהם בעת הבריאה· כידוע שכל כח ועולם קבע בו הבורא יתברך כח ויכולת להנהיג ולהטות את הכח והעולם שתחתיו לכל אשר יהיה שמה הרוח וכו' · ומ"ש שם שמכחישין פמליא של מעלה ר"ל שרק סדור כחות הפמליא של הכוכבים והמזלות קבע הבורא יתברך כח בכחות הטומאה שיהו יכולין להפכם · אבל לא שיהא בכחם לשנות ח"ו מסדר הפעולות הקדושים של כחות המרכבה קדושה · ואדרבה כשמשביעין אותם בשמות של כחות הקדושה · ממילא כרגע מתבטל כל ענייני פעולתם לגמרי · וכמ"ש בתיקון י"ח אלין דידעין בקליפין עבדין אומאה בשמהן ובהויות דקב"ה לאלין קליפין ובטלין גזרה · ועיין ע"ח בפ' הנ"ל · כיון שאין הכח שלהם מעצמם ח"ו · כי אין עוד מלבדו יתב' בעל הכחות כולם · וגם שבאמת הלא הכל מלא רק עצמות אחדותו הפשוט ית' ואין עוד מלבדו שום מציאות כח כלל לא כחות הטומאה ולא שום כח ושום עולם ונברא כלל · ז"ש אין עוד מלבדו אפילו כשפים :

וזהו שמביא שם הש"ס ע"ז עובדא דההיא אתתא דהוות קא מהדרא למשקל עפרא מתותא כרעי' דר' חנינא · אמר לה שקולי לא מסתייע מלתך אין עוד מלבדו כתיב · ופריך והאר"י למה נקרא שמן כשפים שמכחישין פמליא של מעלה · שאני ר"ח דנפיש זכותיה · ודאי שלא היה מחזיק עצמו ר' חנינא דנפיש זכותי' כ"כ מתורתו ומעשיו הטובים המרובים עד שבעבורם היה סמוך לבו שלא ישלוט בו פעולת הכשפים · אבל הענין כמש"ל כיון שבאמת אין בכחות המרכבה טמאה שום כח מעצמם חלילה · אלא שהוא יתב' קבע כחם למעלה מכחות טבעי הכוכבים ומזלות כדי שעל ידי זה יהא ביכולתם לעשות פעולות אף גם לשנות סדרי טבעי המזלות · ובלתו יתב' הם אפס ותהו · ולכן גם ר"ח לא שבטח על זכות קדושת תורתו ומעשיו המרובים · רק שידע ושיער בנפשו שזאת האמונה קבועה בלבו לאמיתה שאין עוד מלבדו יתב' שום כח כלל · והדביק עצמו בקדושת מחשבתו לבעל הכחות

כולם

שער ג

ענין התפשטות דבורו ית' בכל דבר בעולם. כמו שכבר היתה השגה מעין זה בעת מתן תורה דכתיב וכל העם רואים את הקולת. (*) והוא ג"כ בכלל מאמרם ז"ל ס"פ אלו עוברין לא כהעוה"ז העוה"ב. העוה"ז נכתב בי"ה ונקרא בא"ד אבל העוה"ב נכתב בי"ה ונקרא בי"ה והבן. והוא ענין הכתוב (ישעיה ל') ולא יכנף עוד מוריך והיו עיניך רואות את מוריך. וע' ז"א יתרו ל"ד סוף ע"א כנפים כסויין לאתכסאה שמהן וכו' ע"ש היטב כל הענין: ולכן פתח ית"ש ראשית עשרת הדברים אנכי ה' אלקיך. כי זה כל עיקר יסוד האמונה שצריך כל איש ישראל לקבוע בלבו שרק הוא ית"ש הוא הבעל כח האמיתי ונשמת וחיות ושורש העיקר שלו ושל כל הברואים והכחות והעולמות כולם:

הגה"ה

(*) וי"ל עפ"ז מאמרם ז"ל עפ"ז הכתוב (מכילתא לגי' רש"י בחומש) שהיו שומעים את הנראה ורואים את הנשמע. ור"ל שכ"כ נתבטלו מהם אז כל כחות הגשמיות ונזדכך השגתם מאד. עד שכל מציאות עניני המוחשים הגשמים שהיו תחלה רואים אותם ראי' חושי' עתה נתבטלו אצלם מראותם כאיש ראותם והתבונן בהם כלל עד שדרך משל אם היה רוצה מי להבינם עניני המוחשים הגשמיים היה צריך לספר להם להשמיעם לשמע אזן שישנם במציאות. והענינים הרוחניים שתחלה הי' צריך להבינ' עניינם לשמע אזן. עתה ראום בחוש ראותם ונפלאות השגתם:

זהו ענין ופי' של שם אלקים בעל הכחות כולם. אבל עכ"ז לפי פירושו וענינו של זה השם משמע שיש במציאו' גמור גם עולמו' וכחות מחודשים מרצונו הפשוט יתברך שצמצם כבודו והניח מקום כביכול למציאות כחות ועולמות. אלא שהוא יתברך הוא נשמתם ומקור שרש כח חיותם שמקבלים מאתו ית' שמתפשט ומסתתר בתוכם כביכול. כענין התפשטות הנשמה בגוף האדם. שאף שהיא מתפשטת בכל חלק ונקודה פרטית שבו. עכ"ז לא נוכל לומר שהגוף מתבטל נעדר כאלו אינו במציאות כלל. וכן בכל כח ועולם עליון שמתפשט בכל עצמות הכח והעולם שתחתיו. עכ"ז גם הכח והעולם התחתון ישנו במציאות. והוא כפי אשר מצדנו בענין השגתנו כמש"ל: אבל שם העצם הוי"ה ב"ה מורה על הבחי' והענין כפי אשר הוא מצדו יתברך שנתבאר למעלה (ואף שגם שם הוי"ה ב"ה נקרא ג"כ מצד התחברותו ית' ברצונו להעולמות. כי עצמות אדון יחיד א"ס ב"ה בבחי' היותו מופשט מהעולמות לא אתרמיז בשום שם כלל. אעפ"כ העולמות המה בטלים ומבוטלים במציאות נגדו יתברך מצד זה השם המפורש. והוא מעין הבחי' כפי אשר מצדו ית') ולכן נקרא שם העצם שם המיוחד כ"כ:

וזש"ה כי ה' הוא האלקים כו'. ר"ל עם פי מצד השגתנו הוא נקרא בשם אלקים ומצדו ית' נקרא בבחי' שם הוי"ה ב"ה. באמת שכל א' וה' הוא האלקים כו'. כמש"ל פ"ז ענין הצמצום והקו דכלא חדא:

וזהו ג"כ בכלל ענין יחוד פסוק ראשון דק"ש ה' אלקינו ה' אחד. (*) ר"ל לכוין שהוא ית' הוא אלקינו בעל הכחות ומקור שורש נשמתנו וחיותנו ושל כל הברואים והעולמות. ואף שברא והמציא מציאות כחות ועולמות ובריות עכ"ז הוא בבחי' הוי"ה ואחד מצדו ית' שאין הברואים כולם חוצצים ח"ו כלל נגד אחדותו הפשוט יתברך הממלא כל ונקרא גם עתה הוא ואחד:

הגה"ה

(*) ובזה יובן אמרם ז"ל (פסחים נ"ו א') בענין השכמ בשכמל"ו ביחוד ק"ש שתקנו שיאמרוהו בחשאי. משל לבת מלך שהריחה ציקי קדרה וכו' התחילו עבדיה להביא לה בחשאי. ולכאורה יפלא משלם ז"ל הלא שבח גדול הוא: ועפ"י פשוט י"ל דלפי האמת אינו שבח כלל. כמו האם יחשב לשבח למלך ב"ו לומר שהוא מולך על רבי רבבות גמלים ויתושים. והמה מקבלים עליהם עול מלכותו ברצון כ"ש וק"ו אין ערוך כלל שהוא ית' אשר אין ערוך לקדושתו ועוצם אחדותו הפשוט וכל העולמו' כלא חשיבין קמי'. ודאי באמת

וכו׳ · ובפ׳ במדבר קי״ח ב׳ ודמות פניהם וכו׳ · וע׳ ז״ח יתרו במעשה מרכבה ל״ב ע״ג ול״ג ריש ע״א · (ושרש שרשו של האדם הוא מאדם שעל הכסא כנ״ל בשער א׳ פ״ו) ושרשם וחיותם של הד׳ חיות הוא מהעולם שעליהם · וכן עד לעילא ולעילא וע׳ זוהר יתרו פ״ב ב׳ תאנא ברזא עלאה ארבע חיוון אית דאינהו לגו וכו׳ ואינן קדמאי עתיקין דעתיקא קדישא כו׳ תאנא כגוונא דלעילא אית לתתא מנייהו וכן בכלהו עלמין כלהו אחידן דא בדא ודא בדא · וברע״מ ואית חיוון דסחרן לכורסייא דבריאה כו׳ ואית חיוון דיצירה כו׳ ואית ד׳ חיוון דארבע יסודות וכו׳ · וע׳ ע״ה שער קיצור אבי״ע ספ״ח · ושם בסוף השער בענין כחות נפש האדם ע״ש · ושרש כל השרשים דלהון הוא מד׳ אותיות שם הוי״ה ב״ה והן השרשין קדמאין רזא דמהימנותא אבהן דכלהו עלמין שנזכר בזוהר וארא כ״ג סוף ע״ב :

וכן פרטי הכחות והמינים כולם · לכל א׳ יש שורש ושרש לשרש למעלה מעלה · כמאמר׳ ז״ל (ב״ר פ״י) אין לך כל עשב ועשב שאין לו מזל ברקיע שמכה אותו ואומר לו גדל שנאמר הידעת חקות שמים וכו׳ · וע׳ זוהר תרומה קנ״א ב׳ ובפ׳ קדושים פ״ו א׳ הענין באורך קצת · כי אותו הכוכב והמזל הוא פנימיות נפשו וחיותו ושרשו של אותו הצמח שממנו מקבל כח הצמיחה שהיא נפשו כידוע · ושרש ונפש אותו הכוכב והמזל הוא המלאך הממונה עליו שממנו מקבל הכוכב כח הצמיחה להצמיח ולגדל אותו הצמח כמ״ש בזוהר תרומה הנ״ל ועל ההוא כוכבא ממנא חד וכו׳ · ושרש ונפש המלאך הוא מהכח והעולם שעליו · ולכן משביעין את המלאכים בשמות · כי אותו השם הוא נפשו וחיותו ונהורא דילי׳ של אותו המלאך בהעולם והכח שעליו שמאירו ומקיימו · וע׳ זוהר בלק ר״ח א׳ כל אלין מלאכין קדישין דלעילא לא קיימין ולא יכלין למיקם בר בנהורא עלאה דנהר לון וקיים לון ואי פסק מנייהו נהורא דלעילא לא יכלין למיקם · וע׳ ע״ח שער ציור עולמות אבי״ע בהקדמת הרח״ו ושם סוף פ״א ובשער השמו׳ פ״ז שהמלאכים הם בחי׳ כלים והשמו׳ הם העצמות שלהם ופנימיות נשמתם · ולכן הוא פועל בו ומנהיגו לכל אשר יטהו כנשמה שמנהגת הגוף · וכן פז״הד עד לעילא לעילא :

וכן בענין הנשמות שבכל עולם · כל נשמה שרשה ומקור חיותה הוא מבחי׳ הנשמה של העולם שעליה שהיא נעשית ונקראת אצלה נשמה לנשמה · וכן כולם :

והוא ית״ש הוא האלקים בעל הכחות כולם · שהוא נשמת וחיות ושורש השרשים של הכחות כולם · כמ״ש ואתה מחיה את כולם · כל רגע ממש · ולכן נקרא הוא ית״ב׳ נשמתא דכל נשמתין ועקרא ושרשא דכל עלמין :

פרק יא

והענין כידוע בזוהר שהוא ית״ב ודבורו חד · וכל דבור ומאמר של הקב״ה במעשה בראשית שאמר ויהי · הוא הנפש וחיות אותו הדבר שנברא בו וכל רבי רבוות המינים שבו עם המזלות הממונים עליהם והמלאכים הממונים על אותם המזלות ושרשם ושרש שרשם למעלה מעלה שבכל עולם · ומאז והלאה יד כל ימי עולם דברו ית״ב׳ נצב בהם להאירם ולקיימם כל רגע בכל פרטי עניניהם ושינוייהם וסידור מצבם · לכן בכל העשר מאמרות לא נזכר רק שם אלקים שאותו המאמר הוא בעל הכחות של אותו הדבר וכל המינים שבו שנבראו בו · שהוא נפשם המתפשט בפנימיות כל פרטי חלקיהם · רק שעתה נוה עיניהם מראות בעיני הבשר איך ובאיזה אופן דבורו ית׳ מתפשט בהם · ולע״ל כתיב (ישעיה מ׳) וראו כל בשר יחדו כי פי ה׳ דבר · היינו שיזדכך השגתם עד שנזכה להשיג ולראות גם בעין הבשר

ענין

שער ג

דלא לימרו קליי' לאלהי' בנורא · וע' ז"ח רות ס' ע"ב · ובב"ר פ' ל"ו ובתנחומא ר"פ ויחי וכן אתם מוצא בדניאל וכו' מה כתיב באדין מלכא נבוכדנצר וכו' ומנחה וניחחין אמר לנסכא לי' אבל דניאל לא קיבל למה שכשם שנפרעין מעובדי עבומ"ז כך נפרעין מהעבומ"ז עצמה · וכן אמרו שם זה הטע' גם על יעקב אבינו ע"ה שלא רצה ליקבר במצרים הרי שקראו ז"ל ענין זה עבומ"ז · אף שהכוונה היתה לרוח אלהין קדישין דבי' · וי"ל עפ"ז הכתוב לא יהיה לך אלהים אחרים על פני · ר"ל שלא לכוין ח"ו בשום דבר לאיזה בחי' וכח פרטי אפי' אם יהיה אותו הכח בחי' פני היינו אפי' לפרט רו"הק שבאיזה אדם או פרט בחי' הקדושה שבאיזה כח. עליון שבעליונים וכענין מאמרם ז"ל (ר"ה כ"ד ב') על לא תעשון אתי אפי' דמות שמשי המשמשין לפני במרום כגון אופנים ושרפים וחיות הקדש · ועם כי עיקר אזהרת הכתיב על כל העבומ"ז הנ"ל היינו בד' עבודו' דוקא אמנם עתה שעבודת התפלה בהשתעבדות כוונת הלב הוא במקום עבודת הקרבן · ודאי גם ע"ז שייך האזהרה :

וזש"ה זובח לאלהים יחרם בלתי לה' לבדו · היינו שלא לכוין ח"ו בשום עבודה וענין לאיזה כח פרטי מכחות שקבע הבורא יתב' (כי שם אלקים משותף לכל בעל כח פרטי שיהי' כידוע וכמש"ל) · רק לכוין לשם העצם המיוחד לו יתב' לבד שפירושו מהוה הכל היינו כללא ומקורא דכל הכחות כולם כנ"ל (וזהו שמע ישראל ה' אלקינו ה' אחד · ר"ל שכל הכחות פרטים שנמשכים מהוי' ב"ה · המה מאוחדים ונקבלים בבחו יתב"ש כלל מקור אחדותו) · והוא מצד התחברותו יתב' עם העולמות . ולזאת בכל מקום שנאמרה התורה על ענין הקרבנות ביארה בפי' לה' דוקא · וכאמרם ז"ל (סוף מנחות) בא וראה מה כתיב בפ' קרבנות שלא נאמר בהם לא אל ולא אלקים אלא לש' שלא ליתן פ"פ לבעל הדין לחלוק · וע' ז"ח בראשית ו' ע"ד ח' ע"א וע"ב הענין יותר מבואר :

פרק י ולפי

דרכנו בענין הב' בחי' הנ"ל שמלדו יתב' ומלדנו שנתבאר · יבואר עוד הפרש וחילוק שבינהב' שמות ה' ואלקים · כי שם אלקים פי' בעל הכחות כולם · וקצת ביאור ענינו עי' בריש שער א' · וביותר ביאור ענין בעל הכחות · כי כל כח מהתחתון שבתחתונים עד העליון שבעליונים המשכת קיומו וחיותו הוא ע"י הכח שלמעלה הימנו שהוא נשמתו המתפשט בפנימיותו · וכידוע בדברי האריז"ל שהאור ופנימיות נשמת כל כח ועולם הוא עצמו החיצוניות של הכח והעולם שעליו · וכן הולך ע"ז הסדר גבוה מעל גבוה · בין בכללות הכחות · כי כללי כל הברואים וכחות התחתונים · הם מהתמזגות הד' יסודות · ושרש הד' יסודות הם מהד' מלאכים הנקראים ד' מחנות שכינה שסימנם א'ר'ג' מ'ן · והד' מלאכים אלו שרשם מד' חיות המרכבה שהם כללי כל שורשי נפשות כל הברואים התחתונים · שכל האלפי רבוי מיני החיות שרש נפשותם משתלשל מן פני ארי' שבמרכבה · ונפשות כל מיני הבהמות משתלשלים מפני שור · ושל כל מיני העופות מפני נשר · וכמ"ש בזוהר פנחס ר"ח ע"ב רזא דקרבנין כו' פני שור אתפשט לבעירי רואה מני' וכו' ע"ש · ולכן בכל א' מולך עליהם אותו המין שצורתו ושמו הוא כצורת ושם הפנים שבמרכבה כמ"ש ז"ל (חגיגה י"ג א) ובשמות רבה פכ"ג) ארי' מלך בחיות וכו' · ונפש האדם הוא מפני אדם · לכן האדם מתגאה על כולם · כי כן עיקרם וכללם של כל הד' פני המרכבה הוא פני אדם· כמ"ש ומתוכה דמות ארבע חיות וזה מראיהן דמות אדם להנה · וע' בזה בזוהר יתרו פ ב אדם כליל כלהו וכו' · ובפ' תזריע מ"ח סוף ע"א כתיב ודמות פניהם וגו'

שער ג'

לזאת לא נזכר בכל מע"ב רק שם אלקים לבד · ואחר שנגמרו המשכת כל הכחות כפי שגזרה רצונו יתב' לצורך העולם : אז נאמר ביום עשות ה' אלקים שם מלא · וזהו וידעת היום והשבת אל לבבך כי ה' הוא האלקים וכו' · היינו שלא לכוין להשתעבד ולהתדבק בשום עבודה לאיזה כח או כחות פרטים אשר בשמים ממעל ואשר בארץ מתחת · רק לכוין הכל לשם העלם המיוחד הוי"ה ית"ש מקורא וכללא של כלל הכחות כולם שנמשכו ממנו : וזו היתה כל ענין העכו"ם של דורות הראשונים מימי דור אנוש שאז התחילו בעול' ענין העכו"ם כמ"ש אז הוחל לקר' בשם ה' · שהיו עובדים לכחות הכוכבים והמזלות כל א' לכוכב ומזל מיוחד שבירר לעצמו · לא שחשב כל א' שאותו הכוכב הוא אלוה שברא את כל · שהרי מעולם היה שומה בפיהם של העכו"ם לקרותו יה"ש אלהא דאלהין כמשרז"ל · וכן אמר מלאכי הנביא בתוכחתו לישראל כי ממזרח שמש ועד מבואו גדול שמי בגוים כו' כי גדול שמי בגוים אמר ה' צבאות אלא שתחלת טעות דור אנוש היה · שחשבו בשבוש דעתם · כי רם ה' ועל השמים כבודו ואין כבודו להשגיח על ברואי זה העולם השפל ולכן חשבו שהסיר הוא יתב' השגחתו מהם ומסרם לכחות הגלגלים והמזלות שהמה ינהיגו זה העולם כרצונם והיה נחשב אצלם חולין ואיסור גמור וחוצפה גדולה נגדו ית' להתפלל לשמו הנכבד והנורא לבקש מאתו צרכיהם השפלים · לזאת השתעבדו עצמם וכיונו כל עניני עבודתם ובקשתם לכחות הכוכבים והמזלות (ואופן עשייתם הצלמים · וזיבוחם וקטירם אליה · (ע' בתקון ס"ו) · והיו יודעים ג"כ להשביע המלאכים הממונים על המזלות · לדעת טוב ורע ושישפיעו להם ע"י טובות והנאות עה"ז מכחם שנתמנו עליו מאדון כל ית"ש · ומעטים יחידי סגלה היו שהכירו וידעו באמת · שאף שהוא ית"ש מגביהי לשבת : עכ"ז הוא משפילי לראות בשמים ובארץ : ומהם שהיו עובדים לחיות ועופות (כמ"ש מלכים ב' סי' י"ז) ג"כ כוונתם היה להתדבק עצמם עי"ז להכח והמזל העליון של אותה הברי' · שישפיע עליהם מכחו וממשלתו שנתמנה עליו מהבורא יתב' · וז"ש הנשים הארורות לירמי' ומן אז חדלנו לקטר למלכת השמים והסך לה נסכים חסרנו כל כו' (ירמיה מ"ד) · ומהם שהיו משתעבדים ומזבחים ומקטרים לאיז' אדם שראו שכח ממשל' מזלו גדול מאד · בחשבם שע"י השתעבדם ועבודתם אליו יעלה מזלם עם מזלו · ומהם אף שלא היתה כוונת עבודתם להשפעת הנאות עוה"ז · אבל כוונתם היתה להשיג עי"ז איזה השגות בכלים שחמדו להם · כמו חכמת הקסמים וכיוצא איזה השגות · ומהם שהתדבקו לעבודת איזה אנשים כדי להמשיך השפעת אמונת אמון ועניני עתידות · וזהו הכל עכו"ם גמורה · ובכלל לא יהיה לך אלהים אחרים כמ"ש הכל הרמב"ן ז"ל בפירושו על התורה שם · וע' לק"ת ס"פ נח בענין דור הפלגה :

ואפילו להשתעבד ולהתדבק באיזה עבודה לבחי' רו"הק שבאיזה אדם נביא ובעל רו"הק · גם זה נקרא עכו"ם ממש · כמו שמצינו בנבוכדנצר שהשתחוה לדניאל · ג"כ לא בעבור שהחזיקו לאלוה בורא כל · אלא שכיון בהשתחויתו להשתעבד ולהתדבק לרוח הקדש שבו כמ"ש (דניאל ב') באדין מלכא נבוכדנצר נפל על אנפוהי ולדניאל סגיד ומנחה ונחחין וכו' מן קשוט די אלהכון הוא אלה אלהין כו' וגלה רזין · די יכלת למגלא רזא דנא ושם (סי' ד') ועד אחרין על קדמי דניאל כו' ודי רוח אלהין קדישין בי' וכו' · ורז"ל אמרו (סנהדרין צ"ג א') הטעם שלא היה דניאל בעת ציווי ההשתחוי' לצל' שאמר דניאל איזיל מהכא דלא לקיים בי פסילי אלהיהם תשרפון · ונ"ע אמר ג"כ יזיל דניאל מהכא דלא

שער ג

להעסק חקירה במהות ענין הצמצום כפי אשר הוא מצדו יתברך · ורק בענין הקו היינו בהשתלשלות העולמות שכפי השגתנו · בזה הוא שהעמיק הרחיב הדבור · אבל בענין הצמצום דבר בו ברצוא ושוב ולא דיבר במהות ענינו בפרטות · וע' בריש ספר אוצרות חיים ד' ב' ריש ע"ב · ולא גילהו רק מציאותו דרך כלל לבד לחכם ומבין מדעתו · מטעם שודאי ראוי להאדם הישר חכם לבב הקבוע כל הימים בת"ת ומצות אשר נאמנה את אל רוחו · לידע מציאות זה הענין הנורא דרך כלל שאדון יחיד ית"ש מלא את כל ואין עוד מלבדו ית"ב' · להלהיב מזה טוהר קדושת מחשבתו לעבודת התפלה · לכוין לבו באימה ויראה ורתת למקום הוא מקומו של עולם · (ומקומו של עולם הוא הוא כוונת ענין הצמצום · והוא מבואר כנ"ל) · כמאמרם ז"ל שהמתפלל צריך שיכוין לבו למקום · וכן אמרו וכשאתה מתפלל אל תעש וכו' אלא רחמים ותחנונים לפני המקום ב"ה · וכענין שאמר ר"א לתלמידיו (ברכות כ"ח ב') דעו לפני מי אתם מתפללים · וכן ביחוד פסוק ראשון דק"ש בתיבת אחד ראוי להעובד אמתי לכוין בקדושת מחשבתו שהוא ית"ש מצדו הוא אחד כמשמעו גם בכל הברואי' כולם אחדות פשוט לבד כקודם הבריא' וכמ"ש א"ים להלן : גם להיות ירא וחרד מזה מלעבור ח"ו על אחת ממצותיו ית"ב' כי מלא כה"כ · כמש"ה (ירמיה כג) אם יסתר איש במסתרים ואני לא אראנו כו' הלא את השמים ואת הארץ אני מלא · וכענין שאמר דוד המע"ה שויתי ה' לנגדי תמיד : והוא ענין חילול השם הנאמר בכ"מ · כענין שפי' בזוה' פסוק מחלליה וכו' שהוא לשון חלל ופניית מקום · כן הענין כאן שמראה ח"ו כאלו המקום שעומד בו הוא חלול פנוי ממנו יתב' ואינו חושש מלעבור על מצותיו יתב' · וכענין זה מאמרם ז"ל (ספ"ק דקדושין) כל העובר עבירה בסתר כאלו דוחק רגלי השכינה : (ובזה יתישב מאי דקשיא טובא ובעיני כל חכם לב יפלא · מאין התיר האר"י ז"ל לעצמו לדבר ולהזכיר כלל ענין הצמצום · כיון שההתבוננות בו אסורה · ולפמ"ש ענין הצמצום · באמת הענין טהג בכל מקום וזמן גם בזה העולם לשרידים אשר ה' קורא · לידע מציאות זה הענין הנורא מטעמים הנ"ל · וכן ברע"מ ותקונים וקדוש ה' רבינו שמואל בעל שיר היחוד הנ"ל והרוקח ז"ל שהזכירו הענין ברמז למבין · הכל מאלו הטעמים הנזכרי' · וכמבואר למבין ברוקח שם בשורש קדושת היחוד ע"ש) · אמנם הזהר מאד בנפשך · זכור ואל תשכח אשר נתבאר למעלה שאין הדבר אמור אלא לדעת הענין ידיעת הלב דרך כלל בשיעורא דלבא לבד · אבל לא לחקור ולהתבונן ח"ו במהות הענין · וגם להזהר מאד שלא יהא ממשכא לבא לקבוע כל סדר ההנהגה במעשה ע"פי זה הענין הנורא · כי בקל יוכל להולד מזה להתנהג בכמה דברים גם נגד חוקי ויסודי תוה"ק · ולא יעבור כתיב · וכמ"שה וידעת היום והשבת אל לבבך כי ה' כו' · בשמים ממעל וכו' אין עוד · אל לבבך דוקא היינו רק בהובנתא דלבא ושיעורא דלבא לבד · וכענין שאמרו בתפלה יכוין לבו למקום :

פרק ט ומ"ש

וידעת היום כו' · כי ה' הוא האלקים · ההבדל שבין אלו ב' השמות הוא · שאם אלקים נאמר גם על איזה כח פרטי הנמשך ממנו יתב' · ושם הוי"ה נאמר על מקור הכחות כולם שנמשכים ממנו ית"ש · וכינו שאמרו ז"ל בב"ר שהזכיר אחר גמר כל מעשי בראשית שם מלא (היינו הוי"ה אלקים) על עולם מלא · שאם הוי"ה ב"ה הוא מקורא דכלא בי' · ובעת הבריאה נמשך בכל מאמר כח או כחות פרטים ממקורא דכלא להתהו' ולהברא' אותו הדבר וקיומו

לזאת

שער ג

שונים במקומות חלוקים כמו שמנו רז"ל עשר קדושות · וג' מחנות מקודשות · זו למעלה מזו בערך קדושתם · אז מצד קו אור השגתינו התגלות אורו יתב' · הוא שיצדק בו מעלה ומטה · וכל חילוקי המקומות והבחי' שונים ופרטיהם המבוארים בדברי האריז"ל · וכן ענין המקראות אל עליון · ואלקינו בשמים · יושב בשמים · והרבה כיוצא · שמצד השגתנו יצדק לומר שבמקום זה ניכר יותר גם אצלנו התגלות אור אלקותו ית"ש מבמקום אחר שהתגלות אורו יתב' הוא בבחי' הסתר מהשגתנו · וכענין שאמר יעקב אבינו ע"ה בעמדו על מקום המקדש כמו שקבלו רז"ל · אין זה כי אם בית אלקים · ר"ל שבזה המקום מושג גם להשגת האדם שאין בו רק התגלות אור אלקותו יתברך לבד) :

וזהו ענין החלל ומקום פנוי שהזכיר ז"ל · ושכלל ענין הצמצום היה להתגלות הכלים · היינו שגזרה רצונו מטעם הכמוס אתו יתברך · להסתיר אור אחדות עצמותו יתב' בזה המקום שיעור עמידת העולמות והבריות כולם הסתר עצום · להמציא עי"ז ענין נפלא כזה שיתראה ויושג מציאות עולמות וכחות אין מספר דרך הדרגה והשתלשלות · ולהאיר בהם התגלות אורו יתברך אור דק בשיעור ודקדוק עצום ודרך מסכים אין קץ · ועד שיוכלו להמצא דרך השתלשלות ומסכים עצומים גם מקומות אשר אינם טהורים וכחות הטומאה והרע והקליפות בשפל המדרגות התחתונים · ונראה ומתדמה כאלו ח"ו הוא חלל פנוי מאור אחדות עצמותו ית"ש · ואין אנחנו משיגים רק רשימה דקה מועטת ואור מועט כענין קו דרך משל · עד שבהגיעו דרך סדר ההדרגות והמסכים הרבים אל הכחות תחתוני התחתונים כחות הטומאה והרע · אין התגלות אורו יתב' ניכר כלל להשגתנו · וז"ש שם שהקו האור לא הגיע עד קצה התחתון ולא נדבק בתחתיתו ועי"ז ימלא בחי' מעלה ומטה כו' ע"ש · והוא מבואר למבין · והצמצום והקו הכל א' וענין א' · ור"ל עם כי ודאי שגם במקום כל העולמות והברואים הכל מלא גם עתה רק עצמותו ית"ש לבד כקודם הבריאה אמנם הוא בבחי' צמצום היינו בבחי' הסתר לבד מופלא ומכוסה מהשגתינו · כדי שעי' זה הצמצום וההסתר תהא כל השגתינו את העולמות דרך השתלשלות · והמשכת התגלות אורו יתב' בהם בסדר ההדרגה לבד כענין קו דרך משל כנ"ל · וז"ש שם בשער עיגולים ויושר ענף ב' שהקו חוט האור לא נמשך ונתפשט תיכף עד למטה אלא לאט לאט · ר"ל דרך הדרגות רבות מאד בשיעור מדוקדק כפי הצורך להשגתנו ענין העולמות וסדר הדרגתם · והמבין יבין מפי"ז מדעתו כל שורש הענין המבואר שם · כי א"א לפרש ולהסביר היטב כל דבריו ז"ל שם:

פרק ח

ולכן נאסר החקירה והתבוננות במהות ענין הצמצום כמ"ש האריז"ל · כמש"ל שלא הורשינו להתבונן כלל לידע ולהשיג מהות ענין מקומו של עולם איך שהכל מלא רק אחדותו הפשוט יתב' · ואין עוד מלבדו כלל לגמרי מלבדו יתב' · והאמת שהוא בכלל שאלת וחקירת מה לפנים שלמדוהו ז"ל (בר"פ אין דורשין) מכתוב מפורש כי שאל נא לימים ראשונים למן היום אשר ברא אלקים אדם וכו' ואי אתה שואל וכו' · והאריז"ל אשר הורשה והפליא לגלות סודות עמוקים ורמים · כבר פי' הוא ז"ל שפנימיות כוונת הכתוב למן היום אשר ברא אלקים אדם וכו' הוא על עולם אדם קדמאה · וגם בענין איך כתב שאין אנחנו רשאין לדבר ולחקור בענין עצמות פנימיותו · רק בהארות היוצאים ממנו לבד · וגם זאת רק מהארות דס"ג שבו ואילך · ולא בהארות ע"ב שבו · כ"ש שלא הורשינו

להתבונן

יתב׳ · שיתראה לענין ההשגה מציאת עולמות וכחות ובריות נבראים מחודשים · ולזאת חייבים אנחנו לידע ולקבוע בלבנו אמונת אומן בל תמוט · שמצדנו ודאי שיש חילוק מקומות וענינים שונים לענין דינא והלכתא רבתי כמש״ל · כי היא פנת יסוד האמונה ועיקר שורש התורה והמצות כולם :

והוא ג״כ א׳ מהטעמים · שאחר יחוד פסוק ראשון דק״ש אומרים בשכמל״ו · והוא כמ״ש להלן בפ׳ י״א שענין יחוד פ׳ ראשון בתיבת אחד · היינו לכוין שאדון יחיד ב״ה הוא אחד בכל העולמות והבריות כולם אחדות פשוט כמשמעו וכולם נחשבים לאין ואין עוד מלבדו יתברך לגמרי · ושלא נבא להתבונן חלילה על מהות הענין איך ומה · לזאת אנחנו אומרים אח״ז ברוך שכמל״ו שיתבאר שם שהכונה הוא על הבחי׳ שמצד השגתנו שמתראה מציאות עולמות ובריות מחודשים ברצונו יתברך שצריכים להתברך מאתו · והוא המולך עליהם · זהו ברוך שם כבוד מלכותו וכו׳ · (וזהו הענין שפסוק ראשון נקרא בזוהר יחודא עלאה · ופסוק בשכמל״ו נקרא יחודא תתאה · והוא מבואר) :

פרק ז ואלו הב׳ בחי׳ הנ״ל שמצדו יתברך ומצדנו · הן הן עצמן ענין הצמצום והקו הנזכר בדברי האריז״ל · ואשר מבואר שם · שמצד הצמצום לא ידבק בו שום שינוי וחילוק מקום מעלה ומטה פנים ואחור · רק השואה גמורה אמתית · וכל עניני השינויים וחילוק המקומות וכל השמות וכנויים · כולם נאמרים רק מצד בחי׳ הקו · ועי׳ בריש ס׳ אוצרות חיים · ומודעת שכל דברי האריז״ל בנסתרות משל הם · ופנימיות ענין הצמצום והקו · הכוונה על אלו הב׳ בחי׳ הנ״ל שהן בעצם בחי׳ א׳ וענין א׳ לגמרי · כי ביאו׳ מלת צמצום כאן · אינו לשון סילוק והעתק ממקום למקום להתכנס ולהתחבר עצמו אל עצמו כביכול להמציא מקום פנוי ח״ו · אלא כענין שאמרו בב״ר ס״פ מ״ה וצמצמה פניה ולא ראתה המלך · ובאיכה רבתי בריש א״ב דאני הגבר הלכה וצמצמה פניה אחר העמוד · שפירושו שם לשון הסתר וכיסוי (עיין בערוך ערך צמצם) · כן כאן מלת צמצום היינו הסתר וכיסוי · והכוונה · שאחדותו ית״ש בבחי׳ עצמותו הממלא כל עלמין בהשואה גמורה · מכנים אנחנו בשם צמצום · מחמת שאחדותו יתב׳ הממלא כל עלמין הוא מצומצם ומוסתר מהשגתנו · וכענין אכן אתה אל מסתתר (ישעיה מ״ה) · והשגתנו מה שאנחנו משיגים מציאת השתלשלות עולמות זה למעלה מזה בבחי׳ שונים · מכנים אנחנו בשם קו שהוא כענין קו המשתלשל : וז״ש האריז״ל שמצד הצמצום היינו מצד עצמות אחדותו יתב׳ שבהעולמות הממלא את כל · אשר אף שמאתנו הוא מצומצם ומוסתר · אבל בבחי׳ עצמותו לא ידבק ענין מעלה ומטה · רק מצד הקו היינו מצד השגתנו שאנחנו מצדנו משיגים סדר העולמות דרך השתלשלות כענין קו · ידבק מצדנו מעלה ומטה · (ואף גם זאת · שמצד הצמצום · היינו אף שהוא ית״ש צמצם והסתיר מהשגתנו אור עצמות אחדותו הממלא כל · עכ״ז לא ידבק בו מעלה ומטה אף מצד השגתינו אם היינו משיגים הסתר שוה בהשואה גמורה בכל המקומות כענין עיגול המקיף שלא ידבק בו ענין מעלה ומטה וחילוק מקום · אך מצד הקו היינו שמאחר שגזרה רצונו יתברך שגם אחר הצמצום וההסתר · אין ההסתר שוה להשגתנו בכל המקומות בשוה · ואנחנו משיגים השגות שונים בחילוק בחי׳ פרטים דרך השתלשלות כענין קו אור המאיר השגתינו להשיג התגלות אורו יתב׳ בעולמות וכחות חלוקים · שכל עולם וכח היותר עליון ההתגלות אור האלקי בו יותר · וגם השגתינו התגלות אורו יתב׳ בזה העולם · הוא ג״כ בבחי׳ ומדרגות

שער ג

דולה היה מדבר עם משה מבין שני בדי הארון · ארחב"א פעמים שאין העולם ומלואו מחזיקים כבוד אלקותו פעמים שהוא מדבר עם האדם מבין שערות ראשו כו' · וכ"ה בשמות רבה פ"ג · רמזו ג"כ לאלו ב' הבחי' כמבואר למבין :

ולכן נקרא הוא יתברך בכל דברי רז"ל בשם הקדוש ברוך הוא · כי כללו בזה השם הנכבד · אלו הב' בחי' יחד · כי קדוש פירושו מובדל ונעלה · והוא כפי אשר מצדו יתברך שהוא באמת מופרש ומובדל ומאד נעלה מכל עניני החילוקים ושינויים חלילה · רק הכל מלא אחדות גמור לבד בהשוואה גמורה · ומרומם מעל כל ברכה ותהלה ואיננו צריך להתברך ח"ו · ועיין תקונים ת"ע ק"ל סוף ע"א · וגם לא שייך כלל לפי זאת הבחי' שום ענין תוספת ורבוי ברכה · כיון שהכל אחדות פשוט לבד כקודם הבריאה · וכמ"ש (ישעיה מ') ואל מי תדמיוני ואשוה יאמר קדוש · שזה הכתוב נאמר על עצמות אחדותו יתב' כידוע ברע"מ ותקונים · ומצד בחי' השגתנו מציאות הכחות והעולמות · הוא נקרא ברוך כביכול · מצד התחברותו יתב' אליהם · כי הם הצריכים לענין התוספת ורבוי ברכה ושפע ע"י מעשי האדם הרצויים כמש"ל בשער ב' · וזהו הקדוש ברוך הוא · ר"ל שהוא מצדו יתב' קדוש והוא הוא עצמו נקרא ברוך כביכול מצדנו והכל אחד . וע"ז הבחי' שמצדנו הוא שנאמרו המקראות · אל עליון · יושב בשמים · והרבה כיוצא :

פרק ו

והנה כל יסודי תורה הקדושה בכל האזהרות והמצות כולם עשה ול"ת · כולם הולכים ע"פי זאת הבחי' שמצד השגתנו שודאי יש חילוק ושינוי מקומות · שבמקומות הטהורים מותרים וגם חייבים אנחנו לדבר או להרהר ד"ת · ובמקומות המטונפים נאסרנו בהם אף בהרהור ד"ת · וכן כל עניני וסדרי חוב הנהגותינו שנצטווינו מפיו יתב' בתוה"ק · ובלתי זאת הבחי' שמצדינו אין מקום לתורה ומצות כלל · ואף שבאמת שמצדו יתב' המשיג עצמותו הוא מלא את כל בהשוואה גמורה בלא שום חציצה ולא שום חילוק ושינוי מקומות כלל · רק הכל אחדות פשוט כקודם הבריאה ממש · אבל אין אנחנו יכולים וגם לא הורשינו ליכנס כלל להתבונן בינה בזה הענין הנורא · לידע ולהשיג איך אדון יחיד ב"ה מלא את כל וכל המקומות באחדות פשוט ושווי גמור · חליל' וחלילה · וכמ"ש הרוקח ז"ל בשורש קדושת היחוד ז"ל הק' במופלא ממך אל תחקור כו' · ז"ש בריש ברייתא דס' יצירה השב היוצר על מכונו הוא היוצר כל כו' · ובברייתא אחרת ואם רץ לבך שוב למקום שלכך נאמר והחיות רצ"א ושוב · פי' כשתחשוב בלבך על בורא עול' מה הוא ואיך חנייתו בכל מקום ומעשיו · בלום פיך מלדבר ולבך מלהרהר הסר המחשבה מלבך · ואם רץ לבך למחשבה זאת חושה ומהר ואל תהרהר ושוב ליחוד מקומו של עולם לעבודתו וליראתו וכו' · ועל דבר זה נכר' ברית שלא לחשוב באלקותו שאין כל החכמים יכולין לידע עכ"ל · ועי"ש באורך · וכל צבאות המוני מעלה שואלין איה מקו"ם כבודו · שאין יכולין להשיג מהות ענין בחי' מקומו של עולם הנ"ל · והוא מאמרם ז"ל בפ' אין דורשין (י"ג ב') דמדאמרי ברוך כבוד ה' ממקומו מכלל דמקומו ליכא דידע לי' · ומשרע"ה בקשה נפשו להשיג הענין באמרו הראני נא את כבודך היינו בחי' מקום כבודו הנ"ל · ולא ניתן לו · ורק הוא לבדו יתב המשיג עצמותו הוא היודע עצמות מהות זה הענין המופלא ומכוסה · והנסתרות לה' אלקינו · ואנחנו אין רשאין להתבונן אלא במה שהורשינו והנגלות לנו להשגתנו · והוא בהבחי' שמצדינו שנקרא הוא ית"ש בבחי' סובב כל עלמין · מחמת שעכ"ז למלא ברצונו הפשוט כבודו יתב'

שער ג

שעומדים העולמות עתה · ולכך תשית לדברי קדוש ה' רבינו שמואל אביו של הקדוש ר"י חסיד בשיר היחוד שחיבר · ביחוד יום ב' אין קצה כו' ואין תוך מבלעדיך כו' ע"ש · וביחוד יום ג' סובב את הכל ומלא את כל · ובהיות הכל אתה בכל כו' ע"ש עוד בזה:

וז"ש רז"ל בהדברים שדימו התחברותו יתברך להעולמות · להתחברות הנשמה להגוף · מה הנפש טהורה בגוף אף הקב"ה טהור בעולמו (וי"ר סו' פ"ד) ר"ל כענין הנשמה אף שמתפשט' בכל פרטי אברי האדם · הנקיים וגם המלאים לכלוך מטונפת ומזוהמת · ועכ"ז אינם חוצצים כלל לענין טהרתה וקדושתה וטהרתה עומדת · כן הענין· אם שהוא יתב' ממלא את כל · וכל המקומות · מקומות הטהורים והמקודשים ואשר אינם טהורים· אעפ"כ אינם חוצצים כלל ולא גורמים שום שינוי חלילה לקדושת טהרת עצמותו ואחדותו הפשוט יתב': וז"ש (מלאכי ג) אני ה' לא שניתי·* וכמ"ש בתז"ח דף פ"א סוף ע"ד וכל ישראל דקבילו מניה אורייתא אינון עבדין לי' אחד בה ובכל אתוון ושמהן קדישין דילי' ובכל משריין עלאין ותתאין דאתבריאו בהו ובכל בריין עלאין ותתאין · ולעילא מכלהו אחד ולתתא מכלהו ומגאו דכלהו ומלבר דכלהו איהו אחד כו' הכי איהו מגאו דכל עלמין כמו מלבר דכל עלמין לא אשתני כו':

הגה"ה

ולפי מה שיתבאר אי"ה להלן ענין החילוק שבין הב' שמות הוי"ה ואלקים · שהשם אלקים פירושו מורה על הבחי' אשר מצדנו · ושם העצם הוי"ה יתב' מורה על הבחי' שמצדו ית' · לזאת אמר אני ה' לא שניתי · וע' תקונים ת"ע בענין האודנין אמר וארבע אתוון דאינון הוי"ה איהו לא אשתני בכל אתר כד' שינויין אינון במאני דגופא אבל בי' לית שינויא כלל הה"ד אני ה' לא שניתי:

פרק ה

אבל עכ"ז הן הן גבורותיו ונוראותיו ית"ש · שאעפ"כ צמצם כביכול כבודו יתב' שיוכל להמצא ענין מציאות עולמות וכחות ובריות נבראים ומחודשים · בבחי' שונים וענינים מוחלקים · וחילוקי מקומות שונים · מקומות קדושים וטהורים · ולהיפך טמאים ומטונפים והוא הבחי' אשר מצדינו · היינו שהשגתנו אינה משגת בחוש רק ענין מציאותם כמו שהם נראים · שע"פי זאת הבחי' נבנו כל סדרי חיוב הנהגתינו שנצטווינו מפיו יתברך חק ולא יעבור · ומצד זאת הבחי' הוא שדימוהו רז"ל · כביכול כענין הנשמה אל הגוף וכמ"ש בזוהר שהוא יתב' הוא נשמתא דכל עלמין · שכמו שבאדם לא נראה בחוש רק הגוף והנשמה אף שהיא מלאה את כל הגוף · הוא בבחי' הסתר לעיני בשר ונגלית לעיני שכל· כן כפי השגתינו הנגלית · נראה מציאות העולמות והבריות כולם · ושהוא ית"ש מתפשט ומסתתר כביכול בפנימות כולם להחיותם ולקיימם · כענין הנשמה שמתפשטת ומסתתרת בפנימות כל פרטי חלקי אברי הגוף להחיותו · וכל השמות והכנויים והתארים והמדות עליו יתב' שמצינו בתוה"ק · כולם מדברים מצד זאת הבחי' כפי שהוא מצדינו וסדרי חיוב הנהגותינו · שהוא מצד התחברותו יתב' אל העולמות שמצדם ועל ידיהם נמשך כל השינויים של פרטי סדרי ההנהגה כולם כמש"ל בשער ב':

וז"ש בהקדמת התיקונים הנ"ל דע"ס דאצילות מלכא בהון איהו וגרמי' חד בהון איהו וחיוהון חד בהון · מה דלאו הכי בע"ס דבריאה דלאו אינון ואיהו חד לאו אינון וגרמיהון חד ועלת על כולא הוא נהיר בעשר ספירן דאצילות ונהיר בע"ס דבריאה ובעשר כתות דמלאכייא ובעשר גלגלי דרקיעא · ולא אשתני בכל אתר · רמז לב' הבחי' הנ"ל כמבואר · ובב"ר פ"ד אמרו כשהוא רוצה הלא את השמים ואת הארץ אני מלא · וכשהוא רוצה

שער ג

לבנו לקבוע לנו מחשבה זו להתיר לעצמנו להתנהג גם במעשה לפי המחשבה זו · הלא יוכל להולד מזה ח"ו הריסת כמה יסודות התוה"ק ר"ל · ובנקל יוכל להלכד ח"ו ברשת היצר שיראה לו היתרא ע"פי מחשבה זו דרך משל להרהר בד"ת בשאט נפש אף במקומות המטונפים אחר שיוקבע אצלו שהכל אלקות גמור · ורז"ל הפליגו בזה מאד וכרתוהו ברוח קדשם מהיות לו חלק לעה"ב ר"ל · כמ"ש (ברכו' כ"ד ב') שבכלל כי דבר ה' בזה הוא גם המהרהר ד"ת במבואות המטונפים · וממילא נשמע סיפי' דהאי קרא הכרת תכרת וכו' ופירשוהו ז"ל בפ' חלק (צ' ע"ב) הכרת בעוה"ז תכרת לעה"ב · ועוד כמה טעיות שיוכל לבא ח"ו אם היה נקבע ההנהגה במעשה ע"פי זה הדרך · וזה שהביאני להכנס לדבר בזה הענין ולהזהיר ולהרחיק מטעות שיוכל להולד מזה ח"ו · ולהבין על בוריו כל מה שרמזו לנו רז"ל בזה · והנם ככל דרכי ה' הישרים ועת לעשות .

פרק ד ולהשב הדבר על מכונו · נבאר מאמר קדישין רז"ל

שמבואר בע"ח לוקח מהתקונים בכ"מ · שהוא ית"ש ממלא כל עלמין בהשוואה גמורה והרי מליט שגם בעולמו' העליוני' כל עול' חלוק ומשונ' מחבירו בבחי' שונים · בענין התחברותו ית' אליה' · וכמ"ש בהקדמ' התקוני' דעשר ספי' דאצילו' מלכא בהון איהו וגרמי' חד בהון איהו וחייהון חד בהון מה דלאו הכי בע"ס דבריאה דלאו איהון ואיהו חד וכו' · וע' בע"ח שער השתלשלות הי"ס בריש סדר האצילות בקיצור כתב שא"ס ב"ה בבחי' התלבשותו והתפשטותו בכל העולמות אינו נוגע ודבק זולתי בעולם אצילות לבד ולא בבי"ע ולכן מהם ולמטה ישתנה מהותם · וגם בשער דרושי אבי"ע פ"ז כפי' מאמר התקונים הנ"ל כ' שהאצילות כולו ש בחי' הכלים נק' אלהות גמור משא"כ בבי"ע ע"ש · וכן מבואר שם החילוק העצמי שבין האצילו' לג' העולמו' בי"ע בענין האלקו' ע"ש בריש שער ציור עולמות אבי"ע בהקדמ' הרח"ו ובשער השתלשלות הי"ס פ"ג · ושער הצלם פ"א · ושער השמות פ"א · ושער סדר אבי"ע פ"ב וריש פ"ג · וכיוצא כמה חלוקי בחי' וענינים שונים בין העולמות פרטי פרטים · המבואר בכל הזוהר ודברי האר"י ז"ל · וע' היטב בסוף ס' ארבע מאות שקל כסף בענין ידיעתו ית"ש מקודם במעשי האדם · שחילק האר"י ז"ל בזה בין העולמות · ויתר על כן שמצינו כמה מקראות כמו אל עליון יושב בשמים אשר אלמלא מקרא כתוב א"א לאומרם וכן מנו רז"ל עשר קדושות וג' מחנות מקודשות · זו למעלה מזו :

אבל אמיתת הענין · הט אזנך ולבך חביב והלך לבטח ·

כי מבואר בכ"מ בזוהר שאדון יחיד א"ס ב"ה ממלא כל עלמין וסובב כל עלמין והיינו שמצדו ית' נקרא בבחי' ממלא כל עלמין · ומצדנו כפי אשר נצטוינו בתוה"ק בענין הנהגותינו בתורה ומצות · וכפי השגתנו בחוש · נקרא ית"ש בבחי' סובב כל עלמין שבחי' ממלא כל עלמין הוא כבוד אלקים הסתר דבר מצדנו · והענין כי ודאי האמת שמצדו ית' גם עתה אחר שברא וחידש העולמות ברצונו הוא ממלא כל העולמות והמקומות והבריות כלם בשיווי גמור ואחדות פשוט · ואין עוד מלבדו כמשמעו ממש · וכמ"ש מהמקראות מפורשים ובשם הרוקח ז"ל · וכמו שתקנו לנו קדמונינו ז"ל לומר קודם התפלה אתה הוא עד שלא נברא העולם אתה הוא משנברא העולם · ר"ל אף שכבר נבראו העולמות ברצונו הפשוט ית' עכ"ז אין שום שינוי והתחדשות ח"ו ולא שום חציצה מחמתם בעצמות אחדותו הפשוט והוא הוא גם עתה כקודם הבריאה שהי' הכל מלא עצמות א"ס ב"ה גם במקום שעומדים

ומתילא נשמע · שגם בזה הענין עצמו שדימוה ז"ל לא הושוו גם לגמרי · כי אף שאמרו מה הנשמה מלאה את כל הגוף אף הקב"ה מלא את כל העולם · וכן מ"ש במאמר התקונים הנ"ל כנשמתא כו' ולית אבר פנוי מינה · וגם בת"ע בכל אבר איהו הוי"ה וכו' לית אתר פנוי מני' כנשמתא דאשתכחת בכל אבר ואבר דגופא · אין ענין מלוי הקב"ה את העול' כענין מלוי הנשמה את הגוף שעכ"ז גם הגוף ישנו לעצמו חוצץ בפניה · רק שמתפשטת בפנימית כל פרטי חלקיו ותקייםו · שהרי גם בצאת הנשמה מהגוף אין הגוף מתבטל עי"ז מנמציאות · אבל אדון כל ית"ש הוא מלא את כל העולמות והנבראי' ואינם חוצצים חלילה נגדו ית' כלל באמת · ואין עוד מלבדו ית' ממש שום דבר כלל בכל העולמות · מהעליון שבעליונים עד התהום התחתון שבתהומות הארץ · עד שת"כ לומר שאין כאן שום נברא ועולם כלל רק הכל מלא עצמות אחדותו הפשוט ית"ש · וע' רוקח בס' שורש קדושת היחוד ז"ל הבורא אינו צריך למקום יתכן כי היה קדם כל הויות ואין קירות והקורות יכלין לפניו כי לא היה בורא דבר שהוא מזיק כנגדו ·

פרק ג. והוא ענין הכתוב (ירמיה כ"ג) הלא את השמים ואת הארץ

אני מלא · ויותר מפורש במשנה תורה וידעת היום וגו' כי ה' הוא האלקים בשמים ממעל ועל הארץ מתחת אין עוד · וכן אתה הראת לדעת כי ה' הוא האלקים אין עוד מלבדו · והוא ממש כמשמעו שאין עוד מלבדו ית' כלל בשום בחי' ונקודה פרטית שבכל העולמות עליונים ותחתונים והבריות כולם · רק עצמות אחדותו הפשוט ית"ש לבד · והוא פנימיו' אמרם ז"ל בדברים רבה פ"ב ד"א כי ה' הוא האלקים וכו' יתרו נתן ממש וכו' רחב וכו' משה עשאו אפי' בחללו של עולם · שנאמר כי ה' כו' בשמים ממעל ועל הארץ מתחת אין עוד · מהו אין עוד אפי' בחללו של עולם · וזה ג"כ בכלל מאמרם ז"ל שהוא יתב' מקומו של עולם ואין העולם מקומו · היינו שאף כל המקומות שמורגשים לחוש במציאות אין המקומות מקומות עצמים · אלא הוא ית"ש הוא המקום של כל המקומות · שמלדו יתב' נחשבים כולם כאלו אינם במציאות כלל גם עתה כקודם הבריאה :

אמנם כבר הקדמנו בתחלת דברינו · שהמשילו דבריהם ז"ל כגחלי אש · שיהא זהיר מאד בגחלתן שלא ליכוה להתבונן ולחקור יותר מדאי · בדברים שאין הרשות נתונה להתבונן הרבה ויכוה ח"ו · וכ"ה זה הענין הנורא · אין הדבר אמור אלא לחכם ומבין מדעתו פנימיות הענין בשיעורא דלבא לבד ברצוא ושוב · להלהיב בזה טוהר לבו לעבודת התפלה· אבל רב ההתבוננות בזה הוא סכנה עצומה · וע"ז נאמר בס"י ואם רץ לבך שוב למקום כמש"ל פ"ב וכמ"ש אי"ה להלן פרק ו' · ובאמת הייתי מונע עצמי מלדב' בענין זה כלל כי הראשוני' ז"ל הסתירו הענין מאד כמו שתראה דברי קדוש ס' הרוקח ז"ל הובא לעיל שלא דיבר בזה רק ברמז · כי נאמנה את אל רוחם וכסו דבר · אבל שנתי וראיתי · שכך היה יפה להם לפי דורותיהם · אבל עתה הן ימים רבים ללא מורה · וכל דרך איש ישר בעיניו להלוך אחרי נטיית שכלו · וכל יצר מחשבו' לב האד' אלא רק לשוט במחשבתו אל כל אשר יטנו שכלו· והעולה על כולם · שזה תורת כל האדם ונעשה משל גם בפי כסילים· לאמר הלא בכל מקום וכל דבר הוא אלקות גמור · ועינם ולבם כל הימים להעמיק ולעיין בזה : עד שגם נערים מנוערים ממשכא להו לבייהו לקבוע כל מעשיהם והנהגתם בזה לפי שכלם זה · וכמה זהירות יתירה צריך האדם להזהר בזה ולשמור את נפשו מאד במשמרת למשמרת · באם חיו יקחנו

איך כל העולמות וכל צבאם המה בעצם אין · ורק כל רגע המה מתהוים למציאות ממנו יתברך · לזאת בחרו להמשילהו יתברך ולהסביר לאזן שומעת בקרב חכמים · בתיבת מקום · *) שאף שכך גזרה חכמתו יתבר' ליתן מציאותו לעולמו באופן שלאה כל שכל להשיג איך הוא המשכת התהוותם ממנו ית"ש כל רגע · ויוכל להדמות בעיני בשר שהעולם הוא מציאות וקיום בפני עצמו ח"ו · האירו עיני השכל בהמשילם לענין מקום · שכמו שהכלי העומדת על איזה מקום · הנה בהכלי הרי יש לה באמת מציאות בפני עצמה · עכ"ז אם לא היה להכלי מקום שתעמוד עליו · היתה כלא הי'. כן אף שהעולם כולו מורגש ונדמה כמציאות בפני עצמו · הוא ית"ש הוא מקומו : שאלמלא הי' מקום ברצונו להתהוות העולמות · עכ"ז שהיו כולם כלא היו * : וזה"ש בס"י פ"א מ"ח ע"ם בלימה בלום פיך מלדבר ולבך מלהרהר · ואם רץ לבך שוב למקום שלכך נאמר רצוא ושוב · אמר למקום דייקא . היינו שאם ירוץ מחשבת לב האדם להשיג' המושכל איך נמשך התהוותם כל רגע ממנו ית"ש · שוב למקום להשיג ערך המושכל מדמיון המורגש בבחי' מקום כנ"ל · וע' פי' הרמב"ן ז"ל על משנה זו :

* הגה"ה

ודרך דרש נוכל להעמים בפסוקי (איוב כ"ח) והחכמה מאין תמצא · שהחכמה הגדולה על כל חכמה המושגת מאתו ית' הוא החכמה הנפלאה שמאין תמצא כל רגע מציאות · ואיזה מקום בינה היינו שאין במציאות איזה שכל שנוכל לבנות שהשכל ההוא הוא מקום מוכשר שתחול עליו בינה להבין כח הנפלאה הזה וסיים והוא ידע את מקומה :

הגה"ה

גם המשילוהו יתב' בבחי' מקום · שכמו שהמקום ע"י נתקיים הכלי אף אם אינו שוה בערך עם הכלי · וגם המקום אף אם ע"י מתקיימים כמה וכמה כלים שונים זה מזה · אין גורמים ע"ז שום שינוי בהמקום · והמקום מקיים וסובל כולם בהשואה אחת · כך הוא ית"ש מקיים כל העולמות. אף שאין ערך כלל בינו ית' וביניהם · דאף כ"ע חוכמה איהו לגבי' דא"ס · וגם אם

ונע"ז הכוונה דרכו רז"ל הקדושים · להמשיל משלים במענין התחברותו יתב' להעולמות · אף שאין ערך ודמיון כלל בין המשל והנמשל רק באיזה דבר פרטי · ואף גם זאת רק בדמיון מה · וכמ"ש ברע"מ פ' פנחס רכ"ז ב' ורכ"ח א' ואית למנדע כו' כגוונא דא ברא נשמתא כו' ומה רבון עלמין לית לי' שם ידיע ולא אתר ידיע אלא בכל סטר שלטנותי' · אוף הכי לית לה לנשמתא כו' אלא בכל סטר שלטנותא לית אבר פנוי מנה כו' · בכל היכן שמהן וכנויין אתקרי' ע"ש כל עלמין כו' לאתחזאה שולטניה עלייהו אוף הכי נשמתא על שולטנותא דכל אברים דגופא אתקיל לה לגבי · לאו דארמיא לי' איהי בעלמה · דהוא ברא לה וכו' ועוד כו' · ובג"ד איהי אדמיא לגבי' בשולטנותא דילה על כל אברי גופא אבל לא במלה אחרא · וע"ש באורך · וכן כל הדברים שמנו רז"ל שם בענין התדמותו יתב' להנשמה בגוף · הכל הוא רק על ענין התפשטותו ית"ש בהעולמות וממלאם ושליטותו עליהם כנ"ל · שרק בדבר זה לבד מתדמין בעניינם · וכן רמזו בתקונים סוף תל"ח אמרו דאשתמע קלי' ודבוריה מן כרסייה ומלאכייה ושמייא וארעא דישתמודעון לי' בכל עילא ותתא כנשמתא דשלטנותה בכל גופא אפילו באבר זעירא ולית אבר פנוי מינה · דייק באומרו כנשמתא דשלטנותה וכו' · ומזה

כי נראה לנו שנויים השנויים שונים מנגד הבריאה מדרגות שונות זו מזו · ואף כי נמצאים גם כחות הטומאה והס"א בכל מדרגותם · והקיום של כולם הוא רק ממנו יתברך לבד · עכ"ז לית בי' שנוי ית"ש דאיהו לא אשתני ומלבדו ית' הוא מקיימם בדמיון מקום · ואם כי דבר זה אין בשום שכל להשיג איך ומה וסוד פלאי · לזה המליצו רז"ל הנה מקום אתי אתראי ספלה לי פי' שלית מחשב' תפיסא איך הוא בבחי' מקום בלי שינוי · רק הוא יתברך לבדו המשיג עלמותו משיג איך הוא מקומן דכולהו עלמין בלי שנוי · כענין והוא ידע את מקומה · וזהו אתי דייקא · כענין לבא לפומא לא גליה :

שער ג

פרק א

כאן למקו"ם · וכן באבות אמרו וכשאתה מתפלל אל תעש תפלתך קבע אלא רחמי' והתחנונים לפני המקום ב"ה · רמזו ז"ל בתיבת מקום לענין גדול · והענין צריך ביאור להבין עומק כוונתם ז"ל בזה · ולמסבר קראי הרומזים ע"ז :

וכבר אמרו ז"ל באבות שכל דבריהם כגחלי אש · שכמו הגחלת שאף שלא נראה בה רק ניצוץ אש · אם תשים כחך בה להפכה ולנפחה · כל שתנפחה יותר תתלהב ותתפשט בה הניצוץ · עד שתעשה כולה לוחשת ותוכל ליהנות ממנה להשתמש לאורה ולהתחמם נגדה · אבל רק נגדה ולא לאוחזה · שכיון שנעשית לוחשת צריך זהירות שלא תכוה בה · כן בדמיון זה כמשלו כל דברי חכמים · שאף שנראים דברים קלים ופשוטים · אבל הם כפטיש יפוללו · שכל שהאד' מהפך ומסלסל ומדקדק בהם יאורו עיניו משלהבת אורם הגדול · שימצא בתוכם ענינים עמוקים · כאמרם ז"ל הפוך בה וכו' דכלא בה · אבל צריך להזהר מאד בגחלתן · שלא ליכנס להתבונן ולחקור בדברים שאין הרשות נתונה להתבונן בהם יותר מדאי · כאמרם שם והוי מתחמם כנגד אורן של חכמים · היינו שלא להתרחק מלהתבונן כלל בדבריה' כי לא יהנה מאורם כלל · וגם לא יתקרב יותר מדאי שלא יכוה כנ"ל · רק מנגד · כמו שסיים את"ז והוי זהיר בגחלתן וכו' :

והנה כאן בתי' מקום נ"כ · הגם שפשוטו מובן · אבל כשנדקדק בו נמצא שכללו ורמזו בזה עוד ענין גדול · כי ענין מה שהוא יתב' נקרא מקום . פירשוהו ז"ל בב"ר פס"ח ע"פ ויפגע במקום · ר"ה בשם ר"א אמר מפני מה מכנין שמו של הקב"ה וקוראין אותו מקום שהוא מקומו של עולם ואין עולמו מקומו ובשמות רבה ס"פ מ"ה ובתנחומא פ' תשא ויאמר ה' הנה מקום אתי אר"ב"ח וכו' הרי טפלה לי ואין אני טפל לאחרי · וכ"א בשו"ט תהלים מזמור צ' · ולפי פשוטו ר"ל כמו שהמקום הוא סובל ומחזיק איזה דבר וחפץ המונח עליו · כן בדמיון זה הבורא אדון כל ית"ש הוא המקום האמיתי הסובל ומקיים העולמות והבריות כולם · שאם היה יסלק כחו מהם אף רגע אחת · אפס מקום קיום וחיות כל העולמות · וכמ"ש ואתה מחיה את כולם · והוא פנת יסוד אמונת ישראל כמ"ש הרמב"ם ז"ל בריש ספרו · ולכן קורא בזוהר לאדון כל ית"ש נשמתא דכל נשמתין · כמו שהנשמה מחיה ומקיימת הגוף וכמ"ש (סנהדרין ל"א ב') וכי אפשר לחתיכת בשר ג' ימי' וכו' · כן הוא ית"ש הוא לבדו חי העולמי' כולם וכידוע במקומות רבות בתקונים ורע"מ · וע' בריש הקדמה שני' של התקונים במאמר פתח אליהו וכו' · וכן רז"ל דימו קיום כל העולם ע"י כחו יתב' · לקיום הגוף ע"י כחות הנשמה · אמרו מה הנשמה מלאה וזנה את כל הגוף אף הקב"ה מלא וזן כו' · זהו פשטות ענין שהוא יתב' נקרא מקומו של עולם :

פרק ב

אמנם פנימית ענין מקומו של עולם · הוא ענין גדול מאד · כי מה שכנוהו ית"ש מקומו של עולם · אין ערך כלל · לענין מקום הנושא כל חפץ העומד עליו שעצמות התהוות וקיום הכלי יש לה מציאות בפני עצמה · והמקום רק מקבלת אותה שלא תפול ותשבר · וכן ענין חיות וקיום הגוף ע"י הנשמה · הגוף יש לו מציאות בפני עצמו · ואינו מתבטל ממציאותו גם בצאת הנשמה ממנו · אבל העולמות כולם כל עיקר התהוות מציאותם כל רגע הוא רק מאתו ית"ש · ואלו היה מסלק רצונו יתב' מלהוות אותם כל רגע היו לאין ואפס ממש · ורק מחמת שאין בכח שום נברא אף עליון שבעליונים להשיג מהות הענין איך

שער ב

עתה בחי' שורש הנשמה · ואחר התחי' נתבונן בינה בסוד סדרי צרופי האותיות בשורש קדושתם · והוא שאמרו בזוה' בהעלותך קנ"ב א' אורייתא כו' ולעלמא דאתי זמינין לאסתכלא בנשמה לנשמתא דאורייתא **והוא** בחי' שורש נשמות כלל ישראל יחד · מ"ל דאצילות · לזאת נקראת כנסת ישראל (*) :

הגה"ה

(*) **ונקראת** כתי"הק אל אלקי הרוחות לכל בשר · ע' זוהר קרח קע"ו ב' ויאמרו אל אלקי הרוחות כו' דאיהו אתר דנשמתין וכו' תמן סלקין ומתמן אתיין · ורז"ל דרשו אביו ואמו כו' אתו זו כ"י וע' זוהר במדבר קי"ט א' ובריש פ' פנחס ושם ר"מ ע"ב וברע"מ תלא רע"ז ב' ובסוף האד"ז רנ"ו א' ובז"ח רות נ"ט ב' · וע' בע"ח שער המלכי' ריש פ"ז ובפע"ח שער עולם העשי' פ"ב ובשע' הק"ש פ"ה ובשער העמידה סוף פע"ז · והוא ענין הכתוב העמוסים מני בטן וכו' ע' בפע"ח שער ר"ה פ"ג ולכן כלל ישראל יחד נקראין אברין דשכינתא · ע' זוהר פנחס רל"ח ב' ושם רל"ח ריש ע"ב ורנ"ב סוף ע"ב · וזהו ענין הכתוב הלוך וקראת באזני ירושלים כו' זכרתי לך כו' לכתך אחרי במדבר כו' כינה הכתוב כלל ישראל בשם ירושלים · כי היא היתה כנסית כלל ישראל בעלותם לראות פני האדון ה' ברגל · ושם קבלו כלל ישראל שפע תורה קדושה ויראה כ"א לפי שרש אחיזת נשמתו מכנ"י · ולזה נקראת ירושלים של מעלה ז"ש אהבת כלולתיך ר"ל כלילות · **וזהו** ענין שכינה הנזכ' בכל מקום פי' הפשוט של שכינה היינו קביעות דירה · כמאמרם ז"ל (ב"ר פ"ד ובתנחומא בחקתי) מיום שברא הקב"ה עולמו נתאוה שיהא לו דירה בתחתוני' ועיקר קביעת דירתו ית"ש היה בירושלים התגלות קדושתו בלי התלבשות לבושין · והוא שאמרו ז"ל (שבת קמ"ה ב') דאמרי אינשי ביתא שתאי בלא מתא תותבאי · ושיתם ז"ל צריכה תלמוד :

פרק יח

והנה אחר שכבר הורגל וסדור' לו תפלתו בהתקשרות הג' בחי' נר"ן שבכללות נפשו ע"י האותיות ונקודות וטעמים שבכל תיבה כמש"ל פט"ז · יתעלם בטוהר מחשבתו וכוונתו לדבק אח"ז כל הג' בחי' נר"ן בבחי' נשמה לנשמתא הנ"ל שהוא שורש נשמתו (*) · ע"י צרופי האותיות של התיבה בשורש קדושתם העליון וכשיתדבק בזאת המדרגה אז יוכל להחשב כאלו אינו בעולם כלל · וממילא יתבטל בעיניו מכל וכל · כי בחי' זאת היא נעלה ממדרגת האדם עתה כמש"ל · ויכלול עצמו בשורש נשמתו בכלל שורש העליון של כלל נשמות ישראל יחד :

הגה"ה

(*) **ולכן** תקנו שתיכף אחר העמידה ימסור נפשו ורוחו ונשמתו לגמרי למיתה בפסוק אליך ה' נפשי אשא · ולהעלותם עם הנר"ן של ג' העולמות ולכוללו' יחד במ"ל דאצי' כמ"ש בפע"ח בש"ו משער התפלה · והוא עיקר כוונת כל נפילת אפים הנז' בתור' · כמ"ש בזוהר קרח קע"ו ב' הנז"ל בפנים · ת"ח משה ואהרן מסרו גרמייהו למיתה · במה בגין דכתי' ויפלו על פניהם ויאמרו אל אלקי הרוחות כו' ובכל אתר נפילת אנפין להוא אתר הוי כו' · אלקי הרוחות דאיהו אתר דנשמתין דעלמא וכל נשמתין תמן סלקין ומתמן אתיין ולכן צריך לכוין ברעותא דלבא כאלו נפטר מן העולם לגמרי כמ"ש בזוהר ס"פ במדבר ובריש פ' ואתחנן · ועיין היטב בפע"ח בכל פ"ב משער נפילת אפים והבן · ועיין עוד שם בפ"ג ופ"ד ובלק"ת פ' שלח ע"ש :

לכן קבעו אנשי כנה"ג לומר קודם התחלת תפלת העמידה הפסוק אדני שפתי תפתח · כי מי שזוכה למדרגה זו בעת התפלה · הרי מהתקשרות המחשבה זו יוכל להיות גופו כאבן דומם וכאלם לא יפתח פיו · רק שהוא ית' יפתח שפתיו לדבר לפניו תיבות התפלה · ולכן אמר שם אדני דוקא שהוא סוד כנסת ישראל הנ"ל ועיין בפע"ח סוף שער הבריאה בענין זה הפסוק קודם התפלה שאחז"ל עליו שהוא כתפלה אריכתא (ברכות דף ד' ע"ב) · ושרז"ל שמתפלל צריך שיתן לבו למעל' וכעין שפי' ר' יונה ז"ל שם · וכן חסידים הראשונים שהיו שוהי' שעה א' וכו' כדי שיכוונו את לבם למקו' · והוא מבואר :

הגה"ה

ולכן כלל סדר התפלה נחלק לד' · שהן הד' בחי' נר"ן ושרש הנשמה · הקרבנות הם נגד בחי' הנפש ועולם הנפש עשיה כי אם נא ס על העשי בחי' הנפש כמ"ש ונפש כי תחטא כו' והביא כו' ופסוקי דזמר' נגד עול' הרוח עולם המלאכים המשוררים · וק"ש וברכותיה נגד היכלין דבריאה כידוע · עולם הנשמות · ובאמירת פרשיות הקרבנות עד ב"ש · יכוין להעלות כל בחי' הנפשות דעשיה שהוא הפנימיות דעשי' · לכללם ברוחו' דיצירה · ויכלול גם נפשו עמהם לקשרה ברוחו · ומב"ש עד ברכות ק"ש יכלול כל הנפשין דעשיה והרוחין דיצירה וגם בחי' נפשו ורוחו בנשמתין דבריאה · ומברכות ק"ש עד העמידה יכלול ויעלה כל הנר"ן דבי"ע ונר"ן שלו עמהם לכוללם יחד בשורש הנשמה ושורש הכנסיה של כלל נשמות ישראל יחד · וע' קלת מכ"ז בפע"ח ס"א משער התפלה · וזה שרמז שם האריז"ל כמ"ש ועי"כ נכללת השכינה מכולם כו' ע"ש · וז"ש האריז"ל לקבל ע"ע קודם תפל' מצות ואהבת לרעך :

שער ב

ממנו לגמרי · או נפגם ונתקלקל ח"ו · ואז אין התקשרותו בבחי' הנשמה בשלימות כראוי ואם ח"ו הרבה והוסיף לחטוא יותר · אז גם בחי' נפשו נפגמת או נכרתת ח"ו לגמרי מהתקשרותה בבחי' הרוח · וכשהוא חוזר בתשובה · הוא חוזר להשיג אותם כסדר ממטה למעלה היפך מסדר הסתלקותם תחלה · תחלה הוא משיג לבחי' הנפש · ואח"כ בא ושורה עליה הרוח ומתקשרת בו · ואח"כ באים והושפעים עליהם גילויי אור הנשמה · ואז מתקשרים כל אחד בחבירו כראוי · וכזה מבואר הכתוב מאליו :

ואף שבשער א' פ"כ נתבאר · שאם פגם או הכרית ח"ו בחי' נפשו · והוריד כל ע' ספירותיה במצולות הרע · ע"י תשובתו הוא מאציל ומשפיך קדושה ואור עליון מלמעלה של בחי' נשמתו תחלה · וממנה נמשך על רוחו · ואז הרוח מבהיק מזיו האור הגדול הנשפע עליו גם על הנפש · ועי"ז היא מתעלת מעמקי הרע להתקשר בבחי' הרוח כמקדם וכן עד"ז אחר נפגם הרוח ח"ו כמש"ש · וכידוע בדברי האריז"ל שלתיקון איזה פרצוף ובחי' · צריך להמשיך אורות ומוחין חדשים מלעילא לעילא דרך כל הפרצופי' והמדרגות כולם עד אותו הפרצוף והבחי' שצריך לתקנו שאליו נמשכו המוחין · היינו רק כדי להעלות הנפש מעמקי הטומאה שנשקעה בתוכו או לתקן פנימותה · צריך להמשיך קדושה ואור עליון מלמעלה למטה · לגרש ולכלות ברשפי אש השלהבת הזה את הכחות הטומאה שנשקעה בתוכם או למלאות פנימתה · ולהעלותה מטוהרה ומתוקנת שתוכל להתקשר עם הרוח · וכן עד"ז בבחי' הרוח שנפגם · כדי לחזור ולתקנו כבתחלה · אבל אחר שכבר נתקנו ע"י התשובה · סדר כניסתם אח"ז בגוף האדם הוא ממטה למעלה כנ"ל וזהו ושב פי' כשהיה משיב כל בחי' על מקומה · אז היה נרפא :

פי"ז אמנם עוד יש לאלוה מלין לפני העובד אלקים בקדושה · בבחי' יותר פרטית · והוא בבחי' שורש הנשמה היא נשמתא לנשמתא הנזכר בזהר · ונקראת חיה · ואדה"ר השיגה ולבחי' היחידה הנכללת בה · סוד עולם אדם קדמאה · וכמבואר למבין בע"ח סוף שער המוחין שאדה"ר זכה לבחי' חיה יחידה האמיתים במקומם העיקרי · וע' ריש גלגולים ובפי"ז שם · וזהו עיקר כוונתם ז"ל שדרשו בפסוק תוצא הארץ נפש חיה אפי' נפשו של אדה"ר אפי' נפשו של משיח · כי זאת הבחי' היא סוד כ"י ארץ החיים העליונה · (היינו שרש יסוד העפר מהד' יסודין שרשין קדמאין

אכן דכלהו עלמין הנזכר בזוהר ואדרא כ"ג ע"ב ע"ש) · וע' זוהר שמות י"ב א' ובפ' שלח קע"ד ב' רזא דכתיב תוצא הארץ נפש חיה וכו' · ובפ' שמיני ל"ט ב' ואת כל נפש החיה כו' · וע' ס"פ ואתחנן במתני' · וע' רמ"בן ז"ל בפסוק נעשה אדם · כי רוח ה' דיבר בו · ולכן היה אדה"ר מוכן לחיות לעולם · כי היא החכמה תחי' בעליה · ולכן נקראת חיה · וזהו תוצא הארץ נפש חיה · ובחטאו נסתלקה הימנו · וע' מ"ש האריז"ל בפע"ח וריש פ' כ"א ובפ' ל"ה מהגלגולים · ומאז לא זכה אליה שום אדם בעודו בזה העולם · ואיך כשהגיע לזאת המדרגה וירש מעלתו של אדה"ר כמ"ש בז"ח תרומה ל"ה ע"ג ושם בשה"ש כ"ד ע"ד ע"ש וברע"מ קדושי' פ"ג ובמתניתין ס"פ ואתחנן כמו שפירשם האריז"ל בפ' בראשית בדרוש אדה"ר ובגלגולים פי"ח ע"ש וכמ"ש שם פל"ה-לא הוה יכיל עלמא למסבלי' והוכרח להסתלק מזה העולם · וכן אליהו נסתלק מזה העולם כשהשיג קצת מאותה הזיהרא עלאה כמ"ש בפי"ט מהגלגולים וכמ"ש בזוהר ויגש ר"ס ריש פ"ב א"ל קב"ה כו' ועלמא לא יכיל למסבלך עם בני נשא · ואנחנו מקוים להשיגה אחר התחי' אי"ה שיערה עלינו רוח ממרום והוא בחי' שורש המחשבה של אדם · כי בחי' המחשבה הוא כשמדבק מחשבתו לחשוב איזה ענין פרטי · והוא בחי' נשמה כמ"ש ונשמת שדי תבינם (איוב ל"ב) · ואז המחשבה מושגת עכ"פ להאדם עצמו המחשב · אבל שורש מקור הולא כלליות כח המחשבה · הוא טמיר ונעלם לגמרי שאינו מושג גם להאדם עצמו מאין תמצא · והוא בחי' שורש נשמתו · וזאת הבחינה הנעלמה · היא בחי' לגופי האותיות של התיבה · שהוא שורש נשמת האותיות וכח רוחניות בשרשם העליון · ואמיתת מהות סדרי צרופם בשרש העליון אינו מושג לנו עתה · אחר שאין אנחנו משיגי'

שער ב

מהפה אם לא ע"י ליריק הנקודות אליהם לכן האותיות לבד בלא נקודות נקראים בחי' גוף (היינו עם התגין כמ"ש בהג"ה) שהוא בחי' נועשה כידוע · והנקודות הם בחי' רוח שלהם · כנ"ל שהנקודות באים עם האותיות ע"י הדבו' של האדם שהוא בחי' רוח · וכמו שעיקר חיות האדם ע"י בחי' הרוח שבו · שבלאת ממנו הרוח הוא מת אף שחלק מנפשו נשאר בו עדיין כידוע· כן עיקר חיות תנועות האותיות הם הנקודו' · שבלתם א"א להוציא האותיות מהפה · וכמ"ש בכ"מ בתקונים והמשכילים אלין נקודי · יזהירו דנהרין באתוון · והטעמים של התיבות הם בחי' המחשבה וכוונת הלב · שהוא בחי' הנשמה כידוע כי הם תנועות והנהגת הנקודות והאותיות ונטייתם לאיזה צד שהוא דבר התלוי במחשבה בשכל ובז"ח פה"ש נ"ז ע"ד הורי זהב אינון תנועי דטעמי כו' בנין דאינון אתיין מרישא דמלכא למיהב דעתא וסכלתנו לאתוון כלהו · וע"ש עוד בענין הג' בחי' ט' נ' א' באורך · ושם ד' נ"ח ע"ג תנועה דטעמי דאינון תקונא ושלימו ברעותא וסוכלתנו למנדע ידיעה בו כלהו מטלניהון בחכמתא ובסכלתנו כו' · תנועי דאיהו שלימו דכלא אן אינון כב"כ . אלא רזא דא כו' לנו סוכלתנו ומדע כו' הן בזקיפו הן למיזל כו' בלא איהו מנדע וסכלתנו כו' ע"ש · ולכן נקראים טעמים · כמו שהטעם והפי' של כל ענין הוא השכל הנסת' שבענין בתוכו יוכל האדם להבינו במחשבתו ובתיקון י"ח ל"ה ב' ואתוון אינון לגבי נקודין כגופא לגבי רוחא כו' · ומאנא דנקודין איהו נפש · נשמתא איהי כתר על כלהו ומנה כתרין דאינון טעמי הנועה דנקודין ואתוון · ואיהי תליא במחשבתא · ונקודין תליין באמירה · ואתוון בעשיה :

ולכן העובד האמיתי בכוונה רצויה · יכוין לשפוך ולדבק יחד בתפלתו כל הג' בחי' נפש רוח נשמה אשר נפשו כלולה בהם · שבעת שמוציא מפיו כל תיבה מהתפלה שיש בה כל הג' בחי' נר"ן באותיותיה ונקודותיה וטעמיה· יתעלם בטוהר לבו בעוצם התשוקה לקשר ולדבק על ידה ממטה למעלה בסדר התדרגות נפשו ברוחו ורוחו בנשמתו (*) ויתעלו כולם לשרש אותה התיבה בעולמות העליונים וזהו הענין שאמרו בתז"ח ע"ו ריש ע"א והמשכילים כו' אינון דאית בהון שכל לאשתמודע בצלותא איך סלקא כו' באתוון ונקודי וטעמי כו' ע"ש · ושם בדף ע"ח ריש ע"ג ואשר כח בהם לעמוד בהיכל המלך בעמידה דצלותא כו' · כלילא מכלא טעמי ונקודי ואתוון :

ג"ן שהם ענין כפ"ע · והטעם בזה תפור'בע"ח שער ט'נ'ת'א' פ"ו ז"ל שם בקיצור גם בזה יובן ענין תאמר התקוני' כי פעם הוא אומר כי האותיות הם גופא כו' · ובמקומו' אחרים מצאנו כי האותיות נפש כו' · א"כ האותיות נקראים גוף כו' והתגין כו' הם הנפש דהאותיות · וכמו שהנפש אינה נפרדת לעולם מהגוף כך התגין אינן נפרדין מאותיות בס"ת לעולם משא"כ הנקודות וטעמים כו' · כי התגין הם משתתפי' ומתחברין בעצמות האותיות שהם גוף והתגין הם כללות האותיות כו' · ובעבור זה אין התגין רמוזים ונזכרים בתקונים יען כי הם והאותיות משתתפים יחד כו' · כי בהזכיר את הגוף ממילי' הנפש בכלל כי הם משותפים כנ"ל · עכ"ד וע"ש באורך :

הגה"ה

(*) ועי"ז יתוקנו כל הג' בחי' אלו · אף אם פגם ח"ו באיז' מהם ע"י מעשיו או דבוריו או מחשבותיו אשר לא טובים וגרם ח"ו על ידיה' לרחק ולהפריד ההתקשרות שביניהם כמש"ל בשער א' פי"ח · עתה עי"ז יתוקנו להזוג ולהתקשר כל א' בחבירו שעליו כבתחלה · שזהו שורש עיקר ענין התשוב' כמש"ש באורך ע"ש · וזהו ענין הכתו'(ישעי' ו') השמן לב העם הזה ואזניו הכבד ועיניו השע · פן יראה בעיניו ובאזניו ישמע ולבבו יבין ושב ורפא לו · שבסיפי' דקרא הסידור הפוך מסדרי' דרישי' · כי הלב הוא בחי' המחשבה כידוע · והאזנים הם כלי שמיעת הדבור · והעינים הם כלי הראי' לראות עניני המעשים בפועל · והם הג' בחי' נר"ן · ובחטאי האדם המה מסתלקים ממנו מעט מעט כסדר · שמפת שעולה על רעיון האדם לבד מגד הנפש לעבור שום חטא אז מסתלקת בחי' הנשמה תיכף כי היא בחי' גבוה ונעלה מאד ואם ח"ו חטא יותר גם בחי' הרוח מסתלק ממנו

שער ב

להתדבק כביטול בו ית"ש · ז"ש כאן ולעבדו כו' ובכל נפשכם · וכן מ"ש חנה ואשפוך את נפשי לפני ה' · והוא מבואר · וכן י"ל מאמרם ז"ל (תענית ח' ע"א) אין תפלתו של אדם נשמעת אא"כ משים נפשו בכפו · היינו להעלות ולדבק בתפלתו את נפשו למעלה · וכפו פי' שרשו מלשון וכפתו לא רעננה (איוב ט"ו):

ושנאה · וזהו אוהבי ה' שנאו רע · וזהו הללו את ה' מן השמים הללוהו במרומים:

פט"ו ומ"ש ובכל נפשכם · ידוע פלוגתת רז"ל בכמה דוכתי בש"ס · לחד מ"ד תיבה כל פי' כולו · ולחד מ"ד פי' מקצת וכל שהו · וכן הוא הענין כאן שניהם אמיתים · כי כמה בחי' ומדרגות יש בזה · כל אדם לפי כח טהרת לבו ומחשבתו · שהאדם שכחו יפה בטהרת המחשבה והכוונה · יוכל לדבק את כל נפשו מגודל האהבה והתשוקה לו ית"ש · וכל א' לפי כחו · וגם לפי ענין הכנת טהרת לבו אז · כי גם לא כל העתים שוות באדם בטהרת המחשבה · רק זאת ראוי ונכון · שעכ"פ יראה שתהא כוונתו רצויה לדבק לו יתב' באהבתו וטהרת לבו מקצת נפשו בכל תיבה · לכ"א הכתוב ובכל נפשכם דלהוי משתמע לתרי אפי כנ"ל כל א' לפי כחו ומדרגתו והכנתו · ועיקר ההכנה לזה הוא לפי הנהגתו כל היום והלילה בתלמוד תורה ומצות · ומדרגת חנה היתה · ששפכה בתפלתה לפניו ית"ש כל נפשה · לכן אמרה ואשפוך את נפשי כו' ושפיכה פי' לגמרי כידוע בש"ס · (והיינו שלא נשאר לה שום רצון לעניני עה"ז · כי נפש פי' רצון כמ"ש (שמואל א' ד') מה תאמר נפשך ואעשה לך · ורצון הכללי קשור בכלל הנפש):

והנה כל הנ"ל בענין התפלה · שעיקרה שפיכת הנפש לדבקה לו יתב' בכל תיבה היינו שפיכת כלל הנפש לו ית' · בלא כוונה והבחנה בבחי' הפרטי' הכלולי' בנפש · אמנם יש מדרגה יותר גבוה בזה · והוא לכוון בבחי' הפרטים הכלולים בנפש אלא שצריך חינוך להרגיל עצמו ממדרג' למדרגה · שאחר שכבר הורגל בתפלתו איזה זמן בענין שפיכת והתדבקות כלל הנפש · אח"ז יעתיק עצמו לכוון בבחי' הפרטים שנפשו כלולה מהם : והוא

הגה"ה

וצריך שתדע · שאף בהתפללו במדרגת התקשרות פרטי הנפש זה בזה · לא יניח תקומה מהתקשרות כלל הנפש כי הוא פרט הצריך לכלל · וכלל הצריך לפרט · היינו שקודם התפלה העיקר לקשר כלל נפשו ורצונו המקיפים כלל פרטי כחותיו ורצונותיו להכלל באור ה' · ועל כל תיבה ותיבה שמתפלל ידביק פרטי כחות נר"ן ועפ"י כח התקשרות הכללי יומשך קו אור ישר על כל פרט · שיוכלו כל פרטי רצוני להכלל בהתקשרות כח המקיף הכללי · ועיין ע"ח דרושי עגולים ויושר · וזהו ענין המבואר שם שקו האור שנמשך מאור א"ס ב"ה לא הגיע עד קצה תחתית המקיף · ועיין במבוא שערים פ"כ · ויובן ענין המקיפים זה תוך זה הנפשי' דרך המשכת קו האור · היינו שכל כח פרטי לפי מדרגתו צריך לקשרו בכללי · וגם הכלל הוא לפי ערך הפרט · וראשית קו אור המשיכה הוא המשכת מחשבה הכללית לליבא אמצעיתא דכל גופא · שכל תיבה נמשכת מהכלל הלב · והוא מבואר למבין מדעתו:

פרק ט"ז

כי ידוע שנפש האדם בכללה · היא כלולה מג' בחי' פרטים · והם נר"ן · שהם עצמם הג' בחי' מעשה דבור ומחשבה · שזה כל האדם וגם בכל תיבה יש ג' בחי' מעש' דבור מחשב' · כנר"ן והם אותיו' ונקודות וטעמים שבה · כמ"ש בהקדמת התקונים ז' ע"ב טעמי איגון נשמתין · ונקודין רוחין · ואתוון נפשין (*) וכ"א שם בריש תס"ז ע"ש · האותיות הם בחי' מעשה כי מציאת אותיות גרידא בלא נקודות א"א שיהיו אלא בבחי' מעשה היינו מעשה הכתיבה כמו שהם כתובים בס"ת בלא נקודות · כי בדבור א"א להוציאם מהפה

הגה"ה

(*) ואף שבכתבי האריז"ל מחלקם לד' בחי' ט' נ' ת' א' כידוע הכל א' · ועיקרם הם רק ג' בחי' שרשיים · כי בכל ס' התקונים מחלקם רק לג' בחי' ט' נ' א' לבד. ולא נזכרו בו ענין התגין של כל האותיות רק הג' זיונין של שעטנ"ז ג"ץ

שער ב

לא נשארה רק עבודת התפלה במקומה · שגם היא סגולתה לקשר ולייחד העולמות עד לעילא לעילא. כא"ס ב"ה כמבואר במקומות רבות בזוהר · ויותר מפורש בפ' ויקהל רי"ג ב' כד סלה למארי' בצלותא אדבק רעותי' כגונא בגלותא ליחדא אינון רקיעין תתאין דסטרא דקדושה לאעטרא לון בשמא חדא תתאה · ומתמן ולהלאה ליחדא אינון רקיעין עלאין פנימאין למהוי כלהו חד כו · ובעוד דפומי' ושפוותי' מרחשן · לבי' יכוין רעותי' יסתלק לעילא לעילא ליחדא כלא ברזא דרזין דתמן תקיעו דכל רעיונין ומחשבין ברזא דקיימא בא"ס · וכמבואר בפע"ח שכל עיקר כוונת ענין התפלה מראשיתה עד אחר העמידה · הוא תיקון העולמות והתעלותם ממטה למעלה להתקשר ולהתכלל כל א' בהעולם שעליו לעילא לעילא עד א"ס ב"ה · וע"ש פ"ד ופ"ה ופ"ו ופ"ז משער התפלה הענין בכללות · ופ' ברע"מ ריש ס' עקב שזהו החילוק בין ברכות המצות והנהנין לברכות התפלה · שברכות המצות והנהנין הם המשכת השפע להרקא ברכאן מלמעלה למטה · אבל ברכות התפלה הם תיקון העולמות עלאין והתעלותם והתקשרות כל עולם בעולם שמעליו · וע' בפע"ח ריש שער הברכות ובריש כ"ג שם (ומ"ש עוד שם ברע"מ ומעילא לתתא · היינו המשכת השפע מעולה למטה אחר העמידה · וגם זה הוא מצד שחוזרים ומעלים את העולמות כל א' בשלמעלה הימנו · כמ"ש בפע"ח בספ"ה משער התפלה וכריש שער הקדישים כמ"ב וכס"א שם) :

לזאת בעת עומדו להתפלל לפני קונו יתיש יפשיט גופו מעל נפשו (*) היינו שיסיר כל רעיוני ההבלים הבאים מכחות הגוף שנחקקו ונתדבקו בנפשו שלא תהיה עבודת תפלתו רק בהנפש ורעותא עלאה דילי' · והוא · שקודם עומדו בתפלה צריך לבטל ולהסי' מעליו במחשבתו כל תענוגי הגוף והנאותיו וכל עניניו · עד שיוקבע במחשבתו לאחם הגוף כאלו אינו בעל גוף כלל · ורק נפשו לבדה היא המדברת תפלתה · ובדברו כל תיבה שהיא כח וחלק מנפשו · ידביק בה רעותי' אחד ליהן ולשפוך בה נפשו ממש לגמרי · ולהדביקה בשרש העליון של תיבות התפלה העומדי' ברומו של עולם וכמ"ש בזוהר ויקהל הנזכ' בהגה"ה ובעוד דפומי' ושפוותי' מרחשן לבי' יכוין רעותי' יסתלק לעילא לעילא ליחדא כלא ברזא דרזין דתמן תקיעו דכל רעוהין ומחשבתין ברזא דקיימא בא"ס והוא יחשב כאלו הוא מסולק מזה העולם · והוא מדבר עליה למעלה עד שגם אחר התפלה יקשה לו מאד להפנות מחשבתו לענייני זה העולם · ויהא בעיניו כאלו נופל ומטפ' ויורד מאגרא רמא לבירא עמיקתא · וכענין חסידים הראשונים שהיו שוהי' שעה אחת גם אחר התפלה · והוא שכתב ג"כ האר"י ז"ל הטעם ע"ז כדי להשהות עוד במוחין וכו' · והוא ענין מאמרם ז"ל (יבמות ק"ה ב') המתפלל צריך שיתן לבו למעלה · וכ"כ תרבה ותתלהט אהבתו ית' בכח נפשו · עד שיהא חושק ומתאוה באמת שבדברו עתה אותו הדבור הקדוש של איזה תיבה מנוסח התפלה · תהא נפשו יוצאת מהגוף לגמרי · והתעלה להתדבק

הגה"ה

(*) כמ"ש רבינו יונה ז"ל פ' אין עומדין ל"ה ב' בענין המתפלל צריך שיתן עיניו למטה ולבו למעלה וז"ל הק' שם כלומר שיחשו' בלבו כאלו עומ' בשמים ויסיר מלבו כל תענוגי ע"הז וכל הנאו' הגוף · כענין שאמרו הקדמונים כשתרצה לכוין הפשוט גופך מעל נשמתך · ולאחר שיגיע לזו המחשבה · יחשוב גם כן כאלו הוא עומד בבה"מק שהוא למטה מפני שע"י זה תהי' תפלתו רצויה יותר לפני המקום מפי מורי הרב נרו' עכ"ל ר"י · ומודעת שהר"י היה תלמי' קדוש ה' הרמב"ן ז"ל · ודבריו הן המה דברי הרמב"ן ז"ל בפ' אחרי בפסוק את משפטי תעשו וכו' · וז"ל שם והעוזבים כל ענייני עוה"ז ואינם משגיחים עליו כאלו אינם בעלי גוף וכל כוונתם ומחשבתם בבוראם בלבד כאשר הי' הענין בחנוך ואליהו בהדבק נפשם בשם הנכבד יחיו לעד בגופם ובנפשם וזהו ג"כ מה שהביא ר"י בשם הקדמונים פשוט גופך מעל נשמתך היינו שכ"כ יהי' הגוף וענייניו ותענוגיו נבזה בעיניו נמאס · עד שיהא לו תשוקה עצומה להשליך נפשו מנגד ושתהא כל תשוקת נפשו בבוראו ית"ש כאלו אינו בעל גוף אלא כאחד מלאכי המרום המופשטי' מגשם מופרשים ומובדלי' מכל ענייני עולם הזה · וזהו כוונת ר"י ז"ל שיחשוב בלבו כאלו עומד בשמים · היינו שירגיש בעצמו שנתבטלו אצלו כל הרגשות הגוף שהוא עפר מן האדמה · וכל הרגשותיו יהיו בעניני הנפש לקשרה בשרשה בשמים באהבה רבה · עד שאם היו מעמידים נגד עיניו איזה תענוג מתענוגי עוה"ז שנפשו של אדם מתאוה אליו היה מואס בה מכלי' המיאו'

שער ב

הוא ית"ש בפיהם אלו התיבות ספורות וגנוזות בתוכם כל התקונים · לזאת מי הוא אשר עמד בסוד ה' על עומק כוונתו ית"ש · איזה דרך ישכון אורה של כל תיבה פרטית מהם :

אלא העיקר בעבודת התפלה · שבעת שהאדם מוציא מפיו כל תיבה מהתפלה· יצייר לו אז במחשבתו אותה התיבה באותיותיה כצורתה (*) ולכוין להוסיף על ידה כח הקדושה שיעשה פרי למעלה להרבות קדושתם ואורם · כמש"ל בפ"י שלכן נקראת התפלה דברים העומדים ברומו של עולם שכל תיבה בצורתה ממש היא העול' למעלה מעלה כל אחת למקור' ושרשה לפעול פעולות ותקוני' נפלאים · והיא סגולה נפלאה בדוק ומנוסה למרגילים עצמם בזה · לבטל ולהסיר מעליו בזה כל מחשבות ההבלים הטורדות ומניעות טהרת המחשבה והכוונה · וכל אשר יוסיף הרגלו בזה · יתוסף לו טהרה במחשבתו בתפלה· והיא כוונה פשטית :

הגה"ה

והגם שהלכה פסוקה בש"ס שתפלה נאמרת בכל לשון· היינו לצאת ידי מצות תפלה כמו שנתבאר לעיל סוף ש"א שבכל המצות ואפי' מצות תפלה שנקראת עבודה שבלב · עכ"ז עיקרן לעכובא הוא חלק המעשי שבהן · אמנם למצוה מן המובחר ודאי צריך לצרף גם טוהר המחשב' וכוונה שלימה· ולפי גודל טוהר הכוונה כן תגדל מעשה המצוה ובפרט עבודת הלב שבתפלה · עם כי מי שמתפלל בכל לשון יצא י"ח· אבל אין ערוך למי שמתפלל בלה"ק באלו התיבות דוקא העומדי' ברומו של עול' ומדבק כל כחותיו בהם:

פרק יד אמנם ביאור הכתוב הנ"ל בתחלת דברינו ולעבדו כו' ובכל נפשכם · שעבודת התפלה השלימה צריכה שתהיה עם הנפש · הוא ענין גדול ליודעים ומביני' קצת · וכאשר יתמיד האדם תפלתו בזאת המדרגה שיתבאר אי"ה · יתוסף לו טהרה על טהרתו · כי מצינו בכמה מקומות במקרא ובדברי רז"ל שהתפלה נקראת בשם נפש· כי כמה הלכה' גברוותי בעיקרי התפלה איכא למשמע מקראי דחנה · וכתיב בה ואשפוך את נפשי לפני ה' · וכתיב ברכי נפשי את ה'. הללי נפשי את ה' · ורז"ל בפ"ק דברכות (ה' ע"ב) אמרו שנים שנכנסו להתפלל וקדם א' מהם להתפלל ולא המתין את חבירו ויצא טורפין לו תפלתו בפניו · שנא' טורף נפשו באפו וגו' · פרש"י לך אומר אשר גרמת לך לטרוף את נפשך בפניך ומה היא הנפש זו תפלה כמו שנא' ואשפוך את נפשי כו'. והענין שעבודת התפלה היא במקום עבודת הקרבן(*) וכמו שענין הקרבן היה להעלו' נפש הבהמה למעלה · ולכן עיקר הכפר' היה תלוי בזריק' הדם הוא הנפש · וכן הקטרת האימורים עיקרם היה לכוונת העלאת הנפש · כן עיקר ענין התפלה הוא · להעלות ולמסור ולדבק נפשו למעלה · כי כח הדבור של האדם נקרא נפש כמ"ש ויהי האדם לנפש חיה ות"א לרוח ממללא·וכן נראה לעין שבכל דבו' שהאדם מוציא מפיו · יוצא מפיו רוח והבל הלב · והדבור הוא עיקר נפש האדם שזה יתרון האדם מן הבהמה · א"כ כל תיבה היוצאת מפי האדם היא כח וחלק מנפשו :

הגה"ה

שע"י הקרבנות שבמקדש שהי' כולו בדוגמא עליונה עליותיו וחדריו וכל כלית אשר ישרתו בהם · היו מתקשרים ומתייחדים על ידיהם העולמות והכחות העליונים והנהורין של ההיכלות הקדושים כולם כסדר המדרגות לעילא ולעילא עד א"ס ב"ה · כמבואר במקו"ת רבות בזוהר · בפ' בראשית מ"ה ב' · נח ס"ה א' · לך לך פ"ע ב' · ויגש ר"ו ב' · ויחי רמ"ד א' · פקודי רנ"ט ב' · ויקרא ה' ריש ע"ב לו ל"ו ב' · ז"ח נו ל"ח א' · ושם בש"הש נ"א ב' עש"ה בכל אלו המקומות נוראות הענין וע' בפע"ח פ"ה ופ"ז משער התפלה סדר ההעלאה וההתקשרות בפרטיות · ולכן נקרא קרבן כמ"ש בבהיר אמאי אקרי קרבן אלא ע"ש שמקרב הצורות הקדושות וכו' ואמרו לריח ניחח כו' הרוח יורד ומתייחד בצורות הקדושות ההם ומתקרב ע"י הקרבן והיינו לאקרי קרבן עכ"ל · וע' זוהר ויקרא ריש דף ה' ודף ח' ע"א · וברע"מ פנחס רנ"ו ב' ואתקריאת קרבן ע"ש דאתקריבו בה כו' וע' פע"ח פ"ה משער התפלה · ומעת שבעונינו נפסקה עבודת בית קדשינו

ע"ז כלל · אלא שהטיחה דברי תפלתה לפני ית"ש על הצער של מעלה הנעשה מחמת שהיא שרויה עתה בצער · ולכן אמרו שם שגם משה הטיח דברי' כלפי מעלה כו' אל תקרי אל ה' אלא על ה' ולפי פשוטו מי הכריחם לרז"ל לדרוש אל תקרי ולומר שהטיח דברים כלפי מעלה · אמנם לנעליותא הוא דדרשו הכי וכמ"ש · (ואת פני מבין להבין עד"ז מ"ש שם עוד שגם אליהו הטיח דברים כלפי מעלה שנא' ואתה הסבות את לבם אחורנית (מלכים א' י"ח) · והוא כענין נור לבבי וכו' · וע' זוהר תרומה קכ"א ריש ע"ב וכמ"ש (ישעיה נ') ובפשעכם שולחה אמכם השיב אחור ימינו זהו ואתה הסבות את לבם אחורנית · וכן מפורש בפע"ח שער הק"ש פ"ח ע"ש) :

ואם בענין תפלת היחיד על צערו לצרך שתהא כוונתו רק צורך גבוה לבד · כ"ש במטבע ברכות התפלה הקבועה וסדורה מאנשי הכנסיה הקדושים ודאי ראוי שלא לכוין בהם כלל צורך עצמו הנראה מפשוטם · אלא צורך גבוה לבד · להמשיך תוספת רבוי ברכה וקדושה להעולמות מצד התחברותו ית"ש אליהם · כמש"ל באורך .

ואף שגם רז"ל אמרו (ערובין ס"ה א') יכולני לפטור כל העול' מדין תפלה שנא' שכורת ולא מיין · ומה נאמר עתה בדורות הללו · אשר כל איש הוא כשוכב בראש חבל ובלב ימים כל הימים מעול יגיעת הפרנסות · ולזאת אין איש שם על לב לפנות לבו ומחשבתו מבלבולי טרדותיו העצומי' בהבלי זה העולם השפל · להכין עצמו לקראת אלקיו ית"ש · עכ"ז ודאי שכל א' לפי שכלו והשגתו מחוייב לשית עצות בנפשו ולבקש תחבולות מלחמת מצוה · להמלט מבלבול המחשבות אשר לא טרידים שתתכונן דעתו עליו לעבודת התפלה כראוי · כי עבודת התפלה היא לנו עתה במקום עבודת הקרבן שהיה תלוי כלו במחשבתו של הכהן · שבמחשבתו היה יכול לפגלו · וע"י הרחקת מחשבות חו' הקרבן מתעלה לריח ניחוח לפניו ית"ש :

פרק יג והעצה היעולה על זה· היא כמו שאמר המגיד להב"י

בהקדמה ב' שבריש הספ' מגיד מישרים ז"ל ליזהר מלחשוב בשעת תפלה שום מחשבה אפילו של תורה ומצות כי אם בתיבות התפלה עצמם · דוק בדבריו שלא אמר לכוין בכוונת התיבות כי באמת בעומק פנימיות כוונת התפלה · אין אתנו יודע עד מה · כי גם מה שנתגלה לנו קצת כוונות התפל' מרבותינו הראשונים ז"ל קדישי עליונין ועד אחרון הרב הקדוש איש אלקים נורא האריז"ל · אשר הפליא הגדיל לעשות כוונות נפלאים · אינם בערך אף כטפה מן הים כלל נגד פנימיות עומק כוונת אנשי כנה"ג מתקני התפלה · שהיו ק"כ זקנים ומהם כמה נביאים · וכל מבין יבין · דלא איתי אנש על יבשתא שיוכל לתקן תקון נפלא ונורא כזה · לכלול ולגנוז במטבע תפלה קבועה וסדורה בנוסח א' · התקונים של כל העולמות עליונים ותחתונים וסדרי פרקי המרכבה · ובכל פעם שמתפללין יוגרם תקונים חדשים בסדור העולמות והכחות והמשכת מוחין חדשים אחרים · שמעת שתקנוה עד ביאת הגואל ב"ב לא היה ולא יהיה שום תפלה בפרטות דומה לחברתה שקודם לה ואחריה כלל · דלבושין דלביש בצפרא לא לביש ברמשא ודלביש ברמשא כו' כמ"ש בתקונים תכ"ב · וכן כל יום לחברו שלפניו ואחריו · ולכן ארז"ל (חגיגה ט' ע"ב וברבה במדבר פ"ט) מעוות לא יוכל לתקון זה שביטל ק"ש כו' או תפלה כו' · וכמ"ש באורך בפע"ח פ"ז משער התפלה ע"ש · והוא בלתי אפשר אם לא ע"י הנבואה העליונה ורוח קדשו ית' אשר הופיע עליהם הופעה עצומה בעת תקון נוסח מטבע התפלה והברכות · שם

הוא

שער ב

ישועה שבאה לישראל היא של הקב"ה שנאמר עמו אנכי בצרה כו' (ר"ל ומסיים ואראהו בישועתי) הישועה שלך היא שנא' ולכה לישועתה לנו · ובס"ט תהלים מזמור י"ג יגל לבי בישועתך אר"א זה אחד מן המקראו' הקשים שישועתו של הקב"ה היא ישועתן של ישראל · בישועתנו אין כתיב אלא בישועתך כו' ישועתך היא ישועתנו · וע' זוהר אמור צ' ריש ע"ב בענין הכתוב לה' הישועה · וזהו עמו אנכי בצרה · היינו שמן המצר משתתף אותו ית"ש אז אחלצהו וכו' · וכשהאדם אין מרגיש לצערו מיסוריו · מגודל מרירותו מצערו כביכול · המרורות הללו הן הן עצם מירוק פשעיו · ומתכפר בזה עד שיסורי עצמו בדלין הימנו (והן הן הגבורות: קדושות כדרכו ית"ש להמתיק מר במר · והוא תיקון המדות בשרשן) :

להטיב עמנו בכל · כמ"ש שם תפלין דמארי עלמא מה כתיב בהו · ומי כעמך ישראל גוי אחד · כי מי גוי גדול וכו' · וכן כל הפסוקים דשם הם רק שבחי ישראל . וכלהו כתיבי באדרעי והוא כענין את ה' האמרת היום וה' האמירך היום להיות לו לעם סגולה כו' · שכמו שבתפילין שלנו כתובים שבחי הקב"ה כן תפלין שלו כביכול הם שבחים שלנו · ששם הוא ענין ההתדבקות · והוא ענין הכתוב ישראל אשר בך אתפאר סוד התפלין דמארי עלמא · שהתפלין נקראים פאר כמארז"ל וע' זוה' בשלח ס"ב ריש ע"ב · לכן כשאד' מצטער ואז אין ההתקשרות וההתדבקו' כביכול בין האדם לבינו יתברך שמו בשלימותו כראוי · הוא ענין קלני מראשי קלני מזרועי שהם מקומות התפלין ששם היה ראוי להיו' ההתדבקו' הקדוש

פרק יב ולכן

אר"ז (ברכות ס"ג א') כל המשתף שם שמים בצערו כופלין לו פרנסתו · והענין כי מלבד זה הצער שנעשה למעלה כשמקבל עונשו ביסורים ר"ל · אין ערוך ודמיון כלל זה הצער של מעלה כנגד עולם הצע' שגורם למעלה בעת עשותו העון ר"ל · כענין הבן יקיר שנתפתה ביינו ונפל לארץ ונשבר מפרקתו ונופו והוא מסוכן · והאב עצמו אינו מרגיש אז כלל סכנת נפשו · כמ"ש (משלי כ"ג) הכוני בל חליתי הלמוני בל ידעתי · אמנם אביו לבו מתחמרמר מאד ע"ז וכאשר הרופאים קשרו השברים והניחו רטי' ותחבושת מסמנים חריפים · והבן מר צורח על הכאב שלו מהסמנים החריפים האוכלים בשרו · ועם כי אביו מצטער לצעקתו ורבות אנחותיו עתה · אין ערך כלל הצער של עתה נגד הצער והיגון הראשון שהיה לאביו בעת שנפל ונשבר עצמותיו אשר כמעט נתיאש מחייו אז · כן ממש ע"ז האופן · הוא ענין העון ר"ל · שבעת שהאדם עושהו הוא גורם למעלה צער גדול ועצום לאין ערך · והאדם עצמו אינו מרגיש אז בזה כלל · ולא ידע כי בנפשו הוא · כי הוא נחשב אז כמת ח"ו כמאמרם ז"ל (בר"פ מי שמתו) רשעים בחייהם קרויים מתים · ויש עונות שעל ידיהם נפשו נכרתה ח"ו לגמרי מהתקשרות חבל הקדושה · אבל הוא ית"ש אב הרחמן · כביכול בצרתו לו צר · ומרוב רחמיו וחסדיו ית"ש שולח לו יסורין אשר המה רטיה ותחבושת למרק עונו ואז האדם מרגיש כאב יסוריו ומצטער · ובזה מתעורר ג"כ צער למעלה כנ"ל · אמנם אין ערוך כלל זה הצער נגד הצער שגרם למעלה בעת עשותו העון ח"ו ולכן כשכל תכלית תפלת האדם לפניו ית"ש להסיר מעליו צערו · הוא רק על הצער של מעלה המשתתף עמו בצערו · ושב ומתחרט באמת על עונו שגרם על ידו הצער של מעלה· אז היסורין מסתלקין מעליו · ולא עוד אלא שמודדין לו כמדתו וכופלין לו פרנסתו נגד הב' מיני צער שגרם למעלה ועתה מתחרט על שניהם· וזדונות מתהפכין לו לזכיות :

והוא שדרז"ל בחנה (ברכות ל"א ב') והיא מרת נפש ותתפלל על ה' · שהטיחה דברים כלפי מעלה · ר"ל הגם שהיא עצמה היתה מרת נפש עכ"ז השליכה צערה מנגד ולא אכפת לה להתפלל ע"ז

שער ב

עצמו מנגד ומוסר נפשו ברצונו רק על כבוד המלך · שישיג הכתר מלוכה של אותה המדינה ותנשא מלכותו · כן ראוי נאה להאדם הישר לשום כל כוונתו ועיקר מחשבתו בתפלתו רק להוסיף את כח בהעולמות הקדושים · ולעורר בקולו הקול העליון לאמשכא מחיה ברכאן ונהירו לכלא · להעביר רוח הטומאה מן העולם ויתוקן עולם במלכותו ית"ש · ולא על עניניו וצרכי עצמו כלל · ועינינו הרואות נוסח תפלת ר"ה שהוא מסודר מראשו עד סופו רק על כבוד מלכותו ית"ש שתתעלה כבתחלה קודם חטא אד"הר וגם נוסח תפלת כל השנה · אף שלפי פשוטו הנראה רובו ככולו מסודר על עניני צרכי עצמנו · ודאי ברור לכל מבין ומקומו הוא מוכרע שלא כיונו אנשי הכנסי' הגדולה על הנראה מפשוטי פי' המלות לבד וכמש"ל פ"י · ותפלות נגד תמידין תקנום שהיו עולות כליל לאישים כולה לגבוה סלקא ולא היה בהם חלק הדיוט כלל :

ואף דהלכתא גמירא לה בש"ס · שהיחיד רשאי לחדש דבר בתפלתו על צרכי עצמו וצערו. בכל ברכה לפי ענינה · גם בזה צריך שלא תהא תכלית כוונתו על צערו · ולא זו הדרך הנכונה לישרים בלבותם · כי באמת יפלא איך שייך לבקש להתחנן כלל לפניו ית"ש · להסיר מעליו צערו ויסוריו · כמו בענין רפואות הגוף · הרופא משקהו סמנים חריפים · או אם הרופא מוכרח אף גם לחתוך אבר אחד לגמרי שלא יתפשט ארס החולי יותר האם יתחנן אליו החולה שלא ישקהו הסמנים או שלא יחתוך האבר · הלא החולה עצמו שוכרו לכך כן איך ישפוך שיח לפניו ית"ש להסיר מעליו היסורים · הלא המה רטיה וסמא דחיי לכפר עונותיו · כמאמרם ז"ל (שבת נ"ה א') אין יסורין בלא עון · ואם לא אשות כפש החטאת במה תתכפר :

אמנם תכלית הכוונה · צריכה שתהיה רק לצורך גבוה · כי במקום שיש חילול שמו ית' כגון צרת כלל ישראל · באמור עם ה' אלה והמה מוכים ומעונים · מחוייבים לבקש ולשפוך שיח לפניו ית"ש על חילול שמו ית' · ואך למען שמו יעשה · וגם היחיד על צערו אף אם אין חילול השם בדבר · יש מקום ג"כ (*) לבקש לפניו יתברך על גודל הצער של מעלה בזמן שהאדם שרוי בצער למטה · כמאמרם ז"ל במשנה פ"ו דסנהדרין א"ר מ בזמן שהאדם מצטער שכינה מה הלשון אומרת קלני מראשי קלני מזרועי (*) · ואמרו בשמות רבה פ"ב ובחזית בפסוק אני ישנה · תמתי כו' מה התאומים הללו אם חשש א' בראשו חבירו מרגיש · כן אמר הקב"ה עמו אנכי בצרה · ובתנחומא ס"פ אחרי כל ישועתם

הגה"ה

ואלו ב' האופנים · רמוזים התנא שניהם במשנה פ"ג דר"ה · והיה כאשר ירים משה ידו וגבר ישראל כו' · וכי ידיו של משה עושות מלחמה כו' · אלא לומר לך וכו' · כיוצא בדבר אתה אומר וכו' · הנה האופן הא' הנזכ' במקום שיש חילול שמו ית' · אמר שרמז לנו הכתוב במלחמת עמלק שהיה בזה חילול שמו ית' · כידוע מאמרם ז"ל בפסיקתא משל לאמבטי וכו' · וכן אמרו גם שהיה חותך מילות וזורק כלפי מעלה · וז"ש והי' כאשר ירים משה וכו' וכי ידיו של משה וכו' אלא כ"ז שהיו ישראל מסתכלין רק כלפי מעלה לבד · שלא היתה צעקת תפלתם לפניו ית"ש על צערם אלא רק על חילול שם אביהם שבשמים ית"ש · היו מתגברים גם המה · ואם לאו כו' · ואמר עוד שגם במקום שאין חילול השם בדבר · רמז לנו הכתוב בענין נחש הנחשת · אופן וענין הבקשה והתפלה הרצויה לפניו ית"ש · וכי נחש ממית וכו' אלא בזמן שהיו משליכין צער עצמם מנגד לגמרי · והיו מסתכלין ושופכין תחנתם ובקשתם רק על גודל הצער של מעלה שגרמו בעת עשייתם העון ר"ל · וגם הצער של עתה שנעשה למעלה מחמת שהמה שרויים עתה בצער מיסורי העונש בעונם · אז היו מתרפאין כו' :

הגה"ה

ומ"ש קלני מראשי קלני מזרועי · הענין הם תפילין ש"ר ותש"י כי אחז"ל (ברכות וא"ו ע"א) שהקב"ה מניח תפילין · וענין התפלין שלו ית"ש הוא התדבקותו ית"ש בישראל

שער ב

פרק י ולא זו בלבד שבתיבת ברוך אתה שפירושו הוא תוספת רבוי ברכה ושפע שייך זאת הכוונה · אלא שגם בכל תיבה ותיבה מכל נוסח התפלה · שייך ג"כ זאת הכוונה הק' · כי כל תיבה מהתפלה או של איזה ברכה · היא העולה למעלה מעלה ע"י מארי קלין וגדפין דנטלין לה · לפעול פעולתה בשרשה העליון המיוחד לה · והוא נעשה בזה כביכול שותפו של יוצר בראשית · לבנות ולנטוע כמה וכמה עולמות · כמ"ש בתקונים תקון י"ח ל"ה ב' וכד ב"נ אפיק הבלים ודבורים בצלותיה כמה עופין פתחין גדפייהו ופומייהו לקבלא לון · הה"ד כי עוף השמים יוליך את הקול ובעל כנפים כו' · ונטיל קב"ה אינון מלין ובני בהון עלמין דאתמר בהון כי כאשר השמים החדשים והארץ החדשה כו' · ורזא דמלה ואשים דברי בפיך וגו' לנטוע שמים וגו' ולאמר לציון עמי אתה א"ת עמי אלא עמי בשותפי · וכ"ה שם בהס"ט ק"ז ב' · והמשכיל יבין מדעתו שלא לחנם הוצרכו לתיקון תחנה קטנה ותפלה קצרה כזו ק"כ זקנים ומהם כמה נביאים · אלא שהמה השיגו ברוח קדשם וסגנת נבואתם העליונה ונהירא להו שבילין דכל סדרי בראשית ופרקי המרכבה · לזאת יסדו ותקנו מטבע ברכות והתפלות באלו התיבות דוקא · מאשר ראו והשיגו איזה דרך ישכון אורה של כל תיבה פרטית מהם אשר היא נצרכת מאד לתיקון רבוי עולמות וכחות עליונים וסדור המרכבה · וכמאמרם ז"ל העבודה צורך גבוה וזהו ענין מאמרם ז"ל שהקב"ה מתאוה לתפלתן של צדיקים · ובתנחומא פ' תולדות אמרו ולמה נתעקרו האמהות אר"ל שהיה הקב"ה מתאוה לתפלתם · ובזוהר תולדות קל"ז א' ת"ח עשרין שנין אשתהי יצחק עם אתתיה ולא אולידת עד דצלי צלותיה בגין דקב"ה אתרעי בצלותהון דצדיקייא כו' · מ"ט בגין דיתרבי ויתוסף רבות קודשא לכל מאן דאצטריך בצלותהון דצדיקייא · וכתוב מפורש (משלי ט"ו) ותפלת ישרים רצונו :

ולכן קראו רז"ל את ענין התפלה דברים העומדים ברומו של עולם · (ברכו' ו' ע"ב) היינו שהדברים עצמם הם תיבות התפלה עומדים ברום העולמות · ובזוהר ויקהל ר"א א' צלותא דב"נ איהו פולחנא דרוחא · איהי קיימא ברזין עלאין ובני נשא לא ידעין ·. דהא צלותא דב"נ בקעת אוירין בקעת רקיעין פתחא פתחין וסלקא לעילא וע' בע"ב שם ובדף ר"ב ע"א וריש ע"ב נורא"ת נפלאות ענין עליית כל מלה ומלה דצלותא ובריש פ' ואתחנן ר"ס ריש ע"ב ובשעתא דצלותא קיימא כל אינון מלין דאפיק ב"נ מפומיה בההיא צלותא כלהו סלקין לעילא ובקעין רקיעין עד דמטו כו' ומתעטרי כו' :

והוא מעורר בקולו דלתתא את הקול העליון קול גדול הידוע בזוהר · (וכמ"ש בכ"מ בזוהר דצלותא סלקא לאמשכא ברכאן מעומקא דכלא · והוא הקול גדול) : וז"ש הקול קול יעקב · שבקול תפלת האדם מתעורר לעומתו הקול העליון · ולכן דרז"ל (תענית י"ו ב') ע"פ נתנה עלי בקולה ע"כ שנאתיה ואמרו זה ש"צ שאינו הגון ר"ל שאין כוונתו רק קולו לבד ולא גרם קולו לעורר גם הקול העליון עמו · וז"ש נתנה עלי בקולה לבד ע"כ כו' . וזש"ה (יואל ב') וה' נתן קולו לפני חילו · ולזאת קראו רז"ל את ענין התפלה עבודה שבלב · ועכ"ז אגמרו מקראי דחנה שצריך שיחתוך בשפתיו :

פרק יא ומ"ש לפני חילו · רמז זה העיקר הגדול של ענין התפלה שכלל כוונתה הוא · לכוין רק להוסיף כח בקדושת שכמו שהאיש מאנשי החיל משליך כל ענייניו וצרכי

שער ב

שבטבעו הוא מקלקל ומזיק לגופו · יזיק לו אותו המאכל · או גם יחלה ממנו · ואם שם המות הוא ימות ממנו · ובעצמו נתחייב בנפשו · כן הוא בענין העונות של הנפש החוטאת ח"ו · כיון שכן קבע הוא ית' ברצונו טבע סידור מצבם ועניניהם של העולמות שמעשי האדם הטובים או רעים ח"ו הם כענין מאכל ומזון להם · אין שייך ותרעות בזה והוא מוכרח להריק לכלוך הטומאה שהגביר בעונו בהעולמות ע"י א' מב' התקונים הנ"ל :

ועתה תחזה ובין תבין · ענין התוספת ורבוי ברכה · ומה רב עולם לורך עבודתנו הקדושה בכללה אל עצמות קיום העמדת העולמו' ולהמשיך ולהשפיע בתוכם רב ברכות ותוספת קדושה מצד התחברות עצמותו ית' אליהם כפי הרצון העליון ית"ש · כענין האכילה והמזון כנ"ל · וזהו רצונו וכבודו ית' מעמס כמום אתו ית"ש אשר אין ביכלתנו להשיג · וראוי לכל איש מעם הקדש אשר לבו חרד שיהיו מעשיו רצוים לפניו ית' · לצרף זאת המחשבה וטוהר הכוונה הרצויה · בעסק התורה · ומעשי המצות כולם להמשיך ולהוסיף ע"י אותו המזון קדושה ואור חדש בהעולמות ·

פרק ט ובפרט

בעת עמדו להתפלל לפניו ית'· אשר בשעת' המיוחדת לה היא עיקר המזון להעולמות ולנפש האדם עצמו (*) וכמ"ש בזוהר ברשית כ"ד א' מזונא דילי' צלותא דחשיבא לקרבנא . וברע"מ פ' אמור הנ"ל בפ"ז ורבקה אמרה אל יעקב כו' · לאתער' איהו באינון מטעמי' דילי' · ויעקב אתער מתתא מתלבש בצלותין ובעותין כו' · ויאמר מי איפה הצד ציד בכמ' צלותין ובעותין ואוכל מכל ולו' · ובפ' פנחס רל"ה א' ויאכל מציד בנו אלין אינון צלותין, דאזלין ומתתרכין כו' · ובזוהר שם רכ"ו א' וב' ביאר כל סדר הכתוב אכלתי יערי וגו' גם על סדר מטבע התפל' כולה מראשיתה עד סופה ע"ש · וכן ברע"מ שם רמ"ד א' פירשו ג"כ על סדר התפלה באופן אחר קצת ע"ש · ושם רמ"א ב' אר"ש על רזא דא אסיר לב"נ לטעום כלום עד דייכול מלכא עלאה ומה איהו צלותא כו' עד דמלכא עלאה אכיל והיינו ג"ר וג' אחרונות · כיון דאיהו אכיל כו' · ע"ש באורך · והכל על הכוונה הנ"ל · שהוא המשכת תוספת קדושה וברכה ונהירו לכל עלמין · וכמפורש בזוהר ויחי הנ"ל ע"ש היטב · ולריך העובד האמיתי לכוין לזה :

פרק י'

הגה"ה

ועבודת התפלה נגד תמידין תקנוה שהיו ג"כ בשעת' הקבוע להם עיק' המזון הנ"ל כענין את קרבני לחמי · (את הכבש אחד תעשה בבקר · ואת הכבש השני תעשה בין הערבים· כענין סעודת הבקר והערב שהן עיקר המזון) וכתיב כי את לחם אלקיך הוא מקריב והוא אמרם ז"ל בחזית · רעיתי אין רעיתי אלא פרנסתי הן שירעו אותי בשני תמידין כו' · וע' זוה' ויצא קס"ד א' פתח כו' את קרבני לחמי כו' · ובפ' ויחי רמ"ט ב' ורמ"ח א' בינונין ואב יטרף כו'. ובפ' בא ל"ז ב' יבא דודי לגנו ויאכל כו' ע"ש בכל אלו המאמרים באורך· ובפ' ויקרא דף ד' ע"א ושם בדף ז' סוף ע"א ובפ' בלק ר"ב סוף ע"א ובפ' פנח' רמ"א א' דרשו כל ענין הכתוב אכלתי יערי ווי' על סוד ענין הקרבנות ע"ש · ושם בפ' פנחס רנ"ב ב'· וע' שם ר"מ ע"ב ענין נפלא בזה · וכן פרש וביאר שם כל אברי כלי מבשלי ומבשלי האכילה שבאדם שהמה ג"כ בסדרי פרקי המרכבה עולמות וכחות עליונים מכונים בשמות אותן האברים ממש שהן כלי מבשלי ומבררי הקרבן ע"ש היטב כד' רכ"ד ע"א וד' רל"ד ורל"ה בזוהר וברע"מ שם · ובסוד ד' דרגין דקרבן אשה ריח ניחח לה' · ג' דרגין אשה ריח ניחח כסדרן בג' עקרי אברי האכילה כבד לב מוח · אשה בכבד · ריח בלב · ניחח במוח · (ובביאור ענינם אכ"מ להאריך) · שאל ידם מתיישבין בג' בחי' נר"ן שעיקר משכנם הוא בתוך אלו ג' אברים ועוד דרגא עלאה עמירא בחי' נשמתא לנשמתא סוד שרש הנשמה הדבוקה כביכול בו ית' וזהו לה' · ולכן אחז"ל (ברכות נ"ה א') בזמן שבית המקדש היה קיים מזבח מכפר · עכשיו שלחנו של אדם מכפר עליו :

פרק י'

שער ב

צואה כמאמרם ז"ל בפסוק צא תאמר לו (ישעיה ל') וכן אמר ברע"מ פנחס בדף ל"ב ר"ל. ועיי"ש · ושם בפ' תצא רס"ב א' שנקראת אשפה מטונפת וצואה · וכ"א בתקוני' ת"ע קכ"ע א' · וכז"א בס"א פ' בראשית ו' ע"ג בפ' איככ' אטנפס שהוא הס"א מסאבא · ושם בפ' בהר ל"ט ע"ד ואין צואה אלא יצה"ר כו' · וע' בעט"מ להאריז"ל פ' יתרו בזה · וכן הוא מקום יניקתם בשרש העליון ע' בע"ח שער הארת המוחין פ"ה · וזה היה ג"כ ענין עבודת פעור · וכמ"ש במאמר התקוני' הנ"ל ופקודין דל"ת פרנס' לס"מ למאן דעב' עלייהו כו' · וזהו ענין הכתוב אם רחץ ה' את צואת בנות ציון · וז"ש בז"ח פ' אחרי ס"ע א' בענין ירבעם כד עבד תרי עגלי שאמר הקב"ה להמלאכים הרי כל שפע דהוה יהיב לכון אתהפך לכון בזוהמא וגורם בזה פגם וחולי וקלקול גדול ותשות כח ח"ו בהעולמו' לפי ענין ואופן המעשה · ולפי מדרגתו בשרשו בהעולמות · כי אז אותן העולמות שאותן המעשים מגיעים עדיהם · אין ההתפשטו' והתחברו' עצמותו ית' בהם על השלימו' האמיתי כראוי כפי כוונת רצונו ית' · דלא שרי באתר פגים כל עוד אשר עדן חלאתה בתוכה ומצואתה לא רוחץ · ומאחר שכל העולמות בכלל הם מקושרים ומיוחדים כאחד ממילא גם כל העולמות מרגישים מעט במקצת מזה הפגם · ואינם חוזרים לאיתן בריאותם ותקונם האמיתי כמקדם · עד אשר יתרוקנו אלו כחות הטומאה · ע"י קיבול האדם עונשו הראוי לו וכמ"ש ברע"מ פנחס רל"ד סוף ע"א וריש ע"ב שם ע"ש · שעי"ז ממילא מגו יבולשו וכרגע ספו תמו · וע' לעיל בשער א' · ואז ממילא מתרפא הפגם והקלקול של העולמות ונטהרים מחלאת זוהמתם וחוזרים לתקונם הראשון · או ע"י התשובה שלימה אמיתית · שמגעת עד שורשה העליון הנקרא עולם התשוב' עלמא דחירו ונהירו עלאה דכלא · ומשם מתעורר ונמשך אור עליון קדוש · אשר הוא מי מקוה טהרה לרחוץ ולטהר כל לכלוך פסולת כחות הטומאה · והם בטלים וכלים · והוא ענין הכתוב אם רחץ אדני את צואת בנות ציון · וכן וזרקתי עליכם מים טהורים וכו' :

אסירא בר מליצנותא דעכו"ם דשריא · דכתי' (ישעיה מ"ו) · כרע בל קורס נבו כו' כי לא יכלו מלט משא · ולכאורה לפי"ז יפלא מאד סיפיה דהאי ענינא שם שסיים ואני אסבול ואמלט · ומעודי נפלאתי ע"ז · וע"פי דברינו אלה הוא מבואר למשכיל · כמש"ל שכל מה שאנו מדברים בו ית' · הכל הוא רק מצד התחברותו יתברך להעולמות שמסודרים כולם כאחד כמראה דמות אדם כביכול בכל האברים והעניינים שבו ממש · וכל מעשי איש ישראל המה להעולמות כענין המזון לגוף · והמעשי' אשר לא טובים ח"ו · המה נהפכים בתוכם ללכלוך וטינופת והם כחות הטומאה · זהו שאמר הכתוב · שהעכו"ם אינה יכולה להתאפק ולסבול למלט ולהוציא כהוגן משא הזוהמא שמטמאי' אותה אלא קרסו כרעו יחדיו כו' · היינו שאין להם שום כח עצמיי' שיוכלו לגרש ולהוציא מאתם הזוהמא מעצמם · אלא כן הוא ית"ש נורא עלילה · כי תאחז במשפ' ידו ואינו ממהר לשלוח ח"ו בפעם א' כל הכחות הדין והקליפות שהן הטינופות והלכלוך שנעשו בהעולמות שמקבילים ומכוונים לאברי מבשלי האכילה שבאדם · כי היו מחריבין ח"ו את כל העולם אלא שהוא נושאם וסובלם כביכול · וממלטם מהעולמות כהוגן מעט מעט · לפעול הדין בעולם על ידי יסורין מעט מעט בהמשך זמן · כענין הכתוב (עמוס ג') רק אתכם ידעתי כו' · ע"כ אפקוד עליכם את כל עונותיכם · כידוע מאמרם ז"ל על זה (ע"ז דף ד' ע"א) · עד שברבות הימים יתרוקן לכלוך הטינופת הם כחות הטומאה מהעולמות מכל וכל · אחר שיגמר קיבול עונשו של האדם · כמ"ש בפני' שאחר נגמר קיבול העונ' הם כלים מאליהם ואז יחזרו העולמות לאיתן בריאותם ותקונם הראשון · והבן :

פרק ח

וזהו מאמרם ז"ל (ב"ק נ' ע"א) כל האומר הקב"ה וותרן הוא יותרון חיוהי · אשר לכאורה נפלאת · וכבר נתבאר קצת למעלה בשער א' פרק י"ב · ולדברינו כאן הענין יותר מבואר בטוב טעם . שאינו ע"ד הנקמה ח"ו · אלא שכמו שמטבע האדם שאם יאכל מאכל

שבטבעו

יח'. וכמ"ש בפ' עקב שם תקין פתורא למהרך כו' ע"ש. ובפ' בלק ר"ב סוף ע"א כי ממנו תאכל ההוא מגרא תקיפא כו'. דההוא זכאה כביכול איהו מפרנס לה ויהיב לה מזונא כו'. בג"כ כי ממנו תאכל ולית מזונא בהאי עלמי אלא ממנו ע"ש ועי' עוד ברע"מ בהר ק"י ע"א ובפרש' פנחס שם רכ"ד ריש ע"ב ובזוהר שם רכ"ה ריש ע"ב בזה. וכן אחר המגיד להב"י ובפ' בשלח) בענין המן דכל הנבראים צריכים מזון כו'. ואפי' ספירות דאינון נאצלים צריכי כביכול מזונא כו'. והא מזונא דספירן איהי תורה ומע"ט דעבדין לתתא. ע"ש בארוך. וברע"מ משפטים קכ"א א' קדש ישראל לה' ראשית תבואתו כו' וישראל אקריאו חלא רבא והקיף. ומזון לכלא בי'. בי' אורייתא דאיהו מזונא לעילא בי' לאלהא דאיהו מזונא כו'. ואפי' מלאכים לית לון מזונא אלא בישראל. דאי לאו דישראל יתעסקון באורייתא. לא הוה נחית לון מזונא מסטרא דאורייתא דאתמשלא לעץ. הה"ד עץ חיים היא וגו' ולאיבא דאיהי מצוה. והרמ"ק ז"ל רמז הענין בס' אלימה הובאו דבריו בזה בס' שומר אמונים ע"ש. ובתולעת יעקב ובריש ס' דרך אמונה שלו. וזהו ענין מאמרם ז"ל ישראל מפרנסין לאביהם שבשמים:

אבל ש"ג ופסולת ואמרו (סנהדרין נ"ט ב') שהמלאכים היו צולין לו בשר ומסננין לו יין. (ומבין זה הגלוי' והסינון שכ"כ גדלה כח נפשו של אדה"ר סוד אדם קדמאה. יותר מערך כל כחות עליוני העליונים. עד שגם המלאכים צלו לו ראמ"כל שיהא בורא עלאה אם אוכלה אם משאיב שאיב כל שום עכירות המאכל ש'פי ערכו הגבי' מאד'. וגם שמהת היין העליון היה מסינן מכל שמרים שלכי נוגה ערכו. וכענין יין המשומר בענביו). ואחר החטא שעירב רע בטוב במזון העולמות כתיב קוץ ודרדר כו'. ורעין זה וכו ג"כ דור המדבר קודם חטא העגל בענין המן שהפיג גם שאר המאכלים ונבלע באבריהם. כמשרז"ל בפ' יה"כ (ע"ה ב') אלא מה אני מקיים ויתד תהי' לך כו' לאחר שסרחו. וכן אחז"ל (שבת ל' ס"ב) שלע"ל עתידה א"י שתוציא כו'.

פרק ז

וכן נהיפך. המעשים אשר לא טובים ח"ו. הם אל העולמות כענין המאכלים רעים. אשר יתבאר ענינו בע"ה. וכמ"ש ברע"מ פ' אמור ד' צ"ט ב' וד' ק' ע"א. ז"ל ביומא דר"ה נפיק יצחק בלחודוי וקרי לעשו לאטעמא לי' תבשילין דכל עלמא כל חד כפום ארחוי כו' ושכיב על ערסי' דדינא וקרי לעשו ואמר וצודה לי ציד ועשה לי מטעמים כו'. ויהי אך יצא כו' ועשו אחיו בא מצדו טעין טעוני מעובדי דעלמא ועשו גם הוא מטעמים חדיד לשנייה למטען טענות כו'. ויאמר יקום אבי יתער בדינוי ויאכל כמה עובדין בישין דכל עלמא כו'. ובתקונים ת"כ מ"ז ב' ועשה לי מטעמים כאשר אהבתי מפקידין דעשה כו'. ופקידין דל"ת פרנסה לס"מ למאן דעבר עלייהו. ואלין הוה קריב עשו ליצחק ואמר לי' יקום אבי ויאכל מציד בנו. וס"מ בגינייהו הוה קריב לשמאלא לאטעמא לקב"ה מחובין דבני' דאינון מאכלין מרירן כו'. וברע"מ פ' פנחס רל"ב סוף ע"א וההוא לב לאו ארחוי כו' בעכירו דעובדין דעמי'. אלא נקיט כל ברירו כו' וכל זכוון וכל עובדין טבין וכל ההיא עכירו וטנופין ולכלוכא דאינון עובדין בישין אנח לכבד דאתמר בי' עשו איש שעיר כו' ונשא השעיר עליו את כל עונותם. וכ"א עוד שם כענין זה בסוף העמוד ע"ש:

וכשם שמאכל הגוף כאשר איננו טוב ואינו מתקבל אל הגוף. אינו זן וסועד את הגוף. אלא נהפך בתוכו לפסולת וזוהמא וצואה. וגם הוא מתיש ומחליש את כל הגוף. כי עי"ז אין הנפש מתפשט בתוכו כראוי. ולפעמים יחלה מזה. כן הענין. שהמעשים אשר לא טובים ורצויים ח"ו המה נהפכים בתוך העולמות לפסולת ולכלוך כביכול. והוא התגברות כחות הטומאה והקליפות (*). ובזה הרחמן יצילנו. שנקראים קיא צואה

הגה"ה

(*) ובזה יובן אמרם ז"ל (מגילה כ"ה ע"ב) כל ליצנותא אסירא

שער ב

אותם. גזרה רצונו ית' שיהא תלוי בעסק התורה ומעשי המצות ועבודת התפלה של עם סגולה. ובלתם היה הוא יתברך מסלק עצמותו ית' מהם וכרגע היו חוזרים כולם לאפס ואין. ולכן אחז"ל (תענית ג' ע"ב) מ"ד כי כארבע רוחות השמים פרשתי אתכם כו' כשם שא"א לעולם בלא רוחות (*) כך א"א לעולם בלא ישראל. והוא שאמרו בויקרא רבה סוף פ"ד ברכי נפשי את ה' כו' וכי מה ראה דוד להיות מקלס בנפשו להקב"ה. אלא אמר הנפש הזו כו' הנפש הזאת אינה אוכלת בגוף והקב"ה אין לפניו אכילה כו'. וכן אמרו בסגנון זה במדרש תהלים מזמור ק"ג ומה הנפש אינה אוכלת ואינה שותה כך הקדוש ברוך הוא אינו אוכל ואינו שותה. בהזכירם אכילה ושתי' יותר מאשר ההנאות השמיעונו זה הענין הנ"ל. והוא שהגם שהנפש עצמה לא אוכלת ולא שותה. עכ"ז הרי כל עיקר חיבור הנפש עם הגוף כאחד וקיומו מספר ימיו הקצובים. הוא תלוי ע"י המאכל ושתיית הגוף. כן הענין עם כי ודאי שלעצמות אדון יחיד א"ס ב"ה איננו נוגע ח"ו שום מעשה המצות ותורה ועבודה כלל ולא אכפת ליה כלל כמ"ש כך הקב"ה אינו אוכל ואינו שותה. וכמש"ל בהמאמרים הנז' בפ"ד. אמנם כל עיקר ענין התחברותו ית' אל העולמות שמסודרים כאחד כתבנית אדם בכל הפרטים ואברי האביל' כולם. גזרה רצונו ית' שיהא תלוי במעשיהם הטובים של עם קדושו. שהן המה ענין אכילה ושתיה אל העולמו' (*) להעמיד' ולקיימ' ולהוסיף כח קדושתם ואורם ע"י התחברותו ית' אליה' כראוי כפי הרצון העליון ית"ש. הכל לפי רוב המעשה של עם סגול' שהמה המתקני' ומאחדי' העולמות שיהו ראוים לקבל שפעת האור ותוספת קדושתו ית' (*) כענין המזון שהוא מוסיף כח בגוף ומעדן אותו. וזהו ענין הכתוב לכו לחמו בלחמי. שפירשוהו רז"ל ובר"מ צו ל"ג ב' ובפ' עקב רע"א ב' על התור' ע"ש. היינו בלחמי ממש. כביכול לחמו

יב

יתברך

הגה"ה

עיין זוהר ואדרא כ"ג ב'. דארבע יסודין ארמ"ע אינון קדמאי ושרשין לעילא ותתאין ועלאין עלייהו קיימין. ואינון לארבע סטרי עלמא. וע' רע"מ פנחס רכ"ז ב' דעל ד' יסודין טבין דבר נש שלטין ד' מלאכי המרכב' הידועים בד' רוחות העולם. ע"י שרש שרשן שמן ד' אותיות הוי"ה ב"ה ושע"ז נאמר הכתוב מארבע רוחות באי הרוח וכו':

הג"ה

וכמו שבמיני מאכל יש מאכלים שכחם רק לחזק ד' יסודות הגוף שיהיו בכחם הראשון ויש מאכלי' שבכחם להוסיף כח הד' יסודות ברבוי איכות. וכל שמל האדם להוסיף לו כח גופו יתר על כדי קו בריאותו. ואינו מסתפק באכילה מועטת בצמצום כדי קו חיותו. כן גם הנפש לא תמלא באכילה מועטת של תורה ומע"ט. וזה כל האדם לרבות תורה ולהוסיף מצות עד שיומשך תוספת רבוי קדושה וברכה בעליונים ותחתונים. יתר על כדי מדת הקו שנטה הבורא ית"ש בעת הבריאה. (כמבואר בע"ח שכל עבודתינו הוא להמשיך מקיפים בהתרחבות אור גדול. יתר על כדי מדת קו אור היושר שהמשיך הוא יתברך בעת הבריאה לצורך הכרח הויות וקיום העולמות):

הג"ה

וגם אל נשמת האדם עצמו. כמ"ש ז"ל בקהלת רבה סימן ב' פסוק י"ט אין טוב באדם שיאכל ושתה כו'. כל אכילה ושתיה שנא' במגילה הזאת בתורה ובמע"ט הכתו' מדבר. וכ"ה שם בסימן ה' פסוק י"ד ובסי' ח' פסוק י"ב. וכתיב (ישעיה ג) אמרו צדיק כי טוב כי פרי מעלליה' יאכלו. וכן בהיפך ח"ו כתיב ויאכלו מפרי דרכ' ובר"מ צו כ"ט ב' דמזונא דאורייתא איהי מזונא דנר"ן כו' ע"ש. ושם בפ' פנחס רכ"ג סוף ע"א דנשמתא אתפרנסת במלין דאורייתא דאינון נהמא לה כענין נהמא דגופא ממלין דעלמא. ושם רמ"ד סוף ע"ב דנפשא דאתעסקת באורייתא מלחם אביה תאכל כו'. וע' עוד שם רנ"ב ב' בזק. והוא ענין שלחנם של צדיקים לע"ל. וכת"ש דהע"ה תערוך לפני שלחן כו'. וזהו לכו לחמו בלחמי:

הגה"ה

וכ"ה לפי זה הערך ממש. ענין אכילת האדם למשפ נקי וזך מסיג פסולת. כפי ערך מזון העולמות ממעשיו הזכים. אם מעט ואם הרבה. ולכן קודם חטא אדה"ר היו מאכליו מבוררים ונקיי' מכל

שער ב

גדול כחן של נביאים שמדמין צור' ליוצרה שנא' (דניאל ח) ואשמע קול אדם בין אולי. א"ר י' ב"ס אית לן קריא אוחרן דמחוור יתיר מן דין שנאמר ועל דמות הכסא דמות כמרא' אדם כו'. ובבמדב' רבה פי"ט חכמת אדם תאיר פניו א"ר י' גדול כחן של נביאים שמדמין דמות גבורה של מעלה לצורת אדם כו' ע"ש. וכ"ה בקהלת רבה סי' ח' פסוק א' ובתנחומא פ' חקת ולבאורה יפלא. כי אל מי תדמיון וכו'. אמנם הענין כמש"ל שכל השגתנו כביכול אותו ית"ש. הוא רק מצד התחברותו ית' להעולמות. וסדר מצב העולמות והכחות כולם העליונים ותחתונים יחד בכלל. מסודרים כביכול בכל פרטיהם כתבנית קומת אדם. בסידור כל פרקי אבריו וגידיו וכל פרטי הענינים שבו והתאחדותם א' בחבירו. שהוא כולל יחד בתוכו כל הכחות והעולמו'. כמ"ש לעיל בשער א'. והוא ענין השיעו' קומה הנזכר בדבריהם ז"ל במדרשים. וע' בע"ח שער עיגולים ויושר ענף ב' וג' וד' שם וגם בסוף השער בריש מהדורא תנינא. וכתב שם שזה רמז הכתוב ויברא אלקים את האדם בצלמו בצלם אלקים וע' עוד בריש שער הצלם ובשער ציור עולמות אבי"ע שם. ועצמותו ית' מתפשט ומסתתר בתוך כולם וממלאם והוא נשמתא דלהון. כביכול כענין הנשמה המתפשטת ומסתתרת בגוף האדם. לכן הורשנו לתארו יתב' ע"ז האופן (*). וגם הרמב"ם ז"ל כתב במורה בפ' ע"ב מחלק א' שכל זה העולם בכללו נקרא שיעור קומה. והאריך להמשיל כלל חלקי העולם לחלקי אברי האד' וכל עניניו שבו. ושהוא ית' הוא נשמת העולם כענין הנשמה לגוף האדם ע"ש. ודבריו ז"ל ראוים למי שאמרם. שכן מבואר בזוהר תולדו' קל"ד ע"ג ע"ש. ומדבריו ז"ל נשמע לדידן לענין סדר כלל העולמות כולם יחד. ושגורה בפי רז"ל שהאדם הוא איקונין ודיוקן מלכו של עולם ית"ש. כמ"ש בסנהדרין (מ"ו א' וב') לא תלין נבלתו כו' כי קללת אלקים תלוי. תניא א"ר מ' משלו משל למה"ד לשני אחים תאומים כו' אחד מינוהו מלך ואחד יצא ללסטיות צוה המלך ותלאוהו כל הרואה אותו אומר המלך תלוי כו' ופירש"י אף אדם עשוי בדיוקנו של מקום. ובשמות רבה פ"ל מכה איש ומת וכו' משל לאדם שקפח איקונין של מלך כו' אמר המלך לא קראת כו'. שכל מי שהוא נוגע באיקונין שלי הוא אבד כו' כך אם הרג אדם נפש כו' כאילו הוא מעביר איקונין של מלך. ר"ל זה שסיים בסיפ' דקרא הטעם ע"ז כי בצלם אלקים עשה את האדם:

התחברותה לגוף מכ"ש הבורא ית' שאין להשיגו רק מצד התחברותו להעולמות. וגם היא הנותנת. שמאחר שאין להמשילו לשום נברא. שגם כ"ע אוכמא איהו לגבי עלה"ע. ולכל דבר אשר ידמו. לא ישוה. הוכרחו לבאר דרך דמיון לאיזה נברא רוחני וכענין הכתו' יקרה היא מפנינים. ואף שאין דמיון וערך בינה לתוה"ק והפנינים לזה סיים הכתוב עצמו הרי כל חפציך לא ישוו בה:

הגה"ה

(*) וזהו ענין כל התארי' הנזכרים בתורה עליו יתברך. עין יד ורגל וכיוצא. הכל מצד התחברותו ית' להעולמו' שהם מסודרי' ע"ז הסד' בכל אלו האברים. והם שמות עצמיים להכחות והעולמו'. לא מושאלים. וכן גם באד' אינם שמות מושאלים. וגם לא שהם באדם רק לסימן ורמז להענינים העליונים הנעלמים כענינהם של האד' שהוא סימן לאותה הצור' והתבני' שהוסכם לקרותה בזה השם. אלא שגם באדם הם עצמיים. כיון שהוא כלול ומשוכלל ומסודר בצלם דמות תבנית העולמות. ועיין במורה ח"א ובפרשת נפ' כ"ו שם. ובספר עבודת הקודש פ' כ"ו מחלק התכלית. ומה שהשיג על הרמב"ם בפ' ס"ה מזה החלק. ובריש ס' שערי אורה ובפרדס שער הכנויים פ"א. ובשל"ה בהקדמ' תולדת אדם:

פרק ו

וכמו שענין חבור וקיום נשמת האדם בגופו. הוא ע"י אכילה ושתיה. ובלתם תפרד ותסתלק מהגוף. כן חיבור עצמותו ית' אל העולמות שהן סוד האדם הגדול. כדי להעמידם ולקיימם ולא תגעל נפשו

אותם

שער ב

גדול המה לצרף ולזקק להפרי' הסיגים מכל הכחו' והעולמות הברואים · יתצרף ויתלבן וג"כ במשמע לצר' היינו לחבר ולקשר כל הכחות והעולמות הברואים מתוקנים ומסודרי' כפי הכוונה והרצון העליון ב"ה · ומאליו גם בית ישראל עם סגולה יתאחדו בשם המיוחד ית' לחלקו ונחלתו · שרק ע"ז התכלית באו כל המצות והעבודה הקדושה כולה בכללה :

זהו ענין הברכה לו ית' בכל הברכו' והתפלות שפירושו הוא תוספת ורבוי ממש כמשמעו כנ"ל · שזהו רצונו יתב' נוטעם כמום אתו ית' · שנתקן ונייחד ע"י הברכות והתפלות הכחות והעולמות העליונים · שיהו מוכנים וראוים לקבל שפעת קדושת אור עליון · ולהמשיך ולהוסיף בהם קדושת האור ורב ברכות מעצמותו יתב' המתחבר אליהם ומתפשט בתוכם · ומאליו יושפע זה התוספת ברכה והקדוש' גם על עם סגול · שגרמו וסבבו לכל הכבוד הזה · וזה שאמר ר' ישמעאל כשביקש הוא ית' מאתו ישמעאל בני ברכני · יהי רצון שיכבשו רחמיך את כעסך ויגולו רחמיך כו' ותתנהג עם בניך במדת הרחמים ותכנס להם לפנים משורת הדין · ועי' ז"ח רות ס"ז ב' ר"ג פתח ואכלת כו' וברכת את ה' אלקיך כו' · ואר"י גדול כח ברכת המזון שמוסיף כח ברכה בפמליא של מעלה : ולכן אמרו רז"ל (בר"פ כילד מברכין) ובז"ח שם כל האוכל ואינו מברך נקרא גזלן שנאמר גוזל אביו ואמו כו' · ואין אביו אלא הקב"ה כו' · כי הוא גוזל ומונע מהעולמות שפעת הברכה והקדושה שהיה צריך להשפיע בהם ע"י ברכתו · וכן כל המקראות ברכי נפשי את ה' · ברוך אתה ה' אלקי ישראל כו' · וכל כיוצא בו · הכל הוא ע"ז הענין · ומצד רצונו ית' להתחבר אל הבריאה · ע"ז נאמר העבודה צורך גבוה :

ועי' בלשון האר"י ז"ל שהזכרנו בפנים לעיל סוף פ"ב · ועיין עוד בתקונים תכ"ב ס"ג א' ואיהו אתקרי בכל שמהן כו' לאחזאה לכל חד מישראל מאתר דקראן לי' לפום צרכיהון כו' ע"ש וכן בת"ע הנזכר בפנים אמרו לאחזאה בכל אבר כו' לאשתמודע' לב"נ כו' וידע לתקרי לי' בכל אבר כדק' יאות וז"ש בתז"ח ד' פ"א ע"ד ואי' לאשאל למה מצלאין לקב"ה בכמה דרגין · זמנין מצלין לי' בספירה ידיעה ובמדה ידיעא · לזמנין צלותא לימינא כו' לזמנין לשמאלא כו' לזמנין לעמוד' דאמצעי' כו' · כל צלותא סלקא לדרגא ידיעא . אלא ודאי הוי"ה איהו בכל ספירה וספירה כו' · בזמנא דבעי לרחמא על עלמא סליקת לימינא · ובזמנא דבעי כו' · וכלא לגבי הוי"ה דאיהו בכל אתר כו' · וזש"ה לבספרי כה' אלקינו בכל קראנו אליו · אליו ולא למדותיו:

פרק ה אמנם

להבין עיקרו של ענין התוספת ורבוי ברכה בהעולמות ע"י מעשי האדם · ומהות הענין צורך העולמות לזה · הנה רז"ל אמרו · (ברכות י' ע"א) הני חמשה ברכי נפשי כנגד מי אמרן דוד · לא אמרן אלא כנגד הקב"ה וכנגד הנשמה (*) מה הקב"ה נולא כל העולם אף הנשמה מלאה כל הגוף כו' · וכן אמרו בויקרא רבה פ"ד ודברים רבה סוף פ"ב ובמדרש תהלים מזמור ק"ג ובתקונים ריש התקון י"ג · וכמו שביאר ברע"מ פ' פנחס רכ"ז ב' ורכ"ח א' · ועי' בע"ח שער פנימיות וחיצונות סוף דרוש י"א · וחשר"ל במס' ר"ה כ"ד ב' ובעכו"ם מ"ג ב' בבריו' כל הפרצופות מותרים חוץ מפרצוף אדם · ומפ' טעמא דכתי' לא תעשון אתי לא תעשון אותי · וכ"מ בזוהר יתרו פ"ו סוף ע"א ע"ש · ובב"ר ריש פכ"ז אמרו כתיב כי יש אדם שעמלו בחכמה כו' א"ר יודן

גדול

הגה"ה

ועם כי רז"ל המשילו התחברותו יתב' להעולמות · להתחברות הנשמ' להגוף · ה"ל יטעה ח"ו הרואה דבריהם · שהנמשל דומה למשל ח"ו · כי באמת אין ערוך ודמיון ביניהם בשום אופן · כמבואר בזוהר וברע"מ בהרבה מקומו' ומקרא מלא דבר הכתו' ואל מי תדמיון אל · וגם אל מי שיני בכלל · יכין, שאיך אפשר ליקח דמיון מהנבראים על הבורא ית"ש · ולא המשילו ז"ל עצמות הנשמה לעצמות הבורא ית' · רק לדבר זה דימוי שאף שהנשמה היא כח נברא מאתו ית' · שכ"ז א"א להשיג עצמותה לבנות לה שום היאר ופעולה · אם לא מצד התחברותה

שער ב

כל דהו · אנו מדברים לנוכח ברוך אתה ה' כו' · כי העולמות הם הצריכים לענין התוספת ורבוי ברכה מעצמותו ית' המתחבר אליהם · וזהו מלך העולם כמ"ש ברע"מ הנ"ל כד נחית לאמלכא עלייהו ויתפשט על ברייין כו' והמצוה אותנו ומקדשנו הוא עצמותו ית' א"ס ב"ה לבדו הסתו' מכל סתימין · לכן תקנו בלשון נסתר אשר קדשנו וצונו :

פרק ד וטעמו של דבר שנכלל בכל ברכה ב' הבחי' הנ"ל ·

כי יסוד פנת אמונתנו הק' · שכל מגמת כוונת לבנו בכל הברכות והתפלות ובקשו' · אך רק ליחידו של עולם אדון יחיד א"ס ב"ה · אמנם לא שאנו מדברים אליו כביכול על עצמותו יתב' לבד בבחי' היותו מופשט ומופרש כביכול לגמרי מהעולמו' כענין שהיה קודם הבריאה · דא"כ איך נתארהו ח"ו בכל ברכותינו ותפלותינו בשום שם וכנוי בעולם כלל · וגם דאם לא מצד שהראנו ית' שרצונו להתחבר להעולמות ולאמלכא על ברייין כפום עובדיהון · לא היינו רשאי' כלל להתפלל לעצמותו ית' שיתחבר להעולמו' ולהשגחא על ברייין · ולכן מקדימין אנחנו לומר אתה ה' מלך העולם · פי' אחר שרצונך היה להוות העולמות ולהתחבר אליהם לאמלכא עליהון · לזאת בקשתנו שיתברך מקור הרצון לאמלכא כן לעלמין · וגם שלפי בחי' עצמותו ית' בלתי התחברותו אל העולמות אין מקום לתורה ומצות כלל · וע"ז נאמר (איוב ל"ה) אם חטאת מה תפעל בו וגו' אם צדקת מה תתן לו או מה מידך יקח · וכן כתיב (משלי ט') אם חכמת חכמת לך · כי לעצמות אדון כל ב"ה · כל מעשה האדם הטובה היא אם רעה איננה נוגע לו בשום כלל ח"ו · והוא מאמרם ז"ל בב"ר ריש פ' מ"ד אמרת ה' צרופה כו' אמר רב לא ניתנו המצות אלא לצרף כו' · וכי מה אכפת לי' להקב"ה למי ששוחט מן הצואר או מי ששוחט מן העורף כו' · וכ"ה בתנחומא פ' שמיני בפסוק זאת החיה כו' · ובמדרש תהלים מזמור י"ח ע"ש · ובתקונים ת"ע ק"ל סוף ע"א עלת העלות מתעלה על כלא איהו בריך לכלא ולא צריך איהו ברכאן מאחרא דלית עלי' מאן דאשפע לי' הה"ד ומרומם על כל ברכה ותהלה : *) אלא שכל כוונת לבנו בכל הברכות והתפלות · צריך שתהיה לעצמות א"ס ב"ה מצד התחברו כרצונו יתברך אל העולמות שמצדם הם כל התוארים והשמות מתחלפים לפעול ולהמשיך בהם אור ושפעת קדושה מעצמותו ית' כפי התעוררות המגיע אליהם ממעשי האדם של כל איש מעם סגולה · אם בחסד · אם במשפט · אם בצדקה · אם ברחמים · המעט ואם רב · ככה הוא ע"ז האופן והשיעור בדקדוק עצום במדה ובמשקל ענין התחברותו ית' אל הכחות והעולמות לשנות סדר התקשרותם להמשכת שפעת אורם · וכל פרטי הנהגתם · אם לדין ורוגז · אם לחסד ורחמים · וגם שיעור הדין והחסד המעט ואם רב · וז"ש בהמאמרים הנ"ל שלא ניתנו המצות אלא לצרף בהן את הבריות · היינו שצורך גדול ·

הגה"ה

*) ומה שכ' בכוונת התפל' והברכו' לכוון בכל ברכה כוונה מיוחדת לספיר' מיוחד' לא ח"ו לעצמות הספיר' · כי הוא קיצוץ נטיעות ח"ו · כי כמו שמצינו עבודת הקרבן · ארז"ל בברייתא סוף מנחות והוא מהספרי ס' פנחס בא וראה מה כתיב בפ' קרבנות שלא נאמר בהן לא אל ולא אלקים אלא הוי"ה שלא ליתן פ"ש לבעל הדין לחלוק וכמ"ש זובח לאלהי' יחרם בלתי לה' לבדו · ועיין להלן בש"ג פ"ט · כן בעבודת התפלה · חלילה לכוין לשום כח פרטי וספירה מיוחדת אלא לעצמות אדון יחיד א"ס ב"ה כלל הכחות כולם · שמתחבר ברצונו ית' מטע' הכמוס אצלו ית' לפעול באותה ספירה ואותו הכח שהם כסדר ההשתלשלו' שקבע הוא יתב' ברצונו שכל ספירה מיוחדת לענין פרטי שעל ידה פועל ענין זה בהעולמות · (וע' בתשו' ריב"ש סי' קנ"ז אשר השיב הר"ר ן' שושאן בזה להריב"ש ז"ל · ולדברינו אלה יתיישב יותר · והבן) ·

ופ'

שער ב

פ"ג · אלקי אבותיכם שלחני אליכם אותה שעה נתברר משה על עסקיו כו' · באותה שעה היה מבקש משה שיודיענו הקב"ה את השם הגדול כו' א"ל הקב"ה למשה שמי אתה מבקש לידע · לפי מעשי אני נקרא · פעמים אני נקרא באל שדי · בצבאות או באלקים · בהויה · כשאני דן את הבריות אני נקרא אלקים · וכשאני עושה מלחמה ברשעים אני נקרא צבאות · וכשאני תולה חטאיו של אדם אני נקרא אל שדי · וכשאני מרחם על עולמי אני נקרא הויה כו' · הוי אקי"ק אשר אקי"ק אני נקרא לפי מעשי · וברע"מ פ' בא דף מ"ב ב' כי לא ראיתם כל תמונה כו' דהא כתיב ותמונת ה' יביט כו' · דאפילו האי תמונה ל"ל באתרי' אלא כד נחית לאמלכא עלייהו ויתפשט על בריין כו' · דהא קדם דברא דיוקנא בעלמא וצייר צורה הוה הוא יחידאי בלא צורה ודמיון · ומאן דאשתמודע ליה קדם בריאה דאיהו לבר מדיוקנא אסור למעבד ליה צורה ודיוקנא בעלמא וכו' ואפילו בשמא קדישא ולא בשום אות ונקודה בעלמא · והאי איהו כי לא ראיתם כל תמונה כו' · אבל בתר דעביד הא דיוקנא דמרכבה דאדם עלאה · נחית תמן ואתקרי בההוא דיוקנא הויה · בגין דאשתמודעון ליה במדות דיליה כו' אל אלקים שדי צבאות אקי"ק · בגין דישתמודעין ליה בכל מדה ומדה איך יתנהג עלמא בחסד ובדינא כו' · ווי ליה למאן דישוי ליה בשום מדה כו' · אלא דמיונא דיליה כפום שלטנותיה על ההוא מדה ואפי' על כל בריין כו' · כד אסתליק מנה לית ליה מדה ולא דמיון ע"ש · וכפ' פנחס רכ"ה א' ואיהו לא אתקרי הוי"ה ובכל שמהן אלא באתפשטות נהוריה עלייהו וכד אסתלק מנייהו לית ליה מגרמיה שם כלל כו' ע"ש · ובתקונים ת"ע קכ"א ב' האריך בענין פרקי אברי השיעור קומה כביכול · אמר הא"ז שכל הענין הוא לאחזאה בכל אבר ואבר דגופיה שלטנותיה לאשתמודעא לב"נ איך אתנהיג עלמא וינדע למקרי ליה בכל אבר כדקא יאות · ואיך אשתני שמיה לפום ההוא אבר · ואית אבר דאתקרי ביה הויה רחמי · ואית אבר דאתקרי ביה אלקים . ואית אבר דאתקרי בי' כו' · אקי"ק אתוי על עלת העלות כו' · דעלת על כל העלות איהו חד בכל שמהן ולא אשתני בכלהו · דשניין בשמהן איכון ולאו ביה כו' ע"ש · וע' עוד ברע"מ פנחס רנ"ז ב' ורכ"ח א' · וע' בע"ח ריש שער עיגולים ויושר ושם בסוף זה השער ריש המהדורא תנינא ותבין שם ע"פ דברינו :

*) **וזה** כל השגחתו כביכול שמו ית' הכל מצד ענין התחברותו אל העולמות והתפשטותו ית' בתוכם · כמ"ש ברע"מ פ' בא הנ"ל דאפי' האי תמונה לית ליה באתריה · אלא כד נחית לאמלכא עלייהו ויתפשט על בריין יתחזי לכל חד כפום מראה וחזון ודמיון דלהון והאי איהו וביד הנביאים אדמה :

הגה"ה

ובזה יובן מאמרם ז"ל בחזית ע"פ יונתי תמתי ז"ל ר' ינאי אמר תאומתי כביכול לא אני גדול ממנה ולא היא גדולה ממני · ולכאורה נפלאת היא · ולדברינו הוא מבואר · אחר שכל ההשגו' במקצת שמדברי' בו ית' · הוא רק מצד התחברותו יתברך אל העולמות · וכל תחלת כוונתו יתברך בבריאת העולמות והתחברותו אליהם · היה רק בשביל ישראל כי' כמאמר' ז"ל בראשית בשביל ישראל כו' · ז"ש תאומתי לא אני גדול ממנה ולא היא כו' ר"ל בשניהם והבן :

ולכן קבעו אנשי כנה"ג הנוסח של כל ברכות המצות בלשון נוכח ונסתר · תחלתם ברוך אתה הוא לשון נוכח · ומסיימים אשר קדשנו כו' וצונו לשון נסתר · שמצד התחברותו יתברך ברצונו אל העולמות שעי"ז יש לנו קצת השגה

שער ב

ברכני · לא אמר שם שום שבח בברכתו אלא תפלה ובקשת רחמים · וכן בב"מ (קי"ד א') אמרינן וברכך יצא הקדש שא"ל ברכה · ופריך הש"ס ולא והא כתיב ואכלת ושבעת וברכת את ה' כו' · אבל האמת · כי ברוך פירושו לשון תוספת ורבוי · וכענין קח נא את ברכתי כו' · וברך את לחמך · וברך פרי בטנך וכו' · והרבה כיוצא במקרא · שא"א לפרשם לשון תהלה ושבח · אלא לשון תוספת ורבוי · ובזוהר אמר בכ"מ לאמשכא ברכאן כו' · לארקא ברכאן · לאוספי ברכאן · תוספת רבויא דברכאן כו' · ועי' ברע"מ ר"פ עקב ע"א וע"ב שברוך אתה הוי"ה פי' כמשמעו לאמשכא ולארקא חיין ממקורא דחיי לשמי' דקב"ה קדישא כו' · וכתיב ואכלת ושבעת וברכת את ה' אלקיך · ואינון ברכאן אריך בי"ב באינון מלין כו' ע"ש בארוך · וכ"כ בפע"ח שער הקדישים פ"א ז"ל סוד ברוך בכל מיני רבויין · וכ"ה שם סוף שער הבריאה וספ"ב משער העמידה ובר"פ פ"ג שם ובשער השבת ר"פ פי"ב ובשער תפלת ר"ה פ"ג ע"ש · וכ"כ הרשב"א ז"ל בענין ישמעאל בני ברכני ע"ש :

אמנם ענין הברכה לו ית"ש · אין הכוונה לעצמות אדון יחיד ב"ה כביכול · חלילה וחלילה · כי הוא מרומם מעל כל ברכה · אבל הענין כמ"ש בזוהר דקב"ה סתים וגליא · כי עצמות א"ס ב"ה הוא סתים מכל סתימין · ואין לכנותו ח"ו בשום שם כלל אפילו בשם הוי"ה ב"ה ואפי' בקוצו של יו"ד דבי' · (ואף גם מה שבזוהר מכנהו ית' בשם אין סוף אינו כנוי עליו יתברך שמו · אלא הכוונה על השגתנו אותו מצד כחות השפעים מאתו בהתחברותו ברצונו להעולמות · ולזאת כנהו א"ס ולא אין ראשית · כי באמת מצד עצמותו ית"ש אין לו לא סוף ולא ראשית · רק מצד השגתנו כחותיו ית' · הלא כל השגתנו הוא רק ראשית · אבל אין סוף להגיע בהשגה להשיג את כחותיו ית"ש הנשפעים) ומה שמושג אלינו קצת ואנו מכנים ומתארים כמה תארים ושמות וכנויים ומדות · כמו שמצינום בתורה ובכל מטבע התפלה · כולם הם רק מצד התחברותו יתברך אל העולמות והכחות מעת הבריאה · להעמידם ולהחיותם · ולהנהיגם כרצונו ית"ש · (והם אשר קראום בשם השתלשלות הספירות) · ולפי כל שנויי פרטי סדרי ההנהגה שמשתלשל ונמשך לזה בעולם אם לדין · אם לחסד · אם לרחמים · על ידי כחות העליונים והתמזגותם · משתנים השמות והכנויים והתארים · שלכל ענין פרטי מסדרי ההנהגה מיוחד לו כנוי ושם פרטי · שכן מורים פירושם של כל התארים · שהם מצד הכחות הברואים: כמו רחום וחנון פי' רחמנות וחנינה על הברואים · ואפילו השם המיוחד הוי"ה ב"ה · לא על עצמותו יתברך לבד אנו מייחדים לו · אלא מצד התחברותו ית' עם העולמות · כפירושו היה והוה ויהיה ומהוה הכל · ר"ל הוא יתברך מתחבר ברצונו להעולמות להוות ולקיימם כל רגע · *) וז"ש האריז"ל בלשונו הק' הובא בהקדמת פע"ח · שכל הכנויי' והשמו' הם שמו' העצמו' המתפשטים בספירות וע"ש :

הגה"ה

*) ומה שאמר בפרקי ר"א שקודם שברא הקב"ה את העול' היה הוא ושמו לבד · קודם שברא דיקא · ר"ל עולם הבריאה · היה הוא עצמותו ית' ושמו היינו עולם האצילו' לבדו · אבל אלולי שהאציל ית"ש מאתו עולם האצילות · לא היה שייך על עצמותו ית' היה והוה ויהי' :

פרק ג והוא

שאמרם ז"ל בשמות רבה פ"ג

שער ב

פרק א

כתיב לאהבה את ה' אלקיכם ולעבדו בכל לבבכם ובכל נפשכם. ואחז"ל בפ"ק דתענית ובספרי איזו היא עבודה שבלב הוי אומר זו תפלה. הנה האהבה שאמר שצריכה להיות בכל לב. הוא פשוט. כי היא ממצות התלויות בלב. וכן ענין האהבה בכל נפש שאמר. היינו אף גם למסור נפשו עליו ית"ש מעוצם נפלאת האהבה לו ית'. וכמ"ש בפ' ראשונה ואהבת את ה' אלקיך בכל לבבך ובכל נפשך כו'. אמנם בפ' זו חידוש הוא שחידשה. שגם העבודה היא התפלה צריכה להיות בכל לב ובכל נפש. (ולהכי נמי לא כתיב ובכל מאדכם בפ' זו כמו בפ' ראשונה דכתיב בה נמי ובכל מאדך. כי פרשה ראשונה מיירי מענין מצות האהבה לחוד. שייך לומר שתהיה האהבה גם בכל מאד. זה הממון. כמ"ש רז"ל (ברכות ס"א ב') אם יש לך אדם שממונו חביב עליו מגופו לכ"נ ובכל מאדך. אבל בפרשה זו דכתיב בה נמי עבודה היא תפלה. לא שייך עלה כ"כ ובכל מאד): **והנה** מ"ש בכל לבבכם על ענין התפלה. הוא פשוט ומבואר כוונת הכתוב לב' ענינים. הא' היינו לפנות לבו מטרדת המחשבות. ולהטותה אל הכוונה השלימה לתיבות התפלה בלבב שלם ומעומקא דלבא. כמאמרם ז"ל בברייתא ר"פ אין עומדין המתפלל צריך שיכוין את לבו לשמים שנאמר תכין לבם כו'. וכדמשמע להו נמי התם מקראי דחנה וחנה היא מדברת על לבה מכאן למתפלל צריך שיכוין לבו. וכמ"ש דוד המלך ע"ה בכל לבי דרשתיך. ובזוהר בשלח ס"ג ב' כל מאן דמצלי צלותא קמי מלכא קדישא בעי למבעי בעותי' ולצלאה מעומקא דלבא בגין דישתכח לביה שלים בקב"ה ויכוין לבא ורעותא. ולכן אמרו ז"ל (בס"פ תפלת השחר) שהמתפלל צריך לשהות וכו' כדי שתתחונן דעתו עליו. והיינו בכל לבבכם שתתמלא כל הלב רק בכוונת תיבות התפלה. שאם יעלה בלבו איזה מחשבה אחרת. הרי הלב חלוק בב' מחשבות: והב' היינו גם לשרש מלבו בעבודת התפלה תענוגי העולם והנאותיו מכל וכל. ואך להסתכל כלפי מעלה ברוממות הבורא יתברך. כמו שאמרו (יבמות ק"ה ב') המתפלל צריך שיתן לבו למעלה. עד שיהא כל כח לבו משוכה רק למעלה להתענג על ה' לבד בתיבות התפלה. וכענין החסידים הראשונים שהיו שוהים שעה א' כדי שיכוונו את לבם למקום. וכענין שפי' רבינו יונה ז"ל שם ענינה ע"ש ולבך תשיה. וכמו שאמרו בשמות רבה פכ"ב אדם צריך שיטהר לבו קודם שיתפלל. (אמנם כל עיקר ענין טהרת הלב. היא רק למצוה ולא לעכובא גם לענין התפלה אף שנקראת עבודה שבלב. כמו שנתבאר לעיל סוף ש"א שהעיקר בכל המצות היא המעשה. ע"ש):

ולהבין ענין מ"ש הכתוב ובכל נפשכם על עבודת התפלה. צריך לבאר תחלת פי' וענין הברכה כביכול לו ית"ש. שמצינו כמה פעמים במקרא. וברכת את ה' אלקיך. ברוך ה' לעולם כו'. ברכי נפשי את ה'. והרבה כיוצא. וכן בדברי רז"ל מצינו (ברכות ז' ע"א) שאמר כביכול לר"י ישמעאל בני ברכני. וכן כל נוסח מטבע תפלות והברכות כולם שיסדו אנשי כנה"ג. הם פותחים ומסיימים בברוך:

פרק ב

והענין כי מלת ברוך. אינו לשון תהלה ושבח כמו שסובר בפי ההמון. שהרי כשאמר לר"י ישמעאל בני ברכני

שער א

בפרשת בהעלתך משם רבינו נסים גאון ז"ל :

ומעת שבעונינו פסקה הנבואה מישראל אף אם יתאספו כל חכמי ישראל אשר נמסר להם מעשה בראשית ומעשה מרכבה. ויעמיקו שגתם ונוהר שכלם. לעשות אף איזה פרט מאיזה מצוה. או להקדים ולאחר זמנה ח"ו. לא אבה ולא נשמע אליהם. ואף בב"ק אמרו (ב"מ נ"ט ב) לא בשמים היא : ועדיין בימי חכמי התלמוד. היו רשאים לחדש מצות דרבנן כשמצאו סמך מהתור'. כגון נ"ח וכיוצא בה"ל. וכן לגזור גזירות כמו י"ח דבר וכיוצא. וכאשר נחתם התלמוד הקדוש. אנו אין לנו אלא לשמור ולעשות ככל הכתוב בתו"הק שבכתב ובע"פ ככל משפטם וחקותם ובזמנם ופרטיה' ודקדוקיהם בלי נטות מהם נטיה כל דהו. וכשיקיימם איש ישראל כראוי. אף אם לא יכוין וגם לא ידע כלל טעמי המצות וסודות כוונתם. עכ"ז נתקיימו המצות ויתוקנו על ידיהם העולמות ויתרבה בהם קדושה ואור בכל מצוה לפי ערכה ומקורה ועניינה. ויותן עז לאלקים ית"ש. שכן קבע הבורא ית"ש טבעם של העולמות שיתנהגו ע"י מעשי האדם. וכל מצוה היא העולה מעצמה לפעול פעולתה המיוחד לה :

ומי שזכהו ית"ש. להשיג נסתרות תו"הק אשר השאירו לנו ברכה קדישי עליונין חכמי התלמוד כגון רשב"י וחביריו ותלמידיו ושבוהין מימיו בדורות האחרונים כמו הרב הקדוש איש אלקים נורא האריז"ל. אשר האירו עינינו בקצת טעמי וכונת המצות. הוא רק כדי שיתבונן כל א' לפי שכלו והשגתו. עד היכן מגיעים כל פרטי מעשיו ודבוריו ומחשבותיו וכל עניניו בהעולמות והכחות עליונים ותחתונים. ויתפעל ויתעורר מזה. לעשות ולקיים כל מצוה וכל עניני עבודתו לבוראו ית"ש. בתכלית הדקדוק ובאימה ויראה ואהבה עצומה ובקדושה וטהרת הלב. ועי"ז יגרום תקונים יותר גדולים בהעולמות. מאם שיה מקיים המצוה בלא קדושת וטהרת הכוונה. אמנם העיקר בכל המצוה לעיכובא. הוא פרטי המעשה שבהם :

הג"ה דרוש ספרא המתחלת ענין הצלם וכו'. עד דף ח' ע"א שמסיים ואין להכם ויחכם עוד. כולה מהרב מוהרי"ץ נ"י. בן הגאון המחבר ז"ל :

סליק שער א

שער א

מתהלך ומתנהג בכל עניניו · כפי שראה והשיג התקונים העליונים לפי שורש נשמתו :

לכן כשהשיג יעקב אבינו ע"ה · שלפי שורש נשמתו יגרום תקונים גדולים בכחות ועולמות העליונים אם ישא השתי אחיות אלו רחל ולאה · והמה יבנו שתיהן את בית ישראל · יגע כמה יגיעות ועבודות להשיגם שיכשאו לו · וכן הענין בעמרם שנשא יוכבד דודתו שילאו ממנה משה אהרן ומרים :

וזה ג"כ א' מהטעמים שלא ניתנה התורה לנח והאבות הקדושים · שאם היתה ניתנת להם לא היה יעקב רשאי לישא ב' האחיות · ולא עמרם דודתו · אף אם היו משיגים שכן ראוי להם לפי שרש נשמתם · ובאמת זה היה כל בניית בית ישראל עם סגולה · ותיקון כל העולמות עליונים ותחתונים · כענין מאמרם ז"ל וא"ת קין נשא אחותו · עולם חסד יבנה :

פרק כב ומשבא

משה והורידה לארץ · לא בשמים היא · ולבל יתחכם האדם הגדול שהשגתו מרובה · לומר אני שרואה סוד וטעמי המצות בכחות ועולמות העליונים שראוי לי לפי שורש נשמתי או למי וני לפי שורשו לעבור ח"ו על איזה מצוה · או לדחות שום פרט מפרטי המעשה לעשיתה במגרעת אף דקדוק אחד מד"ס · או לשנות זמנה ח"ו · ולזה סיימה התורה ולא קם נביא כמשה · וכמו שלמדו ז"ל אלה המצות שאין נביא רשאי לחדש דבר מעתה וכמו שסמכה התורה (דברים י"ג) את כל הדבר אשר אנכי מצוה כו' לא תוסף עליו ולא תגרע ממנו וגו' · שגם כי יקום בקרבך נביא וגו' ר"ל להוסיף או לגרוע ח"ו · לא תשמע אל דברי הנביא ההוא · אחרי ה' אלקיכם תלכו וכו' : והרי חזקיהו המלך שראה ברוה"ק דנפקין מיני' בנין דלא מעלי · ולכן לא נסיב אתתא (ברכות י' ע"א) וכוונתו לש"ש שלא להרבות רשעי עולם · עכ"ז בא אליו ישעיה בדבר ה' ואמר לו כי מת אתה וכו' · ולא תחיה לעה"ב · משום דלא עסקת בפ"ו · ולא הועיל לו כל עולם לדקותיו הנוראים להביאו לחיי עוה"ב בשביל שסבר להפטר ממצוה א' מתורת משה · אף שכן ראה בהשגת רוח קדשו דיפקין מיני' בנין דלא מעלי · וגם שהיה בשב ואל תעשה · כי טעמי מצות עד תכליתם לא נתגלו עדיין לשום אדם בעולם אף למשרע"ה · רק לאדה"ר קודם החטא והוא היין המשומר בענביו מששת ימ"ב · בהאור שנשתמש ביום ראשון שהיה אד"הר צופה ומביט בו מסוף העולם וכו' · כי התוה"ק אצולה מלמעלה ראש מעל כל ההשגות · ואיך אפשר שיהא הדבר מסור להשגת האדם לשנות מהלכתם וסדר זמנם עפ"י רוחב דעתו והשגתו · וכמו שהשיבו ישעיה לחזקיה בהדי כבשי דרחמנא למה לך מאי דמפקדת אבעי לך למעבד ומאי דניחא קמי קב"ה לעביד :

ועדיין כשהיתה נבואה בישראל · היה נביא רשאי לחדש דבר להוראת שעה לבד · ואף גם לעבור על אחת ממצות ה' כגון אליהו בהר הכרמל וכיוצא · אמנם זה עצמו הוא מאשר נלטוינו בתורת משה אליו תשמעון (דברים י"ח) שהוא ליווי ואזהרה לשמוע אל דברי הנביא גם כשיתנבא בשמו ית' לעבור על איזה מצוה בשעה הצריכה לכך כמו שדרז"ל לבד מעכ"ומז · אבל לא ח"ילה לחדש דבר לקובעו לדורות · שהרי אסתר שהיתה אחת משבע נביאות (מגילה י"ד א') עכ"ז כששלחה לחכמים כתבוני לדורות · השיבוה הלא כתבתי לך שלשים · עד שמלאו לה אח"כ סמך מן המקרא (שם ז' א') · וכן כ"ח ודאי שמלאו להם ג"כ סמך מהמקרא · ועיין במדרש שהביאו הרמב"ן ז"ל

בפרשת

שער א

המשיך אח"ז על רוחו ונפשו · נטהר כל אבריו מראשו ועד רגליו . ע"ד והיה עקב תשמעון וכו' מצות שאדם דש בעקביו . והוא הפרסות של נפש הבהמית . וז"ש (ברכה ויקרא פ"כ וקהלת ז') שתפוח עקבו היה מכהה וכו' (*) : וז"ש דוד המע"ה

הגה"ה

תורת ה' תמימ' משיבת נפש · שע"י עסק האדם בתורת ה' והיא תמימה אצלו כראוי . היא משיבת נפש האדם לשרשה בשלימותה , ושיים שם גם עבדך נזהר בהם בשמרם עקב רב. ונזהר מלשון יזהירו וכו' · היינו שע"י ששמר כל המצות המכוונים נגד כל אברי האדם נזדכך נפשו וגופו · עד שגם בעקבו היה אור וזוהר רב· כענין תפוח עקיבו של אדה"ר היה מכהה וכו · ופנימיות הענין גם עבדך נזהר וכו' עקב רב כי תכלית עלייתה של מדת דוד הע"ה בשרש שרשה העליון . הוא כרד"לא · שהיא מל' דאדם קדמאה · שורש נשמת אדם הראשון . וכענין הכתוב (ד"ה א' י"ז) מי אני ה' כו' כי הביאתני עד הלם (ואין הלם אלא מלכות) ותקטן זאת בעיניך אלקים ותדבר על בית עבדך למרחוק וראיתני כתור האדם המעלה ה' אלקים (ובשמואל ב' ז' כ' וזאת תורת האדם) · ויתיר היא נילוכן דאדני · והמשכיל יבין . ולכן השאיר אדה"ר לדוד שבעים שנותיו האחרונים · ז"ת דמ"ל דא"ק · וראוי היה לחיות עוד ל' שנין· להשלים ג"ר דילה · כענין נאם הגבר הקם ע"ל (שמואל ב' כ"ג) והוא ג"כ שורש נשמת משיח שכתוב עליו (ישעיה נ"ב) ירום ונשא וגבה מאד ודרשו ז"ל ע"ז מאברהם וממשה ומאד"הר (ר"ל אחר החטא) . וזהו נאם הגבר הקם על משיח אלקי יעקב . שאז תתגדל ותתעלה כבוד מלכותו ית' במקום שרשה הראשון :

פרק כא וזאת

תורת האדם · שבעת עסקו בתורה לשמה . לשמור ולקיים ככל הכתוב בה . מטהר את גופו מראשו ועד רגליו · כמדרשם ז"ל (ברכות י"ו א')· למה נסמכו אהלים לנחלים כו' מה נחלים מעלין את האדם מטומאה לטהרה . אף אהלים מעלין את האדם מכ"ח לכ"ז . וכענין שדרשו ז"ל גבי טהרת הטמאים במקוה · כל בשרו במים מים שכל גופו עולה בהם · כך בד"ת כל גופו של אדם עולה בהם · (ושיערו חכמים אמה על אמה ברום שלש אמות . כן הג' עולמות : ונר"ן · מעשה דבור מחשבה בתורה) . וכשם שכל גופו של אדם עולה ומזדכך ע"י עסק התורה והמצות · כך העולמות כולם אשר הן המה שיעור קומת אדם כמש"ל פ"ו הם מזדככים ומתטהרים ומתעלים . והאדם הישר העובד אמיתי לא יפנה דעתו ומחשבתו בעת עבודתו לו ית"ש · אפי' כדי לעלות ולטהר גופו ונפשו . אלא שיעלה טוהר מחשבתו וכוונתו ופנה למעלה לתיקון וטהרת העולמות הקדושים · וזו היתה גם כל ענין עבודתם של האבות וכל הצדיקים הראשונים . שקיימו את התורה קודם נתינתה · כמו שדרז"ל ע"פ מן הבהמה הטהורה כו' ואמרו מכאן שלמד נח תורה· ואמרו (יומא כ"ח ב') קיים א"א את כל התורה (וכ"א בב"ר פנ"ב ובבמדבר רבה פי"ד . ובתנחומא בהר ובמדרש תהלים מזמור א'): לא שהיו מצווים ועושים כך מצד הדין · דא"כ לא היו מעמידים ח"ו על דעתם והשגתם אף שהשיגו שלפי ענין שרש נשמתם ההכרח להם לעבור ולשנו' אף מקצת מאחת מכל מצות ה' · ולא היה יעקב אע"ה נושא ב' אחיות ולא היה עמרם נושא דודתו ח"ו . רק מצד השגתם בטהר שכלם התקונים הנוראים הנעשים בכל מצוה בהעולמות וכחות העליונים ותחתונים · והפגמים הגדולים והחורבן והריסה ח"ו שיגרמו בהם אם לא יקיימום . וכן נח הקריב דוקא מן הבהמה הטהורה כי ראה והשיג הכח והשרש העליון של כל בהמה וחיה . איזה מהם כח שרשו מצד הקדושה והקריבה · ואיזה מהם כח נפשם מצד הטומאה והס"א ולא בחר בה להקריבה לפניו ית' כי לא ירצה· וזהו ויתהלך חנוך את האלקים · את האלקים התהלך נח · האלקים אשר התהלכו אבותי לפניו · שפי' אלקים בעל הכחות כולם · היינו שהשיגו ענייני הכחות העליונים ותחתונים וחקות שמים וארץ ומשטרם · וסדרי הנהגתם והתקשרותם והרכבתם ע"י של ענייני מעשי האדם · וע"כ סדר וענין זה היה כל א' מהם מתהלך

שער א

מעורר בקול דבריו שלו פה למטה ולמעלה . וגורם שיתוסף תוספת קדושה ממנו ית"ש עד שורש הנשמה תחלה · ומשם לנפשו ורוחו · והרוח מדביק אורו הגדול הנשפע עליו · גם על בחי' הנפש . מלד ההתקשרות שנשאר עדיין ביניהם כנ"ל · לכלות ולטהר הכחות הרע ומדרגות הטומאה · ולהוציא ממסגר אסיר כל בחינותיה ולחזור ולקשרם כבראשונה עם בחי' הרוח :

וכן אם פגם וקלקל בחי' רוחו ח"ו · בדבורים אשר לא טובים או בשאר מינות התלויים בבחי' הרוח . וביטול תורה כנגד כולם · והגביר לעומת זה כח רוח הטומאה ר"ל . ואז גם נפשו אינה שליטה כמקדם · כי היא מקבלת שפע חיותה ואורה ע"י הרוח כידוע . הגה ע"י החרטה אמיתית בלב ומתמרמר על גודל חטאו . כענין צעק לבם אל ה' · ומהרהר הרהורי תשובה במחשבה שהיא משכן נגוהי אור הנשמה . (והוא מלכות דתבונה) מעורר ג"כ עד למעלה להשפיע תחלה תוספת קדושה ואור על שרש הנשמה . ומשם לנשמתו והיא מבהקת זיו האורה שנשפע עליה . גם על בחי' הרוח . וזבחי אלקים רוח נשברה ושובר כח רוח הטומאה שהגביר בעונו . ומטהר בחי' רוחו הקדוש להתקשר בבחי' הנשמה כבתחלה · ומשם ממילא יושפע גם על נפשו להשלימה בשלימותה הראשון ·

וכן אם השא ח"ו במחשבה אשר לא טהורה · וגרם בזה שיסתלקו מעליו נגוהי זהר נשמתו שהיתה עד הנה כאלו נרה עלי ראשו · אז ע"י עסק התורה בבינה יתירה בעומק תבונתו · מעורר שיתוסף תוספת קדושה על שורש נשמתו · ומשם לנשמתו להאירה שתאיר עליו אורה . להשכילו בתוה"ק בבינה יתירה בסתרי טהוריה · ומאותו הקדושה והאור משתלשל ונשפע גם על רוחו ונפשו להשלימם בשלימותם .

ולכן אמרו ז"ל (שבת קי"ט ב') כל העונה אמן יש"ר מברך בכל כחו . קורעים לו גזר דינו · ואפי' יש בו שמץ של עכומ"ז מוחלי' לו כי עיקר כוונת זה השבח הוא · שיתגדל ויושפע תוספת ברכה ושפעת אור עליון לכל הד' עולמות אבי"ע (*) · וזהו יהא שמי' רבה מברך . היינו שיתגדל ברכה ותוספת קדוש' ממנו ית"ש . עד לעלם הוא עולם האצילות . ומשם גם לעלמי הם ג' עולמות בריאה יצירה . עלמיא הוא עולם העשיה ·· והם שורש הד' דרגין של האדם שרש הנשמה ונרנ"ן וכשמכוין האדם בקדושת מחשבתו באמירת זה השבח לעורר ולהשפיע על ידו תוספת קדושה וברכה על שרש נשמתו · ומשם על נשמתו ורוחו ונפשו . גורם בזה להתם ולכלה כל עון וחטא אשר חטא באיזו בחי' מאלו הג' והיו כלא היו וזה כל עיק' ענין התשובה האמיתית כנ"ל. לכן מוחלין לו על כל עונותיו :

הגה"ה

(*) **ואמרם** ז"ל בכל כחו. סובל ב' פירושים . או בכל כחו של העונה · או שיתברך השם י"ה בכל כחותיו . כענין ועתה יגדל נא כח אדני. ואמנם ב' הפרושים המה באחד מתאחדים · שבשרש מקור שפע קדושה והברכות · הוא בשם י"ה , וממנו משתלשל ומתחלא עולם הבריאה הוא עולם המחשבה ממילוי הה"י שלשם י"ה ביו"ד. ומעול' הבריאה מתמלא עולם היצירה הוא שרש השתל' הדבור והגיון הלב , ממילוי הה"א באלף , ומעולם היצירה מתמלא עולם העשיה הוא עולם המעשה · ממילוי אות ה' שבשם י"ה באו' ה'· והן המה שורש הנר"ן של אדם . שהם כל כחותיו של העונה . וכל כחותיו של השם י"ה היינו כל מלואיו · וזהו י"ה א שם י"ה רבא מברך וכו' וע' תוספ' ברכו' ג' ע"א ד"ה ועונין וכו':

וזה ג"כ ענין מאמרם ז"ל (עכומ"ז ח' א') שיר שהקריב אד"הר קרנותיו קודמות לפרסותיו · שכיון בהקרבתו לתקן אשר עוות . לבנות הנהרסות . לקרב אשר הרחיק וליחד אשר הפריד . והעלה טוהר קדושת מחשבתו וכוונתו·להאציל תחלה שפעת אור וקדושה על הבחי' ומדרגות העליונות שבו דמיון הקרנים . הם שרש נשמתו ונשמתו . ומשם

המשיך

שער א

אמנם בבחי' הנשמה · שהוא סוד המוחין נ"ר דילי' כנ"ל בפע"ו · שם אין מעשה התחתונים מגיעים כלל לקלקלם או לפוגמם ח"ו . אלא שיכולים לגרום במעשיהם הסתלקותם ה מנו ח"ו כידוע בע"ח שהם אי"ס בסוד תוספת לבד ותלוים במעשי ההתחתונים כי הם באים מההפשטות בחי' התחתונה של אם הבנים בו כידוע . וכמש"ה כונן שמים בתבונה· והוא עולם המשומר ממגע זרים כידוע :

והוא ענין מראה הסלם מוצב ארצה כו' · ולא אמר מוצב בארץ . אלא ארצה שפי' לארץ ומשמעו שראש עיקר שרשו בשמים ממעל . ומשם הוא משתלשל ויורד עד לארץ יגיע· והוא הנשמת חיים של האדם שמהאצלת כביכול מנשימת פיו ית"ש · ומשם משתלשלת ככלם ושלשלת ומתקשרת עם הרוח והרוח בנפש עד רדתה לזה העולם בגוף האדם . וכן מפירש ברע"מ נשא קכ"ג ב' ויפח באפיו נשמת חיים כו' דאתמר בי' ויחלם והנה סלם ודאי איהי נשמת חיים כו' ע"ש . והנה מלאכי אלקים עולים ויורדים בו · כמש"ל באורך שהיא הנפש חיה של העולמות והכחות ומלאכי עליון · שכל עלייתם וירידתם וכל סדרי הנהגתם כל רגע · תלוי רק כפי נטיית מעשיה ודבורה ומחשבתה בגוף האדם כל רגע · (ומ"ש עולים תחלה ואחר כך יורדים · כי כל עיקר תורת האדם · להעלות תחלה כל עולם ממטה למעלה · ואחר כך נמשכים אורות מלמעלה למטה) · עד שאח"כ והנה הוי"ה ב"ה נצב עליו כנ"ל :

ומה נעמו אמרי רז"ל בירושלמי תענית פ"ב· ר"ל בשם ר"י אמר שיתף הקב"ה שמו בישראל· משל למלך שהיה לו מפתח של פלטרין קטנה · אמר אם אני מניחה כמות שהיא · הרי היא אבודה· אלא הריני קובע בה שלשלת שאם אבדה תהא שלשלת מונחת עליה · כך אמר הקב"ה אם אני מניח את ישראל כמו שהן הן נבלעין כו' · אלא הריני משתף את שמי הגדול בהם · והם ז"ל דברו לענין כלל האומה יחידה · אמנם עיניהם ז"ל מטייפן כדרכם בקדש · ורמזו גם על האדם יחידי · ושיחתם ז"ל צריכה תלמוד שהמשילו הענין למפתח ושלשלת כמש"ל שהאדם הוא הפותח והסוגר של הכחות והעולמות פלטרין של מעלה ופלטרין של מטה · שכולם מתנהגים ע"י כח מעשיו בחי' נפש שהוא עיקרא ושרשא דבחי נפש כל עלמין · ואדון כל ב"ה בטובו הגדול להטיב לברואיו· שקד על תקנתינו ואמר אם אני מניחה כמות שהיא שלא יהיה התקשרות בין הג' בחי' נר"ן · אלו האחד שיפול בחי' נפש התחתונה לעמקי מצולות הרע ח"ו · אין שני להקימו והרי היא אבודה שם לעולם ח"ו · כענין הכתוב והאבדתי את הנפש ההיא · ונפש החטאת במה תתכפר · לזאת הפליא עצה ית"ש וקבע הג' מדרגות נר"ן שכל א' מהם תתקשר בחי' הראשונה שלה העליונה בבחי' התחתונה של המדרגה שעליה · כענין השלשלת שכל טבעת ממנה · קצה העליון שלה נאחזת ונכנסת תוך קצה התחתון של הטבעת שעליה · וע"י כן · גם אם יכרת הנפש ותפול לעמקי כחות הטומאה ח"ו · יכולה היא לתקן ולעלות ע"י התקשרות בחי' עליונות שלה בבחי' הרוח · וכן עד"ז בקלקול ופגם הרוח כנ"ל · וז"ש שם אלא הריני משתף את שמי הגדול בהם · שהג' דרגין נר"ן ושרש הנשמה · מקור שרשם הוא מהד' אותיות השם הגדול ית"ש :

פרק כ וביאור פרטות סדר תיקונם והתקשרותם ע"י התשוב'

שכאשר פגם האדם בחי' נפשו · או אף אם גרם ח"ו שנפסקו ונכרתו כל הש' ספירותיה מחכמה ולמטה מהתקשרותה הנ"ל · ותרד פלאים לעמקי מצולות הקליפות ח"ו · אז ע"י וידוי דברים באמת מעומקא דלבא· בעקימת שפתיו בחי' נפש דרוח :

מעורר

שער א

מחסד העליון ב"ה שע"י בחי' הרוח היינו ע"י ודוי דברים מלב שהוא בחי' רוח כנ"ל . יתעלו גם הט' בחי' הנפש להתקשר כולם בבחי' הרוח כמקדם :

אינה נפסקת לעולם : ועי' רמב"ם סוף פ"ב מהלכות גירושין בדין כופין אותו עד שיאמר רוצה אני שהגט כשר אם הדין נותן שכופין אותו לגרש ופי' שם הטעם דלא מקרי אנוס . כיון שאמיתת רצונו לעשות כל המצות אלא שיצרו הוא שתקפו וכיון שהוכה עד שתשש יצרו ואמר רוצה אני כבר גירש לרצונו ע"ש לשונו הק' :

וכן אם פגם וקלקל ח"ו בחי' הדבור שלו ע"י עונות התלוים בדבור בלה"ר וכיוצא . או שארי עונות התלוים בשרשם בבחי' הרוח . וקלקל בזה בחי' הרוח . (והגם שאין בחי' הרוח נכרת כלל. כי לא מצינו בתורה ענין הכרת . רק אצל בחי' הנפש לבד . ונכרתה הנפש ההיא . ונכרתו הנפשות העושות וכיוצא הרבה . וכ"כ בלק"ת פ' בא שם . ובפ"ו מהגלגולים ובסופו שם . עכ"ז ע"י העונות התלויים בשרשם בבחי' הרוח . הוא מקלקלו ופוגמו . ומגביר לעומת זה כח רוח הטומאה ר"ל) . מצד שהבחי' העליונה סוד כתר שלו . קשור ודבוק לעולם בבחי' התחתונה של הנשמה כנ"ל . יוכל הוא להתקן ע"י בחי' הנשמה בהרהורי תשובה במחשבת הלב שהוא בחי' הנשמה :

אבל בחי' הנשמה . אינה נפגמת כלל לעולם . כי מקור שרשה הוא מזול' המשומר ממגע זרים . ודבוקה לעולם בשורש הנשמה כידוע שהם רעין דלא מתפרשין לעלמין ואין מעשי האדם מגיעים עדיה כלל לקלקל ח"ו . ואם האדם חוטא במחשבה אשר לא טובה ח"ו . הוא גורם רעה לעצמו לבד , שיסתלק ויתעלם ממנו גילוי אור הנשמה . אבל לא שהיא נפגמת ח"ו :

פרק יט

וזהו ענין הכתוב (משלי י"ח) רוח איש יכלכל מחלהו ורוח נכאה מי ישאנה . ר"ל המחלה וחלאת העון של בחי' הנפש (שהם רוב העונות תלויות בבחי' הנפש . שהיא התחתונה הקרובה אל הס"א רגליה יורדות מות . וכמ"ש ונפש כי תחטא . החטאים האלה בנפשותם והרבה כיוצא . וע' ע"ח שער העקודים פ"ג ופע"ח שער ק"ש שעל המטה פ"ח) . יכולה היא להתקן וגם לעלות ע"י בחי' הרוח כנ"ל . ואם הרוח נכאה שפגם וקלקל בחי' רוחו ע"י עונות התלוים בבחי' הרוח . אז מי ישאנה תיקונו הוא ע"י בחי' הנשמה שנקראת מ"י כידוע בזוהר .

ואיש תבונות יבין שכלל הדברים הנ"ל בענין הג' בחי' נר"ן של האדם . הם ג"כ עד"ז גם בשורשם העליון של אלו הג' בחי' . שהם קוב"ה ושכינתי' . ואם הבנים . שעונות התחתונים גורמים לשכינת עוזינו רזא דנפש דלעילא . שנודדת מהתקשרותה העליון בסוד גלות . (היינו כשנפשות ישראל משוקעים בתאות רעות ח"ו) וע' ע"ח שער מיעוט הירח פ"ב ובשער סדר אבי"ע פ"ב . ובשער הקליפות כל פ"ג . ובהקדמת פע"ח בכללי ז"א ונוק' . ובשער היחודים פ"א מתקוני עונות . אמנם לא כל עשר בחינותיה רק הט' בחינותיה מחכמה ולמטה כנ"ל בענין האדם . אבל בחי' העליונה סוד כתרה שהיא נקודה השרשית דילה . היא קשורה ודבוקה לעולם בטהרת יסוד בחי' הרוח ואינה נפרדת משם לעולם (ולכן נק' עטרה שהוא כתרה) . וע' בהקדמת פע"ח הנ"ל . ובשער העמידה שם בענין ברכת המינים . וכ"כ רבינו הגדול ז"ל בפי' על ההיכלות בהיכלא תניינא שם . (וע' בע"ח שער המלכים פ"ז ובשער מיעוט הירח ובשער הקליפות ותבין כמ"ש בפע"ח באלו ב' המקומות הנ"ל . וע' עוד בפע"ח שער ר"ה פ"ב ותבין כל הנ"ל) . אבל בחי' הרוח עילאה אינו נפרד ח"ו ממקומו ע"י עונות התחתונים אלא שגורמים בו פגם וקלקול ח"ו בו"ק שלו כידוע .

שער א

שורש הנשמה · סוד כנסת ישראל שהיא שורש הכנסיה של כל נשמות כלל ישראל יחד · וכן עז"ה גם בחי' שרש הנשמה ג"כ מוקשרת למעלה מעלה ממדרגה למדרגה עד עלמות א"ס ב"ה: וז"ש אביגיל לדוד והיתה נפש אדוני צרורה בצרור החיים את ה' אלקיך ר"ל שגם בחי' נפשו תתדבק כביכול בו ית"ש · וכמ"ש בזוהר תרומה קמ"ב ב' כד ההיא רוח סלקא לאתעטרא כו' ההיא נפש מתקשרא בההיא רוח ואתנהירת מניה כו' · ורוח מתקשרא גו ההיא נשמתא · וההיא נשמתא מתקשרא גו סוף מחשבה דאיהי רזא · וההיא נפש אתקשרת גו ההוא רוח עלאה · וההוא רוח אתקשר גו ההיא נשמה עלאה · וההיא נשמה אתקשרת בא"ס · וכדין איהו נייחא דכלא וקישורא דכלא עילא ותתא כלא ברזא חדא כו' · וכדין דא איהו נייחא דנפש לתתא · וע"ד כתיב והיתה נפש אדוני צרורה בצרור החיים את ה' אלקיך · ובפ' אחרי ע"א ב' תאנא כתיב והיתה נפש אדוני צרורה כו' · את אדוני מבעי לי' · אלא כמה דאמרן זכאה חולקיהון דצדיקייא דכלא אתקשר דא בדא נפש ברוח ורוח בנשמה ונשמה בקוב"ה אשתכח דנפש צרורה בצרור החיים כו' · וע' עוד בפ' ויקרא ריש דכ"ה · וזהו ענין כי חלק ה' עמו יעקב חבל נחלתו · כי הם כחלק ה' מדובקים כביכול בו ית"ש ע"י התקשרות הג' בחי' הנ"ל · כחבל הקשור למעלה ומשתלשל ויורד עד למטה :

פרק י"ח

וכל זה מרוב טובו וחסדו הגדול ית"ש · אשר חפץ להצדיקנו להטיב אחריתנו · לזאת הפליא עצה וקבעם בענין זה שכל בחי' מהג' אלו תתקשר בהבחי' שעליה כדי שעי"ז יוכל האדם לעלות ולהתקשר ממטה למעלה מעט מעט · לפי רוב עסקו בתורתו ועבודתו ית"ש וטהרת לבו ואהבתו ויראתו · עד שיעלה ויתדבק בצרור החיים כביכול את ה' אלקיו ית"ש · לפי שרשו ומדרגתו · זאת ועוד אחרת · כי יש כמה עונות שהנפש החוטאת באחת מהנה · נתחייבה כרת או אבדון ח"ו · וענין הכרת הוא · שבחי' הנפש נפסק ונכרת משורשו העליון וינתק החבל שהיה קשור ומדובק בו עד הנה ע"י התקשרות הנ"ל · וכמ"ש בזוהר תרומה הנ"ל ואית נפשא כו' דכתיב בה ונכרתה הנפש ההיא מלפני אני ה' · מאי מלפני דלא שריא עלה רוחא · וכד רוחא לא שריא עלה לית לה שותפו כלל במה דלעילא כו' וע"ש · וע' בלק"ת פ' בא · ובמכילתא פ' בא ובסוף פ' תשא ובספרי פ' בהעלותך ופ' שלח ונכרתה אין הכרתה אלא הפסקה וז"ש (ישעי' נ"ט) כי אם עונותיכם היו מבדילים ביניכם לבין אלקיכ' היינו לבין אלקיכם ממש כנ"ל · ואז נטבעת בעמקי הטומאה והקליפות ר"ל · ע' בע"ח שער כללות אבי"ע ריש פ"א · ובשער היחודים סוף פ"ד ושם פ"א מתקוני עונות · ובלקתנ"ך בישעיה בפ' כי רוח מלפני יעטוף · ובגלגולים ס"פ ל"ה · וכ"כ בכתבי קדשו של רבינו הגדול מוהר"א ז"ל בפי' על ההיכלות בהיכלא תנינא · ולבל ידח ממנו נדח · גזרה רצונו יתברך שלא יוכרתו ח"ו לגמרי כל היו"ד חלקי בחי' הנפש רק הט' בחי' התחתונים מחכמה דילה ולמטה הם הנכרתי' · אבל בחי' העליונה סוד הכתר דילה (*) אינה נכרתת · שמצד דביקותה והתקשרותה עם בחי' הרוח כנ"ל (*) · נדונית כבחי' הרוח שאין בו כרת כמ"ש להלן · והוא מחסד

הגה"ה

(*) היינו שאף אם נפשות ישראל משוקעים ח"ו בתאוות רעות ר"ל עכ"ז יסד רצונו ית"ש להעלות נפשם ע"י בחי' רוחו ית"ש · כענין הכתוב ואני זאת בריתי אותם אמר ה' · רוחי אשר עליך וכו' · לא ימושו וכו' · וכענין יצ"מ · וזהו אנכי ה' אלהיך אשר הוצאתיך מארץ מצרים · וידוע בזוהר שאנכי הוא בחי' כתר · וזהו דרשתם ז"ל (שבת ק"ה א') אנכי אנא נפשי כתבית יהבית · ואמירה נעימה וכו' · והם שני הבחי' · נפש ורוח · והמשכיל יבין :

הגה"ה

(*) היינו רצון הפנימי המכחיר נפש מישראל מלך היראה אינה

שער א

עצמותו ית"ש לבד כבחי' היותו מופרש מהעולמות · אלא מצד התחברותו ית' ברצונו הפשוט להעולמות והסותרו בהם להחיותם · וזהו כלל שורש ענין העבודה והמצות כולם · וזה לבד כל השגתינו · וע' לקמן בשער ב' פ"ד ופ"ה הענין באורך · וכל חיותם וקיומם של העולמות כולם · הוא רק ע"י התורה הק' כשישראל עוסקים בה · כהיא נהורו דכל עלמין ונשמתא וחיותא דכלהון · ואלו הי' העולם מקצהו ועד קצהו פנוי אף רגע א' מעסק והתבוננות בתוה"ק היו חוזרים כל העולמות לתהו ובהו כמ"ש ז"ל בשביל התורה וכו' · כמ"ש וחיי עולם נטע בתוכנו · כי מקור שורשה העליון היא למעלה מכל העולמות · לכן בה תלוי החיות של כולם · ואמרו ג"כ בשביל ישראל כו' · כמו שנתב' שע"י עסק האדם והגיונו בתוה"ק הוא משיג להתנוצצות אור בחי' הנשמה בו להשכילו בעמקי רזין קדישין דילה שאז מכונה בשם ישראל כידוע בזוהר · ועל כל מוצא פי ה' הוא בחי' נשמת האדם נשימת פיו ית"ש · יחיו ויתקיימו ג"כ כל הכחות והעולמות · שהיא ג"כ הגבוה והפנימית מכל העולמות · וזהו קוב"ה ואורייתא וישראל מתקשרן דא בדא · וז"ש בראשית בשביל התורה שנקראת ראשית ובשביל ישראל שנקראו ראשית :

וז"ש שם בשעה שעמדו ישראל על הר סיני לקבל את התורה · היו מבקשים לשמוע הדברות מפי הקב"ה · וכמ"ש ישקני מנשיקות פיהו · שבעת המעמד המקודש זכו כולם שהיה חופף ומאיר עליהם זיו נצוצי זהר בחי' הנשמה מנשמת פיו ית"ש כנ"ל והוא סוד הכתרים שזכו בסיני · ושמחת עולם על ראשם : ועי"כ זכו להשיג סתרי פנימית נשמת התוה"ק · כמ"ש בזוהר בהעלותך קנ"ב א' אוריית' אית לה גופא כו' חכימין עבדי דמלכא עלאה אינון דקיימו בטורא דסיני לא מסתכלי אלא בנשמת' דאיהו עקרא דכלא אורייתא ממש : והוא שאמר בכ"מ בתיד זיין היה להם בסיני ושם המפורש חקוק עליו·שהוא ההשגה עליונה בנשמתא וסתרין דאוריי' שמא מפרש . כי כן היה הענין אז למעלה בשרשו העליון · כנ"ל בפ' העבר סוד בעטרה שעטרה לו אמו · ודרשו ע"ז בחזית ביום חתונתו זה סיני וביום שמחת לבו אלו ד"ת · וזהו בעטרה כו' הם הכתרים הנ"ל שהיו בסיני · חיי המלך · וע' בע"ח שער הכללים סוף פ"ה :

פרק יז ונבאר

ענין התקשרות הג' בחי' נר"ן א' בחבירו · והוא יסוד ועיקר ענין התשובה· וזה כל פרי הסר החטאת מנפש החוטאת· ולטהרה מחלאת טומאתה · ויתבונן האדם · כמה הוא צריך להשגיח ולהתבונן על כל פרטי עניני עבודתו לבוראו ית"ש · שתהא עבודתו תמה ושלימה קדוש' וטהורה · ויראה לפשפש ולמשמש תמיד בכל מעשיו ודבוריו ומחשבותיו שהם הג' בחי' הנ"ל · אולי לא השלים עדיין חפצו ורצונו ית"ש לפי שורש נשמתו · בהשגה · וכל ימיו יוסיף אומץ בתורה ומצות · להשלים נפשו ורוחו ונשמתו מטוהרים כאשר ניתנה · אחר שיראה בעין שכלו איך שחפץ הוא ית"ש בחסדו הגדול להטיב אחריתו · ושוקד על תקנת הנפש החוטאת · שגם אם כבר נטבעה בעומק מצולת הרע · עכ"ז תחזור כל דבר למקומו ומקורו בלתי ידח מנו נדח :

והענין כי ידוע בסדר השתלשלות העולמות שהבחי' העליונה שבכל עולם מתקשר עם הבחי' התחתונה של העולם שעליו · וע' זוהר ויקרא י' ע"ב דכלהו עלמין מתקשרן דא בדא ודא בדא כהאי שלשלת דאתקשר דא בדא · וכידוע בכתבי האריז"ל שהמלכות מלכות של כל עולם ופרצוף · נעשה פנימיות כתר להעולם או הפרצוף שתחתיו · (היינו שבקבלת האדם עול מלכותו ית"ש · להעלות כל מעשיו ודבוריו ומחשבותיו בתורה ומצות למדרגה יותר גבוה · מזה נעשה לו רצון פנימי לשעבד מוחו ודבורו ומעשיו בתו"מ) · בסוד כתר מלכות · וכ"ה הענין בג' הבחי' נר"ן של האדם · כי כל בחי' מדבר שבקדושה כלול מעשר בחי' פרטים · שהם הי"ס שלו · והבחי' העליונה של הנפש · נאחזת ומתקשרת עם הבחי' התחתונה העשירית של בחי' הרוח · ובחי' העליונה של הרוח מתקשרת עם בחי' התחתונה של הנשמה · והנשמה ג"כ מתקשרת ומתדבקת בבחי' שורש

שער א

וז"ש הכתוב (איוב ל"ב) אכן רוח היא באנוש ונשמת שדי תבינם · ר"ל שבחי' הרוח היא משתלשל ומושפע ונכנס בתוך האדם · אבל הנשמה שהיא נשמת שדי ר"ל נשימת פיו יתב' · אין עצמותה מושפע ומתגלה בתוך האדם · כי היא מרומים תשכון בתוך פיו ית' כביכול רק שהיא המאירה לו בחי' בגלוי אורה עליו להשכילו בעמקי מצפוני התוה"ק :

ומ"ש בזוהר והמקובלים ז"ל שבחי' הנשמה משכנה במוח האדם · כוונתם ז"ל על הגלוי זיו אורה המשכלת מוחו ושכלו · לא עצמותה ממש · ועיקר כוונתם ז"ל על בחי' נ"ר של הרוח סוד המוחין · שהן פעמים מתגדלים פעמים מסתלקין ובאים בסוד תוספת למי שזוכה לזה כידוע · לא על בחי' הנשמה העקרית · וכ"כ רבינו הגדול הגאון החסיד מוהר"א ז"ל בביאורו על ההיכלות בהיכלא תניינא · והכל א' · שבחי' התחתונה של הנשמה המתגלגלת בדעו ושכלו להשכילו · היא היא הנ"ר של הרוח במוחין שלו כמ"ש לפנינו אי"ה :

פרק טז

והמשכילים יבינו · שכן הוא הענין גם בשרשו העליון · שרק בחי' התחתונה של אדם הכנים סוד נשמת חיים עלאה · היא נכנסת ומתפשטת בפנימיות האדם העליון בסוד תוספת אחר התיקון ע"י מעשי התחתונים הרצויים · והוא סוד המוחין קדישין נ"ר דיליה · שעיקרו הוא ו"ק כידוע · כמבואר למבין בע"ח שער או"א פ"ח · ובשער פרטי עי"מ · ובשער הזווגים ריש פ"ד · ובסוף שער מוחין דצלם · ובשער דרושי הצלם דרוש ב' עש"ה בכל הדרוש · ובדרוש ח' שם · ובפע"ח פ"ג משער התפלין · ובשער היחודים פ"ה מתיקון עונות והוא שאמרו שהנשמה שורה במוח · כמ"ש שם בשער אנ"ך פ"ו · ובשער המוחין בכל פ"ז ובפ"ח ובפי"ב · ובשער דרושי הצלם ריש דרוש ב' · ויותר מבואר הענין שם בהגהת הרח"ו ז"ל · ובשער הפרצופים ריש פ"א · ובשער פנימיות וחיצוניות דרוש ד' ודרוש ס' · ובשער קליפת נגה ריש פ"א · והוא מבואר למדקדק היטב בכל דרושי הצלם · וקצתה חופף ומקיף ומאיר על ראשו בקירוב מקום · כעין בעטרה שעטרה לו אמו · בסוד הנשימה וההבל היוצא מפה אימא לאור מקיף אליו · כמ"ש בע"ח שער הכללים סוף פי"א ובלקוטי תנ"ך בתהלים בפ' הכל כנ כו' · כמש"ל שבחי' הנשמה היא נשימת הפה העליון · אבל עיקרה היא כולה למעלה גנוזה ונעלמה במקורה העליון בתוך הפה · ומאיר בריחוק מקום :

ובזה יובן כוונתם ז"ל בשמות רבה פמ"א · ע"פ כי ה' יתן חכמה מפיו דעת ותבונה · שאמרו למה"ד למלך שהיה לו בן · בא בנו מבית הספר מצא תמחוי לפני אביו · נטל אביו חתיכה אחת ונתנה לו כו' · א"ל איני מבקש אלא ממה שבתוך פיך · מה עשה נתנו לו כו' · היינו שבקשת הבן יקיר להשיג שיושפע בו מגלוי אור בחי' הנשמה אשר מקורה נעלמה בנשימת פיו ית"ש : ורמזו עוד בלשונם הק' שהמשילו להתינוק הבא מבית הספר דוקא · הודיעו בחכמה שאין מבוא בעולם להשיג בחי' גלוי אור הנשמה · אם לא ע"י העסק והעיון וההתבוננות בתוה"ק בקדושה · כי שניהם ממקור א' באים כידוע למבין (*) :

הגה"ה

(*) ועפי"ז יוכל המעיין להבין עפ"י פשוט · ענין הנזכר בזוהר פ' אחרי ע"ג א' שקוב"ה ואורייתא וישראל מתקשרין דא בדא · ודאי עומק כוונתו לסודות עמוקים · אכ"ז יש להסביר הענין גם בפשטות עפי"ז · והענין כי קוב"ה סתים וגליא · כי עצמות אדון כל א"ס ב"ה אינו מושג ולית מחשבה תפיסא בי' כלל · ומה שמושג לנו קצת מן המעט · הוא רק מצד התחברותו להעולמות מעת שבראם וחידשם · להחיותם ולקיימם כל רגע ולהנהיגם כמ"ש ואתה מחיה את כולם · ולכן נשבחו יתברך בתפלתינו שהוא חי העולמים · כי כל כוונת לבנו בכל התפלות והבקשות אסור להיות רק ליחידו של עולם הוא א"ס ב"ה · אמנם לא מצד עצמותו

עצמותו

שער א

היא בחי' הנשמה שהיא המלמדת לאדם דיעה ובינה בתו"הק · לכן עיקר משכנה הוא במוח כלי המחשבה ושא הבחי' העליונה שבהם · וכן אמרו בב"ר פי"ד חמשה שמות נקראו לה כו' נפש זה הדם כו' · רוח כו' · נשמה זו האופי' דבריותי · ר"ל דעתו ומחשבתו כמו שפי' הערוך ורש"י ז"ל :

פרק טו ובי

יפלא · מלא שם נשמה פירושו הוא נשימה · והרי נראה לעין שנשימת האדם הוא ההבל העולה מהלב ממטה למעלה · וגם כי הרי הוא בחי' אויר חוזר ואינו בחי' עליונה · אמנם הענין שנקראת בלשון נשימה · אין הכוונה בחי' נשימת האדם · אלא כביכול נשימת פיו ית"ש · כמ"ש ויפח באפיו נשמת חיים · וכבר המשילו רז"ל (בר"פ חלק) ענין השתלשלות הרוח חיים באדם לעשיית כלי זכוכית לענין תחיית המתים ואמרו ק"ו מכלי זכוכית שעמלן ברוח בשר ודם כו' ב"ו שברוחו של הקב"ה עאכ"ו · וכ"ה בש"ט תהלים מזמור ב' ע"ש · כי הנדון דומה לראיה · שכשנבחין בנשימת פי האומן בכלי הזכוכית בעת עשייתו · נמצא בו ג' בחי' · בחי' הראשונה הוא כשנשימת ההבל הוא עדיין תוך פיו קודם באו לתוך חלל השפופרת החלולה · אין לקרותה או אלא בשם נשימה והבחי' השנית כשנכנס ההבל ובא לתוך השפופרת ונמשכת כמו קו · אז נקרא רוח · והבחי' הג' התחתונה הוא כשיוצא הרוח מהשפופרת לתוך הזכוכית ומתפשטת בתוכה עד שנעשית כלי כפי רצון המזגג או מכלית רוחו ונקרא אז נפש לשון שביתה ומנוחה :

כן בדמיון זה · הוא ענין הג' בחי' נר"ן שמושפעים כביכול מנשימת פיו ית"ש · שבחי' הנפש היא הבחי' התחתונה שהיא כולה בתוך גוף האדם · ובחי' הרוח הוא בא דרך עירוי מלמעלה · בחלק וקלה העליון שלו קשור ואחוז למעלה בבחי' התחתונה של הנשמה · ומשתלשלת ונכנסת גם בתוך גוף האדם ומתקשרת שם בבחי' העליונה של הנפש · כמ"ש (ישעיה ל"ב) עד יערה עלינו רוח ממרום · אשפוך את רוחי וכו' (יואל ג') · שהוא מושפע באדם דרך שפיכה ועירוי כנ"ל · וכמו שיתבאר עוד להלן אי"ה ענין התקשרותם באורך :

אמנם בחי' הנשמה · היא הנשימה עצמה שפנימיות עצמותה מסתתרת בהעלם ומקורה ברוך כביכול בתוך נשימת פיו ית"ש · שאין עצמות מהותה נכנסת כלל בתוך גוף האדם · ואד"הר קודם החטא זכה לעצמותה · ובסיבת החטא נסתלקה מתוכו ונשארה רק חופפת עליו · לבד משרע"ה שזכה לעצמותה תוך גופו · ולכן נקרא איש האלקים · כידוע שכל ג' עולמות בי"ע · ומבחי' הנשמה דאצין ולמעלה הוא אלקות גמור · כמ"ש בע"ח שער הללם פ"א · ובריש שער ציור עולמות אבי"ע בהקדמת הרח"ו ז"ל · ובשער השמות פ"א · וזולתו לא זכה אליה שום אדם · רק בהירות גלולי אור מתנוצצים ממנה על ראש האדם הזוכה אליה · כל אחד לפי מדרגתו ולפום שיעורא דילי' · וע' רע"מ נשא קכ"ג ב' ויפח באפיו נשמת חיים דא איהי דיוקנא דעל ב"נ כו' · ובז"ח רות ס"ד ע"ג ואי זכי כו' כדין נחתא עלי' רבו יתיר מלעילא כו' · אתער עלי' מלעילא אתערו קדישא ושרי' עלי' דב"נ וסחרא לי' מכל סטרין · וההוא אתערו דשריא עלי' מאתר עלאה הוא ומאי שמי' נשמה שמיה ע"ש · והיא הנותנת להאדם בינה יתירה להשכיל השכליות הפנימים הגנוזים בתו"הק · וכמ"ש בס"ת לך לך ע"ט ב' נשמה אתערת לאיעל בבינה · ובז"ח רות ס"ד א' ואתער בי' בחכמתא עלאה כו' · ועיין בע"ח שער מוחין דקטנות פ"ג ז"ל אמנם לא כל אדם זוכה לזה · ודע כי מי שיש בידו כח במעשיו כו' אז יהיה לו זכירה נפלאה בתורה ויבין כל רזי התורה ט' ויתגלו לו רזי התורה כתקונן ע"כ · וע' להלן הענין בשורשו העליון · ותבין :

שער א

שרש למעלה . והפגם של כל א' מגיע עד שורש נשמתו . כמ"ש בתקונים סוף תמ"ג מאן דפגם לאתא פגים לעילא לאתר דאתגזר נשמתי' . ושם בת"ע קכ"ג א' וכד בר נש עביד חובין כפום ההוא בר נש הכי סליק חובי' לאתר דאתגזר נשמתיה כו' ועונשי' איהו סגי כפום דרגי' . וכ"כ האריז"ל בשער היחודי' ר"ס תיקון עונות . ובפע"ח בהקדמת שער השבת פ"א ובגלגולים . ואינו דומה המטנף חצר המלך למטנף פלטין של מלך . וכ"ש הכסא או בגדי תפארתו וכ"ש הכתר . ואף שכל עולם שהוא יותר גבוה ונעלה אין בכח העון לפעול בו פגם ורושם גדול כ"כ . עכ"ז עונשו גדול יותר . כי מי שהוא ממונה לטהר ולנקות כתרו של מלך אם השאיר עליו אפי' אבק מועט לבד אין ערוך ודמיון לעונשו לעונש הממונה לנקות חצר המלך אף אם השאיר או הניח בתוכו הרבה רפש וטיט . ולכן רבו משפטי ה' אמת בשינוי חילוקי העונשים לאין קץ . לכל א' כפי מדרגת הפגם בשורש נשמתו מאיזה עולם חוצבה . גם לא יהיה שוה עונש שני האנשים . מטעם שלא היתה מחשבת שניהם שוה בעת עשיית העון ושפגם נמשך בהעולמות גם לפי ענין המחשבה בשעת העשייה . ואם האחד הדביק יותר מחשבתו להעבירה . ודאי שהוא ראוי לעונש יותר גדול . כי אז הפגם מגיע ח"ו לעולמות יותר עליונים . ומטעם זה השוגג עונשו יותר קל מהמזיד : ולכן אמרו (יומא כ"ט) שהרהורי עבירה קשין מעבירה. ז"ש היוצר יחד לבם (הייט שרואה יחד מחשבו' לבם כמו שפי' ח"ל במס' ר"ה י"ח א') המבין אל כל מעשיהם . ר"ל שהיוצר עליון ית"ש רואה ומבין מחשבות לבם המצטרף אל מעשיהם . ודן את כל א' כפי ענין מחשבת לבו שהיה בעת עשיית העון :

וכן אמר שלמה המע"ה כי את כל מעשה האלהי' יביא במשפט על כל נעלם כו' . ר"ל שמלבד השוגג על מעשה העון בפועל . עוד יביא האלהים ית"ש במשפט את כל מעשה לגלגל עליה לדונה גם על המחשבה הנעלמה . איך ובאיזה אופן היתה בעת העשיה . וכן אמר (משלי ג') ה' בחכמה יסד ארץ כונן שמים בתבונה בדעתו תהומות נבקעו . כלל כאן דרך כלל את כל העולמות . ארץ הוא עולם האמצעי . שמים הם, כלל העולמות העליונים . ותהומות הם כלל התחתונים . ואמר אח"ז בני אל יליזו מעיניך . ולשון עין מצינו כמה פעמים במקרא נאמר על ענין המחשבה . כמ"ש ולבי ראה כו' . החכם עיניו בראשו . ויליזו מצינו במשנה שהוא לשון עקמימות . כמו נלוז הוא ומליז את אביו שבשמים עליו (סוף כלאים) ז"ש בני חוס נא וחמול על שלמו' היקרים שנבראו בחכמה ובתבונה ובדעת והזהר שלא תגרום ח"ו עיקום וקלקול לכלם במחשבה אחת אשר לא טובה ח"ו .

ואלו הג' בחי' מעשה דבור מחשבה . הן כלל הבחי' פנימיות של האדם . שהם הג' בחי' נר"ן . כי המעשה הוא מבחי' הנפש כמ"ש והנפש אשר תעשה. הנפשות העושות . והרבה כיוצא כי הדם הוא הנפש שהנפש שורה ומתלבש בדם האדם ולכן עיקר משכנה בכבד שהוא כולו דם . ומרוצת הדם בכל פרטי חלקי האברים כלי המעשה הוא הנותן להם חיות התנועה והתעוררות שיוכלו לפעול ולעשות את אשר בכחם . ואם יומנע מרוצת הדם מאבר א' אותו האבר מתיבש ואין בו שום תנועה לעשות שום דבר . והוא אבר מת . והדבור הוא מבחי' הרוח כמ"ש (ש"ב כ"ג) רוח ה' דבר בי וברוח שפתיו (ישעיה י"א) וכתו ת"א ע"פ (בראשי' ב') ויהי האדם לנפש חיה. לרוח ממללא . וכן נראה לעין שבכל דבור שהאדם מוציא מפיו יוצא רוח והבל מהפה . ומשכן הרוח עיקרו הוא בלב . כי רוח והבל הדבור עיקרו וראשיתו הוא עולה מהלב . ומחשבה

היא

שער א

ב"נ מפומי' סלק' ובקע רקיעין וקיימא באתר דקיימא · שכל היוצא מפיו יעשה למעלה ומעורר כח עליון · הן בדבור טוב מוסיף כח בכתות הקדושים · כמ"ש (ישעי' נ"א) ואשים דברי בפיך כו' לנטוע שמים כו' · ובזוהר אמור קי"ה א' דלית לך מלה ומלה כו' ומאן דאפיק מלה קדישא מפומיה מלה דאורייתא · אתעביד מניה קלא וסליק לעילא ואתערו קדושי מלכא עלאה ומתעטרן ברישי' וכדין אשתכח חדותא לעילא ותתא · וע' באורך בפ' ויקהל רי"ז א' נוראות נפלאות ענין הדבור של מילין קדישין דאורייתא · שכל עלמין נהירין מתדוותא ושמחות וגיל שבאנה בהיכלין קדישין עלאין ומעטרן להו בעטרין קדישין · ועיין בפ' קדושים פ"ה סוף ע"א · וכן מבואר במקומות רבות בתקונים שמכל דבור וקול והבל דאורייתא או דצלותא נבראים כמה מלאכים קדושים · ובהיפך בדבור אשר לא טוב ח"ו · הוא בונה רקיעים ועולמו' של שוא לכ"ס ר"ל · וגורם ח"ו הריסת וחורבן העולמות סדרי המרכבה הקדושה הנוגעים לשורש הדבור וע'

אשר אני יכולין לכנותו בשם נקרא אצילות · ואצילות פי' שנים לו · לשון חבור כמו אצלו ולשון התפשטות רוחני · כמו ויאצל מן הרוח (וכמו אצילי ידיו שהם מחוברים בגוף תמיד וגם התחלת התפשטות ידיו) · כי עולם האצילות הוא הכל אלקות גמור · כמ"ש בהקדמת התיקונים באצילות איהו וגרמוהי חד כו' · ובע"ח שער דרושי אבי"ע פ"ו · וברי"ש שער ציור עולמות אבי"ע בהקדמ' הרח"ו · ובשער השתלשלות הי"ס פ"ג · ובשער הכלם פ"א · ובשער השמות פ"א · ובשער סדר אבי"ע פ"ב וריש פ"ג ע"ש · ונקרא אין דלית מחשבה תפיסא מהות ההתאצלו' והחבור דאיהו וחיוהי וגרמוהי חד · ועולם השני נשתלשל וירד מדרגה יותר מהראשון שמושג שכ"פ קצת מציאותו שיוכל להקרא יש · והוא היש מאין לכן נקרא בשם בריאה וכמש"ל · ועולם הג' נשתלשל כסדר המדרגה מהעולם השני ונתעבה יותר שמציאותו מושג יותר · והוא היש מיש · ולכן מתואר בשם יצירה כמו יוצר חומר שהוא יש מיש · ועולם הד' הוא גמר מלאכת כל העולמות שקדמוהו ותיקונם של תכלית הטוב האמתי שכיונה יתש"ב בענין כלל

זהר לו ל"א ב' דהא לית לך טב וביש כו' · ואוי להם לבריות שרואות ואינן יודעות מה הם רואות · כי אין לך דבור שאין לו מקום · כי עוף השמים יוליך את הקול וכמה אלפי מארי דגדפי דאחדין לה וסלקין לה למארי דמדין ודיינין לה הן לטוב או להיפך ח"ו כמ"ש בזוהר לך לך נ"ב א' · ובפ' קדושים הנ"ל ולית לך מלה ומלה וכו' וכמה קסטורין מתחברין עמי' דההוא קלא עד דסלקא ואתער אתר דת"ר ט'·וכמה מתערין עלי' דההוא ב"נ ווי למאן דאפיק מלה בישא בפומי' ע"ש·וכתי' (קהל' ה) למה יקציף האלהי' על קולך וחבל את מעשי ידיך·ואמרו (ערכין) גדול האומר בפיו מן העושה מעשה כו' · ואמרו ז"ל (סנהדרין נ"ב א') כל המחליף בדבורו כאלו עובד עבודה כוכבים : ז"ש ומגיד לאדם מה שחו ר"ל שבע' עמוד האדם לתת דין וחשבון לפניו ית' אז הוא ית' מגיד לו הסוד רזא דמלתא מה שגרם שחו למעלה בעולמות העליונים · כמש"ל שלשון הגדה פי' רזא דמלתא :

פרק יד וכן על ההתעוררות שלמעלה ע"י בחי' המחשבה ·

אמר דוד המע"ה היוצר יחד לבם המבין כו' · ופי' נ"ל המבין כל מעשיהם · ולמעלה בפי"ב פירשנו על בחי' המעשה · ויש לפרשו ג"כ על בחי' המחשבה · והוא כי יתכן ששני אנשים עושין עבירה אחת · ועכ"ז אין עונשן שוה · או מפני שהא' שכלו והשגתו יותר גדולה מחבירו · או שורש נשמתו ממקום גבוה ועליון משל חבירו · והעונש הוא כפי ענין הפגם שגרם

הבריאה כולה : והוא זה העולם התחתון שבו דירת האדם המנהיג העולמות בכח מעשיו · וכמ"ש וירא אלקים את כל אשר עשה והנה טוב מאוד · ואמרו בב"ר פ"ח והנה טוב מאד והנה טוב אדם · וכ"ה שם בפ"ט · ובפ"ד שם אר"שבא מתחלת ברייתו של עולם נתאוה הקב"ה לעשות שותפות בתחתונים · וכ"ס בתנחומא בפ' בחקותי ופ' נשא ע"ש · לכן נקרא עשיה המורה על תיקון הדבר מלשון ויתן אל הנער וימהר לעשות אותו · והרבה כיוצא · וכן אמרו בז"ח שם עשי' הוא תיקון הדבר בנוצ' ומעלה מכמות שהיה כד"א ויעש דוד שם · ע"כ :

אתוקד נורא דגיהנם. זמנא חדא לא אשתכח יצה"ר בעלמא כו' וכל ההוא זמנא כבה נורא דגיהנם ולא אתוקד כלל. אהדר יצר הרע לאתריה שארו חייבי עלמא לאתחממא ביה שארי נורא דגיהנם לאתוקדא. דהא גיהנם לא אתוקד אלא בחמימו דתוקפא דיצר הרע דחייביא: וזש"ה כי פעל אדם ישלם לו. שהפעולה עצמה הטובה היא אם רעה ח"ו היא היא עצמה התשלומין שלו כנ"ל. ועיין זוהר קרח קע"ז א'. וז"ש באבות ששכר מצוה מצוה ושכר עבירה עבירה. וז"ש כי את כל מעשה וגו'. ר"ל המעשה עצמה העומדת ונרשמת כמות שהיא כמש"ל:

ולכן אחז"ל (ב"ק נ' ע"א) כל האומר הקב"ה וותרן הוא יותרו חייו כו'. וכ"ה בירושלמי פ"ה דשקלים ובב"ר פס"ז ובתנחומא פ' תשא ובש"ט תהלים. ולכאורה יפלא. הלא אפי' אדם איש חסד מתנהג במדת ותרנות. אמנם הוא כמש"ל. שאינו ע"ד העונש ונקימה ח"ו. רק חטאים תרדף רעה שהחטא עצמו הוא עונשו. כי מעת הבריאה קבע הוא ית"ש כל סדרי הנהגת העולמות. שיהיו תלוים כפי התעוררות מעשי האדם הטובים ואם רעים ח"ו. שכל מעשיו וענייניו נרשמים מאליהם כל א' במקומו ושרשו. והוא מוכרח לקבל דינו ע"י אותן כחות הטומאה שהגביר במעשיו. כפי ערך וענין הפגם. ובזה ממילא יתוקן הפגם של העולמות ושל נפשו. או ע"י כח התשובה. שמגעת עד שורשה בעליון עולם התשובה עלמא דחירו ונהירו דכלא. ומשם מתאצל ונשפע תוספת קדושה עליונה ואור מבהיק. להאיר ולכלות כל טומאה. ולתקן העולמות כמקדם. וביתרון אור חדש מעולם התשובה המופיע עליהם. לזאת אין שייך ותרנות בזה. וז"ש באבות וכל מעשיך בספר נכתבים. היינו שמעצמן נכתבים ונרשמים למעלה:

פרק יג וכן בענין ההתעוררות שלמעלה

ע"י בחי' הדבור. אמר עמוס הנביא ע"ה (סי' ד') כי הנה יוצר הרים ובורא רוח *) ומגיד לאדם מה שחו. כי אמרו בזוהר (לך לך פ"ו ב'. ויחי רל"ד ב' ורמ"ע א'. יתרו פ' ע"א. תזריע נ' ע"ב. שלח קס"א א'. ובא"ז ריש דף רל"ג ובז"ח שה"ש כ"ה ע"ד) בלשון הגדה שייך על רזא דמלתא. הזהיר כאן את האדם. מאחר שהוא עתה בזה העולם השפל שאינו רואה ומשיג הבנין או ההריסה חס ושלום הנעשה למעלה בהעולמות מכל דבור ודבור שלו. ויכול להעלות על דעתו ח"ו לומר במה נחשב דבור ושיחה קלה שתפעול שום פעולה וענין בעולם. אבל ידע נאמנה שכל דבור ושיחה קלה שלו לכל אשר יבטא בשפתיו. לא אתאביד והוא הולך לבטלה ח"ו וכמ"ש בסנה ק' ע"ב אפילו הבל דפומא אתר ודוכתא אית ליה וקוב"ה עביד מיני' מה דעביד. ואפילו מלה דב"נ ואפילו קלא לא הוי בריקניא ואתר ודוכתא אית להו לכלא. ובפ' מצורע נ"ב א' כל מלה ומלה דאפיק ב"נ מפומי סלקא לעילא ובקעא רקיעין ועאלת לאתר דעאלת. וכר"פ נשא דבכו' מלה דאפיק
ב"נ

הגה"ה

*) ולפי סדר הד' עולמו' אבי"ע הי' ראוי לומר תחלה לשון בריאה ואח"כ יצירה. אמנם הענין. כי לשון יצירה פי' הצטיירות דבר יש מיש. ולשון בריאה פי' דבר מחודש יש מאין. כמו שהסכימו כל המפרשים. (וכן אמרו בז"ח בראשית במד"הנ י"ז ריש ע"א). וז"ש אע"פי שנראה לנו שעתה אחר הבריאה הוא רק יוצר הרים יש מיש. כי ההתחדשות יש מאין כבר הי' בששת ימי קדם. אבל האמת כמאז כן גם עתה בכל עת ורגע הוא בורא אותם ומחדשם יש מאין ע"י חיות הרוח שמשפיע בהם מחדש ברצונו ית' כל רגע. וכן אמרו באבות הוא היוצר הוא הבורא. והוא כנ"ל:

ובמוצא דבר ישכיל המעיין על פי פשוט ענין הד' עולמות שנקראו אצילות בריאה. יצירה. עשיה. כי מודעת שהעולמות נשתלשלו בהדרגה ממדרגה למדרגה. וכל שנשתלשל וירד יותר למטה. נתעבה יותר. וכללות העולמות הם נחלקים לד' חלוקות כוללים בערך מעלתם. (לבד האצילות העליוני' שאין לכנותם אפי' בשם אצילות;) ועולם האצילות מהד' שהאציל הוא ית"ש
אבר

שער א

ר"ל הנוגע למעשיהם · והיינו שהוא היוצרם ית"ש יודע ומבין עד היכן מעשיהם מגיעים ונוגעים בתיקוני העולמות או להיפך חס ושלום · וכן קהלת אמר כי את כל מעשה האלקים יביא במשפט על כל נעלם כו'. ולא אמר כי האלקים יביא במשפט את כל מעשה וגו' · והיינו כי אלקים פי' בעל הכחות כולם · ובעת עמוד האדם למשפט לפניו ית"ש · לא ידונו את המעשה לבדה כפי שהיא · אך יחשבו גם כל מה שגרם וסיבב ע"י מעשיו אם טוב ואם רע בכל הכחות והעולמות · זהו אמרו מעשה האלקים :

ואמר כי את כל מעשה · ולא כי על כל מעשה הענין כמ"ש (איוב ל"ד) כי פועל אדם ישלם לו · והוא כמו שנתבאר למעלה (בפ"ו בהג"ה) שמצוה שעולה על טוהר מחשבת האדם לעשו' מצוה · תיכף נעשה רשומו למעלה בשרשו העליון · לנטות ולנטוע כמה עולמות וכחות עליונים · כמ"ש (ישעי' נ"א) ואשים דברי בפיך וכו' לנטוע שמים כו' · וכמאמרם ז"ל א"ת בניך אלא בוניך כמש"ל · ותחילה מתעורר וממשיך גם עליו אור מקיף מהקדושה העליונה · והוא המסייעו לגומרה · ואחר גומרו המצוה · הקדושה והאור מסתלק לשרשו . וזהו ענין שכר העוה"ב שהוא מעשי ידי האדם עצמו · שאחר פרידת נפשו מהגוף · הוא עולה להתעדן ולהשביע נפשו בצחצחות האורות והכחות והעולמות הקדושים שנתוספו ונתרבו ממעשיו הטובים · וארז"ל כל ישראל יש להם חלק לעוה"ב · ולא אמרו בעוה"ב שמשמעו היה שהעוה"ב הוא מוכן מעת הבריאה ענין ודבר לעצמו ואם יצדק האדם יתנו לו בשכרו חלק ממנו · אבל האמת שהעוה"ב הוא הוא מעשה ידי האדם עצמו שהרחיב והוסיף והתקין חלק לעצמו במעשיו · לכן אמר שכל ישראל יש להם לכל א' חלק הקדושה והאורות והצחצחות שהתקין והוסיף לעה"ב ממעשיו הטובים * · וכן ענש הגיהנם ענינו ג"כ שהחטא עצמו הוא עונשו · כמ"ש (משלי ה') עונותיו ילכדונו את הרשע ובחבלי חטאתו יתמך · תיסר' רעתך כו' (ירמי' ב') · כמו שנתבא' שכאשר האדם עושה אחת ממצות ה' אשר לא תעשינה · הפגם והחורבן נרשם ח"ו תיכף למעלה בשרשו · ולפומת זה אמלאה החריבה הוא מקים ומגביר כחות וחיילי הטומאה והקליפות · הרחמן ית"ש יצילנו · ומשם ממשיך גם על עצמו רוח הטומאה שמלפפתו בעת עשיי' העון ואחר עשותו הרוח טומאה מסתלק למקומו והוא בחייו בגיהנם ממש המקיפו בעת עשיית החטא · רק שאינו מרגיש עדיין עד אחר פטירתו שנלכד אז ברשת אשר הכין הן כחות הטומאה והמזיקין שנבראו ממעשיו ·

הג"הה

אמנם מרובה מדה טובה כו' כהפרש ויתרון רב · כי הצחצחות ותוספ' קדוש' שנתוספו ממעשיו הטובים · הם נצחים וקיימים לעולם · ונפשו מתעדן בהם תענוג נצחי · אבל הכחות הטומאה והמזיקין שנבראו ונתרבו מחטאיו · אחר קיבול כל העונש הנקצב לו · הם מתים וכלים מאליהם כי עצמות חיותן הוא רק מפגם החטא וההריסה שגרם בכחות והעולמות הקדושים · שמזה נמשך להם שפע חיות ובלולי אור תופש דרך צנורות אחוריים שנתקלקלו · כענין אמלאה החרבה · וכיון שקיבל דינו על ידיהם חיל בלע ויקיאנו · ונפסק חיותם ממילא וכלים מאליהם · וזהו הענין שהגיהנם נקרא עלוקה · שהעלוקה מוצצת הדמים הרעים ומזה היא מתה תיכף · כן הוא ענין הגיהנם כנ"ל:

וז"ש רז"ל רשעים מעמיקין להם גיהנם ר"ל שהן עצמן המעמיקים לעצמן הגיהנם ומרחיבין אותו ומבעירין אותו בחטאיהם · וכמ"ש (ישעיה נ') הן כלכם קודחי אש כו' לכו באור אשכם ובזיקות בערתם מידי היתה זאת לכם וגו' · לכן כשתפסו אנשי כנה"ג להיצה"ר · כבה אז גם הגיהנם מעצמו כמ"ש בזוהר תרומה קס"ח ע"ב כגוונא דתייבין מתחממן בנורא דיצה"ר כו' בכל תוקפא ותמוהא כו' ספי' אתוקד

ואז

שער א

פרק יא וזהו הטעם · שהמלאכים המקדישים בשמי מרום ממתינים מלשלש קדושתם עד אחר שאנו משלשים קדושה למטה (כנ"ל פ"ו בהגה"ה) · אף שקדושתם למעלה מקדושתנו · לא שהם חולקים כבוד לישראל אלא שאין בכחם ויכולתם כלל מצד עצמם לפתוח פיהם להקדיש ליוצרם · עד עליית קול קדושת ישראל אליהם מלמטה · כי ענין אמירת הקדושה הוא העלאת העולמות והתקשרותם כל עולם בעולם שמעליו להוסיף קדושתם ולאצול אורם · ועיין בהיכלות דפקודי בהיכלא תנינא רמ"ז סוף ע"ב בענין קדושת המלאכים הבא מכח אמירת קדישתינו ז"ל ואלין דימינא אמרי שירתא וסלקי רעותא לעילא ואמרי קדוש · ואלין דשמאלא אמרי שירתא וסלקי רעותא לעילא ואמרי ברוך כו' · ומתחברן בקדושה בכל אינון דידעי לקדשא למאריהון ביחודא כו' · וכלהו כלילן אלין באלין ביחודא חדא ומתקשרן דא בדא · עד דכלהו אתעבידו קשורא חדא ורוחא חד ומתקשרן באינון דלעילא למהוי כלא חד לאתכללא דא בדא · ועיין בפע"ח בכל פ"ג משער חזרת העמידה מבואר שם כוונת ענין אמירת הקדושה שהוא העלאת והתקשרות עולמות עליונים · להוסיף בהם ע"י תוספת קדושה ואור עליון · (ואולי מזה יצא מנהגן של ישראל שנוהגים להעלות עצמן בעת אמירת הקדושה) · וזה אין בכח שום מלאך ושרף לעשותו בעצמו תחלה כנ"ל · לזאת לא יפתח פיו עד עליית הבל פיהם של קדושת ישראל קבוצי מטה · ואלו היו כל ישראל מסוף העולם ועד סופו שותקים ח"ו מלומר קדושה · ממילא בהכרח היו גם המה נשתקים מלהקדיש קדושתם · ועיין בזוהר בלק ק"צ ע"ב · וזש"ה (יחזקאל א') בעמדם תרפינה כנפיהם · ר"ל כשישראל למטה עומדים שותקים · ממילא תרפינה כנפיהם של המוני מעלה · כי ענין אמירת קדושתם הוא גם בכנפיהם · כמאמרם ז"ל (חגיגה י"ג ב') כתוב אחד אומר וכו' כי מנייהו אמעטן אר"ח א"ר אותן שאומרות בהן שירה כו' ועיין ז"ח בראשית י"ג רע"ב קול המולה כו' · אלא שגם פי' כנפיהם לשון כנופיא :

ולזאת המון צבאות מעלה כתות כתות יש · אחת אומרת קדוש · והם השרפים כמ"ש בהיכלות דבראשית ופקודי בהיכלא תניינא . שם מ"ב א' · ושם רמ"ז סוף ע"א · וכמ"ש (ישעי' ו') שרפים עומדים ממעל לו כו' וקרא זה אל זה ואמר קדוש כו' · והשנית לעומתם משבחים ואומרים ברוך · והם האופנים וחיות כמאמרז"ל ריש ג"ה והאיכא ברוך ברוך אופנים הוא דאמרי לי' · וכמו שסדרו אנשי כנה"ג בקדושת יוצר · שכל כת מקדשת כפי מקורה ושרשה בהעולמות · אבל ישראל קבוצי מטה אומרים שניהם קדוש וברוך · להיותם כוללים כל המקורות והשרשים יחד : וזהו ג"כ ענין אמירת פרק שירה שאמרו ז"ל כל האומר פרק שירה בכל יום כו' · שע"י אמירת האדם אותו שהוא כולל כל הכחות כולם · הוא נותן כח להמלאכים והשרים של כל אלו הבריות שיאמרו אלו השירות · וע"ז הם מושכים חיותם ושפעם להשפיע בכל התחתונים · ועיין בזה בלק"ת בטע"מ פרשת ואתחנן :

פרק י"ב ומה שהנר"ן של האדם אין ביכולתם לקשר העולמות · עד רדתם למטה בגוף האדם כנ"ל · כי לתקן עולם העשיה הוצרכו בהכרח להתלבש בגוף בעולם המעשה · וכן מצינו כמה מקראות המדברים באלו הג' בחי' הנ"ל : בענין ההתעוררות שלמעלה ע"י בחי' המעשה · אמר דוד המע"ה היוצר יחד לבם המבין אל כל מעשיהם · ולפי פשוטו היה ראוי לומר המבין כל מעשיהם · ואמר אל כל מעשיהם

ר"ל

שער א

ולכן בעת קריעת ים סוף. אמר הוא ית' למשה מה תצעק אלי דבר אל בני ישראל ויסעו. ר"ל דבדידהו תליא מלתא. שאם המה יהיו בתוקף האמונה והבטחון ויסעו הלוך ונסוע אל הים כמוך לבם לא יירא. מצילם בביאתם שודאי יקרע לפניהם. או יגרמו עי"ז התעוררות למעלה. שיעשה להם הנס ויקרע לפניהם. **וזהו** לססתי ברכבי פרעה דמיתיך רעיתי. ר"ל כמו בסוסי רכבי פרעה שהיה היפך מנהגו של עולם שהרוכב מנהיג לסוס. ובפרעה אילו הסוס הנהיג את רוכבו כמרז"ל. כן דמיתיך והמשלתיך רעיתי ע"ד הנזכר ממש. שאף שאני רוכב ערבות. עכ"ז כביכול את מנהיג אותי ע"י מעשיך. שענין התחברותי כביכול להעולמות הוא רק כפי ענין התעוררות מעשיך לאן נוטים. וחז"ל רוכב שמים בעזרך. וכן מרז"ל העבודה צורך גבוה:

פרק י **ועפ"ז** יבואר פשר דבר בענין שתי דעות שבין גדולי הראשונים ז"ל. אם האדם מישראל גדול מהמלאך. או מלאך גדול ממנו. וכל א' משני הדעות מביא ראיות משרשות ממקראות מפורשים. ועל פי דברינו הנ"ל יתבאר. אשר באמת אלו ואלו דא"ח. רק בבחי' חלוקים. כי ודאי מלאך גדול מהאדם. הן בעצם מהותו. הן בגודל קדושתו ונפלאות השגתו. אין ערך ודמיון ביניהם כלל. וכמש"כ בז"ח בראשית במד"הנ בפ' ויקרא אלהים לאור יום. השגת המלאכים היא השגה גדולה מאח"כ למטה מהם. בשגה שניה כו'. השגה שלישית היא השגת המדרגה התחתונה אשר בעפר יסודה והיא השגת בני אדם. וגם ע"ז ש המלאכים הקרובים מקבלים כח שפע מאספקלריא של מעלה תחלה. ומהם יורד לשמים ולכל צבאם. ומהם אל האדם ע"ש. ובזוהר תרומה קס"ט ב' מלאכי עלאי אינון קדישין יתיר מינן. אינש בדבר א'. יתרון גדול לאדם מהמלאכים. והוא העלאת והתקשרות העולמות והכחות והאורות א' בחבירו. אשר זה אין בכח כלל לשום מלאך. והוא מטעם הנ"ל. כי המלאך הוא בעצם כח א' פרטי לבד שאין בו כלילות כל העולמות יחד. (וכ"כ בע"ח שער פנימיות וחיצוניות ריש דרוש יו"ד שהמלאך אינו רק בחי' פרטית של אותו העולם שעומד בו. אבל נשמת האדם בכל ג' החלקי נר"ן שלה היא כלולה מכל העולמות ע"ש). לכן אין בכח ויכולת המלאך כלל להעלות ולקשר ולייחד כל עולם בהעולם הנמוי על ראשיהם כיון שאינו כלול ומשותף מהם. וגם עליית עצמותו של המלאך עד מדרגה להתקשר בעולם שעליו. אין תלוי בו בעצמו. לכן נקראים המלאכים עומדים כמ"ש (ישעיה ו') שרפים עומדים. ונתתי לך מהלכים בין העומדים האלה (זכריה ג'). ורק האדם לבד הוא המעלה והמקשר ומייחד את העולמות והאורות בכח מעשיו. מחמת שהוא כלול מכולם. ואז גם המלאך משיג עליה ותוספת קדושה על קדושתו אשר בא בכח מעשה האדם. מפני שגם הוא כלול בהאדם. (ועיין כענין זה בע"ח שער העיבורים ריש פ"ד):

וגם הג' בחי' נר"ן של האדם עצמו. לא ניתן להם זה הכח ההעלאה וההתקשרות של העולמות ושל עצמם. עד רדתם לזה העולם המעשי בגוף האדם. וכמ"ש ויפח באפיו נשמת חיים בגוף האדם אז ויהי האדם לנפש חיה של כל העולמות כנ"ל בפ"ד: **והוא** ג"כ ענין מראה הסולם של יעקב אבינו ע"ה. פי' רע"מ נשא קכ"ג ב' ויפח באפיו נשמת חיים כו' דאתמר ביה ויחלם והנה סלם ודאי איהו נשמת חיים כו' ע"ש. וכמש"ית אי"ה לקמן בפי"ט. ועי"ז והנה מלאכי אלקים עולים ויורדים בו. ר"ל ע"י הנשמת חיים שהיא מוצב ארצה מתלבשת קצה התחתון שלה בגוף האדם.

וזהו

שער א

חיבתכם לפני המקום כו׳ · ובזוהר תרומה קנ״ב ב׳ אימתי איהו ברחמי · א״ל בשעתא דכרובים מהדרן כו׳ ומסתכלן אנפין באנפין · כיון דאינון כחבר׳ מסתכלן אנפין באנפין כדין כל גוונין מתתקנן כו׳ · כמה דמסדרין ישראל תקונייהו לגבי קוב״ה הכי קיימא כולא והכי אתהדר כו׳ · ובפ׳ אחרי נ״ט ריש ע״ב תנא אתיא כו׳ בשעתא דהוו חד באחד משגיחין אנפין באנפין כתיב מה טוב ומה נעים וגו׳ וכד מהדר דכורא אנפוי מן נוקבא ווי לעלמא כו׳ · ובבא ס״פ תרומה ל״ו א׳ בכל זמנא דישראל הוו זכאין כרובים הוו דביקן בדביקו אפין באפין · כיון דהוו סרחן הוו מהדרין אפייהו דא מן דא כו׳ · ועו״ד כרובים פרצופא זמנא דהוו ישראל זכאין הוו אנפין באנפין כו׳ · ועל רזין אלין הוו ידעי אי ישראל זכאין אי לא ס׳ · כתיב עבדו את ה׳ בשמחה הדווהא דתרין כרובין כו׳ כיון דשארי עלייהו אתהדר בחדוה כו׳ ועלמא אתהדר ברחמי כו׳ ועיש באורך :

פרק ט והנה דור המדבר שזכו להיות אוכלי שלחן גבוה לחם מן השמים דבר יום ביומו · ושמלתם לא בלתה מעליהם · ולא היו צריכים לשום עסק פרנסה במילה כלל · לדידה לא מקרו עושין רצונו של מקום אא״כ היו מסתכלין לפי מעלה ביותר גמור ומשעבדין את עצמם רק לתורה ועבודה ויראתו ית״ש יומם ולילה לא ימוש מפיהם דברים כשתבן ממש בלי פנות אל הצד כלל אף שעה קלה לעסק פרנסה · וכמאמרם ז״ל לא ניתנה תורה אלא לאוכלי מן · לכן העמידו אז את הכרובים לפי מה שהיו עושין רצונו של מקום פניהם איש אל אחיו ממש · להראות כי ישר יחזו פנימו ית׳ פנים בפנים עם עם קדושו · אבל בימי שלמה שהיו כלל המון ישראל צריכים ומוכרחים לנטות מעט אל הצד לעסק הפרנסה עכ״פ כדי חיי נפש · שזה עיקר אמיתת רצונו ית׳ לדעת ר׳ ישמעאל דסבר דלרבים עפי צריך למעבד הכי וכמ״ש באבות יפה ת״ת עם ד״א כו׳ וכל תורה שאין עמה מלאכה כו׳ · וכל מילי דאבות מילי דחסידות ניהו · רק שגם בעת עסקם בפרנסה יהא לבם נוהג בחכמה בהרהור ד״ת · לכן העמידו אז בתחלה את הכרובים לפי מה שיהיו עושין רצונו של מקום פניהם מצודדין מעט · ועכ״ז היו מעורים כמעבר איש ולויות בפנים של חיבה · להראות חיבתו ית׳ אלינו · שזה עיקר רצונו ית׳ כנ״ל · (וכסבר כר׳ ישמעאל · ומ״ד שגם בכרובי שלמה · העמידום תחלה לפי מה שיהיו עושין רצונו של מקום · פניהם איש אל אחיו ממש · סובר כרשב״י) · ולבאורה אכתי למה הוצרכו להעמיד ב׳ הכרובים מצודדין · כלא הכרוב הא׳ שרמוז עליו ית״ש היו צריכים להעמידו ישר ממש · אמנם הענין כמ״ש שהתחברותו ית׳ כביכול להשתלמות והכחות עולם וכל סדריהם והתקשרותם · וכן כל סדרי הנהגתו ית׳ אתנו · הוא כפי שיעור התנועה וההתעוררות המגיע אליהם ממעשינו למטה · וכפי זה השיעור משתלשל ונמשך גם אלינו למטה פנים שוחקות ומסבירות · לכן גם הכרוב שרמוז עליו ית״ש היו ג״כ צריכים להעמידו מצודד מעט · כפי שיעור הצדוד של הכרוב שרומז עלינו · מזה הטעם · *

הגה״ה

* ועפי״ז יובן מאמרם ז״ל בפ״ט דשבת (פ״ח א) · ארז״ל מ״ד כתפוח בעצי היער כו׳ למה נמשלו ישראל לתפוח כו׳ · והקשו תוס׳ שם דהא כבר קרא לא ישראל נמשלו לתפוח אלא הקב״ה כדכתיב כן דודי בין הבנים · ולפמ״ש יתיישב בע״ה כי אחר שישראל השיגוהו והתגלותו ית״ש בדמיון התפוח · ודאי הוא מחמת שגם ישראל נתפעלים ומתדמים במעשיהם לענין התפוח · וכדרך שאנחנו מתראים לפניו ית״ש כך הוא ית״ש בא לירא את הפעולות ע״ז ההדרגה והשיעור ממש · לכן שיאל באיזה דבר וענין נתדמו ונמשלו ישראל במעשיהם הראשים להבות אשר ע״י ז השיגוהו ית״ש כענין התפוח :

ולכן

שער א

שאין ישראל עושין רצונו של מקום · וכ"כ תוס' שם דמסתמא העמידום תחלה לפי מה שהיו עושין רש"מ ולכאורה אכתי תקשי למה העמידום תחלה כרובי שלמה פניהם מלודדין ולא איש אל אחיו ממש · והענין הוא · כמ"ש פ' כילד מברכין (ל"ה ב') ת"ר ואספת דגנך כו' לפי שנאמר לא ימוש ספר התורה הזה מפיך כו' יכול דברים ככתבן · ת"ל ואספת דגנך הנהג בהן מנהג ד"א דברי ר' ישמעאל רשב"י אומר אפשר אדם חורש בשעת חרישה כו' תורה מה תהא עליה · אלא בזמן שישראל עושין רצונו של מקום מלאכתן נעשית ע"י אחרים כו' · ובזמן שאין ישראל עושין רש"מ מלאכתן נעשית ע"י עצמן שנא' ואספת דגנך ולכאורה תמוה דמוקי לקרא דואספת דגנך · כשאין עושין רש"מ · והא לעיל מינה כתיב והיה אם שמוע תשמעו אל מצותי וכו' לאהבה וכו' ולעבדו בכל לבבכם וכו' · ועלה קאמר ואספת דגנך · אבל הענין · כי ודאי שאין דעת ר' ישמעאל שיהא הרשות נתונה לאדם לפרוש ח"ו אף זמן מועט מעסק התורה · ולעסוק בפרנסה ויהיה בטל אותו העת מעסק התורה לגמרי ח"ו · אמנם רמזו ר"י בלשונו הק הנהג בהן מנהג ד"א · ר"ל עמהן עם הד"ת · היינו שגם באותו העת ושעה מועטת שאתה עוסק בפרנסה כדי הצורך וההכרח לחיות נפש · עכ"פ ברעיוני מחשבתך תהא מהרהר רק בד"ת · וכן רבא אמר לתלמידיו ביומי ניסן ותשרי לא תתחזו קמאי דיקא · שלא לבא לבית מדרשו · אבל ודאי שתלמידי רבא לא היו בטלים ח"ו לגמרי מעסק התורה גם בביתם באלו הימים . ואמרו שם הרבה עשו כר"י ועלתה בידם · והרבה עשו כרשב"י ולא עלתה בידם · היינו רבים דוקא . כי ודאי שלכלל ההמון כמעט בלתי אפשר שיתמידו כל ימיהם רק בעסק התורה שלא לפנות אף שעה מועטת לשום עסק פרנסת מזונות כלל · וע"ז אמרו באבות כל תורה שאין עמה מלאכה וכו' · אבל יחיד לעצמו שאפשר לו להיות אך עסוק כל ימיו בתורתו ועבודתו יתב"ש · ודאי שחובה מוטלת עליו שלא לפרוש אף זמן מועט מתורה ועבודה לעסק פרנסה ח"ו · וכדעת רשב"י * : והנה פסוק ואספת דגנך וכו' הוא מולא מכלל פרשת והיה שכולה נאמרה בלשון רבי' ופסוק ואספת נאמ' בלשון יחיד · לכן קרי לי' אין עושה רצונו של מקו' כשמפנה עצמו אף מעט לעסק פרנסה:

הגה"ה

ולכן כפ' ראשונה של ק"ש כתיב ובכל מאדך · ובפ' והיה לא כתיב ובכל מאדכם · כי פ' שמע כולה בלשון יחיד נאמרה · ויחיד שאפשר לו · הוא צריך לקיים לא ימיש ספר התורה הזה מפיך דברי' ככתבן ממש · לכן נאמר ובכל מאדך פי' בכל ממונך כמ"ש במשנה סוף ברכות · ר"ל שלא לעסוק בפרנסה כלל · אבל פ' והיה שנאמרה בלשון רבים · לרבים כמעט מוכרחים להתעסק עכ"פ מעט גם בריוח ממון לחיי נפש · לכן לא כתיב בה ובכל מאדכם · (והגם שעדיין לא זו הדרך והמדרגה הגבוה שבגבוהות לפי אמיתת רצונו ית"ש לדעת רשב"י · עכ"ז גם לדידי' לא מקרו ח"ו בזה אין עושין רצונו של מקום כשמפנין עצמם מעט גם לעסק פרנסה ובעת עסקם בפרנסה לבם נוהג בחכמה ומהרהרים בד"ת ויראת ה' · ולר' ישמעאל · זו היא עיקר רצונו ית' בהנהגת כלל ההמון · ופלוגתתם מה היא עיקר רצונו ית והמדרגה היותר גבוה בהנהגת כלל ההמון) :

וידוע שהכרובים · הא' רמז עליו ית"ש והשני על ישראל סגולתו · וכפי שיעור התקרבותם ודביקותם של ישראל אליו ית"ש · או להיפך ח"ו · היה ניכר הכל בענין עמידת הכרובים דרך נס ופלא · אם פניהם ישר יחזו אליו ית"ש · גם הכרובים עמדו אז פניהם איש אל אחיו · או אם הפכו פניהם מעט ומצדדי אצדודי · כן היה ניכר הענין תיכף בכרובים · או אם ח"ו הפכו עורף . גם הכרובים כרגע הפכו הפכו פניהם איש מעל אחיו לגמרי ח"ו · וכענין שאמרו ז"ל ביומא (נ"ד א') שהיו מגללין הפריכת לעולי רגלים ומראין להם הכרובים שהיו מעורין זה בזה ואומרים להן ראו

הא מבהכם

שער א

כמ"ש פירש"י באורך בתו"ה פ' א' ובר"מ פנחס רכ"ט ב' וכ"כ רח"ו ז"ל בשערי קדושה ח"ג שער ב' ובלק"ת פ' הבל ופ' האזינו ע"ש. וז"ש בב"ר פ"ח ויאמר אלקים נעשה אדם בתי נמלך. ר"י בשם ר"ל אמר במלאכת השמים והארץ נמלך רבב"נ אמר במעשה כל יום ויום נמלך. ובקהלת רבה ס' ב' פסוק י"ב את אשר כבר עשוהו אין כתיב כאן עשאו אלא עשוהו כביכול הקב"ה ובית דינו נמנו על כל אבר ואבר שלך ומעמידך על תיקונך. וא"ת שתי רשויות הן והלא כבר נאמר הוא עשך ויכוננך. והוא מבואר:

פרק ז ועתה

מבואר הענין הנ"ל בפ"ה. שהאדם נקרא הנפש ונשמת החיים של כל רבוא עולמות. לא נפש כנפש הנתון ודבוק ממש בתוך גוף האדם. דזה לא יתכן. אמנם היינו שכמו שכל פרטי תנועות ונטיית אבר הגוף. הם ע"י הנשמת חיים שבו כפי תנועות חיותו ונטייתו כן הענין שכל נטיית הכחות והעולמות וסדרי המרכבה. תקונם ובנינם והריסות' ח"ו. הוא רק כפי ענין ההתעוררת ממעשי האדם למטה. ומטעם שהוא כלול ומשוכלל במספר פרטי כחותיו וסדריהם ע"פי סדרי השתלשלות והתקשרות הכחות והעולמו' עליונים ותחתונים כולם. והוא מצד שורש נשמתו העליונה שהיא הגבוה והפנימי' מהעולמות הנבראי' כולם כנ"ל בפ"ה. לכן הוא כולל את כולם. והטעם שנתבאר בפ"ה מחמת שורש נשמתו שהיא גבוה ופנימית מהעולמות. והטעם שנתבאר בפרק העבר מחמת שהוא כלול מכל העולמות. הכל א' כמו שנתבאר:

ולזאת לו לבדו ניתנה משפט הבחירה להטות עצמו ואת העולמות לאיזה צד אשר יחפוץ. או אף אם כבר גרם וסיבב ח"ו בחטאיו הריסת העולמות וסדרי המרכבה וחורבנם וירידתם ח"ו. יש כח וסיפוק בידו לתקן את אשר עיות ולבנו' הנהרסות מצד שהוא כלול ומשותף מכולם.

וז"ש דוד המע"ה ה' צלך על יד ימינך. היינו שכמו שנטיית הצל של איזה דבר הוא מכוון רק כפי תנועות אותו הדבר לאן נוטה. כן בדמיון זה כביכול הוא ית"ש מתחבר לנטות העולמו' כפי תנועה ונטיית מעשי האדם למטה. וכן מפורש במדר' אמר לו הקב"ה למשה לך אמור להם לישראל כי שמי אקי"ק אשר אקי"ק. מהו אקי"ק אשר אקי"ק כשם שאתה הוה עמי. כך אני הוה עמך. וכן אמר דוד ה' צלך על יד ימינך. מהו ה' צלך כצלך. מה צלך אם אתה משחק לו הוא משחק לך. ואם אתה בוכה הוא בוכה כנגדך. ואם אתה מראה לו פנים זעומות או מוסברות אף הוא נותן לך כך. אף הקב"ה ה' צלך כשם שאתה הוה עמי הוא הוה עמך ע"כ. ובזוהר תצוה קפ"ד ב' ת"ח עלמא תתאה קיימא לקבלא תדיר כו' ולעלמא עלאה לא יהיב ליה אלא כגוונא דאיהו קיימא. אי איהו קיימא בנהירו דאנפין מתתא כדין הכי נהרין ליה מלעילא. ואי איהו קיימא בעציבו יהבין ליה האי דינא בקבליה כגוונא דא עבדו את ה' בשמחה. חדוה דב"נ משיך לגבי' חדוה אחרא עלאה. ה"נ האי עלמא תתאה כגוונא דאיהו אתער הכי אמשיך מלעילא כו'. והוא ענין הכרובים שהיו מעורין כמעור איש ולויות פניהם איש אל אחיו ובכרובי שלמה כתיב (דה"ב ג') ופניהם לבית כמו שיתבאר בע"ה:

פרק ה הנה

רז"ל אמרו בענין הכרובים (ב"ב צ"ט א') כיצד הן עומדין. ר"י ור"א. ח"א פניהם איש אל אחיו. וח"א פניהם לבית. ולמ"ד פניהם איש אל אחיו הכתיב ופניהם לבית. ל"ק כאן בזמן שישראל עושין רצונו של מקום כאן בזמן שאין ישראל עושין רצונו של מקום ועי' רש"י. ולמ"ד פניהם לבית הכתיב ופניהם איש אל אחיו. דמצדדי אצדודי. ר"ל קצת לבית וקצת זה לזה. ועי' רש"י ז"ל וכא ליכא לתרוצי כדלעיל כאן בזמן שישראל עושין כו'. דכיון דעיקר עשיית כרובים פניהם לבית. לא היה להם לעשותו לסימן שאין

שער א

ונודע מדרגתו · כי לא כל העולמות שוו בשיעורן בענין הפגם והקלקול · שבתחתון הוא הריסה וחורבן ר"ל · ולמעלה מניעת האור · ובעליון יותר ממנו גורם רק התמעטות שפעת אורו או הקטנתו · וביותר גבוה ונעלם גורם רק התמעטות בגודל לחלות אורו וטהרת קדושתו הנפלאה · וכהנה רבות בחינות שונות :

הוא דבוק כביכול בו יתברך גם בחייו · וזש"ה ואתם הדבקים בה' אלהיכם גם בעודכם חיים כלכם היום · וזה האור מקיף הוא לו לעזר לגמור המצוה · וע"י הגמר האור מתחז' יותר וירים ראש עליון וע"ז אמרו ז"ל הבא ליטהר מסייעין אותו · גם מושכת וגוררת את לבו מזה לסגל עוד כמה מצות · אחר שהוא יושב עתה בג"ע ממש חוסה בצל כנפי הקדוש' בסתר עליון · אין מקום להיצ"הר לשלוט בו ולהסיתו ולהדיחו מעסק המצות · וז"ש שמצוה גוררת מצוה · וכאשר ישים אליו לבו בעת עשיית המצוה · יבין וירגיש בנפשו שהוא מסובב ומלובש כעת בהקדושה ורוח נכון נתחדש בקרבו · וזש"ה אלה המצות אשר יעשה אותם האדם וחי בהם · בהם היינו בתוכם ממש שהוא מסובב אז בקדושת המצוה ומוקף מאוירא דג"ע :

וכן להיפך ח"ו בעת עברו על אחת ממצות ה' אמרו ג"כ במאמרם ז"ל הנ"ל כל המטמא עצמו מלמטה מטמאין אותו מלמעלה · פי' ג"כ כנ"ל שמשורש אותו העון למעלה בכחות הטומאה הוא ממשיך ר"ל רוח הטומאה על עצמו ותוספת עליו וסובבתו · כמ"ש במאמר פ' מי הנ"ל ואי איהו אשתאב לתתא אזער רוח מסאבותא לעילא ואתי ושריא עלי' ואסתאב בי' · דהא לית לך טב וביש קדושה ומסאבותא דלית לה עיקרא ושרשא לעילא · ובעובדא דלתתא אתער עובדא דלעילא ע"ש · ובפ' קדושים הנ"ל ובשעתא דאיהו אחזי עובדא לתתא בארחא עקימא כו' כדין נגיד ונפיק ושריי' עלוי רוחא אחרא כו' ע"ש · וע"ז אמר הכתוב ונטמתם בם היינו בתוכם ממש ח"ו · שהוא קשור ומסובב אז ברוח טומאה ואוירא דגיהנם מלפניו ומאחוריו גם בעודנו חי בעולם · כמרז"ל (ע"ז ה' א') כל העובר עבירה א' בעה"ז מלפפתו והולכת לפניו ליום הדין שנאמר ילפתו כו' · רא"א קשורה בו וכו' · וז"ש דוד המע"ה עון עקבי יסובני (תהלים מ"ט) :

ובזה יובן מאמרם ז"ל בפ' יוה"כ (פ"ו ב') גדולה תשובה שזדונות נעשות להם כזכיות שנא' (יחז' יג) ובשוב רשע מרשעתו ועשה משפט וצדקה עליהם הוא יחי' · ולכאורה אין הראי' מוכרחת · דכרוחא עפי יש לפרש דעליהם הוא יחי' קאי על המשפט וצדקה שעשה אחרי שובו · ולפמ"ש ראייתו נכונה · דלישנא דקרא דייק הכי · דאי קאי עליהם הוא יחיה על המשפט וצדקה · הול"ל בהם הוא יחי' כמ"ש וחי בהם וכמו שנתבאר · ומדקאמר עליהם ודאי דקאי על רשעתו ועונותיו

דבכוכב יהא גבר נהיר וחכי' וכו' האי מאן דבצדק יהא גבר צדקן וכו' · ועכ"ז אינם נותנים חלק מכחם אלא בהתעוררת מעשה הזיווג בפועל · כן הכחות מעולמות עליונים אין נותנים חלקם בחיים אלא לעומת מעשה האדם בפועל ממש במצות ובתלמוד תורה המביא לידי מעשה אז מתעוררים להשפיע מאורם העליון גם למטה בהתמזגות הד' שרשין עלאין בנשמתא בשכל · וכן בלב · במדות · ובמעשה · ועוד כי הדברים ארוכים בפרטי בחי' הללם לפי כתבי האריז"ל · אמנם דרך כלל די בזה · ותן לחכם ויחכם עוד :

נולדים נשמות בני אדם הנמשכים מגבוה שבגבוה לפעול פעולה' בארץ מכחם העליון · ויתכן להמשיך הענין בכתוב (קהלת י"א ה') כאשר אינך יודע כו' כעצמים בבטן המלאה ככה לא תדע את מעש' האלקים אשר יעשה את הכל · פי' מעשה אלקים הוא המעשה אשר נעשה האלקי' אשר יעש' אותם האדם וחי בהם · שהמעשה יעשה את הכל ויעשה נשון תיקון הדבר כמו וימהר לעשות אותו (בראשית י"ח ז') וכמו ולא עשה שפיו (שמואל ב' י"ט כ"ה) · ע"כ :

ועונותיו הקדמונים · שע"י תשובתו בעזיבת מעשיו הראשונים ועשותו אח"כ משפט וצדקה המה יתגברו על מעשיו הראשונים להפך גם אותם לזכיות והיו עילם :

וזהו הענין שקראו רז"ל בכמה מקומות לפגם העון פגם איקונין של מ"ך · ובזוהר יתרו פ"ה ב' ובג"כ מאן דפשע בפקודי אורייתא כמאן דפשע בגופא דמלכא כמה דכתיב ויצאו וראו בפגרי האנשים הפושעים בי בי ממש · ווי לחייביא דעברין על פתגמי אורייתא ולא ידעין מאי קא עבדין · ובתיקונים ת"ע קכ"ט ב' וכל מאן דפשע בפקודא כאלו פשע בדיוקנא דמלכא · כנ"ל שהפגם נמשך ונוגע בפרקי וסדרי הכחות והעולמות השיעור קומה · מלך שכולם נכללו בו וכתנו חלק מעלמותם בבניינו ובריאתו *

הגה"ה

וזהו פעמות ענין הכתוב נעשה אדם לשון רבים · ר"ל שכולם יתנו כח וחלק בבניינו שיהא כלול ומשותף מכולם · כמבואר

שער א

וזהו זיווג הראשון שתלוי רק לפי קדושת אבא ואמא · ומאז והלאה כל התקונים והתוספת המוחין להזדווג להוציא פעולתם בעולם הוא זיווג הבני · תלוי לפי מעשיו·וסדרם אז הוא נ"ל"ס · ומזה תבין הענין בשרשו בעולמות עליונים :

כללמו הזכיר הצלם בכף הדמיון · שאחר שהוסר הצלם ממנו ונחמעט רק על מאה אמה כנ"ל בהגה"ה · לא נשאר רק הדמות ובדמות פעולתו עורר להמשיך צלם · וגם שת היה יכול ע"י דעות פרטי מעשיו לטובה להשלים צלמו עפ"י בחירתו וקבלתו מלכות שמים וקבלת מ"ש במעשה הוא עיקר נקודה הפנימית שגרמה לו כביכול לאלם בריאת כל העולמי' שיוכל להכרתו האדם בעול' המעשי' · וכן נאמר בזוהר על מדת מלכותו ית"ש שאיהי שלימו דכל ספירא · ומשלמת הט' בחינות וזה עשר ולא תשע· וכמבואר בע"ח שעיקר מדת מלכותו ית"ש שתהיה נגדלת להיות בעלת עשר כבחינת פרצוף · ע"כ :

ולכן כל תקוני העולמות נקרא בזוהר וכתבי האריז"ל בשם זיווגים · ולכאורה יפלא שהיא מודעת שהוא רק משל על חבור עניני' רוחני' · כענין אדם המחבר תחלה בשכלו ב' סברות בשכל ומחביר ב' הסברות נולד לו סברא חדשה · ע"פי הקדמת שני הסברות הראשונות · ומה הביאם לקדושי עליון להמשיל דבר רוחני במשל גשמי כזה · אך הענין הוא לסכור פי הדוברים ומרחיבים פה ולשון וממלאים פיהם שחוק על שלומי אמוני ישראל · שאומרים שכל מעשי המצות שעושה האדם למטה גורמים תקונים גדולים בעולמות עליונים · ולכן הראו דוגמא שכמו שלא נוכל להשכיל ולהבין איך שממעשה שפלה כענין זיווג נולד מטפה סרוחה בריה נפלאה וקומה שלימה מלא שכל רוחני להשיג ענינים נפלאים רוחנים וקדושים · כן לא נוכל להבין שורש אמתת תקוני העולמות והכחות עליונים המשתלבים באורות רוחני' ע"י מעשי המצות שהאדם עושה למטה בזה העולם השפל כפי רצונו ה' ית"ש * ועיין כוזרי מאמר ג' סי' כ"ג · וכולי עלמא מודים שכחות המצות העליונים מתעוררים ליתן חלק באדם · כמאמר רז"ל האי מאן דבכוכב

הג"ה

וידוע שאף זיווג הנשיקין אתדבקות רוחא ברוחא אינם מולידים רק נשמות מלאכים שכליי' נבדלים · ומזיווג זו"נ

נגדו · וכאשר קיים כל המצות בשלימות בכל פרטיהם ודקדוקיהם בעיקר המעשה · ונוסף עליהם הצירוף עולם טהרת וקדושת המחשבה · הרי תיקן כל העולמות והסדרים העליונים · ונעשה כולו בכל כחותיו ואבריו מרכבה להם ומתקדשים מקדושתם העליונה · וכבוד ה' חופף עליו תמיד· וע' זוהר תרומה קנ"ה א' כל הנקרא בשמי ולכבודי בראתיו כו' · ולכבודי בראתיו דיקא · ורזא דא כו' אוליפנא דהאי כבוד כו' כלא אתקן לעילא מגו תקונא דבני עלמא כד אינון בני נשא זכאין וחסידין וידעין לתקנא תקוני' כו' ע"ש באורך וע' היטב ברע"מ פרש' פנחס רל"ט א' · וארז"ל האבות הן הן המרכבה · וכן להיפך ח"ו בפגום אי מכחותיו ואבריו ע"י חטאהו אשר חטא · ג"כ הפגם מגיע לפי שרשו לאותו העולם והכח העליון המכוון נגדו בסדרי השיעור קומה כביכול · להורסו ולהחריבו ח"ו · או להורידו · או לפוגמו· או להחשיך ולהקטין לאלות אורו· ולהתיש ולהחלים ולמעט כח טהרת קדושתו ח"ו · הכל כפי ערך החט' ואופני עשייתו וכפי ערך וענין אותו העולם

קדשנו במצותיו · וכן וקדשתנו במצותיך · כי מצות שעולה של רצון האדם לעשות תליה · תיכף נעשה רשומו למעלה במקור שרשה העליון וממשיך משם על עצמו אור מקיף וקדוש' עליונה חופפת עליו וסיבבת אותו · וכתיב מפורש והתקדשתם והייתם קדושים·וכמאמר' ז"ל (יומא ל"ט א') כל המקדש עצמו מלמטה מקדשין אותו מלמעלה ר"ל שמלמעלה נמשך עליו הקדושה משרשה העליון של המצוה כמ"ש בזוהר נו ל"א ריש ע"ב כתר והתקדשתם והיית' קדושים מאן דמקדש גרמי' מלרע מקדשין לי' מלעילא כו' · מקדשין ליה מלעילא כו' דהא קדושה דמארי' שרי' עלי' כו' · אי עובדא דלתתא היא בקדושה אתער קדושה לעילא ואתי ושרי עלי' ואתקדש ביה כו' ע"ש · ובפ' קדושים פ"ו ב' בשעתא דב"נ אחזי עובדא לתתא כארח מישור כו'· נגיד ונפיק ושרי' עליה רוח קדישא עלאה כו' ובההוא עובדא שריי' עלי' רוח קדישא רוח עלאה לאתקדשא בי' · אתא לאתקדש מקדשין ליה דכתיב והתקדשתם כו' · ובפ' נשא ריש ד' קב"ה דמשיך עלי' רוח קדישא עלאה כמד"א עד יערה עלינו רוח ממרום ע"ש · וע"י זה הקדושה והאור המקיף · הוא

שער א

יתי"ש ומקיים באיזה אבר וכח שבו אחת ממצות ה'. התיקון נוגע לאותו שרש וכח העליון שמקבילו. לתקנו. או להעלותו. או להוסיף אור וקדושה על קדושתו מחפץ ורצון העליון יתי"ש. כפי ערך ואופן עשייתו. ולפי רוב ההזדככות וטהרת קדושת מחשבתו בעת עשיית המצוה המצטרפת לטובה למעשה העקרית. וכפי ערך מדרגת אותו העולם והכח עליון.

לכן כשמכניסין האדם לתשפט לפניו ית"ש. צריך חשבונות רבים לאין שיעור. על כל הפרטי פרטים של כל מעשיו ודבוריו ומחשבותיו וכל פרטי הנהגותיו. באופני נטייתם לאן היו נוטים. וזש"ה (שם) אשר עשה האלקים את האדם ישר כנ"ל והמה בחטאם בקשו חשבונות רבים. וע' זוהר אמור ק"ז סוף ע"א והוא מבואר שם ע"פ דברינו. ונמשך הענין כן עד עת מ"ה שאז פסקה אותה הזוהמא מתוכ' כמרז"ל (שבת שם). ולכן אח"כ בחטא העגל ארז"ל (שם פ"ם א') שבא שטן וערבב כו'. היינו שבא מבחוץ כמו בענין חטא אד"הר כנ"ל כי מתוכם נתגרש. וע"י חטא העגל חזרה אותה הזוהמא ונתערבה בתוכם כבתחלה. וזש"ה (הושע ו') והמה כאדם עברו ברית. וז"ש הוא ית' לאד"הר כי ביום אכלך ממנו מות תמות. לא שהיה ענין קללה ועונש. כי נוסי עליון לא תצא כו'. אלא פי' שע"י אכלך ממנו תתערב בך הזוהמא של הרע. ולא יהיה תיקון אחר להפרידה ממך כדי להסיכך כאחריתך. אם לא ע"י המיתה והעיכול בקבר. וזהו ג"כ הענין מ"ש הוא ית' אח"כ הן האדם היה כו' ועתה פן ישלח ידו ולקח גם מעץ החיים ואכל וחי לעולם. והלא חפצו ית"ש להטיב לברואיו ומה אכפת ליה אם יהיה לעולם. אמנם ר"ל שכאשר יאכל מע"הח וחי לעולם ישאר ה"ו בלא תיקון. שלא יתפרד הרע ממנו עד עולם ח"ו ולא ירצה מאורות וטובה מימיו. לזאת לטובתו גירשו מג"ע. כדי שיוכל לבא לידי תיקון גמור כשתפרד הרע ממנו ע"י המיתה והעיכול בקבר. וזהו ענין הד' שמתו בעטיו של נחש (פ' במה אשה) שאף שלא היה להם חטא עצמם כלל. עכ"ז הוצרכו למיתה מחמת התערובת הראשון של הרע ע"י חטא אד"הר בעצת הנחש. וימשך הענין כן עד עת קץ הימין בלע המות לנצח. וגם עיד יתרון שיתבער אז הרע מן העולם מתליאותו. כמ"ש (זכריה יג) ואת רוח הטומאה אעביר מן הארץ:

ומשם נמשך הקדושה ואיזות גם על אותו הכח של האדם(*) וזה שתקנו שבי קיים מצו' בורא המצוה'

הגה"ה

נוסח ברכות המצו' אשר

הפנימים. ולפי המבואר שמקום שליטת היצ"הר הוא בין פנימים למקיפין ע"כ נכשל בעץ הדעת ע"ור קליפת נוגה. והדברים ארוכים. ואפס מקום לבארם פה. ע"כ:

כל שמעשיו מרובין מחכמתו חכמתו מתקיימת כו' *. כי העיקר הוא לגלות תחלה לכוף את יצרו להשתעבד למעשי המצות אף שאין לו עדן מוחין דצמ"ד דצלם וגם הוראת פי' האותיות הוא תחילה לד"יק במעשה. ואח"כ למ"ד הוא בחי' השכל שמקיפין במוחין. ואח"כ המ"ם הוא בחי' נהי"מ דבינה כי אם לבינה תקרא. והוא ענין בן מ' לבינה. ומ' יום של יצירת הולד: והמ"ם סתומה בסוף תיבת אם כידוע שבעיבור היא סתומה. ע"כ): וזה מאמרם ז"ל שזיווג ראשון איט לפי מעשיו של אדם. וזיווג שני הוא לפי מעשיו. כידוע בזוהר (אמור ד' ק"ד) שבע' זיווג ד"וכ קאים עליה חד צולמא. והוא ענין הג' בחי' דצלם הנ"ל. כי התמזגות הד' יסודין ושרשין קדמאין איט שוה בכל בר"ן. שהלבוש מד' יסודין והמוחין מד' שרשין נמשכין לפי ענין קדושת האב ואם בעת הזיווג. ואיט תלוי אז עדיין לפי מעשה הולד שיהי'. ואז סדר המשכתן והזדווגות מזגם הוא המ"ם תחלה הד' שרשין עלאין ואח"כ הלמ"ד המשכת פעולתן שהוא הג' יסודין אר"מ לבד מיסוד העפר. והכל עדיין בבחי' השכלה ומקיף המוחין לבד. ואח"ז מתפשטין במדות ובמעשה גפ"ג והוא צ' כנ"ל.

הגה"ה

ולפי המבואר לעיל כמו שצלם הוא מעלמין סתימין. ודמות הוא מעלמין דאתגליין. ככה היא חכמתו ושכלו של האדם הצלם הסתום בתוכו להוציא דמות כלי המעשה בפועל ממש במעשי המצות וכמו שבתחילת בריאת העולם דמות כלי המעשה במצוה שעלה במחשבה תחלה עוררה להמציא כלי הצלם כן גם עתה מעשי המצות שהאדם מקיים בפועל ממש מעורר להמשיך עליו הצלם משרשין קדמאין. ולזאת בבריאת האדם כתיב נעשה אדם בצלמנו כדמותנו והאדם בהולידו את שת כתיב ויולד בדמותו כצלמו. שבעת בריאת האדם ברא הקב"ה כאות השרשין שהן הצלם שיוכל האדם. לפעול מעשי המצות כדכתיב לעבדה ולשמרה. ודרשו רז"ל זו מ"ע ומל"ת. אבל הבחירה היה בידו. והי' עדן הדמות בכח ולא בפועל. לזאת כתיב נעשה אדם בצלמנו. כדמותנו בכ"ף הדמיון ולכך כתיב אח"כ ויברא אלקים את האדם בצלמו בצלם אלקי' ברא אותו. ולא נזכר דמות. ובני אדם בהולידו את שת ויולד בדמותו כצלמו.

שער א

חגיגה י"ב שאדם הראשון הי' גבוה מהארץ עד לרקיע . וחד אמר מסוף העולם ועד סופו וכמאמרם ז"ל דאידי ואידי חד שיעורא הוא (וכמבואר בע"ח דאדם קדמון עיבר בכל העולמות) ומבואר בזוהר שהאור נגנז באורייתא. ועיין זוהר ל"א ב' שהאור נגנז לצדיקים ומסיים שם והוא טמיר נצדיקי' לצדיקיא דייקא. פי' צדיק בכ"מ הוא במעשה כי דוקא ע"י מעשה המצות בפועל ממש מעוררי' אור העליון הגנוז בתורה. ושם הן השרשין עלאין שבכללם׳ לזה אז"ל (אבות פ"ג משנה ט')

שהתקינו (ברכות נ"ד א' ועיין רש"י שם וס"ג א' ד"ה ויברכו את שם) ואמרו בזוהר ויצא קנ"ח ב' כל ברכאן דתרין עלמין באתגליא ובאתכסיא. ושם כל דא כלא חד כו' דכתיב ברוך ה' אלקי ישראל מן העולם ועד העולם. וזהו מסוף העולמות רומזי עד סוף עולם הגשמי כי כחדא נחשבין כאחת. ולכך במקדש ראשון שהיתה השראת שכינה בשלימות ועלמין סתימין היו מתחברין עם המצות וראו כולם שהמ' כחדא היו אומרי' רק עד העולם. וכבית שני שחסר החמשה דברים ולא כולי עלמא השיגו האחדות. וקלקלו המקלקלין. התקינו לומר מן העולם ועד העולם. להורות עכ"פ שלא זה העולם הוא עיקר אלא טפל. ובלשון חכמים הורו עוד למשיגים שעלמא דאתכסי' הוא חדא עם עלמא דאתגלי'. לפיכך לא אמרו מן עולם ועד עולם אלא מן העולם ועד העולם. כי כחדא נחשבין כאחת. וכן קומת אדם הראשון היה מסוף העולם ועד סופו. ולפי המבואר עלמא דאתכסי' הצלם ועלמא דאתגלי' הדמות היו מאירים ובאים לו כחדא ובקשר אמיץ. וזהו אחור וקדם צרתני לשון צורת הצלם. שהיו מקושרים מוחין הפנימיין בהמקיפין. והמקיפין במקיפין שעליהם. וזהו מן הארץ עד לרקיע כידוע שהשמים המה מקיפין ור"א לא הזכיר המקיפין אלא דרך כלל. ור"י א"ר הזכיר גם המקיפין העליונים. והוא מ"ש דצלם השרשין עלאין. וזהו דרשתו ולמקצה השמים ועד קצה השמים. כי ר"א אמר סתם עד לרקיע מקיף הנגלה. והוא הוסיף עוד שגם מקצה הרקיע שנקרא אח"כ שמים עד קצה שמי השמים העליונים. (ועיין פי' רמב"ן על החומש על פסוק ויקרא אלהים לרקיע שמים. ומה שכתב שם אבל יותר נכון וכו') וע"ז אמרו בגמרא אידי ואידי חד שיעורא הוא. ועיין תוס' שם. וכיון שסרח והוסר ממנו הצלם המקיפין נתמעט קומתו על מאה אמה. (עיין בעין יעקב חגיגה שם. ובמהרש"א ח"א שם) הוא ענין ג' כלי הצלם הפנימית. וכל חד כלול מג' יסודין הפועלים. וגופו התשלמת בדמותו כל הבחי' משלים לעשר. וידוע שכמו שלספירות אין שיעור כן כל א' כלול מעשר הוא מאה. ושם כי בתחלה היו המקיפין כחדא עם הפנימים

כולן. קשורין ותלוין במקור שרשן העליון בסדרי פרקי המרכבה ושיעור קומה של העולמות כולם. שכל מצוה פרטית בשורשה כוללת רבי רבוון כחות ואורות מסדרי השיעור קומה. כמ"ש בזוהר יתרו פ"ה ב' כל פקודי אורייתא מתאחדן במלכא קדישא עלאה. מנהון ברישא דמלכא. ומנהון בגופא. ומנהון בידי מלכא. ומנהון ברגלוי כו'. והענין יותר מבואר בתקונים ת"ע קכ"ט ב' ע"ש. ובזוהר תרומה קס"ה ב' פקודי אורייתא כלהו שייפין ואברין ברזא דלעילא. וכד מתחברן כלהו כחד כדין כלהו סלקן לרזא חד. ושם בד' קס"ה ב' בהאי שמא כלילן תרי"ג פקודי אורייתא דאינון כללא דכל רזין עלאין ותתאין כו'. וכלהו פקודין כלהו שייפין ואברין לאתחזאה בהו רזא דמהימנותא. מאן דלא ישגח ולא אסתכל ברזין דפקודי אורייתא. לא ידע ולא אסתכל היך מתתקנן שייפין ברזא עלאה. שייפין דגופא כלהו מתתקנן על רזא דפקודי אורייתא ע"ש. וכ"כ האריז"ל בשער היחודים פי"ב ובעשות האדם רצון קונו

יתי"ש

והענין מבואר למבין בע"ח שער קליפת נוגה פ"ב אלא שקיצר שם בענין. ועיין היטב בגלגולים פ"א. ואמרז"ל (שבת קמו א) כשבא נחש על חוה הטיל בה זוהמא. ר"ל בתוכה ממש. ומאז גרם עי"ז ערבוביא גדולה במעשיו. שכל מעשי האדם המה בערבוביא והשתנות רבים מאד. פעם טוב ופעם רע. ומתהפך תמיד מטוב לרע ומרע לטוב. וגם המעשה הטוב עצמה כמעט בלתי אפשר לרוב העולם שתהי' כולה קדש זכה ונקיה לגמרי. בלי שום נטיה לאיזה פניה ומחשבה קלה לגרמי'. וכן להיפך בהמעשה אשר לא טובה. ג"כ מעורב בה לפעמים איזה מחשבה לטוב לפי דמיונו. וגם הצדיק גמור שמימיו לא עשה שום מעשה אשר לא טובה ולא שח מימיו שום שיחה קלה אשר לא טובה ח"ו. עכ"ז כמעט בלתי אפשר כלל שמעשיו הטובים עצמם כל ימי חייו. יהיו כלם בשלימות האמיתי לגמרי ולא יהיה אפי' באחת מהנה שום חסרון ופגם כלל. וזש"ה (קהלת ז') כי אדם אין צדיק בארץ אשר יעשה טוב ולא יחטא. ר"ל שא"א שלא יהיה עכ"פ קצת חסרון במעשה הטוב עצמה שעושה. כי חטא פי' חסרון כידוע.

לכן

שער א

דעלמ' דלתתא·וכלא מתחקקא בב"נ דאיהו קאים בצלם אלהי' כו' דכתיב · ויברא אלהים את האדם בצלמו ע"ש·ובפ' תזריע מ"ח א' תאנא כיון דנבראת אדם כו' · ובריש פר' במדבר ר"א פתח ויברא אלקים את האדם בצלמו וגו' ת"ח כו' · ובאדר"ז קל"ה א' כמראה אדם כו' · ושם בד' קמ"א סוף ע"א דיוקנא דכליל כל דיוקנין כו' · וברע"מ פ' פנחס רל"ח ב' ויאמר אלקים נעשה אדם כו' עד והיינו נעשה אדם בצלמנו כו' · וכן אמרו זה בארוכה יותר בארוך בתז"ח פ"ע נ"א ע"ש · ובז"ח יתרו במעשה מרכבה ל"ב ע"ג דיוקנא דאד' דדא איהו דיוקנא דכליל כל דיוקנין כו' · ושם רף ל"ג ריש ע"א · ושם בש"הש כ"ח ב' ויאמר אלקים נעשה אדם בצלמנו כו' · ע"ש היטב בכל המקומות הנז' · וע' בע"ח שער הצלם פ"א ובל"קת ופ' תשא ופ' האזינו · וזה כל האדם שכל כח פרטי שבו מסודר נגד עולם וכח א' פרטי מסוד שיעור קומה של כלל הכחות והעולמות · שמסודרים כביכול כתבנית קומת אדם כמ"ש א"יה בשער ב' פ"ה · ובו' המלות

כולן

והענין כי קודם החטא · אם כי ודאי שהיה בעל בחירה גמור להטות עצמו לכל אשר יחפוץ להטיב או להיפך ח"ו · כי זה תכלית כוונת כלל הבריאה · וגם כי הרי אח"כ חטא · אמנם לא שהיה ענין בחירתו מחמת שכחות הרע היו כלולים בתוכו · כי הוא היה אדם ישר לגמרי כלול רק מסדרי כחות דקדושה לבד·וכל עניניו היו כולם ישרים קדושים ומזוככים טוב גמור · בלי שום תערובות ונטי' לצד ההיפך כלל · וכחות הרע היו עומדי לבד וענין כס"ע חוץ ממנו · והי' בעל בחירה ליכנס אל כחות הרע ח"ו כמו שהאדם הוא' בעל בחירה ליכנס אל תוך האש · לכן כשרצה הס"א להחטיאו הוצרך הנחש לבא מבחוץ לפתותו' · לא כמו שהוא עתה שהיצר המפת' את האדם הוא בתוך האדם עצמו · ומתדמה להאדם שהוא עצמו הוא הרוצה ונמשך לעשות העון ולא שאחר חוץ ממנו מסיתהו · וכחטאו שנמשך אחר פתוי הס"א· אז נתערבו הכחות הרע בתוכו ממש · וכן בהעולמות · וזהו עץהדעת טוב ורע· שנתחברו · ונתערבו בתוכו ובהעולמות הטוב והרע יחד זה בתוך זה ממש · כי דעת פי' התחברות כידוע :

הוי' ב"ה הרי ממשיך עליו שם ה' ׳ דהא ישראל מתקשראן באורייתא ואורייתא בקב"ה · ובזוהר פ' שמיני ל"ה ב' · ר' חייא אמר תורה שבכתב ותורה שבע"פ אוקמוהו לי' לבר נש בעלמא הה"ד נעשה אדם בצלמנו כדמותנו · הרי שהתורה נקראת צלם ודמות · לפי שבארנו ענין צלם עלמין סתימין ודמות עלמין דאתגליין · כך התורה כלולה מרזא עד סוף והוא מה שנאמר בזוהר פ' אמור ל"ח ע"ב · אורייתא כלא סתים וגליא · כגוונא דשמא קדישא סתים וגליא · בגין דאורייתא כלא שמא קדישא היא ועל דא איהי סתים וגלי' · פי' כמו שהוא ית"ש נקרא אל מסתתר מפני שנבראו העולמות במדריגות רבות · לגבי' אין שום שנוי · ורק לגבי דידן הוא מסתתר שיתראו לעינינו פעולותיו במדריגות שונות ושנשיג אחדותו ית"ש בסתר המדריגה התחתונה · וכל הסתתרו הוא כדי שרק עי"ז יגלה כבוד אחדותו אלינו בזה האופן דוקא · כאשר יבא בשערים הבאים · כנודע שהצלם אור בהיר הוא הנעלם שיוכל להגלות כל ידי כרזנקן כמבואר בזוהר ברא"מ נש"ו ע"א דאתהפי' לגו וכו' · דאיהו הושבחתא דילי' ותושבחתא דכלהו עיין שם · וזהו סתים ופי"ז הוא גלי' כן תורה"ק עם שנכון בה כל הלכתו' עליונו' שבעליוני' כמלאו בה מדריגות שמה שרשי' לכלי המעשה דבור מחשבה נגד נר"ן של אדם · ומוסתרים בתוכה סתרי סתרין ונגלים לנו ע"י הנגלות תלמוד שמביא לידי מעשה המצות · כדי שע"י התורה והמצות תושב"כ ושבע"פ נוכל להמשיך עלינו ובתוכנו צלם מעלמין סתימין · ודמות פעולות גופינו מעלמין דאתגליין · לכך אמר גם היא סתים ועי"ז היא גליא · כרצונו ית"ש שנשיג הסתום ע"י הגלוי · וזה רק מלדינו כדי לאכפייא ס"א במעשי המצות · ומצילא המאור שבה מאיר לנו השרשין עלאין · וזהו דרשתם ז"ל חגיגה י"ב ע"א ומדרש רבה בראשית פ' י"א אור שבא' הקב"ה ביום ראשון אדם מביט בו מסוף העולם ועד סופו וכו' ונגנזו לצדיקים לעתיד לבא · פי' מסוף העולם ועד סופו הוא כל המציאות מריש העולמות עד סוף עולם המעשה (*) הי' מאיר ובא כאחד כענין דרשת' ז"ל שם

הגה"ה

ובענין מן העולם ועד העולם

חגיגה

שער א

כלי מוחו ממולאים במחשבה תורה ובכל לבבו יהגה יומם ולילה כד״ת · ובכל גופו יעסוק במצות מעשיות שהיא שורש כל השרשין עלאין שקדמה לבריאת עולם :

מאש הגאוה הוא נמא לכל מיני התאוה ר״ל וכדרך הנמאים לרוות למאוגם במים · כן ממציא לו לרוות נמאון התאות כיסוד המים שבמות להמציא לו מהשבות איך להוציא תאות לבו מכח אל הפועל · כענין שכתוב (ישעיה נז כ) כי השקט לא יוכל ויגרשו מימיו רפש וטיט · והן המים מטונפים ובוזים שמוריד לו תמותא מחשבותיו והרהוריו הרעים · ומעורר לו יסוד הרוח · מפאפי ריאה דנשבין על לבא להוציא דברים לה״ר רכילות ניבוס וכדומה · ויסוד העפר מנא לאפקא הילהין דג׳ יסודין · וע״י נגלו פעולות מחנה א״ר״ס · ולאשר אין אדם מת והני תאותו בידו לגלות מתענג אל לבו כנבע העפר :

ובאשר האדם מנביר ברשין דיליה שבקדושה · הנה יסיד האש בכלבו תגביה לבו בדרכי ה׳ יהתדבק בשרשו · ובוער כרשפי אש שלהבה יה ולמא לתורה ועבודה כענין שנאמר צמאה לך נפשי · וכתיב הוי כל צמא לכו למ ים ומתעורר יסוד המים שבמוחו · וממציא לו שכל טוב בתורה ועבודה · ולהתענג על ה׳ בצלותיו · וכמבואר ברע״מ פנחס רכ״ז כ׳ קול ה׳ על המים מספרא דמיא · דאיהו מוחא דאמן סליק בכנפי ריאה · קול ה׳ חוצב להבות אש מספרא דלבא ומתחבר ע והם יסוד הרוח שבכנפי הריאה דנשיב על לבא שאחבת כל מיני מיקין שבמוחא · וזהו קלא דכליל מאשא רוח ומיא · לקיים והגית בו יומם ולילה · ויסוד העפר הוא מנא לאפקא הילהין דברין קדישין · בדבור ומעשה · וניכר בו עלנות ובכיות בלא לעבור ח״ו על רצון הש״ית אף כאיסור קל · ועצבות על עונותיו · ובכל עצב כגוונא דא יהיה מותר שמאשא עלאה דלבא מתעורר בינה דבמוחא דמינה מתערין דינין להבין דבר מתוך דבר כמה קלקולים גרם במחשבה · דבור ומעשה · ואיך הוא רחיק מה׳ · ורבה התשובה · וכל מה שמרבה לחפש דרכיו ולהקיר מתעוררים גבורות קדושות · ומתמרמר במרירות על נפשו על שנתלכשה בלבוש · מה״ד יומא אשר לא טובים · ומתעורר מיא שבמוחא להוציא דמעה ע״ז · ומתמתקות הגבורות בחסד ה׳ בשנפתחים שערי דמעה שהמה הוא יו״ד משם הוי״ה ב״ה נמתקים הקי״ע דינין שמק״כ צרופי אלקים שבמנין דמעה ושורש הראשון שלו נמתק בשרשו בטינא סקיהא · כמ״ש עיני נגרה ולא תדמה עד ישקיף וירא ה׳ משמים · ע״כ ·

והן הן עלם רצון הקב״ה להמציא הד׳ שרשין עלאין כדרשתם ז״ל בראשית בשביל התורה שנקראת ראשית ובשביל ישראל שנקרא ראשית וכשמקיים תורה ומצות במחשבה דבור ומעשה לשם הוי׳ קלרה כדרכו בכל כתבי קדשו בנסתרות · כמ״ש בעצמו בהקדמתו שם שהוא מגלה טפח ומכסה אלפים אמה) · שלא כדמשמע לכאורה מדבריו ז״ל שם שהאדם אל העולמית הוא נפש ממש כמו הנפש הניתן ודבוק בתוך גוף האדם אשר איזה דבר שהנפש עושה הוא רק ע״י כלי הגוף · שבאותו רגע ממש גם הגוף עושהו · דזה ודאי לא יתכן (*) :

הגה״ה

ונם שלפי זה · יתחייב היה שבעת אמירתינו קדושה למטה·ממילא באותו רגע ממש גם המלאכי׳ היו מקדישים במרום אתנו כאחד · ורז״ל אמרו בפ׳ ג״ה צ״א כ׳ אין מ״הש אומרים שירה למעלה עד שיאמרו ישראל למטה שנאמר ברן יחד ככבי בקר והדר ויריעו כל·בני אלהים ולישנא דוהדר ויריעו עפי משמע שהמה לא יתחילו כלל להקדיש ליוצרם עד אשר יגמרו ישראל שילוש קדושתם למטה· וכן סדרו אנשי כנ״הג בברכת קדושת השם אתה קדוש וכו׳ ואח״כ וקדושים בכל יום יהללוך · הגם דמלישנא דהזוהר פ׳ תרומה קכ״ט ריש ע״ב ושם קס״ד ריש ע״ב לכאורה משמע שהמלאכים מקדישים קדושתם אתנו יחד בהדא ממש · הייט משום שקדושתם תכופה ממש תיכף אחר סיום אמירתינו · כחדא קרי לה :

אבל עיקרו של דבר כי הוא ית״ש אחר שברא כל העולמות · ברא את האדם אחור למע״ב בריאה נפלאה כח מאסף לכל המחנות · שכלל בו כל נתאוה אורות הנפלאות והעולמות והיכלין העליונים שקדמו לו · וכל תבנית הכבוד העליון בסדר פרקי המרכבה (*)· וכל הכחו׳ פרטים הנמלאי׳ בכל העולמות עליונים ותחתונים· כולם נתנו כח וחלק מעלמותם בבנייני ונכללו בו במספר פרטי כחותיו שבו · כמ״ש בזוהר יתרו ע״ה ב׳ קוב״ה כד ברא לי׳ לב״נ סדר בי׳ כל דיוקנין דרזין עלאין דעלמא דלעילא · וכל דיוקנין דרזין תתאין דעלמא ·

הגה״ה

וזה היה קודם החטא לא היה כלול את רק מכל העולמות וכחו׳ הקדושה לבד · ולא מכחות הרע· אבל אחר החטא נכללו ונתערבו בו גם כחות הטומאה והרע · וממילא עירב אות׳ ע״ז גם בהעולמו׳ מזה הטעם שהוא כלול ומשותף מכולם והם מתעוררים ומתתקנים כפי נטיית מעשיו · והוא ענין עץ הדעת טוב ורע :

שער א

ומלך שרש העליון של הנשמת חיים שלו הוא קדש לעובדא דמרכבה גם מעולם הכסא. וגם כי הנשמת חיים היא סוד נשימת פיו ית"ש כביכול כמש"ית אי"ה להלן פ' ט"ז ע"ש. לכן העולמות מתנהגים ע"י מעשי האדם כי המה כפי נטייתם מעוררים שרש נשמתו העליונה שמעליהם שהיא הנפש חיה שלהם בהתנועעו ינועו ובעמדם תרפינה. ז"ש כאשר נופח באפיו הנשמת חיים שהיא גבוה מהעולמות ופנימיותם. אז ויהי האדם לנפש חיה להעולמות. וכ"כ רח"ו ז"ל בשער הקדוש' ח"ג ש"ב שנשמ' האדם היא הפנימי שבכולם:

בב"ר פ"ב ובויקרא רבה פ"ט. שלא רצה הקב"ה להטיל קנאה במע"ב. וביום א' ברא שמים וארץ. בשני רקיע בשלישי תדשא הארץ וכן עד"ז בד' וה'. בששי בא לבראות את האדם. אמר אם אני בורא אותו מן העליונים אין שלום בעולם. ואם אני בורא אותו מן התחתונים כו'. אלא הריני בורא אותו מן העליונים ומן התחתונים. עפר מן האדמה ויפח באפיו נשמת חיים. ולכאורה הלא עתה תתגב' הקנא' יותר משאם היה בורא אותו מן התחתונים לבד שעתה יש בו חלק מן העליונים והוא כולו למטה עם החלק העליון שבו. אך הענין הוא. שהאדם השלם כראוי עיקרו הוא נטוע למעל' בשרש נשמתו העליונה ועובר דרך אלפי רבואות עולמות עד שקצהו השני הוא נכנס בגוף האדם למטה. זהו כי חלק ה' עמו יעקב חבל נחלתו שעיקרו קשור ונטוע למעלה חלק הוי"ה ממש כביכול ומשתלשל כחבל עד בואה לגוף האדם (ועיין לקמן פ' י"ז). וכל מעשיו מגיעים לעורר שורשו העליון כענין החבל שאם ינענע קצהו התחתון מתעורר ומתנועע גם ראש קצהו העליון. (ודעת לנבון נקל. שכן הוא הענין גם בשורש הדברים למעלה בסוד האדם העליון כביכול. ע' אד"ר קמ"א ב' בפסוק וייצר ה' אלקים את האדם כו' על סוד האדם העליון. ובי"ס וכל דא למה בגין לאשתלפא ולעיילא בי' סתים דסתימא עד סופא דכל סתימין. הה"ד ויפח באפיו נשמת חיים נשמתא דכל חיי דעילא ותתא תליין מההוא נשמתא ומתקיימין בה. ויהי האדם לנפש חיה לאתרקא ולעיילא בתקונין כג"ד ולאשלפא להויא נשמתא מדרגא לדרגא עד סיפא דכל דרגין. בגין דיהוי ההיא נשמתא משתכחא בכלא ומתפשט' בכלא כו' ע"ש):

פרקו אמנם עדיין הענין צריך ביאור. (כי הוא ז"ל דיבר בקדשו דרך קצרה

דצלם כנ"ל. אמנם רצון הקב"ה הוא שיהיו כל פעול' השרשין עלאין בנר"ן מוסתרים בתחלה בעלמותן ולא יפעלו תיכף בכלי הגוף מיום הולדו עד יגדל הנער(*). וכנראה בחוש שכל מה שנגדל הולד בכלי הגוף כן נגדל שכלו ודבורו. ומעשיו. ואמנם בעוד יסודות הטובים שלו שבפנימיותו מוסתרים ושרשין עלאין מקיפין. ולא שלחו הארתן לפנימיות. יש מקום שישלטו עליו כחות הרע ח"ו. (כנודע בע"ח שבמקום שורש שליטת הס"א הוא בין פנימים למקיפין) ועיר פרא אדם יולד מסטרא דד' חיון דורסין מסאבן על ד' מרירן. מרה חיורא. מרה סומקא מרה ירוקה. מרה אוכמא. דאינון לקבלייהו דיסודין דכיין כנ"ל ברע"מ פנחס דף רל"ד ב'. ואף כי אית חיון שכליות דסחרין לכורסייא. ואית לעילא מינייהו. וגבוהים עליהם. אמנם הלא השרשין הנה בשרשם בבחי' מקיפין ולא נכנסו עדן והם וגבוהים עליהם. ומשליטת סטרא דמסאבא נמשכים המדות רעות מהד' יסודין דבעירין מיסוד האש מתעורר גאוה וכעס (*) מיסוד הרוח דבורים רעים. מיסוד המים צמח תאות רעות. ומיסוד העפר מנא לאפקא חיליהון במחשבה דבור מעשה בגוף למעשים רעים. ולמעשים טובים הגוף עצל וכבד ועצב בטבעו. כמו שהאריך הרח"ו בשער הקדוש'. וכשרצה הקב"ה לזכות את ישראל לפיכך הרבה להם תורה ומצות שע"י יוכלו לאכפייא לס"א ולעור' השרשין עלאין הנמשכים משם הוי"ה ב"ה. לזכך כל גופו שיהיו כל

גימל כלי

הגה"ה

וכידוע בע"ח שער מוחין דקטנות שלכן נק' ז"א שאף שיש לו כל כלי המוחין. אמנם פעולת המוחין דכלי הצלם אינם פועלי' פעולתם ומוסתרים בעלמותם. וכענין לשון הנאמ' בזוהר בלק קפ"ה א' איהו קדישא ורב ועלאה על כל עלמין. אזעיר נהוריה וקמיט קדישתיה לגבי דבר נש. ע"כ:

הג"ה

וזהו המבואר בזוהר דינא דחייביא בגהינם הא אוליפנא דאיהו למידן תמן חייבי עלמא וגהינם איהו נור דליק יממא ולילא כגוונא דחייביא מתחממין ביצ"הר הכי איתוקד גהינם. דכתיב אם היא עד אבדון תאכל כי מהאש יצאו והאש תאכלם. כי עיקר משכן היצ"הר הוא בלב. ולבא אשא. וכאשר בוער בלב האדם אש זרה אשר לא צוה ה'. בגאוה וגבהות הלב תועבת ה'. אזי

מאש

שער א

תגועות אברי גופו יהא ניכר שהמה נמשכים בלתי לה' לבדו · וכל כלי הגוף שיסוד העפר הוא מגא לאפקא חיליהון דשרשין עילאין שלש אמות אמ״ש במעשה :

וכל אשר ירבו השלש יסודות אמ״ש להתקשר בשרשין דילהון כנ״ל·יתרבה אורן בפנימיותן ובהקיפן ויזדככו כל הגוף שמעפר שלא יהא שום עגלות וכבדות באברי הגוף · ויהיה רץ כצבי וקל כנשר לעשות רצון הקדוש ב״ה · כענין שכתוב בזהר פנחס רכ״ה א' · לב איהו זכיך מכלא · מינה כל טב וכל בריאותא דשייפין כלהו · וכל תוקפא וכל חדוה וכל שלימו דאצטריך לכל שייפין · ובזוהר ויקהל קנ״ח ב' · ת״ח בשעתא דבר נש שוי רעותי' לגבי פולחנא דמארי' ההוא רעותא סליק בקמייתא על לבא דאיהו קיומא ויסודא דכל גופא · ולבתר סליק ההוא רעותא על כל שייפי גופא ורעותא דכל שייפי גופא ורעותא דלבא מתחברן כחדא · ואינון משכין עלייהו זיהרא דשכינתא לדיירא עמהון · והכוא ב״נ איהו חולקא דקב״ה :

ולפי מה שקדם · הד' שרשין עלאין הן המה הצלם והדפוס רוחני שעל ידן ימלאו רשום פרטי אברי האדם על תמונת שלשה הכלים מוח לב וכבד · שהמה נר״ן · ושיתראה על ידן פעולת המחשבה דבור מעשה כפי רצון העליון · והם נמשכים מאד״בע אותיות הוי״ה ב״ה · ושיות כי אור השרשין עלאין בשרשו רב מאוד · המה רק עומדין ומקיפין על האדם שכל מה שיזדכך פנימיות כלי גופו יוכל אורן להשתלשל ולכנס יותר בפנימות . והוא מ״ם דצלם הוא הד' שרשין עלאין · וכל שורש נחלק לעשר בחי' כנודע · והלמ״ד דצלם הוא מקיף דשלש אמות דעבדי עבידתיהון לפי התמצותן במוחא · והצדי״ק הוא מוחין כנימים לפי השלש אמות שנכנסין בגוף בשלשה כלים מוח ולב וכבד · וזהו מה שמבואר בענין חיים שצדי״ק מתפשט בכל גוף ז״א בע' פרקין · ולמ״ד בחאי ז״א :

ומה שקדם הג' תחלה ואח״כ הלמ״ד ואח״כ המ״ם · הנה אם היה רצון הקב״ה שהשרשין עלאין יפעלו פעולתן כסדרן במגא דלהון בגופו של אדם מיום הולדו · היה נקל לו לאדם לזכו' למוחין דצלם

שכל עולם הוא מהנהג בסידור מלבו וכל פרטי ענייניו כפי נטיית כח העולם שעליו · שמנהיגו כנשמ' את הגוף· וכן הולך ע״ז הסדר גבוה מעל גבוה · עד הוא ית״ש נשמת כולם · ע' זוהר בראשית ך' ע״א וכל עלמא כו' עילא ותתא מרישא רזא דנקודה עלאה עד סופא דכל דרגין כלא איהי דא לבושא לדא ודא לדא כו' דא לגו מן דא ודא לגו· מן דא כו' ובא״ז רל״א ב' וכלהו נהורין אחידן נהורא דא בנהורא דא ונהורא דא בנהורא דא ונהרין דא בדא כו' · נהורא דאתגליא אקרי לבושא דמלכא נהורא דלגו לגו כו' ע״ש · ופרטות הענין מבואר בע״ח שער פנימיות וחיצוניות דרוש ב' ובפע״ח בהקדמת שער השבת פ״ז ופ״ח ובשער השבת פכ״ד · שחיצוניות של כל פרצוף ועולם מתפשט ומתלבש בהפרצוף והעולם שתחתיו ונעשה לו לפנימיות ונשמה · וכל העולמות כללים ונחלקים לד' כידוע · שהן האופני' והחיות · וכסא כבודו · ואצילות קדשו ית״ב' · ונשמת כל אחד הוא העולם שעליו · כמ״ש (יחזקאל א') ובהנשא החיות לו' ינשאו האופנים לעומתם כי רוח החיה באופנים · בלכתם ילכו ובעמדם יעמודו וגו' · והחיות ג״כ מתנהגים ע״י עולם הכסא שעל־הם כמשארז״ל שהכסא נושא את נושאיו · ובז״ח יתרו מעשה מרכבה ל״ג א' דחיות נטלין לדנטלין לון כו' כרסייא קדישא כנ״ל לתו'·ונשמת החיים של הכסא · הוא סוד שרש העליון של כללות נשמות ישראל יסוד שהוא יותר גבוה ומאד נעלה גם מהכסא · שהוא האדם שעל הכסא כמ״ש שם ועל דמות הכסא וכו'(*) · וז״ש בזהר יתרו ע' ע״ב בענין הפסוק אחור וקדם צרתני אחור לעובדא דבראשי' וקדם לעובדא דמרכבה · שמלך הגוף הוא אחור למע״ב

ומלד

הג״ה

כי עיקר האדם הוא נשמתו · (ולזאת נקרא הגוף בשר איש כתיב) נגד הנשמה · כי רק בחי' עקביי' מהשורש נכנס לתוך גוף האדם · וכזה יובן מאמרם ז״ל בכ״ר

דלם

ועשו לי מקדש כו' ככל אשר אני מראה אותך וגו' וכן תעשו ארז"ל דרשו (סנהדרין ט"ז) וכן תעשו לדורות. ולדרכינו י"ל ג"כ שר"ל אל תחשבו שתכלית כוונתי הוא עשיית המקדש החיצוני · אלא תדעו שכל תכלית רצוני בתבנית המשכן וכל כליו · רק לרמז לכם שממנו תראו וכן תעשו אתם את עצמיכם שתהיו אתם במעשיכם הרצויים כתבנית המשכן וכליו · כולם קדושים ראויים ומוכנים להשרות שכינתי בתוככם ממש · וזהו ועשו לי מקדש ושכנתי בתוכם דייקא · ככל אשר אני מראה אותך את תבנית המשכן וגו' · תכלית כוונתי שכן תעשו את עצמיכם · וכן אמר הוא ית"ש לשלמה אחר גמר בנין המקדש (מלכים א' ו') הבית הזה אשר אתה בונה · אם תלך בחקתי כו' ושכנתי בתוך בני ישראל דייקא · לזאת כשקלקלו פנימיות המקדש שבתוכם · אז לא הועיל המקדש החיצוני ונהרסו יסודותיו ר"ל · וזה שאמר השם ליחזקאל (מ"ג) הגד את בית ישראל את הבית ויכלמו מעונותיהם כו' · ואם נכלמו מכל אשר עשו צורת הבית ותכונתו ומוצאיו ומובאיו וכל צורותיו ואת כל חקותיו וכל צורותיו וכל תורותיו · הודע אותם וכתוב לעיניהם וישמרו את כל צורתו ואת כל חקותיו ועשו אותם · והוא מבואר · וכתרגומו ואם יתכנעון מכל דעבדו בתחויהון צורת ביתא ותיקוני' כו' :

ובזה יובן הכתוב וייצר ה' אלקים את האדם עפר כו' ויפח באפיו נשמת חיים ויהי האדם לנפש חיה · ופשוטו של מקרא ודאי הוא כתרגומו והוה באדם לרוח ממללא · ור"ל שכאשר היה הגוף לבדו היה עדיין עפר ממש בלא שום חיות ותנועה · וכאשר נפח בו נשמת חיים · אז נעשה איש חי להתנועע ולדבר · ועיין רמב"ן בפי' התורה · אמנם בקרא ויהי באדם לא כתיב אלא ויהי האדם לזאת יש מקום לפרשו ע"פי שנתבאר · שהאדם בנשמת החיים שבתוכו · הוא נעשה נפש חיה לרבוי עולמות אין מספר · שכמו שכל פרטי הנהגות הגוף ותנועותיו הוא ע"י כח הנפש שבקרבו · כן האדם הוא הכח ונפש החיה של עולמות עליונים ותחתונים. לאין שיעור · שכולם מתנהגים על ידו כנ"ל :

פרקה **ומה** שעלתה ברצונו ית"ש להרכיב את האדם התחתון לראשי העולמות עליונים · שיתנהגו ע"י · כי ידוע בזוהר וכתבי האריז"ל בסדר השתלשלו' והתקשרות העולמו'

והיותר מובחר לקבל ולתפוס שכל עמוק הוא מי שטבעו התגברות המרה ירוקה ומרה שחורה · כי מרה ירוקה הוא מיסוד האש דסליק לעילא לעומק רוחניות השכל · ועיי' אורה שבמוחא מהגלם להצטייר צורה במיא שבמוחא ונשרשי' הציורי' השכליות במגא דיסוד העפר שבמוחו · ונקבע קביעות חזק בדעתו כענין הדעת להכר היטב כל הכחות מן הקנה אל הקנה · שיהא כל כלי מוחו ממולאים במחשבת תורה להבין כל רצונות השי"ת · ומחשבת עבודתו ית"ש · וגדולתו והוי"ר · ועיי"ז יומשך בשכלו לרצונו ית"ש שיהיו כל מחשבותיו בלתי לה' לבדו בתורה ועבודה עד שלא יעלה שום מחשבת פגול אשר לא ירצה : י

ועוד משהשלים מזג היסודות לכלי הלב · ואף שבלב אינם בדקות כ"כ כמו במוח · כי תנועתם בלב המה מורגשים יותר · כי מוחא שקיט וניית · ובלב פועלים היסודות בכח יותר חזק · אמנם כך הי' רצון השי"ת שיהי' מזגם מתגלה יותר בכלי הלב כי שם הוא מקור חיות כל האברים · ושיהיה פעולות האברים נמשכים אחר ציור הלב נתמזגו היסודות בכח יותר חזק · שיוכל לעורר בכח חזק את האברים היותר מגושמים לציורם הרוחני · ובלב מתגבר יסוד האש יותר להגביה לבו בדרכי ה' ולהמשיך כל כחות הגוף מגשמיות העולם להשתמש בקודש · בתורה ועבודה והוי"ר · כטבע האש להפוך כל גשמיות לאעלא לון לעילא · וכח האש שבלבבו מעורר יסוד הרוח להוציא כל רוח ממללא דילי' בתורה ותפלה כפי שהבין במוחו · והוא קלא דכליל מאש ורוחא ומיא · כמ"ש ברע"מ פ' פנחס ד' רכ"ו ע"ב · קול ה' על המים · מסטרא דמיא דאיהו מוחא דתמן סליק בכנפי ריאה · קול ה' חוצב להבות אש מסטרא דלבא כד נפיק מפומא אתקרי דבור ונמלא כל דבורו בתורה ותפלה · וכלי הלב וה' מוצאי הפה · המה מוכנא לאפקא מיליהון דשלם אתוות אמ"ש לפי מזגם שיהא בלתי לה' לבדו · ודבורו נם ולא בדברים בטלים :

ומן הלב נמשכים התמזגותם לכל כלי המעשה לקיים בפועל ממש כל מצות ה' · באהבה ויראה מסטרא דמיא · ובשמחה של מצוה מסטרא דאשא · ובזריזות נפלאה מסטרא דרוח · עד שכל

שער א

אבל להם נשון בהנו נרו שדרך השמש נקבלים אורות רוחניות השמים ליתן האורה בתוך הארץ ממדריג׳ למדריגה ועיין בזוהר תרומה קל״ו ע״ב וקל״ז ע״א · ונוהכח או הרצון ההוא נשתלשלו ונגלמו כחות היסודות ממדריגה למדריגה עד שמשפיעים שפעם גם בכל האצילות התחתונה הלזו ומתראים ע״פי דמות פרטים משונים כפי רצון הקב״ה שימלא בריאת האדם בגוף מעפר ושע״י שלש היסודו׳ אמ״ש שהן הגלם ודפוס רוחני ימלאו כל כלי גופו באופן שיוכל האדם לפעול על ידיהן פעולות פרטים כפי רצונו ית״ש · וע״י פרטי מעשי המצות שיעשה האדם בארץ הלזו הנשמה יתכשרו היסודות שלו לשרשן הקדמאין דלעילא כפי רצונו ית״ש · והגוף היא מנא לאפקא חיליהון דהנך שרשין שע״י פעולותיו באיזו יגלה שתשוקת היסודות שבנפשו הוא להתנשא לראש · כענין שאמר דהע״ה · לך ה׳ הגדולה וכו׳ כי כל בשמים ובארץ לך ה׳ הממלכה והמתנשא לכל לראש · לא אמר ממך ה׳ הגדולה אלא לך ה׳ · היינו שאף כל הכחות המתגלים בארץ מתחת המה נמשכות לך ה׳ · וגם כי מגהון נחתין לתתא לארץ · היינו כי כל דאחיד בשמיא ובארעא · הנה לך ה׳ הממלכה · ומתנשא לכל לראש · אף בארץ :

והנה רצון הקב״ה היה להמציא ע״י השלש אמות אמ״ש שימלאו כלים נמלאים מדליגות מדריגות · ושבכל מדריגה יתמזגו היסודות באופנים שונים · ושע״י כל כלי וכלי לפי בחינתה יוכר בבחי׳ שונות שתשוקתן להמשך למעלה וגם להשפיע למטה להכלי שלמטה הימנה · בכדי שגם בכלי התחתונה שבתחתונות ימלאו הכוונה הראשונה שהיא מתנשא לראש · לזאת נמצא התמזגותם באדם בשלשה כלים · במוח · בלב · ובכבד · והן כמה כלי הנפש רוח ונשמה שבאדם · ובכל אלו מהג׳ כלים מתגלמים השלש אמות אמ״ש להתראות כאן בגלוים שונים · היינו בכלי המוח ניכר התמזגות השרשן ע״פי המחשבה :

והוא שמידעת בזוהר שלפי התמזגות ד׳ יסודין בכלי המוח · ככה תהא גלוי השכל בו ·

והזוהר

היא בעצמותה כשרה ורק שלא תנקב הריאה · שיוכל קול התורה להשמע לקיים והגית בו יומם ולילה · ע״כ :

באורך · א״כ בעת אשר יתור האדם לחשוב בלבבו מחשבה אשר לא טהורה בניאוף ר״ל · הרי הוא מכנים זונה סמל הקנאה בבית ק״הק העליון נורא בעולמות העליונים הקדושים ח״ו · ומגביר ר״ל כחות הטומאה והס״א בבית ק״הק העליון · הרבה יותר ויותר ממה שנגרם התגבהות כח הטומאה ע״י טיטוס בהכניסו זונה בבית ק״הק במקדש מטה · וכן כל חטא ועון אשר כל איש ישראל מכני׳ בלבו ח״ו אש זרה · בכעס או שארי תאוות רעות ר״ל · הלא הוא ממש כענין הכתוב (ישעיה סד) בית קדשנו ותפארתנו אשר וכו׳ היה לשריפת אש · הרחמן ית״ש יצילנו · ח״ש הגם ליחזקאל (מ״ג) את מקום כסאי כו׳ אשר אשכון שם בתוך בני ישראל לעולם ולא יטמאו עוד בית ישראל שם קדשי כו׳ בזנותם כו׳· עתה ירחקו את זנותם כו׳ ושכנתי בתוכם לעולם :

א׳ ושם רל״א ב׳ ובז״ח תרומה ל״ב ע״ג ע״ש באורך · ולכן אמרו ז״ל (ברכות נ״ה א) יודע היה בצלאל לצרף אותיות שנבראו בהם שמים וארץ · ולכן האדם ממש הקדש שכולל ג״כ כל סדרי בראשית וסדרי המרכבה כלל הבריאה כולה · הוא ג״כ דוגמת ותבנית המשכן והמקדש וכל כליו · ומכוון בסדר התקשרות פרקי אבריו וגידיו וכל כחותיו · וכן מחלקי בזוהר כלל תבנית המשכן וכליו · שהמה רמוזים כולם באדם אחד כאחד ינשו כסדר :

לזאת הרי כי ודאי עיקר ענין הקדש והמקדש ושריית שכינתו ית׳ הוא האדם שאם יתקדש עצמו כראוי בקיום המצות כולן שהם תלויין ג״כ בשורשן העליון בפרקי אברי השיעור קומה כביכול של כלל כל העולמות כולם · (וע׳ זוהר תרומה קס״ב ב׳ ואת המשכן תעשה כו׳ · הא הכא רזא דיחודא כו׳ עש״ה) אז הוא עצמו המקדש ממש ובתוכו ה׳ ית״ש · כמ״ש (ירמיה ז׳) היכל ה׳ היכל ה׳ המה · וכמאמרם ז״ל ושכנתי בתוכם בתוכו לא נא׳ אלא בתוכם כו׳ וזה שארז״ל (כתובות ה׳ ע״א) גדולים מעשי צדיקים יותר ממעשה שמים וארץ דאלו במעשה שמים וארץ כתיב אף ידי יסדה ארץ וימיני טפחה שמים · ואלו במעשה צדיקים כתיב מקדש אדני כוננו ידיך · פתחו במעשי צדיקים וסיימו ראייתם ממקדש · כי כן באמת שהצדיקים ע״י מעשיהם הרצויים לפניו יתברך · הן הם מקדש ה׳ ממש · וי״ל שע״ז הכתוב

ועשו

שער א

כח לכ"כ ושיעום להחריב המקדש של מטה המכוון עד המקד' של מעלה· כמו שאחז"ל (איכ'רבתי) קמחא טחינא טחינת · הרי כי עונותינו החריבו גם מעלה עולמות עליונים הקדושים · והאנו החריבנו רק גם מטה· וזהו שהתפלל דוד המע"ה יודע כמביא למעלה בסבך עץ קרדומות · ביקש שיחשב לו כאלו למעלה בשמי מרומים הרס · אבל באמת לא נגעו שם מעשיו כלל כנ"ל : גם על זאת יחרד לב האדם מעם מקדש שהוא כולל בתבניתו כל הכחות והעולמות כולם (*) כמ"שית א"ה להלן בפ"ו ובשער ב' פ"ה · שהן המה הקדש והמקדש העליון · והלב של האדם אמצעיתא דגופא הוא כללית הכל נגד הבית ק"ק אמצע הישוב אבן שתיה · כולל כל שרשי מקור הקדושה' כמוהו ורמזוהו ז"ל במשנה פ' תפלת השחר יכוין את לבו כנגד בית ק"הק · ובזוהר שלח קס"א סוף ע"א ת"ח כד ברא קב"ה ב"נ בעלמא אתקין לי' כגוונא עלאה יקירא ויהב לי' חילי' ותוקפי' באמצעיתא דגופא דתמן שרי' לבא כו' · כג"ד אתקין קוב"ה עלמא ועביד לי' חד גופא כו' ולבא שארי באמצעיתא כו' דהוא תוקפא דכלא וכלא ביה תליין כו' · וההיכל לבית קה"ק דתמן שכינה וכפורת וכרובים וארון והכא הוא לבא דכל ארעא ועלמא ומהכא אתזנו כו' ע"ש באורך

הג"ה

(*) כי המשכן והמקדש היו כוללים כל הכחות והעולמות וכל הסדרי קדושות כולם · כל בתיו וגנזכיו עליותיו וחדריו וכל כלי הקדש · כולם היו כדוגמ' עליונ' צלם דמות תבנית העולמות הקדושים וסדרי פרקי המרכבה · המה יסד דוד ושמואל הרואה · הכל מיד ה' עליה' השכיל כל מלאכו' התבנית · ואמרו ז"ל בפ' איזהו מקומן (נ"ד ב') מ"ד כו' וכי מה ענין נויות אצל רמה אלא שהיו יושבין ברמה ועוסקין' בנויו של עולם כו' · ז"ש בתנחומא ר"ס פקודי שהוא שקול נגד בריאת העולם · ומונה שם בסדרן כלל הענייני' שהיו בבריאה שהמה היו ג"כ במשכן · ולכן אמר הכתוב בבצלאל ואמלא אותו רוח אלקים בחכמה ובתבונה ובדעת' כי באלו הג"ד נבראו העולמות כמ"ש (משלי ג') ה' בחכמה יסד ארץ כונן שמים בתבונה וכו' וע' זוהר פקודי רכ"א א'

בית

תלאה פרשי מידלא עיבא · עכ"ז מניחים מקום גבוה שלהם באויר ויורדים למקום נמוך לעפר · ואף כי ברוחניים אין לומר מעלה ומטה · ובפרט בכח העליון הנאצל · אמנם ענין מעלה ומטה נאמר גם לא על שנוי מקום · כמו והיית רק למעלה ולא תהיה למטה (דברים כח יג) שפירושו שיהיו עליונים במעלות רוחניות ולא ירדו למטה ממדריגתם · (*) כענין מעלין בקודש ולא מורידין · כמו כן ענין כחות דסלקין לעילא פי' שנמשך לרוחניות למדריגה העליונה שבעליונות ודנחתין לתתא פי' למדרגות התחתונות · כי אף בעולם האצילות ולמעלה כל בחי' מתדבק בפנימיותה למדריגה שעליה וגם משתלשלת להשפיע קיום למדריגה שלמטה הימנ' · וכמו ד"מ טבע האש לכלות כל גשמיות לרוחניות· כידוע ענין הקרבנות ועכ"ז מוליד רוח · וטבע תנוע' הרוח להוליד אש· ועכ"ז נכנס בגשם ומקיימו · וטבע המים להמשך אחרי הרוח בתנועה כל דהו ועכ"ז יורד למקום נמוך לעפר ומצמיח כל מיני גשמים · כן היה רצון הש"ית שימצא כח שישתוקק תמיד להתדב' בשור' שרשו ושישפיע שפע גם לקיום מדריגות שלמטה והן הנה השמים וצבאיה והארץ וצבאיה (ועיין רמב"ן בפי' על החומש בזה) כי אף שתשוקת צבא השמים רוחנים להדבק במדרגות עליונים · כענין שנאמר השמים מספרים כבוד אל · עכ"ז בכל הארץ יצא קום ובקצה תבל מליהם · היינו השפעתם בארץ · לשמש שם

הג"ה

(*) ויתכן לומר דרך דרש והיית רק למעלה · הוא תנאי וצווי היינו שהוא ית"ש מבטיח לנו כל הברכות האמורות למעלה באופן שכשנהי' רק למעלה בקודש · ולא נרד למטה למדריגת עמי הארץ · ומבאר אח"כ מהו המעלה בקדש כי תשמע אל מצות ה' אלקי' כו' לשמור ולעשות וזהו המדריגה העליונה שבעליונים ולא תסור מכל הדברי' כו' · כי בסור מכל הדברים · אם לימין ירד מטה מטה ח"ו ללכ' אחרי אלהים אחרים :

הג"ה

נסהגאת' בזוהר אורייתא בלא דחי' ורהיטא לא פרח' לעילא · פי' שמי שאין לו תשוקה והאהבה לד"ת כראוי · וגם אינו ירא מלפרוש הימנה כפורש מן החיים · אף שלומד לפרקים א"א שתתקיים תלמודו בידו במדריגה עליונה כראוי גם דרך דרש נוכל לומר שמ"ה שהמשילו אהבה ויראה לתרין גדפין כמו עוף שנשברו אגפיו עכ"ז

היא

תחילה מעורר שכלו להמציא כלם ודפוס באופן שיוכל לעשות ע"י הכלם הדמות פרטי שרוצה · וממציא דפוס פנימי שע"י תעשה פנימית הכלי כפי הבית קבול שרוצה· וגם דפוס חיצוני המקיף דופני הכלי להגביל הדפנות בעובים ומדתם כפי רצונו · ושניהם כאחד המה כלם ודפוס א' · אך זה נכנס לפנימית הכלי לעשות חללה כפי המדה · וזה סובב ומקיף להעמיד דפנותי' כפי המדה · (*) ככה ד"מ כשרצה הבורא ית"ש לברוא אדם מעפר שיהא הכלי להשתמש לפי רצונו ית"ש · הזמין תחילה כלם ודפוס שתוכל להעשות דמות האדם בגוף ואברים שע"י יוכל לפעול פעולות פרטים כפי רצון השי"ת · וברא ד' שרשין שמהם המציאו כלם פנימי ומקיף · רותחים :

הגה"ה

ובמו דמיתי לקאת מדבר וכו' (תהלים ק"ב) פי' שכמ' שפעולו' הקאת להתרחק מישוב ולצעוק יום ולילי בקול נהי . כן התרחק הוא ממקומו והי' צועק ונאנח יום ולילה . והתגברות מזג המרה שחורה של הקאת גורם לה עצבות לזעוק . ועצלות לישב בתקומה במדבר · כן מרובי צרותיו גברה עליו המרה שחורה לברוח מחברת בני אדם ולזעוק נהי כמו שאמר שם כי אפר כלחם אכלתי ושקווי בבכי מסכתי כטבע חולי מרה שחורה שיש לו תאוה לאכול פחמים וגחלים ולבכות תמיד · ואף שלא נראה בדמות פעולותיו כלל התבודדית ובכי ואכילת עפר · ומהות פנימיות מזגו והתגברות מרה הוכמא לא נראה בחוש · ועכ"ז בשכל מושג שפנימיות המרה שחורה מדאגה שנכנס בו ככר וצרות הדאגית שסבביהו והקיפוהו עוד מבחוץ · הן המה הכלם והדפוס רוהני שע"י היו פעולותיו בדמות פרטי כזה לבכות ולזעוק ולהתבודד · ע"כ

ועתה נבחין בבחי' כלם ודמות הכללי ברותחיו' · שכאשר רצה הבור' ית"ש ברצונו הפשוט לברוא העולם שיגלה דמות כל פרטי העולם כמו שהן האציל כח א' שהפלוסיפים קוראים אותו היולי · ואנחנו נקראהו · או כח או אור · או רצון · היינו שכך רצה שיתגלה רצונו ע"י שני כחות א' שיומשך למעלה ד"מ · והשני יומשך למטה ד"מ · ולמען לא יתפרדו המציא אמצעים ביניהם כמו ענין האש שסליק לעילא ועפר היורד למטה · אך הנה אויר הוא קרוב לטבע האש לעלות למעלה · וגם יוכל לירד למטה · ומים אף שנמשכי' לאויר כמשרז"ל

תלתא

בזוה"ק דאוקי ב"נ עבדין פגימו לעילא כו' · וכן להיפך כנ"ל · וזש"ה תנו עוז לאלקים · ובזוהר ר"פ בא ויהי היום ויבאו כו' להתיצב על ה' כד בעאן לקיימא על איכון עובדין דישראל על ה' ודאי קיימין · דהא כד ישראל עבדין עובדין דלא כשרן כביכול מתישין חילא דקב"ה · וכד עבדין עובדין דכשרן יהבין תוקפא וחילא לקב"ה · וע"ד כתיב תנו עז לאלקים במה בעובדין דכשרן · ולכן אמר לאלקים · וכן באלקים נעשה חיל · עפי' בעל הכתוב כולם וכנ"ל :

פרק ד וזאת

תורת האדם כל איש ישראל אל יאמר בלבו ק"ו · כי מה אני ומה כחי לפעול במעשי השפלים שום ענין בעול' אמנם יבין וידע ויקבע במחשבות לבו · שכל פרטי מעשיו ודבוריו ומחשבותיו כל עת ורגע · לא יתאבדו ח"ו · ומה רבו מעשיו ומאד גדלו ורמו · שכל א' עולה כפי שרשה לפעול פעולתה בגבהי מרומים בעולמות ולאצלות האורות העליונים · (*) ובאמת כי האיש החכם ויבין את זאת לאמיתו · לבו יחיל בקרבו בחיל ורעדה · בשומו על לבו על מעשיו אשר לא טובים ח"ו עד היכן המה מגיעים לקלקל ולהרוס בחטא קל ח"ו · הרבה יותר ממה שהחריב נ"נ וטיטוס · כי הלא נ"נ וטיטוס לא עשו במעשיה' שום פגם וקלקול כלל למעלה כי לא להם חלק ושורש בעולמות העליונים שיהו יכולים לנגוע שם כלל במעשיהם · רק שבחטאינו נתמעט ותש כביכול כח גבורה של מעלה· את מקדש ה' עמאו כביכול המקדש העליון · ועי"כ היה להם

הגה"ה

וקרוב לשמוע שגם זה בכלל כיונתם ז"ל באמרו דע מה למעלה ממך · ר"ל אם כי אינך רואה בעיניך הסניגים הנוראים הנעשים ממעשיך · אבל תדע נאמנה · כי כל מה שנעשה למעלה בעולמו' העליוני' נבוהי גבוהי' הכל ממך הוא על פי מעשיך לאן ניסים על פיהם יצאו ויבואו :

כח

שער א

פרק ג **כן** בדמיון זה כביכול · ברא הוא ית״ש את האדם והשליטו על רבי רבוון כחות ועולמות אין מספר · ומסרם בידו שיהא הוא המדבר והמנהיג אותם עפ״י כל פרטי תנועות מעשיו ודבוריו ומחשבותיו · וכל סדרי הנהגותיו · הן לטוב · או להיפך ח״ו · כי במעשיו ודבוריו ומחשבותיו הטובי׳ הוא מקיים ונותן כח בכמה כחות ועולמות עליונים הקדושים · ומוסיף בהם קדושה ואור · כמ״ש (ישעיה נ״א) ואשים דברי בפיך כו׳ לנטוע שמים וליסוד ארץ · וכמאמרם ז״ל א״ת בניך אלא בוניך · כי המה המסדרים עולמות העליונים כבונה המסדר בנינו · ונותנים בהם רב כח · ובהיפוך ח״ו ע״י מעשיו או דבוריו ומחשבותיו אשר לא טובים · הוא מהרס ר״ל כמה כחות ועולמות עליונים הקדושים לאין ערך ושיעור · כמ״ש (שם מ״ט) מהרסיך ומחריביך וכו׳ · או מחשיך או מקטין אורם וקדושתם ח״ו · ומוסיף כח למומת זה במדורות הטומאה ר״ל:

וזהו ויברא אלקים את האדם בצלמו בצלם אלקים כו׳ · כי בצלם אלקים עשה וכו׳ · שכמו שהוא ית׳ שמו הוא האלקים ׳בעל הכחות שנמצאים בכל העולמות כולם · ומסדרם ומנהיגם כל רגע כרצונו · כן השליט רצונו יתברך את האדם שיהא הוא הפותח והסוגר של כמה אלפי רבואות כחות ועולמות · עפ״י כל פרטי סדרי הנהגותיו בכל עניניו בכל עת ורגע ממש · כפי שרשו העליון של מעשיו ודביריו ומחשבותיו · כאלו הוא ג״כ הבעל כח שלהם כביכול · ואמרו ז״ל באיכה רבתי (בפסוק וילכו בלא כח כו׳) ר״ע בשם ריב״ס אומר בזמן שישראל עושין רצונו של מקום מוסיפין כח בגבורה של מעלה כד״א באלקים נעשה חיל · ובזמן שאין ישראל עושין רצונו של מקום כביכול מתישין כח גדול של מעלה דכתיב צור ילדך תשי כו׳ · ובכ״מ

בזוה״ק

בו עולים תרי ויורדים תרי וכו׳ . עפר מנא דכלא · והוא שלפי פנימיות מזג האש והרוח שבנפש האדם דסליקין לעילא בטבעם ככה נמשך פנימיות פרטי כחות האדם למעלה . ולפי פנימיות מזג יסוד המים והעפר שבנפש האדם ככה נמשכים פרטי כחותיו למטה · ואם כי אופן התמזגות פנימיות היסודות שבנפש האדם אינם מושגים לחוש איך ומה. אמנם בהאיר אור התמזגות במנא דלהון יסוד העפר שורש הגוף · אזי הגוף מפיק · לבר אילהון דשלש אמות א״מ״ש ע״פי פעלו . כמבואר בזוהר ואר״א הנ״ל : וכח התמזגות שרשין דנ׳ יסודי א״ר״מ הן המה שרשים שמהם נמשכים כל כשולו׳ הגוף · אך המה נסתרים ואינם מושגים : ואף גם כאשר רואים אנחנו פעולות הגוף הנמשך מהתמזגות הנ׳ מרות · הנה אין היסודות נגלות לנו לחוש : רק מהפעולות הנגלות לנו · נוכל לתפוס ערך התמזגותם ברוחניות כמבואר בזוהר יתרו בפסוק ואתה תחזה · ותקוני זוהר · וז״ח · ולזאת אמרו בזוהר וכתבי האריז״ל שלש מבחי׳ עלמין סתימין וקמות מבחי׳ עלמין דאתגליין · גם מאמרם שצלם דוכרא ודמות נוקבא והוא כח פועל ונפעל · וזהו בצלמנו כדמותנו · כמו שהקב״ה נסתר מצד עצמותו ולית מחשבה תפיסא בי׳ · רק נגלה פעולותיו הטובות נגלה לנו טובו בכל מילי דמיטב · כן הנפש רוח נשמה שבאדם אינה מושגת למחשבה רק ע״פי פעולותי׳ ע״י הגוף · ואף גם זאת אין רואים אותה רק מושגת מאליה · כמ״ש רז״ל (ברכות ד׳ יו״ד ע״א) · הני חמשה ברכי נפשי וכו׳ מה הקב״ה רואה ואינו נראה אף הנשמה רואה ואינ׳ נראית · ועיין תומר דבורה שע״ז סיבב כל דברי קדוש ה׳ הרמ״ק ז״ל כמ״ש פ״א בהתחלתו וז״ל האדם ראוי שידמה לקונו ואז יהיה בסוד הצורה העליונה צלם ודמות שאלו ידומה בגופו ולא בפעולו׳ הרי הוא מכזיב הצורה עכ״ל :

וזהו מה שכתוב בע״ח שעיקר ירידת הנשמה להגוף הוא לברר בחי׳ הצלם · והענין הוא כמו שצלם פירושו דפוס (עיין פי׳ רש״י על פסוק בצלמנו כדמותנו) כמו ד״מ מי שמצייר במחשבתו איזה דמות פרטי לעשות סוף המעשה שבמחשבתו ·

תחלה

שער א

לארץ · או מתגלה ע"י יסוד העפר כל הצמחים בהתמזגות כל הג' יסודות כנ"ל · וכל שנוי טבעי כל הצמחים שבעולם · מתהום ארעא עד שמי רום הכל הוא משנוי התמזגות הד' יסודין · שהן השרשין קדמאין · והתמזגותם הן פנימיות נפש כל דבר · ומאיכות התמזגותם בפנימיותם נמשך הבדלי הפרטי' רבים שבכל דבר בתמונת ממשו · וגוון מראיתו בדומם · וכן שנוי הצמחים בטעמם · ותמונתם וגוונם · וכן שנוי טבעי כל הבעלי חיים · תמונת איבריהם מראיהם וצורתם ופעולתם · משתנות לפי התמזגות נפשם ודמם מד' מרות דאינון הד' יסודין · וכל ההמזגות הד' יסודות נמשך משליטת הכוכבי' המסודרים במשמרותיהם ברקיע כמאמרז"ל אין לך כל עשב בארץ שאין לו מזל ברקיע שמכה ואומר לו גדל · והכוכבים בממשלותם מקבלים ע"י מלאכים בשליחותם מד' חיות המרכבה והכל נמשך משם הוי' ב"ה כמבואר בע"ח באריכות · היינו שכל הד' שרשין קדמאין הן הוי' אחת · שרצון ה' יתברך שמו היה לברוא כל העולם בהתהוות הוי' כזו שבכל המציאות ימצאו כח הד' שרשין · גם כל כחות האדם בטבעו ונטיית שכלו ונטיית רצונו משתנים לפי השתנות מזג ד' שרשין דילי' · וכמבואר ברע"מ פנחס דף רל"ד ע"ב · אית חיון טבעיות ממנן על גופין דאינון מארבע יסודין ואינון דכיין · ולקבלייהו ארבע חיון דורסין מסאבין על ד' מרירן · מרה חיורא · מרה סומקא · מרה ירוקה · מרה אוכמא · ואית חיון שכליות דסחרין לכורסייא · ואית לעילא מנייהו · וגבוהים עליהם · והד' שרשין דאדם שלעילא הן המה הצלם שמהם נמצאים כל צורות הכחות באדם · כמבואר בזוהר חדש מדרש הנעלם בראשית ד' ט' ע"א · וז"ל שהבורא ית"ש ברא את האדם וברא אותו בצלם ובצורה והכינו מארבעה דברים מובדלים זה מזה · מאש מרוח ממים ומעפר וכו' :

וכמבואר בת"ז תקון ל"ח דף ל"ד ע"ב · סליק באשא ורוחא · ונחית במיא ועפרא ברזא דסלם והנה מלאכי אלקי' עולים ויורדי'

במה שהוא ית"ש משפיע בהם ברצונו יתברך כל רגע כח ושפעת אור חדש · ואלו היה הוא ית' מסלק מהם כח השפעתו אף רגע אחת · כרגע היו כולם לאפס ותהו · וכמו שיסדו אנשי כנה"ג המחדש (*) בטובו בכל יום תמיד מעשה בראשית · היינו תמיד ממש כל עת ורגע · וראייתם מפורשת כאמור לעושה אורים גדולים · שלא אמר עשה אלא עושה :

הגה"ה

ואף שאין חידוש ניכר לעין אמנם הד' יסודין עלאין דאינון השרשין קדמאין ואבהן דכולא כנז' בזוהר וארא כ"ג ע"ב · שהם שרש כל מעשה בראשית ופנימיות כולם · והם ד' אותיות הוי"ה ב"ה · התמזגותם והרכבתם כל עת ורגע בשרש שרשם אינו מושג כלל · והוא ית"ש מחדשם כל רגע לפי רצונו · וענין התמזגותם כל רגע הם התתר"ף צרופי השם ב"ה על פי השתנות נקודותיהם · תתר"ף רגעי השעה · וכן משתנים עוד כל שעה לצרופים אחרים · וגם אין מדת יום שוה למדת לילה · לא כל יום דומה לחבירו שלפניו ואחריו כלל · ז"ש המחדש כו' מעשה בראשית דיקא :

וזהו שנקרא הוא ית"ש האלקים בעל הכחות כולם · (*) שכל כח פרטי הנמצא בכל העולמות · הכל הוא ית"ש הבעל כח שלהם שמשפיע בהם הכח וגבורה כל רגע · ותלוים בידו תמיד לשנותם ולסדרם כרצונו ית' :

הגה"ה

ואף שהוא שם משותף לכל בעל כח שנמצ' בעולם · וכל שרי מעלה ומטה נקראים אלקים · כמ"ש אלהי העמים · כי כל העמים ילכו איש בשם אלהיו · ועיין זוהר ויקרא ה' ע"א וכפ' בלק ר"ח א' כענין ויבא אלקים דכתיב באבימלך ולבן ובלעם פי' השר שלו · כי הם ממונים עליהם להנהיגם · וכן דייני מטה נקראים אלקים ובסבא ל"ו א' ושמא חד מכל שאר שמהן וכו' ע"ש · אמנם כולם אין הכח שלהם מעצמם · רק מאת שקבע בהם הוא ית' כח וגבורה להיות מושלים וכו' · לכן נקרא הוא ית"ש אלקי האלקים · וכן כתיב כי גדול ה' מכל האלהים · השתחוו לו כל אלהים · וגם העובדי כוכבים קוראים אותו יתברך אלהא דאלהין ולכן נקראי' אלהים אחרים ר"ל שאין הכח שלהם מעצמם רק מכח הגבוה ממנו והגבוה ממנו מושך ג"כ כחו מהכח שעליו · עד שבעל כח האמיתי של כולם הוא ית"ש · ולכן נאמר (ירמיה י"א) וה' אלקים אמת · שהוא הבעל כח האמיתי של כולם שכולם מקבלים כחם ממנו ית"ש · ז"ש ויפלו על פניהם ויאמרו ה' הוא האלהים :

שער א

פרק א

כתיב ויברא אלקים את האדם בצלמו בצלם אלקים ברא אותו וכן כתיב כי בצלם אלקים עשה את האדם. הנה עומק פנימיות ענין הצלם, הוא מדברים העומדים ברומו של עולם והוא כולל רוב סתרי פנימיות הזהר. (*) אמנם כאן נדבר במלת צלם בדרך הפשטנים הראשונים ז"ל על פסוק נעשה אדם בצלמנו כדמותנו:

והוא כי מלת צלם ודמות כאן אינו כמשמעו כי כתוב מפורש (ישעי' מ) ומה דמות תערכו לו. אלא פירושו דמיון מה באיזה דבר. כמו דמיתי לקאת מדבר. כי לא נעשו לו כנפים וחרטום ולא נשתנה צורתו לצורת הקאת. רק שנדמה אז במקרה פעולתיו שהיה נע ונד כמו הקאת מדבר שהוא צפור בודד ומעופף ממקום למקום. כ"ה לפי הפשטנים הראשונים ז"ל. וכן עד"ז הוא ענין מלת צלם. כי המה דומים במשמעם בצד מה:

פרק ב

אמנם להבין ענין אמרו בצלם אלקים דיקא. ולא שם אחר. כי שם אלקים ידוע פירושו שהוא מורה שהוא ית"ש בעל הכחות כולם. כמ"ש בטור א"ח סימן ה'. וענין מה שהוא יתברך נקרא בעל הכחות. כי לא כמדת ב"ו מדת הקב"ה. כי האדם כשבונה בנין ד"מ מעץ אין הבונה בורא וממציא אז מכחו העצים רק שלוקח עצים שכבר נבראו ומסדרם בבנין ואחר שכבר סדרם לפי רצונו. עם שכחו הוסר ונסתלק מהם. עכ"ז הבנין קיים. אבל הוא ית"ש. כמו בעת בריאת העולמות כולם. בראם והמציאם הוא יתברך יש מאין בכחו הבל"ת. כן מאז כל יום וכל רגע ממש. כל כח מציאותם וסדרם וקיומם. תלוי רק

במה

הג"ה

ענין הצלם שחילקם האר"י ז"ל לג' בחי' צ' ול' ומ': הוא כידוע דשרשין הקדמאין דכלא הוא שרש הד' יסודות אש רוח מים עפר. ועיקר הפועלים הם הג' יסודות א"מ"ר נק' בס"י ג' אמות א"מ"ש שהם אמות דכלא ופעולתם של אלו הג' הוא ע"י יסוד העפר שהוא מתפעל ומקבל מהם. והם ג' אותיות יק"ו של השם ב"ה וה' אחרונה כפולה. והם מ' דצלם כל א' בכ"ע. והפועלים הם ג' ל' דצלם. ועדיין הם בבחי' השכל והמוחין הג'. ובהתפשטותם אח"ז בלב ובמעשה הם נפ"נ. והוא שרש המדות במלכות דתבונה המתפשטת בז"א ועלם המדות חג"ת ואח"כ המדות במעשה ממש והם נה"י והוא צ' דצלם. ועי' בזוהר וארא כ"ג ע"ב דהא קב"ה כד ברא עלמא עבד לי' לבר נש בדיוקנא דיליה ואתקין ליה בתקונוי וכו'. אר"ש ת"ח ארבע אינון קדמאי רזא דמהימנותא. ואינון אבהן דכלהו עלמין ורזא דרתיכא עלאה קדישא. ואינון אש רוח מים עפר. אלין אינון רזא עלאה. ואלין אינון אבהן דכלהו עלמין וכו'. (שם כ"ד ע"א) ת"ח ארמ"ע אלין קדמאין ושרשין דלעילא ותתאין ועלאין עלייהו קיימין. ואלין אינון ד' לד' סטרי עלמא וכו'. עפר איהו קר ויבש ועל דא מקבל עלי' כלהו. וכלהו עבדי' בי' עבדתיי' ומקבלא מכלהו לאפקא בחילהון והוא כנ"ל שעיקר הפועלים בעולם ובנפש הם הג' יסודות אש רוח מים. וע"י יסוד העפר נגלה כח פעולות הג' יסודין בעולם. וכן בנפש נגלה ע"י גוף האדם שיסודו מעפר פעולת כח הג' יסודות א"ר"מ שבנפש. כמבואר בזוהר הנ"ל וכלהו עבדי בי' עבידתיי' וכו' לאפקא בחילהון. וכנראה בחוש שהארץ מוציאה צמחים. מהם תולדות אש. כענין ממגד תבואות שמש. ומהם תולדות המים לחים וקרים. כענין וממגד גרש ירחים. ומהם תולדות הרוח. כענין מקוירא קא רבו. זיקא דבתר מטרא כמטרא שמשא דבתר מטרא כתרי מטרי. כידוע שטבע האש והרוח להגביה עוף. ומים יורדין למקום נמוך לעפר. ואם גם יסוד רוח ואש מתקשרים ביסוד המים. וגם המה נותנים שפעם ומשכים

אף לארץ

דברי כבוד אחי רב חביבי הרב המופלג וחריף ירא ה' ומפורסם כש"ת מ' **יוסף** ·

במה אכף ואקדם על כל יקר שראו עיני בדברי קדוש ה' מר אבא הגאון וצדיק נ"ע · ומה אוסיף לדבר על דברי אחי הגדול הרב נ"י · אשר בדעת שפתיו ברור מללו בהקדמתו אומנם לאשר משמיא העירוני לבא הלום בעת הלקח ארון האלקים אבא מארי הגאון זללה"ה · וחזינא שנתן נפשו או על דבריו שנאמרו **ביראת ה' לחיים** · וגם עתה כי באתי על יום פטירת מר אבא זללה"ה · משמיא אסתייע לבא בעת גמר הדפסת הקונטרסים · מהודא ומשבח אנא למרא עלמא · שהחייני והגיעני לחזות בנועם אמריו כי יצא לאור בחסד ה' · כה יגדיל חסדו שעינינו תחזינה כי יצא לאור דבריו אשר המה בכתובים · וישים חלקנו בתורתו כרצון יראי ה' · נאום **יוסף** בהגאון מוה' **חיים** זללה"ה ·

יום ה' **ב'ז'ה'** סיון יום העלות מר אבא ז"ל · **ורב שלום** לפ"ק

והואיל ואתינא לבית אולפנא של כבוד מר אבא הגאון נ"ע · בשעתא דעסקי בבי מדרשא במס' יבמות באתי בדבר שנתחדש ·:

יבמות דף צ"ד ע"ב ואע"ג דאזיל אשתו וגיסו למדינת הים · ועיין תוס' ד"ה ואע"ג דאזיל דמתרצי שם מאי דמשמע להגמרא דמתני' איירי באזיל אשתו וגיסו · ועיין תוספות ד"ה אשת גיסו אסורה וכו' מוהר בשני' ההיא לאו באזיל אשתו וגיסי איירי וכו' · ושלא לאוקמי רישא וסיפא בתרי גווני ולתרץ מאי אשמועינן מתניתין במה שמתה ראשונה מותר בשניה · נראה לומר דמיתורא דייק הגמרא דאיירי באזיל אשתו וגיסו ואשמעינן בבא זו דאף דאסורה לגיסו מותרת לו ולא אמרינן כשם שאסורה לבעל אסורה לבועל · מחמת שהיתה קימא עלי' באיסורא דאחות אשה תחלה · ועיי' תוס' כתובות ד' ג' ע"ב ד"ה ולדרוש להו דאונס שרי וכו' ומתוך כך התיר ר"ת וכו' ואין נראה לריב"ם וכו' · ועיין ברא"ש שם מבואר שהרי"בם והרא"ש מחולקים בסברא זו · והרא"ש מקיים פסק ר"ת בהכרעת סברא זו מגמרא דסוטה · (וע"ד פלפולא נוכל לומר שר' יוסי פליג ע"ז במתניתין · ועיי' גמרא יבמות צ"ה ע"ב פיסקא ר' יוסי אומר כל שפוסל וכו') :

הקדמה

ואתם בית ישראל · לאו ראו הדרך הישרה שידבק בה האדם · שימו לבבכם לכל הדברים שנאמרו **ביראת ה׳ לחיים** ולאויינהן למי שאמרן · ולמי שנאמרו · ויהא רעוא דינשתמעו הני מילי מעליותא בין יראי ה׳ · לאחוז קירות לבב אחב״י לתורת חסד · ועבודה שלמה · ותפלה זכה · ופעולת צדיק לחיים שמסר נפשו בחייו על תורה ועבודה · תוסיף אומץ לכל האיש החפץ חיים · בתורה ועבודה בכל לבבם ונפשם · ולעורר אולר הטוב בחסד ורחמין נפישין על נפשות בית ישראל שי׳ ונפש נענה **יצחק** בהגאון המחבר מוה׳ **חיים** זללה״ה מוואלאזין

אזהרה

גם אם לא נאמר · לא חשידי מ״ו שארית ישראל לעשות עולה · ואף כי נאמר · אמנם למען לא יעלה על לב איש שום היתרא על איזה אופן שיהיה · הנני מודיע שאינני מרשה להדפיס ספרי כבוד מר אבא הגאון נ״ע בלתי רשות מאתי בשום אופן · כפי פקודת הקיר״ה והשומע יתברך באלקי אמן :

ולחתום בברוך · הנני קובע ברכה בפני עצמה · ובהודאה · לכל אחב״י היקרים שי׳ · בכל מקומות מושבותיהם · מחזיקי עץ החיים · והתומכים מאושרים · שתוכם רצוף אהבה לעשות נחת רוח לנשמתו של מר אבא הגאון זלה״ה ומאמצים כח להקים שמו על בית אולפנא דידי׳ · ואני תפלה · מי שהטיב · ומי שמטיב · ומי שיטיב · לקבוע **כן צדקה להזכרת נשמת חיים** לבית תלמודו כולם יהיו נזכרים בזכירה אחת לכל מעלות לבבם לטובה וברכה · וזכות ה״ת דרבים יהוי בסעדא דידהון שכל הברכות שברך כבוד מר אבא הגאון ז״ל לפני ה׳ טרם נעלה מאתנו · את כל טהורי לב וטהורי ידים המוסיפים אומץ · יחולו על ראשם להתברך בברכה משולשה · רחבה וגדושה · איש איש כברכתו · יבורך מעשי ידיהם בנועם ה׳ כנפשות כלל אחב״י הישרים והיקרים שי׳ ונפש נענה :

יצחק בהגאון **מוהר״ח** ז״ל ·

היום יום ג׳ **ז״ך** אייר · אשר **ב״ם** יברכו ב״י · **ורב שלום** לפ״ק :

הקדמה

הללו · להשרים יראת ה' ותורה ועבודה זכה בלב ישרי לב המבקשים דרכי ה' · אלה הדברים אשר דבר לי :

ואחרי הדברים האלה · הלא דמוע תדמע עין כל הירא את דבר ה' · כאשר יכנים בלבו דברים הללו היוצאים מן הלב בעקב ענוה ויראת ה' **לחיים** · ואם האדם הגדול בתורה · ועמלו היה בתורה · כל ימיו עשה נחת רוח ליוצרו · נדמה לו שאין בו יראת ה' · אכן מה נעני אבתרי' :

ועם כי בי הוא · שלא נדרזתי לקיים מילי דאבוהא · להזדרז לאשר ציווני · (ונענשתי ע"ז כפליים בפרי בטני על חטאת נפשי · א' שלשנה האחרת י"ד סיון תקפ"ב יום פטירת מר אבא ז"ל · נולד לי בן זכר והכנסתיו לברית · ונקרא על שם נפש החיים · ואיננו כי לקח אותו אלקים ביום שלישי למילה · ושנה זו ה' כסליו יום ש"ק היה פ' ויצא יצא ממני הדר כבן שמונה יפה תואר נחמד והטוב · וכבר היה יודע לישא וליתן בגמרא כיתר שמחה נפתלי הערך · צדיק הוא ה' כי פיהו מריתי · והוא רחום יכפר עון · ולא יוסיף לדאבה עוד) · אמנם לא מלבי ח"ו · ברם הורעת השעה בעו"ה היא שגרמה · כי מיום שהורס העטרה · טובה בעינינו לא ראינו · ונשארתי כאיש נדהם רצון לבב · מאבר השתרג · ומשתרגי · ולא מצאתי לי עת לפטור עצמי ממלאכת שמים שלוויתי ממנו על בית אולפנא דידי' · כאשר מודעת לכל · ולפום שיעורא דילי שיערתי רצון מר אבא ז"ל · שאולי לא יהא ניחא לי' לדחות מעשה גדול ת"ת דרבי' מפני מצוה זו :

וגם דמיתי לחבר מילין דאגדתא דילי' לדרושיו על פרקי אבות שהיה דורש שבת בשבתו במילין בסימין · ושמו נאה לו **רוח חיים** . כאשר מלאים רוח עצה ורוח בינה ודעת וחיים הם למוצאיהם :

וגם לקבץ כל השו"ת ולסדרם · לקרותם בשם **נשמת חיים** · כי בדבריו נותן נשמה ותבונה למבינים כענין ונשמת מי יצא ממך (איוב כ"ו) (וקונטרסים הללו קראתים **נפש החיים** כחתימתו של מר אבא ז"ל בתשובותיו וכל מכתביו) ברם לית אתר פנוי לזה · מרובי הטרדות והעבודה המוטלת עלי · ה' ירחיב · ובין דא לדא אשתהי עד האידנא . ואם שגיתי ה' יכפר · (וגם חוו לי דעת קדושי' · תרי הגאונים הגדולים אשר בק"ק ווילנא יע"א · שהסכמתם שלא לאחר המוקדם בדעת כבוד מר אבא הגאון נ"ע . עדי יוקבצו השו"ת דאתבדרן בעלמא :

ועתה אחרי שמן השמים עוררוני לעשות רצון צדיק כבוד מר אבא הגאון נ"ע יהא רעוא להפק רצון יראי ה' המתאווים לתורת **חיים** · ויהי נועם ה' לכונן מעשי ידינו להוציא לאור מה שהנס עוד בכתובי · ומשמיא ישלמו כל כ"ד הרב המופלג מבקש מטמוני יראת ה' כש"ת מ' **אברהם שמחה** שי' · שטרח ויגע בפעולת צדיק **לחיים** בעסק הדפסת הקונטרסים האלו · והטיבה ה' לטובים שהטיבו מטובם לסייע · והמתעסקים בגופם כולם ישאו ברכה מה' · וזכותי דכבוד מר אבא הגאון זללה"ה יהוי בסעדא דכל המתפלים לעשות רצונו הטוב · להביא עליהם ברכת טוב ומטיב :

וחתם

שמבקשים ממנו כלי גדול ויש לו דומה עליו · ככלי קטן · קטן ואין לו דומה עליו ככלי גדול והענין, שכל מי שהוא עניו יותר, אינו מרגיש ענותנותו, ואדרבה נחשב בעיניו למתיהר, ואת חביריו מחשיב לענוים, ומשרע"ה העניו מאד מכל האדם, ודאי הי' מחזיק עצמו למתיהר, ואת כל ישראל החזיק לענוים נגדו, וזהו לגבי משה שהיה עניו ביותר והחזיק את ישראל לענוים, אמר שאצלם יראה מלתא זוטרתי, כי היא עקב ענוה, כמאמרם ז"ל מה שעשתה חכמה וכו' עשתה ענוה עקב לסוליתה, ורק לגבי דידי' נחשב לו יראה לדבר גדול, מחמת שנחשב בעיניו ליהיר עוד, ואולי לזאת תביא הגמרא משל השני מכלי קטן ואין לו, למען דרוש חיבת מעמך שבקרא :

הקדמה

ומודעת שלבו ראה הרבה חכמה · והגדיל תורה · והוסיף עבודה · וממעשיו המרובים · אף חכמתו נתקיימה לו בכל מדע · לחדש חדושי תורה בנפ"ת המתוקים מדבש (והנם בכתובים פסקי פסקי מה שכתבו תלמידיו · כי לא הוה ניחא לי' לכתוב על ספר בעצמו כל דבר שאינו הלכה למעשה) והרבה להשיב ש"ות מנעוריו ועד שיבה לכל גדולי רבני מדינתינו וגאוני זמנינו · וכולם נקבעו הלכה למעשה · (ועם כי בעו"ה המון גנזי ש"ות שנגזם · נשרפו בעו"ה באש שנשלח ממרום יום ד' י"ד אייר בשנת תקע"ה · ונשרפה ר"ל כחצי העיר וגם הוא הי' נוהם שהיו בתיו לאכול אש · ורק על בית אולפנא דידי' · רחמי ה' מתלקחת בתוך האש שאכלה סביביו וקלותיו · והוא נשאר כאוד מוצל מאש · וגם הספרים כלולו · ברוך שעשה נס במקום הזה · אמנם הרבה מהם נשארו ביד התלמידים שהעתיקו להם · והרבה מבדרן בעלמא · ה' יהא עוזר לאספם ולחברם יחד) · ועם כי חזינא לדעתי' דמר אבא ז"ל דיהיב דעתי' עליהון לקבלם יחד · אמנם על כולם לא נצטויתי מאתו להדפיסם · רק על דא נצטויתי מפורש יוצא מפיו · יום העלותו השמימה בנוראות דברים · להתחזק בכל כחי לחזק בית אולפנא דידי' שלא תמוש תורה ח"ו · וגם על הקונטרסים הללו נתן קולו עלי מקירות לבבו · שלא אשנה מדבריו כאשר המה כתובים · ככה צוויתי להדפיסם בזרוז :

וניתי ספר ונחזי עניותנותי' · שהניח דעתו מחבירים גדולים · והמעיט עצמו למיהב דעתי' על הקונטרסים הללו המעטים וכמוכים לפי ערכו הגבוה · כי מודעת שדבר ה' היתה אל **אליהו** חסידא נ"ע · ונגלו לו תעלומות חכמה · כאשר כבר יצא אור דבריו בדפוס · ועוד עשר ידות לו בנסתרות בכתובים · כמו שהאריך מר אבא הגאון נ"ע בהקדמתו לספרא דצניעותא · (ושמעתי ממר אבא הגאון ז"ל · שכל כתבי הקדש בנסתרות ממרן אלי' ז"ל · נכתבו קודם שהגיע לארבעים · כי מאז בינה יתירה התוספת לי' שלא היה הזמן מספיק להכתב כל מה שנגלה לו) · ומר אבא ז"ל קלט סלת מכל בית נכואת רבו ז"ל · להבין מדעתו ראשי פרקים פנימיות דרך עץ החיים להאר"י ז"ל · והיו חקוקים על לוח לבו · ומענותנותי' סייף ועייל מעט מזעיר בקונטרסים הללו · ופתח כמחט סדקית למי שלבו פתוח לפתוח פתח כפתחו של אולם · וברוחב בינתו חקק וחצב הדברים שקלן והזירן וצרפם לדרך התורה ועבודה ויראת ה' · להורות הדרך ילכו · והמעשה אשר יעשון · וכאשר מצודו נפשו אותה לזכות את הרבים בדבר השוה לכל נפש · כן היתה מגמת נפשו קשורה בזה בחד קטירא בעלותה למרום :

ומי שלא ראה העוז והענוה דילי' ביום הלקחו מאתנו · לא ראה עוז וענוה · שמעת תפלת השחר עד עת צאת נשמתו למרום · כל שעה ושעה החליף כח · רגע היה משפיל גיפו בדבריו כאשר הרגיש שישוב העפר אל הארץ כשהי' · ופניו שחורות כעורב · וכרגע הי' מתאזר עוז בדביקות נפלא ופניו היו מאירים כאור פני מלך **חיים** · לקשר נפשו ברוחו שתשוב אל האלקים אשר נתנה בטהרה עד רוחו ונשמתו אליו ית"ש נאספו בנשיקה · והיו צרורים בצרור **החיים** את ה :

וטרם לקח אותו אלקים · אותיום אזעיר גרמיה וקמיט פניו בנמיכת קול ורוח ממללא מנשמת **חיים** · וכה היו דבריו ז"ל · אף ברי יצטריך להדפים הקונטרסים חיש מהר · ואתה בני ידעת · שאף שללמוד לא זכיתי · זכוני מן השמים ללמד לאחריני · ולעשות קיום לת"ת · כן אם שלא זכיתי ליראה את ה' *) · אולי אזכה מן השמים · שיתקבלו דברי בקונטרסים הללו

---

*) **ומי** שידע שמענותנותו היה נחשב בעיניו עוד ליהיר, לא נפלאת היא מה שנדמה לו שלא הבין יראת ה', כענין מאמר חז"ל (ברכות ל"ג ב') אטו יראה מלתא זוטרתי היא וכו', אין לגבי משה מלתא זוטרתי היא, משל לאדם

הקדמה

דרש בפרקיה · ומעשיותיו לא מלאו לבו להוכיח לבריאתא · והוכיח במישור לעצמו בכל דבריו · והי' כבא ללמד ונפלא למד *) ורובי מוסריו היו להשפיל גבהות הלב :

ועם כי רובי דבריו בדרשותיו היו עומדים ברומו של עולם · מיוסדים ע"פ זוהר וכתבי האר"י ז"ל (כאשר המעיינים הבינו בדברים) · הוא ז"ל מענות צדקתו · הלבישם והפשיטם וגנזם · לבל יגדיל דבריו כדורש בנסתרות · להמתיקם כדבש וחלב תחת לשונו · וכבשם תחת לבושו · מלדורשן להדיא כהמון ורבים שלא מלא כריסם בתלמוד להטהר במעשיהם ברוח נכון ביראת ה' · לבל יכשלו בהבלי הבלי השוא · ולפי הוראת השכל שהיה נראה לי להוציא איזה דברים מבלי הלפנים · הי' קורא על עצמו לא המדרש עיקר אלא המעשה (ומתחלה נשמע כוונתי על סיפא דמשנה זו וכל המרבה דברים וכו' (לשון רבי המלך) שממלל מלין לבד עלתה להגדילם בעיני השומעים · (ועיין מדרש שמואל שם) :

בכל דרכיו · הי' ממעט כבוד עצמו להרבות כבוד שמים · הן במילי דאורייתא · בפרט בעניני הכלל · מודעת שהשליך נפשו מנגד ועסק הרבה יתר על כדי כחו · ואף כי זקן היה · היו ידיו אמונה עד בא השמש · ואף ככלות כח רח"ל גם על משכבו בחליו · רעיוניו סליקו · ועיניו היו נשואות השמימה לשתף שם שמים בצערא דהכלל והפרט · בגנוחי ואנחות בשברון מתנים · ואנחותיו הרבות כזה היו שוברות כל גוף השומע · (והי' רגיל להוכיח אותי על זאת שאינני משתתף בצערא דאחרינא · וכה היה דברו אלי תמיד · שזה כל האדם לא לעצמו נברא · רק להועיל לאחריני ככל אשר ימצא בכחו לעשות) ודן והורה · אהב שלום ורודף שלום · אוהב את הבריות · ומקרבן לתורה **)

וזה היה דרך הלוכו בקדש מעודו · הן בתורה · והן בדרכי ה' הישרים שהיה מורה · הניח כבוד עצמו ובחר לו ללמד באשר ייטב להם לאחריני · אשר כקטן כגדול ישמעון · בכל רובי תורותיו אשר זכה וזיכה את הרבים · לא הניח ידו מלהגיד לבני עירו אחר תפלת השחר · פרשה מסדרא דשבוע יום יום · וכל הנכנסין לבית המדרש יצא מלא דבר כאשר כל אחד קלט לפי דרכו · אוהב הפשט קלטו עומק פשוטו במקרא · ודורשי הרשומות · דרוש דרשו ממה שלקחה אזנם · מה שנזרקה מפיו מדי דברו בקדרה · וכל השומעים שמחו במתק שפתיו אשר ברור מלל כקורא הפרשה לפני תשב"ר · וכ"כ היתה מצוה זו חביבה בעיניו · שהניח כל דבריו בקדש והוה רהיט לבי מדרשא · בעוד שכל הצבור מתפללין וקטן וגדול שם הוא · וחדותא שלימתא הוה חדי מינה · באמרו שלאגמורי דבר הצריך תלמוד · לאו כולי עלמא גמירי · וזאת התורה כל אפיין שוין באכנתא · ומטיב לכולם · ועלך לגו באזי · ילמדו ענוים דרכו :

ומודעת

---

*) **ואולי** כן כוונת הכתוב (ישעיה נ) ה' אלקים נתן לי לשון למודים וכו' יעיר לי אזן לשמוע כלמודים, היינו שה' ית"ש נתן לי לשון למודים בתוכחת מוסר לאחריני, והוא ית"ש העיר אזנו שילמד גם הוא מוסר לעצמו · כלמודים שמלמד לאחריני :

) **ובכוונא שהורגלנו להגיע תפלת שהמע"ה (מלכים א' ח' כ"ז), כי האמנם ישב אלקים על הארץ, ר"ל שכמו שקרוב להאמין שאיש חסד עם כי הוא עשיר נכסים וגדול כבודו לאדירי עם, בחכמה וגבורה ועושר, יבחר לו מקום לישב בשפל, ולהיות את נדכאים ארץ מלחה, לא תקים ורש, ומים אין לשתות, למען יוכל גמול כל מיני חסדים טובים כחפץ לבו רק להיטיב בכל מילי דמיטב. ככל החזיון הזה אמר שהמע"ה שם, יאמן נא דבר כו' כי האמנם (לשון אמונת אומן) ישב אלקים על הארץ, שתמלא ידך לגמול כל חסדים טובים, אשר יחפוץ איש לרעהו תעשה חסד בגבורה להציל עשוק מיד עושקו, איש אשר יסיג גבול רעהו תשיבהו על אדמתו, כי יצמאו למים, ונתת להם מטר רעב כי יהיה ונתת לחם לקצירי ומריעי תפלה ארוכה, לכל נגוע לבב תחבוש לעצבותו ומלאה הארץ דרכי טובך להטיב בכל מיני הטבה :

הקדמה

עוד מדרך הענוה האמיתית · שיהיו כל ענייני הגוף נבזה ונמאס בעיניו באמת עד שלאפס ותהו יחשבו מבלי הרגיש לא ענג ולא נגע · ורק בדרכי ה׳ יגבהו · שיהא לבם פתוח לתורה ועבודה וקדושה · ואך בה׳ ישמחו כי ישיהו לבם מדור נאה לו ית״ש ככתוב (ישעי׳ כט) ויספו ענוים בה׳ שמחה · וכמאמר הרגיל תמיד בפינו בעמדנו בתפלה לאמר · ולמקללי נפשי תדום ונפשי כעפר לכל תהיה · ואח״כ פתח לבי בתורתך ואחרי מצותיך תרדוף נפשי · הן כל מכירי כבוד מר אבא הגאון ז״ל · המה יעידו ויגידו מענותנותו הגדולה · אשר אם היה נעלב לא העליב · והיה שפל רוח בפני כל אדם · ובתענוגי הגוף · אף למעוטא דמעוטא היה חושש · ושם דרכיו לבלי הרגיש תענוג · ואף כי הגיעו ימי הזקנה שנתייסר ביסורים של אהבה · במאדו ונפשו קבלם בשמחה ובצהלת פנים · מבלי הוציא אנחה (כמאמר חז״ל (ברכות סב ע״א) קבלה דיסורי שתיקותא) · ודעתיה הוה בדיחא עליה כל שני דקביל עלי׳ יסורים · ורק ע״ז היה מצטער אותו צדיק על שהוכרח לכלכל גופו לפי מאכלו · ובמספרים היו עיניו יורדים סיף סיף (ועיני ראו ולא זר) · ועם כי לבו היה דוי ע״ז · היה שמח ביסוריו הממעטים לו הרגש התענוג · עד שלא שם לבו לא לענג ולא לנגע :

וכל רואי השמש בגבורתו · המה ראו כן תמהו · שעם כל כניעת גופו ונמיכת רוחו למילי דעלמא · כן נהפך לבבו במילי דשמיא · ללבוש עוז והדר · ועד זיבולא בתרייתא · לבו היתה שומה לעשות מחדיצאה לתורה ועבודה וג״ח · ומה מאד גבה לבו בדרכי ה׳ ללחום מלחמתה של תורה · וכל מצוה שבתל בדוח חכמה וגבורה · גמרה ברוח דעת ויראת ה׳ · ודבר אחד מדבריו לא שב · והוציא לאור מחבבתו המוכה לפני רבבות עם . והכל בשובה ודברים מחוכמים אשר בנחת היו נשמעים :

עיקר הענוה · שלא להרגיש מעשין הטובים שפעל · וערך מעלותיו שהשיג · וכל אשר יגדלו פעולותיו ומעלותיו ושכלו ירבה להכיר גדולתו ית״ש · כן רוח האלקים תוסיף את כח הרגש חסרונו · ותדמים הרגש עלמות מעלותיו · וכשרואה שמתיקר בעיני אנשים לכבדו · מצטמק ורע עליו המעשה *) ומחשב לו חסרונותיו להקטין עצמו לבלתי רום לבבו · (כמו שמצינו בדל (יומא פ״ו א׳) כד הוה חזי אמבוה כו׳) :

ומי שלא ראה דרכי כבוד מר אבא הגאון ז״ל בזה · לא יאומן כי יסופר · כל תחבולותיו ועלילותיו אשר שם שם לו בזה · רגיל על לשונו היה · שכל חדושים שמחדש · כן בגפ״ת · או בש״ות · ושיערה דעתו דחדי לבי׳ מפלפולי׳ · הוא חושש לנהגה מד״ת · והיה קרוב בעיניו שהחדוש אולי אינו לאמתה של תורה · כמאמרם ז״ל (ר״פ אלו דברים) כל המתיהר חכמתו מסתלקת הימנו (ודרך בדיחותא היה אומר · שזהו נחשב אלו לשיהד · שמשחד עצמו בחדותא דמסתיי׳) · והיה מתיגע לסתור דברי עצמו ולחזור לשנות דבריו · ולשקול בפלס שכלו איך להעמיד על האמת בסברה ישרה · ובשקול דעת נכונה והרואה יראה ויבין מחכמתו שנתקיימה לו · איך היה מקטין שכלו בעיניו ודעתו היה שפלה עליו · כמאמרם ז״ל (תענית ז׳ א׳) אין ד״ת מתקיימין אלא במי שדעתו שפלה עליו :

היה אוהב תוכחת מוסר · וכל דבריו היו כאש · והוה להיט מפומי׳ שלהבת י״ק באהבה · ורשפי אש בירא · וכל אזן שמעה הי׳ נמס לבבו כהמס דונג · ונמשך אחרי מיליו דחסדאין באגדתא דהוה

דריש

---

*) **ודרך** דרש אולי הוא כוונה שניי׳ במה שאמר ר״א לתלמידיו (ברכות כח ב) הזהרו בכבוד חבריכם , שצריך זהירות שלא יוגבה לבו מהכביד שחבריו נוהגים בו :

ואולי

הקדמה

נ"ע *) ומה טוב ונעים הי' שבת אחים גם יחד בתורה ועבודה · ושניהם כאחד למדו תורה מהרב הדומה למלאך ה' צבאות עיר וקדיש מן שמיא רבינו הגדול רשכבה"ג הגאון מרנא ורבנא **אליהו** החסיד זצוק"ל מק"ק ווילנא · והוא ז"ל האציל מרוחו עליהם · רוח חכמה וכו' · אשרי עין ראתה כל אלה · הרואים ראו ושמחו · והשומע ישמע למשמע אזן תאבה נפש :

ויותר מלמודו הי' גדול שמושו שמשמש את רבו החסיד נ"ע · ובימים הרבים שעמד לפניו · אנהיר לי' שבילי דאורייתא בנגלה ונתיבות פליאות בנסתר · הוא הוא דחזא רבי' מקמי' **) וגלי' לי' מסכתא ונהירו דחכמתא · וכימים אשר למד לפניו באימה וביראה ברתת ובזיע · מן נהר דינור דהוה נגיד ונפיק מן קדמוהי · כן כאשר לימד והודיע לבניו ותלמידיו הימים אשר עמד לפניו · אימתי' דרבי' הוה עלי' במורא נפלאה כאלו עומד לפניו במרום · וכאשר פתח בשמעתתא ודכיר עתי' דרבי' · הוי מרתע כלא גופי' וזיוסי שנין עלוהי מאש המתלקחת בלבבו · בהגינו דרכי צדקתו וחסידותו וטהרת קדושתו · ואור תורתו נקנת לו · כאשר הי' כתר יפה בהמעלות שהתורה נקנית בהם · ומאדרת **אליהו** הלבש ענוה ויראה :

וגדולה ענוה של כבוד מר אבא הגאון נ"ע · ונתלבש בכל דרכי' ונתיבותי' · וקצות דרכיו לספרה · באשר מדרך ענוה · להיות את דכא · או לרומם את דכא אתו (סוטה ה' ע"א) · הן שהי אלה ראתה בו עין כל יקר · שמעודו ועד שיבה נתן נפשו להחיות רוח שפלים במאדו וצדקת פזרונו · ולהיות את נדכאים · וגם עדיו כי באו אביוני אדם · ששו ושמחו כי קרבם ימין · והרחיב לבבם בפיוסי דברים · ובדברי חן שהוצק בשפתותיו :

עוד ;

---

*) **ונודע** כיהודה וגדול שמו בישראל · וקצות דרכו בקצרה הנם כתובי' על ספר תולדות אדם ח"א וח"ב שחבר הרב המובהק הדרשן הגדול מהו' **יחזקאל פייוויל** מ"מ דקהלא רבתי מווילנא , ועוד ה"ב אצלו בכתובים, יהי ה' אתו להדפיסו · ואבא מארי ז"ל היה גדול בשנים מאחיו הגאון מוהר"ם זלמן נ"ע ז' שנים וט' ימים , ונולד שנת **תקי"ט** בחודש סיון יו"ט שני של חג השבועות יום שנתנה תורה לישראל , ונתעלה מאתנו בן ע"ב ביום חנוכתו י"ד סיון ה' לסדר ויהי בנסוע הארון · שנת **כל הכתוב לחיים** :

) **ואולי ענין הנאמר בעירובין (י"ג ב') ואלו חזיתיה מקמיה וכו' והיו עיניך רואות את מוריך , הוא כענין הכתוב (שמות ל"ג) וראית את אחורי ופני לא יראו , עפ"י מדרש שמות פ"ג אקי"ק אשר אקי"ק על שם מעשי אני נקרא (וסוף פרטי המעשים כלולים במחשבה הקדומה) , ולזאת נקרא' המחשבה פנים. שקודמת , והמעשה מאוחרת , ובמחשבה עצמה יש מחשבה קדומה וכוללת, והיא פנימית, ומחשבה מאוחרת המתפשטת מהפנימי' לדבור או למעשה · (והוא דעת המתפשט בפנימית המדות) והיא היא הנכרת מתוך מעשה , או דבר המאוחר , כעקימת שפתיו דהוי מעשה , אבל פנימית המחשבה הקדומה , א"א להכירה בציבור , כענין דבש וחלב תחת לשונך (ע' חגיגה י"ג א'), והוא דעת העליון , כענין לא קאים איניש אדעתיה דרבי' (עכו"ם ה' ע"ב) , ואינה נתפסת להתלמיד אלא בהארת פנים של רבו , לתלמיד חכם ומבין מדעתו , וכל זה הוא כמחשבות שבלב איש , אבל בו ית"ש אמר לא מחשבותי מחשבותיכם כתיב (ישעיה נ"ה) · כללות מחשבתו לית מחשבה תפיסא בשום אופן , אף לעליונים , ורק מחשבתו המתפשטת לקיום מעשיו , נכרת ממעשיו לכל נביא ונביא כפי מדרגתו , וזהו וראית את אחורי, את לרבות המחשבה המתפשטת לקיום המעשה וניכרת ע"י כח מעשיו , ונקראת ע"ש המעשה , ופני לא יראו אף על ידי כח מעשיו המאוחרים אל הקודם (וכהוראת מלת יראו דגירי) : י"ד

ודרך

הקדמת בן מרן הגאון המחבר נ"ע

מלפנים זאת · שכל מחבר חבור · מקדים הקדמה בראש ספרו · מהם נהגו להודיע מה ראו על ככה לבוא במגלת ספר · מהם מודיעים תכלית כוונת תועלת החבור · מהם עקבותיהם עקב ענוה ויראת ה' הקודמת לחכמתם · להשפיל עצמו על ד"ת לבל יתרברב במחברתו : **ואם** לבנו ייעדנה לקבעו בדפוס · הנה בן יכבד אב למלל גבורת אביו המחבר · ולהשמיע תהלת החבור · איש איש לפי מהללו :

ואנכי במה אקדם · נער אנכי לא ידעתי דבר שיותקו מלי בספר · ואף כי לא בי הוא לכוין לב במה אחל · אם כה אומר להשמיע תהלות דברים שנאמרו **ביראת ה' לחיים** · ותכליתם · הלא דבר שפתים אך למחסור *) בדבר אשר עין בעין יראו · ויהיו נדברים בין יראי ה' · אשר קרבת אלהים יחפצון · וכל קוראי ספרו אשר יקראוהו באמת · לעומתו יאמרו ברוך שחלק מחכמתו ליראיו :

ואם אתן אומר בשבח הראוי לכבוד מר אבא הגאון צדיק המפורסם נ"ע · עירום אנכי מלהבין בין להעריך דרכי תורתו וצדקתו · ולא עמדי הוא להכיר ולהבירו לאחרים · זקני ת"ח וגאוני גדולי רבני מדינתינו נ"י · שלהם נודע כח מעשיו בנגלה ובנסתר · להם נאה לספר שמו וזכרו · כי רב הוא · ועל ספריו כולם יכתבו: **והאומנם** צדק דרכיו ארץ מלאה ומעשיו הכריזוהו ·

ומי כל בשר אשר לא שמע קל משרוקיתא · שבחא דעבד בארעא · וחבנא ותיקפא אהיבת ליה באורייתא קשוט · ועובדין טבין וקשוט דעבד · התקנת כרכו יתירא להאוית כמלכיי' · בחילא דאלהא דשמיא :

הוא הגבר שהקים עולה של תורה **בזמם** במדינתא בתורת חסד · ופיהו פתח בחכמה למאות תלמידים · וזכה להגדיל תורה · לאגמורי · ולמסבר · אזן וחקר ותקן · ובנה לו בית תלמוד גדול עומד על שלשה עמודים · **תורה ועבודה וג"ח** :

ורא נפלאות היא שזכה וזכה את הרבים · כי מנעוריו נשא עולה של תורה בשקידה נפלאה · ובהיותו למעלה מבר ארבעסר · קבע למודו עם אחיו הגדול הגאון מ' **שמחה** ז"ל · והוו גרסי יממא ולילי · וזקנינו ספרו לנו · שכאשר לא היה להון אור הנר מצוי · אור הלבנה הוה יפה להון לגירסא דלילא · וקבעו אז דרכה של תורה מרב רבנן גאון הגאונים אדו' דבי עלאה רבנא **ארי' ליב** נ"ע · בעל שאגת ארי' : **)

וכד היה כבר עשרים וחמש · הוה גמיר בבלא תלמודא · ופוסקים ראשונים ואחרונים · והיה לומד תורה עם אחיו הגאון וצדיק דמי לבר אלהין מ' **שלמה זלמן** נ"ע

---

*) **ואולי** יתכן פי' הכתוב ודבר שפתים אך למחסור (משלי י"ד) שלדבר שנראה בהשקפה שיש בו איזה פתרון · צריך דבר שפתים להתמיקו אבל באין מחסור , למה זה רוב דברים :

) **והגאון בעל ש"א ז"ל, היה כמה שנים אב"ד פה ק"ק, והיה מודע למשפ' אבא מארי ז"ל, ובהיותו פה חבר חבורי היקר ש"את ש"א, ובנסעו מפה להדפיסו, הי' אז אבא נ"ע עדן קטן בשנים, ואחרי עברו דרך פה אחרי הדפיס ספרו הנ"ל, נתאכסן בבית א"ז ז"ל כמה שבועות · ויתן את פני השלך וקבע תורתו פה · והי' אז אבא מארי ז"ל כבר תמיסר, ומאהבה שאהבו, ואת אחיו הגדול נ"ע, קבע להם מעתה שיהא סדורם · ונודע

בית

הסכמות

מדי דברו בו יראו ויבינו מה רב כחו ושקידתו בהלכה · ללמד חכמה ומוסר השכל הקדש קדש לה' ראשית בכורי פרי חכמתו וצדקתו אשר ראה ראשית לו ראשית חכמה יראת ה' · ופקד את כבוד בנו הרב המאו"הג הנ"ל לתת לו משפט הקדימה על כל דבריו הקדושים הנחמדים אשר בכתובים אשר ודאי יהיו לנס ולתפארת · אך כאשר כל דרכיו הי' צדק לצדקות ד' פזורות בישראל הישר דרך בית אל · לכן אמרתי לעורר לבבות אחב"י להחזיק בעץ החיים ולהיות חלקם בחיים · מבלי ירוסף ח"ו עמודי השמים · ויתברכו בכפלי כפליים · עדי נעלה לציון וירושלים · ולשומע יונעם ויתברך מה' מלא וגדוש · כ"ד המדבר לכבוד התורה והצדק · היום יום ו' עש"ק ט"ז סיון שנת מצמיח הישועה לפ"ק פה ווילנא:

נאום **אברהם אבלי** בלאא"מ הרב הג' מו' שלמה זללה"ה:

דהלכתא · היינו העמדת תלמידים הרבה לזכות רבים בתורה ע"י תסתיים השמעתא אליבא דהלכתא · כדאמרו ז"ל (ערובין ר"פ כיצד מעברין) בני יהודה דגלו מסכת נתקיימה תורתן בידם וכו' דוד דגלי מסכת וכו' ופי' רש"י שם ובגיפין כ"ס א' · והמזכה את הרבים אין חטא בא על ידו וכו' מכולם · ומתורץ תמיהת התוס' שם ד"ה זה ת"ה · ובעסקו הגאון ז"ל בתורה לשמה · זכה שכל מחשבות לבו ותשוקתו היו לזכות את הרבים ומסר נפשו על זה · כן הצליח ה' חפצו בידו שהקימו מזימותיו ויצאו לאור עולם · וע"ד בקשת ר' אלכסנדרי בתר צלותיה (ברכות י"ז א') יהי רצון שתעמידנו בקרן אורה וכו' (היינו שעוסק בתורה לשמה כעין בקשת רב ספרא הנז' שם לעיל מינ' וכענין דרשת רחב"י במס סוטה שם בפ' כי נר מצוה ותורה אור) ובזה אל ידוה לבנו · ע"ד מאמרם ז"ל ר"פ כיצד מעברין (כ"ד א') רבא רמי כתיב תאות לבו נתת לו וכתיב וארשת שפתיו וגו' זכה תאות לבו נתת לו · ר"ל בעסק התורה לשמה שהיא נקראת עץ חיים (כמאמרם ז"ל יומא (ע"ב ב') זכה נעשית לו סם חיים) מתמלאי' חפציו · כמאמרם ז"ל (ברכות ל"ב ב') ע"ש תוחלת ממושכה מחלת לב · מאי תקנתיה יעסוק בתורה שנאמר ועץ חיים תאוה באה · ז"ש ר' אלכסנדרי ואל ידוה לבנו ומ"ש ואל יחשכו עינינו · ע"ד מאמרם ז"ל (ב"ב ע"ה א') עשן בחופה למה א"ר ח שכל מי שעיניו צרות בת"ח בעוה"ז מתמלאות עיניו עשן לעוה"ב · לכ"א שבעסקינו בתורה לשמה ומנעימים זה לזה אל יחשכו עינינו לעוה"ב: וגם עתה אחרי אשר נתעלה מאתנו ש"ב הגאון ז"ל הנ"ל קם בנו הבן יקיר לי הרב המאו"הג המפורסם מ' יצחק נ"י אב"ד ור"מ דק"ק וואלאזין · ומתחזק בנפשו ומאדו להקים שם אביו ז"ל על בית תלמודו הגדול ויכוננהו כראוי · יהי ה' אתו שתתקיים בידו כרצונו ית"ש וכרצון כל יראי ה' הדבקים בתורת ה' להגדילה ולהאדירה · ודרכו בקדש של ש"ב הגאון ז"ל הי' שתמיד הי' דואג וכואב ומצטער בצערן של ישראל · צער הכלל · והפרט מכל איש אשר ידע נגעי לבבו ותמיד הי' חונן ומלוה · אוהב שלום ורודף שלום · והלוכו בקדש בעקבות רבו רבינו הגדול מרכן שמו בכל תפוצות ישראל הגאון החסיד מוהר"א נ"ע מווילנא יע"א · למסור נפשו לקיים כל מילי דרבנן · וכמודעת לי גם מפי איש אמונים מעשה פרטית גדולה היא אלי · ומצינו בחכמי הש"ס שהשתבחו עצמם בזה כמ"ש (ס"פ איזהו נשך) אמרו לי' רבנן לרב אשי קא מקיים רבינא כל מה דאמור רבנן וכו' · ובערכין (ט"ז א') תיתי לי דקיימית וכו' · ובמקום גדולתו שם נמצא ענותנותו הגדולה בכל עניניו· וגם ברצותו להשאיר אחריו ברכה · לא שת לבו לרוני תורתו · ורצה לעשות נ"ר ליוצרו ית"ש להיות ממצדיקי הרבים · וצוה את בני הרב המאו"הג מוהרי"ץ הנ"ל · בראשית חכמה ידפיס דברי מוסריו ביראת ה' לחיים · הנעימים ומושכין לבות בנ"א לתורה ועבודת הלב · ושלהבת יראתו ואהבתו ית"ש הגם כי נפשי יודעת דמוסר היא לגביה דרב ז"ל · והנה בן יכבד אב קם ונתעורר לקיים בדפוס כיון · ועל הטוב יזכר שם ידידי הרב המופלג הוותיק מוה' **אברהם שמחה** נ"י אשר התאמץ וגם הרבה בזה · וזכות שארי הגאון יעמוד לנו ולכל ישראל אכי"ר: ומשמיא יהא רעוא שיוציא בנו חביבי הנ"ל לאור בדפוס עוד דברי קדשו של מר אביו הגאון ז"ל · אשר עדן בכתובים · גם לקבץ את אל אחת כמה שו"ת היקרים של מר אביו ז"ל בהלכו' המחודשות·לרוות הצמאי'·לדלות דבר ה' זו הלכ' ברורה מבאר מים חיים·וגם שעתה כמעט נדרתי בעדי מליתן הסכמה· אמנם אדעתא דגברא רבא כוותיה דש"ב הגאון ז"ל · לא נדרנא · וגם מפני יקרא דחיי כבוד בנו חביבי הנ"ל · יצאתי מגדרי לגדור כראוי שלא להסיג גבולו של בנו חביבי הנ"ל להדפיס ספרו זה של ש"ב הגאון ז"ל · לא מניה ולא מקצתו ולא ע"י שום אופן ותחבולה בעולם בלתי רשות בנו · כפי פקודת הקיר"ה 22 אפריל 1828 כחוק הניתן להמחברים פעטערבורג 8. ולשומע יונעם ותבא עליו ברכת טוב · כ"ד המדבר לכבוד התורה ולומדיה · היום יום א' עו"ב סיון שנת תקפ"ד פה ק"ק ווילנא יע"א ·

שאול בהגאון מוהר"ר **יוסף** זללה"ה:

הסכמות

הרב הגאון המפורסם בתורה ובחסידות גר ישראל כקש"ת מו' שאול זצ"ל ·

נודע ביהודה · ובישראל גדול שמו של ש"ב רב חביבי הרב הגאון המפורסם בתורתו וצדקתו מופת הדור מוה' חיים זלה"ה · אב"ד ור"מ דק"ק וואלאזין · ונהירנא כד היה מפיק מפומיה זקוקין דנור בתוה"ק · ומרגלא טבין מאוצר יראת ה' הקודמת לחכמתו שנתקיימה · וגדל בתורה ועמל בתורה לשמה נעשות נ"ר ליוצרו ית"ש · ואזן וחקר עשה אזנים לתורה ומעשים טובים · לקרב את הבריות לתורה ויראת ה' · ולהרים דגלה של תורה · תכנה בית תלמוד גדול · ומעיין מים החיים יוצא מבית תלמודו להשקות עדרי צאן קדשים שנאספו אליו יום יום · בעומק הלכות מרובות · והעמיד תלמידים הרבה · זכה וזכה את הרבים · וזכה מנה שתורת אמת היתה בפיהו · ונליא ליה מסכת · וידיו הי' רב לו בנגלה ובנסתר · ולאסוקי שמעתא אליבא דהלכתא · בכל תשובותיו אשר הרבה להשיב לכל אשר יבקשו תורה מפיהו בדבר ה' זו הלכה בתוכו · ואהני ליה ואהני לעלמא כולא כאשר למד ולימד לשמה · כמאמרם ז"ל על העוסק בתורה לשמה שכל העולם כולו כדאי הוא לו · וכענין מאמרם ז"ל ברבה ריש מגילת רות ע"פ אני מדבר בצדקה רב להושיע · באיזו צדקה ר' אלעזר ור' יוחנן · ח"א בצדקה שעשיתם את עולמי על שקבלתם את תורתי וכו' · וח"א בצדקה שעשיתם עם עצמיכם על שקבלתם את תורתי וכו' ע"ש · וי"ל דל"פ · מר קאי אלשמה · ומר קאי אשלא לשמה דעביד צדקה לגרמי' · ואזיל ר"י לשיטתי' בפ' חלק (נ"ט ב') כל העוסק בתור' לשמה וכו' ר' יוחנן אמר אף מגין על כל העולם כולו · וכדאמרי' (פסחים ס"ח ב') ברב ששת דאמר חדאי נפשאי לך קראי לך תנאי ופריך איני והאר"א וכו' ומשני מעיקרא כי עביד איניש אדעתיה דנפשיה קא עביד כמשז"ל בריש פ' מקום שנהגו שמתוך שלא לשמה בא לשמה · וחלילה וחלילה לעזוב את התורה בשביל שלא זכה ללמוד בתחלת למודו לשמה · כמו שמביא ש"ב הגאון ז"ל הנ"ל ראיות נכונות וברורות על זה מכמה מאמרים : גם לעת זקנותו של ש"ב הגאון ז"ל שנתייסר ביסורים ר"ל · ועד יום העלותו מאתנו · היתה שעשועיו בעיון תורת ה' בלבון הלכה לאמיתה · ונתקיים בו כל מאמרם ז"ל בסוטה (כ"א א') על הת"ת · הגיע לפרשת דרכים ניצול מכלם · ואמרינן שם מאי פרשת דרכים אר"ח זה ת"ח ויום המיתה · ופרש"י שם ז"ל והוא ת"ח ביום מותו וידע שלא פירש וכו' · וכן מ"ש שם רנב"י זה ת"ח ויראת חטא · נתקיים ביראת ה' לחיים · וכמאמרם ז"ל ברבה קהלת ע"פ טובה חכמה עם נחלה טובה חכמה כשהיא נחלה · ע"ד דמכריז ר' ינאי חבל על דלית ליה דרתא וכו' (יומא ע"ב) · גם מ"ש מר זוטרא שם זה ת"ח דסליקא ליה שמעתתא אליבא דהלכתא

הרב הגאון המפורסם סיני ועוקר הרים כקש"ת מו' אברהם אבלי זצ"ל ·

מי האיש החפץ חיים · השב לב בנים אל האב אבינו שבשמי' · זה הדרך יבור לו ברה מאירת עינים · זה דרך היחיד ועין העדה · לתורה ולתעודה · ה"ה כבוד הרב הגאון הגדול בנגלה ובנסתר פאר הדור מ' חיים זצוק"ל אב"ד ור"מ דק"ק וואלאזין · תלמיד רבינו הגדול רבן של ישראל הגאון החסיד מוהר"א מווילנא נ"ע · כאשר שמו הגדול נו"ע ונתפרסם כשמן אפרסמון · והרואה יראה בהקדמת בנו ממלא מקומו הרב המאור הגדול הריף ובקי המפורסם מ' יצחק נ"י · באמירה נעימה בתושבחתא דהאי מרגניתא דלית ליה טימי כבוד אביו הגאון זצוק"ל · ויותר שהי' חכם · עוד לימד ואזן וחקר הרבה להגדיל תורה ולהאדירה · הוא הגבר הוקם על עולה של תורה · להחזיר ליושנה העטרה · אשר בעו"הר בדורות הללו אשר נתמעט כבוד התורה וירד שפל מעלות · ואין מתעורר ומחזיק להחזיק כבוד התורה · הוא האיש אשר הרפנסו ומאדו להושיב ישיבה נשגבה ורמה · רמה קרנו קרן דתור' · בהנכי"י · אזרי אשר נתקיים כמעט ח"ו עתידה תורה שתשתכח מישראל · ינע להחזירה · ותמנו השקה עדרים לפתח כאבני חפץ ולקדר בהרים · וכמה הגיעו להוראה ומורים · וגם כהיום בנו הרב המאו"הג הנ"ל מתאמץ בכל עוז ומקיים מילי דאבות להחזיק הישיבה הלז בעתים הקשים · ועבודת הקדש אשר ישא עליו · רבה היא מאד · ומשמים זכו שמלא את ב"ד מלא דבר להיות לעזר במילי דישיבה · ה"ה הרב המופלג השנון ירא ה' מרבים מ' אברהם שמחה נ"י בהרב המונהק המפורסם מ' נחמן זללה"ה אחי הגאון המנוח ז"ל · והרב הגאון ז"ל עדן בחיים חיותו הראה חביבות ופנים מאירות לב"א מוהרר"א שמחה הנ"ל · יהא רעוא שחפצו ית"ש תתקיים ביד בנו הרב המאו"הג נ"י · יתגדל תורה ויאדיר · ושמר את דרך החיים כאשר אביו הגאון הנ"ל זצוק"ל שם שקידתו על הישיבה עם סדרתו העצומה במילי דלנטרא · ואשר ישאלו אותו איש איש משאליו כאשר ישאל איש וכו' · וכל דבר הקשה להלכה ולמעשה · מפיהו תורה יבקשו · והשיב לשואל דברים אשר ישאל על שלחן מלכים מלכי רבנן להעלות : ועם כל זה הקדים יראת חטאו לחכמתו המתקיימת · וחיבר לעת זקנתו חבור נחמד מאד להלל · בהלולא דרבנן קשישאי דעבדין עובדין טבין ומטיבין לאחרינא לרעות בטוב · ולשמור דרך החיים אשר יחיה בהם האדם · ותפקחנה עיניהם באכלם מפריו פרי עץ חיים אשר הגאון הנ"ל שתל בשתילי סתום ופתוח פתח שער לדופקי בתשובה · שמגעת עד כסא הכבוד העליון למעלה למשכיל במושכלות ובלימודות · וירבץ ברב בקיאותו אשר הבית מים התלמוד ומאמרי זו"הק ועץ חיים ופרי עץ חיים · אשר

מדי

שחוטה במקצת אז אינו די בשחיטת כל דהוא לומר שעשה בה מעשה אך צריך שישחוט מעט יותר כדי שיהיה ניכר שנעשה שינוי בשחיטת הבהמה על ידו ולכן אף אם היה הקנה פגום פחות מחציו והוא השלים לחציו לא אסרה כי המעשה שעשה אינו ניכר עדין להקרא מעשה והרי הוא כאלו לא עשה בה ולא כלום ורק אם השלים את רוב הסימן אז אמרינן שעשה בה מעשה והרי כולהו בהדי הדדי קאתו, ודו"ק.

בב"ק דף י"ט: (אמתניתן) דהיה דליל קשור ברגליו אמר רב הונא ל"ש אלא שנקשר מאליו, אבל קשרו אדם חייב ופירש רש"י חייב הקושר נזק שלם דהוי בור ואם נתקל בו אדם חייב בנזקו. והתוספות כתב ולאו דוקא קשרו אלא כל היכא דלא אצנעיה כקשרו דמי, ונ"ל לפרש חלוקי דיעות בין רש"י ותוספות בסוגיא זו: רש"י סובר אם פשע אדם אחד שלא אצניה או אפילו הניח בר"ה אם קשר אדם אחר חייב הקושר אע"פ שבעל הדליל פשע בשביל[illegible] ועדיף מההופך את הגלל ברשות הרבים והוזק בהן אחר חייב ההופך כשנתכוין לזכות בה (שם דף כט:) אעפ"י שאדם אחר הניח את הגלל ברשות הרבים והוי בורו, משום שנתכוין ההופך לזכות בו אעפ"י שלא הגביה ג' טפחים נעשה הגלל בורו והכא בפעולת הקשירה נפק הדליל מרשותו של בעליו וממילא חל החוב על הקושר. אעפ"י שלא נתכון לזכות בו.

אבל התוספות סוברים שפעולת הקשירה אינה מוציא את הדליל מרשות בעליו הראשון כמו בענין הגלל לא מהני מעשה הפכתו לחוד כשלמטה מג' כמשמעת הגמרא שהצרכו ענין „מתכוין". מבאר פה התוספות שהניחו ג"כ ולכן פירש הת' קשרו לאו דוקא אלא כל היכא דלא אצנעיה פושע הוא וחיב. במסקנת הגמרא אוקמי מתניתן בדאדייה אדויי ופירש"י ואפילו קשרו אדם פטור הקושר דלא נתקל אדם בבורו ומקשין התוספות למה לא יתחייב משום אשו כאבנו סכינו ומשאו שהניחם בראש גגו ונפלו ברוח מצויה והתרנגול הוי כמו רוח מצויה, אולם דעת רש"י היא שהתרנגול אינו דומה לרוח מצויה מפני שעל בעל התרנגול מוטל החוב לשמרו ולכן פטור הקושר. ולדברי התוספות איירי מתניתן בדאדייה אדויי דוקא בדליל הפקר או דחבריה ואצנעיה וכשלא אצנעיה חייב גם בעל הדליל משום אשו.

מסקנת הגמרא דכי איתמר דרב הונא בדליל הפקר לדעת רש"י אם פשע אחד ואם קשרו אדם חייב הקושר דקשירה מילתה היא וקניה בהגבהה והתוספות סבירא ליה דקשירה לאו מילתה היא ולכן אמרו דלאו דוקא קשרי אלא משום שהיה במקום מוצנע והניחו במקום התורפה, ואפילו לא הגביהו ולא קנה חייב המניח.

אברך את ה' על המוגמר ותפלתי להמלמד תורה לעמו ישראל שיזכני לשכלל ולשפר את בנין בהמ"ד וישיבת הגר"א שברחוב קווינסי מספר 712 לגדל בני ישראל לתורה ולתעודה. וזכות הגאון המחבר זצוק"ל יעמוד לי ולזרעי עד עולם אמן. כעתירת המו"ל.

הצעיר **שלום אלעזר ראגאזין.**

שלמים של מים שמראה היין יחסר את המים משיעוריה ולכן גורס רש״י בלישנא בתרא גם ברישא חסר קורטוב ודו״ק.

ודברי רש״י בד״ה ומראיהן כמראה מים וכו׳ ובד״ה והכא נמי וכו׳ דרבנן תרתי בעי שיעורא וחזותא אין כאן מקומם אלא איזה תלמיד טועה הניחם שם לבלבל את הלומדים כי איפכא מסתברא אם רבנן בעי גם חזותא הלא אם מראיהן כמראה מים היו צריכים לפסול את המקוה אלא הטעם בסיפא הלא פסלו את המקוה הוא דאע״ג דמראיהן כמראה מים אין כח בחזותא דמיא לבטל את החלב והחלב הוא חלב כמו שהוא והלא אין בו שיעור ג׳ לוגין מים ולכן לא פסלי, אלא דברי רש״י דרבנן תרתי בעי וכו׳ קאי ארישא על ד״ה לא פסלוהו דאע״ג דאיכא ג׳ לוגין שלמים כיון דחזותייהו דחמרא לא פסלו, דרבנן בעי שיעורא וחזותא ולא שחזותא דחמרא מבטל את המים שלא יהיו מים אלא יין כדברי ר׳ יוחנן בן נורי כי הלא בסיפא אמרי רבנן דחזותא דמיא אינו מבטל את החלב אלא המים הם מים כמו שהם לרבנן רק חזותיהו דחמרא דומה הוא כאילו אין בו שיעור שלשה לוגין אבל קצת דוחק הוא לרש״י לומר כן שאם יש שם שלשה לוגין שלמים של מים ותזותא דחמרא אינו מבטלם מדוע זה מפחות את השיעור ולכן הוא אומר ולבי מהסס.

בחולין דף כ״ח ע״ב בענין מחצה על מחצה כרוב, א״ר קטינא ת״ש חלקו לשנים והן שוין שניהם טמאין לפי שאי אפשר לצמצם הא אפשר לצמצם טהורין אמאי טהורין זיל הכא איכא רובא וזיל הכא איכא רובא ומקשין התוספות מאי קא קשיא ליה אם אמרינן הכי אגמריה רחמנא למשה לא תשייר רובא כדלעיל הרי אין כאן רובא וטהורין ומתרצי דלא הרי שחיטת חצי סימן דאמרינן כרובא דמיא לנתיצת חצי כלי חרש דתלוי הדבר בחשיבות חצי המעשה שעשה דאם שחט חצי סימן דאמרינן כרובא מפני שבשחיטת חצי הסימן יצתה הנשמה מכל העוף ואם כן המעשה שעשה בחצי האחד ניכרת גם בחציה השני והרי יש כאן שיעור הכשר שחיטה והחצי הנשאר לא כלום הוא אבל בתנור אם חלקו לשנים הרי הם שני חצאים שוים ואם חציו כרובו זיל הכא איכא רובא וזיל הכא איכא רובא ואמאי טהורין ומתרץ הגמרא תרי רובא בחד מנא ליכא ואם אי אפשר לצמצם אמרינן שבחד איכא רובא ובחד מיעוטא ומספיקא שניהם טמאים אבל אם אפשר לצמצם על כל חד וחד אמרינן דאע״ג דכרובא דמי אבל מפני שנחתך ממנו החצי שהוא כרובו זה הנשאר איננו הכלי דמעיקרא ושניהם טהורין.

בחולין דף מ׳ ע״ב, הכא במאי עסקינן כגון שהיה חצי קנה פגום מקשין העולם והא אי אפשר לצמצם שיהיה הקנה פגום בחציו לא פחות ולא יותר שאם היה פגום פחות מעט מחציו כיון שהשלים לחציו אסרה ואזדך מחתך בעפר הוא ואם היה פגום מעט יותר מחציו הרי היתה נבלה מעיקרא והוא לא עשה ולא כלום ונראה לי לפרש דברי דגמרא כך שהרי צריכים אנו לומר שהא דאמרינן שאם עשה בה מעשה כל דהוא אסרה היינו שהבהמה היתה במצב כזה שיהיה ניכר שהוא עשה בה מעשה ולכן אם הבהמה היתה חיה והוא שחט בה רק מה שהוא ניכר הוא שהוא עשה בה מעשה ואסרה אבל אם הבהמה היתה

הקדמת המו"ל:

כאשר הגאון החסיד המחבר זצוק"ל צוה לפני מותו לבנו הגאון מהרי"צ זצ"ל להזדרז בהדפסת הספר „נפש החיים" לפני יתר חבוריו מצד השתוקקתו הגדולה לזכות את הרבים בדבר המועיל ליראת שמים ולאהבת התורה כידוע לכל גודל תועלת ספר דנא, וכאשר הקודמים כבר ספו ותמו, ונשארו רק אחד בעיר ושניים במשפחה, לכן אמרתי לעשות דבר טוב למלאות רצון הצדיק קדוש עליון בעל המחבר זצוק"ל לזכות את הרבים.

ואברך הטוב והמטיב שזכתי בטובה כפולה ומכופלת כי הכנסת הספר מוקדש לטובת הת"ת וישיבת רבינו הגאון החסיד אליהו מווילנא זצוק"ל וזה חלקי מכל עמלי בטפחות ימי הלדי.

ויען שזיכני ה' להוציא לאור את ספר **„נפש החיים"** מהגאון החסיד ר' חיים מוואלאזין זצ"ל, אמרתי בלבי להביא בדפוס מפרי רעיוני איזו חדשים מאשר חנני ה' ואקוה שיהי' לרצון לפני הלומדים והתלמידים.

בחולין דף כו' א', רבא אמר הא מני ר' יוחנן בן נורי וכו' ומפרש רש"י שתי לשונות ועל לשון ראשון הוא אומר ולבי מהסס ונתחבטו בו קמאי בדברי רש"י שקשה להולמן וגם הגהת רש"א אינו מובן והפשט הנכון להבנת דברי רש"י בלשון ראשון לפי עניות דעתי כך הוא: הנה ברור הדבר שהמים פוסלין את המקוה ופירא ניקח בכסף מעשר שני אבל בעת שהדבר הניקח בכסף מעשר דיו שיהיה רק פירא ולא יותר הנה לפסול את המקוה אינו די שיהיה מים לבד אבל צריך שיהיה שיעור שלשה לוגין ולכן לרבנן שלשה לוגין שלמים של מים. (לפי לשון ראשון של רש"י אין הגירסא חסר קורטוב). שנפל לתוכן קורטוב יין ומראיהן כמראה יין לא פסלוה דרבנן סברי דכיון דבעינן שיעוריה בעינן נמי חזותא כלומר: כמו דבעינן ג' לוגין מים לפסול את המקוה בעינן נמי שיתיה מראיהן כמראה מים אבל כאן שמראיהן מראה יין דומה היא כאלו אין בו שיעור מים ולכן לא פסלוה ואם שלשה לוגין מים חסר קורטוב שנפל לתוכן קורטוב חלב ומראיהן כמראה מים לא פסלוה מפני שהחלב שהוא פירא בעינו עומד ואינו מצטרף להשלים את השיעור ולא פסלוה ור' יותנן בן נורי סבר הכל הולך אחר המראה ופליג אסיפא ואמר דחזותא דמים מבטל את החלב והרי הוא כאלו כלו מים והרי יש בו שלשה לוגין מים ופוסל את המקוח והנה בסיפא פליגי רי יוחנן בן נורי ורבנן בדינא, דלרבנן מראה המים אינם מבטלים את החלב והחלב הוי פירא כמו שהוא ואינו מצטרף לשיעור והרי אין בו שיעור ג' לוגין מים ולא פסלו את המקוה ולר' יוחנן בן נורי מראה המים מבטל את החלב לגמרי והרי הוא כאלו כולו מים ולכך פסול את המקוה וברישא פליגי בטעמא דלרבנן מראה היין אינו מבטל את המים רק מפני חזותא דיין דומה הוא כאלו אין בו שיעור מים ולכן לא פסלוה ולר' יוחנן בן נורי מראה היין מבטל את המים לגמרי והרי הוא כאלו כולו יין ולכן לא פסלוה ועל זה אמר רש"י ולבי מהסס משום שלא נראה לו לומר דלרבנן אם היה בו שלשה לוגין

יראת ה'

לחיים

קונטרסים מכתבי קודש של הגאון אמתי המפורסם בתורתו, וצדקתו ומעשיו המכריזים עליו · פאר הדור ומופתו · חסיד ועניו · כקש"ת מו' חיים נ"ע האב"ד ור"מ דק"ק וולאזין · אשר יקרא בחתימתו בכתיבתו'

בשם

נפש החיים

וכמאמרם ז"ל בירושלמי דשקלים דף ו' תני רשב"ג אין עושין נפשות לצדיקים שדבריהם הן זכרונן וזכר צדיק לברכה ·

ועתה נדפס פעם רביעי ע"י הצעיר
שלום אליעזר ב"ר **ישראל** ז"ל המכונה **ראגאזין**
רב ומו"צ בב"המד' ישיבת הגאון החסיד רבנו **אליהו**
מווילנא זצוק"ל, 712 קווינסי סטריט, ברוקלין, נ. י.

RABBI S. L. ROGOZIN
712 Quincy St.
Brooklyn, N. Y.

ACTIVE PRESS, Inc.
Printers-Linotypers
33 East First St.
New York